FRANK CAPRA
Here is Hollywood's greatest director looking at some of the 329,460 ft. of film he shot for *You Can't Take It with You*. The 11,530 ft. of it you will soon see on the screen will have been cut, edited and scored under his minute supervision. For such pictures as *It Happened One Night*, *Mr. Deeds Goes to Town* and *Lost Horizon* have made Frank Capra so famous that he is allowed complete say over his productions, has more box-office appeal than many movie stars.

Page 42 from *Life Magazine*, September 19, 1938.

Rex Hardy, Jr., *Life Magazine*. © 1938 Time Inc.

FRANK CAPRA

*a guide to references
and resources*

*A
Reference
Publication
in
Film*

Ronald Gottesman
Editor

FRANK CAPRA
a guide to references and resources

CHARLES WOLFE

G.K. HALL &CO.
70 LINCOLN STREET, BOSTON, MASS.

All rights reserved.
Copyright 1987 by Charles Wolfe.

Library of Congress Cataloging-in-Publication Data

Wolfe, Charles, 1949–
 Frank Capra : a guide to references and resources.

 (A Reference publication in film)
 Includes indexes.
 1. Capra, Frank, 1897–   —Criticism and
interpretation. 2. Capra, Frank, 1897–   —Bibliography.
 I. Title. II. Series.
PN1998.A3C2683   1987   791.43′0233′0924   86-27095
ISBN 0-8161-8507-7

This publication is printed on permanent/durable acid-free paper
MANUFACTURED IN THE UNITED STATES OF AMERICA

For my parents

Contents

The Author		x
Preface		xi
I.	Biographical Background	1
II.	Critical Survey	21
III.	The Films: Credits, Notes, and Synopses	37
IV.	Writings about Frank Capra	187
V.	Writings by and Interviews with Frank Capra	375
	Articles and Books	375
	Published Interviews	383
	Interviews on Film and Videotape	404
VI.	Other Film-Related Activity	407
VII.	Archival Sources	423
VIII.	Film Distributors	445
Author Index		451
Film-Title Index		459

The Author

Charles Wolfe received a Ph.D. in film from Columbia University in 1978, and since that time has been teaching in the film studies program at the University of California, Santa Barbara. His writings on film have appeared in <u>Sight and Sound</u>, <u>Quarterly Review of Film Studies</u>, <u>Wide Angle</u>, <u>Film/Literature Quarterly</u>, <u>Journal of Film and Video</u>, and the <u>Village Voice</u>.

Preface

A central premise of any book in this series is that a collection of films can have a certain unity traceable to their director. A related premise is that this unity is not wholly a function of the films themselves, but is dependent upon a network of commentary—criticism, biography, testimony, publicity—that surrounds and supports them. Within the discipline of film studies, the adequacy of the first premise has in recent years come into question, but the companion premise suggests a way of refining our notion of directorial authorship by considering the history of its specific applications. It focuses our attention on the ways in which a director has been written and spoken about, and thus on the ways in which a director becomes an object of popular or critical interest. It invites us to consider the director in question not as the source of all meaning but as a figure upon whom meaning is mapped.

Frank Capra—the biographical figure (behind the scenes) and the name (above the title, among other places)—is a particularly instructive object of study from this perspective, for during the 1930s he was a central factor in the formulation of the idea that a Hollywood director might be considered an "author." Thus to examine the evidence surrounding Capra's career is in part to examine the origins of a book of this kind. This is primarily a reference guide to existing materials on Capra, and I hope that it will prove useful to researchers embarked on a wide variety of projects. But what has sustained my interest over the course of several years work on the book, and has governed many of my decisions along the way, has been the broader historical questions framing its value as a scholarly guide in the first place. How have we come to recognize "Capra"? What social functions has this figure, and the films figured by him, served? Within the limited space of the biographical sketch (Section I) and the critical survey (Section II), I have explored these questions. I hope that the remaining sections of the book will help future scholars and critics pursue similar questions at greater length and in more detail.

The reference material collected here is of three kinds: (1) credits, notes, and plot synopses for the fifty-six films Capra

Preface

directed, produced, or supervised, and background information concerning all other projects he worked on;(2) annotated bibliographies to writings about and by Capra, and interviews with Capra; and (3) a guide to holdings on Capra at archives around the world and to the nontheatrical distribution of prints of his films in this country. A few notes concerning my selection and organization of this material are in order.

The chronology of the filmography in Section III is based on the sequence in which films were made, not necessarily the sequence of release. I have noted, however, the year of release in parentheses next to each title. Thus Arsenic and Old Lace, which was filmed in 1941, can be found prior to the government documentaries, but still bears the date "1944," the year that Warner Brothers finally distributed the film. The only exception to this occurs for those films made in 1928, Capra's first, whirlwind year at Columbia. Because I have not been able to determine precisely the sequence in which these films were made, I have listed them in order of their date of copyright at the Library of Congress. Previous filmographies have given widely divergent release dates for many of Capra's films, perhaps because of the practice of previewing works before they are officially distributed. (On some occasions, however, it appears as if dates were simply plucked out of the air.) For the sake of clarity, I have taken the New York opening as the release date and treated previous screenings of the films as previews, a system in concert with Columbia's release pattern in the 1930s. Major previews of the films (for example, the screening of Mr. Smith Goes to Washington for members of Congress in 1939) are described in the notes section following the credits. All these dates have been cross-checked by consulting newspaper advertisements for the day in question.

Credits have been drawn from various sources: prints of the films, previous filmographies, reviews, publicity material, copyright records, and, whenever possible, production cast sheets. They are therefore composite, rather than "official," listings. When an official credit is dubious, or when I have been unable to verify a claim for an unofficial credit, I have indicated this in the notes section. The same section also provides information concerning published scripts and literary source material; major awards won by the film; and production, distribution, and exhibition information that is not generally known. Synopses have been based on recent screenings of the films, unless otherwise noted. Films that I was unable to see are marked by an asterisk.

Background information and credits for other film-related work by Capra is provided in Section VI. Here I have tried to reconstruct the chronology of Capra's involvement in other projects over the course of his career, from his early apprenticeship as prop man, editor, and writer in San Francisco and Los Angeles through the various abandoned projects of the 1960s. This material has been primarily gleaned from trade reports, and it provides an interesting complement to the offi-

Preface

cial Capra filmography, a view of the false starts and detours of a career that a listing of completed works masks.

The annotated bibliography is divided into two parts: Section IV covers published writings about Capra, and Section V covers published writings by Capra, published interviews with Capra, and those filmed interviews with Capra that have been broadcast or are available for rental. (Recorded interviews held by archives, which must be used on their premises, are listed in Section VII.) These bibliographies are based on a thorough search for material in four languages: English, French, Italian, and German. Articles that I came upon during the course of my research that are in other languages are also included, but it is only for the four named here that I can make a claim for exhaustiveness.

Even for these, I make this claim with some trepidation; anyone who has attempted to compile an exhaustive bibliography for a famous figure knows the elusiveness of the goal. In particular, there are limits to the reviews included here, especially for foreign countries and for newspapers outside the New York-Los Angeles axis in the United States. (Scholars should keep this in mind when making bold assertions about the "critical reception" of a given film.) However, I can claim with confidence that the listings here subsume all existing Capra bibliographies, as well as the bibliographical information on Capra supplied in the following indexes: The New Film Index (MacCann); The Critical Index (Gerlach); Retrospective Index to Film Periodicals (Batty); Film Literature Index (1973 through 1981); International Index to Film Periodicals (1972 through 1981); Film lexicon degli autori e delle opere; Index to Critical Film Reviews (Bowles); A Guide to Critical Reviews (Salem); Cumulated Dramatic Index; Chicorel Index to Film Literature; Motion Picture Directors (Schuster); Cinema Booklist (Rehrauer); Reader's Guide to Periodical Literature; British Humanities Index; and The New York Times Index. They also incorporate references obtained from a comprehensive search for reviews in Variety; the Nation, the New Republic, the New Yorker, Time, and Newsweek. Moreover, they are based on an exhaustive check of clipping files held at the following libraries: Margaret Herrick Library, the Academy of Motion Picture Arts and Sciences; Louis B. Mayer Library, the American Film Institute; Theatre Arts Library, University of California, Los Angeles; Film Study Center, the Museum of Modern Art; and the Library for the Performing Arts at Lincoln Center, New York. Because I last researched these clipping files in 1982, I have used December 1981 as the cutoff date for all bibliographic material. All entries marked by an asterisk are based on information from secondary sources, as described in the annotations.

Material referred to in the bibliographies include books, essays, reviews, trade reports, and magazine articles, as well as general news coverage. My guideline in selecting material was whether the writing provided a critical or historical perspective on Capra's films or career; if it did, I included it, and when in doubt, I favored inclusion over exclusion. I have not included, however, news reports on

Preface

specific productions unless (1) Capra is interviewed, or (2) he figures importantly in the article. (If the production information itself is particularly revealing, I have included it in the notes for the film in Section III.) I have interpreted the notion of "interview" broadly: some interviews are direct transcriptions of question-and-answer sessions with Capra; others are journalistic accounts in which quotations are integrated into a general report; others do not quote Capra directly at all, but describe the gist of his response. Interviewers and reporters obviously have great power to shape the material presented, and with the last two formats this should especially be kept in mind. Occasionally the formal interviews will be accompanied by introductory remarks by the interviewer about Capra. When these constitute a critical approach, I have entered the interview in both Section IV and Section V, with separate annotations, and have cross-indexed the two entries.

Section VII surveys the Capra holdings of fifty-seven archives and libraries in eighteen countries, listed by city. I have tried to be as specific as possible in describing these collections and, whenever possible, to supply information concerning access to the material. I was able to check out myself the holdings of the Academy of Motion Picture Arts and Sciences; the American Film Institute; the UCLA Theatre Arts Library; Doheny Library, University of Southern California; the Library for the Performing Arts, Lincoln Center; the Museum of Modern Art; and the Library of Congress. In all other cases, I have relied upon information provided by archivists by telephone or by mail.

Needless to say, the completion of a project of this scope would not have been possible without the cooperation and assistance of numerous people and organizations, and I would like to acknowledge some of them here. Kit Parker Films generously allowed me to screen several early Capra films that I had not previously seen. (They have also played a crucial role in the reconstruction of works that were once considered "lost," and all film scholars are in their debt for that.) Twyman Films likewise allowed me to screen their print of Lost Horizon so that I could refresh my memory of it. Research funds were provided by the Academic Senate, University of California, Santa Barbara. Kathryn Uthe and the staff of the Inter-Library Loan Department at UCSB were patient and painstaking in assisting me in my search for written material; without that assistance my annotations would have been much less complete.

Staff members at all the archives and libraries I visited were helpful, but I would like especially to thank Charles Silver of the Film Study Center, Museum of Modern Art; Emily Sieger and Barbara Humphreys of the Motion Picture, Recorded Sound Division, the Library of Congress; Dorothy Swerdlove and Monte Arnold of the Billy Rose Theatre Collection, Lincoln Center for the Performing Arts; Robert Knutson and Janet Lorentz of Special Collections, USC; Anne G. Schlosser of the Louis B. Mayer Library, American Film Institute; and

Preface

Robert Rosen and Charles Hopkins of the UCLA Film Archive. Jeanine Basinger, curator of the new Capra archive at Wesleyan University, responded to my requests for information with speed, thoroughness, and warmth; future Capra scholars are indeed fortunate that this collection will be in her hands.

The survey of archival sources included in this volume also benefited greatly from the assistance of archivists in foreign countries who took the time to provide me with detailed reports. Among these correspondents I especially would like to thank Lars Olgaard of Det Danske Filmmuseum, Copenhagen; Jon Stenkler of the Norsk Filminstitutt, Oslo; Nicole Schmitt of the Centre National de la Cinématographie, Paris; Marika Junstrom of the Svenska Filminstitutet, Stockholm; Roberto Radicati of the Museo Nazionale del Cinema, Turin; and Linda Woods of the Library Services Department of the British Film Institute.

I am deeply grateful for the cooperation of Frank Capra himself: he gave me information that no one else could, put me on the track of material I would not have otherwise located, and answered with graciousness and good humor questions that probably seemed pedantic. I am also grateful to Robert Potter and Paul N. Lazarus, Jr., whose wonderfully sharp recollections gave me a more detailed picture of past events.

Ronald Gottesman was as thoughtful and supportive an editor as his reputation promised; critics and scholars everywhere are in his debt for his work on this and other series. Patrizio Rossi assisted with a difficult translation. Alexander Sesonske offered encouragement at a crucial moment. The typing of Kathryn Carnahan was impeccable (as always), and she caught more than a few errors in the manuscript, for which she has my thanks.

Among the many friends and colleagues who listened to me talk about my labors, and gave me good advice, I would particularly like to express my gratitude to Albert J. LaValley, Karen Wingo, Michael Renov, and Andrew Martin (who also compiled the list of film distributors). Ronald Magliozzi might best be described as my New York contact on this project, and deserves credit as a substantial contributor. Two people closer to home—Patrice Petro and Nataša Ďurovičová—came to my rescue at key stages in the project, helping me locate material, assisting me with translations, reading sections of the manuscript, and above all providing a perspective on what I was doing. I cannot imagine having finished this work without them.

Finally, I am deeply indebted to Deborah Scott Wolfe—collaborator on all projects, large and small—for her sound judgment and constant support, and to Christopher and Timothy who helped simply by being around.

October 1984

I. Biographical Background

Frank Capra was born 18 May 1897 to Salvatore and Sara Nicolas Capra, Sicilian peasants from the village of Bisaquino, thirty miles inland from Palermo. Six years later his parents immigrated to America with their four youngest children (Frank was the sixth of seven), crossing the continent to Los Angeles to join their eldest son, who had run away from home several years before. In his accounts of his early years in Little Sicily--the urban ghetto into which the family settled--Capra has consistently emphasized the intensity of his ambition to escape the oppressive poverty and illiteracy that surrounded him. Like the rest of his family, he was expected to go to work as soon as they settled in America, and he sold newspapers on street corners in downtown Los Angeles from the age of six. Unlike his brothers and sisters, however, he insisted on attending, and staying in, school. Excelling in math and science, Capra finished Los Angeles Manual Arts High School at the top of his class and enrolled-- despite protest from most of the family--in Throop Polytechnic Institute (soon to be known as Cal Tech). Paying his way through college with various part-time jobs and scholarships, he was awarded a bachelor of science degree in chemical engineering in 1918. Upon graduating, he served a brief wartime stint as an instructor in ballistic mathematics in the Coast Artillery in San Francisco.

Capra's escape route out of the ghetto, however, was not to be as straight and purposeful as his initial successes portended. In 1915 his family had placed a down payment on a lemon grove a few miles east of Los Angeles and had lived there for two years while Frank was in college. But his father was killed in a well-pump accident in 1917, and the property was lost; his mother was forced to return to Little Sicily and a job in a cannery to support herself and her youngest daughter. Unable to find employment as a chemical engineer amid the postwar recession, Capra joined them in the ghetto he detested. There he was stricken by a severe stomach ailment (fifteen years later he was to learn his appendix had burst), and his mother, having no faith in scientific medical treatment, nursed her science graduate at home. After six weeks in bed he began to recover and weakly set off on his own, eventually regaining his strength while working at an orchard his brother now owned in the San Fernando Valley. He also found employment for two months as a live-in tutor for the scion of the "Lucky" Baldwin family, a job that not only permitted him to put his education to use but brought him into direct contact for the first time with the ways of the wealthy. For the next three years Capra led an itinerant life, peddling Elbert Hubbard self-improvement books, Hartsook photographs, and blue-sky mining stocks, and playing poker and performing on the guitar in various cities and small towns throughout the West.[1]

In December 1921 Capra bluffed his way into motion pictures by convincing an actor and dilettante producer of "literary" short subjects in San Francisco that he was from Hollywood. Improvising as he went, Capra directed a twelve-minute adaptation of Rudyard Kipling's poem "The Ballad of Fisher's Boarding House" with sufficient skill to have the film sold to Pathé for a substantial profit. His appetite for filmmaking whetted, Capra spent the next two years learning what he could about the profession in San Francisco, first as an assistant in a photo lab, and then as a prop man, editor, and writer for Bob Eddy, a Hollywood producer who was filming Toonerville Trolley comedies in the San Francisco area. Capra's connection with Eddy brought him back to Los Angeles, a few miles away from his childhood home, where he landed a job as a gag writer for Hal Roach's "Our Gang" series in 1924. Six months later he moved on to the Mack Sennett Studio and, after a brief apprenticeship as a general gagman, was promoted to staff writer working primarily on comedies for Harry Langdon and Ralph Graves.[2] When Langdon left Sennett to make independent features in 1926, he took Capra with him and promoted him to director on The Strong Man and Long Pants before a disagreement ended their collaboration on a bitter note.[3] Capra struggled to keep his new career alive by traveling to New York to direct a financially strapped independent feature, For the Love of Mike, but the film was not widely distributed. In 1927 he returned to the writers' stable at Mack Sennett Studio and contemplated resuming his studies at Cal Tech in pursuit of a doctoral degree.[4]

Before the year was out, however, Capra was hired by Columbia Pictures to direct low-budget features, and for the next ten years the fortunes of Capra and Columbia were to be intertwined. With no exhibition circuit to guarantee a showcase for its films, Columbia had established its economic base in Hollywood by marketing inexpensive productions through regional sales offices, but by the time of Capra's arrival, studio head Harry Cohn was experimenting with classier productions as well.[5] Impressed with Capra's efficiency, versatility, and brashness, Cohn entrusted the newcomer with a foundering A production Submarine, starring Jack Holt and Ralph Graves--and the popular and critical success of the finished film advanced Capra up the studio's directorial ladder. Unintimidated by the technology of sound, Capra oversaw Columbia's transition to talkies in 1929, first with the insertion of dialogue passages into his silent melodrama, The Younger Generation, and then as director of the studio's first full-length dialogue film, The Donovan Affair. As Cohn slowly engineered Columbia's bid for major recognition, he began to give Capra longer

Biographical Background

production schedules and to orchestrate more elaborate publicity campaigns for his films. <u>Flight</u>, made in 1929 to capitalize on the great success of <u>Submarine</u>, for example, was given a prestigious roadshow release, and <u>Dirigible</u>, which teamed Holt and Graves together for a third time in 1931, was premiered in Los Angeles at Grauman's Chinese Theatre, the first such affair for a Columbia film. In 1933 Capra's <u>The Bitter Tea of General Yen</u> was selected to inaugurate a new all-movie policy at the year-old Radio City Music Hall in New York and went on to garner Academy Award nominations in four of the top five categories. <u>It Happened One Night</u>, released in February 1934, was the box-office surprise of the year (the fifth biggest money-maker among all Hollywood productions)[6] and was still in distribution the following spring when it swept the Oscars, winning all five of the top awards, including best direction.

By mid-decade Capra had carved out a position of considerable power for himself within the Hollywood studio system. A star director at a studio that had few celebrities under contract, Capra was able to exercise control over the writing, casting, and editing of his films. Moreover, he had established close working relationships with a variety of Columbia craftsmen (cinematographer Joseph Walker, editors Maurice Wright and Gene Havlick, art directors Harrison Wiley and Stephen Goosson, sound engineer Edward Bernds), many of whom remained loyal to Capra from project to project, and he had been free to cultivate partnerships with writers of his choice (Jo Swerling early on, and then Robert Riskin, with whom Capra formed perhaps the most celebrated director-writer team in Hollywood). He had earned a reputation for being able to create an atmosphere of collaboration on the set and for sensitively handling actors and actresses. Reviewers spoke of the magic touch he brought to most the ordinary scene.[7] By his own account, moreover, winning an Oscar for directing <u>It Happened One Night</u> had fulfilled a professional ambition he had nurtured for many years.

In the wake of these achievements, however, came a grave personal crisis. A fear of future failure, Capra claims in his autobiography, led to a psychosomatic illness of life-threatening dimension; visited by an anonymous Christian Scientist, who reprimanded him severely for wasting his talents at a time of international peril, he was gradually restored to health. Despite the sudden halt in Capra's work schedule, nothing was reported of the illness in 1935,[8] but the impact of this conversion experience seems evident in an article Capra wrote for <u>Esquire</u> shortly thereafter. Entitled "A Sick Dog Tells Where It Hurts," the piece is a detailed attack on the movie industry, with Capra himself numbered among the accused. Critics had referred to him as a "giant" in the field, he noted, but he was only a "pigmy among pigmies"; his training in the sciences had left him ill-prepared to explore cinema's potential as an art. The emergence of film art, moreover, was blocked by business expediency: studios, owning talent to ensure product and owning theaters to ensure a market, had standardized what should be a creative process. Producers, Capra advised, had to learn to value the quality of films over the profits of stockholders; studios had to divest themselves of theater chains that held

Biographical Background

the public captive to bad movies; censorship had to be abolished so that filmmakers could work in freedom. But the next move was less in the hands of the businessmen than in those of creative talent: writers, actors, and directors had to reject the security of long-term contracts, accept only quality projects, and, if necessary, go into business making films for themselves. Directors, Capra argued, were in the best position to lead moviemaking out of the factory wilderness, but unfortunately most directors were "fat, forty, and rich," lacking the courage to assert their artistic independence. He himself, Capra ironically noted in closing, had displayed scant courage in recently signing a new long-term contract at Columbia.[9]

Despite the self-indictment, the attack was not without a self-serving aspect. By linking the aesthetic and social value of films inextricably to personal expression, Capra was positing the necessity for directorial autonomy in the filmmaking process. It was an idea that was to shape his conception of his career to follow. Beginning with his next film, Capra writes in his autobiography:

> my films had to _say_ something. And whatever they said had to come from those ideas inside me "that were hurting to come out." . . . Was this a new form of arrogance, perhaps a superior form? Many fellow workers thought so. But, believe it or not, it was a change in the polarity of goals: from "using" films, to serving them; from "what is good for Capra," to what is good for the profession.[10]

Capra thus saw himself as reconciling social consciousness with personal ambition: a principle of "one man, one film" was to go hand in hand with the making of socially valuable films for a popular audience--for "the people."

For the rest of the decade, Capra would have had little reason to consider the possible ambiguities contained in this notion. The next four films he selected to make--<u>Mr. Deeds Goes to Town</u>, <u>Lost Horizon</u>, <u>You Can't Take It with You</u>, and <u>Mr. Smith Goes to Washington</u>--were all popular successes and attracted wide coverage by the media. That <u>Mr. Smith</u> survived attacks from the Washington press corps, and an attempt to suppress the European distribution of the film by the American ambassador to London, Joseph P. Kennedy, to attain great success both at home and abroad only reinforced Capra's notion that his films served the public at large rather than the social or political establishment. Respect within the Hollywood community ran deep: collectively the films were nominated for twenty-eight Academy Awards, and won six, including best direction honors for <u>Mr. Deeds</u> and <u>You Can't Take It with You</u>. Capra also assumed an active role in studio politics, managing to wear different hats during heated labor disputes without getting shot in the crossfire. Elected president of the Academy of Motion Picture Arts and Sciences in 1935, he opposed the efforts of the studio chiefs to use the organization as a company union, a maneuver that had led many of his colleagues to abandon the Academy entirely, but remained loyal to an institution that had

Biographical Background

brought the industry--and Capra himself--a certain prestige. In May 1938, while still serving as AMPAS president, he was also elected president of the emerging Directors Guild; in 1939 he used the threat of a strike by guild members, as well as a possible boycott of the Academy Awards (at which he was scheduled to be master of ceremonies), to win recognition for the union as the directors' sole bargaining agent.

Capra's critique of Hollywood in Esquire, moreover, could have functioned as a blueprint for his own bid for independent production. In 1937 Harry Cohn falsely advertised a routine Columbia release, If You Could Only Cook, as a Capra film in England. Already engaged in a protracted salary dispute with Cohn, Capra decided to sue Columbia for breach of contract and requested financial compensation and release.[11] Ignored by the other studios while the case was pending, Capra tried to organize an independent production company with directors William Wellman, Gregory La Cava, and Wesley Ruggles, but the plan collapsed for lack of financial backing.[12] Eventually Capra and Cohn resolved their differences out of court and Capra fulfilled his contract, but upon completing Mr. Smith Goes to Washington in the summer of 1939, he left Columbia to form Frank Capra Productions with Riskin. Capra's clout in the industry enabled him to strike a production-distribution deal with Warner Brothers, Vitagraph (Warner's distributor), and the Bank of America, in which he as producer was granted complete control over the making and marketing of his next film.[13] He and Riskin spent the next fifteen months writing, producing, filming, and distributing Meet John Doe.

Over the next decade a host of similar companies--controlled by directors, writers, or actors, but dependent upon the production facilities and the distribution systems of the major studios--were to emerge in Hollywood, and in this sense Capra was on the cutting edge of changes in the way films were produced in Hollywood. But Frank Capra Productions was not to constitute the personal breakthrough he hoped for. The problem in part stemmed from the financial structure of the company which had left him vulnerable to debilitating taxation. Riskin, moreover, was eager to branch out on his own, and after the release of Meet John Doe his partnership with Capra was dissolved. The making of Meet John Doe, furthermore, had bogged down on the matter of a credible closing scene; production at one point had been suspended while writing continued, and a further revision was made after the film's initial release. According to Capra, personal doubts concerning his success resurfaced. Even as he had become a powerful figure in Hollywood, he had cultivated his memory of being an outsider, a Poverty Row scrapper at a second-class studio like Columbia, for example, rather than at a "palatial" major, a "class-structured" studio like MGM.[14] Now he worried that he had lost touch with his audience, had become bored, grown stale.

World War II was to offer a temporary antidote to these concerns. In June 1941 Capra journeyed to Washington and offered his services to the Signal Corps Army Pictorial Service. He then returned to

Hollywood for two months of unsuccessful negotiations with United Artists for partnership in that company.[15] He signed a one-picture contract with Warners to direct an adaptation of Joseph Kesselring's popular stage play, Arsenic and Old Lace, without pretending to commit his talents to the service of mankind. Discussions with Warners and 20th Century-Fox for future independent productions also continued, but America's entry into the war was to decide Capra's fate for the next few years.[16] The day after Pearl Harbor he was inducted into the army on the set of Arsenic and Old Lace, and he left for Washington two months later. Backed by General George C. Marshall, the army chief of staff, Capra quickly consolidated power as head of the Morale Branch's newly formed film unit, and by June he had assembled a crew of professional writers, directors, and editors (both enlisted and civilian) in Los Angeles, where he oversaw the production of the army's orientation film series, Why We Fight, as well as several related indoctrination projects. In September 1943 he was appointed commanding officer of a special unit formed under the aegis of the Public Relations Office to improve photographic coverage of the battlefront. He traveled widely in this post and remained on special assignment for the duration of the war. In 1943 Winston Churchill awarded Capra the Order of the British Empire, and a Distinguished Service Medal was presented by General Marshall prior to Capra's discharge in June 1945. Capra's tenure in the army thus provided yet another path to reconciling ambition and social mission. He conceived of his shift from commercial to wartime filmmaking--as the titles to the second and third sections of his autobiography suggest--as a displacement of his "Struggle with Success" by "The Great Struggle," a propaganda battle of epic scale and grave historical consequence. In his most recent accounts of this period, however, Capra has also emphasized the degree to which the war was a profoundly disturbing experience; the carnage he witnessed during 1943 and 1944 led him to question the unambiguous argument for war he had so willingly and forcefully presented in the Why We Fight series. No longer, he claims, could he argue for social causes with the same conviction or handle the pressures of film production with the same confidence.[17]

In terms of popular reputation, it would have been difficult to forecast these long-range difficulties for Capra at the time of his return to Hollywood in the summer of 1945. Although he had been out of circulation for several years, and many of his prewar collaborators were no longer at his fingertips, his name still carried weight at the box office, and the opportunities for independent production were more abundant than ever.[18] Two months prior to his discharge, Capra and Samuel Briskin (a former producer at Columbia who had worked as a production manager in Capra's film unit during the war) had incorporated an independent company, Liberty Films. Now back in Hollywood, Capra signed on two other prominent directors just out of the service-- William Wyler and George Stevens. They had no difficulty attracting distribution offers from the major studios, and in 1946 they struck a deal with RKO in which each director was to make five films and RKO was to provide production facilities and handle the distribution of the fifteen projects.[19]

Biographical Background

Capra, moreover, once again took up the cause of reforming the industry, this time in the pages of the New York Times Magazine. In an article titled "Breaking Hollywood's 'Pattern of Sameness,'" Capra reiterated his complaint of ten years before that assembly-line production methods resulted in complacent, unimaginative filmmaking. But his commentary was less accusatory than in 1936, less pitched in terms of a Manichean struggle between creativity and compromise, between honor and disgrace. The industry, he proposed, was being changed from within by a generation of filmmakers who had returned from the war to discover that Hollywood was isolated behind a "wall of mirrors." And while he generously allowed that the standard studio production would still have appeal, there now would be space for these new filmmakers to work independently as entrepreneur-artists within the studio system, making films that bore a personal stamp.[20]

News coverage of Capra's first film under the Liberty banner, It's a Wonderful Life, was extensive, in part because it was the company's debut film, in part because it marked the return to commercial filmmaking of both Capra and actor Jimmy Stewart, a celebrated air force pilot during the war.[21] But upon its release in December 1946, It's a Wonderful Life performed sluggishly at the box office, and by the spring of 1947 Liberty Films was in financial trouble. To fulfill a prewar contract with Samuel Goldwyn, William Wyler had spent a year on The Best Years of Our Lives. The film had eclipsed It's a Wonderful Life in all the major categories at the Academy Awards in the spring, but the profits went to Goldwyn rather than to Liberty, and Wyler's next project was only in the planning stage. George Stevens, moreover, had spent a year on an aborted project, One Big Happy Family, and his next work was a year away from completion. With profits declining in the industry overall, Capra and Briskin convinced their colleagues to accept an offer from Paramount to sell Liberty Films--including the services of the partners on their remaining contracted projects--for an estimated $4 million in company stock. Following the release of Capra's State of the Union (completed at MGM rather than RKO) and Stevens's I Remember Mama, the four partners went to work for Paramount.[22]

The sale made all four men wealthy, but Capra came to regret the deal deeply, considering it a betrayal of his ethos of autonomy and a primary symptom of a new failure of nerve as a filmmaker. Moreover, a retrenchment program and budget limit introduced at Paramount shortly after his arrival made it difficult for Capra to get productions off the ground. After negotiating with Paramount executives on various projects for close to a year, Capra completed two modest comedies with Bing Crosby (Riding High [1950], Here Comes the Groom [1951]). With a third film owed Paramount, his contract was abrogated by mutual consent in 1951.[23] Frustrated, he reluctantly withdrew from the industry, selling off various story ideas that he owned to his colleagues and retreating with his family to an avocado ranch in Fallbrook, California.[24] He entered a brief period of self-exile from Hollywood, tending the orchard (his father's favorite occupation), serving on various commissions and advisory committees, and, in the style of a Jefferson Smith, leading his neighbors in a fight to protect local water rights to the Santa Marguerita River.[25] But the itch to make films remained.

The resentment Capra harbored for the direction his career had taken was exacerbated by political events as well. Capra had always kept his political affiliations private; he had, for example, never publicly endorsed a candidate or championed a political party. He viewed political issues as, first and foremost, moral issues, with the triumph of the disenfranchised over their oppressors the logical cause of all who embraced Christian humanist values. Rabidly committed to "individualism" (albeit tempered by social consciousness), he found political heroes more attractive than political organizations and was suspicious of systematic governmental action. Thus in the 1930s Capra would find Franklin D. Roosevelt an inspiring leader--energetic, charming, and compassionate, despite his privileged background, toward the underdog--yet at the same time see little to celebrate in the New Deal. He worked well with writers to the left of him politically (including Riskin and Sidney Buchman), yet he had also taken measures while in the army to ensure that "Communist propaganda" did not find its way into the Why We Fight scripts. If his films had frequently depicted the rich and powerful in America as buffoons or villains, by the late 1930s they also contained their share of patriotic sentiment, and the Why We Fight series had been recognized as perhaps the most compelling assertion of traditional American values the war years had to offer. Thus Capra was startled to discover in 1952 that he had been identified in Washington as a Communist sympathizer and denied security clearance for work on a government project. A flimsy case could be constructed: Capra had visited the Soviet Union in 1937; he had worked with screenwriter Sidney Buchman, now blacklisted for his past affiliation with the Communist party, on Mr. Smith Goes to Washington, and the film had been circulated in Russia after the war as a document of American political corruption; he had gotten footage from the Soviet Union during the war for the making of The Battle of Russia; State of the Union, released in the wake of the first round of congressional hearings by the House Un-American Activities Committee into "subversion" in Hollywood, had been described by a journalist as Communist propaganda; Capra had opposed the existence of a Hollywood blacklist.[26] Amid the cold war hysteria, Capra thus was labeled a security risk. Capra considered the existence of this new government dossier as tantamount to an accusation of treason and worked feverishly to clear his name. He finally succeeded when he undertook the role of State Department representative at the 1953 India Film Festival, where, acting as a cold warrior himself, he countered Communist propaganda at the event.

Meanwhile Capra kept his hand in filmmaking by accepting an offer from Bell Telephone to work on a series of science documentaries to be broadcast on television and later distributed to schools. Having long maintained an interest in popular science and technological gadgets, Capra approached the assignment with enthusiasm, enjoying the contact

Biographical Background

it brought him with leading scientists as well as with a new audience of young people. Work on the project also brought him back to Los Angeles, close to the scene of his earlier triumphs in the industry, and upon completing the series he decided to try to rekindle his career as a feature filmmaker. In August 1957 he set up a coproduction deal with Frank Sinatra for the making of A Hole in the Head, and while waiting for Sinatra to become available for shooting, he briefly returned to Columbia at the invitation of Harry Cohn to work on an adaptation of Thomas Mann's Joseph and His Brethren. (For years a troubled project at the studio, it was canceled following Cohn's death a few months later.) He also resumed an active role in the industry: twenty years after his first term as president of the Directors Guild, he was reelected to that post in 1959 and oversaw the merger of the screen branch with that of radio and television.

But Capra's return to active filmmaking was not to be long-lived. "Independent" production was now standard operating procedure in Hollywood, but not in the way he had originally envisioned: production and distribution deals were contingent upon the employment of "bankable" stars, and his own name was now insufficient to obtain financing. Sinatra had held up the making of A Hole in the Head for thirteen months, and a subsequent attempt by Capra to collaborate with Sinatra, Bing Crosby, and Dean Martin on a biography of Jimmy Durante collapsed in 1960 when Capra sensed that the production was slipping out of his control. He managed to arrange a second coproduction deal, this time with Glenn Ford, to remake Lady for a Day as Pocketful of Miracles in 1961, but the making of the film was fraught with tension and animosity, with Capra losing more battles to his bankable star than he won. He struggled for the next few years with a half dozen projects, all unrealized, and decided to retire for good in 1967 after spending three years on Marooned without filming a scene.

That these were difficult times for the proud and once powerful director is clear from his autobiography (written during 1969 and 1970); disaffection from Hollywood and a profound sense of bitterness pervade his account of the previous decade. There is a strong dose of self-recrimination as well. If the film industry had in his estimation deteriorated, he himself no longer possessed the stamina to fight for something different. Moreover his reconciliation of ambition and conscience in the 1930s had been predicated on the notion that the instincts of the audience were sound—that viewers knew what they needed as well as what they enjoyed—but contemporary moviegoers had evidenced a taste for vulgarity and violence that appalled him. Through his inability to get films made—even to know what kind to make—he had failed both his audience and himself.

Despite the acrimony and frustration evidenced in these passages, however, Capra closes his autobiography on an upbeat note, recounting how the death in 1969 of his eldest brother, Ben, a man of no fame but many friends, had prompted him to make peace with retirement, find a broader perspective on his life, and write a book about it. This ending is reminiscent of the final, optimistic turn taken by so many of Capra's scripts, and it provides formal closure for a narrative that had opened with Ben's journey to America and the subsequent migration of the Capra family to the "promised land." Yet however formal the peroration, the optimism of the conclusion did in fact presage a turn of events in Capra's life. As if the venting of his anger in the autobiography had been in some sense therapeutic, he was relieved of debilitating migraine headaches, an affliction that had first struck him during the filming of Pocketful of Miracles in 1961. In addition, the publication of the book launched Capra on a new career lecturing at colleges and universities around the country. He had treated student demonstrators (among other groups much in the news at the time) harshly in his autobiography, but direct contact with them gave him a new respect for their energy and commitment, and if mass demonstrations seemed to him dangerously "conformist," he nevertheless was sympathetic toward the opposition to the war in Vietnam. He also had the satisfaction of discovering among students a new audience for his films from the 1930s and 1940s, and in turn became a lively advocate of opportunities for new young filmmakers. He took up the cause of film studies programs, envisioning their struggle to survive in academia as yet another version of the struggle of the outsider and underdog against the establishment.[27] Now in his mid-eighties, Capra remains highly visible at festivals and testimonials, and has received a variety of honors both inside and outside the industry over the last few years, including an honorary doctoral degree from Wesleyan University in 1981, and the American Film Institute's Life Achievement Award in 1982. He now enjoys the kind of sustained recognition that seemed to elude him two decades ago.

Elements of Capra's biography have long been a matter of public record--and public fiction--and as such have had a social impact complementing that of the films. During the course of the 1930s, Capra fleshed out a persona that abetted his power in the industry, played well in the popular press, and strongly shaped expectations concerning his work. Capra's autobiography, moreover, can be read as an attempt to revive this persona, complicating it through revelations of a darker, pessimistic aspect, a side barely visible in the "Capra" of the 1930s and 1940s. Two profiles of that persona seem to me particularly important: "Capra-as-author" and Capra-as-immigrant." We might then briefly consider, by way of closing this biographical sketch, how each has functioned within the broader framework of publicity and popular culture in America, and how they have influenced, as biographical background sets, critical readings of Capra's films.

Capra not only sought control of productions early on at Columbia; he sought public recognition for his labors as well, and by the end of his first year at the studio his films were clearly billed as "Frank Capra Productions." (Occasionally he added an "R" as a middle initial, flirting with a pen name that sounded a bit more high-toned. He abandoned the affectation in 1933.) In the wake of his Academy Award nomination in 1934, and his winning of that prize in 1935, Columbia began to feature Capra prominently in studio adver-

Biographical Background

tising. The evidence would also suggest that producers at other studios considered Capra's emerging celebrity good business for the industry overall; at the time of the release of Mr. Deeds Goes to Town, for example, Irving J. Thalberg of MGM and Jesse Lasky of Paramount both provided laudatory comments on Capra's achievement which Columbia incorporated into its advertising copy.[28] Like the Academy Awards, which above and beyond the victories of competing studios celebrated the achievements of the studio system, praise for Capra helped advance the notion that work of distinction could be accomplished in Hollywood.

Beginning with Lost Horizon in 1936-37, publicity concerning Capra intensified. With $2 million invested in the project (an unprecedented sum for the studio), Columbia launched a promotional campaign that stressed Capra's direct supervision of all aspects of the lavish production. The theme was picked up by the press and carried over into both favorable and unfavorable reviews of the film upon its release.[29] By 1938 a special place for Capra as a filmmaker controlling all aspects of his work within the context of the studio system had been clearly established in popular commentary on the movies. The Saturday Evening Post published a profile in May which ran beneath the headline "Capra Shoots as He Pleases."[30] Capra was on the cover of Time in August, the lead figure in a story on the role of the director in Hollywood.[31] In November, as part of a feature article on the making of You Can't Take It with You, Life ran a photo spread entitled "How Frank Capra Makes a Hit Picture." A series of photographs depicted Capra not only on the set directing the cast but conferring with Cohn and Riskin, supervising the set design and the score, studying the rushes, and physically cutting the film himself.[32] By December, Howard Barnes in the New York Herald Tribune was proposing that Capra was "the most important figure in motion pictures today," having advanced the fundamental character and quality of filmmaking by defining "the importance of the director in the complicated business of turning out a photoplay."[32] Capra's decision to become an independent producer-director in 1939 simply confirmed what the press was already saying about him.

Yet if Capra-as-author was excellent publicity for Hollywood, it also aggravated tensions along the fault line separating the talent groups from the studio executives. The case of If You Could Only Cook illustrates this handsomely; Cohn's use of Capra's name clearly indicated that he considered the director's credit to be, in the final analysis, a possession not of Capra but of the studio, one that Cohn might deploy at his own discretion to stimulate box-office receipts. (The incident also illustrates the power of marketing over critical perception: Graham Greene, although not very taken by the film, nevertheless dutifully noted in it the existence of "a few agreeable Capra touches.")[34] The legal implications of the case were never resolved, but other studios appeared to have backed Cohn in the controversy by blocking Capra from jumping his contract. In turn, the incident appears to have strengthened Capra's determination to establish himself as an independent producer-director and likely prompted

Biographical Background

his active lobbying on behalf of the Directors Guild, both in its general bid for industry recognition and in its specific campaign to guarantee the right of all directors to a preproduction review of scripts and, postproduction, to control of the assembly of the first cut.[35]

Capra, in short, came to assume a unique position within the Hollywood studio system. His success provided him with a platform to challenge certain structural relations within the industry. But that challenge, in turn, seems to have been circumscribed by his devotion to an institution that had provided him with a medium and a mass audience. His forays into documentary filmmaking--essentially digressions in his career rather than radical breaks--kept him close to Hollywood production facilities and placed him, as "author," in the service of his sponsoring agencies. His primary interest, moreover, remained the making of commercial features. Even when he operated as an independent producer-director, he financed his films through conventional sources, used studio office space and production facilities, and distributed his work within existing channels of first-run theatrical release. He might vigorously attack the business practices of the motion picture moguls, but would no less vigorously defend Hollywood against the accusation that it unfairly dominated foreign markets,[36] and he remained loyal throughout his career to the Academy and the image it conveyed of a community committed to the "arts and sciences" of motion pictures.

Capra's rebellion was fundamentally an internal protest concerning the disposition of power within a corporate bureaucracy. Independent production, he took pains to point out, was a vehicle for bringing a greater variety of subjects and styles to commercial film production--the difference between "a strictly Hollywood product" and an "American" film made in Hollywood. The nuance of difference between the two, he proposed, was important, and he sought to establish this nuance as a criterion of value.[37] He argued for a Hollywood that might function as a precorporate industrial system, one in which craftsmanship would be favored over mass production, independents over monopolies, open markets over block booking, and individual expression over the crass formulas of an efficient economic machine. For critics, Capra-as-author thus played a crucial role in the construction of the notion of what a successful, yet self-respecting and in some sense "autonomous" filmmaker in Hollywood might be thought to be like. In doing so, from a longer perspective, Capra-as-author served as a bridge between the critical interest in the American cinema of D.W. Griffith (who, perhaps not coincidentally, was brought back into the limelight by Capra at the 1936 Academy Awards ceremony) and the rediscovery of the Hollywood director as artist by way of the critical practices of auteurism in the 1950s and 1960s.

Capra-as-immigrant also emerged as an important component of Capra's popular reputation of the 1930s. Drawing upon myths deeply rooted in American culture, journalists circulated--with varying degrees of accuracy--tales concerning Capra's improbable rise to fame.

Biographical Background

His early years in the ghetto became the source material for stories of a bright, cocky ethnic kid beating the odds and getting an education. His years traveling around the West proved fertile for extravagant stories of his life on the road, simultaneously honing his skills as a huckster and getting to know rural and small-town America.[38] His extraordinary success in the film industry fit the popular notion that Hollywood was one of the last arenas in America where Cinderella or Horatio Alger fantasies might be fulfilled. "His stories cannot match his story," read the caption under Capra's photograph on the cover of Time in 1938, encapsulating a common cliché of commentary on Capra: that his biography was perhaps the most astonishing scenario of all.[39]

The immigrant success story so heavily promoted during this period contained within it an ambiguous aspect: on the one hand Capra was celebrated for the shrewdness and moxie that had lifted him out of the ghetto: on the other, for his common touch, his empathy with the plight of the common man. The ambiguity was perhaps essential to the rags-to-riches myth, in which the exemplary figure is typically cast as at once unique and ordinary. But in the case of Capra, it also raised the question of the director's allegiance to the subject matter of his fiction, of the authenticity of his "voice." Was Capra a folk-teller, expressing through a mass medium the frustrations and aspirations of the people from whom he had emerged? Or was he simply a savvy survivor who had risen to uncommon heights by divining the tastes of the people and telling them what they wanted to hear? Most articles suggested that he was something of both, although the approach to this paradox varied. In the pages of the New Yorker, the irony that a highly paid Hollywood director would find personal success in championing the poor and humble was not lost on Geoffrey T. Hellman, author of a somewhat patronizing profile on Capra in 1940.[40] Writers for middle-class publications, on the other hand, were more likely to play down any discrepancy between Capra's success and his bond with the average American, and indeed often presumed that bond to be the essential ingredient of that success. If Capra was the highest paid and most celebrated director working in Hollywood, Mary Hamman assured the readers of Good Housekeeping in 1941, he was "still essentially the Capra of the park bench, with his humanity, his sense of values, and his ideals intact."[41] Or, in a more sensationalistic vein, Alva Johnston, in his 1938 profile for the Saturday Evening Post, glorified Capra's years on the road as, on the one hand, the journeys of a "tin horn gambler and petty financial pirate" and, on the other, the mark of Capra's assimilation of grass-roots American values.[42]

Critics over the years have often used the concept of Capra-as-immigrant in a fashion not dissimilar to that of the popular journalists, although the larger question involved is typically not the personality of the successful immigrant so much as what his success suggests about social responses to the films. From this perspective, Capra-as-immigrant provides a convenient rationale for grounding sociological criticism in biographical detail, with Capra's background

Biographical Background

set forth as proof that the aspirations of the director were in some sense aligned with that of his audience. In some cases this has involved a flattening out of the possible ambiguities of the immigrant legend. Richard Griffith, for example, sets up his social reading of the films by noting that Capra's background had allowed him to "absorb" America's "psychological atmosphere more completely because he looks on it with an objective, therefore a visual, eye." Here the immigrant outsider's detachment (which curiously translates for Griffith into a special visual sense) becomes the very condition ensuring the complete internalization of the values he observes.[43] Jeffrey Richards offers a refinement of Griffith's premise when he proposes that Capra turned a "completely fresh eye" on the American scene and "distilled the quintessence of the American dream," a "national philosophy" he then embraces as his own. Moreover, by defining that dream as one and the same with the ideals of the middle class, Richards, like Griffith before him, can go on to treat Capra's films as direct, unmediated expressions of middle-class anxieties and fantasies, of a lingering attachment (in Richards's version of this sociological reading) to populist mythology at a time of social upheaval.[44]

Other critics, however, have emphasized the ambiguities in Capra's immigrant success story as a means of accounting for ambivalences or contradictions within the films. As an "immigrant starveling," Harold J. Salemson argues, Capra was aware of "social evils and wrongs" and was able to dramatize these in his works. Yet the "immigrant ragazzo up from poverty to Hollywood's fabulous luxuries" could not bring himself to endorse radical solutions to these problems and thus fell back on conventional panaceas, undermining the social power of his work.[45] Andrew Bergman, working with a somewhat more dynamic model, drafts from Capra's "erratic background" two personae--an innocent immigrant dreamer who works his way through college, and a traveling con man who hustles his way through rural America--and attributes the attractive quality of the films to the play between these polar selves. "Capra's comedy," Bergman thus proposes, "was a wide-eyed and affectionate hustle--the masterwork of an idealist and door-to-door salesman."[46] Charles Maland echoes this sentiment when he proposes Capra gave expression in his films to the contrary pull in American culture between "individual achievement and moral responsibility to others."[47]

Capra-the-immigrant plays no less a role in The Name Above the Title, where the protagonist's ambition to escape the ghetto and make his mark on the world dominates the first half of the saga. Featured as well in this narrative is a drama between an immigrant hustler and an immigrant dreamer, with the drama turning on the events of 1935 and the director's discovery of a social purpose. Capra's autobiography can thus be read as a maturation plot in which Capra-as-immigrant eventually gives way to Capra-as-author. ("You may also sense a story," Capra writes in his preface. "A cheap, egotistical punk grows into a man.")[48] For Capra-as-immigrant, the struggle for directorial autonomy is simply a struggle for recognition, with the director as

Biographical Background

consummate showman, able to "juggle many balls in the air," and success itself the very content of his work. For Capra-as-author, directorial autonomy is a claim to a voice, a voice that in turn can only be authenticated by the audience for whom--as well as to whom--it speaks. That audience--and that voice--is wholly "American." The migratory youth thus acquires a home and a social philosophy.

The danger of criticism built on these biographical constructions is that the constructions themselves can be taken as empirical fact, as fully explanatory and determining in accounting for the films, with the autobiography serving as a master code to their "true" meaning. But if allusions to biographical details have persisted in Capra criticism during the past decade--during which time, at least in academic circles, the practice of biographical criticism has been held in general disdain--it is perhaps because of an intuition that this particular biography, no less than the films attached to his name, can yield up an insight into the inner workings of American ideology in the first half of the twentieth century. Capra's biography--or better yet, biographies--invite a consideration of the broader cultural context in which they have been written. Capra-as-immigrant becomes the figure (in the sense both of "character" and "metaphor") through which Capra-as-author (a precondition of looking to the biography for clues in the first place) assumes a social dimension, and cultural patterns can be charted. Here biography must be understood not as the key to the films, establishing a closed circuit of exchange between "work" and "author," but as a complementary text that can help situate the works along a historical axis, illuminating distortions, displacements, and omissions as well as simple correspondences. If for no other reason than this, the time for a full-scale Capra biography is long overdue.

Notes

1. Profiles of Capra in the 1930s often featured extravagant accounts of this period on the road, but Capra in his autobiography covers it in a single sentence. He confirmed the activities I list here, however, in my interview with him on 23 July 1981.

2. It has often been falsely reported that Capra worked as an extra on Harry Carey westerns on location in northern California and at Universal in Los Angeles, and as a writer at Columbia before joining Mack Sennett. These appear to be traceable to a highly inaccurate biographical sketch of Capra by Jim Tully in 1937 (see entry 339).

3. According to Capra, he was fired by Langdon following a disagreement over the script for their next project, and his agent countered subsequent attacks by Langdon in the press with a publicity campaign that did little to revive Capra's young career (interview with author, 24 July 1981). After he had become successful in the 1930s, Capra was indirectly accused of harming Langdon's career

Biographical Background

through this counterattack. See Katharine Albert, "What Happened to Harry Langdon" (entry 139).

4. Upon his return from New York, Capra was also served with divorce papers, ending a four-year marriage to Helen Howell, an actress whom he had met on the set of Eric von Stroheim's Greed in San Francisco in 1923.

5. See Edward Buscombe, "Notes on Columbia Pictures Corporation 1926-41," pp. 75-76 (entry 962); Bob Thomas, King Cohn, pp. 53-57 (entry 784). By 1932 Columbia was regarded as the largest of the independents and was making a bid for major status. To ensure first-run markets for its films, deals were struck with R-K-O and Warners (theater-owning majors), and ambitious production schedules were announced. See "Studios Demand More Hokum," New York Times, 3 January 1932; sec. 10, p. 5; "Notes from Hollywood Studios," New York Times, 7 August 1932, sec. 10, p. 3.

6. Daily Variety, 1 January 1935, p. 36.

7. Otis Ferguson: "Every turn of a familiar plot has had a certain alchemy practiced on it" ("Frank Capra's Latest," entry 214). Andre Sennwald: "Somehow no scene which he photographs is quite ordinary" ("The Screen," entry 210). For a "fanzine" approach to the notion of Capra as a "modern Merlin," see Kirtley Baskette's "Hollywood's New Miracle Man" (entry 188).

8. The Los Angeles Times did report in December 1934 that Capra had suffered a relapse following an appendicitis operation and had been rehospitalized, but this would have been prior to the Academy Award ceremonies in which It Happened One Night swept the Oscars ("Capra to Work at Palm Springs," Los Angeles Times, 5 December 1934, sec. 1, p. 19). The specific chronology of events during this period is somewhat vague in Capra's autobiography.

9. Capra, "A Sick Dog Tells Where It Hurts," pp. 87, 130 (entry 1161).

10. Capra, The Name Above the Title, p. 185 (entry 1176).

11. In his autobiography Capra suggests that the fraudulent use of his name was the sole issue in this case, but reports at the time indicated that a salary dispute was also involved. Capra's lawsuit in September 1937 allegedly claimed that Columbia owed him $100,000 in salary, and that he had notified the studio that he considered his contract terminated on 16 February 1937. The false use of his name on If You Could Only Cook was introduced as further evidence of breach of contract. According to Bob Thomas in King Cohn, Capra's anger at Cohn originally stemmed from his decision not to pay Capra any salary after he completed Lost Horizon on the grounds that Capra had spent too much time on the film and had not yet begun work on another. The February date cited in the lawsuit would corroborate this, as it precedes by a

Biographical Background

month the long-delayed release of <u>Lost Horizon</u>, which had cost Columbia $2 million. See "Release, $100,000 Sought by Capra," <u>Motion Picture Herald</u>, 14 September 1937, p. 34; Thomas, <u>King Cohn</u>, p. 124 (entry 784).

12. Bosley Crowther, "Such Guys as Capra and Wellman," <u>New York Times</u>, 17 October 1938, sec. 9, p. 5.

13. The financing from the Bank of America is particularly interesting in light of the fact that the bank's president, A.P. Giannini, was an early financier of Columbia Pictures and, according to Capra, the figure upon whom the character of Tom Dickson in <u>American Madness</u> was based. See Capra's interview with Richard Glatzer (entry 1286). Information concerning the contract with Warners comes from the Warner Brothers-Burbank files on <u>Meet John Doe</u>, held by the Special Collections Department, University of Southern California.

14. Capra, <u>The Name Above the Title</u>, pp. 86, 161 (entry 1176).

15. It was originally rumored that A.H. Giannini (brother of A.P. Giannini—see note 12) would finance the Capra-Riskin partnership with United Artists handling the distribution of the films, but no deal with Capra was ever struck. UA stockholders Mary Pickford, Douglas Fairbanks, and Alexander Korda also tried to lure Capra and Riskin into a partnership in 1939, but a lawsuit by the departing Samuel Goldwyn blocked their efforts. Following the release of <u>Meet John Doe</u> in 1941, Selznick and Capra jointly negotiated with UA for acquisition of Fairbanks's stock under a plan whereby each of the newcomers would have equal control along with Pickford, Korda, and Charles Chaplin. Capra pulled out after several months of negotiations, however, claiming that too many people other than the partners had become involved in the talks and that tax problems related to the deal had not been resolved. See <u>Variety</u>, 21 June 1939; <u>Variety</u>, 20 August 1941; Douglas W. Churchill, "News of the Screen," <u>New York Times</u>, 14 June 1941, p. 17; Churchill, "Murder in Hollywood," <u>New York Times</u>, 9 November 1941, sec. 10, p. 5; Tino Balio, <u>United Artists</u> (Madison: University of Wisconsin Press, 1976), pp. 176-77, 182.

16. Warners worked especially hard to sign Capra, offering him $250,000 for each film he produced and directed and $50,000 for each additional film he produced only. The contract also would have given him freedom in selecting script material, as long as the properties were not "of a political or controversial nature." Capra never signed. See the Warner Brothers-Burbank production files of <u>Arsenic and Old Lace</u>, Special Collections, University of Southern California.

17. Capra interview with George Bailey, "Why We (Should Not) Fight," pp. 10-12 (entry 1284); Capra interview with Walter Karp, "The Patriotism of Frank Capra," p. 35 (entry 1307).

18. Capra says in his autobiography that possibilities for independent productions had dried up by the time of his return from the army

Biographical Background

(The Name Above the Title, pp. 371-72, entry 1176), but actually, within the industry at large, they had increased. See Janet Staiger, "Individualism versus Collectivism," Screen, 24, Nos. 4-5 (July-October 1983), 70-73.

19. Thomas Brady, "Unrest in Hollywood," New York Times, 20 June 1946, sec. 2, p. 3.

20. Capra, "Breaking Hollywood's 'Pattern of Sameness'" (entry 1168).

21. See my article, "The Return of Jimmy Stewart: The Publicity Photograph as Text," Wide Angle, 6, No. 4 (1984).

22. Thomas M. Pryor, "Sounds of Alarm," New York Times, 26 January 1947, sec. 2, p. 5; "The Price of Liberty," Time, 26 May 1947, p. 88; Thomas F. Brady, "Hollywood Agenda," New York Times, 8 April 1951, sec. 2, p. 5.

23. Brady, "Hollywood Agenda," p. 5.

24. Capra married Lucille Warner Reyburn in 1932, the second marriage for both, and one that endured until Lucille Capra's death in July 1984. Their children include Frank, Jr. (born 1934), a motion picture producer and past president of Avco Embassy Pictures, Lulu (born 1937), a professor of literature and philosophy at Michigan State University; and Tom (born 1941), a vice president of the Satellite News Channel. A fourth child, John, died at the age of three in 1938.

25. Los Angeles Times, 25 November 1953, p. 15.

26. For Capra on the footage from the Soviet Union, see his interview with John F. Mariani (entry 1298). For Capra's defense of State of the Union against accusations that it was "leftist" while still in production, see his 1947 interview with Philip K. Scheuer, "'State of the Union' to Pace Election" (entry 1125). W.R. Burnett reported on Capra's support of blacklisted screenwriters in Ken Mate and Pat McGilligan's "Burnett," Film Comment, February 1983, p. 65.

27. Capra interview with Arthur Bressan and Michael Moran, "Mr. Capra Goes to College," p. 26 (entry 1275); Capra interview with James Childs, "Capra Today," p. 23 (entry 1276); Capra interview with George Bailey, "Why We (Should Not) Fight," pp. 11-12 (entry 1284).

28. New York Times, 16 April 1936, p. 19.

29. See, for example, "All Over the Lot" (entry 219); "$2,000,000 Worth of Scenes from Lost Horizon" (entry 236); James Reid, "Lost Horizon--Facts about a Fantasy" (entry 268); W.T. Borden, "Frank Capra of the Cinema," (entry 303); Harrison Forman, "The Hollywood Star You Never See on the Screen" (entry 318); and Michael Orme, "The World of the Kinema" (entry 334).

Biographical Background

30. Alva Johnston, "Capra Shoots as He Pleases" (entry 378).

31. "Columbia's Gem" (entry 343).

32. "Movie of the Week: You Can't Take It with You" (entry 349).

33. Howard Barnes, "The Screen" (entry 363).

34. Graham Greene, "The Cinema" (entry 251).

35. See Capra's 1939 letter to the New York Times, "By Post from Mr. Capra" (entry 1165).

36. Thomas M. Pryor, "Sounds of Alarm," New York Times, 26 January 1947, sec. 2, p. 5.

37. Capra wrote in the French journal Cinémonde in 1946: "While mass production by the major movie companies usually gives standardized results, the individual system of creation by independent producers permit them to imprint a personal stamp on each of their works. From this great variety of subjects and styles it will follow that a film directed in the city of 'stars' will not always be strictly a Hollywood product, but rather an 'American' film made in Hollywood, which is very different. The nuance is important" (my translation). See "Il faut un film avant de la commercer" (entries 1169, #1180).

38. See especially Alva Johnston's "Capra Shoots as He Pleases" (entry 378).

39. Time cover, 8 August 1938.

40. Geoffrey T. Hellman, "Thinker in Hollywood" (entry 432).

41. Mary Hamman, "Meet Frank Capra Making a Picture" (entry 467).

42. Alva Johnston, "Capra Shoots as He Pleases" (entry 378).

43. Richard Griffith in Paul Rotha's The Film Till Now, p. 440 (entry 630), and Griffith's Frank Capra, p. 3 (entry 649).

44. Jeffrey Richards, "Frank Capra and the Cinema of Populism," pp. 22-23 (entry 806).

45. Harold J. Salemson, "Mr. Capra's Short Cuts to Utopia," pp. 25-34 (entry 623).

46. Andrew Bergman, We're in the Money, pp. 134-35 (entry 816).

47. Charles Maland, Frank Capra, p. 182 (entry 1128).

48. Capra, The Name Above the Title, p. xi (entry 1176).

II. Critical Survey

The films of Frank Capra have come to represent in popular culture a particular view of American life: comic, optimistic, and sentimental; celebrating the vitality, ingenuity, and sound instincts of the common man; prescribing small-town good neighborliness as an antidote to the greed, ostentation, and atrophied moral sensibility of urban elites. Longfellow Deeds and Jefferson Smith are often cited as American archetypes: idealistic young men from the countryside, naive to the ways of the city, but roused to do battle against corrupt powerbrokers and restore the lost faith of the cynical. Capra's films are routinely described as fables of social mobility and community, fictions that eased America through the upheavals of the Great Depression and entry into World War II and then fell out of fashion amid the cynicism of the postwar period. Popular commentaries may differ as to whether the films rekindled essential American values or countered genuine social ailments with simplistic--even dangerous--bromides, but a therapeutic model for their aesthetic function is generally assumed without further scrutiny.

Much of the critical literature on Capra over the past two decades, however, has cast the films in a different light, one that illuminates a skepticism behind the comedy, a pessimism behind the sentiment. Stress has been placed on the suffering and suicidal bent of the central characters; on the restless and volatile mobs populating the backdrop to the stories; on the depiction of a vast media network of seemingly unlimited power; on abrupt shifts in mood; on a sense of irresolution clouding endings that are presumably "happy." Some of this criticism has carried with it a polemical charge, a conscious attack on the shibboleths of Capra commentary. But the notion that Capra's work is in need of rethinking has also been evident in criticism that simply assumes that the operation of the films is not a simple process and the values they trade in are somewhat ambiguous. Even those critics who have taken the comic thrust of Capra's work as its defining trait typically call attention to a disquieting aspect that, if not wholly negating the quality of affirmation for which the films are more familiarly known, constitutes at the very least a compelling countertheme.

Capra's films first attracted critical attention in the 1930s, it is interesting to note, not for their subject matter but for their style. "The Capra touch"—a commonplace term by mid-decade—conceptualized the relation between Capra and the actors and action as primarily tactile, the trace of which could be found in idiosyncratic gestures, bits of business, minor details. The story material behind It Happened One Night and Broadway Bill, many reviewers observed at the time, was not unique; what seemed to distinguish the films was Capra's treatment of this material: the behavioral charm of his actors, deft pacing, and a tone that was at once casual and vibrant. For a critic like Otis Ferguson (who cut his teeth as a film reviewer during the year these two films were released), Capra's work suggested the degree to which movies of the sound era were at their best a director's medium, demonstrating how a facility with incidental action, with inflection and timing, might mark the triumph of the popular art of movies over literary sources.[1] Perhaps the most eloquent and original of Capra's early defenders, Ferguson (who was also a jazz critic) used musical metaphors to describe the effect, praising Capra's direction of It Happened One Night for its "phrasing," its "smoothness of technical attack," and "a precision and instinct for where the swing of words or of the body should be" that made everything "natural and irresistible."[2] A few years later, surveying American film comedy of the 1930s from the vantage point of the early 1940s, Ferguson described Capra's particular skill as a "trick of building a whole thing out of little ordinary things, all caught in the shifting eye of the camera . . . and all joined to make a pattern of life as we all know it."[3]

But by this time Ferguson was waxing nostalgic, for Capra's reputation was now primarily that of a director willing to tackle "big themes." During the course of the late thirties, the tables gradually had turned on the earlier assessment of Capra as unassuming comic stylist. That Lost Horizon and You Can't Take It with You were adapted from celebrated literary works made the question of Capra's subject matter somewhat more pressing; that they were also utopian fantasies, depicting ideal societies overseen by benevolent patriarchs, made the question of Capra's own "philosophy of life" seem relevant as well. With each film in the Deeds-Smith-Doe trilogy, moreover, topical social problems were pushed further into the foreground; if the intrusion of a dispossessed farmer in Mr. Deeds Goes to Town had come fairly late in the drama, political corruption in government was central to Mr. Smith Goes to Washington from the outset, and the depiction of American fascism in Meet John Doe seemed to leave little room for analysis of the "Capra touch."

Critical reaction to this change in Capra's work varied. Ferguson and Alistair Cooke (who worried in his review of Mr. Deeds that Capra was "starting to make movies about themes instead of about people,")[4] were greatly dismayed that Capra had sought to sail the high seas of social philosophizing.[5] Most others were sympathetic, although occasionally they expressed concern that Capra played more to emotion than logic. Sidney Meyers[6] and Irving Lerner,[7] writing from the political Left, praised the introduction of social issues in films like Mr. Deeds, but registered alarm at what they thought was a dangerous fascination with spectacle and escape in Lost Horizon. Meet John Doe occasioned critics from various quarters to laud the film for its social frankness, but many questioned the tensile strength of what by now appeared to be a Capra formula--as seen in the Deeds-Smith-Doe trilogy--to support a topic of this kind, and almost all were dissatisfied with the ending. Capra critics tended to be respectful, but ambivalent; responding to the films as they appeared year by year, reviewers rarely presented--either individually or as a composite group--a clear critical line on Capra's work overall.[8]

After World War II, however, Richard Griffith set forth a historical overview that was to greatly influence Capra commentary to follow. In a section on Capra for Paul Rotha's The Film Till Now in 1949 (reprinted in slightly modified form as the introduction to a monograph on Capra for the British Film Institute a year later), Griffith proposed that although Capra was a filmmaker of economy and forcefulness, his claim to "significant popularity" resided in his "temperamental affinity to the middle-class outlook." Capra's films summoned up a "fantasy of goodwill"--a dream of America as a great small town, free of class identities--which he had absorbed from the work of middle-class writers like Damon Runyon and Clarence Budington Kelland (whose short stories had been the basis for Lady for a Day and Mr. Deeds Goes to Town). On the one hand, Griffith argued, Capra's films had depicted the social crisis of the prewar years with "striking naturalism"; on the other they had offered a fantastic solution: the arrival of a messianic innocent who evokes the "goodwill" of the people and triumphs. "Such a blend of realistic problem and imaginary solution," Griffith concluded, "epitomised the dilemma of the middle-class mind in the New Deal period."[9]

Working from a postwar critical perspective that was sociological and realist, Griffith simplified matters in three related ways. First, he isolated discussion of Capra's style, of his mastery of the medium of motion pictures, from the matter of the director's "significant popularity." Griffith thought Capra (for whom he had worked on the Why We Fight series as a research assistant) possessed a talent as an editor that rivaled that of D.W. Griffith or Sergei Eisenstein, and he expressed hope that intellectuals would come to appreciate this aspect of Capra's work, but he centered his interpretation of the films on the literary model he was certain Capra had drawn on. Second, Griffith's interpretation gave priority to how dramatic crises were resolved. For the average spectator, the social dilemma the films first posed purportedly dissolved under the spell of the fantasy; if the intellectual critic had doubts about the logic of these resolutions, none was imagined to be had by the middle-class viewer anxious to be free of all "realistic" thought. The use of the term fantasy in this context suggested rosy evasion, baseless optimism. Third, at a time when the 1930s were receding into history and Capra's career as a filmmaker seemed on the wane, Griffith offered a cultural reading of the films that framed them within the context of the New

Deal. It turned Capra's films into quaint historical objects. Small wonder then that cultural historians, as well as many historians of film, frequently fell back on Griffith's analysis. It provided a theory as to why Capra's career had risen and fallen, gave it a clear shape, and a catchphrase--"fantasy of goodwill"--to signal the place of the films in the museum of popular culture.

But film critics soon found other ways to talk about Capra's work, approaches that often gave precedence to precisely those elements Griffith had factored out. Indeed, the gap between popular commentary on Capra and critical analysis can in part be attributed to these changes in critical methods, in the ways in which films--most importantly films from the "classical" Hollywood period--have been conceptualized as objects of study. As Capra's films have been revived and made available for close scrutiny, new critical writing has thus opened them up to different kinds of readings.

Crucial in this regard has been the influence of auteur criticism. Capra was not included among the first cluster of Hollywood directors singled out by auteur critics in France, America, and England for special attention, in part perhaps because no battles needed to be fought concerning his authorial status, in part also (if the early commentary of Andrew Sarris is a guide) because of the films' reputation as sociological curiosities, dated fantasies from the thirties.[10] But in scattered pieces in the 1960s and an outpouring of criticism in the 1970s, auteurist appraisals of Capra challenged this interpretation. By divorcing the question of the "personality" of the director from the sociology of the audience, critics no longer felt obliged to justify the trajectory of Capra's popularity and looked for other patterns instead.

They found, for example, a trail of autobiographical clues in the films. As I have discussed in the previous section, critics from the 1930s on often turned to biographical detail in discussing Capra's work, but always in terms of Capra's affinity with or deviation from the popular audience, as a means of anchoring sociological analysis in the social milieu of the author. Auteur critics, on the other hand, looked for a hidden subtext, a personal dimension the popular audience was unlikely to notice. Thus in 1962, at a time when many reviewers were treating Pocketful of Miracles as a period piece from another age, Steven P. Hill analyzed the film closely in terms of the kind of self-referential details and intertextual allusions that auteurists were boldly deciphering in the late films of Alfred Hitchcock, Howard Hawks, and John Ford, and claimed that in a "symbolic, perhaps unconscious way" Pocketful was as autobiographical as the work of the Italian director Federico Fellini.[11] The publication of The Name Above the Title in 1971 clearly helped to fuel speculation of this kind. With its dramatizations of the emotional peaks and valleys of Capra's life, with its confessions of ambition, humiliation, and guilt, the book encouraged critics to treat the wild turns in the fate of Capra's protagonists, and their recurring admissions of failure or blame, as privileged elements, as private disclosures by the director.

Critical Survey

Stephen Handzo, for example, offered autobiographical readings of <u>Mr. Smith Goes to Washington</u> and <u>It's a Wonderful Life</u>, and made a related point concerning <u>State of the Union</u> simply by placing the confession of Grant Matthews at the close of that film side by side with a similar confession by Capra at the close of <u>The Name Above the Title</u>.[12] In more recent years, Richard T. Jameson has made a case for <u>Ladies of Leisure</u> as a metacommentary on Capra's relationship with Barbara Stanwyck,[13] and Richard Glatzer (among others) has reread <u>Meet John Doe</u> as an autocritique, as an assertion of Capra's private doubts about the populist symbol making of his previous films.[14]

Auteur critics, moreover, refocused attention on matters of style, on the director's "handprint," the Capra "touch" that had been dropped from critical discussion at an early moment. Writing of <u>Mr. Deeds Goes to Town</u>, Stephen Handzo asserted that "surely, the face of Gary Cooper and <u>voice</u> of Jean Arthur are the film's real content," and surveyed Capra's improvisational acting, his atmospheric lighting, his deployment of editing techniques like the reaction shot.[15] Of the same film, Jean-Loup Bourget proposed that Capra's politics resided, at least in part, in directorial and camera strategies that, whatever the rhetorical statements contained in the script, emphasized spontaneous behavior within a collective context.[16] Indeed, as early as 1962, William S. Pechter challenged Richard Griffith's isolation of the topic with the following analysis:

> [Capra's] films move at a breath-taking clip: dynamic, driving, taut, at their extreme even hysterical; the unrelenting, frantic acceleration of pace seems to spring from the release of some tremendous accumulation of pressure. The sheer speed and energy seem, finally, less calculated than desperate, as though Capra were aware, on some level, of the tension established between his material and what he attempts to make of it. Desperation--in this quality of Capra's films one sees again the fundamental nature of <u>style</u> <u>as</u> <u>moral</u> <u>action</u>; Capra's desperation is his final honesty. It ruthlessly exposes his own affirmation as pretense, and reveals, recklessly and without defense, dilemma. (emphasis mine)[17]

Here Pechter assumed the possibility of a counterpuntal relationship between author and subject: the style of a film might now be read as cutting across, even working against, the narrative line, undermining the scenario of the "fantasy of goodwill" Capra had borrowed from popular fiction. Capra's use of the convention of the happy ending, Pechter claimed, seemed perfunctory, its tone at odds with the rest of the work; what endured instead were indelible images of greed, corruption, manipulation, and the frustrations of small-town American life. Was this Capra's intention? Probably not, Pechter thought, but the very style of the films betrayed a gulf between intention and final result. Pechter accepted Griffith's conclusion that in Capra's work realistic social observation abutted fantasy and that the convention of the happy ending, for the critical observer, at times seemed insufficiently motivated. But Pechter turned Griffith's argument on its

head: the gaps the alert viewer could detect between the imagery of
"American madness" and the rhetorical assertions of optimism, between
narrative impasse and a whirlwind path to a comic closure, were now to
be read as evidence not of wishful thinking but of ambivalence or
irony, above all, as honesty.

Auteur critics also tended to place new weight on quiet passages,
those charged by eroticism or melancholy rather than those involving a
broader social portrait. With the gradual revival of many of Capra's
early works--romantic comedies and melodramas--during the course of
the 1970s, some critics began to mount an alternative canon, with the
early work greatly favored over that of Capra's "socially conscious"
period. But this revival also prompted a reassessment of the later
films as well, an interest in those moments of romance and despair
that frequently punctuated, and flavored, the topical projects. The
rediscovery of Capra's work in France during the 1970s owed much to
this line of inquiry: surveying that reassessment in 1978, Claude
Beylie proposed that the "smoothing optimism" attributed to Capra
concealed another figure whose true register was perhaps romanticism
"sustained through a sparkling, sculpted mise-en scène," comedies
"infiltrated by purely tragic motifs," and argued his case with a
discussion of The Miracle Woman, The Bitter Tea of General Yen, and
State of the Union.[18] The "authentic" Capra that auteurists sought to
identify was more likely to be somber and confessional than exuberant
and optimistic. Darker moments were no longer treated as scenes of
dramatic convenience--a way of intensifying the sense of relief comic
closure would provide--but as projections of the director's own hesi-
tations and qualms. "It is in the moments where he finds himself
completely helpless before a state of affairs that he secretly knows
cannot be repaired," wrote Olivier Eyquem in 1974, "that Capra speaks
to us most sincerely and most truly."[19]

There was a cultist side to this, as critics of auteurism (and
even avid practitioners) frequently noted--a hint of revelation, of
the discovery of an unheralded voice from the shadows of the screen.
But there was a more radical implication as well: that there might be
in fact more than one "Capra," each the construction of the spectator-
critic working with the film, a function of contemporary predispo-
sition and available critical method. To the extent that auteurist
readings were set forth as alternative rather than fixed interpretations, criticism was opened up rather than closed off. By placing
the films within a new context (the auteur's complete body of work)
and positing the existence of subtexts (detectable in autobiographical
allusion, in style), auteurists broke with the sociological framework
of postwar criticism of Capra. Ahistorical in its thrust, criticism
of this kind nevertheless redressed the tendency of previous Capra
commentary to bind the "essential Capra" within a limited time frame
and corpus where the social import of his work could be more unproble-
matically drawn, where it could be cited as an illustration of thirties America, legible at a glance.

Moreover, the crossbreeding of auteurism and genre criticism--under the rubric of what was often termed "structuralism"--set the stage in the 1970s for the return of the popular audience as a concept important to film analysis. Here the director was taken not as a biographical figure but as a "structure" to be mapped from those films bearing his name, a structure that in turn took on meaning only in relation to an understanding of the generic formulas with which he worked. The formulas themselves were understood as complex, having been drawn into shape to accommodate various sets of antinomies; their longevity, their enduring popularity, was considered a symptom not of banality but of the potential richness of the structure, its capacity to engage and contain deeply rooted tensions in culture. Formulas functioned as a grammar shared by audience and author, as the very grounds for communication between these two entities.

In certain instances, the social complexion of that audience was left undefined. Indeed, in the most elaborately developed study of Capra in the structural-auteurist mode--Leland Poague's The Cinema of Frank Capra--the audience was broad enough to subsume all of Western civilization. The conventions bequeathed Capra were nothing less than the comic mythos that Northrop Frye had charted for the history of literature. Thus Poague was able to bypass the specific contingencies not only of the 1930s but of American culture in its broadest sense; to the extent the films shared in Frye's comic mythos--an unending struggle between the forces of sterility and fertility--they could be seen as "natural" forms, given "realistic" expression through a photographic medium.[20] Other critics, however, worked with a less abstract notion of genre and audience, with the social ground for popular culture in the twentieth century, and specifically for Hollywood genres. In the case of Capra, this typically included forms of comedy: romantic, domestic, screwball. Attention shifted away from the topical political issues of the Deeds-Smith-Doe trilogy, only to locate the "deeper" ideology of heterosexual romance, marriage, and family.[21] Robin Wood imported the notion of deep structure, for example, as a way of establishing a background set of unresolvable tensions (contradictions, then, not just antinomies) manifest in film genres and in the works of different directors within those genres. By contrasting It's a Wonderful Life with John Ford's My Darling Clementine, Wood sought to define both the points of connection and the boundary lines in the series "Ideology/Genre/Auteur."[22]

Meanwhile, cultural readings of Capra's work had been developing along another front--that of American studies. Here scholars and critics had been attracted to Capra's films as artifacts and sought to situate them within indigenous American traditions. Thus patterns of social relationships in the films were linked to the political culture of populism (Jeffrey Richards).[23] The folk heroes of the Deeds-Smith-Doe trilogy were matched against various American archetypes: the Yankee hero (Wes D. Gehring),[24] the "genteel" hero (Robert Sklar),[25] the Jeffersonian yeoman farmer crossbred with Tom Sawyer (John Raeburn).[26] Rhetorical modes were linked to an American pessimistic jeremiad followed by a reaffirmation of middle-class values (Charles

Maland).[27] In a certain sense this line of inquiry was indebted to Richard Griffith's analysis; indeed in the case of Richard's discussion of populism the link to Griffith was clearly drawn. But these critics widened the framework of their analysis beyond the sociology of the depression to encompass long-range patterns in American culture. By speaking not of "fantasy" but of "folklore" or "myth," the films were no longer conceptualized as quick fixes aimed at soothing depression anxieties, but as variations on a complex ritual. Verisimilitude, which had been a central concern of both the stylistic criticism of Ferguson and the sociological criticism of Griffith, was not an issue here. Fictions were not presumed to either reflect or evade social reality, but to give it symbolic form.

It has not been until recently, however, that the symbol-making function of the "classical" cinema--its specific characteristics as a representational and discursive system--has been incorporated into this kind of analysis. Cultural critics had tended either to ignore the film medium--as if symbols were transmitted through but not transformed by it--or to treat the cinematic as a set of techniques at the disposal of the director to enhance "content." Latent in the auteurist concern for style as content, as a producer of meaning, was another model for analyzing the film text. Integrating in various combinations the critical vocabularies of semiology, narratology, rhetoric, and psychoanalysis, critics have singled out several of Capra's more famous works for close analysis. Steve Neale, for example, has examined how Populist political positions are inscribed within the system of address of "classical" texts like the Deeds-Smith diptych,[28] and Kaja Silverman has traced patterns of male subjectivity in It's a Wonderful Life through the "interpellation" (after Louis Althusser) of both character and viewer within a "celestial suture" (after Jacques Lacan).[29] Speech, the "democratic voice" from the screen, in Mr. Smith Goes to Washington, has been the topic of detailed studies by Nick Browne[30] and Charles Affron[31] in attempts to define the relationship between political and cinematic "representation," and the process by which "dead" political texts are made to seem "present," brought to "life." Browne also has returned to the question of authorship--and implicitly the auteurist notion of an autocritique--reading Mr. Smith as in part an allegory of Capra's contradictory desire to speak with his own voice through a media apparatus, of his self-perceived democratic martyrdom. Similarly Dudley Andrew has closely examined how Capra's effort to speak "independently" as the author of Meet John Doe is echoed in the film across two registers: in the plot, in which John seeks to speak authentically and autonomously within a media network, and discursively in an allegory of narration involving the film's implied author and the various subvoices (montage specialist Slavko Vorkapich, the various actors) this narrator must control.[32]

Much of this new critical work, as these brief synopses suggest, draws heavily on previous interpretations of the films--on Capra as author, on populist political culture, on Christian mythology and comic form--but treats these as part of the play of various discourses

Critical Survey

within the unfolding text rather than as the ground upon which the "meaning" of the text resides. Meaning becomes a function of shifting positions made available to the spectator by the text in coordination with other contextual discourses. For Browne and Andrew, "Capra" is one of these contextual elements--not necessarily the center of the text, but always seeking to center it.

To the extent that films like Mr. Deeds and Mr. Smith now hold a privileged position in the history of cinema as exemplars of both political symbol making and classical Hollywood style, they are likely candidates for an analysis in which ideological and textual questions converge. Perhaps more revealing of how critical priorities have changed since the late 1940s, however, has been the new emphasis placed on Meet John Doe and It's a Wonderful Life, films that under the sociological and realist model of Griffith were considered key evidence of Capra's failure as a director to deal plausibly with social reality. Indeed, it is precisely those elements with which earlier critics found fault--the unresolved contradiction in Doe between the necessity and invariable corruption of symbol-making activities (like politics) in the age of advanced media systems; the recourse to a "celestial" narrator and narrational agent (an angel no less) in Wonderful Life to resolve the problems of mortals--that recent critics have found most interesting, for they provide the grounds for an oblique interrogation of representation and enunciation in cinema. The protagonist's ambivalent identity in Meet John Doe (as authentic folk hero or fake) is not simply treated as a problem of John's moral "character," but as touching on the more basic question of "character construction" within the fiction--the agglomeration of traits around a figure--through "scriptwriting" and "directing" (by Ann Mitchell), through "producing" (by mogul D.B. Norton), and through the technology of photography and media broadcasting. The crisis of representation on which the film ends (John's silence, the desperate attempt of Ann and the John Doe Club members to "speak their piece" in his presence to forestall his suicide) is in a sense taken up at the beginning of It's a Wonderful Life where another Capra hero on another Christmas Eve is about to leap to his death. The metaphor for cinema in the later film, however, is not the contemporary media but a divine "medium," a heavenly viewfinder and voice-over narrator through which and through whom the "biography" of a character is constructed, and a heavenly agent who can become flesh on earth and unleash an expressionist nightmare which compels that character to claim his "life" fully as his own. From this perspective, the observation by earlier critics that Wonderful Life resorts to a deus ex machina needs to be applied somewhat differently. It is not the sudden or unexpected quality of celestial intervention that makes this term apt--heavenly forces do not appear at the last moment, but provide a narrational frame from the outset, a teleology for the telling of the tale--but rather its suggestion that this intervention is negotiated through a mechanical support, the machine of cinema. Perhaps, in this instance, a deus in machina.

Critical Survey

Where does this leave a Capra critic today? In a position, I think, to undertake a rereading of Capra's entire body of work—from the low-budget, silent films at the beginning of the career to a Panavision, Eastmancolor costume drama at the close—a rereading aimed not at introducing into the critical literature yet another, more authentic "Capra" but at isolating and identifying the specific functions of the director's "authorial voice" within (a) changing conditions of production, and (b) changing conventions and discursive strategies of the classical Hollywood film. This would involve, for the first time, a systematic investigation of the silent and early sound work, for it is here that we will be able to trace Capra's negotiation of the transitional stages toward a fully vocal cinema, those first attempts to marry the discrete components of an image and sound track, and to locate rhetorical strategies that inscribe the spectator/auditor within the constructed unity of a sonic as well as a visual space. It will require a more detailed account of Capra's pre-Production Code comedies and melodramas—and those more eccentric projects like Rain or Shine that seem to oscillate between the two genres—where sexuality and spectacle were often intertwined. It will benefit greatly from closer scrutiny of the wartime documentaries—which Meet John Doe and It's a Wonderful Life bracket—where the guarantee of unity is located not at the level of any legible diegesis, but with the voice-over narration that at once plays off and oversees the flood of disparate images and invites the spectator to occupy its own centering position through the use of the collective "we." It will be illuminated by a study of the altered context of production, distribution, and exhibition during the forties and fifties: the relationship between Hollywood and Washington, interaction with radio and television, and the changing demographics of the audience, an entity Capra had always taken as "the people," without further discrimination.

Through all these shifts and changes, I suspect, we will also come to a clearer notion of what seems to me the central thrust of Capra's work as a director: an ongoing effort to render through cinema the experience of an "authentic" moment for the spectator, an effort implicitly (and on occasion explicitly) contradicted by the very conditions of mediation—the institutional structures of the industry, the material processes of cinema—that made Capra's work possible. It is this search for authenticity and immediacy that underlines Capra's satire of the rich and his celebration of the "democratic" hero, that informs the desires of the protagonists of the romances and melodramas and the alienated "common people" in Meet John Doe. It allows most of the films to assume something of the air of a spiritual quest, even if that quest in some instances seems closer to the ridiculous than the sublime. It is a sentiment with certain appeal in an age that saw the expansion of corporate capitalism, of rationalized labor and hierarchical managerial bureaucracies, and the secularization of culture. But to think of the films simply in therapeutic terms (even if we assume the anxieties to run deeper than those prompted by the Great Depression) is to miss their disturbances, their unsettling moments, and their nagging paradoxes. Immediacy within a highly mediated system: the political films simply push to the foreground the contradiction posed by Capra's work overall. If this dilemma now seems most compelling, it is perhaps because in the modern age its traps have become even more intricate than those designed by D.B. Norton, the media magnate turned putative dictator in Meet John Doe.

With this in mind, the question of Capra's relative optimism or pessimism--alternative assessments that have appeared to satisfy the purposes of different observers at different times--might be reposed so as to account for an ongoing tension within the work between different dramatic modes (comedy and melodrama) and stylistic strategies (transparency and artifice). On the one hand, there is that "natural" comic style of which a critic like Ferguson was so fond, constructed through the behavior of the actors--their spontaneity, offbeat humor, digressive quality--but also through strategies of effacement (continuity editing, lip-synchonized sound, a "natural" mise-en-scène), through the construction of an experience of unity and community in which the psychical and social barriers to the "pursuit of happiness" are dissolved. On the other hand, there is the broad streak of melodrama--disillusionment, martyrdom, forces in conflict, communities broken down into unruly mobs--where Capra's editing patterns are disruptive and discontinuous (more critics than Griffith have compared them to Eisenstein's),[33] and his mise-en-scène highly stylized and dense.

The key event upon which the transition from one mode to the other turns in Capra's work is typically an act of persuasion: the protagonist exhorting or cajoling, at times by way of public confession, in an attempt to win over an audience.[34] From The Strong Man through State of the Union, these scenes are the centerpieces of Capra's dramas, and through them comic victory is often claimed in the face of unlikely odds. But the power to persuade is double-edged. The systems through which persuasion, if it is to be a political tool, must circulate are subject to corruption: newspapers, radio, even-- prophetically in State of the Union--television, distort "true" speech, limit access to power, pass off contrived and manufactured events as precisely those kinds of "authentic" and "natural" experiences the films otherwise prize. Moreover, it is not simply the "media," in a technological sense, that are at fault; implicated here are symbol-making processes of all kinds. Sitting in the shadows of the Lincoln Memorial, Jeff Smith decries the fancy words carved into stone, wants to flee those words and the people who engrave them in monuments, seeks escape from "the whole rotten show." Language often houses deception; even in direct communication dissembling and misinterpretation abound. And if the effects of that dissembling can be comic--as they are for Capra's glib shysters in Rain or Shine and Lady for a Day--they can also be the source of despair. Thus the counterpoint to fast talk, quick wit, even passionate argument: the protracted silence and paralysis of the hero in American Madness, Mr. Deeds, Mr. Smith, Meet John Doe, and even in minor--but visually arresting--scenes for the comic protagonists of It Happened One Night and Broadway Bill. In each of these, the hero's renewed faith in relationships that are guileless, transparent, is signaled by a decision to speak or to act, by the protagonist's willingness to articulate a community for others.

If we are to take the equivocation of these films on this point as a defining trait, as I think we should, then The Bitter Tea of General Yen emerges more clearly as a central work. Here, as is often true in Capra's films, dramatic conflict--and moral argument--is cast in terms of a collision of styles: the sincerity, frankness, and zeal of Megan Davis, an American missionary in China, as opposed to the aestheticism, polish, and restraint of the princely warlord General Yen, who holds Megan hostage in his lavish palace. (It is a collision that carries over as well into the divergent acting styles of Barbara Stanwyck and Nils Aster, to compelling dramatic effect.) But unlike the occupants of the penthouses and mansions of Capra's films set in America, whose manners are symptoms of arrogance and sterility, Yen gives off mixed signals that undermine Megan's self-righteousness and brash American confidence. His introduction, as an elegant passenger in a limousine that fatally strikes a rickshaw boy, establishes him as at once brutal and refined, cold and sensitive in the extreme; he functions as an Oriental Other through which contradictory values that set up the drama in Capra's other work--idealism and cynicism, spiritualism and materialism, self-sacrifice and greed--are fused in a single, disturbing character. Megan is a surrogate for the audience in our efforts to interpret, read, fix this character, and her dream of Yen in the double role of demonic rapist and heroic knight gives the lie to Occidental fantasies, for Yen is neither kind of aggressor.

What Yen comes to argue for in his philosophical debate with Megan is the transcendence of social identity, not simply the dissolving of class or generational tensions--typically the goal of the Capra comedies--but transport to a world where there is "no General Yen and no Megan Davis, just you and I." Like that of his more recalcitrant counterpart in Meet John Doe, the Colonel (Walter Brennan), Yen's cynicism seems grounded on the fundamental notion that all social discourse is a trap, and Mah-Li's treachery--deceiving Megan with her pious manner as she betrays Yen in her native tongue--proves his point. But if the Colonel only aspires to travel to the "North Country" with John, Yen pursues the full implication of the argument: that the burden of human signification will be relieved only with death. Here the drift of so many other Capra heroes toward suicide is allowed to be played out, cushioned, as it were, by an Oriental pantheism and sense of ceremony that makes death a seductive affair.

In an epilogue to this death scene, Jones, Yen's mercenary American adviser accompanying Megan back to her mission weaves into a desultory eulogy speculation concerning the plausibility of the General's pantheism. Is Yen's spirit, Jones wonders, now visible in the wind that pushes a sailboat or plays around Megan's hair? Can immortality, we might ask, be read from these "natural" signs, signs of Yen's presence--for the viewer watching this shadow play--at a

Critical Survey

double remove? Without committing himself, Jones seems to be working, like most Capra witnesses, toward conversion. The viewer, however, is left with a close-up of Megan: below what seems to be lacquered hair her high fur collar is gently ruffled by the breeze; her gaze is distant; she wears a faint, set smile. Megan's vivid reactions to Yen--including her subjective fantasy about him--have been available to us throughout the film, but now she offers no response to the question posed by Jones. Once voluble, she is silent; once animated, she is still. Her image no longer cues us, but is itself an ambiguous sign. On this moment of hesitation, in which interpretation is suspended for the viewer, the film closes. Into this moment, into the space of this shot, several "Capras" might be written, but which one would suffice?

Notes

1. For Ferguson's development of this idea, see especially "Frank Capra's Latest" (entry 214), and "Mr. Capra Goes to Town" (entry 249).

2. Otis Ferguson, "It Happened Once More" (entry 198).

3. Otis Ferguson, "While We Were Laughing" (entry 436).

4. Alistair Cooke, review of It Happened One Night (entry 309).

5. Otis Ferguson, "Capra and Tibet" (entry 316), "The Earth, the Egg, Etc." (entry 317), "Boys of All Ages" (entry 370), and "Mr. Capra Goes Someplace" (entry 411).

6. Sidney Meyers, "Mr. Capra Goes to Town" (entry 259), and review of Lost Horizon (entry 330).

7. Irving Lerner, "The Screen" (entry 257a), and "The Screen" (entry 328a).

8. Lewis Jacobs's commentary on Capra in his 1939 book, The Rise of the American Film (entry 417), might be considered an exception to this. But perhaps because Jacobs was writing in advance of the release of Mr. Smith Goes to Washington, he was able to treat Capra simply as an American humorist with a strong sense of characterization, dismiss Lost Horizon as an excursion into sophomoric philosophy, and avoid the thornier issues that critics a few years later had to face. His discussion of Capra's comic style is fairly close to that of Otis Ferguson, yet Jacobs seeks to maintain a distinction-- which he had drawn several years earlier in an article on Hollywood directors (entry 215)--between Capra's "craftsmanship" and "cutting, composition, and rhythm in a more profound sense," which Jacobs saw as the province of European directors.

9. Richard Griffith in Paul Rotha's The Film Till Now, pp. 449-54 (entry 630), and Griffith's Frank Capra, pp. 3-5 (entry 649).

10. See Andrew Sarris's 1963 capsule commentary on Capra in Film Culture (entry 764). Sarris, having been recently converted to auteurism by the writers of Cahiers du cinéma in France, was rebelling against his own sociological criticism of the late 1950s. It is also perhaps fitting that whereas Cahiers for the most part ignored Capra, its rival French journal, Positif, which was more likely to favor American directors with a reputation for "social comment," devoted an entire issue to Capra at the time of the publication of his autobiography in 1971.

11. Steven P. Hill, "Le confessioni del 'filibustiere' Frank Capra" (entry 757). A translation of this article has been published in Focus Magazine (University of California, Santa Barbara), 2, No. 2 (June 1982), 6-9.

12. Stephen Handzo, "Under Capracorn: A Decade of Good Deeds and Wonderful Lives" (entry 876), and "Capra: Big Man on the Columbia Lot" (entry 1038).

13. Richard T. Jameson, "Stanwyck & Capra" (entry 1143).

14. Richard Glatzer, "Meet John Doe: An end to Social Mythmaking" (entry 986). Also see Morris Dickstein, "It's a Wonderful Life, But . . ." (entry 1122), and Charles Maland's discussion of Meet John Doe in his Frank Capra, pp. 113-14 (entry 1128).

15. Handzo, "Under Capracorn: A Decade of Good Deeds and Wonderful Lives," p. 9 (entry 876).

16. Jean-Loup Bourget, "Capra et la 'screwball comedy,'" p. 53 (entry 821).

17. William S. Pechter, "American Madness," p. 77 (entry 759).

18. Claude Beylie, "Sur trois films de Capra" (entry 1070; translation mine). Also see Bernard Cohn's "Un Général, une blonde, un banquier, des clowns, des explorateurs" (entry 827).

19. Olivier Eyquem, "Frank Capra," p. 28 (entry 935; translation mine).

20. Leland Poague, The Cinema of Frank Capra, pp. 13-119 (entry 989). Also see Poague's "As You Like It and It Happened One Night: The Generic Pattern of Comedy" (entry 1053).

21. For recent work in this vein, see Thomas Schatz's chapter on screwball comedy in Hollywood Genres, pp. 150-85 (entry 1151), and Robert Self's and Lois Self's "Adaptation as Rhetorical Process: It Happened One Night and Mr. Deeds Goes to Town" (entry 1152).

22. Robin Wood, "Ideology, Genre, Auteur" (entry 1065).

23. Jeffrey Richards, "Frank Capra and the Cinema of Populism" (entry 806).

24. Wes D. Gehring, "McCarey v. Capra: A Guide to American Comedy of the '30s" (entry 1078).

25. Robert Sklar, "The Imagination of Stability: The Depression Films of Frank Capra" (entry 992).

26. John Raeburn, "Introduction," in Frank Capra: The Man and His Films, pp. xii-xiii (entry 990).

27. Maland, Frank Capra, pp. 184-86 (entry 1128). For a sustained reading of Capra's work against the backdrop of postromantic expression in American literature, philosophy, painting, and film, see Raymond Carney's American Vision: The Films of Frank Capra, forthcoming from Cambridge University Press.

28. Steve Neale, "Propaganda" (entry 1051).

29. Kaja Silverman, "Male Subjectivity and the Celestial Suture: It's a Wonderful Life" (entry 1153). Also see Brenda Wineapple, "The Production of Character in It's a Wonderful Life" (entry 1157); Peter Valenti, "The Theological Rhetoric of It's a Wonderful Life" (entry 1155).

30. Nick Browne, "The Politics of Narrative Form: Capra's Mr. Smith Goes to Washington" (entry 1101). Also see Brian Gallagher, "Speech, Identity and Ideology in Mr. Smith Goes to Washington" (entry 1140).

31. Charles Affron, Cinema and Sentiment (Chicago: University of Chicago Press, 1982), pp. 118-31.

32. Dudley Andrew, "Meet John Doe" (entry 1134a). Meet John Doe has also been the topic of papers presented by Nick Browne at film conferences in Urbino, Italy, in 1983 and Toronto in 1984.

33. See, for example, Graham Greene, "The Cinema" (entry 73); Arthur Knight, The Liveliest Art, pp. 128-29 (entry 694); and Stanley Cavell, Pursuits of Happiness: The Hollywood Comedy of Remarriage, pp. 40-41 (entry 1139).

34. Charles Affron briefly discusses the "persuasive narrativity of voice" in Capra's work as a prelude to his analysis of Mr. Smith Goes to Washington in Cinema and Sentiment, pp. 116-18.

III. The Films: Credits, Notes, and Synopses

1   **FULTAH FISHER'S BOARDING HOUSE (1922)**

   Fulta Fisher's Boarding House, The Ballad of Fisher's Boarding House[1]

Production Company:	Fireside Productions, Inc.
Producers:	G.F. Harris, David Supple
Director:	Frank R. Capra
Screenplay:	Walter Montague, from the poem "The Ballad of Fisher's Boarding House" by Rudyard Kipling[2]
Photography:	Roy Wiggins
Cast:	Mildred Owens (Annie of Austria), Olaf Skavlan (Hans), Ethan Allen (Salem Hardieker), Gerald Griffin (British sailor), Oreste Seragnoli (Luz)[3]
Filmed at Montague Studios, San Francisco, in December 1921	
Distributor:	Pathé Exchange, Inc.
Copyright:	27 April 1922 by Pathé Exchange, Inc. (LU 17797)
Released:	2 April 1922 (Strand Theatre, New York City)[4]
Running time:	12 minutes

Notes

1. Although the title of the film is listed as Fultah Fisher's Boarding House in all Capra filmographies, copyright for the film was filed under the title of Kipling's poem, "The Ballad of Fisher's Boarding House." To confuse matters further, the title on the print held at the Library of Congress is Fulta Fisher's Boarding House, with the "h" dropped from "Fultah." Future researchers should be alert to the fact that material on the film may therefore exist under these alternative titles.

2. Kipling's poem was originally published in Departmental Ditties and Other Poems (1899) and reprinted in Departmental Ditties and

The Films: Credits, Notes, and Synopses

Ballads and Barrack Room Ballads (Garden City, N.Y.: Doubleday, Page & Co. 1913).

3. With the exception of Mildred Owen, none of the actors was professional, and Capra suspects that they used fictitious names. (See Victor Scherle and William Turner Levy's The Films of Frank Capra [entry 1062], p. 36.)

4. Credits on the print filed at the Library of Congress listed the year of release as 1921, but this conforms with no other records.

Synopsis

An unidentified man opens a book as he sits by the fire. He turns to the title poem by Rudyard Kipling. The scenes to follow illustrate the verse.

We are introduced to a motley assortment of sailors residing at Fisher's waterfront boarding house: Hans, the blue-eyed Dane, who wears a silver crucifix for protection; Jake Without-the-Ears; Pamba, the Malay; Carboy Gin, the Guinea Cook; Luz, from Vigo Bay; Honest Jack, the bartender; and Salem Hardieker, a lean Bostonian. They all gather in the evening to drink.

Joining their number is Anne of Austria, a notorious prostitute. She dances with several of the men, but by port law, she officially belongs that week to Salem Hardieker. While sitting in Salem's lap, her eye is drawn toward Hans, who sits alone at a nearby table. She leaves Salem to flirt with Hans, but he politely rebuffs her, reminding her that she is Salem's girl. Spurned, Anne loudly accuses Hans of calling her names, provoking a fight between Hans and Salem. The two combatants are seen in "a dance of shadows on the wall." Suddenly the shadow of a third figure appears and Hans is stabbed with a knife. The blow has been delivered by Luz, who bears Hans a grudge. Luz sneaks away. Stunned, Anne cradles Hans in her arms. Hans dies. Removing the silver crucifix from his chest, Anne clasps it and weeps. As everyone watches, she runs to the foot of the stairs and strips off her jewelry in favor of the crucifix. She exits a reformed woman.

We return to the man by the fire. He closes his book.

2   **THE STRONG MAN (1926)**

L'athlète incomplet or L'homme fort (France), La grande sparata or L'atleta innamorato (Italy), Der starke Mann (Germany)[1]

Production Company: Harry Langdon Corporation
Director: Frank Capra
Screenplay: Arthur Ripley, Hal Conklin, Robert Eddy [and Frank Capra]
Comedy Construction: Clarence Hennecke
Titles: Reed Heustis

The Films: Credits, Notes, and Synopses

Photography: Elgin Lessley, Glenn Kershner
Lighting: Denver Harmon
Editor: Harold Young
Production Manager: William H. Jenner
Technical Director: Lloyd Brierly
Assistant Director: J. Frank Holliday
Cast: Harry Langdon (Paul Bergot), Priscilla Bonner (Mary Brown), Arthur Thalasso (Zandow the Great), Gertrude Astor (Gold Tooth, or Lily of Broadway), William V. Mong (Parson Brown, or Holy Joe), Robert McKim (Roy McDevitt, or "Mike" McDevitt),[2] Brooks Benedict (bus passenger)
Filmed at the United Lot in Burbank, California, in May-June 1926
Distributor: First National Pictures, Inc.
Copyright: 31 August 1926 by First National Pictures, Inc. (LP 23063)
Released: 5 September 1926 (Strand Theatre, New York)
Running time: 78 minutes (24 fps)

Notes

1. One of the working titles for The Strong Man was The Yes Man, and the film was referred to as that in early trade coverage and advertising.

2. Alternative names for these characters appear on different prints.

Synopsis

"Where once a Belgian orchard bloomed" is now a battlefield of World War I. A soldier, Paul Bergot, repeatedly fails to hit his target while practicing with a machine gun; when he reverts to a slingshot he strikes the target in a single try. Grazed by an enemy bullet, Paul retaliates with his slingshot, using biscuits and onions for ammunition, and his assailant, a rotund German soldier, is forced to retreat. But Paul is caught off guard when he pauses to read a romantic letter from an American pen pal, Mary Brown, and gazes at the photograph she has enclosed. The German soldier sneaks up from behind and carries Paul off.

After the Armistice, the German immigrates to America as "Zandow the Great"--a strongman--with Paul in tow as his assistant. They successfully pass through Ellis Island, despite some mishaps with a luggage clerk, and Paul naively sets out in search of Mary Brown. A woman he pursues on the streets of New York angrily rebuffs him before a crowd of bystanders. Among the spectators is Lily, a stylish moll who has been handed a stolen bankroll by a friend in crime. Trailed by a detective, Lily surreptitiously slips the bankroll into Paul's pocket, but after the coast is clear she has trouble retrieving it. So she pretends to be Mary Brown and soon has the elated Paul in a taxi on the way to her apartment.

In the taxi Lily gropes for the money. Paul is so shocked by what he takes to be a sexual overture that when they reach her apartment building he skittishly refuses to follow her in. So Lily collapses on the sidewalk in a feigned fainting spell, and Paul is obliged to carry her up a grand staircase to her room, an arduous task accomplished only by sitting on the stairway and pushing himself up step by step. Finally alone with Paul in her room, Lily knocks him out, but he revives in time to defend his honor as she tries to undress him. At knife point Lily finally wins a kiss from him; while he is thus engaged, she secretly slits open the jacket and gets the bankroll. Mission accomplished, she collapses on her bed, as if sated. As he exits, Paul asks that she not let word of his kiss get around. Hearing mention made in the hallway of a "Madame Browne" who runs an art studio next door, Paul enters the studio, hope aroused, only to find himself face-to-face with a nude female model. In his fervor to escape, he smashes through a screen partition, flips over the staircase bannister, and somersaults to the bottom of the steps.

Zandow books his strongman act in the distant border town of Cloverdale. Once a sanctuary of tranquility, the town has been corrupted by the arrival of bootleggers who have transformed the town hall into the Palace Music Hall, complete with dancing girls and free-flowing liquor. Battle lines are drawn between McDevitt, the tough-talking proprietor of the Music Hall, and Parson Brown, the only man of influence in Cloverdale who McDevitt cannot buy out. The feisty old parson leads his parishioners on a march around the Music Hall, while inside McDevitt threatens to make the parson's blind daughter, Mary, the main attraction of his show. In the backyard of the parsonage, Mary feeds cake to children gathered at her feet, and tells them the story of a heroic Belgian soldier who, after winning the war, comes to America in search of his pen pal not knowing she is blind.

Enroute to Cloverdale, Paul contracts a cold and annoys the rest of the passengers in the bus with his sneezing, coughing, and assorted remedies. When Paul accidentally substitutes Limburger cheese for camphor rub, he is kicked out the back door of the moving vehicle. He tumbles down a steep slope, only to crash through the roof of the bus as it follows a hairpin curve down the hillside. He is no less amazed than the rest of the passengers.

Arriving in Cloverdale, Zandow joins the merriment inside the Music Hall while Paul begins work backstage. In search of water, he is instructed to see Mary Brown at the parsonage well. After a flurry of ecstatic but indecisive movements, Paul proceeds to the well in hopes of finding his true love. Sighting Mary, he strikes a pose for her and asks if she's glad to see him. The blind girl tearfully turns away. The scene advances to a short time later. Mary laughs as Paul recounts—and acts out—the story of his search. Hesitating slightly, he finally kisses her.

The strongman act is scheduled to begin, but Zandow has become too drunk to perform. Pressured by the rowdy customers, McDevitt

The Films: Credits, Notes, and Synopses

commands Paul to appear on stage in Zandow's stead. Despite the outlandishness of his appearance in Zandow's oversized costume, Paul manages to survive the first part of the act by improvising a routine. But he is panicked by the idea of the finale, in which he is to be shot from cannon and land on a distant trapeze. Just then Parson Brown leads his parishioners on another march around the Music Hall, calling for God's destruction of these "Walls of Jericho." Inside, Paul naively requests that the audience honor what he takes to be a funeral procession with silence. A drunken spectator responds with a mock prayer in which he insults Parson Brown and requests Mary's appearance on stage. Incited by this, Paul tries to attack the drunk, but is overpowered and tossed up onto the trapeze. From this vantage point he swings out over the crowd, pelting his enemies with bottles and temporarily covering the now brawling mob with a stage backdrop. Returning to the cannon, he then unleashes a volley which propels the pistol-waving McDevitt out the window into a garbage can. Additional volleys drive the crowd out into the street and collapse the walls of the Music Hall. Parson Brown and his parishioners rejoice. After firing a final blast, Paul crawls into a fetal position and falls asleep.

Cloverdale is again a tranquil town, protected by the "majesty of the law" in the person of Paul Bergot as town cop. Setting out on his beat, he asks Mary not to follow him, but yields to her when she starts to cry. As they walk down the street, he stumbles over a rock. Mary helps him back onto his feet, and they go off together.

3 LONG PANTS (1927)

Sa dernière culotte (France), Lange Hosen (Germany)

Production Company:	Harry Langdon Corporation
Director:	Frank Capra
Screenplay:	Story by Arthur Ripley, adapted by Robert Eddy
Comedy Construction:	Clarence Hennecke
Photography:	Elgin Lessley, Glenn Kershner
Cast:	Harry Langdon (Harry Shelby, the boy), Gladys Brockwell (his mother), Alan Roscoe (his father), Priscilla Bonner (Priscilla, his bride), Alma Bennett (Bebe Blair, the vamp, his downfall), Betty Francisco (his finish), Ruth Waterburg (nightclub singer)[1]
Filmed in Burbank, California, in October-December 1926	
Distributor:	First National Pictures, Inc.
Copyright:	22 March 1927 by First National Pictures, Inc. (LP 23766)
Released:	26 March 1927 (Mark Strand Theatre, New York City)
Running time:	60 minutes (24 fps)[2]

The Films: Credits, Notes, and Synopses

Notes

1. Donald C. Willis in The Films of Frank Capra (see entry 950) includes in the credits Frankie Darro in the role of "Harry as a small boy," but no such figure exists in current prints of the film. Darro's name is also mentioned in the brief credits appended to the New York Times review of the film by Mordaunt Hall (see entry 69). A passage with Darro as young Harry may have been cut from the film.

2. The original version of Long Pants reportedly included an additional ten-minute passage in Technicolor. Tom Waller, discussing the film prior to its release, describes the passage as follows: "It shows Langdon, gorgeously costumed, as the gallant lover of a beautiful maiden in a fairy castle. It depicts Langdon fighting a duel with his fist as the weapon against a long sword wielded by a huge knight. In the end the fist wins and just after Langdon marries the Fairy Princess, amid much pomp and splendor, he wakes up--the adolescent youth on the broken spring bed in the small town farmhouse of his mother and father" ("'Long Pants' promises to be Harry Langdon's Greatest Film," Moving Picture World, 84, No. 4 [22 January 1927], 266). This would suggest that the Technicolor passage was an extension of the black-and-white fantasy imagined by Harry in existing versions. Subsequent reviews of the film in 1927, however, do not mention this Technicolor segment; it may have been deleted before the film's official release.

Synopsis

Harry Shelby, armed with classic works of romantic literature from the Oak Grove Public Library, retreats into his attic to read in private. Provoked by an injunction by the god of Olympus to be bold in love, Harry imagines himself to be a prince in a fairy-tale kingdom, chasing a princess and climbing her balcony to kiss her. Outside Harry's home, two girls laugh and talk gaily. Harry whistles and waves to one as she passes by his window. "Little boys should be seen and not heard," she replies, departing haughtily. Returning to his book, he measures himself, clad in childish short pants, against the literary image of a Grecian god's stately glory.

Through the trapdoor of the attic, Harry sees and hears his parents in the kitchen below discussing whether or not he is ready for long pants. His mother fears Harry will be prompted to take to the streets, but his father insists that the time has come for Harry to try long pants on for size. When he does, the legs are too long. His father is confident the boy will grow into them, but his mother weeps. Alone in his new manly outfit, Harry practices embracing and kissing an imaginary lover.

An "answer to a maiden's prayer" arrives in the figure of vampish Bebe Blair, whose car gets a flat tire in Oak Grove near Harry's house. While she sullenly waits for her chauffeur to fix the tire, she reads two letters. The first, a typed note from Marty, warns her

The Films: Credits, Notes, and Synopses

that the cops are hot on her trail for smuggling "snow," a crime too severe for him to risk helping her. The second is a handwritten love note, unsigned. "Don't be downhearted," it reads. 'I haven't deserted my Baby Face. Believe me, as soon as I get back we'll be married." Leaving home in his new long pants, Harry is stopped in his tracks by the sight of Bebe. He backs off, comes forward, hesitates. A copy of <u>Desire under the Elms</u> slips from his arms. He mounts a bicycle, but a porch pillar intrudes between his body and the handlebars; he smacks head on into the pole. Recovering, he rides over to Bebe and attracts her attention by posing astride the crossbar with a leg swinging jauntily. He circles the car, performing stunts on the bike; she teasingly calls him a wonderful boy. He clambers into the car and she kisses him. His body lists to the left and then topples over to the ground. Summoned home by his mother, a dazed Harry kisses Bebe goodbye. She urges the chauffeur to drive her away "before that boob gets back."

On the phone for Harry is Priscilla, a neighborhood girl, who reminds him that they are to be partners at the Egg Festival tomorrow. When the Shelbys leave Harry alone to talk in private, he quickly hangs up and races back outside. Bebe is gone. But Harry discovers the love note, and mistakenly assumes it is from Bebe to him. He races home to tell his parents that he may soon be married. They mistakenly assume that Priscilla is the intended bride.

Marriage to Priscilla is thus arranged. On the day of the wedding, Harry begs his father to let him back out of the ceremony. But Mr. Shelby instructs him to forget about Bebe, drawing his attention to the society notices concerning the wedding in the local paper. Unconcerned with the notices, Harry instead discovers a front-page story about Bebe; imprisoned in the city jail, she has been deserted by her former pal. Mr. Shelby insists that it's too late to cancel the wedding, but Harry imagines escorting Priscilla through an idyllic forest and shooting her dead. After telegraming Bebe that he is coming to rescue her, harry sneaks over to Priscilla's window and invites his bride to take a walk in the woods. She accepts.

Deep in the woods, Harry instructs Priscilla to look off in the distance, but when he reaches for his gun she invariably turns her head back around. Suggesting a game of hide-and-seek, he has her cover her eyes, but every attempt to shoot her goes awry. He throws a horseshoe over his shoulder for good luck, but it rebounds off a tree and knocks him over. A series of complications follow: his hat is jammed over his eyes; he is ensnared in barbed wire; he is caught in a bear trap tied to a sapling which flails him. Finally, Priscilla rescues him. Ready for another game, she picks up a pistol and innocently uses the news photo of Bebe for target practice.

Despite his failures, Harry takes off for the city, arriving at the jail just as Bebe escapes. He hides her in a large storage crate and carts it off on his back through the traffic. Pausing to rest, he props the crate on two boxes and hides underneath. But the sight of a

The Films: Credits, Notes, and Synopses

woman fixing her garter sends him bolt upright, upsetting the crate. Moving on, he stops again at the stage entrance of a theater. A dog steals his shoe. While he retrieves it, a mannequin cop is placed on the crate by a stagehand. Assuming the cop to be real, Harry tries to distract him by acting out a series of imaginary crises: a distant fistfight, a holdup, and his own death by seizure. A store owner douses Harry with water to revive him. Harry sees the mannequin being removed, but while wiping his face doesn't notice that a real cop has taken its place. So he throws a brick at this cop, and a chase ensues. Making it back to the stage door, he hastily retrieves the wrong crate. Sitting atop it to cover an opening from the view of another cop, Harry's bottom is bit by an alligator. Racing back to the stage door, he finally frees Bebe, who steals a change of clothes for both of them in the theater. She dresses Harry and then robs a passing gentleman of his watch and wallet. Harry naively accepts the items as gifts.

Marty calls his newest girlfriend at her dressing room in the tawdry nightclub where she works, warning her that Bebe has escaped and knows that they squealed on her, and promising to pick her up after her last show. She locks her closet door before leaving to perform, but Bebe and Harry are already hiding inside. When the showgirl returns, a vicious fight between the women breaks out. Victorious, Bebe tosses her battered victim out of the ransacked dressing room and belts down a couple of drinks; immobile, Harry watches all this in silence. When she puts her arm around him, he scampers for the door and declares their romance over. Marty returns, and he and Bebe kill each other in a final shoot-out. As sensation seekers crowd into the room, Harry sits paralyzed.

Released from jail in the wake of this gun battle, Harry hurries home. Inside his house the Shelbys and Priscilla are saying grace before dinner. Harry quietly joins them. When they look up, they rush to embrace him, knocking over the table and spilling the dishes on their prodigal son and fiancé.

*4 **FOR THE LOVE OF MIKE (1928)**

<u>Pour l'amour de Mike</u> (France)

Producer:	Robert Kane
Director:	Frank Capra
Screenplay:	J. Clarkson Miller, from the story "Hell's Kitchen" by John Moroso[1]
Photography:	Ernest Haller
Production Manager:	Leland Hayward
Assistant Director:	Joe Boyle
Cast:	Ben Lyon (Mike), George Sidney (Abraham Katz), Ford Sterling (Herman Schultz), Hugh Cameron (Patrick O'Malley), Claudette Colbert (Mary), Richard "Skeets" Gallagher

The Films: Credits, Notes, and Synopses

    (Coxey Pendleton), Rudoph Cameron (Henry Sharp), Mabel Swor (Evelyn Joyce)
Filmed at the Hearst-Cosmopolitan Studio in New York City and on location in Connecticut in the spring of 1927
Distributor: First National Pictures, Inc.
Copyright: 1 August 1927 by First National Pictures, Inc. (LP 24252)
Released: 22 August 1927 (Hippodrome, New York City)
Running time: 75 minutes (24 fps)

Notes

1. According to Capra, Leland Hayward wrote a scenario for the film (see The Name Above the Title, p. 73). Benny Rubin also claims to have worked as a gagman on this project (see Victor Scherle and William Turner Levy's The Films of Frank Capra [entry 1062], p. 47).

No prints of this film are known to exist.

Synopsis

    Herman Schultz, delicatessen owner, Abie Katz, tailor, and Patrick O'Malley, street cleaner, live in separate rooms on the same floor of a tenement in Hell's Kitchen, New York City. A baby boy is abandoned on the landing. Despite their inexperience with infants, they adopt the boy and name him Mike.

    Sacrificing and skimping, they rear the boy as if he were their own. When he has finished high school they urge him to go on to college, but Mike thinks he has been a burden long enough and wants to find a job. Mary, a pretty Italian neighbor who works as cashier in Shultz's store, sides with the three "fathers" and persuades Mike to enter Yale. By his senior year he has reached the peak of collegiate success, socially popular and captain and stroke of the varsity crew.

    On Mike's twenty-first birthday, the tree fathers arrange a banquet at the local Tammany Club. They invite prominent politicians and businessmen from the community in hopes that Mike will impress the guests and be offered a job after graduation. But Mike is delayed when an amorous girl coaxes him to come to a cocktail party at her apartment. When he finally arrives at the banquet, he is drunk and insults the guests for dining without him. The guests leave in a huff, and Mike quarrels with his fathers about their lack of courtesy. "You're not my fathers anyway," he finally declares. O'Malley, boiling over with disappointment and disgust, knocks Mike out.

    The next day Mike is treated coolly by his fathers and Mary. Downhearted, he returns to college and begins gambling beyond his means. Mike soon owes a crooked gambler $5,000, and pays off $10,000 more with a bad check. Just before the big Yale-Harvard crew race, the gambler appears on the scene and threatens to have Mike sent to

The Films: Credits, Notes, and Synopses

jail unless he throws the race to Harvard, on whom the man has heavily bet.

The day of the race Mike is delighted to discover that his fathers and Mary have come to New Haven to watch him. They bet on his team and seem to have forgiven him for his escapade at the banquet. He rows Yale to victory. At the boat landing the gambler confronts the three fathers with the bad check and again threatens jail, but the men push him into the water. Mike paddles his boat back to the crew house, having won the acclaim of his college, the forgiveness of his fathers, and Mary's heart.

(This synopsis is drawn primarily from material submitted to the Library of Congress by First National Pictures for the purpose of securing copyright.)

5   THAT CERTAIN THING (1928)

Production Company:	Columbia Pictures Corporation
Producer:	Harry Cohn
Director:	Frank R. Capra
Screenplay:	Elmer Harris[1]
Titles:	Al Boasberg
Photography:	Joseph Walker
Editor:	Arthur Roberts
Art Director:	Robert E. Lee
Assistant Director:	Eugene De Rue
Cast:	Viola Dana (Molly Kelly), Ralph Graves (Andy B. Charles, Jr.), Burr McIntosh (A.B. Charles, Sr.), Aggie Herring (Mrs. Maggie Kelly), Carl Gerard (Secretary Brooks), Sydney Crossley (valet)
Filmed at Columbia Pictures Studio in the fall of 1927	
Distributor:	Columbia Pictures Corporation
Copyright:	2 February 1928 by Columbia Pictures Corporation (LP 24942)
Released:	18 April 1928 (Trivoli Theatre, New York City)[2]
Running time:	69 minutes (24 fps)

Notes

1. Capra in his autobiography claims to have first presented the idea for the story to Harry Cohn (see The Name Above the Title, p. 83).

2. Most Capra filmographies list 1 January 1928 as the release date, but I have found no reviews prior to the New York opening at the Tivoli.

46

The Films: Credits, Notes, and Synopses

Synopsis

Plucky Molly Kelly supports her widowed mother and two kid brothers in their tenement apartment. Her mother wishes she would marry Jim Callahan, the streetcar conductor who lives in the building, but Molly is holding out for a millionaire. Jim is waiting for her in the hallway when she leaves for work, but she gives him the brush-off.

Behind the cigar counter at the Stratford Hotel, Molly waits on a customer who requests her most expensive cigars. She speculates aloud that he must be a millionaire. He is not, but he is secretary to A.B. Charles, the restaurant king. "Give him my love," says Molly with irony.

The secretary delivers the cigars to an agitated boss. Rumor has it that Restaurant #65 is cutting the ham too thick, so A.B. orders the secretary to have them cut it thinner. His son, Andy B. Charles, Jr., stumbles home from a night on the town. Trailing Andy up to his bedroom, A.B. overhears his son brag that he's put one over on "the old crab." He informs his son that the time has come for him to work at one of the restaurants. Andy remains aloof and unmoved.

As they close up shop for the day, a coworker teases "Miss High Hat" Molly about not meeting her millionaire today. "I might bump into him any moment," Molly replies, undaunted. Rushing out the door to catch her bus, Molly collides with Andy. He apologizes, but Molly is snappish. Quickly gathering up her belongings, she runs after her bus, leaving a handkerchief behind. Andy pursues her in his car. Folding the handkerchief in a magazine, he tosses it up to her on the upper deck of the bus. She dismisses him as fresh, but soon discovers among her possessions his billfold. Noting it belongs to A.B. Charles, Jr., son of the restaurant king, she now begins to pursue him. Catching up to his car at the first stop, she returns the billfold and feigns an injured ankle from their collision. Andy lifts her into his car and drives her home.

At her doorstep, Molly prolongs their parting. Andy finally asks her out dancing that night. Elated, Molly races through the building, borrowing clothes for her date. A dressmaker offers his daughter's most glamorous gown. Andy arrives that night in a Rolls-Royce driven by a chauffeur, and the entire neighborhood watches as Cinderella Molly descends the tenement staircase for her night with Prince Charming.

The fairy-tale romance proceeds dizzily. Andy proposes they get married that night, and a dazed Molly accepts. She calls home to give the good news to Mother, who promptly faints. Molly awakens the next morning in a fancy hotel. Her bridegroom overwhelms her with lavish gifts, but the dream is quickly shattered. The gifts have all been charged to Andy's father and must be returned. Moreover, he has been disinherited for marrying a gold digger. Overhearing that reinstatement is possible if Andy leaves her and pleads that he was a victim of

The Films: Credits, Notes, and Synopses

her cleverness, Molly returns home alone. Neighbors viciously mock her; clothing she has borrowed is torn from her back.

Safe inside their apartment, Mrs. Kelly consoles Molly, noting that the family has been cursed with bad husbands. But Molly insists she loves Andy and has only left him for his own good. When Andy appears at the door, however, she tries to convince him that she was only interested in his money all along. Spotting Jim in the hallway, she announces that were she to marry for love, Jim would be the man. But Andy doesn't believe her. Insulted by Jim, he knocks his rival through the stairway railing. He settles into Molly's apartment, sleeping on the floor.

Andy goes to work digging ditches to prove himself an able provider. But with the first blow of his pick he breaks a water pipe and is fired. Noon hour comes. The workers file across the street to eat at one of his father's restaurants. Seeing Molly approach with a box lunch for him, Andy returns to the ditch and pretends he has worked all morning. The lunch she has provided is more than he can eat, but the workers all return from the restaurant hungry. So Andy hands out an extra sandwich. When the workers express their preference for this heartier fare, Andy decides to start a box-lunch business.

The box lunches sell as quickly as they are made. Soon business has expanded into the Molly Box Lunch Company, an assembly-line production with Andy overseeing the workers and Molly running the office. They have put all their cash into capital investment, but Andy assures Molly that within a week they will be on easy street financially.

A.B. learns that the Molly Box Lunch Company has cut his profits in half, with further damage expected. He decides he'll stamp the company out. Arriving at the factory, he wanders amid the impressive facilities. Unaware of who runs the company, he is surprised to find Andy on the premises. Andy informs him the company does $500,000 in business a day and that his father will surely be out of business in six months. A.B. demands to see the proprietor. Quickly preparing Molly for the ruse, Andy ushers his father into her office. Although very nervous, Molly plays the part of a tough, busy executive. A.B. offers $5,000 for the company. Molly, coached through a window by Andy, counters with a demand for $100,000. A.B. argues he could reproduce the factory for a fraction of the cost. But not their sandwich with a secret, she replies. After loudly ringing the bells of empty cash registers, Andy enters with a moneybag filled with the day's receipts. Molly makes light of these profits. Intimidated, A.B. offers to meet Molly's price if she promotes his son to manager. Feigning reluctance, she agrees. A.B. tells Andy that if he would marry a girl like Molly, he would give his son another $100,000. Their wedding rings visible, Andy and Molly hand him a pen. After he as written this second check, Molly empties the moneybag; it was filled with worthless washers. A.B. is amused. He has only one question: what is the secret of their sandwich? "Cut the ham thick," Molly replies.

The Films: Credits, Notes, and Synopses

Father exits. The couple kiss.

6 SO THIS IS LOVE (1928)

Un punch à l'estomac (France)

Production Company:	Columbia Pictures Corporation
Producer:	Harry Cohn
Director:	Frank Capra
Screenplay:	Adapted by Elmer Harris from a story by Norma Springer; continuity by Rex Taylor
Photography:	Ray June
Editor:	Arthur Roberts
Art Director:	Robert E. Lee
Assistant Director:	Eugene De Rue
Cast:	Shirley Mason (Hilda Jensen), William Collier, Jr. (Jerry McGuire), Johnnie Walker ("Spike" Mulligan), Ernie Adams ("Flash" Tracy), Carl Gerard (Otto), William H. Strauss ("Maison" Katz), Jean Laverty (Mary Malone)
Filmed at Columbia Pictures Studio in January-February 1928	
Distributor:	Columbia Pictures Corporation
Copyright:	6 March 1928 by Columbia Pictures Corporation (LP 25044)
Released:	17 April 1928 (Loew's Theatre, New York City)[1]
Running time:	60 minutes (24 fps)

Notes

1. Most Capra filmographies list 6 February 1928 as the release date, but I have found no reviews prior to the New York opening at the Loew's, where it played for one day on the lower half of a double bill.

Synopsis

As Hilda Jensen, a counter girl at a German delicatessen, washes the front window of the shop, her eye is caught by a freshly mounted poster of Spike Mullins, a champion boxer. She gazes at the picture longingly. Brash and cocky, Spike meanwhile entertains friends outside the athletic club. Instructed by his manager to sell tickets to the boxer's benefit, Spike arranges for ruffians to throw bricks through the store windows of uncooperative shopkeepers. He and the manager stop at the delicatessen for a bite to eat. Excited by Spike's presence, Hilda loads his sandwich with various meats and accidentally sprays him with a bottle of beer. Spike feigns anger, but is mildly amused.

At work in his studio across the street is Jerry McGuire, a dress designer, secretly in love with Hilda, but too shy to tell her.

The Films: Credits, Notes, and Synopses

Summoned to his employer's clothing store to meet with a client, Jerry discovers Hilda hanging from an awning after the ladder on which she was standing to wash the store windows gave way. His attempt at rescuing her ends with both of them entangled on the sidewalk, much to Hilda's amusement. When he reaches the store, Jerry is faced with the task of robing a massive, matronly woman who, to his dismay, repeatedly grabs him in support as he encircles her with fabric. Spike arrives peddling the benefit tickets and Jerry's boss, Mr. Katz, seeing the ruffians, reluctantly buys two. He passes them on at a reduced rate to Jerry, advising him to ask Hilda to the dance.

Jerry nervously does so, offering her the choice of Katz's collection of dresses to wear for the evening. She excitedly accepts. They arrive at the dance a handsome couple, but Hilda's attention is soon drawn to Spike, who whisks her away from Jerry and dances her off into a private room where he makes advances. When Jerry tries to intervene, Spike knocks him across the room. Spike asks Hilda if she is Jerry's girl. No, she replies, stunned. So Spike carries Jerry outside by the seat of his pants and dumps him in a puddle, much to the amusement of bystanders.

Jerry stumbles home, humiliated. Hilda sneaks out of the benefit and follows him to his apartment, where she gently tends to his wound. She discovers that she is the model for all his sketches. Jerry confesses his love for her. At first embarrassed, she soon responds warmly. But Spike, who has missed her at the dance, angrily arrives on the scene. To spare Jerry further punishment, Hilda leaves with Spike. A man, who has followed Spike from the dance and listened outside Jerry's door, offers to teach Jerry how to defend himself. With guarded hope, Jerry accepts.

In training, Jerry is graceless but energetic. His confidence buoyed, he calls on Hilda at the deli and flexes his muscles for her. She warns him that Spike might visit, but Jerry claims he is no longer afraid. When Spike appears in the doorway, Hilda pretends Jerry is a customer rather than a suitor. She accepts a ticket from Spike to his bout that night. Jerry contemplates slugging Spike, but chickens out. He leaves the deli disgusted with himself.

That night Spike's scheduled opponent injures himself before the fight and Jerry's trainer volunteers his pupil as a substitute, citing Jerry's hatred for Spike as special incentive for a great fight. The promoter agrees but Jerry himself is reluctant. Spike considers the match-up a joke and asks his manager to let him eat, but the manager refuses. Panicking, Jerry escapes from his dressing room but in the corridor runs into Hilda. She urges him not to fight, but the sight of her inspires him with new resolve. She, in turn, is moved by Jerry's heroism and embraces him. She then visits Spike who, famished, recalls the first sandwich she made for him. Hilda gets an idea and promises to return with some food.

The Films: Credits, Notes, and Synopses

A battered, unconscious boxer from the previous bout is carried into Jerry's dressing room. Distraught, Jerry considers packing a horseshoe inside his glove, but decides against it. He is rewarded by his trainer with a hearty embrace and more words of encouragement. Meanwhile, Hilda returns to Spike's room and he dismisses his entourage. She unloads a basket of food: pickles, meats, milk, eggs, pie, and a creamy cheese spread to coat his stomach "like velvet." When he is thoroughly stuffed, she coaxes him to finish off what remains and then tops off the feast by giving him an ice-cream cone and a cigar. Spike's manager and entourage clamor to get into the room. Hilda returns to Jerry and advises him to hit Spike in the stomach during the bout.

Jerry enters the arena. Trying to climb the ropes into the ring, he falls on his face, so he crawls underneath instead. Spike arrives, cockily smoking his cigar. When Spike offers Jerry his glove for a handshake at the center of the ring, Jerry instinctively flinches. The fight begins. Quickly knocked down twice, Jerry woozily imagines the arena has emptied except for Hilda, who cheers him on. He gets to his feet, but barely survives the round. Spike, however, begins to feel the effects of his dinner; in the second round some blows to his stomach leave him moaning on the mat. Declared the winner, Jerry continues to swing at anyone who comes near. Hilda enters the ring and calms him down. The arena empties. Jerry asks Hilda if he's good enough for her. When she feigns uncertainty, he playfully jabs her. She falls into his arms.

*7   **THE MATINEE IDOL (1928)**

   Bessie à Broadway (France), Il teatro di Minnie (Italy)

Production Company:	Columbia Pictures Corporation
Producer:	Harry Cohn
Director:	Frank R. Capra
Screenplay:	Adapted by Elmer Harris from the story "Come Back to Aaron" by Robert Lord and Ernest S. Pagano; continuity by Peter Milne
Photography:	Phillip Tannura
Editor:	Arthur Roberts
Art Director:	Robert E. Lee
Assistant Director:	Eugene De Rue
Cast:	Bessie Love (Ginger Bolivar), Johnie Walker (Don Wilson/Harry Mann),[1] Lionel Belmore (Col. Jaspar Bolivar), Ernest Hilliard (Wingate), Sidney D'Albrook (J. Madison Wilberforce), David Mir (Eric Barrymaine)
Filmed at Columbia Pictures Studio in February-March 1928	
Distributor:	Columbia Pictures Corporation
Copyright:	5 April 1928 by Columbia Pictures Corporation (LP 25136)
Released:	23 April 1928 (Hippodrome, New York City)[2]
Running time:	66 minutes (24 fps)

The Films: Credits, Notes, and Synopses

Notes

1. Benny Rubin claims to have doubled for Johnnie Walker during a dance sequence in the film (see Victor Scherle and William Turner Levy's The Films of Frank Capra [entry 1062], p. 58).

2. Most Capra filmographies list 14 March 1928 as the release date, but I have found no reviews prior to the New York opening at the Hippodrome.

No prints of this film are known to exist.

Synopsis

   Don Wilson, star blackface comedian, is about to open the season in a new Broadway revue. A novelty act is needed to complete the bill. Anticipating the strenuous season ahead, Don decides to take a short vacation upstate with his producer, Wingate, and a few friends.

   Their car breaks down in a small town. Intrigued by a poster advertising the Great Bolivar Stock Company, the vacationers decide to make a call on the hick tent show. But Don, irked at the delay, stays behind to try to get the car fixed. The only mechanic in town is away at the stock company show, so Don puts on work clothes and sets to work on the car himself. Wingate, however, has the keys to the toolbox, and Don has to go to the show to retrieve them.

   At the stock company tent, Don inadvertently falls in line with a group of local men auditioning for a small role in a Civil War melodrama. When Ginger Bolivar, star of the show and daughter of its impresario, hears Don deliver the line "I love you," she hires him for the part. She quickly coaches him for that evening's performance; he is to play a Confederate soldier who will die in her arms.

   The amateur production greatly amuses the sophisticated visitors from New York, who meanwhile wonder what has happened to Don. When Don appears on stage for his brief death scene, they burst into laughter, leading Ginger to believe that Don cannot act. Wingate is convinced that the show would work as the novelty act in his revue and immediately signs up the Bolivar troupe. Ginger suggests that she be allowed to replace the terrible actor she had hired for the performance that night, but Wingate insists the entire cast be included. Don tries to convince Wingate that they are playing a cruel trick on these well-meaning amateurs, but Wingate considers the act too hilarious to pass up, especially with Don as the dying soldier.

   Under the name of Harry Mann, Don joins the Bolivar company at an East Side boarding house. He takes lessons from Ginger, who advances only slight hope for his future as an actor. J. Madison Wilberforce, Ginger's leading man, resents her attention to the new ham actor since he views the leading lady as his future bride. And indeed Don is

The Films: Credits, Notes, and Synopses

falling in love with the vivacious, independent Ginger. He again protests to Wingate that the laughter of the New York audience will be heartbreaking for Ginger and her father, but Wingate refuses to yield.

The night before the opening, Don holds a masquerade party. Ginger is introduced to the masked matinee idol. She is flattered by his attention to her, but cuts short his attempt at wooing. Back at the boarding house, she finds "Harry Mann" waiting up for her and delights him with her description of Don Wilson's technique in love-making. She tells "Harry" that although he is an awful ham she loves him just the same.

The opening night audience finds the Bolivar act hilarious. As Don predicted, Ginger is crushed. She slips out into the alley and starts home in the rain. Don, who has made a quick change to black-face for his next act, follows her. In the rain his makeup washes away; when he catches up to her she sees that Harry Mann and Don Wilson are the same person. Ginger is more hurt than ever, but Don has no chance to explain; Wingate and his assistants arrive and drag Don back to the theater to perform.

Later Don goes to the boarding house to talk with Ginger, but is confronted instead by her father. Enraged at the deception, he slaps Don and denounces him. Don makes no attempt to defend himself.

The Great Bolivar Stock Company returns upstate to their tent show. Ginger holds another audition for the part of the soldier in the Civil War melodrama. Don turns up, fourth in line. She passes him by, but he gets back at the end of the line. When it's his turn again, she instructs him to say "I love you." After he delivers the line, she thinks for a moment and then invites him inside the tent. There she makes him repeat the line over and over. They embrace.

(This synopsis is drawn primarily from material submitted to the Library of Congress by Columbia Pictures for the purpose of securing copyright.)

8 THE WAY OF THE STRONG (1928)

Production Company:	Columbia Pictures Corporation
Producer:	Harry Cohn
Director:	Frank R. Capra
Screenplay:	William Counselman; continuity by Peter Milne
Photography:	Ben Reynolds
Cast:	Mitchell Lewis (Handsome Williams), Margaret Livingston (Marie), Alice Day (Nora), Theodore von Eltz (Dan), William Norton Bailey (Tiger Louie) |//
Filmed at Columbia Pictures Studio in the spring of 1928	
Distributor:	Columbia Pictures Corporation
Copyright:	7 August 1928 by Columbia Pictures Corporation (LP 25517)

The Films: Credits, Notes, and Synopses

Released: 19 June 1928 (?)[1]
Running time: 61 minutes (24 fps)

Notes

1. I have no reason to believe that this "official" release date is any more accurate than those listed in Capra filmographies for other films from his whirlwind period of production in 1928, but I have not been able to determine when or where the film actually premiered. Neither Variety nor the New York Times reviewed the film, nor is there an announcement or advertising concerning the film in these papers, or in the Los Angeles Times, during the week of June 19.

Existing prints of this film have been struck from a 35mm Danish nitrate print under the supervision of Kit Parker Films, with the titles translated into English by Barbara Thornbury. As a consequence, the names of the characters have been slightly altered: "Handsome Williams" is now "Pretty Boy Williams," "Tiger Louie" now "Denver Louis," and "Marie" now "Mary."

Synopsis

Police arrive at the smoldering remains of a bootlegger's truck, destroyed by a rival gang. A man who has survived the wreck refuses to talk.

At his headquarters, Tiger Louie scolds his underlings for not protecting his truck. One man questions whether even the machine guns Louie has provided can stop his chief rival, Handsome Williams. Louie throws the man out. His moll, Marie, has landed a job as a barmaid at William's speakeasy, the Handsome Club. Louie instructs her to report back when Williams leaves the hangout. Marie tries to flirt with Louie, but he rebuffs her.

At the Handsome Club, William's disfigured face is reflected in a slot machine mirror. He smashes the mirror and orders it removed from the club. A woman with an open cosmetic compact is warned that if Williams sees his face in the mirror he'll go crazy. Sampling the whiskey he has just stolen from Louie, Williams finds it distasteful. He phones Louie and tells him to provide better booze. Louie is not amused. Williams goes to the piano, where Marie has been singing, and mocks Louie for not being able to take a joke. Dan, an ex-concert pianist now on the skids as a speakeasy piano player, asks his boss why he doesn't quit before he gets killed. Williams assures him he is too fast to get shot. But when a young woman openly laughs at Williams's face, and customers join in the laughter, he retreats up a stairway to his apartment, humiliated.

Williams descends a back stairway and exits out onto the dark city streets. Marie trails him. He stops to listen to Nora, a beautiful young blind woman, play the violin. This is his nightly habit, a news vendor tells Marie. She quickly phones Louie to report

The Films: Credits, Notes, and Synopses

Williams's location. Moments later, Louie's car pulls up to the curb and a machine gun is fired. Williams saves himself by ducking down a stairwell, but Nora passes out. He carries her back to his apartment.

When Nora revives, she is frightened. Williams calms her by giving her the violin and asking her to play. At Williams's command, the customers are silent. Dan spontaneously accompanies Nora on the piano. When she is finished, Williams is weeping. Over dinner, she accepts his invitation to perform full time at the club.

The Handsome Club is transformed into a quiet, respectable restaurant. Dan, now clean-shaven and well dressed, performs with Nora. Jealous, Marie reminds Williams that he is lucky Nora cannot see his face. Briefly hurt by the remark, he is soon caught up again in the performance, which concludes to hearty applause. A drunk tries to pull Nora to his table. When Dan leaps to defend her, the drunk's companion joins in the struggle. Williams throws the rowdy customers out of the club, while Dan escorts Nora upstairs.

When Williams returns with a small bouquet of flowers, Dan reluctantly leaves so his boss can court Nora freely. Williams confesses he loves her; she insists on touching his face to "see" what he looks like. Dan returns, and Williams has Nora touch the pianist's face instead of his own. She is pleased to find the face handsome. Williams makes Dan promise he will never tell Nora about the deception. Dan agrees; he owes his boss too much to cross him.

Marie convinces Tiger Louie that they can stop Williams's theft of their liquor by kidnapping Nora. Williams and Nora return from a day at the amusement park. Exhausted and happy, she falls asleep on the couch. Secretly measuring her finger for a ring, Williams discovers that the barrel of his pistol is about the same size. He goes to a jewelry store and pulls out the gun. The jeweler thinks he is being held up, but Williams pays for the ring from his bankroll. Seeing his face in a mirror behind the counter, he smashes the mirror and pays for it as well. Back at the club, Dan covers Nora with a blanket and props up her feet. Awakened, she touches his face and embraces him. Meanwhile, Marie leads Louie's thugs up the back stairway into the room. They overwhelm Dan and kidnap Nora. After purchasing more gifts, Williams returns home to find Nora gone and Dan bloodied on the floor. When Dan explains what has happened, Williams orders his men to leave Louie's booze alone.

From a summer home in the country, Louie phones Williams to tease him about the kidnapping. Angered, Williams decides he must find Nora. Dan begs Williams to let him help, confessing that he, too, loves her. Williams attacks Dan violently and has to be restrained by some of his men. Meanwhile at the summer home, Louie traps Nora in her room for the sadistic pleasure of frightening her. Outside the room, Marie protests. Louie responds with a warning shot through the door just above her head. Nora becomes hysterical. So Marie calls

Williams, informing him of Nora's location. Dan again offers to help, but Williams shoves him aside.

Disguised as an iceman, Williams leads his gang on the rescue mission. At the summer home, Nora runs to the third-story window, as if to jump, but Louie stops her. The ice wagon pulls up outside. A Chinese cook lets the iceman into the kitchen, but soon finds himself at Williams's gunpoint. Hiding behind an armored shield, Louie opens machine-gun fire from the second floor, but Williams climbs up to the upper landing and knocks his rival out of position. A wild fight ensues. A telephone receiver is knocked off the hook, and the battle is heard by an operator, who summons the police.

Meanwhile Dan arrives to find Nora at the third-story window, calling for Williams. Dan scales the building and rescues her. Touching his face, she believes Williams has saved her. Inside the house, the battle has wound down. Louie is dead. Williams, Nora, and Dan escape before the police arrive. But Marie is shaken by Louie's death and tells the cops that Williams is responsible. The chief orders Williams captured, dead or alive.

In the getaway car, Nora is unconscious. Dan, shot in the shoulder as he fled the house, soon passes out also. Williams stops to get water to revive them. Waking, Nora touches Williams's face and is horrified. She grabs Dan and, touching his face, feels safe. Police sirens approach. Williams gives Dan the engagement ring, telling him that if he is half as good to Nora as Williams himself would have been, they will be even. Dan and Nora walk away.

Williams gets back in the car and is chased by the police over the country roads. Glancing in the rearview mirror, Williams sees his face one more time. He smashes the mirror and then takes his pistol and shoots himself. The car careens off the road into a lake. As the cops arrive on the scene, the car disappears underwater.

*9   SAY IT WITH SABLES (1928)

Production Company:	Columbia Pictures Corporation
Producer:	Harry Cohn/A Frank Capra Production
Director:	Frank Capra
Screenplay:	Story by Frank Capra and Peter Milne; continuity by Dorothy Howell
Photography:	Joe Walker
Editor:	Arthur Roberts
Art Director:	Harrison Wiley
Assistant Director:	Joe Nadel
Cast:	Francis X. Bushman (John Caswell), Helene Chadwick (Helen Caswell), Margaret Livingston (Irene Gordon), Arthur Rankin (Doug Caswell), June Nash (Marie Caswell), Alphonz Ethier (Mitchell), Edna Mae Cooper (maid)

The Films: Credits, Notes, and Synopses

Filmed at Columbia Pictures Studio in the spring of 1928.
Distributor: Columbia Pictures Corporation
Copyright: 1 September 1928 by Columbia Pictures Corporation (LP 25600)
Released: 8 August 1928 (Loew's-New York, New York City)[1]
Running time: 70 minutes

1. Most filmographies list 13 July 1928 as the release date, but the only play date I have been able to verify is the 8 August showing at the Loew's-New York. The film was not reviewed in <u>Variety</u> or the <u>New York Times</u>, but was reviewed by <u>Film Daily</u> on 12 August and by <u>Exhibitors Herald</u> on 8 December.

No prints of this film are known to exist. The Library of Congress, however, does have a three-minute trailer.

<u>Synopsis</u>

John Caswell, a wealthy banker, decides to remarry for the benefit of his motherless son. As a consequence, he breaks relations with his mistress, Irene Gordon, a gold-digging adventuress. Police tell Irene to get out of town.

John marries Helen, a proper society woman. His son, Doug, grows up and goes off to college. Doug returns on a vacation with news that he has found a wonderful girl. John asks his son to bring her to dinner. John happily complies with the request, but the woman turns out to be none other than Irene Gordon. John tries to buy Irene off, but she only laughs. This is her revenge, she tells him; she intends to marry Doug.

In an effort to break up the romance, John tells his son of his past relations with Irene. At first Doug refuses to listen. When the truth finally dawns on him, he leaves for Irene's, swearing that if she does not admit to the truth he will kill her. John follows his son to Irene's apartment and finds her dead from a revolver shot. To protect his son, he arranges the room so as to make it appear that Irene committed suicide.

Detective Mitchell, investigating the incident, discovers an earring in the dead woman's hand. Thinking that Irene's new sable coat may provide a clue, he traces the purchase of the coat back to Doug.

The detective arrives at the Caswell home as the family assembles for breakfast. Frightened by questioning, Doug confesses to having killed Irene, but Mitchell does not believe him. He searches the house and finds the mate to the earring in Helen Caswell's jewel case. Helen proposes a scenario whereby a woman is responsible for Irene's death. She could have gone to the apartment to secure certain letters that would ruin her son's life; in a subsequent encounter, Irene could

The Films: Credits, Notes, and Synopses

have threatened the woman with a revolver and been killed accidentally when the weapon went off.

Mitchell declares the theory farfetched; the evidence clearly points to suicide. But before he leaves, he places the two earrings on Helen's vanity. She realizes that he understands what truly occurred.

(This synopsis is drawn primarily from material submitted to the Library of Congress by Columbia Pictures for the purpose of securing copyright.)

10   **SUBMARINE (1928)**

L'Epave vivante (France), Femmine del mare (Italy)

Production Company:	Columbia Pictures Corporation
Producer:	Harry Cohn/An Irvin Willat Production[1]
Director:	Frank Capra
Screenplay:	Adapted by Winifred Dunn from a story by Norman Springer; continuity by Dorothy Howell[2]
Photography:	Joe Walker
Editor:	Arthur Roberts[3]
Art Director:	Harrison Wiley
Assistant Director:	Buddy Coleman
Theme Song:	"Pals, Just Pals" by Herman Ruby and Dave Dreyer[4]
Cast:	Jack Holt (Jack Dorgan), Ralph Graves (Bob Mason), Dorothy Revier (Bessie), Clarence Burton (submarine commander), Arthur Rankin (boy sailor)

Filmed at Columbia Pictures Studio and on location in San Pedro, California, in the summer of 1928

Distributor:	Columbia Pictures Corporation[5]
Copyright:	15 November 1928 by Columbia Pictures Corporation (LP 25833)
Released:	30 August 1928 (Embassy Theatre, New York City)
Running time:	93 minutes[6]

Notes

1. Irvin Willat was initially assigned to direct Submarine, but was taken off the project after three weeks of shooting. Capra thus received his first chance to direct an A picture at Columbia. He claims to have retained none of Willat's original footage (see The Name Above the Title, pp. 91-92).

2. The idea for the story came from two naval accidents: the sinking of a S-44 cruiser during battle maneuvers off the coast of California, and a submarine disaster in the Atlantic a short while later. The

The Films: Credits, Notes, and Synopses

navy, which had come under attack from the press for the accidents, served as consultants in the making of the film, leading one critic to speculate that the film might be seen as taking the navy's point of view on the accidents (see Robert J. Landry's review in <u>Variety</u>, entry 80).

3. Ben Pivar is listed as the editor in Victor Scherle and William Turner Levy's <u>The Films of Frank Capra</u> (entry 1062), but this is confirmed by no other source.

4. An orchestral score and effects track was added to an otherwise silent film during this period of transition to sound. Unfortunately, only the last section of the original sound-on-disk-recording survives. Current prints of the film, restored under the supervision of Kit Parker Films, include a new score by Carl Shrager; the sound switches to the original score and effects track for the last reel.

5. New prints of <u>Submarine</u> have been struck from a version originally released in the United Kingdom, where distribution of Columbia's films was handled by Film Booking Office. These prints, therefore, misleadingly describe the film as a FBO release.

6. Credits appended to Robert J. Landry's review of the film in <u>Variety</u> (see entry 80) list the original running time as 103 minutes. Thus, 10 minutes may be missing from existing versions.

<u>Synopsis</u>

Just off the coast of the Philippines, a U.S. Navy mine sweeper clears out the remains of a sunken ship from a harbor. After working on the wreck underwater, Jack Dorgan, the navy's crack diver, surfaces and announces that a depth charge can now be dropped. But when his foot becomes caught in a towline, he is pulled overboard with the bomb. His best friend, Bob Mason, dives into the water and cuts Jack free in the nick of time.

On shore leave, Jack and Bob are ready for a night on the town. Jack tries to pick up a Philippine woman, but fails. Bob, however, succeeds. Jack complains loudly to Bob that his friend always steals his girls. But when Bob gets into a fight with a soldier who claims prior rights to the woman, Jack takes Bob's side. After the brawl, they leave the bar smiling with the woman between them.

A few weeks later, Jack is sent home to California with the Pacific fleet while Bob stays behind. Jack tells Bob that at least he won't have to worry about his friend stealing his girls. Bob warns Jack that should he see a girl wearing dice-patterned garters, Bob's trademark, Jack is to leave her alone. Both try to make light of their separation, but they are clearly sorry to split up.

A year later in San Diego, Jack meets Bessie at the Palais Ballroom. The evening passes. They stay until the ballroom closes for

The Films: Credits, Notes, and Synopses

the night. He asks her if she can cook. "And how," she replies. As he helps her with her wrap, he proposes marriage.

Three months later, however, Jack is frying eggs for dinner while his wife primps before the mirror in the bedroom. She wants to go to the Palais Ballroom for dinner and dancing, but he reminds her he is leaving at midnight for a week-long assignment and suggests they spend the time together. At first she resists his embrace, but then gives in. At 11:10 he is packed and ready to go. If she gets lonesome, he tells her, remember he's thinking of her. "Don't worry," she calls after him, "I won't be lonesome."

On leave in San Diego, Bob complains to a barber that he has had no luck with women since he split up with his buddy. He goes off to the Palais Ballroom where he meets an unescorted Bessie. She accepts his invitation to dance, and then takes him to the table where Jack had first courted her. Bob asks her if she is married; she silently shows him a ringless finger. The evening passes. As the ballroom closes, he tells her he has a week to play. "I love to play," she replies.

So Bob and Bessie "play" on the beach, while Jack is hard at work at sea amid a violent storm. A week later, as they lie by a bonfire, Bob laments to Bessie that their week together is over. She seems sad, but insists she must go.

At the San Diego dock, Bob sees Jack with a bunch of young sailors returning from sea. As Jack lectures the sailors, Bob pelts him in the neck with BBs. Jack starts after his assailant, but when he sees it is Bob his anger turns quickly to glee. He invites Bob home to meet his new wife.

Bob meets Bessie. He is shocked; she is terrified. Summoned by his superior to file a report of his trip, Jack leaves Bob and Bessie alone, jokingly warning his wife about his pal's former habit of snitching Jack's girls. Alone with Bob, Bessie cautiously flirts with him, but he slaps her. She collapses, and he carries her to the couch. She renews her advances; Bob starts to succumb. Just then Jack returns and, despite Bob's apology, knocks his pal to the floor. Bob apologizes again and departs. Jack is distraught. Bessie embraces him.

Out on maneuvers, Bob's submarine collides with a destroyer and sinks to the ocean floor. Bob rescues a young sailor from the control room before it fills up with water. They settle with the rest of the crew in the torpedo room and await help. Unable to withstand the absence of oxygen below a certain depth a navy diver fails to get an airline to the sub. On shore, anxious mothers, wives and children stand vigil. In the sub, Bob tries to entertain the sweltering crew with card tricks while the commander rations the depleting supply of oxygen. The commander confesses to Bob he sees no chance of rescue. Only Jack Dorgan could reach them, says Bob.

The Films: Credits, Notes, and Synopses

When a second diver fails to make it to the sub, officials summon Jack. But Jack hesitates. Bessie has assured him that she never led Bob on, and she herself seems unconcerned about Bob's fate. Meanwhile, the crew is fading. A young sailor dies in Bob's arm. A desperate man turns the oxygen tank fully on, and the tank is soon depleted.

Discovering that Bessie has a pair of Bob's dice-patterned garters, Jack finally decides to accept the rescue mission. As Jack hurries by ship and plane to the site, the commander in the sub counts out a bullet for each sailor, instructing them to die like men. Jack descends into the water, vowing to stay down with the sub if he doesn't reach the men in time. Inside the sub, Bob requests to be the first man shot. Just as the commander inside raises his pistol, Jack reaches the sub. A knock on the wall by Jack stops the commander from shooting. An airline is lowered, and Jack hooks it up to the vessel. The men inside crawl to the spigots to breath the new air. Lifted back up to the ship, Jack requests a chaw. A huge hunk of tobacco is stuffed in his mouth; he smiles and passes out.

As Bessie sits at the table in the Palais Ballroom with a new sailor, Jack and Bob land ashore in a dinghy. Where do they go from here? Bob asks, holding out his palm. Jack spits in Bob's palm; Bob wipes his hand on Jack's jacket. Laughing, they walk off together.

*11   **THE POWER OF THE PRESS (1928)**

Production Company:	Columbia Pictures Corporation
Producer:	Jack Cohn/A Frank Capra Production
Director:	Frank Capra
Screenplay:	Adaptation and continuity by Frederick A. Thompson and Sonya Levien; from a story by Frederick A. Thompson
Photography:	Chet Lyons, Ted Tetzlaff
Editor:	Frank Atkinson
Art Director:	Harrison Wiley
Cast:	Douglas Fairbanks, Jr. (Clem Rogers), Jobyna Ralston (Jane Atwill), Mildred Harris (Marie), Philo McCullough (Blake), Wheeler Oakman (Van), Robert Edeson (city editor), Edwards Davis (Mr. Atwill), Del Henderson (Johnson), Charles Clary (district attorney)
Filmed at Columbia Pictures Studio, probably in the summer of 1928[1]	
Distributor:	Columbia Pictures Corporation
Copyright:	20 December 1928 by Columbia Pictures Corporation (LP 25940)
Released:	25 November 1928 (Broadway Theatre, New York City)[2]
Running time:	62 minutes

The Films: Credits, Notes, and Synopses

Notes

1. From existing sources, it is difficult to determine when the film was shot. Some filmographies list the film before <u>Submarine</u>, and although it is certain that the film was released and copyrighted after <u>Submarine</u>, it may have been filmed before. (The fact that the film has no sound track, in contrast to <u>Submarine</u> and all of Capra's films to follow, makes this all the more plausible.) Capra does not mention the film in his autobiography.

2. Most Capra filmographies list 31 October 1928 as the release date, but I have found no reviews of the film prior to its New York opening at the Broadway Theater on 25 November 1928.

Although <u>The Power of the Press</u> was screened at film festivals in Venice and West Germany in 1966, in America it was thought to be "lost." The American Film Institute, however, has recently acquired a print from a private collector; it may be available soon for study. Moreover, Kit Parker Films is in the process of preparing a 16mm print of the film which will be available for rental. Raymond Rohauer also claims to have "35mm original material" for the film (see Scott Isler, "Presenting Raymond Rohauer . . . Part Two," <u>Marble</u>, January-February 1976, p. 3).

Synopsis

It is a quiet night at the <u>Times</u>, a big-city newspaper. The front-line reporters are all out on their beats. The rewrite and desk men are busy with late copy. Clem Rogers, an aggressive, ambitious cub reporter recruited from the sticks, tries to create a masterpiece out of a dry weather report. When the city editor complains about the lack of front-page news, Clem begs for a chance to do some real reporting, extolling his talents at the expense of the paper's star reporter, Johnson. Just then the editor receives a phone call: the district attorney has been murdered. No other reporters are available, so Clem is given the assignment until Johnson can be reached.

Elated, Clem rushes to the D.A.'s home, the scene of the crime. In his haste, however, he misplaces his hat and police card and is barred by the cops. He tries crashing the gate, but to no avail. Johnson arrives and, to Clem's chagrin, refuses to identify him. So Clem goes to the rear of the house in search of another entrance. There he spies a girl escaping out a back window. He follows her. She drops her purse without knowing it, and Clem picks it up. She drives away in a roadster. Clem learns from Van, another man who is following her, that she is Jane Atwill, daughter of the reform candidate for mayor.

Clem returns to the <u>Times</u>. His story tops that of Johnson. The presses are halted and a new story is written under Clem's by-line. The next morning the city is electrified by the sensational scoop in

The Films: Credits, Notes, and Synopses

the paper. Clem moves to a star reporter's desk. Much to Johnson's disgust, Clem gloats.

Jane Atwill is arrested. She admits that she was with the D.A. when he was shot, but claims she does not know who fired the gun. She is released on bail, but her father's campaign appears finished. Angry, she goes to the <u>Times</u> and convinces Clem that his article has falsely implicated her in the crime. When Clem tries to force the editor to print a retraction, however, he is fired. Johnson and a fellow reporter happily give Clem a "grand bounce" out of the office.

Meanwhile Van reports to his boss, Blake, the rival candidate for mayor. Blake is pleased with the effect of the scandal, but is concerned that his own reputation will be tarnished if the public learns of his mistress, Marie. So he is having her held prisoner in an isolated house under close watch.

Clem sees Van outside Blake's office. He puts his hand on Van's shoulder; startled, Van pulls out his gun as he spins around. When he sees Clem, Van relaxes, but Clem's suspicions are aroused.

Clem calls on Jane. She shows him a portfolio the D.A. handed her right before he was shot. It contains several photographs, including a portrait of Marie. But the contents mean nothing to Clem or Jane. Nevertheless, Clem has an idea.

Clem visits Van at a speakeasy. Feigning intoxicated camaraderie, Clem lets Van see the portfolio. Skillfully, but not unobserved, Van extracts the picture of Marie before returning the portfolio. Clem staggers out of the speakeasy, muttering that he must return to the office with his big scoop. He quickly rejoins Jane. When they discover that Marie's photo is missing, they try to phone her. But she has moved and her whereabouts are unknown.

Clem gets another idea. Imitating the voice of Blake's bootlegger, he calls Blake and offers to deliver a case of Scotch to Marie. Appreciating the gesture, Blake reveals Marie's hiding place. Clem takes Jane's roadster to the hideout, where he makes his way past a guard into the house. Irritated at her incarceration, Marie welcomes him. But Clem tries to trick her by telling her that Blake and Van have accused her of the murder. Meanwhile Blake learns that his bootlegger never called him. Suspecting a ruse, Van assembles his men and heads for the hideout.

Van arrives just as Marie is signing a statement accusing him of killing the D.A. Holding Clem and Marie at gunpoint, he forces Clem to write a suicide note. Marie leaps for the window. Van fires, and she collapses. But when he comes near her, she leaps to her feet and pulls a curtain over him. She and Clem bind him with cord. Clem calls the <u>Times</u> at once. The editor agrees to listen to Clem's story, but Van frees one of his hands and disconnects the phone. Clem binds Van more securely, but is now unable to phone in the story.

The Films: Credits, Notes, and Synopses

While Marie decoys the gang outside, Clem carries Van to the roadster. She makes it back to the car just before the thugs realize what is happening. A chase follows, with Clem bent on reaching the <u>Times</u> in time to get his story in the morning edition on election day.

Clem and Marie arrive at the office, dragging Van between them. The presses are stopped, photos of the trio are taken, and a new story written. The truth reaches the public before they vote. Jane's father is elected mayor, and Clem takes Jane as his bride.

(This synopsis is drawn primarily from material submitted to the Library of Congress by Columbia Pictures for the purpose of securing copyright.)

12 THE YOUNGER GENERATION (1929)

<u>Loin du ghetto</u> (France), <u>La nuova generazione</u> (Italy)

Production Company:	Columbia Pictures Corporation
Producer:	Jack Cohn/A Frank R. Capra Production
Director:	Frank R. Capra
Screenplay:	Sonya Levien, from the play <u>It Is to Laugh</u> by Fannie Hurst;[1] dialogue by Howard J. Green
Photography:	Ted Tetzlaff
Sound Cameraman:	Ben Reynolds[2]
Editor:	Arthur Roberts
Art Director:	Harrison Wiley
Technical Director:	Edward Schulter
Production Manager:	Joe Cooke
Assistant Director:	Tenny Wright
Sound:	Recorded by Western Electric (sound-on-disk) with the Columbia Symphony Orchestra
Musical Conductor:	Bakelienikoff
Cast:	Jean Hersholt (Julius Goldfish, Papa), Ricardo Cortez (Morris Goldfish), Rosa Rosanova (Tilda Goldfish, Mama), Lina Basquette (Birdie Goldfish), Rex Lease (Eddie Lesser), Martha Franklin (Mrs. Lesser), Julia Swayne Gordon (Mrs. Striker), Julanne Johnston (Irma Striker), Jack Raymond (Pinsky), Syd Crossley (butler), Otto Fries (tradesman), Bernard Siegel (Kruger), Walter Brennan

Filmed at Columbia Pictures Studio and at sound stages in Santa Monica, California, in the winter of 1929

Distributor:	Columbia Pictures Corporation[3]
Copyright:	18 March 1929 by Columbia Pictures Corporation (LP 227)
Released:	9 March 1929 (Colony Theatre, New York City)
Running time:	75 minutes

The Films: Credits, Notes, and Synopses

Notes

1. It Is to Laugh by Fannie Hurst opened at the Eltinge Theatre in New York City on 26 December 1927. As described in the New York Times review (27 December 1927, p. 42), the play seems very close to the film adaptation, with the exception that the final curtain fell with the death of Papa Goldfish.

2. Ben Reynolds is not mentioned in any Capra filmographies, nor is he credited on the film, but Capra cites him as the sound cameraman in his autobiography (see The Name Above the Title, p. 101).

3. Existing prints of The Younger Generation have been struck from a version originally released in the United Kingdom, where distribution of Columbia's films was handled by Film Booking Office. These prints therefore misleadingly describe the film as a FBO release.

A transitional talkie, The Younger Generation contains four lip-synchronized dialogue passages: (1) Morris announces his plans to change his name, upsetting his father; Birdie and Morris quarrel; Eddie arrives, joins the argument, and is evicted by Morris. (2) Mama tries to comfort Papa; Morris arrives with news of the robbery; Birdie arrives with her new engagement ring; a detective comes in search of Eddie. (3) Papa visits Mrs. Lesser for news about Birdie; a boy reads a letter from Eddie; Papa and Mrs. lesser sing together. (4) Mama refuses Morris's offer of gifts; Birdie comforts Mama as the baby cries; Morris inquires after Eddie's finances; Mama announces she is going to live with Birdie. The dialogue in all other scenes is conveyed through titles, but an orchestral score and selected sound effects are heard throughout these "silent" passages.

Synopsis

Amid a bustling crowd along Delancey Street in New York's Lower East Side, Papa Goldfish jokes with his friends about his lack of concern for money. At home, Mama Goldfish removes freshly baked bread from the oven. Her young daughter, Birdie, is hungry, but Mama slaps her hand for taking the largest piece. The largest is always reserved for Birdie's brother, Morris. When Mama leaves to find Morris, however, Birdie gives the piece to the boy next door, Eddie Lesser, who entertains her from his nearby tenement window with a song he has written.

Mama finds Morris selling newspapers, and praising him for his industry, sends him home for the bread. Morris returns to find his piece gone. When Birdie shyly offers him what is left of her own, he slaps her. Eddie climbs in the window to defend her. In the scuffle that follows, Morris accidentally knocks oil onto the hot stove, setting the apartment ablaze. Meanwhile Mama has found Papa and is chiding him for his indolence. Hearing the fire trucks, they rush home to see their tenement ablaze. Birdie runs to her father, but Morris has not been found. Moments later he emerges from the burning

The Films: Credits, Notes, and Synopses

building with a bundle of goods. "Now we can have a fire sale," he cheerily announces.

Years pass. Morris parlays a secondhand furniture store run with his father into an imported antiques shop on Fifth Avenue with himself as sole proprietor. The Goldfishes now live in luxury. But Papa at night dreams of being back on Delancey Street, laughing with his friends. He wakes up to find out from the butler that Morris now requires him to bathe before dressing. The old man refuses and returns to bed. When Birdie mocks Morris's social pretensions, Mama angrily defends him. So Birdie comforts her father, playfully kissing him, and coaxes him to take his bath. Once downstairs, he strikes up a friendship with a delivery man who overhears Papa's attempt to get the butler to laugh and joins in on the joke. They proceed to play a spirited game of poker, with Papa winning all the groceries.

At dinner, Morris announces that for business reasons he is changing his name to Maurice Fish. Acrimonious words are exchanged between him and Birdie, while Papa looks on, hurt and confused. When Eddie Lesser, now a piano player, arrives to see Birdie, tensions escalate. Morris ejects Eddie on the grounds that he does not entertain "East Side bums" in his house. Eddie warns Morris before going that the day will come when he will welcome anyone in his home.

Depressed by the loss of the family name, Papa huddles before the fireplace, a tiny figure within the ornately furnished room. Mama places an embroidered shawl over his shoulders to warm him, but she does not understand how her husband could be cold in such a nice house. Meanwhile Eddie, distressed over his forced separation from Birdie, tries to make some fast money by acting as decoy in a jewelry store heist. Morris returns home with news of the robbery; Birdie follows, sporting an engagement ring from Eddie. Mama and Morris are quick to oppose the marriage. When a detective arrives looking for Eddie, Morris is more than happy to help in the search. Papa comforts a weeping Birdie, playfully kissing her to get her to smile.

Birdie offers to marry Eddie immediately if he turns himself in and serves his time. He agrees. She stands by him proudly at the police station and bids him an emotional farewell at the prison. When she returns home, however, Morris immediately evicts her, claiming that their parents are too ashamed of her to even say good-bye. Papa, in fact, pines for Birdie. Mama, however, worries that Morris's social standing has been tarnished.

Two years later, Morris has climbed still higher up the ladder of success. He maintains the barrier between his sister and parents by confiscating Birdie's plaintive letters. Nevertheless, the future looks brighter for Birdie and Eddie; they now have a baby boy, and Birdie has sold one of Eddie's songs for $1,000.

Papa sits morosely in the huge living room. The butler lowers the venetian blinds and slats of shadows fall across the old man's

The Films: Credits, Notes, and Synopses

face. Rousing himself from this entombment, Papa heads for Delancey Street in search of Birdie. He learns from Mrs. Lesser not only that Birdie is well but that he is a grandfather. He weeps for joy and sings a folk song with Mrs. Lesser.

Mama covers for Papa's absence at a dinner party by telling Morris his father is sick. She journeys to Delancey Street where she finds Papa celebrating with a throng of old friends, who shower him with flowers. When she brings Papa home, they are stopped by the doorman because of their parcel of flowers and told to go up the back way. Papa protests vehemently. Morris arrives on the scene with his dinner guests, an upper-crust girl and her mother. To save face, he pretends his parents are servants, dismissing them coldly. Led to his bedroom by Mama, Papa bitterly claims he should die if he lies again in the fancy bed. So she takes him back out on the street, where they rest briefly on a park bench as the night wind moans. Despite Mama's protest, he insists on moving on. But when he tries to stand up, he collapses in pain.

Mama brings Papa home and, with Morris's help, puts him to bed. Barely conscious, Papa calls for Birdie. Morris phones her. Birdie arrives for a tearful reunion with her father. She shows him his grandson. As the family gathers at the bedside, they laugh together; even Morris manages to smile. Papa dies in peace.

Now a widow, Mama sits alone in a rocking chair. Morris arrives and offers her a trip to Europe and any gifts she wants, but she is unmoved. Birdie and Eddie arrive with the baby, and Birdie puts the embroidered shawl around her mother's shoulders. The music store Birdie and Eddie now run is doing good business. Mama announces her decision to move in with Birdie, refusing Morris's offer to have them all live together with him.

Abandoned, Morris stands by the fireplace as the butler lowers the blinds. Shadows cross Morris's face. He puts the embroidered shawl over his shoulders and turns to sit before the fire in the empty living room.

*13   **THE DONOVAN AFFAIR (1929)**

       L'affaire Donovan (France), Il mistero Donovan (Italy)

Production Company:	Columbia Pictures Corporation
Producer:	Harry Cohn/A Frank R. Capra Production
Director:	Frank R. Capra
Screenplay:	Continuity by Dorothy Howell, from the play The Donovan Affair by Owen Davis;[1] dialogue and titles by Howard J. Green[2]
Photography:	Teddy Tetzlaff
Editor:	Arthur Roberts
Art Director:	Harrison Wiley
Assistant Director:	Tenny Wright

The Films: Credits, Notes, and Synopses

Sound: Movietone
Cast: Jack Holt (Inspector Killian), Dorothy Revier (Jean Rankin), William Collier, Jr. (Cornish), Agnes Ayres (Lydia Rankin), John Roche (Jack Donovan), Fred Kelsey (Carney), Hank Mann (Dr. Lindsey), Wheeler Oakman (Porter), Virginia Browne Faire (Mary Mills), Alphonse Ethier (Capt. Peter Rankin), Edward Hearn (Nelson), Ethel Wales (Mrs. Lindsay), John Wallace (Dobbs)
Filmed at a rented sound studio in Los Angeles in the spring of 1929
Distributor: Columbia Pictures Corporation
Copyright: 10 May 1929 by Columbia Pictures Corporation (LP 381)
Released: 27 April 1929 (Roxy Theatre, New York City)[3]
Running time: 83 minutes

Notes

1. Davis's play opened at the Fulton Theatre in New York City on 30 August 1926.

2. <u>The Donovan Affair</u> was Capra's first all-talking film, but titles were used in a silent version released to theaters not yet equipped for sound.

3. Capra filmographies usually list 11 April as the release date, but I have found no reviews of the film prior to its opening at the Roxy on 27 April.

Kit Parker Films is restoring a 16mm version of this film.

Synopsis

Jack Donovan, gambler and philanderer, has aroused the animosity of an uncommon number of people. Having failed to pay off some heavy track debts, he is marked for slaying by his creditors. One of their number, Porter, is elected to do the job. Donovan is also involved in affairs with two women: Lydia Rankin, ex-actress and young second wife of Captain Peter Rankin; and Mary Mills, servant at the Rankin estate. Hard pressed for money, Donovan blackmails Lydia by threatening to tell her husband of the affair. Mary, moreover, fearful that Donovan's affection has waned in favor of Lydia, is deeply jealous.

Donovan has unintentionally provoked the hostility of David Cornish as well. In love with Lydia's stepdaughter, Jean, Cornish suspects that Donovan visits the estate to see her. Because she is protecting Lydia to spare her father unhappiness, Jean cannot tell Cornish the truth. One night Lydia, clad in Jean's cloak, meets Donovan outside the house. Spying them, Cornish believes the assignation is between Donovan and Jean. When Donovan starts to leave,

The Films: Credits, Notes, and Synopses

Cornish gives him a beating and threatens to kill him if he sees Donovan with Jean again.

All these figures gather at the estate one evening for Captain Rankin's birthday dinner party. Even Porter, an old friend of the Captain's, is present. Rankin, who himself has begun to suspect an affair between his wife and Donovan, slips a revolver in his pocket before he goes down to greet the guests. During dinner, Donovan shows the guests a mysterious ring which supposedly shines in the dark like a cat's eye and holds peculiar power over women. Several of the guests are skeptical. Donovan asks that the lights be turned off so that he may prove his claim. Nelson, a quiet and well-mannered butler, turns the lights off. The ring shines, much to the amazement of all. Suddenly a dark shadow obliterates the reflection of the glass. A groan is heard and then a fall. The lights are turned on. Donovan is slumped in his seat with a carving knife buried in his back. A doctor among the guests pronounces Donovan dead.

Inspector Killian and Carney, his assistant, arrive at the scene. Everyone speaks at once, causing great confusion. When order is established, Killian asks to see the ring. To everyone's surprise, it has disappeared. The inspector orders that everyone be searched. A revolver is found on Porter. Identifying Porter as a former criminal, Killian accuses him of the crime. Porter emphatically denies participating in the murder, but volunteers to give the inspector a hint as to who is truly guilty. Meanwhile Killian discovers the ring in his own pocket. When Porter describes the surprising luminosity of the ring, Killian is skeptical. The lights are turned off for a second demonstration, and Porter goes on with his story. As he is about to announce his conclusion, Porter ceases to speak. The lights are quickly turned on. Porter is dead--the carving knife thrust in his back--and the ring has once again vanished. The inspector is irate that a murder has been committed under his nose.

A police officer arrives with evidence located in Donovan's apartment. It is a letter, seemingly in a woman's hand, torn into pieces. Killian asks Nelson, the butler, to piece the letter together. Nelson secretly hides some of the pieces. At Killian's request, Nelson then gets the women present to write a few words so that their handwriting can be compared with that in the letter. Nelson hides one of the samples he collects. None of the other samples matches the original, leaving Killian at a dead end.

Suddenly there is a disturbance outside. Dobbs, a wooden-legged gardener, is caught snooping around the grounds. Although he insists he knows nothing about the murder, he admits that he is searching for the ring. It once was his own, he claims, but someone stole it. Suspicions against Dobbs are dropped when it is ascertained that the carpet near the chair where the dead men were murdered bears no marks of the gardener's wooden leg.

The Films: Credits, Notes, and Synopses

Killian, attentive to every movement in the room, sees Jean burn a spot of blood off Cornish's cuff with a cigarette. The inspector accuses Cornish of the crime. Cornish insists he is innocent, claiming that when the lights were off the first time, he felt somebody brush by him. But Cornish admits that he knows more about the crime than he has told and has only withheld the information because he, too, had a grievance against Donovan and might well have killed the man himself had not someone beaten him to it. Now that he is in a pinch, however, Cornish will tell what he knows about the complicated affair.

Cornish asks that the lights be turned off again, and everyone sits where they were before. With the stage thus set, he will attempt to explain how the murder was accomplished. Killian is to stand beside him to protect him. Cornish's requests are followed. As Cornish is about to mention a name, a struggle and a cry are heard in the dark. The lights are turned on to reveal Nelson struggling in the arms of the inspector. In Nelson's gloved hand is the carving knife. He confesses. He killed Donovan because he suspected him of having an affair with Mary Mills, whom Nelson had loved for many years although she did not love him. Nelson then killed Porter to prevent him from telling what he might have known about the first crime.

(This synopsis is drawn primarily from material submitted to the Library of Congress by Columbia Pictures for the purpose of securing copyright.)

14 **FLIGHT (1929)**

Diavoli volanti (Italy)

Production Company:	Columbia Pictures Corporation
Producer:	Harry Cohn/A Frank R. Capra Production
Director:	Frank R. Capra
Screenplay:	Scenario by Howard J. Green, from a story by Ralph Graves; dialogue by Frank R. Capra
Photography:	Joseph Walker, Joseph Novak; aerial photography by Elmer Dyer
Assistant Cameraman:	Paul Perry
Editors:	Gene Milford, Ben Pivar, Maurice Wright
Art Director:	Harrison Wiley
Technical Sound Engineer:	John Livadary
Sound Mix Engineer:	Harry Blanchard
Sound Recorders:	Dean Daly, Eddy Hahn
Sound Equipment Supervisor:	Ellis Gray
Assistant Director:	Buddy Colemen
Adviser:	Capt. Francis E. Pierce
Cast:	Jack Holt (Panama Williams), Ralph Graves ("Lefty" Phelps), Lila Lee (Elinor), Alan Roscoe (major), Harold Goodwin (Steve

The Films: Credits, Notes, and Synopses

Roberts), Jimmy De La Cruze (Sandino, Lobo)
Filmed at Columbia Pictures studio and on location at the North Island Marine Base, San Diego, and in the foothills near La Mesa, California, in the summer of 1929

Distributor: Columbia Pictures Corporation
Copyright: 4 December 1929 by Columbia Pictures Corporation (LP 884)
Released: 13 September 1929 (George M. Cohan Theatre, New York City)[1]
Running time: 110 minutes

Notes

1. Most Capra filmographies inaccurately list the release date as 18 September 1929.

Flight was a major Columbia release, with a $2.00 admission at its Broadway opening and a well-publicized road-show campaign aimed at competing with films from the major studios.

Synopsis

Lefty Phelps is brought off the bench in the closing moments of a dramatic New Year's Day football game and runs with the ball in the wrong direction, losing the game for his school. Jeered by the fans and the subject of derisive headlines in the afternoon papers, Lefty seeks refuge in a men's room. When he overhears Panama Williams, a Marine Corps flyer who has witnessed the play, speculate that the player was bribed to throw the game, Lefty angrily assaults his accuser. Impressed by the young man's fervor, Williams immediately apologizes and offers his friendship.

After he graduates, Lefty enlists in the Marine Corps flying school where Panama is an instructor. Panama lectures the new recruits, not recognizing Lefty. But when Lefty reintroduces himself, Panama tells him he now has a perfect opportunity to erase his past by proving himself in the air, and he takes special interest in the young man's progress as a flyer. Lefty soon falls in love with a young nurse on the base, Elinor. Unfortunately, Panama has long wanted to propose to the nurse himself, but hasn't been able to summon the nerve. Neither Lefty nor Panama is aware of the other's feelings about her.

On the day of his first solo flight, Lefty is teased mercilessly by a fellow recruit, Steve Roberts, who reminds him of his bonehead play on the football field. Upset, Lefty crashes the plane during takeoff. Panama rescues him from the burning aircraft, injuring his hands in the process. Lefty is taken to the hospital, where Elinor nurses him back to health and bolsters his ego. Although Lefty has flunked flying school and been grounded, Panama gets him assigned as a mechanic on a mission to Nicaragua. Before they leave, Panama shows

The Films: Credits, Notes, and Synopses

Lefty a photograph of his girlfriend--it is Elinor. Lefty says nothing of his own love for her and tears up his photo of Elinor when his mentor has gone.

Elinor is sent to Nicaragua with a crew of nurses. But when she arrives at the air base, lefty receives her very coolly. As Panama gets ready for a date with Elinor that evening, he senses Lefty's depression, but attributes it to the boy's failure as a flyer. Worried that Lefty will get himself in trouble that night at the local cantina, Panama orders him to stay and work at the camp. Lefty is unhappy, but the tension between them is relieved when they briefly roughhouse with one another. Panama playfully spanks his young friend.

Despite Panama's orders, however, Lefty sets off for the cantina that night. Panama, after once again failing to propose to Elinor, retrieves Lefty from the cantina, sneaking him back into camp past the guards. Elinor comes to their tent to make sure Lefty is safe. When she hears what Panama has done, she gives him a friendly kiss, which he interprets as a sign of romantic affection.

The next day Panama asks Lefty to propose to Elinor on Panama's behalf, figuring that the college-educated youth will know the right words to use. Lefty reluctantly does so. The proposal convinces Elinor that the time has come to tell Panama of her love for Lefty. But when she does, Panama thinks he's been double-crossed. He slaps Lefty.

Their confrontation is interrupted by an alarm. Native rebels, led by their bandit leader Lobo, are attacking a Marine outpost; aerial support is needed. Panama is picked to ride as observer/gunner for the major. Lefty is similarly teamed with Steve Roberts. The mission is successful, but Lefty's plane is shot down in a swamp. After returning to the camp to refuel, the major leads an aerial search party, but Panama, still angry at Lefty, reports in sick rather than make the rescue flight. Meanwhile in the swamp, Roberts is paralyzed with a broken back. Despite their former animosity, Lefty tries to help his wounded comrade. The major's rescue mission fails.

Elinor convinces Panama that Lefty never betrayed him. So Panama requests permission to go on a search mission alone. Meanwhile Roberts dies. Lefty covers the body with a parachute silk and sets the airplane aflame. He stands at attention during the spectacular cremation. He then hears a plane and looks up; it is Panama. While landing the plane, Panama is shot in the leg by the natives. So Lefty takes over the controls and skillfully gets the plane airborne. Elated by his triumph, he performs a series of daredevil aerial stunts, much to the chagrin of the major on the ground below. The plane loses a wheel. Panama tries to take over the stick to bring the plane down, but Lefty won't let him. Lefty lands it safely.

The Films: Credits, Notes, and Synopses

Sometime later, Lefty has been awarded his wings and is now an instructor at the Marine flying school. He lectures the new recruits in the same manner Panama once lectured him. Elinor, now his wife, appears in a fancy new car. Panama stands nearby, alone.

15   LADIES OF LEISURE (1930)

Femmine di lusso (Italy)

Production Company:	Columbia Pictures Corporation
Producer:	Harry Cohn/A Frank R. Capra Production
Director:	Frank R. Capra
Screenplay:	Adaptation and dialogue by Jo Swerling, from the play Ladies of the Evening by Milton Herbert Gropper;[1] titles by Dudley Early[2]
Photography:	Joseph Walker
Editor:	Maurice Wright
Art Director:	Harrison Wiley
Musical Director:	Bakaleinikoff
Chief Sound Engineer:	John P. Livadary
Sound Mix Engineers:	Harry Blanchard, Edward Bernds[3]
Assistant Director:	David Selman
Cast:	Barbara Stanwyck (Kay Arnold), Ralph Graves (Jerry Strong), Lowell Sherman (Bill Standish), Marie Prevost (Dot Lamar), Nance O'Neill (Mrs. Strong), Juliette Compton (Claire Collins), George Fawcett (Mr. Strong), Johnnie Walker (Charlie), Charles Butterworth (party guest)

Filmed at Columbia Pictures Studio and on location at Malibu Lake, California, in December 1929 and January 1930.

Distributor:	Columbia Pictures Corporation
Copyright:	1 May 1930 by Columbia Pictures Corporation (LP 1295)
Released:	2 April 1930 (R-K-O Orpheum, Los Angeles)[4]
Running Time:	98 minutes

Notes

1. Ladies of the Evening by Milton Herbert Gropper opened at the Belasco Theatre in New York City on 23 December 1924.

2. Titles were used in a silent version of the film for release in theaters not yet equipped for sound.

3. Although Bernds did not receive official credit, he reportedly filled in as soundman during on-location shooting at Malibu Lake and then stayed on for the rest of the filming. Bernds subsequently worked for Capra throughout the 1930s (see entry 1137, pp. 36, 65).

4. Ladies of Leisure's New York premiere was a heavily publicized opening at the Capitol Theatre on 23 May, by which time the film had

The Films: Credits, Notes, and Synopses

enjoyed successful runs in major cities around the country, including Los Angeles, Detroit, Chicago, and Pittsburgh. Most Capra filmographies inaccurately list 5 April 1930 as the release date rather than 2 April.

Ladies of Leisure was originally released in both silent and sound versions. Columbia did not retain material for the silent version, but a rare print has been preserved by the American Film Institute.

Synopsis

A party is in full swing at the Manhattan penthouse-studio of artist Jerry Strong, but Jerry seems detached from the revelry around him. His fiancée, Claire, asks him what's wrong. Jerry passes his ailment off as a headache, assuring Claire that he isn't angry she has borrowed his place for the party. Bill Standish, a mutual friend, inquires of Claire if she and Jerry are quarreling. Claire complains that Jerry wants her to be a "lily," when in fact she is an "orchid." Once the two are married, Billy replies coyly, Jerry will discover that there are no lilies left in the world. Claire feigns shock. Bill returns to his occupation of the evening: painting the backs of willing young women.

Later that evening Jerry goes for a drive in the country. His car gets a flat tire. When he stops to change it, he spots a young woman trying to dock a rowboat along a nearby stream. She is Kay Arnold, a professional "party girl," who has escaped the evening's festivities aboard a nearby yacht. She accepts a ride with Jerry back to New York. Borrowing his coat to keep warm, she locates his wallet in the coat pocket. After cheering him up with some funny faces, Kay falls asleep on Jerry's shoulder.

The next morning at breakfast, Kay entertains her roommate, Dot, with the details of her adventure with Jerry. He has propositioned her by asking her to pose as a model, Kay claims. Dot gets a call from a client who wishes to engage the services of both her and a friend. Kay turns down the job: she has work to do at Jerry's.

The same morning, Jerry has an elegant breakfast with his upper-class parents. His crusty father is upset about last night's party and criticizes Jerry for the company he keeps. Jerry denies responsibility for either the party or the partygoers, but he covers up for Claire, of whom his father is fond. When Mr. Strong contrasts Jerry's dabbling with paint to his own successful career as a railroad baron, Mrs. Strong quickly defends her son's work. Outnumbered, Mr. Strong departs. Jerry tells his mother that he thinks he's found a girl who, beneath her mask, embodies a quality he seeks to paint on canvas—hope.

The first session between Jerry and Kay turns into a playful sparring match. Jerry tries to get her to assume an inspirational pose, to "look up," and asks her to exchange her excessive makeup and

The Films: Credits, Notes, and Synopses

gaudy clothes for a simpler, more natural appearance. But Kay wittily resists. Claire arrives with Bill, and the two women size each other up. Claire wants Jerry to leave immediately for dinner and a party, but he decides to continue working with Kay.

The next day Kay dresses in the kind of clothes Jerry has suggested. She confesses to Dot that she hasn't yet hooked Jerry and can't figure him out. Meanwhile, Bill visits Jerry in search of booze and warns him that Kay is a gold digger. Jerry disagrees, pointing out that although she first took his wallet, she returned it. Kay arrives while Jerry has stepped out, and Bill offers to take her on a cruise to Havana. When Jerry returns, he excitedly resumes working with Kay. She tells him of Bill's proposal, but Jerry doesn't seem jealous. Instead his attention is focused on getting her to appear as she did that first night when she slept on his shoulder.

Bill calls on Kay at her apartment. Kay isn't in, but Dot fills in for her. She admits openly to Bill that she and Kay are career gold diggers. Meeting with Kay later, Dot expresses concern that her roommate is losing her professional detachment with Jerry. Kay protests adamantly.

During a break in the next session with Jerry, however, Kay is openly moved by his description of starry nights in Arizona. Look up at the stars, he coaxes her. She protests that they are too far away. But seeing her framed by the window against the black sky, he is inspired to capture her expression at that very moment on canvas. They work long into the evening. Tired, she agrees to spend the night. She undresses by the window, while he undresses in his room. She watches his door, but he emerges only to cover her with a blanket while she feigns sleep. Kay is touched by the gesture, and relieved.

In the morning Kay cooks and serves breakfast; she is unsure of, but clearly enjoys, her domestic role. Jerry's father arrives and firmly suggests that Jerry marry Claire. Jerry refuses. The visit ends bitterly when Mr. Strong challenges Kay's virtue and tries to buy her off. Jerry and Kay decide to leave for Arizona.

Jerry tries to patch up his relationship with his father, but his father disowns him. His mother offers her support, but then secretly calls on Kay and tries to bribe her. When she realizes that Kay is truly not interested in money, Mrs. Strong argues that Jerry would be ruined socially by the marriage and appeals to Kay's love for her son. Kay tearfully promises to give Jerry up.

Kay sinks into depression. When Dot steps out to buy some liquor to cheer them both up, Kay calls Bill and offers to go with him to Havana. He arranges to pick her up shortly. But while she is ironing her clothes for the trip, Jerry arrives with tickets for Arizona. Kay stalls for time, claiming she still has to pack. When he leaves, she hurries down to Bill's waiting limousine. She promises her new benefactor she will be cheerful if liquor is provided.

The Films: Credits, Notes, and Synopses

Dot returns in time to see them drive off. She tries to call Jerry, but without success. As Kay and Bill board ship, Dot reaches Jerry's building. The doorman tries to call him, but the line is busy. Now at sea, Kay stands at the boat rail, staring at the water as if drawn to it. Dot climbs the apartment stairs, reaching the top floor just before Jerry is about to descend in the elevator. He radios the ship at once. But while Kay is being paged, she leaps into the water.

Rescued, Kay wakes up to Jerry's voice. They are reunited.

16   RAIN OR SHINE (1930)

Luci del circo (Italy)

Production Company:	Columbia Pictures Corporation
Producer:	Harry Cohn/A Frank Capra Production
Director:	Frank Capra
Screenplay:	Dialogue and continuity by Joe Swerling and Dorothy Howell, from the play by James Gleason and Maurice Marks[1]
Photograph:	Joseph Walker
Editor:	Maurice Wright
Art Director:	Harrison Wiley
Musical Score:	Bakaleinikoff
Song:	"Sitting on a Rainbow" by Jack Yellen and Dan Daugherty
Chief Sound Engineer:	John P. Livadary
Sound Mix Engineer:	E.L. Bernds
Assistant Director:	Sam Nelson
Cast:	Joe Cook (Smiley Johnson), Louise Fazenda (Frankie, the princess), Joan Peers (Mary Rainey), William Collier, Jr. (Bud Conway), Tom Howard (Amos K. Shrewsbury), Dave Chasen (Dave), Alan Roscoe (Dalton, the ringmaster), Adolph Milar (Foltz, the lion tamer), Clarence Muse (Nero), Edward Martindale (Mr. Conway), Nora Lane (Grace Conway), Tyrell Davis (Lord Gwynne), Nella Walker
Filmed at Columbia Pictures Studio in the spring of 1930	
Distributor:	Columbia Pictures Corporation
Copyright:	14 August 1930 by Columbia Pictures Corporation (LP 1491)
Released:	7 August 1930 (Globe Theatre, New York City)[2]
Running time:	87 minutes

Notes

1. The play opened at the George M. Cohan Theatre in New York City on 9 February 1928. A musical comedy, with a book by James Gleason and

The Films: Credits, Notes, and Synopses

Maurice Marks, music by Milton Ager and Owen Murphy, and lyrics by Jack Yellen, it was stripped of its songs during the course of its adaptation to the screen (not an infrequent occurrence at this time). "Sitting on a Rainbow" (the tune of which is very close to that of "Singin' in the Rain") is heard in the background, but not performed. The film does retain, however, the verbal comedy of Joe Cook, Tom Howard, and Dave Chasen, all of whom had appeared in the original Broadway play.

2. <u>Variety</u> reviewed the film on 23 July 1930, based on an unannounced preview held at the Globe Theater on 17 July (see entry 114), but <u>Rain or Shine</u> was not commercially released until 7 August. Capra filmographies usually list the release date as 15 August, but this is inaccurate.

<u>Synopsis</u>

The lead wagon of the John T. Rainey circus runs aground in the mud on a rainy night. Manager Smiley Johnson uses the strength of the elephant he is riding to free the vehicle. The caravan starts moving again.

Smiley calls on Mary Rainey, who has recently inherited the show from her father. A stack of unpaid bills has her troubled, but Smiley distracts her with some cheerful fast-talking and tears up the bills. In another wagon, Dalton, the ringmaster, and Foltz, the lion tamer, plot to buy out the circus. Dalton is certain that local authorities in the next town will attach the show for indebtedness, at which point he and Foltz can make their move. Back in Mary's cabin, her boyfriend, Bud Conway, stops by to say good night. Noting that their next booking is in his hometown, Bud promises Mary that his parents are influential enough to ensure the show's success there. Smiley returns, and is jealous to find Bud with Mary. When Bud departs, Smiley expresses doubt about the youth's usefulness as a circus worker, but Mary praises the stability someone like Bud represents. The wagon tilts, propelling Mary into Smiley's arms. Instead of taking advantage of this accident, however, he nervously talks nonsense.

The next day, the circus parades down the main street of town in bright sunshine. Smiley cons a creditor, A.K. Shrewsbury, out of $60, and grants the man special status as a partner who doesn't pay bills. Hungry, the lions and tigers are edgy. Smiley solves the problem by promising free tickets to any kid who brings him a piece of meat. Shrewsbury returns to make another stab at collecting payment, but Smiley distracts the old man with the show's provocative Oriental dancer. Shrewsbury ends up writing Smiley a blank check.

Bud returns from a visit with his parents, sporting a new suit and a new car. He informs Mary that his father is holding a dinner party in her honor at the country club that night. Unaware of Dalton's scheme, Bud invites the ringmaster to join them. Mary excitedly invites Smiley, extracting from him a promise that he will behave properly amid "high society."

The party that night starts out smoothly. Mary graciously accepts the welcome and compliments of her elegant hosts. Smiley runs into Shrewsbury and staves off the creditor's attempt to back out of his "partnership" with yet another convoluted argument. Impressed with Smiley's verbal gymnastics, Shrewsbury in turn tries to spin a similar spiel for an inebriated British aristocrat, but loses more money in the process.

During dinner, decorum begins to unravel. Teaming with Dave, a frizzy-haired stooge who hangs around the circus, Smiley transforms the passing and serving of food into anarchic comic play. After Shrewsbury delivers a drunken appeal for cash from Bud, Mr. Conway leaves the party, convinced that Mary is simply after his son's fortune. Humiliated, Mary accuses Smiley of intentionally ruining the party.

The next day, the circus sells out at the box office. Smiley is urgently summoned by Mary, but is delayed by Shrewsbury, to whom he delivers another rambling lecture. When Smiley finally reaches Mary, he finds her distraught over Bud's failure to return to the circus. Vowing to marry Bud, she demands that Smiley keep her boyfriend on the payroll. When Smiley refuses, she tearfully fires him. He exits and wanders sadly through the lively crowd outside the tent. Mary promotes Dalton to the position of manager, commending him for his fine manners at the party the night before.

As the first performance is about to begin, the local sheriff arrives and attaches the box-office receipts. The performers have already made their grand entrance into the tent, but they refuse to continue unless they immediately receive their back salaries. Unable to convince them that they will be paid after the show, Mary gamely performs her bare-back act alone. When the band walks out, however, the audience grows restless.

Smiley, on his way out of town, meets Bud, who informs the ex-manager of the sheriff's action. Smiley leaps into Bud's car and they race back to the circus, arriving as Mary is about to succumb to Dalton's offer to buy out the show. Smiley goes into the ring and, with assistance from Mary and Dave, temporarily placates the audience with a series of astonishing acrobatic stunts. But he soon runs out of tricks and the crowd turns ugly. A riot ensues. Circus members enter into the fray with relish, but a fire breaks out. Some angry customers hoist Mary to the roof of the Big Top, endangering her life. Wetting himself down, Smiley scales the big top from the outside and cuts his way through the canvas in time to rescue her before she is engulfed in flames. He carries Mary down a rope to the ground and takes her to Bud's car. Bud drives her away.

The Films: Credits, Notes, and Synopses

Hours later, amid the smoldering ruins, Smiley and Shrewsbury meet again and strike up another comically desultory conversation. That night, Smiley is back atop the lead elephant as the caravan moves on through the rain.

17 **DIRIGIBLE (1931)**

Dirigible (Italy)

Production Company:	Columbia Pictures Corporation
Producer:	Harry Cohn/A Frank R. Capra Production
Director:	Frank R. Capra
Screenplay:	Adaptation and dialogue by Jo Swerling, from a story by Cmdr. Frank Wilber Wead, U.S.N.; continuity by Dorothy Howell
Photography:	Joseph Walker
Aerial Photography:	Elmer Dyer
Editor:	Maurice Wright
Technical Effects:	Ned Mann, W.J. Butler
Sound Engineer:	E.L. Bernds
Assistant Director:	Sam Nelson
Cast:	Jack Holt (Jack Bradon), Ralph Graves (Frisky Pierce), Fay Wray (Helen Pierce), Hobart Bosworth (Dr. Louis Rondelle), Roscoe Karns (Sock McGuire), Harold Goodwin (Hansen), Clarence Muse (Clarence), Alan Roscoe (commander of the USS Lexington), Emmet Corrigan (Admiral Martin), Selmer Jackson (Lieutenant Rowland)

Filmed at Columbia Pictures Studio and on location at the Lakehurst Air Force Base, Lakehurst, N.J., and a balloon school in Arcadia, California, in the fall and winter, 1930-31

Distributor:	Columbia Pictures Corporation
Copyright:	24 March 1931 by Columbia Pictures Corporation (LP 2077)
Released:	3 April 1931 (Central Theatre, New York City)[1]
Running time:	102 minutes

Notes

1. On 7 April Dirigible had its Los Angeles premiere at Grauman's Chinese Theatre, a prestigious opening and the first of its kind for Columbia. (Capra, noting the significance of the event in his autobiography, inaccurately gives 18 April as the date.)

Synopsis

The navy informs dirigible commander Jack Bradon that he may be needed on an expedition to the South Pole. But the organizer, Dr. Rondele, must be convinced of the advantage dirigibles hold over conventional aircraft.

The Films: Credits, Notes, and Synopses

Navy Day at Lakehurst, N.J. gives Jack the opportunity to make his case. Dr. Rondele is impressed when Jack demonstrates how, in the event of an emergency, his dirigible crew can easily parachute to safety. Meanwhile, celebrated pilot Frisky Pierce flies over Pennsylvania on the last leg of a solo coast-to-coast flight. Jack calls Frisky from the dirigible and warns him not to pull any stunts when he arrives amid the balloons at Lakehurst. Frisky laughs his old friend off. Moments later, his plane is sighted. Frisky performs some aerial stunts, flies through the dirigible hanger, and lands his plane to a tumultuous reception. He has broken the coast-to-coast flight record.

At home alone, Frisky's wife, Helen, waits by a dinner table set for two. Jack arrives with the trophy Frisky has won and tells her that Frisky has likely been delayed by reporters and well-wishers. Weary of her husband's fame, Helen is unconsoled. Jack notices a photograph of himself, inscribed by him to Helen, on the mantle next to Frisky's awards. He removes it, claiming it is out of place amid the souvenirs of Frisky's conquests. Helen retrieves it; to her it represents not conquest, but friendship.

Frisky arrives, accompanied by a cluster of officers. Jack skillfully herds the officers back out the front door. He interrupts Frisky's reunion with Helen to offer his friend a position on the expedition. Frisky is interested, but Helen retreats to the bedroom, upset. After Jack goes, she reminds her husband of a romantic letter she gave him to read when he landed. He apologizes for forgetting to open it and tries to make light of her frustration by charming her. But when she begs him not to join the expedition he refuses.

The next day, Frisky and Jack show Dr. Rondele how Frisky's plane can be hooked onto the dirigible while in flight. Frisky almost spoils the delicate maneuver by topping it off with some loops around the blimp, but Dr. Rondele is sufficiently impressed to hire them both. While the three map strategy at a restaurant, Jack receives a message from Helen asking him to meet her at his office. There she begs Jack to find a reason to take Frisky off the assignment. He reluctantly agrees. Grateful, Helen kisses him good-bye.

At a bon voyage party for the expedition, Jack takes Frisky aside and asks him to withdraw from the flight. When Frisky refuses, Jack threatens to go to the admiral and accuse Frisky of unprofessional grandstanding in the air. Frisky gives in, but departs in anger, convinced that Jack is jealous of his fame.

The next day the dirigible sets off over Manhattan. The horns of ships in the harbor below blast a celebratory farewell. Over the Caribbean, however, the dirigible runs into a violent storm. Collapsing in midair, the dirigible plummets to the ocean. The expeditionary force must be rescued at sea.

The Films: Credits, Notes, and Synopses

Back home, Dr. Rondele plans a second expedition, this time using conventional aircraft with Frisky in charge. Jack tries to offer his good wishes, but Frisky treats him coldly. At a party on the eve of departure, Helen writes a letter for Frisky to open when he reaches the South Pole, informing him that she has gone to Paris to get a divorce and marry Jack. Cockily assuming it is a love note, Frisky displays the envelope to the crowd at the party. Later that night, Helen makes a final attempt to get him to stay, but he brushes her off. After he goes, she knocks all his trophies off the mantle and weeps.

The expeditionary force sails to a point nine hundred miles north of the pole and sets up camp. From here, Rondele, Frisky, and two assistants take off on a flight to the polar cap. The rest of the party is instructed to set sail north should the plane not return within twelve days. Meanwhile at home, Helen and Jack wait together. Receiving a telegram from Frisky in which he tells her he still has the letter, Helen prays for his safety.

The expeditionary plane approaches the polar barrier. Finding it difficult to climb to a sufficient altitude, Frisky orders the plane lightened, and much of the food they are carrying is tossed overboard. They clear the barrier by a small margin. The crew cheers heartily and passes the news on to the camp. When Helen hears of Frisky's safety, she asks Jack to follow her to Paris where she will get a divorce.

When Frisky attempts to land on the South Pole, however, the plane flips over and ignites in flames. Dr. Rondele is severely injured. Greatly humbled by the accident, Frisky is forced to organize a journey by sled back to the camp. At home, Helen is badly shaken by news of the accident. Jack requests permission to take his new dirigible on a rescue mission.

Dr. Rondele dies and is buried in the ice by Frisky. The three remaining explorers continue their trek across the Antarctic. When one of the assistants, Stark, suffers frostbite, Frisky has to amputate the man's feet. That night, Stark tells a lengthy story about a girl with whom he had a chance to spend a night, but whom he never even kissed. Seeing the other two are asleep, Stark covers Frisky with his parka and drags himself away into the darkness to die.

The next day, Jack's dirigible picks its way through the icecaps as Frisky plunges onward with the remaining survivor. Frisky's eyesight is fading rapidly. Their sled topples over the side of a precipice. To save his partner, Frisky cuts the tie-rope, sacrificing the sled. His colleague begins to go mad. When they discover Stark's frozen corpse, both survivors collapse. But they are soon spotted by Jack in the dirigible and hoisted to safety.

The Films: Credits, Notes, and Synopses

Aboard a navy ship carrying them home, Frisky asks Jack to read Helen's letter aloud since Frisky still cannot see. Jack ad libs a statement of devotion to substitute for Helen's original message, and Frisky is genuinely moved by the sentiment. Jack then pretends the letter is accidentally blown out the window.

In New York City a ticker-tape parade is held for the heroic Jack. Frisky is joyously reunited with Helen at home. She fears he has read her letter, and thus is greatly relieved to hear him recite the message Jack has composed instead. She laughs, and they embrace. Below on Fifth Avenue, Jack rides alone in the back seat of a car, cheered by the crowd.

18   THE MIRACLE WOMAN (1931)

La donna del miracolo (Italy)

Production Company:	Columbia Pictures Corporation
Producer:	Harry Cohn/A Frank R. Capra Production
Director:	Frank R. Capra
Screenplay:	Jo Swerling, based on the play Bless You, Sister by John Meehan and Robert Riskin; continuity by Dorothy Howell[1]
Photography:	Joseph Walker
Editor:	Maurice Wright
Sound Engineer:	Glenn Rominger
Cast:	Barbara Stanwyck (Florence Fallon), David Manners (John Carson), Sam Hardy (Hornsby), Beryl Mercer (Mrs. Higgins), Russell Hopton (Dan Welford), Charles Middleton (Simpson), Eddie Boland (Collins), Thelma Hill (Gussie), Aileen Carlyle (Violet), Al Stewart (Brown), Harry Todd (Briggs)
Filmed at Columbia Pictures Studio in the spring of 1931	
Distributor:	Columbia Pictures Corporation
Copyright:	13 July 1931 by Columbia Pictures Corporation (LP 2345)
Released:	14 August 1931 (Mayfair Theatre, New York City)
Running time:	91 minutes

Notes

1. Bless You, Sister opened at the Forrest Theatre in New York City on 26 December, 1927. According to the New York Times, John Meehan was principal author, with Robert Riskin primarily involved in producing the play along with his brother A.E. (Everett) Riskin (see the New York Times, 27 December 1927, p. 24). Although Robert Riskin was under contract at Columbia by the time the film version was made, he did not work on the screenplay.

The Films: Credits, Notes, and Synopses

In contrast to <u>Dirigible</u>, for which Columbia launched a major publicity campaign, <u>The Miracle Woman</u> was released without fanfare. This may have been the result of Columbia's fears concerning the controversial nature of the subject; according to reviewer Creighton Peet, the film was heavily censored in several states, including New York (see entry 131).

Synopsis

At a small-town church, parishioners file inside to hear the farewell sermon of their elderly minister, whom they have dismissed. His daughter, Florence, ascends to the pulpit in his stead and delivers her father's incomplete address. The old man, she tells them, has died moments before, his spirit broken by the dismissal. She assails the affluent congregation for their ingratitude toward a poorly paid pastor who dutifully served them, and whose burial she cannot afford. Challenged by the church deacon to respect the house of God, Florence launches into a passionate attack on the hypocrisy and immorality of the parishioners. As they flee the church, she descends from the pulpit and pursues them to the door, enraged. After closing the door behind them, she begins to weep. Inside the church, a remaining figure applauds her. He is Hornsby, a stranger passing through town, and he would like to talk to her. Florence throws him out, but he follows her to the parsonage and coaxes her to let him promote her talents as an evangelist. "You'll get famous, and get rich," he assures her. "And what's more—get even."

Sister Florence Fallon becomes a popular evangelist, broadcasting her message daily to poor city dwellers from her Temple of Happiness. John Carson a young blind man depressed by his failures as a songwriter, is stopped from committing suicide when he hears her cite the achievements of handicapped artists such as Beethoven and Milton. His spirits renewed, John decides to attend a revival meeting at the temple with his landlady, Mrs. Higgins.

That night, spotlights illuminate the front of the temple; a neon cross glows brightly on the roof. Inside, a band and chorus perform lively, upbeat tunes. Backstage, Hornsby assesses the attendance for the evening. With a brass fanfare the curtains part to reveal a cage filled with roaring lions. The chorus hums "Onward Christian Soldiers," and Florence descends a ramp in a flowing, diaphanous gown. Entering the cage, she attributes her safety to the power of her faith and urges someone from the audience to join her. John cheerfully volunteers. Learning he has lost his eyesight in the war, Florence uses him as the pretext for an inspirational sermon and promises that God will restore his vision. The audience joins hands to celebrate this "miraculous" event. John is skeptical, but is nonetheless charmed by her.

A week passes. Hornsby berates a motley group of confederates he has hired, for their terrible performance the night before. When they are gone, Florence complains that the sincerity of her performance suffers when she works with obvious fakes. Hornsby warns her to keep her professional distance and not fall for her own message. She claims she feels imprisoned, so Hornsby recommends a party that evening. He gets her to relax on the dressing room couch and starts to make a pass. But the sales manager Welford, interrupts with news of bigger profits.

That evening Florence, sexily dressed, steps out. She is detoured from the party, however, when she finds John waiting outside in the rain. She offers to take him home. He invites her up to his apartment, where he entertains her with musical toys, card tricks, and ventriloquism with a dummy. Speaking through the dummy, John expresses his gratitude for her having saved his life. Touched, she hires him as a hymn writer and kisses him good night. When Florence finally arrives at Hornsby's party, he scolds her and then tries to flirt with her. But he is again interrupted by Welford, now drunk, who threatens to tell the press about their racket unless he gets a third of the profits.

Florence and John continue to see each other on the sly. Welford is killed under "mysterious" circumstances, and Hornsby enlists Florence's support in fending off inquiries from the police. Jealous over her relationship with John, Hornsby forcibly embraces her. Angered, she frees herself from him. A secretary interrupts the quarrel.

John makes a birthday dinner for Florence at his apartment. Speaking through the dummy, he tries to tell her he loves her, but fails. Florence understands anyhow and embraces him. When she returns to her apartment that night, Hornsby awaits her. He has arranged a prolonged vacation for the two of them on the Riviera under the guise of a spiritual trip by Sister Fallon to the Holy Lands. She resists the proposal, but he threatens her with exposure, disgrace, and arrest.

John is saddened to hear of Florence's trip. As they sit together at the beach, she tries to maintain a cheerful air, but can sustain the act no longer. She earnestly prays for John's eyesight to return and then gives up, confessing to John that she has been a fake all along. John tries to convince her that she has changed him already. But Hornsby, who has tracked them down, takes Florence away.

With Mrs. Higgins's assistance, John sneaks into Florence's dressing room at the temple and memorizes the arrangement of the furniture. That night, a tearful Florence prepares for her final performance. Mrs. Higgins bursts into the dressing room with word that John has been cured. John follows, pretending that he sees everything in the room. Florence soon catches on to the ruse, but is so moved by his attempt to restore her faith that she vows to Hornsby that she will confess all that night. After she leaves, Hornsby knocks John unconscious.

The Films: Credits, Notes, and Synopses

On stage before a packed house, Florence begins to confess her wrongdoings. Hornsby orders the lights shut off. An electrical fire is sparked; the temple is soon an inferno. Florence exhorts the throng to stay calm, but they push madly for the exits. John awakes and stumbles to his feet amid the flames and smoke. Florence calls him and then collapses. He finds her and carries her to safety. The crowd prays for them as they are carried on stretchers to an ambulance.

Some time later, Hornsby walks down the city street, haranguing a boxer he now manages. He spies Florence, now a member of the Salvation Army. She opens a telegram from John: he is leaving the hospital; there's a chance for his eyesight, but he doesn't care; he loves her, and proposes that his dummy be best man at their wedding. Hornsby comments from afar: "And she gave up a million bucks for that! The poor sap." But Florence's face is radiant.

19   **PLATINUM BLONDE (1931)**

Blonde platine (France), La donna di platino (Italy)

Production Company:	Columbia Pictures Corporation
Producer:	Harry Cohn/A Frank R. Capra Production
Director:	Frank R. Capra
Screenplay:	Adapted by Jo Swerling from a story by Harry E. Chandler and Douglas W. Churchill; continuity by Dorothy Howell; dialogue by Robert Riskin[1]
Photography:	Joseph Walker
Editor:	Gene Milford
Art Director:	Steve Goosson
Sound Engineer:	Edward Bernds
Technical Director:	Edward Shulter
Assistant Director:	C.C. Coleman
Cast:	Robert Williams[2] (Stew Smith), Loretta Young (Gallagher), Jean Harlow (Anne Schuyler), Louise Closser Hale (Mrs. Schuyler), Donald Dillaway (Michael Schuyler), Reginald Owen (Dexter Grayson), Walter Catlett (Bingy Baker), Edmund Breese (Conroy, the editor), Halliwell Hobbes (Smythe, the butler), Claude Allister (Dawson, the valet), Bill Eliot (dinner guest), Harry Semels (waiter), Olaf Hytten (Radcliffe), Dick Cramer (speakeasy proprietor), Wilson Benge (butler); Tom London, Hal Price, Eddy Chandler, and Charles Jordan (reporters); Dick Pritchard
Filmed at Columbia Pictures Studio in the summer of 1931	
Distributor:	Columbia Pictures Corporation
Copyright:	22 October 1931 by Columbia Pictures Corporation (LP 2572)

The Films: Credits, Notes, and Synopses

Released: 30 October 1931 (Strand Theater, New York City)
Running time: 82 minutes

Notes

1. According to Stephen Handzo (see entry 973), eleven writers contributed to the script, although only five received credit. Robert Riskin was called in on the last stage of the screenplay, marking the beginning of his long collaboration with Capra.

2. "Robert Williams wins stardom overnight" read a Columbia advertisement for the film the day before its release (New York Times, 29 October 1931, p. 27). The studio was clearly hoping to launch Williams as a star, and many reviewers of Platinum Blonde commented on his gift for screen comedy. But Williams died of peritonitis on 4 November, four days after the premiere (see Film Daily, 5 November 1931, p. 2).

Synopsis

In the bustling newsroom of the Post, call goes out for ace reporter Stew Smith. He is huddled off in the corner with Gallagher, his female colleague and sidekick, at work on mastering a hand puzzle. His editor, Conroy, offers to relieve Stew's boredom with an assignment. The scion of the prominent Schuyler family has been threatened with a breach-of-promise suit by a chorus girl. A payoff is in the works. Stew, who "knows how to act in a drawing room," is to worm his way into the family mansion and get a story.

In the drawing room of the mansion, a fretful Mrs. Schuyler meets with her wayward son, Michael, her voluptuous daughter, Anne, and her lawyer, Grayson. The butler announces the presence of reporters. Mrs. Schuyler wants them dismissed, but Grayson offers to handle them. Bingy Baker, Stew's rival from the Tribune, has first crack, and soon leaves with a $50 bribe from Grayson. But Stew is less easily put off. He quickly tricks Mrs. Schuyler into admitting a $10,000 payoff has been arranged, and refuses Grayson's bribe for silence. Anne flirts with him, a tactic that at first seems to work. But Stew promptly asks for a phone and calls in the story. Mrs. Schuyler is flabbergasted; Anne is keenly angered.

At a speakeasy that night with Gallagher, Stew confesses he is attracted to the high-class Anne and plans to go back and see her. When Gallagher betrays signs of jealousy, Stew warns her not to turn "female" on him and asks her to pick up the tab.

Calling on Anne the next day, Stew produces a love letter written by Michael which he has lifted from the chorus girl during an interview. Anne raises the bribe to $5,000. Stew convinces her he has other things on his mind besides money and invites himself to lunch. He tells her about a play he is writing and banters with her over the

The Films: Credits, Notes, and Synopses

meal. Anne begins to find him amusing. They are about to kiss when Mrs. Schuyler arrives on the scene. She strongly disapproves of his presence. Stew departs.

Anne, however, becomes obsessed with the notion of transforming the reporter into a gentleman. Against the counsel of Grayson, who is attracted to Anne himself, she decides to pursue the relationship. A month later, Anne and Stew are the subject of society gossip. During an elegant party at the Schuylers' they slip outside to the garden and Stew obliquely proposes.

News of their elopement reaches the <u>Post</u> newsroom by way of a front-page story in the <u>Tribune</u>. Conroy is outraged that the paper has been scooped, and warns Stew not to let it happen again. His colleagues tease him about his marriage to a society dame, but Gallagher is crushed. Finding her alone in the speakeasy, Stew seeks her approval. A city police chief joins them. Stew describes his plan to take Anne away from the mansion and live off the money he will make as a playwright. Scoffing at the notion, the chief predicts Stew will be "Mr. Schuyler," a bird in a gilded cage. Upset by the encounter, Stew tries to get Gallagher to agree that he's a lucky guy. She does so halfheartedly.

Meanwhile, Anne promises her mother that once she gets Stew away from the newspaper she will make him socially acceptable. Stew resists Anne's plan to have him move into the mansion, but she silences him with a kiss. The next morning he wakes up in an opulent bedroom. A valet has brought him a canary in a gilded cage. Stew dismisses the servant along with the bird. Anne arrives with a pair of diamond-studded garters, an item of clothing Stew has long opposed. He tries to refuse them, but again she seduces him. In his garters, he is the laughing stock of the newsroom.

Gallagher lands an assignment covering a Schuyler party. A neophyte as a social reporter, she nevertheless dresses up for the occasion. She finds Stew alone in the garden. Bored, he is elated to see her and takes note of her new dress and hair style. But Anne appears and dismisses the reporter from the garden. Stew apologizes to Gallagher for Anne's rudeness and expresses surprise that he had never thought of her as a woman. Bingy Baker crashes the party and offers Stew a job writing a column for the <u>Tribune</u>. The catch is that it must be signed "by Anne Schuyler's husband." Stew slugs Bingy in the jaw.

"Cinderella Man Grows Hair on Chest" reads the morning headline in the <u>Tribune</u>. Mrs. Schuyler is livid at the impropriety. But Stew holds his ground: he will not be called a Cinderella Man. When Grayson testily suggests that the name is appropriate, Stew announces he is counting the lawyer's cracks, and when they add up to twenty he will sock him in the nose.

The Films: Credits, Notes, and Synopses

Stew refuses to attend the season's next social function, claiming that the people bore him. Anne berates him for his lack of gratitude and goes off to the party with a flier of recent acquaintance. Stew calls out in the empty mansion just to hear his voice echo. Smythe, the butler, responds to the call, only to be coaxed into testing the echo of his own voice as well.

Stew phones Gallagher and asks her to help him with the play he is writing. She soon arrives with some chaperones, a gang of colleagues, including Bingy, with whom Stew makes up. As their friends romp downstairs, Stew and Gallagher work on the play in his bedroom. She persuades him to change the subject to his own situation, and for the first time his writing is unblocked.

The Schuylers return home to find the ballroom filled with drunken commoners. Even Smythe is soused. Discovering Stew upstairs with Gallagher, Anne accuses him of abusing his rights in her home. The limits of his rights as her husband thus defined, Stew decides that it is time to leave, and delivers a parting salvo to his mother-in-law before doing so. Outside the mansion he donates his studded garters to a panhandler.

The next morning Stew is at work on his play in his apartment while Gallagher fixes breakfast. She suggests that his speech to Mrs. Schuyler the night before would make a fine second-act curtain. Grayson arrives with an offer to buy a divorce; he ends with a sock in the jaw for his twentieth crack. This confrontation with Grayson is then written into the play to kick off the third act. But how will the play end, Gallagher wonders aloud: with a return to the wife and an apology? Not on your life, replies Stew: the protagonist will end up with a character Gallagher has suggested, whom he has loved all along without knowing it. Acting out this resolution, Stew and Gallagher embrace.

20   **FORBIDDEN (1932)**

    Amour défendu (France), Proibito (Italy), Sehnsucht ohne Ende (Germany)

Production Company: Columbia Pictures Corporation
Producer: Harry Cohn/A Frank R. Capra Production
Director: Frank R. Capra
Screenplay: Adaptation and dialogue by Jo Swerling, from a story by Frank Capra[1]
Photography: Joseph Walker
Editor: Maurice Wright
Sound Engineer: Edward Bernds
Cast: Barbara Stanwyck (Lulu Smith), Adolphe Menjou (Bob Grover), Ralph Bellamy (Al Holland), Dorothy Peterson (Helen Grover), Thomas Jefferson (Wilkerson), Charlotte V. Henry (Roberta, age eighteen), Myrna Fresholtz

The Films: Credits, Notes, and Synopses

(Roberta, age two), Oliver Eckhardt (Briggs), Harry Holman (lovelorn columnist), Halliwell Hobbes (florist), Flo Wix (Mrs. Smith), Claude King (Mr. Jones), Robert Graves (Mr. Exner), Frankie Raymond, Gertrude Pedlar, Wilfred Noy

Filmed at Columbia Pictures Studio and on location at Laguna Beach and Venice, California, in the fall of 1931

Distributor: Columbia Pictures Corporation

Copyright: 5 January 1932 by Columbia Pictures Corporation (LP 2737)

Released: 9 January 1932 (Rialto Theatre, New York City)

Running time: 87 minutes

Notes

1. Capra claims in his autobiography that his "original" story for Forbidden was greatly indebted to Back Street by Fannie Hurst (see The Name Above the Title, p. 134).

Synopsis

Lovelorn and struck by spring fever, Lulu Smith is late for work at her small-town library. Children taunt her with a refrain of "old lady four eyes." When an elderly male colleague starts to tease her, she launches an attack on the stifling library and town. Lulu decides to withdraw all her savings and embark on a romantic cruise to Havana.

The first night aboard, she descends the grand stairway to the dining room dressed in elegant furs and jewelry. But when a young man tries to arrange for her to join him, she is frightened back up to her cabin. There she discovers a man in a tuxedo, Bob Grover, sprawled on her bed. Drunk, he has confused his room for hers. He apologizes: he has been trying to relax from an overlong stretch with his nose to the grindstone. Sympathetic, Lulu accepts his apology and a compliment concerning her beauty as well. Shortly after he leaves, her phone rings. He invites her to dinner. Lulu descends the grand stairway again, this time escorted by Bob.

In Havana their romance blossoms. Lulu enjoys the casinos and nightclubs. He confesses to a gnawing ambition to be president. Her ambition, she replies, is him. He somberly suggests they learn more about each other, but she deflects him from this line of inquiry.

Lulu takes a clerical job at a newspaper in the city where Bob works as a lawyer. Arriving at her apartment for dinner in a Halloween mask, Bob gives her a mask to wear as well, and they play a mock love scene together. A tickling match, however, suddenly turns serious: Bob wonders if she is truly happy; she admits that she fears the spell of her Cinderella fantasy will be broken. They are inter-

The Films: Credits, Notes, and Synopses

rupted by a call from Al Holland, a reporter at the paper who has been courting Lulu crudely. He proposes over the phone. She coyly begs for time to consult her lawyer. Bob uses the occasion to tell Lulu that he has an invalid wife he cannot leave. Lulu offers to pretend the wife doesn't exist, but Bob refuses to let her sacrifice her own life in this way. Accusing him of using duty as an excuse to reject her, Lulu forces him to leave.

Lulu gives birth to a baby girl and names her Roberta. Two years pass. Bob has been appointed city district attorney. His wife, Helen, begs him to join her on a health trip to Vienna, but he can't spare the time. Al Holland, now city editor of the newspaper, feuds with the new D.A. and is looking for a scandal to sink him.

After a long search, Bob discovers Lulu's new address. He knocks on the door. Her first reaction is to lock him out, but she then calls after him and they are tearfully reunited. Lulu introduces Bob to his daughter. One day Al discovers Lulu in the park with Roberta, and Lulu pretends she is the girl's governess. Bob arrives, and Roberta calls him daddy. Bob announces he has adopted the child, but Al is suspicious. To protect the cover, Bob brings Roberta home to live with him and Helen, and hires Lulu as governess. Helen is delighted, but upsets Lulu by asking the young governess about her references and experiences. Admitting she has none, Lulu hurries out the front door. Bob runs after her. Amid a rainstorm, in and out of a taxi, they quarrel. He insists she stay on as governess, but she refuses to maintain the lie. He's been poison, she raves, and she must start a new life while there is still time. Abandoning him on a park bench, she then returns to coax the morose Bob to go home. He begs her not to leave him. She gives in, requesting a new place to live.

Al hires Lulu to write the paper's "advice to the lovelorn" column. When he tries to pump her for information about Bob's child, she makes fun of his appetite for scandal. Her first letter is from a girl in love with a man fifteen years her senior. "If you love him," Lulu writes, "stick with him."

Years pass. Bob's political career advances. Roberta is now a debutante, engaged to the scion of a wealthy family. Al, now managing editor, is still proposing to Lulu, but she insists that he is already married to the paper. Attending a state political convention, Lulu watches from afar as Bob is publicly hailed for his integrity as a husband, father, and citizen. He is nominated for governor. That night, she receives him in her apartment with a red carpet, strewing his path with roses. But Bob is in no mood for false accolades, and vows to come clean about the past. Lulu tries to convince him that his career cannot be sacrificed, but Bob is adamant. So Lulu marries Al to keep Bob from committing this rash deed. Bob returns to the political arena.

The Films: Credits, Notes, and Synopses

On the night of the election, Al confronts Lulu with information concerning her relationship with Grover, including Roberta's papers from the hospital and a recent love letter from Bob. Lulu accuses him of thievery. "I'd commit murder for a story like that," he replies, and calls the paper to tell them to hold the front page. She fights for the letter. He slaps her viciously, sending her sprawling. Rising with a bloodied mouth, she goes to the bedroom and returns with a pistol. He backs her into the room and closes the door. Lulu fires through the door. She then emerges from the room and fires several more bullets into his body. She burns the evidence in the fireplace. Bob's victory message is broadcast over the radio.

Time passes. Reporters keep a death vigil at the governor's mansion, where Bob is ailing. He has pardoned Lulu, and an aide is concerned about the reporters' reaction. But Bob dismisses the complaint and requests to see Lulu. While he waits he writes out his will; in it he bequeaths her half his estate and reveals their past relationship. Lulu arrives in black. Bob recalls their first meeting when he was flat on his back as well; Lulu promises to run away with him to Havana if he gets well. He dies. As the reporters scramble to phone in the story of Bob's death, Lulu leaves the mansion. Out on the busy city street, she throws his will and confession into a trash can and becomes lost in the crowd.

21   AMERICAN MADNESS (1932)

La follia dalla metropoli (Italy)

Production Company:	Columbia Pictures Corporation
Producer:	Harry Cohn/A Frank Capra Production
Director:	Frank R. Capra[1]
Screenplay:	Robert Riskin
Photography:	Joseph Walker
Editor:	Maurice Wright
Art Direction:	Stephen Goosson
Sound:	Edward Bernds
Assistant Director:	C.C. Coleman
Cast:	Walter Huston (Tom Dickson), Pat O'Brien (Matt Brown), Kay Johnson (Phyllis Dickson), Constance Cummings (Helen), Gavin Gordon (Cyril Cluett), Robert Ellis (Dude Finlay), Edwin Maxwell (Clark), Arthur Hoyt (Ives), Burton Churchill (O'Brien), Robert Emmett O'Connor (inspector), Sterling Holloway (Oscar), Jeanne Sorel (Cluett's secretary), Walter Walker (Schultz), Edward Martindale (Ames), Anderson Lawlor (Charlie), Ralph Lewis (judge), Pat O'Malley (Dr. Strong), Harry Holman
Filmed at Columbia Pictures Studio in the spring of 1932	
Distributor:	Columbia Pictures Corporation

The Films: Credits, Notes, and Synopses

Copyright: 18 July 1932 by Columbia Pictures Corporation
                          (LP 3155)
Released: 4 August 1932 (Mayfair Theatre, New York
                          City)
Running time: 75 minutes

Notes

1. According to soundman Edward Bernds, Allan Dwan was the first director assigned to American Madness, but he was taken off the picture after a week to ten days of shooting. "Dwan even made Walter Huston look bad," Bernds writes, "and we wondered how long it would take Cohn and [Sam] Briskin to wake up to the fact. When [Capra] took the picture over, threw out everything that had been shot before and started over again, I fully realized, for the first time, what directing was about" (see entry 1003). This would suggest that the original idea for the film was Cohn's or Robert Riskin's rather than Capra's. If it was Cohn's, the link Edward Buscombe has attempted to establish between A.H. Giannini—partner with Harry and Jack Cohn on the voting trust of Columbia and brother of "populist" banker A.P. Giannini—and the politics of American Madness would be strengthened. (see entry 962).

American Madness's central dramatic incident, a bank run, was obviously a topical concern, and Columbia exploited this angle in their publicity for the film. A three-column ad appearing in the New York Times on the day after the opening read:

> Last night the first great story of today thundered across the Mayfair screen! Daring, sensational theme closest to everyone's heart. A dramatic thunderbolt challenging the nation! It hurls a smashing answer to the burning questions of the hour! Its story x-rays on every emotion. More than a love story, more than a great drama . . . in fact GREATER THAN A MOTION PICTURE!

Bordering the ad was a high-angle view of the bank-run sequence with Tom Dickson (Walter Huston) staving off the angry depositors (New York Times, 5 August 1932, p. 11). Columbia's publicity department knew what they were selling—most reviewers of American Madness noted the timeliness of the subject matter and the dramatic power of the mob scenes—but the film may have hit too close to home in Baltimore, where it reportedly opened the day after a major bank run, and closed in two days (see "No Kidding Matter," Variety, 23 August 1932).

Synopsis

A new day begins at the Union National Bank. Tellers gathered at the bank vault conspire not to laugh at the routine morning joke of their supervisor, Matt Brown. And Matt's joke indeed meets an icy silence. "Six reasons banks fail," he complains to the six tellers, and the ice is broken. Great sums of money are distributed for the

The Films: Credits, Notes, and Synopses

day's business. Matt asks a friend to loan him $10 to cover a shortage. The friend turns him down, reminding Matt that a depression is on.

On the main floor Matt receives a playfully furtive kiss from Helen, secretary to the bank president, Tom Dickson. The board of directors arrive, led by the stern Mr. Clark, and march into the conference room. As they wait for Dickson, they condemn the president for lending money to small businessmen. If the board enacts a merger with the New York Trust, Clark proposes, Dickson will be rendered powerless. The house gossip, Oscar, spreads a rumor that Dickson is about to be fired, causing Matt to worry about an expected promotion.

Dickson arrives, greeting his employees in an informal, folksy fashion. When he tries to sustain his lighthearted manner with the board, however, Clark is not amused. Dickson passionately defends bank policy, arguing that granting loans based on character rather than collateral is historically sound, and that keeping money in circulation is essential to a recovery from the depression.

Meanwhile, head cashier Cyril Cluett is visited by a local gangster, Dude Finlay. Faced with a $50,000 gambling debt, Cluett agrees to assist the gang in robbing the bank that night. Phyllis Dickson pays a call on her husband, but his is still meeting with the board. Feeling neglected, she visits Cluett, who in the aftermath of his confrontation with Finlay is sneaking a drink. Phyllis teases Cluett about his reputation as a playboy; he takes her teasing as flirtation. Before she can fend him off, they are caught in a compromising embrace by Matt.

Elated by his veto of the board's planned merger, Dickson summons Matt to his office and promotes him to assistant cashier. Dickson has given Matt, an ex-conn, a fresh start, and hopes someday he will succeed him as president. But Matt, stunned by what he has witnessed in Cluett's office, remains cheerless. Phyllis enters, and Dickson showers her with flattery. But he promptly responds to an urgent business request for the evening, forgetting the anniversary party his wife has arranged. When she protests, he brightly promises her a night on the town tomorrow. Moments later he schedules a meeting for the next night as well. Phyllis suffers in silence.

That evening, as Matt closes the vault, Cluett surreptitiously disconnects the burglar alarm and adjusts the time clock for the late-night heist. Abandoned and bored, Phyllis Dickson accompanies Cluett to the theater and afterward goes to his apartment. As soon as Cluett shuts the door, he makes a pass. Phyllis escapes his grasp, only to discover Matt waiting inside. Matt urges them both not to hurt Dickson, who has been like a father to him. When Matt questions Phyllis as to what she sees in Cluett, Cluett slugs him, and then draws a gun and forces Matt to leave. Phyllis departs with Matt.

The Films: Credits, Notes, and Synopses

At midnight the gang robs the bank, killing a night watchman as they escape. In the morning detectives are on the scene. Oscar, claiming to have discovered the corpse, describes his experience with great relish. Matt, an ex-con with access to the vault clock, is the chief suspect. The inspector interrogates him roughly. Dickson intervenes on Matt's behalf, requesting that the inspector take it easy until the police have checked out Matt's alibi. As word of the robbery spreads around town, the $100,000 theft is magnified into one of several million dollars. Depositors begin to arrive at the bank; Dickson orders that all withdrawals be met. Meanwhile, Matt's alibi collapses when his landlady, through circuitous logic, establishes that he did not return home until after 1 A.M. Dickson pleads with Matt to explain where he was the night before. Caught between saving himself and exposing Dickson to the truth, Matt remains silent.

The crowd forming inside the bank grows increasingly unruly. Dickson calms them by promising to keep the bank open until 4 P.M.; in fact he only has funds to pay out money for an hour longer. Board members refuse to transfer their own assets to help Dickson ride out the crisis and suggest that he resign. Dickson claims he will declare bankruptcy first, making sure that the depositors are paid before the board gets a penny. He calls some acquaintances in search of financial support, but to no avail.

Receiving a tip about Cluett, the inspector sets up a ruse: in Cluett's presence, he pretends to receive a call linking the head cashier with Finlay. Cracking under pressure, Cluett flees to the locker room where the police apprehend him. To clear his name of the murder charge, Cluett tells of his date with Dickson's wife the night before. Profoundly insulted, Dickson has to be restrained from attacking Cluett. But when he calls Phyllis to prove Cluett wrong, his wife's hesitation corroborates the alibi. Shaken, Dickson yields without protest to Clark's proposal that he option all of his own stock. When Matt reluctantly confirms the fact that he had seen Cluett with Phyllis, Dickson asks to be left alone. He contemplates suicide. The tellers begin to run out of money. The mob is ready to riot.

Arriving on the scene, Phyllis tries to convince Dickson of her fidelity and begs him not to give up on the bank. But he remains withdrawn and unmoved. Matt and Helen make last-minute calls to small businessmen Dickson has helped over the years. One by one, they appear at the bank, loudly announcing their intention to deposit money. The mood of the crowd begins to change. Dickson springs back to life. Gleefully rounding up members of the board so they can witness the dramatic show of faith on the main floor, he soon convinces them to commit their own assets to the recovery as well. Armored trucks bring the new money. The crowd cheers and then slowly disperses.

The next morning, Matt arrives at the bank vault and cracks a joke about the tellers having a "run for their money" the day before.

The Films: Credits, Notes, and Synopses

Dickson makes his same folksy entrance. He orders Helen and Matt to take the day off and get a marriage license. Moreover, they are to book a honeymoon cruise--not for themselves, but for Dickson and his wife.

22 THE BITTER TEA OF GENERAL YEN (1933)

L'amaro tè del Generale Yen (Italy)

Production Company:	Columbia Pictures Corporation
Producer:	Walter Wanger/A Frank Capra Production
Director:	Frank R. Capra
Screenplay:	Edward Paramore[1], from the novel by Grace Zaring Stone
Photography:	Joseph Walker
Editor:	Edward Curtis
Musical score:	W. Frank Harling
Sound Engineer:	E.L. Bernds
Assistant Director:	C.C. Coleman
Cast:	Barbara Stanwyck (Megan Davis), Nils Asther (General Yen), Gavin Gordon (Dr. Bob Strike), Toshira Mori (Mah-Li), Walter Connolly (Jones), Richard Loo (Captain Li), Lucien Littlefield (Mr. Jackson), Clara Blandick (Mrs. Jackson), Willie Fung (military prisoner), Ray Young (engineer), Emmett Corrigan (Bishop Harkness), Moy Ming (Dr. Lin), Robert Wayne (Reverend Bostwick), Knute Erickson (Dr. Hansen), Ella Hall (Mrs. Hansen), Arthur Millette (Mr. Pettis), Helen Jerome Eddy (Miss Reed), Martha Mattox (Miss Avery), Jessie Arnold (Mrs. Blake), Miller Newman (Dr. Mott), Arthur Johnson (Dr. Schuler), Jessie Perry (Miss Reid), Adda Gleason (Mrs. Bowman), Daisy Robinson (Mrs. Warden), Doris Louellyn (Mrs. Meigs), Lillianne Leighton, Harriet Lorraine, Nora Cecil, Robert Bolder (missionaries), Milton Lee

Filmed at Columbia Pictures Studios and on location in the San Fernando Valley in the fall of 1932

Distributor:	Columbia Pictures Corporation
Copyright:	15 December 1932 by Columbia Pictures Corporation (LP 3486)
Released:	11 January 1933 (Radio City Music Hall, New York City)[2]
Running time:	88 minutes

The Films: Credits, Notes, and Synopses

Notes

1. Grace Zaring Stone, The Bitter Tea of General Yen (Indianapolis: Bobbs-Merrill Co. 1930), 322 pp. A photoplay edition of the novel was published by Grossett and Dunlap, New York, in 1933.

2. Prior to its release, The Bitter Tea of General Yen was previewed at the Ritz Theatre, Los Angeles, on 18 November 1932, and at the RKO-Hill Street, New York City, on 7 January 1933. Its opening at Radio City Music Hall four days later marked the conversion of that theater —which had opened as a showcase for live entertainment two weeks before—into a continuous-run motion picture house under the direction of S.L. Rothafel. (Rothafel also operated the famous Roxy Theatre in New York and opened a new RKO Roxy in Radio City at the same time he took over the Music Hall.) With the exception of Lost Horizon in 1937, Capra was to open all of his subsequent films for Columbia at the Radio City Music Hall.

Capra has often claimed that The Bitter Tea of General Yen was banned in England and throughout the British Commonwealth for its treatment of miscegenation, and as a result the film lost money for Columbia. However, records at the British Board of Censors indicate that although deletions were made before it passed the board in December 1932, it was never banned. It opened at the Regal Theatre, London, in March 1933.

Synopsis

Refugees from the ravaged city of Chapei, China, pour into Shanghai on a stormy night. Meanwhile, American missionaries gather for a major social event: the marriage of a young missionary, Bob Strike, and his childhood sweetheart from New England, Megan Davis. Separated from Bob for the last three years, Megan has just landed in Shanghai. She is detained on her way to the ceremony when her rickshaw boy is struck down by a limousine bearing the elegant warlord, General Yen. Megan boldly scolds Yen, but he responds with diffidence: the boy would be fortunate to die since "life at its best is hardly endurable." Megan's anger subsides only when she notices that Yen himself has been injured; she gives him her handkerchief for his wound. Her driver then hurries her on to the reception where she is introduced to the guests and dresses for the ceremony.

Bob arrives shortly thereafter, flushed with excitement over his work with the refugees amid the civil war. He and Megan are joyously reunited, but he quickly announces the wedding must be postponed until he has rescued some orphans trapped in Chapei. The guests contend that he will never obtain a safe conduct pass from General Yen, but Bob will not be deterred. Megan enthusiastically offers to go along.

Meeting with Yen, Bob acquires what he believes to be a pass. But Yen's note, written in Chinese, in fact mocks the missionary for leaving the arms of his bride and is signed "General Nobody." In

The Films: Credits, Notes, and Synopses

Chapei, soldiers laugh at the supposed pass. Bob and Megan seek refuge in the orphanage, but the soldiers steal their car. So Bob tries to get the orphans to the train station on foot. When a battle flares up around them, Megan is separated from the others. She awakens to find herself in the lavishly appointed train compartment of General Yen, who has rescued her. His concubine, Mah-Li, serves Megan tea containing a potion. After observing Mah-Li prepare the general for sleep, Megan dozes off.

At his summer palace, Yen meets with his American financial adviser, Jones. Jones urges Yen to send Megan back to Shanghai, but Yen refuses. In a luxurious bedroom in the palace, Megan is awakened by the sound of a firing squad outside her window. Horrified, she rejects the elegant breakfast Mah-Li serves. Yen halts the executions to calm Megan. He explains that the prisoners would in any case die of starvation, but Megan is unassuaged and demands to be returned to Shanghai. He ambiguously replies that he will always be her humble servant, but a second meeting with Jones clarifies his intentions: since Megan has been reported dead, he can hold her hostage without fear of retaliation.

Days pass. Megan repeatedly refuses Yen's invitations to dine with him. She tries to bribe Mah-Li to relay her letters to Bob Strike, but Mah-Li gives the letters to Yen instead. On a beautiful summer evening, Megan wanders out on her balcony and watches as women arrive to visit the soldiers. Couples pair off. Near a brook, two lovers embrace. Megan smiles and relaxes. Leaning back in a wicker chair, she begins to dream. In the dream, Yen appears as an Oriental monster who breaks into her room and seizes her violently. Suddenly an Occidental hero in a white fedora and black mask leaps through the window and disposes of the monster in a single blow. She takes off his mask: the hero is Yen in another disguise. As the two descend onto her bed, she wakes up. The real General Yen appears on the balcony and gently courts her, describing with eloquence the beauty of Chinese art and the aesthetic sensibility of the Chinese people. Megan resists his advances, but listens intently.

Megan observes a rendezvous between Mah-Li and the general's bodyguard, Captain Li. Mah-Li tries to bribe Megan not to inform Yen of her infidelity. Megan refuses the bribe, but begs Mah-Li to help her escape. The key to Megan's freedom, Mah-Li advises, is Jones, whom Mah-Li greatly fears. Megan decides to attend dinner in order to meet him. Mah-Li dresses her in a richly jeweled gown and makes her over as an Oriental beauty. But Megan opts for her native dress for dinner.

At the meal Jones is talkative. He strongly hints that Yen is being betrayed romantically and politically by Mah-Li and Captain Li, and expresses concern for the safety of the fortune he has stashed in a railway freight car. Yen says little, but after dinner strips Mah-Li of her jewelry and gives it to Megan. Megan scolds Yen and Jones for their cruelty and, after Jones leaves with Mah-Li, criticizes the

The Films: Credits, Notes, and Synopses

general for employing the self-serving American. Jones will not betray him, Yen replies, because their interests coincide. In contrast, Megan's fiancé would clearly betray her for his God. Megan departs angrily.

Learning that Mah-Li's life is in danger, Megan begs Yen to show mercy. Yen mocks the pleasure Megan derives from her missionary role, but accepts her offer to serve as hostage in answer for Mah-Li's loyalty. Mah-Li appears grateful, but soon tricks Megan into an act of unwitting espionage during a religious ceremony. That night, Yen's money train is ambushed and seized. Jones is enraged: not only is the fortune lost, but Yen's authority is irreparably damaged. Yen himself, however remains serene. If Mah-Li's betrayal has doomed him as a leader, it has also sealed his conquest of Megan.

Despite his bitterness, Jones offers to help Megan as a fellow American. But Megan rejects his protection and stoically goes to Yen when she is summoned. Yen is insulted by her supposition that the price he requires is sexual. Instead, her forfeit as hostage was to be her life, and he has contemplated their deaths as a mutual escape to a celestial garden. Hearing this, Megan pulls herself from his arms and runs to her room. Yen rings for a servant, but all have abandoned him. In her room, Megan dresses herself in Chinese finery and makes herself up at the mirror. Yen ritualistically prepares tea, adding poison to the cup. Megan enters. Copying the gestures she had earlier observed Mah-Li perform, she prepares the general for sleep. She weeps in his lap and clasps his hand as he drinks the poison.

Megan and Jones sit on the deck of a ship returning to Shanghai. His tongue loosened by drink, Jones rambles. He recalls Yen's theory that things never die, only change, and proposes that Yen may himself be the wind playing around Megan's hair. Silent throughout, Megan stares off into the distance.

23   LADY FOR A DAY (1933)

<u>Grande dame d'un jour</u> (France), <u>Signora per un giorno</u> (Italy)

Production Company:	Columbia Pictures Corporation
Producer:	Harry Cohn/A Frank Capra Production
Director:	Frank Capra
Screenplay:	Robert Riskin, from the short story "Madame La Gimp" by Damon Runyon[1]
Photography:	Joseph Walker
Editor:	Gene Havlick
Art Director:	Stephen Goosson
Costumes:	Robert Kalloch
Musical Director:	Bakaleinikoff
Sound:	E.L. Bernds
Assistant Director:	C.C. Coleman
Cast:	Warren Williams (Dave the Dude), May Robson (Apple Annie), Guy Kibbee (Judge Blake),

The Films: Credits, Notes, and Synopses

                                      Glenda Farrell (Missouri Martin), Ned Sparks (Happy McGuire), Jean Parker (Louise), Walter Connolly (Count Romero), Barry Norton (Carlos), Robert Emmett O'Connor (inspector), Nat Pendleton (Shakespeare), Hobart Bosworth (governor), Samuel S. Hinds (mayor), Halliwell Hobbes (butler), Wallis Clark (commissioner), Irving Bacon (dupe), Dad Mills (blind man)

Filmed at Columbia Pictures Studio in the spring of 1933
Distributor: Columbia Pictures Corporation
Copyright: 15 September 1933 by Columbia Pictures Corporation (LP 4259)
Released: 7 September 1933 (Radio City Music Hall, New York City)
Running time: 95 minutes

Notes

1. Damon Runyon's "Madame La Gimp" originally appeared in Cosmopolitan, 83 (October 1929), pp. 62-65, 200-202. It is also collected in two of Runyon's anthologies: Guys and Dolls (New York: Frederick A. Stokes Co., 1931) and Guys and Dolls: Three Volumes in One (Philadelphia and New York: J.P. Lippincott & Co., 1950). Robert Riskin's screenplay for Lady for a Day is available in Four-Star Scripts, edited by Lorraine Noble (Garden City, N.Y.: Doubleday, Doran & Co., 1936).

Lady for a Day was nominated for four Academy Awards: best picture, best direction, best writing-adaptation, and best actress (May Robson). According to Lorraine Nobel in her introduction to the screenplay (see above), the film also was honored for best direction and best adaptation by the Hollywood Reporter based on a general poll of the film industry. Capra remade the film in 1961 as Pocketful of Miracles (see entry 55). The negative to Lady for a Day disappeared while being transferred between two labs in the early 1950s, and prints are rare. In the early 1970s, Capra toured college campuses with his own print; I saw the film on such an occasion, and have refreshed my memory of it by consulting the screenplay. The only archive officially holding a print is the Swedish Film Institute.

Synopsis

    Apple Annie, a frowsy, tough-talking fruit peddler, works the Broadway theater district at night. Times are hard and business is slow, but Annie plays mother hen to her fellow panhandlers, tipping them off as to where the hit shows are playing and assuring them that prosperity is on the way back. Annie is summoned to Missouri Martin's nightclub where kingpin gambler Dave the Dude buys a lucky apple. His acerbic sidekick, Happy, scoffs at such superstition, but Dave is convinced the ritual brings him good fortune and pays Annie handsomely. Annie then bums a ride to the luxurious Hotel Marberry where a

The Films: Credits, Notes, and Synopses

porter sneaks out some hotel stationery for her. At home, over a bottle of gin, she uses the stationery to write to Louise, her illegitimate daughter who has been raised in a Spanish convent. Over the years, Annie has manufactured a fantasy life for herself as Mrs. E. Worthington Manville, a New York society lady residing at the Marberry. As she writes, the gin takes effect, and Annie falls asleep in a drunken stupor.

A mail ship arrives from Spain. Annie waits anxiously outside the Marberry for her daughter's letter, only to learn that the porter has been fired for trying to sneak out her letter. Annie desperately barges into the hotel lobby and creates a scene retrieving the letter. The news from Louise is greater cause for panic: she announces her imminent arrival in New York for a week's visit, accompanied by her fiancé, Carlos, and his nobleman father, Count Romero, who wishes to meet the Manvilles before consenting to the marriage. Annie collapses on the sidewalk. When she revives, she is crazy with fear.

In need of another lucky apple, Dave the Dude has been looking for Annie with no success. The Broadway panhandlers bring Dave word of Annie's predicament, and he follows them to Annie's apartment where she is holed up, drunk. Pressed by the panhandlers, Dave reluctantly agrees to set Annie up for a week at the Marberry in the suite of an out-of-town friend. Missouri assembles a contingent of beauticians to transform Annie into an elegant society matron. "Judge" Henry G. Blake, a courtly, well-spoken pool shark, is enlisted to pose as her husband.

As the excited panhandlers watch from a distance, the reunion of mother and daughter at the dock goes off smoothly. Introductions are made, with Dave brought into the family circle as a black-sheep uncle. Dave's gang encircles them to guard against trouble. A suspicious society reporter is kidnapped by Happy and his thick-headed cohort, Shakespeare. When two detectives move in to interrogate Dave the Dude, Happy deflects their attention by getting his henchmen to start a brawl.

The visitors are kept busy for several days with long drives through the city, and Dave gets ready to resume gambling, an activity from which he has been too long detained. But Count Romero, anxious to determine the true social standing of the Manvilles, insists on meeting their friends. So the judge promises a reception on the night of the Spaniards' departure. Louise confesses to her mother that she fears her dream won't come true, but Annie assures her all will work out.

The judge proposes that Dave's gang be recruited to appear at the reception as society gentlemen, together with Missouri's showgirls as ladies. Happy is incredulous, but Dave, desperate for a scheme, snaps at the idea. The night before the reception, he rehearses his unlikely performers. Frustrated by their frequent mistakes, he urges them to try harder or else Annie's heart will be broken. Dave's

The Films: Credits, Notes, and Synopses

speech moves everyone present, including Missouri and Happy. Meanwhile two more society reporters have had to be kidnapped. Their editors pressure the authorities to find out what's going on. Because he was seen at the dock at the time of the first disappearance, Dave the Dude is a suspect. Detectives appear at his apartment during the rehearsal, forcing Dave to send everyone home. Although the police have nothing on Dave, the inspector orders round-the-clock surveillance.

The night of the reception, the judge holds down the fort at the Marberry, checking out the orchestra, comforting a nervous Annie, and beating Count Romero at billiards with a $50,000 dowry at stake. At Missouri's nightclub, final touches are put on the performances of the mugs and the showgirls. Missouri casts herself in the show as Dave's wife. But cops outside are watching Dave's every move, trapping the gang inside.

Dave goes to the commissioner and admits to the kidnapping, but asks the cops to lay off for just one night. The commissioner refuses to make a deal. He calls the mayor, who is host that evening of a society ball with the governor and the newspaper editors in attendance. Goaded by the editors into dealing directly with Dave, the mayor has the suspect sent to him. At Missouri's Shakespeare tries to keep everyone practicing. But Dave calls and tells him the gambit is off. Everyone is disappointed for Annie.

It is growing late at the Marberry; the Cinderella scheme seems about to unravel. Annie decides to confess the truth. But as she starts to speak, voices are heard in the corridor and the orchestra begins to play. The butler announces the arrival of the mayor, who enters and greets Annie as if they were old friends. Society people from the mayor's ball follow, including the governor. They sustain the charade, impressing the count.

Later that night, a police escort leads a fleet of limousines to the dock. Amid the fairy-tail atmosphere, antagonisms melt. The governor decides to postpone his investigation of City Hall; the mayor decides to lay off the commissioner; the commissioner, in turn, will ease up on the inspector. And the editors decide to cover up their hot kidnapping story. Louise, Carlos, and the count are given a gala send-off, their illusions intact and the marriage assured. Dave invites Missouri home to his apartment for the first time. And Apple Annie reverts to her old self, turning her attention back to her army of panhandlers.

24 IT HAPPENED ONE NIGHT (1934)

New York-Miami (France), Accadde una notte (Italy), Es geschah in einer Nacht (Germany)

Production Company: Columbia Pictures
Producer: Harry Cohn/A Frank Capra Production

The Films: Credits, Notes, and Synopses

Director:	Frank Capra
Screenplay:	Robert Riskin, from the story "Night Bus" by Samuel Hopkins Adams[1]
Photography:	Joseph Walker
Editor:	Gene Havlick
Art Director:	Stephen Goosson
Costumes:	Robert Kalloch
Musical Director:	Louis Silvers
Sound:	E.L. Bernds
Assistant Director:	C.C. Coleman
Cast:	Clark Gable (Peter Warne), Claudette Colbert (Ellie Andrews), Walter Connolly (Alexander Andrews), Roscoe Karns (Oscar Shapely), Alan Hale (Danker), Charles S. Wilson (Joe Gordon), Ward Bond (bus driver), Eddy Chandler (bus driver), Jameson Thomas (King Westley), Wallis Clark (Lovington), Arthur Hoyt (Zeke), Blanche Friderici (Zeke's wife), Harry Holman (auto camp manager), Maidel Turner (camp manager's wife), Harry C. Bradley (Henderson), Irving Bacon (station attendant), Harry Todd (flag man), Frank Yaconelli (Tony), Henry Wadsworth (drunken boy), Claire McDowell (mother), Ky Robinson, Joseph Crehan, Frank Holiday and James Burke (detectives), Mickey Daniels (vendor), Oliver Eckhardt (Dykes), George Breakston (boy), Rev. Neal Dodd (minister), Edmund Burns (best man), Ethel Sykes (maid of honor), Tom Ricketts (old man), Eddie Kane (radio announcer), Eva Dennison (society woman), Fred Walton (butler), Matty Rupert (newsboy), Milton Kibbee, Sherry Hall, Hal Price, and Charles D. Hall (reporters), Earl Pingree and Harry Hume (policemen), Ernie Adams, Kit Guard, Billy Engle, Allen Fox, Marvin Loback, Dave Wengren, Bert Starkey, Rita Ross, Kate Morgan, Rose May, Margaret Reid, Sam Josephson, Ray Creighton, John Wallace, Mimi Lindell, Blanche Rose, Jane Tallent, Charles Wilroy, Patsy O'Byrne, Harry Schultz, Bert Scott, Emma Tansey, Marvin Schector, William McCall, and S.S. Simon (bus passengers)

Filmed at Columbia Pictures Studio and on location in California during the last week of November and the first three weeks of December 1933

Distributor:	Columbia Pictures Corporation
Copyright:	17 February 1934 by Columbia Pictures Corporation of California (LP 4497)

The Films: Credits, Notes, and Synopses

Released: 22 February 1934 (Radio City Music Hall, New
                         York City
Running time: 105 minutes

Notes

1. Samuel Hopkins Adams's "Night Bus" appeared in Cosmopolitan (August 1933). It is reprinted in Stories into Film, edited by William Kittredge and Steven M. Krauzer (New York: Harper & Row Publishers, 1979). A version of the screenplay checked against a transcript of the dialogue in the finished film was published in Four-Star Scripts, edited by Lorraine Noble (Garden City, N.Y.: Doubleday, Doran, & Co. 1936). A version of the screenplay including scenes deleted from the finished film can ge found in Twenty Best Film Plays, edited by John Gassner and Dudley Nichols (New York: Crown Publishers, 1943; New York and London: Garland Publishing, 1977).

It Happened One Night received Academy Awards for best picture, best direction, best writing-adaptation, best actor (Clark Gable), and best actress (Claudette Colbert), and was named best picture of the year by the National Board of Review. According to Jay Leyda, a Russian stage version of the film entitled New York-Miami Bus was the most popular play to run in Leningrad during the siege of 1942 (see Kino: A History of the Russian and Soviet Film [New York: MacMillan, 1960], p. 380). In 1956, It Happened One Night was remade by Columbia as You Can't Run Away from It, directed by Dick Powell, starring June Allyson and Jack Lemmon.

Synopsis

   Heiress Ellie Andrews stages a hunger strike on her father's yacht off the cost of Florida. To spite him, she has married a playboy-aviator, King Westley. Her father intends to hold her prisoner until he has had the marriage annulled but she jumps overboard and swims to Miami. Andrews launches a massive search.

   In Miami, Ellie catches a bus for New York. The seat beside her is taken by Peter Warne, a brash, inebriated reporter who has just been fired by his editor in New York for writing a story in free verse. When the bus pulls out, Peter stumbles into Ellie's lap before settling down beside her; she is clearly unhappy with the arrangement. At the first rest stop Ellie's suitcase is stolen. Peter tries to catch the thief, but fails. He encourages Ellie to report the loss to the bus company for compensation, but she wants to be left alone. When they reboard the bus she selects a different seat, but a fat man sleeping beside her snores loudly and leans against her. Soon Ellie is back next to Peter, although is still careful to keep her distance. When they arrive in Jacksonville in the morning, she discovers that she has been sleeping on Peter's shoulder.

   Ellie decides to freshen up at a hotel, but dallies too long and misses the bus. Recognizing her picture in the morning paper, Peter stays behind to wait for her. Ellie tries to buy his silence, offending Peter; he labels her a spoiled brat who always buys her way. That night they catch the next bus to New York. Ellie finds herself beside Oscar Shapely, a fast-talking bore on the make. Peter rescues her by pretending to be her husband. Ellie is grateful, but then promptly taken aback by his effort to assume control of her dwindling funds.

Heavy rains wash out a bridge up ahead, forcing the passengers to spend the night at a nearby auto camp. To save money, Peter checks the two of them into a single cabin as husband and wife. Ellie is suspicious, but Peter insists he is only interested in her value as news, promising to get her to King Westley in exchange for an exclusive story about her trip. If she leaves him, however, he will notify her father. Ellie agrees to stay. Peter hangs a blanket on a rope between their beds as a "Wall of Jericho" for privacy. Ellie is reluctant to go to her side, but changes her mind when he starts to undress.

Refreshed and cheerful in the morning, Ellie rapidly adjusts to the rusticity of outdoor washrooms. Peter cooks breakfast; as they eat she describes the frustrations of her sheltered youth. Detectives making the rounds in search of the heiress arrive at the cabin door. Following Peter's lead, Ellie fools the police by pretending she is a plumber's daughter having a row with her husband. Afterwards both are exhilarated by the charade.

On the road again, Ellie and Peter join the rest of the bus passengers in a rousing version of "The Daring Young Man on the Flying Trapeze." Carried away by his own singing, the driver steers the bus off the road. A woman traveling with her young son collapses from hunger, and Ellie gives the boy Peter's last $10 to buy food. Shapely, meanwhile, has noticed Ellie's picture in the paper and tries to blackmail Peter. Peter frightens him off by pretending to be a gangster, but decides that he and Ellie must now make it north on their own. They hike a long distance, and he carries her piggyback across a pond, before settling down for the night near a farmhouse on a bed of hay under a bright moon.

The next day Peter tries to get Ellie to eat some raw carrots, but she resists. He confidently demonstrates three sure-fire methods of hitchhiking by thumb, none of which stops a car. Ellie takes his place and, lifting her hem above her knee, brings the next car to a halt. The driver merrily serenades them, but turns out to be a theif; when they stop at a roadside inn, he drives off with their luggage. Peter pursues him, returning a short while later with both his luggage and the car. He and Ellie drive on.

Frustrated in his effort to locate his daughter, Andrews decides to drop his opposition to the marriage if Ellie returns. He asks Westley to make the announcements to the press so that Ellie will believe it. She reads the news that night, three hours outside of New York, but dismisses Peter's offer to push on to the city. Instead she

The Films: Credits, Notes, and Synopses

decides to spend the night at an autocamp, where Peter erects a new "Wall of Jericho" for their last night together. From her side of the cabin she asks Peter if he has ever thought about love. He replies that the kind of genuine girl he's looking for doesn't exist anymore, but then describes a Pacific island where he would take his dream girl if he found her. Ellie comes around the curtain and asks him to take her with him. Peter advises her to go back to her bed. She apologizes and returns to her side. Moments later he asks her if she has meant what she said, but she is asleep. He tiptoes out of the cabin, exchanges his hat for some gasoline, and heads for the newspaper office in New York, where he knocks out a story on Ellie's annulment and engagement to himself. His editor buys the story for $1,000, money Peter thinks he needs to propose to Ellie properly.

Back at the auto camp, Ellie is awakened by the managers and informed that her "husband" has left without paying. She has no money, so they kick her out. She contacts her father and accepts his offer. When word of the agreement reaches the newspaper office, Peter's front-page story is ditched in favor of an updated report. Unaware of this turn of events, Peter is on his way back to the auto camp when he glimpses Ellie riding with her father and King Westley in the opposite direction, accompanied by a police escort. He tries to catch up with them, but his engine overheats and a tire goes flat.

Peter, drunk, returns the $1,000 to his editor, who stuffs the money back in his reporter's pocket and tells him to come back when he's sober. At the Andrew's mansion plans are underway for an elaborate wedding. Ellie confesses to her father that she loves Peter, who she is certain despises her and her way of life. But her faith in his gallantry vanishes when, learning that he has written her father concerning a debt, she assumes that Peter is after the $10,000 reward her father had posted for his daughter's return. So Ellie gets drunk.

On the day of the wedding Peter is summoned to the mansion. He tells Andrews he is only interested in $39.60 to cover his expenses. Peter fends off Andrews's further inquiries, but finally admits to loving Ellie. On the way out, he exchanges a few bitter words with the bride, who in turn refuses to speak with her father. King Westley arrives by aerogyro and is swamped by the press. As father and daughter advance down the aisle, Andrews tells Ellie the truth about Peter and advises her to flee in a getaway car he has provided. At the last possible moment, Ellie breaks for the car and escapes.

Andrews gets his long-awaited annulment by buying off Westley for $100,000. At an auto camp, a trumpet blast signals the toppling of the "Wall of Jericho" between Ellie and Peter.

25   **BROADWAY BILL (1934)**

   La course de Broadway-Bill (France), Strettamente confidenziale (Italy), Strictly Confidential (Great Britain)

The Films: Credits, Notes, and Synopses

Production Company: Columbia Pictures Corporation
Producer: Harry Cohn/A Frank Capra Production
Director: Frank Capra
Screenplay: Robert Riskin, from a story by Mark Hellinger[1]
Photography: Joseph Walker
Camera Operator: George Kelly
Editor: Gene Havlick
Sound Engineer: Edward Bernds
Microphone: Irving Libbot
Electrician: Bob Charlesworth
Props: George Rhein
Gaffer: George Hager
Best Boy: Al Later
Head Grip: Jimmy Lloyd
Assistant Director: C.C. Coleman
Cast: Warner Baxter (Dan Brooks), Myrna Loy (Alice Higgins), Walter Connolly (J.L. Higgins), Helen Vinson (Margaret Brooks), Lynne Overman (Happy McGuire), Raymond Walburn (Colonel Pettigrew), Clarence Muse (Whitey), Margaret Hamilton (Edna), Douglass Dumbrille (Eddie Morgan), George Meeker (Henry Early), Helen Flint (Mrs. Early), Jason Robards (Arthur Winslow), Helene Millard (Mrs. Winslow), Frankie Darro (Ted Williams, Dan's Jockey), Harry Holman (rube), Charles Levison and Ward Bond (Morgan's henchmen), Edmund Breese (presiding judge), Harry Todd (Pop Jones), George Cooper (Joe), Charles C. Wilson (Collins), Paul Harvey (James Whitehall), Edward Tucker (Jimmy Baker), Bob Tansill (Whitehall's jockey), Clara Blandick (Mrs. Peterson, secretary), Gladys Gale (head nurse), Inez Courtenay (Mae, nurse), Claude Gillingham (J.P. Chase), James Blakely (intern), Alan Hale (orchestra leader), Forrester Harvey (horse trainer), Charles Middleton (veterinarian), Lucille Ball (switchboard operator), Irving Bacon (hot dog stand owner), John Ince (mayor), Herman Bing (waiter), Edward Keane (head-waiter), Kit Guard (cab driver), Stanley Blystone (jailer), Bess Flowers (secretary), Ernie Adams (patient), Sam Flint (judge), Eddie Kane (assistant judge), Ky Robinson and Frank Holliday (deputy sheriffs), Harry C. Bradley (book-keeper), Tom Ticketts (Johnson, the butler), Harrison Greene (auctioneer), Eddy Chandler (onlooker), A.R. Haysel (Mike),

The Films: Credits, Notes, and Synopses

                         Pat Moriarty (policeman), Harry Semels (conductor), Joan Standing (secretary), Frank Yaconelli (Spaniard), William H. Strauss (pawnbroker), Robert Allen, Dick Summer, and Frank O'Connor (reporters), Jack Mulhall, Edmund Burns, Pat O'Malley, Arthur Rankin, Dennis O'Keefe

Filmed at Columbia Pictures Studio and on location at the Tanforan Racetrack near San Francisco in the summer of 1934

Distributor: Columbia Pictures Corporation
Copyright: 24 November 1934 by Columbia Pictures Corporation of California (LP 5123)
Released: 29 November 1934 (Radio City Music Hall, New York City)
Running time: 90 minutes

Notes

1. Screenwriter Sidney Buchman, who was later to work with Capra on Mr. Smith Goes to Washington, claims to have done rewrite work on the script after Robert Riskin had departed the project. According to Buchman, Capra did not like the original ending scheduled to be shot at the Tanforan racetrack, and at the last moment came up with the idea of having the horse die after winning the race (see Bertrand Tavernier's 1969 interview with Buchman [entry 799], p. 40).

Although Broadway Bill was not as honored at the time of its release as Capra's work before it (It Happened One Night) or after (Mr. Deeds Goes to Town), it was for the most part favorably received by reviewers and seems to have enjoyed reasonable success at the box office. It is rarely mentioned, however, in surveys of Capra's career, which typically move directly from the grass-roots success of It Happened One Night to Capra's excursion into social and political commentary with Mr. Deeds Goes to Town. Broadway Bill's neglect may in part result from its relative unavailability; Capra remade it as Riding High for Paramount in 1950, at which time the original negative material was lost. Viewing prints, however, are held both at the UCLA Film Archive and in the American Film Institute collection at the Library of Congress.

Synopsis

    J.L. Higgins, president of the Higgins National Bank, calls for a business dinner with his three sons-in-law, each of whom heads one of the subsidiary industries Higgins controls. But Dan Brooks, chief of the paper box division, cannot be reached at his office. He is out at the stables training Broadway Bill, the racehorse he adores, with help from his young sister-in-law, Alice. Alice urges him to abandon her father's business for his first love, racehorses. Bill's groom, Whitey, echoes her advice. A messenger arrives with word of the meeting that night; Dan tosses rocks after the messenger in frustration.

The Films: Credits, Notes, and Synopses

Dressing for dinner, Dan tries to convey to his wife, Margaret, his excitement over Bill and the frustrations he feels as her father's parasite. Tonight, Dan proposes, he and she should sit under the moon and throw rocks at the family mansion. Dismissing this all as nonsense, Margaret reminds Dan that he is the likely heir to her father's position in the company.

They arrive late for dinner, and Dan is received coolly by his father-in-law. J.L. announces his acquisition of a lumber yard, the presidency of which will be reserved for Alice's future husband. Alice retorts that no husband of hers would ever accept such a job. Following a formal meal, J.L. presents a business report. All companies are thriving save the paper box division, which Dan has neglected. So J.L. orders that Broadway Bill be sold. Dan decides at once to quit the business and take leave of the family circle. Alice applauds, but Margaret refuses to go with him.

Dan rejoins his old friends on the horse-racing circuit. He enters Bill in a $25,000 handicap only two weeks off, spending all his cash, and some of Whitey's, on the nomination fee. There are other financial obstacles ahead, but Dan approaches the future with boundless optimism. He fast-talks an old farmer into feeding and sheltering Bill as an investment in the horse's future, and he and Whitey move into the barn with the horse. A scheme to touch an old friend, Colonel Pettigrew, for the $500 entry fee for the handicap backfires when the charming charlatan turns out to be after a few bucks himself, and they both are forced to bluff their way out of a restaurant where they have met without the cash to pay the bill. But the colonel then raises $50 stake money for a preliminary race by courting his spinsterish landlady.

On the day of the preliminary, however, Bill bolts the padlock and is disqualified from the race. He and Dan are the laughing stock of the track. Diagnosing Bill's problem as homesickness, Dan asks Margaret to send him Skeeter, a rooster of which Bill is fond. Margaret ignores the request, but Alice brings Dan the rooster and begs to stay for the big derby. Dan agrees, and teases her about how she's grown up. With Skeeter around, Bill returns to top form. The farmer, meanwhile, becomes suspicious and demands payment on his feed bill. Dan, with the help of the colonel and his sidekick Happy, again talks his way out of the crisis, sketching a portrait of imminent wealth for the old man.

Befriending Whitey, Alice sings a spiritual with him. She domesticates the barn, cooking dinner and stocking shelves with canned goods. The latter inspire Dan to compose a song about split pea soup and succotash. But the playful spell is broken by a thunderstorm. While the owner of Gallant Lady, the prize horse in the race, calmly tends the animal in a well-equipped stable, Dan, Alice, and Whitey work desperately to keep Bill dry in the leaky barn. But the horse gets soaked and in the morning has a high fever. The veterinarian

The Films: Credits, Notes, and Synopses

doubts Bill will recover in time for the race, but Alice nurses him back to health in a few days.

Dan is still short the entry fee for the handicap. Whitey tries to raise the sum by shooting craps but is beaten up for using loaded dice. The colonel and Happy bilk a rube at the racetrack for $25 in exchange for a betting tip, but the colonel falls prey to subsequent rumors spread by the rube and bets on the loser himself. Meanwhile Alice pawns some clothing and jewelry. She passes on the money she raises through Whitey so Dan won't find out.

Dan gets drunk at a party the night before the race. As he staggers back to the barn with Alice, he improvises some romantic lyrics to his "split pea soup" song, but she asks him not to sing. At the barn he discovers that Bill has been seized by the sheriff against a claim for unpaid feed bills. Seeing Bill mistreated by a guard, Dan assaults the officer and ends up in jail. When Alice visits the next day, Dan is so deeply depressed he is ready to return to the paper box company.

A $2 bet placed on Bill by a famous millionaire sets off national interest in the horse. Rumors magnify the size of the bet to $250,000, and widespread betting by ordinary people lowers Bill's odds from 100-1 to 60-1. Big-time gambler Eddie Morgan is pleased. As Bill's odds drop, those on Eddie's horse rise, and he stands to make a killing. When Eddie hears that Bill has been scratched from the race because of the feed bill, he visits Dan in jail and pays off his debts. Dan is elated. The odds continue to shift: Bill is 6-1, Eddie's horse 20-1. Having bribed the jockeys of both Bill and Gallant Lady to lose the race, Eddie places his bets.

On the day of the race, Dan and Alice cheerfully sing Dan's song. Gallant Lady's jockey is suspended and replaced right before the race, but Bill's jockey still has been bribed to lose. The race begins. As the jockeys fight for position, Bill's rider tries to hold his horse back, but Bill springs to the front of the pack. At home, J.L. finds himself caught up in a radio broadcast of the race. Down the stretch, Gallant Lady and Broadway Bill vie for the lead. Bill wins by a nose. But then he collapses and dies from the excitement. A mournful Dan returns to the barn, where Alice comforts him.

The next day Bill is buried at the racetrack. J.L. appears to take Alice home. Margaret has refused to come, expecting Dan to return on his own. Instead he goes off with Whitey.

Two years later the Higgins family has assembled for another dinner meeting. In light of Margaret's divorce, J.L. announces, he has sold the paper box division. Moreover, he intends to sell the ironworks and perhaps the bank itself. Thus the companies will return to the people who founded them, and his sons-in-law can make good on their own. A car horn blows incessantly outside, and a window is shattered by a rock. The butler announces Dan has returned to insist

The Films: Credits, Notes, and Synopses

that "the princess be released from the dark tower." Alice races outside to join Dan and Broadway Bill II. J.L. gives Alice his blessing. After surveying the shocked and silent children around his table, he decides to join the free-spirited youngsters himself.

26   MR. DEEDS GOES TO TOWN (1936)

L'extravagant Mr. Deeds (France), E' arrivata la felicità (Italy), Mr. Deeds geht in die Stadt (Germany)

Production Company:	Columbia Pictures Corporation
Producer:	Frank Capra
Director:	Frank Capra
Screenplay:	Robert Riskin, from the story "Opera Hat" by Clarence Budington Kelland[1]
Photography:	Joseph Walker
Special Effects:	E. Roy Davidson
Editor:	Gene Havlick
Art Director:	Stephen Goosson
Costumes:	Samuel Lange
Musical Director:	Howard Jackson
Sound:	Edward Bernds
Assistant Director:	C.C. Coleman
Cast:	Gary Cooper (Longfellow Deeds), Jean Arthur (Babe Bennett), Lionel Stander (Cornelius Cobb), Douglass Dumbrille (John Cedar), George Bancroft (MacWade), Raymond Walburn (Walter), H.B. Warner (Judge Walker), Warren Hymer (bodyguard), Edward Gargan (second bodyguard), Wryley Birch (psychiatrist), John Wray (farmer), Gustav von Seyffertitz (Dr. Frazier), Irving Bacon (Frank), Walter Catlett (Morrow), Franklin Pangborn (tailor), Barnett Parker (butler), Margaret Matzenauer (Madame Pomponi), Muriel Evans (Theresa), Ruth Donnelly (Mabel Dawson), Spencer Charters (Mal), Emma Dunn (Mrs. Meredith), Arthur Hoyt (Budington), Stanley Andrews (James Cedar), Pierre Watkin (Arthur Cedar), Christian Rub (Swenson), Jameson Thomas (Mr. Semple), Mayo Methot (Mrs. Semple), Russell Hicks (Dr. Malcolm), Edward Le Saint (Dr. Fosdick), Charles [Levison] Lane (Hallor), George Cooper (Bob), Gene Morgan (waiter), Margaret Seddon (Jane Faulkner), Margaret MacWade (Amy Faulkner), Harry C. Bradley (Anderson), Edwin Maxwell (Douglas), Paul Hurst (first deputy), Paul Porcasi (Italian), George F. Hayes (farmers' spokesman), Billy Bevan (cabbie), Bud Flannigan [Dennis O'Keefe]

The Films: Credits, Notes, and Synopses

(reporter), George Meeker (Brookfield), Dale Van Sickel (lawyer), Eddie Kane (Henneberry), Jay Eaton (writer), Jack Mower (reporter), Charles Wilson (court clerk), James Millican (intern), Harry Holden (guard), Lee Shumway (bailiff), John Picorri and Edward Keane (board members), Janet Eastman and Mary Lou Dix (shop girls), Lillian Ross and Patricia Moore (hat check girls), Peggy Page (cigarette girl), Bessie Wade, Bess Flowers, Flo Wix, Ann Doran, Cecil Cunningham, Beatrice Curtis, Beatrice Blinn, Pauline Wagner, Frank Hammond, Charles Sullivan, Hal Budlong, Ethel Palmer, Juanita Crosland, Vacey O'Davoren

Filmed at Columbia Pictures and Twentieth Century-Fox Studios[2] in January-February 1936
Distributor: Columbia Pictures Corporation
Copyright: 8 April 1936 by Columbia Pictures Corporation of California, Ltd. (LP 6259)
Released: 16 April 1936 (Radio City Music Hall, New York City)
Running time: 115 minutes

Notes

1. "Opera Hat" by Clarence Budington Kelland was serialized in American Magazine, 119, Nos. 4-6 (April-June 1935) and 120, Nos. 1-3 (July-September 1935). The working title for the film during shooting was A Gentleman Goes to Town.

2. According to soundman Edward Bernds, the Mandrake Falls sequence was shot on Fox's New England street set (see Victor Scherle and William Turner Levy's The Films of Frank Capra [entry 1062], p. 137).

Capra won his second Academy Award for directing Mr. Deeds Goes to Town. The film also was nominated by the Academy for best picture, best writing-screenplay, best actor (Gary Cooper), and best sound recording. It was named best picture of the year by both the New York Film Critics and the National Board of Review. A television series based on Mr. Deeds Goes to Town was aired by ABC-TV from 26 September 1969 through 16 January 1970. Monte Markham starred as a small-town newspaper editor who inherits a multimillion-dollar corporation.

Synopsis

Millionaire Martin W. Semple is killed in a motor accident in Italy. His lawyer, John Cedar, and press agent, Cornelius Cobb, journey to Mandrake Falls, Vermont, to meet Semple's nephew and heir. He is Longfellow Deeds, a twenty-eight-year-old bachelor who plays the tuba in the town band, serves as a volunteer fireman, and, while owning a local tallow works, earns most of his income writing poetry for special-occasion postcards. Deeds appears unimpressed by news of the $20 million inheritance. Hoping he has a patsy on his hands, Cedar persuades the small-town youth to come to New York. After an emotional send-off by a throng of cheering friends, Deeds leaves Mandrake Falls for the first time in his life.

The heir's arrival in New York is big news, but Cobb shields Deeds from the press. Ace reporter Babe Bennett, lured by an offer of a month's paid vacation, promises her frustrated editor, MacWade, a front-page scoop. Meanwhile Deeds grows uneasy amid the entourage of servants and advisers in the Semple mansion. He startles the opera company's board of directors by announcing he will no longer fund their yearly deficit and, sensing a scam, forcefully evicts a lawyer representing an alleged common-law wife of his uncle. Solidifying his doubts about Cedar, whose hand he finds oily, Deeds demands to see the financial records.

That night Cobb offers to supply Deeds with female companions, but unlike his late uncle, a notorious playboy, Deeds's ideal woman is a "lady in distress." Sneaking out of the mansion alone, he soon thinks he has found one. Babe Bennett has waited for him and now collapses on the sidewalk in the rain. When he rushes to help her, she feigns exhaustion from having searched all day for a job. Unaware that photographers are trailing, Deeds takes Babe to dinner at Tullio's, home of New York's literati, and rapidly falls in love with the role Babe plays—ingenue "Mary Dawson."

A group of writers at a nearby round table invite the greeting card poet from Mandrake Falls to join them so they can have some laughs at his expense. At first Deeds is honored, but then detecting their mockery he denounces their bad manners. With the consent of the delighted Babe, he knocks together the heads of the worst offenders. An inebriated member of the group is so taken by this bold gesture that he offers to take Deeds on a tour of the city.

In the morning, Babe has her front-page story complete with photos: Deeds is cast as a "Cinderella Man" on a drunken binge in the city. She promises MacWade more stories like it. Waking up with a hangover, Deeds learns of the headlines and wants to punch the editor. Cobb advises him to stop talking to outsiders instead. Deeds agrees, but makes an exception for "Mary Dawson," whom he is sure he can trust.

That evening Deeds goes sightseeing with Babe. At Grant's Tomb he pays homage to the Ohio farmboy who became general and president. Confessing to being hurt by the news story, Deeds thanks Babe for her sympathy, a quality he finds in short supply in the city. The irony is not lost on Babe; on a secluded park bench she admits that she was once a small-town girl with a father much like Deeds. She and Deeds strike up an improvised rendition of "Sewanee River." Deeds interrupts the duet to chase a passing fire engine. That night Babe has

The Films: Credits, Notes, and Synopses

trouble writing her story. A romantic phone call from Deeds only deepens her guilt. But Deeds is elated. For fun, he coaxes all the servants in the mansion to call out in unison. Their echoes harmonize.

Mme. Pomponi, an opera star, sponsors Deeds's social debut at the mansion, but he tosses the affected guests out early and goes to visit Babe. Distressed by her predicament, Babe has been packing to leave town. Now she takes a long walk with Deeds and listens to him describe the girl of his dreams. He obliquely proposes by having her read aloud a love poem he has written and gives her until tomorrow to respond.

The next day Deeds excitedly arranges a luncheon date with "Mary" at the mansion. Babe tells MacWade that she is quitting her job and is willing to risk everything on telling Deeds the truth, but before she has a chance to do so, Cobb brings Deeds word of the real "Mary Dawson." When Deeds calls Babe to check out the story, she can only weakly confess to the truth. Shocked and bitter, he decides to leave the city at once and give up the fortune.

As Deeds descends the staircase with his luggage, he is confronted by a dispossessed farmer who castigates Deeds for spending his wealth frivolously while poor people starve. When Deeds labels the man just another moocher, the farmer pulls out a pistol, threatening to shoot Deeds, and then breaks down and apologizes. Deed feeds the farmer the lunch intended for Babe and announces a plan to use his wealth to stake unemployed workers and tenant farmers with a ten-acre farm, a horse, a cow, and some seed. A mob of eager applicants soon swarm the mansion where Deeds works full time running the program.

Meanwhile, Cedar prompts some distant relatives of Semple to legally contest the disposition of the estate on the grounds that Deeds is insane. Just as a spokesman for the crowd at the mansion formally thanks Deeds for giving them hope, the sheriff's office delivers a warrant for Deeds's arrest. Taken to the county hospital, he slips into a deep depression. Cobb tries to rally his spirits, but Deeds refuses to speak with anyone, including a distraught Babe.

His insanity trial begins. Poor people jam the courtroom to support him, but Deeds remains withdrawn, rejecting counsel or a chance to speak in his own defense. Cedar lays the groundwork for the prosecution, describing Deeds's agrarian plan as fantastic and capable of fomenting mass social upheaval. Babe's news stories and photographs are introduced as key evidence. Called to testify, Babe declares the charges a frame-up, but is ruled out of order for her outburst and forced to return to her seat to calm down. Two elderly sisters from Mandrake Falls testify that Deeds has always been "pixilated." Witnesses to his drunken night with the writer confirm his crazy behavior. A noted Austrian psychiatrist diagnoses him as clearly manic-depressive. Cobb begs Deeds to fight back, but gets no

The Films: Credits, Notes, and Synopses

response. After a short recess, the judge rules that for Deeds's own safety he is to be committed to an institution.

Babe suddenly interrupts the proceedings. Deeds's silence, she argues, is a logical response to persecution, and she herself is largely to blame. Challenged by Cedar, she admits to loving Deeds. Deeds begins to stir. When MacWade, Cobb, and members of the crowd echo Babe's support, Deeds takes the stand and demolishes Cedar's case point by point. His playing the tuba is no more bizarre than the other nervous habits he has witnessed in the courtroom, including "o-filling" by the judge and "doodling" by the psychiatrist. His behavior on the bender is excusable as the folly of a youth who had never been drunk. Everyone in Mandrake Falls is "pixilated," as the elderly sisters readily admit. His agrarian plan is a common-sense response to the plight of the poor. Moreover, since Cedar offered to settle the case out of court, his motive are suspect. Cedar labels the last point a lie; Deeds concludes his defense by punching Cedar in the jaw. After another recess, the judge reverses his decision, declaring Deeds the sanest man ever to walk into the courtroom. The cheering crowd carries Deeds out on their shoulders.

Babe sits in the courtroom, empty now save for the elderly sisters. Fleeing his supporters, Deeds rushes back inside. He lifts up Babe. They kiss.

27 **LOST HORIZON (1937)**

Les horizons perdus (France), Orizzonte Perduto (Italy), Das verlorene Paradies (Germany)

Production Company:	Columbia Pictures Corporation
Producer:	Frank Capra
Director:	Frank Capra
Screenplay:	Robert Riskin, from the novel by James Hilton[1]
Photography:	Joseph Walker
Aerial Photography:	Elmer Dyer
Special Effects:	E. Roy Davidson, Ganahl Carson
Editors:	Gene Havlick, Gene Milford
Art Director:	Stephen Goosson
Set Director:	Babs Johnstone
Costumes:	Ernest Dryden
Musical Score:	Dimitri Tiomkin
Musical Director:	Max Steiner
Choir Director:	Hall B. Johnson
Choral Voices:	The Hall Johnson Choir
Technical Adviser:	Harrison Forman
Assistant Director:	C.C. Coleman, [Arthur Black][2]
Cast:	Ronald Colman (Robert Conway), Jane Wyatt (Sondra), John Howard (George Conway), Thomas Mitchell (Henry Barnard), Edward Everett Horton (Alexander P. Lovett),

The Films: Credits, Notes, and Synopses

Isabel Jewell (Gloria Stone), H. B. Warner (Chang), Sam Jaffe (high lama),[3] Margo (Maria), Willie Fung and Victor Wong (bandit leaders), Noble Johnson (leader of porters), Hugh Buckler (Lord Gainsford), John Miltern (Carstairs), John Burton (Wynant), John T. Murray (Meeker), Max Rabinowitz (Sieveking), John Tettener (Montaigne), David Torrance (prime minister), Boyd Irwin, Sr. (assistant foreign secretary), Leonard Mudie (foreign secretary), David Clyde (steward), Neil Fitzgerald and Derby Clark (radio operators), Val Durand (Talu), Dennis D'Auburn (aviator), Milton Owen (Fenner), George Chan (Chinese priest), Richard Loo (Shanghai airport official), Lawrence Grant (first man), Wryley Birch, Ruth Robinson, Margaret MacWade, and Carl Stockdale (missionaries), Beatrice Curtis, Mary Lou Dix, Beatrice Blinn, and Arthur Rankin (passengers), Ernesto Zambrano, Richard Master, Alex Shoulder, and Manuel Kelili (servants), Barry Winton, Robert Corey, Henry Mowbray, Wedgewood Nowell, and Eric Wilton (Englishmen), Chief John Big Tree, Eli Casey, Richard Robles, and James Smith (porters), Clement Horton, Charles Dempsey, Robert Lugo, Morning Gonzales, George Kaluna, Delmar Ingraham, Ira Walker, Tom Campbell, Glen Howard, Antonio Herrara, Pat Tapia, Joe Shoulder, Ed Thorpe, James Spencer, Joe Molino, Harry Lishman

Filmed at Columbia Pictures Studio and at the following locations in California: Los Angeles Metropolitan Airport (the burning of Baskul); Lucerne Dry Lake (refueling at the Tibetan border); Ojai Valley (Valley of the Blue Moon); Sherwood Forest (Bob and Sondra's idyll in the woods); a Los Angeles ice house (snow scenes). Principal photography began 23 March 1936 and continued until August. Additional filming was done during the fall of 1936.[4]

Distributor: Columbia Pictures Corporation
Copyright: 2 March 1937 by Columbia Pictures Corporation of California, Ltd. (LP 6952)
Released: 3 March 1937 (Globe Theatre, New York City)[5]
Running time: 132 minutes[6]

Notes

1. James Hilton's novel was published by William Morrow & Co., New York, in 1933 (277 pp.) and has been frequently reprinted. Screenwriter Sidney Buchman claims that Capra asked him to rewrite a section

The Films: Credits, Notes, and Synopses

of the film after an unsuccessful preview, and that he did so without receiving credit (see Bertrand Tavernier's 1969 interview with Buchman [entry 799], p. 41).

2. In his autobiography Capra mentions Arthur Black as an assistant director on Lost Horizon. Black was to work in this capacity on most of Capra's films to follow, but he did not receive official credit until You Can't Take It with You in 1938 (see The Name above the Title, p. 197).

3. The casting of the part of the high lama has been a source of controversy over the years. Rumors circulated prior to the film's release that numerous actors had been tested for the part, and that Capra had shot all of the lama's scenes twice, using another actor in addition to Sam Jaffe; Walter Connolly is often cited (see, for example, Life's preview of the film on 14 December 1936 [entry 236]). According to Capra, however, only two other actors besides Jaffe were considered for the part: A.E. Anson was tested, but died two days later; Henry B. Walthall was asked to make a screen test, but died before he had a chance to do so. Sam Jaffe was then tested and hired for the part. By this time production was into its third month, but no scenes with another lama had been filmed. Connolly's name, Capra suggests, has probably been bandied about because Capra had considered him for the role of Barnard. Recent research has led Rudy Behlmer to propose, however, that the lama's scenes were reshot with Connolly after principal photography was completed, and a decision was then made to stick with Jaffe. Jaffe's original scenes were condensed and reshot with the actor in different makeup designed by Jack Dawn of M-G-M, and the new footage was used in the film. (For Capra's most recent account, see Victor Scherle and William Turner Levy's The Films of Frank Capra [entry 1062], pp. 146-50. Also see Rudy Behlmer's America's Favorite Movies: Behind the Scenes [New York: Frederick Ungar Publishing Co. 1982], pp. 22-39.)

4. Capra first became interested in filming Hilton's novel in December 1934, and an initial draft of the screenplay was prepared by the following May. But production was held up ten months until Ronald Colman was available for the central role. In the interim Capra filmed Mr. Deeds Goes to Town.

5. In his autobiography Capra mistakenly locates the New York opening at the Radio City Music Hall. The premiere at the Globe in New York, and at the Four Star Theatre in Los Angeles on 10 March, were on a reserve-seat basis, marking Columbia's first venture into prestige exhibition of this kind.

6. Capra claims that his first version of the film was close to three hours long, but that he eliminated the first two reels following a disastrous preview in Santa Barbara in November 1936. Assuming that Capra shot the opening as it is described in the final draft of the screenplay (dated 23 March 1936), the discarded section included the following scenes: (1) At the British Foreign Office word arrives that

The Films: Credits, Notes, and Synopses

Conway has been found, causing great excitement. (2) News stories circulate, providing information about Conway's background. (3) Conway suffers amnesia aboard the SS Manchuria on the way home, and finds a certain pleasure in the loss of memory; upon hearing Chopin played at a concert, however, he recovers his memory of Shangri-La and the high lama, and begins to relate his tale to Lord Gainsford beginning with the burning of Baskul. The script also contains a scene aboard the ship at the end of the film in which Gainsford tries to convince Conway not to return to Shangri-La, but is unable to stop him. This is followed by Gainsford recounting the story at the club, as it exists in the current versions. Following the premiere of the 132-minute version in New York and Los Angeles in March 1937, additional footage was cut from the film for its roadshow release, including scenes in which Chang comforts a despairing Gloria and Barnard and Lovett get drunk at a picnic with native women. By the time of Lost Horizon's general release in September 1937, several romantic scenes involving Bob and Sondra also had been excised, shortening the film to 117 minutes. Then in April 1942, Columbia released another version, 108 minutes long, entitled Lost Horizon of Shangri-La. To accommodate the changing concerns of the war years, an introductory title transformed the local revolution in Baskul into an attack by Japan on China. Moreover, pacifist remarks by Conway were excised, and strands of the romantic subplot trimmed. This 108-minute version eventually was sold to television, where local stations butchered it further. Prints as short as 98 minutes have popped up in 16mm distribution as a result. Since 1969 the American Film Institute has been involved in restoring the 132-minute version. Columbia turned over its nitrate studio print (the 117-minute version), and the National Film Archive in London supplied a sound track from the 132-minute version. By incorporating images from several variant prints, including a French TV print located in Quebec, all but 6 minutes have been restored. On 18 October 1979, the A.F.I. screened their restored version at Mann's Chinese Theatre in Hollywood, projecting black footage during those passages where only the sound track survives. A version incorporating production stills instead of black footage is now being prepared. (See Edward Conner, "Revisiting Lost Horizon," Screenfacts, 1, No. 2 [1963], 50-60; Todd McCarthy, "AFI Screens Results--So--of Search for 'Lost Horizon' Scenes," Daily Variety, 22 October 1979, pp. 4, 9; and Lawrence F. Karr, "The American Film Institute and the Library of Congress," Quarterly Journal of the Library of Congress, 37 [Summer/Fall 1980], 358-59.)

Lost Horizon received Academy Awards for best art direction and best film editing. It was also nominated by the Academy for best picture, best supporting actor (H.B. Warner), best musical score, best sound recording, and best assistant direction. A stage musical of Hilton's novel entitled Shangri-La opened at the Winter Garden in New York City on 13 June 1956 and ran for 21 performances. Ross Hunter produced a musical version of Capra's film for Columbia in 1973 with Liv Ullman and Peter Finch in the lead roles.

The Films: Credits, Notes, and Synopses

Synopsis (based on the 117-minute version)

Baskul, China, the night of 10 March 1935. Robert Conway, England's "man of the East," supervises the evacuation of ninety white people whose lives are endangered by a local revolution. Conway himself finally escapes aboard a plane with four other passengers: Alexander P. Lovett, a fidgety paleontologist; Henry Barnard, an American businessman who delights in teasing Lovett; Gloria Stone, a tubercular American prostitute drifting through the Orient; and Conway's sycophantic brother, George. George offers a toast to Bob, whom he is certain will be appointed foreign secretary upon returning home, but Bob is too weary to be impressed. Everyone falls asleep.

In the morning they discover their plane has been hijacked by an armed Mongolian, and they are heading toward interior Asia rather than Shanghai. After stopping to refuel at a village outpost, the plane climbs up over the Tibetan mountains. George and Gloria begin to break down under the strain of the mysterious journey. Thousands of miles from civilization, the plane runs out of fuel. A crash landing is made in the mountains, killing the pilot. Bob is about to set out alone on foot in hopes of reaching India when a party of Tibetans, led by the English-speaking Chang, suddenly appears. Chang guides the Westerners along a treacherous path to his lamasery, the spectacular Shangri-La, tucked away amid the mountains of the fertile, idyllic Valley of the Blue Moon.

The visitors are sumptuously clothed, quartered, and fed. After dinner, Lovett and George express their eagerness to return home. Chang explains that contact can be made with the outside world only through the uncertain arrival of porters bearing supplies, but that the visitors will be made comfortable for the duration of their stay. Alone with George later that night, Bob observes that the rescue mission must have been planned, but he doesn't know why. This notion only aggravates George further. Bob, on the other hand, finds himself strangely calm and intrigued.

The next day Bob learns from Chang the story of the founding of the lamasery by a Belgian priest, Father Perrault, who arrived in the valley in 1713. Chang describes the perfect health and extraordinary longevity of the inhabitants, and the absence of crime--or the necessity even for laws--in a world without want, envy, or struggle. Bob is attracted to Sondra, a white woman brought to the lamasery as an infant and raised by the high lama. He pursues her on horseback through a lush forest to a waterfall. As she swims nude in the pond above, Bob makes a mock-figure from her clothes and discreetly departs. Meanwhile, George is fascinated by Maria, an enigmatic young woman of mixed parentage. Barnard discovers a gold deposit and excitedly plans to make a potential fortune from it. He also comforts an ailing Gloria. A skittish Lovett carries a sword for protection in his room; his own reflection in a mirror frightens him.

The Films: Credits, Notes, and Synopses

That night at dinner, Gloria appears for the first time without makeup and Barnard confesses that he is a notorious swindler on the lam. George, meanwhile, has become stir-crazy, and fires a gunshot at Chang. Bob presses Chang for more information about their "imprisonment," but Chang sidesteps the inquiry with extraordinary news: the high lama is granting Bob a rare interview. Ushered into the inner sanctum, Bob is astonished to discover that the high lama is in fact the long-lived Father Perrault, now weakening, but luminous in the half-light of his private quarters. The high lama expresses his admiration for the spiritual wisdom Conway has revealed in his writings, and relates a vision of an impending apocalypse in which Shangri-La will serve as the repository of wisdom upon which a new world may be built. Profoundly affected by the meeting, Bob, however is of little help to his anxious worldly colleagues.

In the morning Bob wanders through the valley, acquainting himself with the farmers, shepherds, and children. He talks at length with Sondra about Shangri-La; both confess that the other has filled a long-awaited dream of romantic happiness. Meanwhile Lovett begins to adjust to Shangri-La, volunteering to instruct the children in geology. Barnard abandons his gold scheme in favor of designing a new plumbing system. Gloria has entrusted herself entirely to Barnard's care. Only George remains deeply disturbed. Noting George's attraction to Maria, Chang informs Bob that she arrived at the lamasery in 1888 and will revert to her normal age should she venture outside the valley.

Porters finally arrive at the edge of the valley. George is excited, but Lovett, Barnard, and Gloria refuse to leave with him. Requesting a second meeting with Bob, the high lama places the future of Shangri-La in the younger man's hands and then peacefully dies. A funeral procession, marked by an endless ribbon of torchlights in the night, winds toward the palace. Bob tries to convince George of the dream Shangri-La has to offer, but in vain. Then his own faith is shaken when Maria contradicts Chang's story about her: she claims to have been captured two years before and held prisoner by Chang ever since. The promise of long life, she insists, is a trick; she would rather die escaping than stay in the valley alive. Confused, Bob agrees to go along with them. Seeing Bob depart, Sondra desperately races after him, but she is too late.

During the arduous journey, the trio fall behind the porters, who mock the Westerners and take pot shots at them for sport. One shot sets off an avalanche, burying the porters. True to Chang's prophecy, Maria becomes wizened and dies. Horrified, George leaps to his own death. Bob finally wanders into a village, but suffers amnesia. Reports in London announce that on his way home Conway's memory returned and he has jumped ship. Months later, Lord Gainsford describes how he has pursued Conway around the world, and the incredible feats the man has performed in his fanatical pursuit of Shangri-La. Finally, amid the Tibetan mountains, the weather-beaten figure of Robert Conway comes upon the entrance to the Valley of the Blue Moon.

The Films: Credits, Notes, and Synopses

28   **YOU CAN'T TAKE IT WITH YOU (1938)**

Vous ne l'emporterez pas avec vous (France), L'eterna illusione (Italy), Der Lebenskünstler (Germany)

Production Company:	Columbia Pictures
Producer:	Frank Capra
Director:	Frank Capra
Screenplay:	Robert Riskin, from the play by George S. Kaufman and Moss Hart[1]
Photography:	Joseph Walker
Editor:	Gene Havlick
Art Director:	Stephen Goosson
Associate Art Director:	Lionel Banks
Costumes:	Bernard Newman, Irene
Musical Score:	Dimitri Tiomkin
Musical Director:	Morris Stoloff
Sound Engineer:	Edward Bernds
Sound Recording:	Garry Harris
Dialogue Director:	C.C. Coleman
Assistant Director:	Arthur Black
Cast:	Lionel Barrymore (Martin Vanderhof), Jean Arthur (Alice Sycamore), James Stewart (Tony Kirby), Edward Arnold (Anthony P. Kirby), Spring Byington (Penny Sycamore), Samuel S. Hinds (Paul Sycamore), Ann Miller (Essie Carmichael), Dub Taylor (Ed Carmichael), Mischa Auer (Kolenkhov), Donald Meek (Poppins), Halliwell Hobbes (Mr. DePinna), H.B. Warner (Ramsey), Mary Forbes (Mrs. Anthony P. Kirby), Lillian Yarbo (Rheba), Eddie Anderson (Donald), Charles Lane (Henderson), Harry Davenport (judge), Irving Bacon (Henry), Clarence Wilson (John Blakely), James Burke and Ward Bond (detectives), Josef Swickard (professor), Ann Doran (Maggie O'Neill), Christian Rub (Schmidt), Bodil Rosing (Mrs. Schmidt), Pierre Watkin, Edwin Maxwell, and Russell Hicks (attorneys), Byron Foulger (Kirby's assistant), Ian Wolfe (Kirby's secretary), Chester Clute (Hammond), James Flavin (jailer), Dick Curtis (strong-arm man), Edward Keane (board member), Edward Hearn (court attendant), Pert Kelton and Kit Guard (inmates), Eddy Chandler and Edgar Daring (plainsclothes policemen), Robert Greig, John Hamilton, and Major Sam Harris (diners)

Filmed at Columbia Pictures Studios in the summer of 1938
Distributor: Columbia Pictures Corporation

The Films: Credits, Notes, and Synopses

Copyright: 6 September 1938 by Columbia Pictures Corporation of California (LP 8269)
Released: 1 September 1938 (Radio City Music Hall, New York City)
Running time: 127 minutes

Notes

1. The play by Kaufman and Hart opened at the Booth Theatre in New York City on 14 December 1936. It won the Pulitzer Prize for the 1936-37 dramatic season and was still enjoying a two-year run on Broadway when the film version was released in September 1938. (Columbia paid $200,000 for the rights to the play, reported at the time to be a record price.) The play has been published in several anthologies: The Pulitzer Prize Plays, edited by Kathryn Cordell and William Howard Cordell (New York: Random House, 1938); Twenty Best Plays of the Modern American Theatre, edited by John Gassner (New York: Crown Publishers, 1939); Six Plays by George S. Kaufman (New York: Random House, 1958); and Three Comedies of American Family Life, edited by John Mersand (New York: Pocket Books, 1961).

You Can't Take It with You received Academy Awards for best picture and best direction. It was also nominated for best writing--screenplay, best supporting actress (Spring Byington), best cinematography, best film editing, and best sound recording.

Synopsis

Wall Street banker Anthony P. Kirby returns from Washington with word that the government will not block his attempt to form the world's largest corporation, an armaments firm dealing in all types of weapons. His son, Tony, a reluctant vice president, ironically notes that only the slingshot trade has been overlooked. One obstacle remains. To squeeze out his chief competitor, Ramsey, Kirby has bought up the neighborhood surrounding his rival's factory, blocking expansion. But eccentric Grandpa Vanderhof refuses to sell his home. Kirby orders his realty operator, Blakely, to get the property any way he can.

Blakely tries to intimidate Vanderhof by making him wait outside Blakely's office. In the interim, Grandpa entices one of Blakely's clerks, Poppins, to come live with the Vanderhofs and work full time on his hobby of building mechanical toys. Blakely finally emerges from his office and offers Vanderhof $100,000, but the old man brushes the offer aside and advises the realtor to take a vacation to cure his twitching eye. Grandpa departs for a graduation ceremony with Poppins in tow.

Late afternoon at the Vanderhofs'. Granddaughter Essie prances in toeshoes with a plate of homemade candies. Her mother, Penny, types away on a play, while her father, Paul, builds fireworks in the basement with DePinna, a former iceman who stopped at the house one day and stayed. The black maid, Rheba, cooks dinner; her boyfriend, Donald, soon arrives and starts setting the table. Essie's husband, Ed, arrives with a trick toy for Donald, and strikes up a tune on the xylophone as his wife dances. Grandpa then ushers in Poppins, who is awed by the scene.

Granddaughter Alice, however, has lingered late at the office with her boss, and boyfriend, Tony Kirby, Jr. A call from Rheba interrupts their tryst; Alice announces she won't be home for dinner. Tony's mother walks in on the couple and, shocked by what she sees, hurries off to her husband to complain. Alice is willing to resign, but Tony obliquely proposes marriage, assuring Alice that his parents can be won over.

Outside the Vanderhof home, neighbors who have received eviction notices are promised by Grandpa that they will all be safe as long as he doesn't sell. A short distance away, Blakely plots with two detectives to smear the old man. In the cellar workshop, Poppins proposes that Ed publicize a celebration of the Russian Revolution in Essie's candies in order to boost firework sales. Alice arrives home and excitedly announces that Tony will be calling on her that evening. When she is alone with Grandpa in her bedroom, however, Alice confesses that she is confused. Grandpa calms her with stories of his own hysteria while courting her late grandmother. Alice's room had once been hers, and he hasn't been able to sell the house because his wife's fragrance still lingers in it. Alice gives Grandpa a new harmonica, which he promptly puts to use in a musical session with Essie and Ed.

The doorbell rings. The family is poised to meet Tony, but the caller is an I.R.S. agent after Grandpa's back taxes. Tony soon arrives and watches in amazement as Grandpa parries with the agent. The scene grows progressively uproarious. Exhausted, the agent departs. As Tony leaves with Alice, he also meets Kolenkov, Essie's Russian dancing teacher, who has come in time to bum dinner. Grandpa pronounces a homespun blessing over the meal.

Tony and Alice abandon their original plan to attend the ballet and instead go to a park. Noting that her family seems to have found the secret to happiness, he describes his own dream—the harnessing of the kinetic energy in grass—a dream deferred by his decision to follow six generations of Kirbys and become a banker. Some kids come by and teach Tony and Alice the Big Apple, and then the couple are off to a posh restaurant where the Kirbys are holding a dinner party. Mrs. Kirby snubs Alice. Alice urges Tony to invite his parents to her home so they can meet her family, but he deflects the request by feigning an involuntary scream. Alarmed, Alice screams herself. To justify her scream, Tony loudly announces that they have seen rats. They leave the place in shambles.

Tony arranges for his parents to dine at the Vanderhofs', but brings them a night ahead of schedule in hopes that they will get an

The Films: Credits, Notes, and Synopses

honest view of the family's way of life. Walking in on a typically bizarre scene, the Kirbys are embarrassed and shocked. The Vanderhofs quickly rally, offering to expand their menu of frankfurters with canned salmon and beer. When Grandpa pulls out his harmonica, Tony notes that his father was once an amateur champion, but Kirby is in no mood for frivolity. Civility finally breaks down when Kolenkov demonstrates a wrestling hold on Kirby and breaks the man's glasses. Alice bitterly calls the fiasco to a close. Suddenly G-men arrive. Tipped off by Blakely, they search the house, linking the fireworks in the basement to "subversive" messages in Essie's candy. All the fireworks are accidentally set off at once. Everyone is arrested.

In the women's jail, Mrs. Kirby, distressed by her present company, assails Alice for ambitiously exploiting her son. In the men's jail, Mr. Kirby frets over the possible loss of his deal, but Vanderhof counsels him to forget about money and cultivate his friends. When Blakely appears, Kirby and Vanderhof quickly realize they are antagonists on the sale of the house as well. Kirby accuses the old man of using Tony to get information; Vanderhof angrily labels the tycoon a failure as a man, a human being, and a father. He then apologizes and slips a harmonica into Kirby's pocket.

At night court, Grandpa is fined $100 for possession of fireworks and disturbing the peace. He refuses an offer by Kirby's lawyers to pay the fine; his friends, who have packed the courtroom, raise the money instead. To save the Kirby's embarrassment, Grandpa tells the judge that they were visiting to inquire about the property. A relieved Mrs. Kirby quickly endorses this explanation, but Alice steps forward and tells the truth. Tony concurs, but Alice turns on him as well, asserting that his family is not good enough for her. Bedlam breaks out as the press storm the front of the courtroom.

Alice flees the city, leaving Tony frantic and the Vanderhof clan depressed. She writes Grandpa from Connecticut, explaining that she cannot return home. So Grandpa decides to sell the house and follow her. He settles with Blakely for a low price.

As neighbors receive new eviction notices, Kirby gleefully prepares to close his master deal and announces that Tony will be president of the new company. Ramsey appears, broken in health and spirit, and warns Kirby that his new power won't bring him happiness. Struck by pain, Ramsey staggers out. Then Tony arrives and tells his father he is quitting to pursue his own interests. Kirby is stunned. A message comes over the intercom that Ramsey has died of heart failure. Summoned to the board meeting, Kirby receives a standing ovation. But he immediately takes the elevator down to the ground floor and exits the building.

As the Vanderhofs pack, Tony hovers, looking for a clue to Alice's whereabouts. Alice arrives on the scene and reproaches Grandpa for moving out on the neighbors--and on Grandma. Again scolding Tony, she locks herself in her room. Kirby arrives and asks

The Films: Credits, Notes, and Synopses

Grandpa's advice as a father. Grandpa proposes a duet on the harmonica to think by. As they play, the barren living room fills up with family and friends. Tony and Alice come downstairs; Kirby signals to them his consent. He wrestles Kolenkov and coaxes his wife to do the Big Apple. Everyone dances.

Later, as the Kirbys dine with the Vanderhofs, Grandpa's prayer ties up the loose ends of the plot: Kirby has sold back the house; Alice and Tony are married; perhaps even Mrs. Kirby will loosen up in time.

29 **MR. SMITH GOES TO WASHINGTON (1939)**

<u>Monsieur Smith au Sénat</u> (France), <u>Mr. Smith va a Washington</u> (Italy), <u>Mr. Smith geht nach Washington</u> (Germany)

Production Company:	Columbia Pictures Corporation
Producer:	Frank Capra
Director:	Frank Capra
Screenplay:	Sidney Buchman [and Myles Connolly],[1] from the story "A Gentleman from Montana" by Lewis R. Foster[2]
Photography:	Joseph Walker
Montage Effects:	Slavko Vorkapich
Editors:	Gene Havlick, Al Clark
Art Director:	Lionel Banks
Costumes:	Robert Kalloch
Musical Score:	Dimitri Tiomkin
Musical Director:	Morris Stoloff
Sound Engineer:	Edward Bernds
Electrician:	George Hager
Second Unit Director:	Charles Vidor
Assistant Director:	Arthur S. Black
Technical Adviser:	Jim Preston
Cast:	James Stewart (Jefferson Smith), Jean Arthur (Clarissa Saunders), Claude Rains (Sen. Joseph Paine), Edward Arnold (Jim Taylor), Thomas Mitchell (Diz Moore), Harry Carey (president of the Senate), Guy Kibbee (Gov. Hubert Hopper), Eugene Pallete (Chick McGann), Beulah Bondi (Ma Smith), H.B. Warner (Senator Agnew, majority leader), Pierre Watkin (Senator Barnes, minority leader), Charles Lane (Nosey), Astrid Allwyn (Susan Paine), Ruth Donnelly (Emma Hopper), Moyonne Walsh (Jane Hopper), Billy Watson, Delmar Watson, Harry Watson, Garry Watson, John Russell, and Baby Dumpling [Larry Simms] (the Hopper boys), William Demarest (Bill Griffith), H.V. Kaltenborn (broadcaster), Kenneth Carpenter (announcer), Jack Carson

The Films: Credits, Notes, and Synopses

(Sweeney), Dick Elliot (Carl Cook), Russell Simpson (Allen), Joe King (Summers), Paul Stanton (Flood); Porter Hall (Senator Monroe), Grant Mitchell (Senator MacPherson), Stanley Andrews (Senator Hodges), Walter Soderling (Senator Pickett), Frank Jaquet (Senator Byron), Ferris Taylor (Senator Carlisle), Carl Stockdale (Senator Burdette), Alan Bridge (Senator Dwight), Frederick Burton (Senator Dearhorn), Harry Bailey (Senator Hammett), Wyndham Standing (Senator Ashman), Robert Walker (Senator Holland), Wright Kramer (Senator Carlton), Victor Travers (Senator Grainger), John Ince (Senator Fernwick), Sam Ash (Senator Lancaster), Philo McCoullough (Senator Albert), Frank O'Connor (Senator Alfred), Harry Stafford (Senator Atwater), Jack Richardson (Senator Manchester), Edmund Cobb (Senator Gower), Helen Jerome Eddy, Ann Doran, and Beatrice Curtis (Paine's secretaries), Rev. Neal Dodd (Senate chaplain), Louis Jean Heydt (soapbox speaker), Vera Lewis (Mrs. Edwards), Dora Clement (Mrs. McGann), Laura Treadwell (Mrs. Taylor), Douglas Evans (Frances Scott Key), Allan Cavan (Ragner), Maurice Costello (Diggs), Lloyd Whitlock (Schultz), Arthur Loft (chief clerk), Frank Puglia and Erville Anderson (handwriting experts), Eddie Fetherston, Ed Randolph, Milton Kibbee, Vernon Dent, Michael Gale, Ed Brewer, Anne Cornwall, James Millican, Mabel Forrest, Nick Copeland, and Dulce Caye (Senate reporters), Dub Taylor, William Arnold, George Chandler, Donald Kerr, Clyde Dilson, William Newell, Gene Morgan, George McKay, Matt McHugh, Evelyn Knapp, Jack Gardner, Eddie Kane, Hal Cooke, James McNamara, Jack Egan, and Ed Chandler (reporters), Robert Emmett Kean (editor), Hank Mann and Jack Cooper (photographers), Count Stefenelli and Alex Novkinsky (foreign diplomats), Robert Middlemass, Alec Craig, and Harry Hayden (speakers), Flo Wix and Emma Tansey (committeewomen), Lloyd Ingraham (committeeman), Frank Austin (inventor), Olaf Hytten (butler), Dickie Jones (page boy), Snowflake (porter), Arthur Thalasso (doorman), Dave

The Films: Credits, Notes, and Synopses

Willock (Senate guard), Wade Boteler (family man), George Cooper (waiter), Gino Corrado (barber), Lafe McKee (Civil War veteran), Harlan Briggs (Edwards), John Dilson (committee secretary), Walter Sande and Dick Fiske (committee reporters), Harry Depp (hat salesman), Linda Winters [Dorothy Comingore], Frances Gifford, Lorna Gray, Mary Gordon, Bessie Wade, Wilfred Lucas, Tommy Bupp, Layne Tom, Jr., Edward Wearle, Adrian Booth

Filmed at Columbia pictures Studio in the spring of 1939; second unit photography shot on location in Washington D.C.

Distributor: Columbia Pictures Corporation
Copyright: 10 October 1939 by Columbia Pictures Corporation (LP 9164)
Released: 19 October 1939 (Radio City Music Hall, New York City)[3]
Running time: 128 minutes

Notes

1. According to a letter from Columbia Pictures to the Academy of Motion Picture Arts and Sciences, Myles Connolly worked on the construction of the script and provided dialogue continuity without credit. (See the production file for Mr. Smith Goes to Washington at the Academy's Margaret Herrick Library.) The final screenplay, credited to Sidney Buchman, has been published in The Best Picture, 1939-1940, edited by Jerry Wald and Richard Macaulay (New York: Dodd, Mead & Co., 1940) and Twenty Best Film Plays, edited by John Gassner and Dudley Nichols (New York: Crown Publishers, 1943; New York and London: Garland Publishing, 1977). The shooting script for two sequences appeared in TAC Magazine, No. 2 (November 1939), 4-9. A photoplay edition of Mr. Smith Goes to Washington was published by Grossett & Dunlap, New York, in 1939.

2. In 1941 plagiarism suits were filed against Columbia Pictures by Louis Ullman and Norman Houston who claimed that Mr. Smith Goes to Washington was based on their own written work. Capra testified at the trial that he had seen only a one-page synopsis of the story by Lewis Foster and that he had been moved by its similarity to Mr. Deeds Goes to Town. Moreover, he had originally wanted Gary Cooper to play the key role, but opted for James Stewart when Cooper was unavailable. Columbia won the case. (See "Capra Links 'Mr. Deeds,' 'Mr. Smith,'" Los Angeles Herald-Express, 6 June 1944, p. B1.)

3 On 3 October Mr. Smith Goes to Washington was previewed at the Dyckman Theatre in New York for the National Press Club and also at the Pantages Hollywood in Los Angeles. The Press Club then sponsored a gala preview of the film at Constitution Hall in Washington, D.C., on 17 October with most members of the Senate and House of Representatives in attendance. Congressional reaction was hostile, and the

The Films: Credits, Notes, and Synopses

House allegedly accelerated hearings on an anti-block-booking bill in retaliation against Hollywood. (See "'Mr. Smith' in Washington Stirs Senators—And How!" Los Angeles Times, 22 October 1939, sect. 1, p. 7.) In his autobiography, Capra describes at length the anxieties of the Washington preview and the subsequent pressures to suppress the film. The furor in Washington, however, also created a backlash effect among many critics in New York and Los Angeles who stressed in their reviews the obvious patriotic sentiment in the film.

Mr. Smith Goes to Washington received an Academy Award for best writing—original story (Lewis R. Foster). It was also nominated for best picture, best direction, best writing—screenplay, best actor (James Stewart), best supporting actor (Harry Carey, Claude Rains), best art direction, best editing, best musical score, and best sound recording. James Stewart won the New York Film Critics Award for best actor. In 1941 and 1942, the film had extended runs in Marseilles and Toulouse in France prior to a Vichy ban on all American and British films. Georges Sadoul reported unprecedented public acclaim for the film during this period (see Sadoul's 1945 review, entry 556). A television series based on the film, with Fess Parker as Jefferson Smith, was aired by ABC-TV from 29 September 1962 through 30 March 1963.

Synopsis

The death of a U.S. senator from the West jeopardizes a graft scheme involving a federal dam project in his home state. The governor is pressured by political boss Jim Taylor, a tycoon who secretly has purchased land at the site, to appoint a party stooge to fill the Senate seat. A citizens' group lobbies for another candidate, and the governor's own children press him to appoint local Boy Ranger leader, Jefferson Smith. Wavering between the competing claims of Taylor and the citizens' lobby, the governor flips a coin to decide. The coin lands on its edge, next to a news article about Smith. So the governor appoints the hero of his children, a young man steeped in American history and American ideals. The state's senior senator, Joseph Paine, beholden to Taylor and fearful of scandal, convinces the boss that Smith's naïveté will make him easy to control in Washington, and Taylor okays the appointment.

At a send-off dinner, Smith expresses his deep admiration for Paine, disclosing that the senator was a close friend of his late father's many years before. Paine is struck by this revelation and, during the train ride to Washington with Smith, recalls the youthful idealism he shared with the young man's father, an editor of a small independent newspaper who was slain defending a "lost cause."

A welcoming committee greets Smith at the station in Washington, including Paine's socialite daughter, Susan. But Smith seems uncomfortable and, sighting the Capitol Dome, slips away on his own for a five-hour tour of national monuments culminating in a worshipful visit to the Lincoln Memorial. Meanwhile Clarissa Saunders awaits Smith's arrival at his Senate office, lamenting her assignment as the

The Films: Credits, Notes, and Synopses

Boy Ranger's secretary. Her friend and confidante, reporter Diz Moore, renews a longstanding marriage proposal, a possible escape route from politics, but she wearily declines. Smith finally appears, dewy-eyed and glowing from his tour.

Saunders decides to quit her job in style and hands Smith over to the press in exchange for some World Series tickets. The reporters easily trick him into posing for photographs which, plastered on the front page of the morning papers, make him look like a fool. Paine lures Saunders back to work with the promise of a bonus and orders her to keep Smith clear of real politics. After Paine staves off an attack on Smith's reputation on the Senate floor, the oath of office is administered to the new senator. Filled with righteous anger over his treatment by the press, Smith violently storms the press club in search of his abusers. But the reporters quickly subdue him by explaining that he is indeed a fool, ignorant of the Senate rules and powerless.

To placate his young colleague, Paine encourages Smith to draft a bill for his dream project--a National Boy's Camp in their home state. Saunders is assigned to help him. Softened up by Smith's genuine faith in the spirit of liberty and the wonders of the wilderness, Saunders works late into the night helping him draw up the bill. Paine's plan backfires when Smith's proposal encroaches on land involved in Taylor's graft scheme. Susan Paine, with whom Smith is smitten, is enlisted to entertain the young senator on the day a deficiency bill sealing the graft scheme is read in the Senate.

Angered and frustrated by his ruse, Saunders gets drunk with Diz. She offers to marry him and goes to her office to clean out her desk. Smith is there, dazed by his day on the town with Susan, and Saunders spills the whole story to him. Diz forgoes the marriage proposal and takes Saunders home.

Paine is anxious to protect Smith from further disillusionment, but defers to Taylor when the boss arrives in town to bring Smith in line with a bribe. Smith refuses to believe Taylor's assertion that Paine himself has sold out, but Paine admits to the truth, defending compromise as a strategy that has enabled him to serve the people in honest ways. He begs Smith to save them both from ruin by remaining silent about the project.

Instead Smith rises to speak during the Senate debate on the deficiency bill the next day. He is preempted by Paine, who accuses his colleague of buying up land at the site to profit from the Boy's Camp bill. When Smith tries to respond, he is booed by spectators. At a Senate hearing false testimony and forged documents support Paine's allegations. His spirit broken, Smith leaves the hearing without testifying on his own behalf. That night he returns to the Lincoln Memorial, his attitude no longer reverent but bitter, and his bags packed to go home. Finding him at the monument, Saunders con-

The Films: Credits, Notes, and Synopses

vinces him to stay and fight like the great patriots of the past, offering to coach him in Senate strategy.

The next morning Smith fends off a Senate vote to expel him by initiating a filibuster. Paine rebuts Smith's charges concerning Taylor's graft scheme and exits the chamber, followed by the rest of the senators. Content to speak to the people back home by way of this forum, Smith presses on with his filibuster. But Jim Taylor uses his power over the media at home to suppress favorable reports about Smith and mold public opinion against him. A quorum call by Smith returns the senators to the floor, where they are forced to listen to Smith's emotional appeal for justice, punctuated by humor and amply padded with selections from the Declaration of Independence and the Constitution. Learning of Taylor's manipulation of the news, Saunders arranges for the Boy Rangers to publish the truth in their paper, but the kids are brutally stopped by Taylor's henchmen.

Twenty-three hours into the filibuster, all of official Washington has gathered at the Senate chamber to watch Smith, now on the verge of exhaustion. As Saunders looks on in agony from the gallery, 50,000 telegrams from Smith's constituents urging him to yield the floor are brought into the chamber by Paine. Smith desperately rummages through the telegrams and then turns to Paine and recalls his father's championship of lost causes. Refusing to yield, Smith collapses. Paine rushes out of the chamber, where he is barely restrained from shooting himself. He returns to publicly confess his guilt. Jubilation is unleashed in the chamber. Saunders cheers from the gallery, and the president of the Senate puts down his gavel, content to let the celebration proceed.

30   MEET JOHN DOE (1941)

L'homme de la rue (France), Arriva Joe Doe or I dominatori della metropoli (Italy), Gestatten: John Doe (Germany)

Production Company:	Frank Capra Productions[1]
Producers:	Frank Capra and Robert Riskin[2]
Director:	Frank Capra
Screenplay:	Robert Riskin, from a treatment entitled "The Life and Death of John Doe" by Richard Connell and Robert Presnell, based on Connell's story, "A Reputation"[3]
Photography:	George Barnes
Editor:	Daniel Mandell
Montage Effects:	Slavko Vorkapich
Special Effects:	Jack Cosgrove
Art Director:	Stephen Goosson
Production Design:	William Cameron Menzies
Gowns:	Natalie Visart
Musical Score:	Dimitri Tiomkin
Musical Director:	Leo F. Forbstein
Choral Arrangements:	Hall Johnson

The Films: Credits, Notes, and Synopses

Sound: C.A. Riggs
Assistant Director: Arthur S. Black
Cast: Gary Cooper (Long John Willoughby, "John Doe"), Barbara Stanwyck (Ann Mitchell), Edward Arnold (D.B. Norton), Walter Brennan (the Colonel), James Gleason (Henry Connell), Spring Byington (Mrs. Mitchell), Irving Bacon (Beany), Rod La Rocque (Ted Sheldon), Gene Lockhart (Mayor Lovett), Harry Holman (Mayor Hawkins), Warren Hymer (Angelface), Sterling Holloway (Dan), Regis Toomey (Bert Hansen), Ann Doran (Mrs. Hansen), J. Farrell MacDonald ("Sourpuss" Smithers), Frank Austin (Grubbel), Carlotta Jelm and Tina Thayer (Ann's sisters), Mike Frankovich, Selmer Jackson, Knox Manning, and John B. Hughes (radio announcers), Edward Earle (radio emcee), Andrew Tombes (Spencer), Pierre Watkin (Hammett), Stanley Andrews (Weston), Mitchell Lewis (Bennett), Charles C. Wilson (Charlie Dawson), Vaughan Glaser (the governor), Aldrich Bowker (Pop Dwyer), Mrs. Gardner Crane (Mrs. Brewster), Pat Flaherty (Mike), Bennie Bartlett (Red, the office boy), Sarah Edwards (Mrs. Hawkins), James McNamara (sheriff), Emma Tansey (Mrs. Delaney), Lafe McKee (Mr. Delaney), Edward Keane (relief administrator), Edward McWade (Joe, a newsman), Guy Usher (Bixler), Walter Soderling (Barrington), Billy Curtis (male midget), Johnny Fern (female midget), John Hamilton (Jim, governor's associate), William Forrest (governor's associate), Charles K. French (fired reporter), Harry Davenport (ex-owner of <u>Bulletin</u>), Edward Hearn (mayor's secretary), Bess Flowers, Mary Benoit, and Mildred Cross (secretaries), Hank Mann (Ed, a photographer), James Millican and Jack Gardner (photographers), Garry Owen (sign painter), Cyril Thornton (butler, Paul Everton (Republican), Ed Stanley (Democrat), Forrester Harvey (bum), Ed Kane (tycoon), Alphonse Martel (foreign dignitary), John Ince (doctor), Gail Newbray (telephone operator), Richard Kipling (police commissioner), William Gould (sergeant), Earl Bunn, Eddie Cobb, and Jack Cheatham (policemen), Isabel La Mal, Alfred Hal, George Melford, and Henry

The Films: Credits, Notes, and Synopses

Roquemore (Chamber of Commerce), Lew Davis (electrician), Eddie Fetherston (reporter), Kenneth Harlan (publicity man), Forbes Murray (legislator), Frank Mayor (attendant), Suzanne Carnahan [Susan Peters] and Maris Wrixon (autograph hounds), Frank Meredith, Jack Mower, Cliff Baum, and Don Turner (guards), Melvin Lang, Wyndham Standing, and Frederick Vogeding (associate relief administrators), Gene Morgan (mug), the Hall Johnson Choir

Filmed at Warner Brothers Studio and at the following locations: Wrigley Field, Chicago (the convention); Griffith Park, Los Angeles (John and the colonel by the bridge); Pasadena, California (Norton's mansion); and a Los Angeles icehouse (City Hall roof). Principal photography began 16 July 1940 and ended 12 September 1940. Process shots were filmed 14 November and Second Unit work shot on 18 November. An ending was filmed on 3 January 1941 and retakes of an earlier scene involving Ann and her mother shot on 24 January. Following the film's release, Capra shot new footage for the ending on 23 March.

Distributor: Warner Brothers, through Vitagraph, Inc.
Copyright: 5 May 1941 by Frank Capra Productions, Inc. (LP 10453)
Released: 12 March 1941 (Rivoli and Hollywood theaters, New York City; Warners-Hollywood and Warners-Downtown theaters, Los Angeles; Paramount and Beach theaters, Miami; and Criterion Theatre, Oklahoma City)
Running time: 125 minutes

Notes

1. After contemplating independent production for several years, Capra finally took the plunge in 1939 when he formed Frank Capra Productions, Inc., with Robert Riskin. Negotiations for a distribution deal with United Artists broke down in December 1939, and Capra and Riskin moved on to Warner Brothers where the John Doe project was developed in 1940. Although the film was produced at Warners, Capra and Riskin had complete control and retained the rights to the finished work. Some prints of the film circulating today open with the credit "Sherman S. Krellberg Presenting." Krellberg, who operated a New York-based reissue company called Goodwill Pictures, bought the rights to reissue Meet John Doe in 1946. He had nothing to do with the original production of the film. The rights to Meet John Doe are now in the public domain.

2. Riskin's contribution as a producer to Frank Capra Productions, Inc., has perhaps been neglected. In January 1941, while Capra was attempting to put the finishing touches on Meet John Doe, the New York Times reported that Riskin was in New York working on distribution and

The Films: Credits, Notes, and Synopses

promotion packages for the film. Riskin, moreover, had had experience producing short film subjects in the later teens, and producing his own plays on Broadway in the 1920s (see Theodore Strauss, "Mr. Riskin Hits the Road," New York Times, 26 January 1941, sec. 10, p. 5).

3. Richard Connell's "A Reputation" first appeared in Century Magazine, August 1922, and later was reprinted in a collection of short stories by Connell, Apes and Angels (New York: Minton, Blach & Co., 1924).

Capra has frequently commented on the problems he and Riskin faced in devising a suitable ending to Meet John Doe, and records at Warner Brothers confirm his assertion that he proceeded to shoot the film without a fixed ending in mind. Production was suspended on 12 September 1940, then on 3 January 1941 Capra assembled Gary Cooper, Barbara Stanwyck, Edward Arnold, James Gleason, Mitchell Lewis, and Stanley Andrews in a Los Angeles icehouse to film an ending on the City Hall roof. (Multiple endings may have been shot that day; in his autobiography Capra claims to have filmed four different endings prior to the picture's release, and this is the only occasion before the release date he worked at this location.) The version of Meet John Doe that was released on 12 March 1941 concluded with Ann convincing John not to jump and D.B. Norton offering to publish John's letter on the front page of the Bulletin. Most critics, although praising the film in general, found the ending weak and Norton's change of heart especially unbelievable. Within two days, Norton's final comment had been excised from prints in both cities. (Vestiges of his transformation, however, can still be seen in an earlier passage where he watches Christmas Eve carolers outside his mansion.) Then on 23 March, eleven days after the release of the film, Capra shot additional footage to alter the ending: members of the John Doe Club (played by Regis Toomey, Ann Doran, and J. Farrell MacDonald) drive to City Hall on Christmas Eve; there they convince John not to jump. Gary Cooper, James Gleason, and Walter Brennan were all on hand for this reshooting, but Barbara Stanwyck, Edward Arnold, Mitchell Lewis, and Stanley Andrews were not. Although stand-ins were used in long shots, all dialogue and reaction shots involving these latter actors were taken from footage shot on 3 January and spliced together with the new material, forging the ending that appeared on all subsequent prints of the film. (Production information has been drawn from the Warners-Burbank files on Meet John Doe held by the Special Collections Department at the University of Southern California.)

Synopsis

D.B. Norton, an oil tycoon with political ambitions, transforms the Bulletin (a "free press means a free people") into the New Bulletin ("a streamlined newspaper for a streamlined era"). Most of the old staff are fired, including columnist Ann Mitchell, who for her final column fabricates a letter from and anonymous "John Doe." Unemployed and dispirited, her fictional Doe announces his intention to jump off City Hall to protest the state of the world. The letter creates a

The Films: Credits, Notes, and Synopses

public sensation. Recalled by her new editor, Henry Connell, Ann eagerly proposes that someone be hired to play the role of John Doe, and that the suicide drama be drawn out until Christmas Eve. When a rival paper charges that the letter is fraudulent, Connell reluctantly agrees to her scheme. She blackmails him to hire her back with a $1,000 bonus.

A throng of down-and-out men jam the newspaper office, hoping to land a job the mayor has promised the authentic John Doe. From these men, Ann selects Long John Willoughby, a former bush-league pitcher whose arm has gone bad. Feeding him, and promising him money to get his arm fixed, Ann gets John to sign a contract to play the role of Doe. With boyish curiosity, he settles into lavish quarters at a hotel, ignoring a warning from his antisocial traveling companion, the Colonel, that these compromises will corrupt him.

An ambitious Ann swings into action. At a photo session she exploits John's natural anger with umpires to get a picture of a protesting Doe for the front page. When the governor threatens Norton with a libel suit if Doe is not produced for questioning, Ann proposes that John deliver a speech over the tycoon's radio station, an occasion that might also be used to impart whatever message Norton desires. Pleased with the idea, Norton retains Ann as the speechwriter, answerable only to him. At home with her mother and sisters, whom she supports, Ann struggles to write the speech. Her mother reminds her of the inspiring message of good-neighborliness contained in the diary of Ann's late father, and Ann bases the speech upon it. Meanwhile John is offered $5,000 by a rival paper to reveal the truth during the broadcast.

John's debut is a slickly organized affair. Just prior to the broadcast, Ann gives him the speech, urging him to deliver it with the sincerity of her father—and of her imaginary John Doe. John goes to the microphone also armed with a speech provided by the rival paper, but on the air he forgoes the bribe and reads Ann's speech straight, gaining confidence as he speaks. When he is finished, he escapes with the Colonel for the wilderness of the Columbia River country.

John Doe Clubs sprout up all over America as a result of the speech. Recognized in a diner in the small town of Millville, John is immediately mobbed and taken to the town hall. Norton and Ann soon arrive, anxious to get John to head the club move movement. John at first wants no part of this, but heartfelt testimony from local club members who have put Doe's good-neighbor ideal into practice persuade John to reconsider. Disgusted, the Colonel takes off on his own.

Norton's machinery shifts into high gear. The movement spreads like wildfire, and a national convention is planned. Settling into his role as Doe, John grows increasingly devoted to Ann. He relates to her one of his dreams in which he appears as her father and rescues her from a marriage to Norton's playboy nephew, Ted. Ann, in turn, is enamored of her creation, John Doe, and her conscience about exploit-

The Films: Credits, Notes, and Synopses

ing John has been pricked. But any guilt she feels is blunted on the eve of the convention when Norton gives her a mink coat and jewelry, and informs her of his final move for power. The next night John is to announce the formation of a John Doe party and to endorse Norton for president.

The night of the convention, John stops by Ann's apartment hoping to propose. Finding only Ann's mother at home, he anxiously tells her of his fear that Ann loves John Doe rather than himself. Mrs. Mitchell is sympathetic, and agrees to prepare Ann for John's marriage proposal.

Connell intercepts John on the way to the convention, taking him to a bar to talk. His tongue freed by liquor, Connell reveals his deep sense of patriotism and informs John of Norton's fifth column movement. When Connell shows John a copy of the speech Ann has written for him to deliver, John is stunned. He rushes to Norton's mansion where he witnesses Norton toasting Ann before a cabal of national power brokers assembled to consolidate political strategy. Sensing John's shock, Norton warns his puppet that if his followers learn he's a fake, they will destroy him. But John defiantly argues that the movement is larger than any one person, including himself. The battle lines drawn, John escapes the mansion for the convention. Norton summons his paramilitary police force in pursuit. Ann races to John's car and begs him to let her help, but he closes the window on her.

Gathered on a rainy night beneath umbrellas, the conventioneers cheer John's arrival. Numb, he mouths the words of "My Country 'Tis of Thee" along with the crowd, but the stillness of a silent benediction that follows is punctured by the sound of Norton's army arriving. Newspapers declaring John a fake are rapidly distributed, and Norton seizes the microphone to accuse John directly. John tries to reply, but the microphone wires are cut. As the crowd gradually turns against him, a riot is provoked by Norton's men. The Colonel helps his old friend escape through the hostile mob. Connell and Ann, powerless to help, hear news of the event at a police station.

Briefly reunited with the Colonel, John nevertheless sinks into a deep depression. Soon he is wandering the city streets alone, haunted by memories of past events.

On Christmas Eve, Ann is certain that John will try to vindicate himself by making good on the original suicide threat and leaves her sickbed for City Hall. Others share her suspicion: Connell and the Colonel guard the doors at the building; Norton arrives with his associates and ascends the stairs; and members of the Millville Club drive to the scene. Already on the fourteenth floor, John slips a letter to Connell into a mail chute and walks out on the roof ledge, where he takes from his pocket a letter to "John Does everywhere." Norton emerges from the shadows and warns John that his men are on hand below to cover up any bid for martyrdom. Ann steps forward, confesses her love, and begs John to let them start the movement over

The Films: Credits, Notes, and Synopses

again, this time honestly. In light of Christ's death, she argues, his own death is unnecessary. She collapses in his arms. Then the club members apologize for their hasty betrayal and urge him to stay on as their leader. John finally gives in, joining her supporters, including Connell and the Colonel. As they depart, Connell calls to Norton: "The people--try and lick that."

31 **ARSENIC AND OLD LACE (1944)**

<u>Arsenic et vieilles dentelles</u> (France), <u>Arsenico e vecchi merletti</u> (Italy), <u>Arsen und Spitzenhäubchen</u> (Germany)

Production Company:	Warner Brothers
Producer:	Frank Capra
Director:	Frank Capra
Screenplay	Julius J. and Philip G. Epstein, from the play by Joseph Kesselring[1]
Photography:	Sol Polito
Editor:	Daniel Mandel
Special Effects:	Byron Haskin, Robert Burks
Art Director:	Max Parker
Gowns:	Orry-Kelly
Makeup:	Perc Westmore
Musical Score:	Max Steiner
Music Director:	Leo F. Forbstein
Orchestral Arrangements:	Hugo Friedhofer
Sound:	C.A. Riggs
Dialogue Director:	Harold Winston
Assistant Directors:	Russ Saunders, Jess Hibbs[2]
Cast:	Cary Grant (Mortimer Brewster), Priscilla Lane (Elaine Harper), Raymond Massey (Jonathan Brewster), Peter Lorre (Dr. Einstein), Josephine Hull (Abby Brewster), Jean Adair (Martha Brewster), John Alexander (Teddy Brewster), Jack Carson (Officer O'Hara), Edward McNamara (Officer Brophy), James Gleason (Lieutenant Rooney), Edward Everett Horton (Mr. Witherspoon), Grant Mitchell (Reverend Harper), Garry Owen (taxi driver), John Ridgely (Saunders), Vaughan Glaser (Judge Cullman), Chester Clute (Dr. Gilchrist), Charles Lane (reporter), Edward McWade (Gibbs), Leo White (man in phone booth), Spencer Charters (license clerk), Hank Mann (photographer), Lee Phelps (umpire)

Filmed at Warner Brothers Studio between October 20 and December 16, 1941[3]

Distributor:	Warner Brothers
Copyright:	6 October 1944 by Warner Brothers Pictures, Inc. (LP 12898)

The Films: Credits, Notes, and Synopses

Released: 1 September 1944 (Strand Theatre, New York
                             City)[4]
Running time: 118 minutes

Notes

1. Kesselring's play, produced by Howard Lindsay and Russell Crouse, opened at the Fulton Theatre, New York City, on 10 January 1941. Random House published the play the same year (New York: 1941, 187 pp.). It is collected in two anthologies: S.R.O.: The Most Successful Plays in the History of the American Stage, edited by Bennett Alfred Cerf and Van H. Cartmell (Garden City, N.Y.: Doubleday, Doran & Chapman; Toronto: McClelland & Stewart, 1944); and Best Plays of the American Theatre, edited by John Gladhorn (New York: Crown Publishers; Toronto: Ambassador Books, 1947).

2. Some filmographies list Saunders, others Hibbs. Capra mentions Hibbs in his autobiography (The Name Above the Title, p. 311).

3. In his autobiography, Capra implies that the film was shot in four weeks, but the shooting schedule lasted more than seven.

4. In order to protect the stage run of the play, Warner Brothers agreed to delay the release of the film. The original agreement with Kesselring called for a 1 January 1943 release date in the United States and Great Britain, and a release date one year later in the rest of the world, but Warner's ended up withholding the film in the United States until September 1944. (According to Willmar Andersson [see entry 311], the film was delayed three times by censors in Sweden on the grounds that mentally retarded people would find the film repulsive and might suffer.)

In contrast to Meet John Doe, which was produced by Frank Capra Productions, Inc., on the Warner Brothers lot, Arsenic and Old Lace was made under a one-picture contract with Warners whereby Capra received $100,000 and 10 percent of the gross receipts over $1,250,000, and Warners retained the rights to the film. During the course of the production, however, negotiations were underway between Capra and Warners for a multipicture deal. Offers to Capra were made by United Artists and 20th Century-Fox during this period as well, but the war intervened. In 1947 Capra was awarded the Belgian Challenge International du Cinema Trophy for his direction and production of Arsenic and Old Lace. (Production information has been drawn from the Warners-Burbank files for this film held by the Special Collections Department at the University of Southern California.)

Synopsis

Reporters looking for a story at the Manhattan Marriage License Bureau spy a newsworthy applicant: Mortimer Brewster, noted drama critic and author of treatises on the fraud and failure of marriage. His cover exposed, Mortimer escapes to a phone booth with his fiancée,

The Films: Credits, Notes, and Synopses

Elaine, and tries to convince her of the absurdity of their decision to marry. Confined with her in the booth, however, he succumbs again. Soon they are back in line for a license.

At the Brewster home in Brooklyn, Mortimer's elderly Aunt Abby has tea with Elaine's father, Reverend Harper, who is worried about Mortimer's public position on marriage. Two local cops, O'Hara and Brophy, arrive to pick up some toys from Mortimer's middle-aged brother, Teddy, who thinks he is Teddy Roosevelt. When all the visitors are gone, Aunt Abby excitedly informs her sister, Aunt Martha, of a recent conquest whose remains now reside in their window seat. Teddy is ordered to dig another Panama Canal lock in the cellar for this "yellow fever" victim.

Mortimer and Elaine stop by to tell their families about the wedding before taking off for Niagara Falls. But Mortimer's plan for a quick departure is spoiled when he discovers a corpse in the window seat. Assuming mad Teddy to be the murderer, he tries to break the news gently to his aunts. But the sisters proudly own up to the deed --and eleven others like it. Lonely old men, responding to the sisters' ad for a rented room, have been poisoned with homemade elderberry wine and give a Christian burial in the basement.

Shocked, Mortimer plots to use Teddy as a scapegoat and arranges to have him committed to a sanitarium. Meanwhile another potential victim arrives and the aunts go to work; the man's life is saved only through Mortimer's last-minute intervention. Witherspoon, the director of Happy Dale Sanitarium, reports that Teddy can be admitted. Exacting a promise from his aunts that they will let no one into the house, Mortimer sets off to obtain a signature of committal from the local judge.

While Mortimer is gone, his long-lost brother, Jonathan, a demented brute on the run from the law, sneaks into the Brewster home. He is accompanied by Dr. Einstein, an alcoholic plastic surgeon whose work on Jonathan's face has left his subject looking like Frankenstein's monster. In need of a sanctuary to hid a corpse and remodel Jonathan's face, the visitors inform the frightened Brewster sisters they intend to stay for a while.

After dinner Einstein visits Teddy's Panama Canal in the basement and finds it a perfect site to stash Jonathan's corpse. When the house is dark, on orders from the aunts, Teddy removes the victim from the window seat and takes it down to the basement. Moments later Jonathan and Einstein sneak their victim in through the window. Interrupted by the arrival of Elaine, Jonathan hides the body in the window seat. Fearing Elaine has seen too much, he tries to strangle her. Teddy, emerging from the cellar, identifies Elaine as his daughter, Alice Roosevelt, and goes on to bed. As Elaine is about to be led to the cellar, Abby and Martha descend the stairs in mourning clothes and Mortimer arrives at the front door.

The Films: Credits, Notes, and Synopses

Mortimer and Jonathan quickly renew childhood hostilities. Elaine vies for Mortimer's attention, but he is busy on the phone with Witherspoon, who announces that a doctor's signature is also needed for Teddy's committal. Elaine leaves in a huff. Discovering a second corpse in the window seat, Mortimer blames Aunt Abby. But Jonathan betrays himself by diving to the window seat when Aunt Martha comes to inspect it. Mortimer orders him to leave or he will call the police.

O'Hara stops by to see why the lights are still on. Recognizing Mortimer as a drama critic, he insists on describing a play he has written. Hoping to frighten Jonathan, Mortimer gleefully listens. But when Jonathan threatens to reveal the presence of the other corpses in the basement, Mortimer hurries O'Hara out of the house and leaves in search of a doctor to sign Teddy's form.

Abby and Martha measure their number of victims against those of Jonathan; their nephew, who also has twelve, is jealous of being tied with his elderly aunts. Mortimer returns with the doctor. While Teddy is examined, Mortimer tries to convince Elaine that their marriage should be annulled in light of the insanity in his family. She coaxes him into a kiss. But when the doctor interrupts, she slams the window on Mortimer's fingers. The doctor agrees to commit Teddy.

As Jonathan schemes to kill Mortimer, his thirteenth victim, Mortimer tricks Teddy into signing the commitment papers under the ruse that he is authorizing a secret proclamation. Einstein tries to warn Mortimer about Jonathan's intentions, but Mortimer responds with a lengthy description of a play in which an ostensibly bright character unaccountably ignores threats against his life, is caught unaware, and is bound and gagged. Following this modus operandi to the letter, Jonathan binds and gags Mortimer and then applies the dreaded Melbourne Method, where the victim's struggling intensifies his strangulation. His nerves shot, Einstein proposes a drink of elderberry wine. He and Jonathan are about to drink when Teddy blows his bugle, alarming the neighborhood.

Arriving on the scene, O'Hara takes advantage of Mortimer's captivity to describe the rest of his play. Jonathan sneaks up with a knife behind O'Hara, but Einstein knocks out his partner before he can attack. More cops appear and identify Jonathan as a wanted criminal. Jonathan announces that thirteen corpses are in the basement and then slugs O'Hara as the officer escorts him to the cellar to see. Lieutenant Rooney arrives on the scene. Noting that Jonathan is an escaped lifer from an Indiana penitentiary, he suspends O'Hara and scolds the other cops for falling for a dumb story about the corpses. He also declares Teddy's papers invalid since Teddy has signed Roosevelt's name instead of his own, but Mortimer convinces Teddy that Brewster is a code name for Roosevelt and gets the proper signature. When Witherspoon arrives, Teddy takes him to be President Taft and prepares to depart with him for Africa.

The Films: Credits, Notes, and Synopses

Aunt Abby and Aunt Martha insist on going to Happy Dale with Teddy, but almost ruin their chances by admitting to the murders. Mortimer coaxes everyone to humor the crazy old ladies by feigning complicity with them, and the strategy works. The aunts are committed, with Dr. Einstein serving as approving physician. Receiving a description of Jonathan's accomplice that fits Einstein perfectly, Lieutenant Rooney is blind to the obvious and thanks the good doctor for helping them out.

Mortimer signs the papers for his aunts as next-of-kin, provoking Aunt Abby to reveal that he is their stepnephew, the son of a sea cook rather than a Brewster. Mortimer is elated to learn that madness is not in his blood. Elaine, sneaking into the house by way of the storm cellar, emerges from the basement shrieking that the thirteen corpses truly exist. Silencing her with a kiss, Mortimer escorts her out of the madhouse. They depart for Niagara Falls.

ARMY ORIENTATION FILMS (1942-45)

Credits for the orientation films made by Capra's army film unit during World War II are especially difficult to establish because assignments within the unit were somewhat fluid and official credits were not provided by the army when the films were first presented. Current filmographies are sketchy and contradictory, and conflicting claims have been made in recent years by various people associated with the group. I have synthesized available information, resolving discrepancies whenever possible.

Responsibility for assembling the unit initially fell to Capra, who began hiring both military and civilian personnel in the spring of 1942, but enlisted men were assigned to his staff as projects developed. Moreover, once the unit was set up in Los Angeles in June 1942, assistance was provided on many of the projects by technicians in several Hollywood studios who did not receive credit. Among the long-term members of the unit, the following appear to have been central: Edgar Peterson, a civilian documentary filmmaker whom Capra met in Washington, D.C., and the first civilian Capra hired; Anatole Litvak, a fellow Hollywood director (and recent emigré from Europe) who served as second-in-command of the unit in Los Angeles: and writer Anthony Veiller. Other writers included Eric Knight, Robert Heller, Leonard Spigelgass, Alan Rivkin, William L. Shirer, Bill Henry, James Hilton, John Whittaker, John Gunther, Ted Geisel, Claude Binyon, Carl Foreman, and Irving Wallace. Sam Briskin, former general manager at Columbia Pictures and later partner with Capra on Liberty Films, was hired as a "production manager," but his specific role remains unclear. Richard Griffith headed a research staff (including Leon Levy, Palmer Williams, and Elinor Grey) that located film footage in New York and Washington to match the requirements of the scripts. William Hornbeck served as chief editor, backed by Henry Berman, John Hoffman, and Merrill White. Joseph Biroc was also part of the unit, probably as a cameraman. (Veiller, Hornbeck, and Biroc all worked with Capra on

The Films: Credits, Notes, and Synopses

feature films after the war.) Composer Dimitri Tiomkin, a frequent colleague of Capra's, scored all the films except Prelude to War. The Santa Ana Army Air Force Orchestra, under the direction of Meredith Willson, performed the music. Walter Huston and Anthony Veiller were the principal narrators. Walt Disney Productions produced the animation.

According to Capra, all the orientation films were produced at the unit's makeshift headquarters in the old Twentieth Century-Fox studios on Western Avenue in Los Angeles. In September 1943 the 843rd Signal Service Photographic Detachment was officially shifted from the Special Services Division, Army Service Forces, to the Army Pictorial Service of the Signal Corps based in Astoria, Long Island, but the West Coast headquarters remained open under the direction of Litvak. Capra was reassigned to the Public Relations Office; his work on Tunisian Victory in 1943 fell outside the jurisdiction of the West Coast unit.

All the films produced by the unit were distributed through military circuits: 35mm prints were shown in post theaters at home; 16mm prints at bases abroad. Viewing the Why We Fight series was required of all army personnel before going overseas; the total attendance at these films by July 1945 was estimated at more than 45.5 million. The orientation films were also shown on a voluntary basis at navy, air force, marine, and coast guard training centers, and at war plants around the country. Theatrical release in America was given to Prelude to War, The Battle of Russia, The Negro Soldier, and Two Down, One to Go. Many of the films also had extensive exposure overseas. With the exception of The Battle of China, all the Why We Fight series was translated into Spanish, Portuguese, and French, and shown to Allied forces around the world. Most of the films were shown to civilian audiences in British theaters and were distributed in South America through the Office of the Coordinator for Inter-American Affairs, headed by Nelson Rockefeller. Prints of The Battle of Russia, translated into various dialects, were shown throughout the Soviet Union, accompanied by a prologue by Joseph Stalin.

The best-documented account of the work of the Capra unit is Thomas Bohn's An Historical and Descriptive Analysis of the "Why We Fight" Series (New York: Arno Press, 1977). Also see The Signal Corps: The Test (December 1941 to July 1943), edited by George Raynor Thompson, Dixie R. Harris, Pauline M. Oakes, and Dulany Terret (Washington, D.C.: Department of the Army, 1957), pp. 414-61; The Signal Corps: The Outcome (Mid-1943 through 1945), edited by George Raynor Thompson and Dixie R. Harris (Washington, D.C.: United States Army, 1966), pp. 555-59; and Capra's own account of this period in The Name Above the Title, pp. 314-67.

32   **PRELUDE TO WAR (1942)**

Producer: Special Services Division, Army Service
                         Forces, U.S. War Department

The Films: Credits, Notes, and Synopses

Supervisor:	Frank Capra
Director:	Frank Capra
Script:	Eric Knight, Anthony Veiller
Musical Director:	Alfred Newman
Narrator:	Walter Huston
Distributor:	Office of War Information, Motion Picture Bureau in cooperation with the War Activities Committee, Motion Picture Industry
Military release:	30 October 1942
Theatrical release:	13 May 1943 (Strand Theatre, New York City)
Running time:	53 minutes

Notes

Upon completion in October 1942, Prelude to War was shown to Secretary of War Henry L. Stimson, Army Chief of Staff Gen. George C. Marshall, and President Franklin Roosevelt, all of whom reportedly were impressed by the film. Stimson and Marshall, with Roosevelt's blessing, immediately pushed for its general distribution to civilian audiences, but were blocked for several months by the Office of War Information's Motion Picture Bureau, headed by Lowell Mellett. Arguing that theater owners were reluctant to show a government film of such length, Mellett proposed that strong opposition from the industry might jeopardize the working relationship previously established between Washington and Hollywood. He claimed, moreover, that the film's emotionalism and bias violated standards for domestic propaganda established by the OWI and was supported on this point by Nelson Poynter, head of the Hollywood office of the Bureau of Motion Pictures. Pressure to distribute the film nevertheless continued, and in late April Mellett stopped his blocking action. Prelude to War had a brief engagement at the Strand Theatre in New York beginning 13 May 1943. Then on 27 May 250 prints were distributed free of charge to commercial theaters around the country by the OWI and Hollywood's War Activities Committee. Reviews were generally favorable, but according to exhibitors the film was not a box-office success (see Richard Steele's "The Greatest Gangster Movie Ever Filmed: Prelude to War," Prologue: The Journal of the National Archives, 11, No. 4 [Winter 1978], 221-35). Prelude to War received an Academy Award for best documentary in 1943 and an award from the National Board of Review the same year. It was honored by the New York Film Critics as part of the entire Why We Fight series in 1944.

Synopsis

The first film in the Why We Fight series, Prelude to War seeks to explain the necessity of American involvement in World War II by focusing on international events leading up to this confrontation. The earth is depicted as divided into two worlds--one free, one slave. Members of the free world (the Allies) share a belief in the equality of all men, a notion traceable to the spiritual teachings of Moses, Mohammed, Confucius, and Christ and given fullest political expression in America under the U.S. Constitution. People in the slave world

(the Axis powers) surrendered their freedom to three tyrants--
Mussolini in Italy, Hitler in Germany, Hirohito in Japan. With mass
populations at their disposal, these tyrants developed powerful military forces and now conspire to threaten the free world. Ominous
signs of this could be seen in the 1930s, but most Americans did not
want to become involved in a foreign crisis, in part because they
faced economic problems at home, and in part because the ramifications
of the foreign crisis were not fully understood. Depicted as comic
buffoons by the American media, the tyrants meanwhile mapped a strategy for world domination through propaganda and territorial expansion, and implemented the first stages of this plan successfully. It
now must be recognized that peace for Americans will depend on peace
throughout the world. Japan's two-phase invasion of the Asian continent and Italy's conquest of Ethiopia are briefly outlined in this
film; German strategy is reserved for the next episode in the series.

33 **THE NAZIS STRIKE (1943)**

Producer:	Special Services Division, Army Forces Services, U.S. War Department
Supervisor:	Frank Capra
Directors:	Frank Capra, Anatole Litvak
Script:	Eric Knight, Anthony Veiller, Robert Heller
Editor:	William Hornbeck
Musical Director:	Dimitri Tiomkin
Narrators:	Walter Huston, Anthony Veiller
Running time:	42 minutes

Synopsis

The second film in the Why We Fight series, The Nazis Strike,
deals with German expansion into Eastern Europe during the 1930's,
climaxing with the invasion and conquest of Poland. A history of
maniacal leadership in Germany is constructed: Bismarck in 1863,
Wilhelm II in 1914, and Hitler in 1933. The most recent plan for
conquest, masterminded by Hitler upon his rise to power in 1933,
involves a three-step strategy to capture seven-eights of the world
population: (1) conquest of Eastern Europe, (2) conquest of the
heartland of the Continent, and (3) conquest of the Continent, or
"world island," leading to domination of the world. While Nazi
stooges acquire power in Belgium, Czechoslovakia, and Austria, and a
German Bund rises to support the Nazi cause in America, Germany rearms
itself, violating the Treaty of Versailles. Remilitarizing the Rhineland to protect its western border, it then begins its assault on
Eastern Europe. On 19 March 1938, Austria is overrun. At the Munich
Conference in September 1938, the British allow Hitler to swallow up
the Sudetenland, ostensibly in exchange for "peace in our time." On
14 March 1939, the Nazis invade and conquer the rest of Czechoslovakia
as well. After signing a nonagression pact with the Russians, who are
disillusioned with the West and in need of time to arm themselves,
Hitler invades Poland in the early hours of 1 September 1939, catching
the Polish Air Force flat-footed. A pincer assault is made on Warsaw,

The Films: Credits, Notes, and Synopses

where the people nobly defend the city during twenty days of death and horror. But Warsaw finally falls, and Poland lies a defeated land. With the invasion of Poland, France and England have declared war on Germany; Hitler's strategy against these countries remains to be explained in the next episodes.

34 DIVIDE AND CONQUER (1943)

Producer:	Special Services Division, Army Service Forces, U.S. War Department
Supervisor:	Frank Capra
Directors:	Frank Capra, Anatole Litvak
Script:	Anthony Veiller, Robert Heller
Editor:	William Hornbeck
Musical Director:	Dimitri Tiomkin
Narrators:	Walter Huston, Anthony Veiller
Running time:	58 minutes

Notes

This film should not be confused with a fourteen-minute Warner Brothers "Service Special" by the same title, directed by Lewis Seiler and released in July 1942.

Synopsis

The third film in the Why We Fight series, Divide and Conquer recounts Germany's expansion across Western Europe during 1940. Between Germany and its primary targets, France and England, lie small neutral nations, which are promised friendly relations by Hitler and then betrayed. Denmark, a springboard to Norway, is taken in one day. Weakened internally by the traitorous collaborator, Major Quisling, Norway then falls prey to German merchant ships which enter the fjords like Trojan horses. A battle ensues, but Germany's superiority in the air quickly proves decisive. France, instead of adopting the aggressive combative stance of General Foch in World War I, assumes a defensive position along the Maginot Line. On 10 May 1940, Hitler responds with a coordinated attack along the borders of Luxembourg, Belgium, and Holland. Four days later the Dutch surrender, but the Nazis bomb and destroy Rotterdam anyhow. The Belgians hold out for only two days; refugees from bombed villages are met by the invading army and used as weapons of war. Then, as Allied forces swing up through Belgium in response, a massive attack is made through the Ardennes Forest into France, a blitzkrieg that quickly moves all the way to the Atlantic Ocean. British, French, and Belgium troops are miraculously rescued at Dunkirk, but France is weakened. Mussolini in Italy exploits that weakness by attacking from the South, and France surrenders on 16 June. As part of the armistice, French youth are taken back to Germany as slaves and hostages. Hope for France resides in North Africa, where Charles de Gaulle, with aid from America and England, is gathering retaliatory forces.

The Films: Credits, Notes, and Synopses

35   KNOW YOUR ALLY: BRITAIN (1943)

Producer:	Special Services Division, Army Service Forces, U.S. War Department
Supervisor:	Frank Capra
Director:	Anthony Veiller
Script:	Anthony Veiller, Eric Knight
Editor:	William Hornbeck
Musical Director:	Dimitri Tiomkin
Narrators:	Walter Huston, Anthony Veiller
Running time:	45 minutes

Notes

In May 1942 Capra proposed that the 834th Photographic Signal Corps Detachment produce a comprehensive series of documentaries designed to acquaint American soldiers with the people of Allied and enemy nations, but only three films were eventually made: Know Your Ally: Britain, Here Is Germany (see entry 42), and Know Your Enemy: Japan (see entry 43).

Synopsis

The British are introduced as a people who have learned to live together as good neighbors on a small piece of land. Events in Europe during the late 1930s forced them to wake up to the deadly threat of Hitler and Nazi expansion. During 1940-41 they sustained bombing raids on London, but they never yielded; instead they buried their dead, kept a pledge to support Greece, and assumed the offensive.

Nazi propaganda aimed at dividing the Allies by playing up the differences between England and America is countered. Although people in each country may play different sports and have different tastes and accents, they both possess a free, representative government and enjoy the freedoms of speech, press, and religion inherited from England and its Magna Carta and Petition of Rights. Royalty still serves a symbolic role in England, but political power is vested in the individual voter, and labor unions are a major political force; the right to social security, for example, was won in advance of Americans. The Nazis have accused the British of entering the war only to protect her empire, but where is this empire? England has given freedom to Canada, Australia, New Zealand, and South Africa, and will give it to India as soon as the war is over. The Nazis have suggested that the British let other countries fight for them, but in fact they have sustained heavy casualties and their forces constitute a major portion of the Allied air and naval strength.

Unlike Americans, Englishmen are reticent, and, in sharp contrast to the boastful Germans, they never brag. But the travelogue view of England as a quaint country has masked the fact that it is an industrial power where men and women have been fighting nobly on the front line. American soldiers can expect to find themselves in a country

The Films: Credits, Notes, and Synopses

where food and commodities are in short supply. England, however, is preparing for a world free of want and fear after the war, for a time when, in Winston Churchill's words, the British and American people will walk in majesty and peace.

36   **THE BATTLE OF BRITAIN (1943)**

Producer:	Special Services Division, Army Service Forces, U.S. War Department
Supervisor:	Frank Capra
Director:	Anthony Veiller
Script:	Anthony Veiller
Editor:	William Hornbeck
Musical Director:	Dimitri Tiomkin
Narrators:	Walter Huston, Anthony Veiller
Running time:	54 minutes

Synopsis

The fourth film in the Why We Fight series, The Battle of Britain tells the story of the Nazi assault on Britain, and Britain's successful defense of its island, during 1940-41. Captured German newsreels depict Hitler at Paris and Dunkirk and then at Calais, scanning the channel as he contemplates his assault. A three-step plan is mapped: (1) knock out the Royal Air Force through a blitz, (2) gain control of the coast by pulverizing it with bombs, and (3) invade with ground forces from high-speed barges and close in on London, establishing a position for a eventual attack on America. In the face of such an assault, Britain would have been outnumbered in men and machines, but Hitler did not count on the spirit of people in a democracy.

On 8 August 1940 the Battle of Britain commences. RAF fighter planes battle the Nazis in the air, successfully blocking the first step in Hitler's plan. Germany shifts its attack from the coast to industrial centers, but British morale remains high and RAF air tactics are effective. Postponing his invasion, Hitler decides to demoralize the British by bombing civilian populations. On 7 September a month-long bombing of London begins, but the Germans sustain costly losses as the RAF outfight them in the air. On 6 October the Germans switch to night attacks, dropping incendiary bombs which leave blocks of London in flames, but the British retaliate with a counterattack on German territory, using the few bombers they possess. In revenge, the Nazis drop a million pounds of bombs on Coventry, but the British bury their dead and return to the factories. Christmas night, London is hit by a massive attack setting off the greatest fire in the city's history. But the people refuse to surrender and hold on through the spring when the threat of invasion finally fades. Britain has lost forty thousand men, women, and children, but not a single Nazi soldier has set foot on British soil and the myth of German invincibility has been punctured. Having tasted defeat for the first time, Germany turns eastward toward Russia, the subject of the next episode in this series.

The Films: Credits, Notes, and Synopses

37   THE BATTLE OF RUSSIA (1943)

Producer:	Special Services Division, Army Service Forces, U.S. War Department
Supervisor:	Frank Capra
Director:	Anatole Litvak
Script:	Anatole Litvak, Anthony Veiller, Robert Heller
Editor:	William Hornbeck
Musical Director:	Dimitri Tiomkin
Narrators:	Walter Huston, Anthony Veiller
Distributor:	Twentieth Century-Fox Film Corporation, under the auspices of the War Activities Committee, Motion Picture Industry
Theatrical release:	12 November 1943 (Globe Theatre, New York City, and the Fox Ritz and Egyptian theaters, Los Angeles)
Running time:	80 minutes

Notes

The Battle of Russia received an award from the National Board of Review in 1943, was nominated for an Academy Award for best documentary the same year, and was honored by the New York Film Critics as part of the entire Why We Fight series in 1944.

Synopsis

     The fifth film in the Why We Fight series, The Battle of Russia focuses on Russia's defense of its eastern frontier against Nazi aggression. A history of Russian resistance to foreign invasion is briefly recounted: the repelling of the Germans in 1242, of Charles XII of Sweden in 1704, of Napoleon in 1812, and of the Germans again under Kaiser Wilhelm in 1914. The recent Nazi attack is then described and depicted in detail. In 1934 Russia joins the League of Nations and warns its European neighbors to arrest German aggression under Hitler with collective force, but to no avail. Hoping to buy time to rearm, the Russians sign a nonaggression pact with the Nazis on 21 August 1939. After Germany is blocked by Britain on their western front, however, they turn eastward toward Russia. Reactionary leaders in the Balkans sell out to Hitler for protection, and Yugoslavia and Greece are overpowered. Meanwhile, the Russians brace for an attack, which comes on 22 June 1941 at six points along a two-thousand-mile front. By December, 500,000 square miles of Russian land has been taken. But Russian strategy is to bend without breaking, yielding territory but sucking the enemy in deeper and blunting the invader's wedge formation. Moreover, the Russian people see the war not simply as a matter of territory but as a struggle for life and death; every Russian is a soldier participating in a total war. And while generals win campaigns, people win wars.

The Films: Credits, Notes, and Synopses

The struggle for survival comes to center on three major cities. the first is Moscow, where cultural landmarks like the Tchaikovsky and Tolstoy museums are damaged yet survive. Civilians are killed, girls are raped, but the Moscovites swear vengeance on these actions and hold on until the spring of 1942, shattering the myth of Nazi invincibility. The second city is Leningrad, cut off from the rest of Russia in September 1941 and subject to a seventeen-month siege. During the long winter months, disease and famine set in. Then a miraculous rescue mission is effected across frozen Lake Lagoda. Supplies are brought in and the wounded and ill taken out of the city. Soldiers in trenches finally begin a counterattack, and with the spring thaw the city breathes again. Nazis enter Leningrad only as defeated prisoners of war. The third city is Stalingrad, crucially located on the Volga River. Hitler has promised his soldiers they will winter in Stalingrad, but the Russians resist, leading to 162 days of bloody battle. As the Germans are drawn toward the city, Russian armies from the north and south circle behind the enemy and cut them off. The Nazi defeat is devastating: 24 generals are captured, 330,000 men lost. Russia has broken the back of the invincible German army. The lesson for Germany is that the united people of the Allied nations will successfully counter Nazi aggression.

38 THE NEGRO SOLDIER (1944)

The Negro Soldier in World War II

Producer:	Special Services Division, Army Services Forces, U.S. War Department
Supervisor:	Frank Capra
Director:	Stuart Heisler[1]
Script:	Carlton Moss[2]
Editor:	William Hornbeck
Musical Director:	Dimitri Tiomkin
Cast:	Carlton Moss (minister), Bertha Wolford (mother)
Distributor:	Office of War Information, in cooperation with the War Activities Committee of the Motion Picture Industry
Theatrical release:	21 April 1944 (the Gotham, Rialto, Victoria and Trus-Lux/Broadway theaters, New York City)
Running time:	43 minutes[3]

Notes

1. William Wyler was originally assigned to direct the film. After completing research in Alabama with writers Carlton Moss and Marc Connelly, however, Wyler was reassigned to direct air force documentaries.

The Films: Credits, Notes, and Synopses

2. The first script for the project was written by Marc Connelly, the second by Jo Swerling and Ben Hecht. Both these versions were rejected by army authorities.

3. Because exhibitors were reluctant to show the full forty-three minute version, a shorter twenty minute version was made available to theaters in July 1944.

On the day of its release to commercial theaters, The Negro Soldier was the subject of a lawsuit filed in federal court by Jack Goldberg, president of The Negro Marches On, Inc., who alleged that the government film unfairly competed with his own production, We've Come a Long, Long Way. Goldberg also alleged that The Negro Soldier used footage belonging to his corporation. The NAACP backed the War Department and War Activities Committee in the controversy and heavily promoted The Negro Soldier in the press. Goldberg lost the case. Although The Negro Soldier never had as broad a commercial run as Prelude to War and The Battle of Russia, it was a popular film in nontheatrical circuits. (For a well-documented account of the production and distribution of the film, see Thomas Cripps and David Culbert's "The Negro Soldier (1944): Film Propaganda in Black and White," American Quarterly, 31, No. 5 [Winter 1979], 616-40.)

Synopsis

Inside a large Gothic church, the minister deviates from his prepared text to introduce some of the soldiers in the congregation and to reflect on the role of black Americans in the current war with Germany. Joe Louis's recovery of the heavyweight championship from Max Schmeling serves as a metaphor for the present struggle against Nazism and the racist ideas of Hitler's Mein Kampf. The minister recounts the heroism of blacks throughout American history: at the Boston Massacre, Concord Bridge, and Bunker Hill; beside George Washington crossing the Delaware and at Valley Forge; as pioneers helping to build the nation in the earliest years and rebuild it after the Civil War; in the Spanish-American War; in Cuba; in Panama; and in World War I, where their bravery inspired the French to raise a monument in their honor. "Living monuments" are noted as well: Booker T. Washington and George Washington Carver; judges, explorers, doctors, musicians, financiers, educators, curators, and artists. Negro colleges are quickly surveyed, as are the successes of athletes in college and at the 1936 Olympic Games in Berlin. The tree of liberty, the minister argues, has born these fruits, a liberty the Japanese, who falsely claim to be the saviors of colored nations, do not respect. As the minister lists the branches of the American armed services in which blacks now serve, a woman interrupts to remind him of the infantry. She reads a letter from her son in which he describes his training in boot camp, his exposure to Negro literature, his romance with a beautiful WAC, and his recent selection for officer training. The minister picks up on this last theme with a discussion of ROTC programs at Negro colleges in which men are being trained to fight a war that is not yet completed. The minister prays that they

The Films: Credits, Notes, and Synopses

have the strength to be worthy of their heritage, and the congregation rises to sing "Onward Christian Soldiers." Over a montage of troops marching, "Joshua Fit de Battle ob Jericho" is heard, followed by "My Country 'Tis of Thee."

39   **THE BATTLE OF CHINA (1944)**

Producer:	Army Pictorial Service, Signal Corps, U.S. War Department
Supervisor:	Frank Capra
Directors:	Frank Capra, Anatole Litvak
Script:	Eric Knight, Anthony Veiller, Robert Heller
Editor:	William Hornbeck
Musical Director:	Dimitri Tiomkin
Narrator:	Anthony Veiller, Walter Huston
Running time:	67 minutes

Synopsis

The sixth film in the Why We Fight series, The Battle of China concerns China's heroic struggle against recent occupation by Japan. Throughout history a peace-loving nation, rich in culture and resources, open to progressive elements from the West, China is not subject to Japan's mad dream of conquest. Under the Tanaka Plan formulated in 1927, Japan plots to (1) conquer Manchuria for raw material, (2) absorb China piece by piece for manpower, (3) sweep the Indies for its riches, and (4) move eastward to crush America. Fragmented politically in numerous territories, China is unable to respond to the Japanese invasion of Manchuria in 1931. When the Chinese unify in 1937, Japan strikes at Shanghai, initiating a war of terrorization and mass murder in that city, and then begins a sweep across the continent. The rape, torture, and massacre that follow, however, only further strengthen the Chinese resolve to resist. Short on weapons, they must yield territory to buy time. Thirty million Chinese traverse mountains and rivers in the largest migration in human history. They scorch their own land, blow up their roads and factories, and move two-thousand miles westward, bringing with them schools, machinery, libraries, and hospitals. The Japanese pursue them with bombers, but the Chinese are prepared, having built factories and homes underground, and air support is provided by America's General Chennault and his "Flying Tigers." To bring supplies to their factories, the Chinese perform an astonishing feat, carving the Burma Road out of the mountains. They break a dam along the Yellow River to flood out their pursuers, and guerrillas emerge in rural areas to form pockets of resistance to Japanese occupation. Meanwhile, America wakes up to Japanese aggression. While we sustain initial losses in 1942, the Chinese lose the Burma Road. But today, in 1944, a better story is unfolding, with America on the offensive, working with the Chinese to protect the new Lido Road. Thus the youngest and oldest nations of the world join forces, in alliance with Great Britain, to fight a war that must be won.

The Films: Credits, Notes, and Synopses

40   TUNISIAN VICTORY (1944)

Producers: The British Army Film Unit and the U.S. Army
                            Signal Corps
Directors: Hugh Stewart (British Army Film Unit), Frank
                            Capra (U.S. Army Signal Corps)
Script: J.L. Hodson (British Army Film Unit), Anthony
                            Veiller (U.S. Army Signal Corps)
Narrators: Leo Glenn (British Army Film Unit), Anthony
                            Veiller (U.S. Army Signal Corps)
Soldiers' Voices: Bernard Miles (British), Burgess Meredith
                            (American)
Produced in Great Britain in 1943
Distributors: British Ministry of Information; Metro-
                            Goldwyn-Mayer in the United States
Theatrical release: 16 March 1944 (London); 23 March 1944 (Rialto
                            Theatre, New York City)
Running time: 76 minutes

Notes

Tunisian Victory was initially conceived by the British Ministry of Information as a sequel to Desert Victory, their highly acclaimed documentary on the first stage of the North African campaign. Meanwhile in America, Capra and John Huston had been assigned the task of reenacting battle scenes from America's North African campaign, for which there was no available footage. After filming these scenes in the Mojave Desert and at Orlando, Florida, Capra, Huston, and writer Anthony Veiller went to the Signal Corps film center in Astoria, New York, to work on a script for the film. In September 1943, the British and American projects were combined into one. A series of similar "victory films" based upon collaborative coverage of the war was scheduled to follow, but Tunisian Victory was the only venture of this kind undertaken by the Signal Corps. (British and American filmmakers did collaborate two years later on The True Glory, co-directed by Garson Kanin and Carol Reed, but this was made under the auspices of the British Ministry of Information and the U.S. Office of War Information.) Huston claims that the reenacted scenes he and Capra filmed were "transparently false," and it is uncertain whether any of this material was included in the final version of Tunisian Victory. According to Hugh Stewart, Capra's British counterpart on the project, only three minutes of reenacted footage appeared in the final film, and this depicted hard-to-film night battles that occurred at Hill 609 and Wadi Zig Zaou. These sequences in Tunisian Victory greatly resemble the dramatic night battle at El Alamein in Desert Victory (see "'Tunisian Victory' Now Being Filmed," New York Times, 28 April 1943, p. 20; A.H. Weiler, "Field Report on Tunisian Victory," New York Times 5 March 1944, sec. 3, p. 3; and John Huston, An Open Book [New York: Alfred A. Knopf, 1980], pp. 102-4).

150

The Films: Credits, Notes, and Synopses

Synopsis

<u>Tunisian Victory</u> opens with the gathering of British and American ships at sea in the Atlantic Ocean in November 1942. British and American narrators alternately describe a secret Allied operation, code-named Acrobat, to remove Axis forces from North Africa and prepare a base for a subsequent invasion of Italy. The voices of two ordinary soldiers--one American ("Joe McGinnis"), one British ("George Metcalf")--are also heard, describing events from the point of view of an infantryman. Successful invasions of Casablanca, Algiers, and Oran unite British and American forces with those of the Free French, but the eastward drive toward Tunisia falls short of its objective and the Allied ground forces retreat to the protection of the hills to wait out the winter and rearm. Christmas is spent far from home, but the soldiers enjoy a good meal and have time to relax and get to know the Arab children. Following a meeting between Roosevelt and Churchill near the encampment, General Eisenhower is named commander of the Allied campaign, and battle lines are drawn for the spring offensive. When it commences, British forces from the east meet Allied forces from the west, cornering the Nazis along the eastern coastline of Tunisia. A coordinated attack splits the enemy forces into four isolated pockets; the Germans yield in the greatest mass surrender in modern history. George and Joe discuss the waste the war has caused, and define the differences between themselves and the German soldier in terms of their willingness to think for themselves rather than follow leaders blindly. They agree to keep in touch after the war and work together to build a better world. Africa is now free, the British narrator concludes, and Europe is that much closer to freedom.

41   WAR COMES TO AMERICA (1945)

Producer:	Army Pictorial Service, Signal Corps, U.S. War Department
Supervisor:	Frank Capra
Director:	Anatole Litvak
Script:	Anatole Litvak, Anthony Veiller[1]
Editor:	William Hornbeck
Musical Director:	Dimitri Tiomkin
Narrators:	Walter Huston, Lloyd Nolan
Running time:	67 minutes

Notes

1. Capra claims also to have written the script for this film (see "Additions and Corrections: Frank Capra," <u>Film Dope</u>, No. 8 [October], pp. 24c-24d).

<u>War Comes to America</u> was originally planned as a two-part film, the first part to cover events leading up to America's involvement in the war, and the second to cover the war years themselves. In April 1945, however, the army decided not to make the second half. The titles on existing prints describe the film as "Part One."

The Films: Credits, Notes, and Synopses

Synopsis

The seventh and final film in the Why We Fight series, War Comes to America surveys life in America leading up to the war years and seeks to define American values. An early history of the Republic is briefly recounted: immigrants arrive from all lands to build a new nation based on the principle of the equality of all men. America emerges as a country of enterprising, inventive people, committed to the democratic ideal of the greatest good for the greatest number, and enjoying the highest standard of living on earth. The press is free, churches are regularly attended, government officials are elected. When mistakes are made, such as Prohibition, the people repeal bad laws. Economic depression may strike, but Americans never lose faith in the future. They hate war, but are willing to fight if the principle of freedom is endangered.

In the 1930s, however, Americans were too preoccupied with their own problems to see what was happening in Europe and Asia. While Japan invades Manchuria, Hitler rises to power in Germany, and Mussolini attacks Ethiopia, American neutrality remains entrenched. Britain and France vainly attempt to assuage Hitler's hunger for conquest, and Nazi spies enter American life, but Americans only slowly awake to the problem. When war breaks out, President Roosevelt steers a course toward American involvement, pushing for changes in the neutrality laws and the establishment of Lend-Lease. As the country's defenses are strengthened, Americans debate whether or not they should intervene. The true extent of the threat being posed to their liberty is not driven home until Japan's dastardly attack on Pearl Harbor, executed while a peace mission is supposedly in progress in Washington. Roosevelt requests a declaration of war, and the struggle commences.

42 HERE IS GERMANY (1945)

Know Your Enemy: Germany

Producer:	Army Pictorial Service, Signal Corps, U.S. War Department
Supervisor:	Frank Capra
Script:	Gottfried Reinhardt, Anthony Veiller, William L. Shirer, Ernst Lubitsch
Editor:	William Hornbeck, Merrill White
Musical Director:	Dimitri Tiomkin
Narrators:	John Beal, Anthony Veiller
Running time:	52 minutes

Notes

An earlier version of Here Is Germany, entitled Know Your Enemy: Germany, was made by Hollywood director Ernst Lubitsch in October 1942, but Lubitsch's film was rejected by the army. The project was

The Films: Credits, Notes, and Synopses

not resumed until 1944, at which time Gottfried Reinhardt, Anthony Veiller, and William L. Shirer worked on a new script. (Reinhardt is also credited as the director of the second version in the American Film Institute's Study Guide on Capra [see entry 1099], but I have found no other source to confirm this.) Sections from Lubitsch's script were retained in the final version, most notably the device of tracing Germany's history through the ancestry of a fictional soldier, "Karl Schmidt." For a discussion of the relationship between Lubitsch's script and the later film, see David Culbert's "Notes on Government Paper Records" in <u>Scholars' Guide to Washington, D.C., Film and Video Collections</u> (Washington, D.C.: Smithsonian Institution Press, 1980), pp. 235-43. Unfortunately, Culbert confuses matters further by mixing up <u>Here Is Germany</u> with <u>Your Job in Germany</u> (see entry 44), a later instructional short for American occupation forces.

Synopsis

Drawing on a variety of German films, ranging from costume dramas to newsreels, <u>Here Is Germany</u> reconstructs German history from the era of Frederick the Great to the present, painting a portrait of a people conditioned to undertake wars of conquest. Noting that Germans may appear to us an educated, cultured, and industrious people, the narrator proposes that the military aggression and despicable atrocities committed by the Nazis bespeaks another side to the German personality. "Karl Schmidt," the typical Nazi soldier today, has been shaped by values handed down from generation to generation; his goose-step--and the lust for power it has come to signify--is the same as his father's under the kaiser in World War I, and his grandfather's under Bismark in the 1860s. Unfortunately, instead of heeding the lesson of the past and demanding an unconditional surrender, the Allies in 1918 settled for an Armistice, allowing the leaders of the old Germany to remain in power behind the scenes and the German people to delude themselves with the notion that they had been defeated politically by democratic leaders at home rather than militarily by the enemy they had provoked. Moreover, the ineffectiveness of the Treaty of Versailles and the League of Nations allowed Germany to rapidly rearm, and Karl Schmidt, impoverished by the depression, was ripe for manipulation. Backed by militarists, industrialists, and reactionaries, Adolf Hitler and his cadre of misfits employed the resources of modern media to indoctrinate Karl Schmidt even more thoroughly than his father and grandfather. This is why the Germans have been capable of such barbaric atrocities in their conquest of Europe. It is also why the Allies will this time demand the complete destruction of the existing military, industrial, and political structure of Germany, and will oversee the reeducation of its people. While the Allies may have rid Germany of Hitler, Karl Schmidt will have to rid himself of Bismark and the kaiser, and the historical tradition they represent. Only then can a beautiful, industrious, and cultured Germany flourish and join the peaceful nations of the world.

The Films: Credits, Notes, and Synopses

43   **KNOW YOUR ENEMY: JAPAN (1945)**

Producer:	Army Pictorial Service, Signal Corps, U.S. War Department
Supervisor:	Frank Capra
Directors:	Frank Capra, Edgar Peterson, Leonard Spigelgass, Joris Ivens
Script:	Irving Wallace, Edgar Peterson, Carl Foreman, Albert Hackett and Frances Goodrich, John Huston, Joris Ivens, Howard Duff
Editors:	William Hornbeck, Helen van Dongen
Musical Director	Dimitri Tiomkin
Narrators:	Walter Huston, Jean Beal, Anthony Veiller
Running time:	63 minutes

Notes

Recent research by William J. Blakefield suggests that the production history of Know Your Enemy: Japan was the most troubled and complicated of all projects undertaken by Capra's Signal Corps film unit. An initial script was prepared by Warren Duff, but this was shelved by the General Staff when the unit was transferred to Los Angeles in June 1942. After receiving permission to proceed again on the project in the spring of 1943, Capra hired Dutch documentary filmmaker Joris Ivens to direct it. Ivens brought in Helen van Dongen, with whom he had collaborated on earlier films, as an editor, and Carl Foreman was assigned to the project as a writer. After viewing over a hundred Japanese fiction films and all available Japanese newsreels back to 1932, Ivens and Foreman distilled a scenario that argued that fascism's roots were in bushido culture and depicted the Japanese people as victims of a fascist military state. In September 1943 the General Staff rejected the new script and requested that Ivens be removed from the project. According to Ivens, his dismissal was prompted by his contention that the emperor should be treated as a war criminal at a time when American officials were mapping out a policy of support for the Emperor after the war, but Ivens's reputation as a documentarian of the political Left may have in and of itself made him suspect in the eyes of the General Staff. (Capra subsequently found work for Ivens at United Artists as a consultant on The Story of G.I. Joe.) Work on Know Your Enemy: Japan resumed under the supervision of Leonard Spigelgass, and Foreman collaborated on a series of scripts with Irving Wallace, who had experience as a journalist in Japan to draw on. In February 1944, however, work once again came to a halt, with Foreman and van Dongen leaving the project for good. In April, a new effort to get the film off the ground was undertaken by Edgar Peterson, with Irving Wallace as writer. In May, Capra also hired Hollywood screenwriters Albert Hackett and Frances Goodrich, who synthesized previous material into a forty-four-page script; this script in turn was handed back to Peterson and Wallace. In January 1945, John Huston replaced Peterson, but stayed only long enough to write a new section of the script with Wallace. After the tentative approval of both the script and a rough cut of the film by the Pen-

The Films: Credits, Notes, and Synopses

tagon in February, Capra became actively involved in the project, making final revisions based upon suggestions by the military. (In an interview with Sam. L. Grogg, Wallace has claimed that Ted Geisel also worked as a producer on Know Your Enemy: Japan, and that Geisel was responsible for a final draft of the script, but detailed research by Blakefield has revealed no such contribution by Geisel. Geisel might have been working on Your Job In Germany [see entry 44] during this period.) A final print was assembled in the summer of 1945. After the dropping of atomic bombs on Hiroshima and Nagasaki, however, the War Activities Committee in Hollywood decided not to distribute Know Your Enemy: Japan to commercial theaters. It circulated through military channels between 9 August and 28 August, but then was withdrawn from distribution because of a change in government policy toward Japan. Thus, although Know Your Enemy: Japan, which during the course of its various revisions had become highly racist, may well have reflected the attitude of the War Department prior to the decision to drop the bomb, the dropping of the bomb itself seems to have made the film "nonoperational" as a statement of public policy (see William J. Blakefield, "A War Within: The Making of Know Your Enemy--Japan,: Sight and Sound, 52, No. 2 [Spring 1983], 128-33; Gordon Hitchens's 1972 interview with Joris Ivens [entry 877], pp. 206-7; and Sam L. Grogg's 1974 interview with Irving Wallace [entry 936], pp. 59-62).

Synopsis

A prologue cites the loyal contribution of Americans of Japanese descent to the war effort and then proposes that this film will tell "the story of the Japs in Japan to whom the words liberty and freedom are still without meaning." The Japanese soldier is depicted as small in stature, lacking precision, but tough and proud. For him, religious and political faith merge in the worship of the emperor, believed to be a direct descendant of the sun, and through whom all ordinary people share in a divinity of race and blood. Since 1870, the national religion of Shinto has been twisted by the state into a doctrine of "Hakke Ichiu" whereby the emperor is considered supreme over all races of the world. Hence the blind commitment of the Japanese to world conquest. A soldier who surrenders shames his family and ancestors; a soldier who dies in battle is enshrined as a warrior god.

A brief history of Japan is then charted. Invading Mongols fuse with other races to populate the islands. A feudal society emerges in which the emperor himself has little political power; samurai, operating under the code of bushido, live as aristocrats off the fat of the land. In the sixteenth century, China is plundered and the Christian influence at home is eradicated. For two-hundred years the country is closed off from Western influence, but with the arrival of Commodore Perry, Japanese warriors realize that their weapons are inadequate and their people are not as unified as those in the West. So peasants are permitted to join the military and Westernization is introduced. But these democratic principles are imposed from the top

The Films: Credits, Notes, and Synopses

down, by decree rather than popular demand, and without ethical principle. Regimentation and racism are internalized, and unity of thinking rigorously taught and enforced. The history of the twentieth century has consequently been one of aggression, culminating in the Tanaka blueprint for world conquest outlined in 1927. Spies come to America to collect information; industrialists at home exploit cheap labor to earn profits for a war machine; boys are molded into fanatical soldiers. Newsreel footage of Japan's victory in the Philippines depicts the barbarism of the conquering army. Now that victory has been won in Europe, the narrator concludes, it is time to concentrate on this foe, building on past victories in the Pacific to destroy Japan's power to wage war.

44   YOUR JOB IN GERMANY (1945)

Producer:	Army Pictorial Service, Signal Corps, U.S. War Department
Supervisor:	Frank Capra
Director:	Ted Geisel
Editing:	William Hornbeck, Elmo Williams
Musical Director:	Dimitri Tiomkin
Narrator:	John Beal
Running Time:	15 minutes

Notes

Your Job in Germany is frequently confused with Here Is Germany (see entry 42) in Capra filmographies. A further confusion emerges in the second edition of the U.S. government's National AudioVisual Center film catalogue, where Your Job in Germany is said to have been later released by Warner Brothers under the title Hitler Lives? But while Hitler Lives?--an Academy Award-winning documentary short in 1945-- included substantial footage from Your Job in Germany, it was aimed at domestic audiences. Produced by Warner Brothers, Hitler Lives? was written by Saul Elkin, supervised by Gordon Hollingshead, and narrated by Knox Manning. The distribution of Your Job in Germany was limited to American occupation troops. A prologue attached to the film suggests that it typically was shown immediately following the screening of footage depicting German atrocities.

Synopsis

Victory over Germany is declared, but victory, the narrator warns, does not ensure a lasting peace. Germany may appear to be a defeated and peaceful people, but occupation soldiers are advised to be suspicious, for they are up against the dark legacy of German history. Chapter one of that history is the story of Bismarck and the forging of a German empire in the 1860s and 1870s at the expense of Denmark, Austria, and France, followed by a period of deceptive tranquility. Chapter two unfolds under Kaiser Wilhelm, whose aggressive policies spark World War I. Upon defeating Germany, American soldiers naively think well of the German people and their culture, and blame

The Films: Credits, Notes, and Synopses

the war simply on the kaiser. This misperception sets up chapter three, the story of Hitler's Third Reich and World War II, a contest narrowly won by the Allies at an incalculable price in wealth and human life. In order to prevent chapter four, the occupation soldier must remember that the German lust for conquest is not dead, but has merely gone undercover. The Gestapo, storm troopers, and Nazi party officials have simply gone into hiding; and it must be kept in mind that even people who seem quite ordinary were only recently part of the Nazi network. Most dangerous of all is the German Youth who were raised on Nazi propaganda and still believe they were born to be masters. Therefore, no fraternization with any of the German people is allowed; on cannot clasp in friendship the hand that committed the horrifying atrocities of the past war. Someday the German people may be cured of their belief that they are a master race, but they must prove this beyond a shadow of a doubt before they can take their place among respectable nations. The vicious German cycle of war followed by a phony peace must be broken once and for all. This is the job of the occupation soldier in Germany.

45 TWO DOWN, ONE TO GO (1945)

Producer:	Army Pictorial Service, Signal Corps, U.S. War Department
Supervisor:	Frank Capra
Director:	Frank Capra
Script:	Anthony Veiller
Editor:	William Hornbeck
Musical Director:	Dimitri Tiomkin
Caricatures:	Arthur Sysk
Narrator:	Anthony Veiller
Color:	Technicolor
Distributor:	Office of War Information in cooperation with War Activities Committee of the Motion Picture Industry
Released:	10 May 1945
Running time:	9 minutes

Notes

This nine-minute Technicolor film was commissioned by Chief of Staff Gen. George C. Marshall to be shown to military and civilian audiences following victory in Europe. Originally it was to explain both the army's plan for redeploying forces in the Pacific and its point system for army discharge, but the latter topic appears to have been dropped from the finished film. It was completed in the summer of 1944, far in advance of V-E Day, and received its official title on 8 September. By the end of the year, 1,363 prints had been distributed to theaters, bases, and command posts around the world. On 10 May 1945, two days after the armistice, the film began to be shown to military units at home and abroad, and to civilian audiences in approximately eight-hundred first-run theaters. Within five days, 95 percent of all troops at home had seen it, and 97 percent of the troops overseas had

The Films: Credits, Notes, and Synopses

seen it within two weeks (see <u>The Signal Corps: The Outcome (Mid-1943 through 1945)</u>, edited by George Raynor Thompson and Dixie R. Harris [Washington, D.C.: United States Army, 1966], pp. 557-58).

Synopsis

The film opens with documentary footage of the liberation of Italy and Germany by the Allies. A Japanese flag emerges from the Pacific to dominate the globe. Caricatures of Hitler, Mussolini, and Hirohito fill the screen; the first two are marked out with an X, but Hirohito remains. Chief of Staff Gen. George C. Marshall briefly describes the success of the Allies in the African and European campaigns. Military strategy to first attack the Nazis is justified on the following grounds: (1) supply routes to Europe were shorter; (2) two years were needed to rebuild a Pacific fleet following Pearl Harbor; (3) Allied forces were already fighting in Europe, providing immediate support for our effort; (4) air bases were already established in England; (5) the Axis powers had Russia and England on the ropes. Pacific troops played a crucial role during this period, holding the Japanese at bay while the full force of American efforts was concentrated on Europe. A narrator briefly introduces us to the Japanese people. Authorities, we are told, are preparing to lose 10 million lives in the war with America, and the masses are fanatically dedicated to the Emperor's cause. Gen. Marshall returns to remind the viewer that peace will not be enjoyed until Japan is completely crushed.

46   IT'S A WONDERFUL LIFE (1946)

<u>La vie est merveilleuse</u> (France), <u>La vita è meravigliosa</u> (Italy), <u>Das Leben ist wundervoll</u> (Germany)

Production Company:	Liberty Films, Inc.[1]
Producer:	Frank Capra
Director:	Frank Capra
Screenplay:	Frances Goodrich, Albert Hackett, and Frank Capra, from the story "The Greatest Gift" by Philip Van Doren Stern; additional scenes by Jo Swerling[2]
Photography:	Joseph Walker, Joseph Biroc
Editor:	William Hornbeck
Art Director:	Jack Okey
Set Decorations:	Emile Kuri
Special Effects:	Russell A. Cully
Costumes:	Edward Stevenson
Makeup:	Gordon Bau
Musical Score and Direction:	Dimitri Tiomkin
Sound:	Richard Van Hessen, Clem Portman
Assistant Director:	Arthur S. Black
Cast:	James Stewart (George Bailey), Donna Reed (Mary Hatch), Lionel Barrymore (Henry C.

The Films: Credits, Notes, and Synopses

Potter), Henry Travers (Clarence Oddbody), Thomas Mitchell (Uncle Billy), Beulah Bondi (Mrs. Bailey), Samuel S. Hinds (Mr. Bailey), Todd Karns (Harry Bailey), Karolyn Grimes (Zuzu Bailey), Carol Coomes (Janie Bailey), Larry Simms (Pete Bailey), Jimmy Hawkins (Tommy Bailey), Lillian Randolph (Annie), Gloria Grahame (Violet Bick), Frank Faylen (Ernie), Ward Bond (Bert), H.B. Warner (Mr. Gower), Frank Albertson (Sam Wainwright), William Edmunds (Mr. Martini), Argentina Brunetti (Mrs. Martini), Sheldon Leonard (Nick), Frank Hagney (Potter's bodyguard), Mary Treen (Cousin Millie), Charles Williams (Cousin Eustace), Virginia Patton (Ruth Dakin), Sarah Edwards (Mrs. Hatch), Hal Landon (Marty Hatch), Bobbie Anderson (George as a boy), Jean Gale (Mary as a girl), Jeanine Anne Roose (Violet as a girl), Ronnie Ralph (Sam as a boy), Danny Mummert (Marty as a boy), Georgie Nokes (Harry as a boy), Ray Walker (Joe, luggage shop), Tom Fadden (tollhouse keeper), Charles Lane (Lester Reineman, rent collector), Almira Sessions (Potter's secretary), Carl "Alfalfa" Switzer (Freddie), Marian Carr (Mrs. Wainwright), Stanley Andrews (Mr. Welch), Charles Halton (Carter, bank examiner), Harry Holman (Partridge, high school principal), Edward Keane (Tom, of Bailey Building and Loan), Harry Cheshire (Dr. Campbell), Bobby Scott (Mickey), Ed Featherstone (bank teller), J. Farrell MacDonald (house owner), Garry Owen (bill poster), Ellen Corby (Mrs. Davis)

Filmed April-July 1946 at the RKO Studios and the following locations in California: Arcadia, Westwood Ice Rink, Cheviot Hills, Beverly Hills High School, and Mt. Lassen.

Distributor: RKO Radio Films
Copyright: 6 February 1947 by Liberty Films, Inc. (LP 833)
Released: 21 December 1946 (Globe Theatre, New York City)
Running time: 129 minutes

Notes

1. Liberty Films was incorporated by Frank Capra and Samuel Briskin on 10 April 1945. Several months later they went into partnership with William Wyler and George Stevens, and struck a deal with RKO

The Films: Credits, Notes, and Synopses

whereby that studio would advance the cost of using its facilities and handle the distribution of Liberty's films. Each of the three directors—Capra, Wyler, and Stevens—were scheduled to make five films in this fashion. But Capra took his next project, State of the Union, to M-G-M, and the four partners sold Liberty Films to Paramount in May 1947.

2. Capra claims in his autobiography that when he bought the rights to the story, screenplays based on it had already been written by Marc Connelly, Clifford Odets, and Dalton Trumbo, and that he preserved some of the Odets material in the first part of the film (The Name Above the Title, p. 376) Philip Van Doren Stern's "The Greatest Gift" is reprinted in The Other Side of the Clock, edited by Stern (New York: Van Nostrand Reinhold Co. 1969), pp. 182-92.

Capra received the 1946 Golden Globe award for his direction of It's a Wonderful Life. The film also was nominated for Academy Awards that year for best picture, best direction, best actor (James Stewart), best editing, and best sound recording. It lost in the first four categories to William Wyler's The Best Years of Our Lives. In 1977 It's a Wonderful Life was remade as a television movie, It Happened One Christmas, by Marlo Thomas.

Synopsis

On Christmas Eve in Bedford Falls, prayers are heard in several homes for George Bailey, a man about to take his own life. In heaven, Joseph relays a message to God. Clarence Oddbody, a second-class angel with the "I.Q. of a rabbit" but the "faith of a child" is appointed George's guardian. If successful on this mission, Clarence will earn his long-deferred wings. Before Clarence departs for earth, Joseph relates to him the significant events of George's life.

We see George as a boy, playing with friends on a half-frozen creek. When his younger brother, Harry, slips into the icy water, George rescues him; in doing so he loses his hearing in one ear. Several weeks later he returns to his part-time job at Gower's Drugstore. Violet Bick and Mary Hatch flirt with him over the counter; when Violet leaves, Mary whispers into his deaf ear that she will love him until the day she dies. Oblivious to her confession, George announces his own plan for an adventurous life in exotic locales, complete with harems. Mr. Gower, badly shaken by news of his son's death in the war overseas, accidentally fills a prescription with poison. Commanded to deliver the pills, George goes to his father at the Bailey Building and Loan for advice. But his father is engaged in a heated argument with Henry C. Potter, a crippled financier bent on destroying Bailey's community-minded bank. When Potter calls George's father a failure, the boy excitedly protests and is ushered out of the office. Back at the drugstore, George is cuffed on his bad ear by Gower for not delivering the pills. But when George explains the mistake, Gower breaks down and embraces the boy in gratitude.

The Films: Credits, Notes, and Synopses

We next see George as a young man, preparing for his first trip abroad. On his last night at home, he discusses his future with his father over dinner. Harry, fresh out of high school, will take over George's job at the Building and Loan while George attends college in the fall. Then when George graduates, Harry will go to college. Mr. Bailey hopes George will return to the Building and Loan, but worn down himself by his struggles with Potter, he appreciates his son's ambition to do something more with his life. Later that night at Harry's graduation dance, George is reintroduced to Mary Hatch, now nineteen, and steals her away from her dance partner. His diminutive rival retaliates by opening the gymnasium floor beneath the dancer's feet, and everyone ends up in the swimming pool below. Walking home afterward, George and Mary pass the old, deserted Granville house, which she finds romantic. George tosses a rock at a window for good luck, wishing for a life of world travel and great deeds as a civil engineer. Mary breaks a window as well, but is silent about her wish. Their courtship is interrupted by news from Uncle Billy that George's father has had a stroke. When Mr. Bailey dies, George gives up his trip abroad to straighten out business at home. Potter, now on the board of directors, tries to dissolve the bank; the board agrees to block him if George assumes his father's position as president. To save the bank, George stays in Bedford Falls while Harry goes off to college.

Four years later, George awaits Harry's return to the bank and his own freedom to travel. But Harry arrives home with a bride, whose father has offered him a promising position in the family company. That night Mrs. Bailey coaxes George to call on Mary Hatch. Instead he heads toward Main Street, where he meets Violet Bick. George's invitation to walk through the grass in bare feet, swim in the moonlight, and climb Mount Bedford to see the sunrise is scoffed at by Violet's friends. So George ends up at the Hatches, where Mary, forewarned by Mrs. Bailey, has set the stage for a romantic evening. George, bitter and testy, is a reluctant suitor. When an old friend, Sam Wainwright, calls from New York and offers George a "chance of a lifetime" in a new plastics company, he explodes in anger. He shakes Mary violently and then clings to her tightly.

George and Mary are wed. As they are about to leave for a honeymoon in New York and Bermuda, a bank run strikes the Building and Loan. Potter exploits the crisis by offering investors a chance to sell their shares at half-price. But George and Mary save the bank by dividing their honeymoon money among the various shareholders and convincing them not to panic. That night they honeymoon at the old Granville house, redecorated with travel posters by Mary, with help from their friends Bert, a cop, and Ernie, a cab driver.

George directs his energy toward developing Bailey Park, a tract of new homes sold below cost so that poor people can escape Potter's ghetto. But even as George and Mary proudly help the Martini family dedicate their new home, George's frustrations are rekindled by the appearance of affluent Sam Wainwright, passing through on his way to

The Films: Credits, Notes, and Synopses

Miami. Potter tempts George to sell out, promising him a high-salaried job and trips to New York and Paris. Almost succumbing, George catches himself and repudiates Potter harshly. He returns home to find that Mary is pregnant.

Years pass. Mary restores the Granville house while George works hard at the bank, fighting Potter day after day. The family grows. George, who is 4-F because of his ear, serves on the home front during the war, while Harry becomes a war hero.

Christmas Eve, 1945: George proudly spreads the word around town that Harry is receiving the Congressional Medal of Honor that day in Washington. While depositing funds at Potter's bank, Uncle Billy gleefully gives the old man a copy of the news story about Harry. But he accidentally passes on $8,000 to Potter as well. A bank examiner at the Building and Loan asks to see the records. Uncle Billy and George desperately search for the missing money, but cannot find it. George goes home that night fearing scandal and ruin. Preparations by Mary and the children for the evening's festivities only aggravate his frustration. Upon hearing that his daughter Zuzu has caught a cold on the way home from school, he berates her teacher over the phone for not dressing her properly. The incessant playing of a carol on the piano by daughter Janie sends him into a rage. Everyone freezes. He apologizes and departs into the wintry night. Mary advises the children to pray.

George goes to Potter for financial help. Relishing George's dilemma, the old man instead swears out a warrant for George's arrest for misappropriation of funds. At Martini's bar, George prays for help; just then he is recognized by the husband of the schoolteacher, who slugs George in the jaw. Helped to his feet by his friends, he wanders back out into the night. He ends up on a bridge and pauses at the railing, ready to jump.

Just then Clarence, appearing out of nowhere, leaps into the water. George instinctively dives in and saves him. Drying off in the tollhouse, Clarence announces he is George's guardian angel, but George is thoroughly skeptical. When George wishes aloud that he had never been born, Clarence grants him his wish and George takes a nightmarish tour of a transformed "Pottersville." Martini's is owned by bartender Nick, who doesn't recognize George. Nor does old man Gower, a rummy who has served twenty years in jail for poisoning a child. Main Street is a strip of honky-tonk clubs and flashing neon lights, with the Building and Loan a dime-a-dance hot spot. Violet, a prostitute under arrest, doesn't know George. Nor does Ernie, who drives him to the ghostly Granville house. At Ma Bailey's Boarding House, his mother won't let him in the front door. Uncle Billy, George learns, has lived in an insane asylum since he lost his business. Bailey Park is a cemetery where Harry is buried, having drowned as a boy in the ice pond. Mary is a spinster librarian, who becomes terrified when George tries to approach her. Surrounded by a hostile crowd, George tries to escape; Bert pulls a gun and fires after him.

The Films: Credits, Notes, and Synopses

On the verge of madness, George races back to the bridge and pleads to be returned alive to his wife and kids.

    Snow begins to fall. A friendly Bert stops to tell him everyone has been looking for him. George runs down the street of a restored Bedford Falls, past Potter's window, shouting "Merry Christmas." Back at home, he welcomes the bank examiner and sheriff warmly. He is reunited first with his children and then with Mary. A procession of family and friends enter the house; everyone has chipped in to help repay the debt, and Sam Wainwright, contacted by Gower, is wiring another $25,000. Having just arrived in Bedford Falls, Harry enters and offers a toast to George, "the richest man in town." As everyone sings "Auld Lang Syne," George thanks Clarence, who has vanished having earned his wings.

47   **STATE OF THE UNION (1948)**

    The World and His Wife (Great Britain), L'Enjeu (France), State dell'Unione (Italy)

Production Company:	Liberty Films, Inc.[1]
Producer	Frank Capra
Associate Producer:	Anthony Veiller
Director:	Frank Capra
Screenplay:	Anthony Veiller and Myles Connelly, from the play by Howard Lindsay and Russell Crouse[2]
Photography:	George J. Folsey
Editor:	William Hornbeck
Art Directors:	Cedric Gibbons, Urie McCleary
Set Decorators:	Emile Kuri, Edwin B. Willis
Costumes:	Irene
Makeup:	Jack Dawn
Hair Styles:	Sydney Guilaroff
Special Effects:	A. Arnold Gillespie
Musical Score:	Victor Young
Sound Engineer:	Douglas Shearer
Assistant Director:	Arthur Black, Jr.
Cast:	Spencer Tracy (Grant Matthews), Katharine Hepburn (Mary Mattthews), Van Johnson (Spike MacManus), Angela Lansbury (Kay Thorndyke), Lewis Stone (Sam Thorndyke), Howard Smith (Sam I. Parrish), Maidel Turner (Lulubelle Alexandar), Raymond Walburn (Judge Alexandar), Charles Dingle (Bill Hardy), Florence Auer (Grace Orval Draper), Pierre Watkin (Senator Lauterback), Margaret Hamilton (Norah), Irving Bacon (Buck Swenson), George Nokes (Grant Matthews, Jr.), Patti Brady (Joyce Matthews), Carl "Alfalfa" Switzer (bellboy), Tom Pedi (barber), Tom Fadden (waiter), Charles Lane (Blink Moran), Art

The Films: Credits, Notes, and Synopses

Baker (Leith, radio announcer), Arthur O'Connell (first reporter), Rhea Mitchell (Jenny), Marion Martin (blonde girl), Tom Johnson (wrestler), Stanley Andrews (senator), Dave Willock (pilot), Russell Meeker (politician), Frank L. Clarke (Joe Crandall), David Clarke (Rusty Miller), Dell Henderson (Broder), Edwin Cooper (Bradbury), Davison Clark (Crump), Frances Pierlot (Josephs), Brandon Beach (editor), Howard Mitchell and Boyd Davis (doctors), Maurice Cass (little man), Frank Austin (crackpot), Roger Moore (photographer), Sam Ash (editor), Mahlon Hamilton (Brooklynite), Eddie Phillips (television man), Eve Whitney (secretary), Franklyn Farnum

Filmed at Metro-Goldwyn-Mayer studios beginning September 29, 1947
Distributor: Metro-Goldwyn-Mayer
Copyright: 23 March 1948 by Liberty Films, Inc. (LP 1534)
Released: 22 April 1948 (Radio City Music Hall, New York City)[3]
Running time: 124 minutes

Notes

1. For the second and final film to be made under the banner of Liberty Films, Capra moved operations from RKO to M-G-M. Capra suggests in his autobiography that RKO backed away from State of the Union because of the size of the budget, and that M-G-M took on the project because Spencer Tracy, under contract to them, wanted to play the lead role (The Name Above the Title, p. 388). Although Anthony Veiller, Myles Connelly, and William Hornbeck were familiar colleagues for Capra, most of the craftsmen working on the film were from M-G-M.

2. The play by Howard Lindsay and Russell Crouse was produced by Leland Hayward and opened at the Hudson Theatre, New York City, on 14 November 1945. It was published in 1946 by Random House (New York, 226 pp.). Capra bought the rights to the play in December 1945 for $300,000 plus 50 percent of the gross receipts under a ten-year lease arrangement. (see A.H. Weiler, "By Way of Report," New York Times, 29 December 1945, sec. 2, p. 5).

3. MGM News reported on 30 January 1948 that State of the Union had been previewed in four cities to test the reaction of different kinds of audiences: a manufacturing center, a university town, a farming district, and a location where matinees attract "predominantly female audiences." Unfortunately, no specific towns were mentioned. State of the Union was also previewed at the Capital Theatre in Washington, D.C., for President Truman and assorted public officials prior to its release in New York.

The Films: Credits, Notes, and Synopses

Synopsis

Sam Thorndyke, a newspaper magnate suffering a painful terminal illness, bequeaths his operations to his daughter, Kay. His last request is that she use her power to wrest control of the Republican party away from the politicians who blocked his path to the White House. Loyal to her father, and ambitious herself, Kay accepts the mission. When she departs, Sam takes his life with a pistol.

At the Washington office of the Thorndyke Press, Kay plots strategy with Spike MacManus, her chief political reporter, and Jim Conover, an old political pro. Kay proposes organizing a campaign around a dark-horse candidate, Grant Matthews. An airplane manufacturer and self-made industrialist with a prolabor record, he has just made the cover of Time by speaking out passionately on current affairs. Jim is skeptical about working with an amateur, but Kay is convinced Grant will be easy to control once he is bitten by presidential fever.

Summoned to Conover's Washington home, a retreat for disenfranchised Republicans, Grant makes light of the idea of his candidacy. But when queried about his past speeches, he spontaneously launches into an attack on the political establishment and a spirited plea for national unity amid postwar divisiveness. Jim's private investigators report that rumors are circulating about possible affairs between Grant and Kay, and between Grant's wife, Mary, and a certain "major." So Jim suggests that Mary accompany Grant on a speaking tour while Kay stays out of sight. Agreeing to make the tour, Grant calls home and, after wishing his son happy birthday, invites Mary to come down to Washington.

As she packs to leave, Kay fans the flame of Grant's ambition, urging him to run for the presidency even at the risk of destroying their relationship. She then convinces Jim to commit himself to the campaign, promising him the party's chairmanship should they win and a permanent job should they lose. She leaves a pair of her glasses on Grant's night table before going. Mary arrives later that night and quickly learns from Jim the true purpose of the invitation. At first rejecting the scheme, she finally agrees to it, admitting to Jim that Grant would make a fine president if the idea does not go to his head. Grant returns from a walk to the White House; awed by the legends of its past occupants, he worries that he is not presidential timber. As Mary mends his coat, he admits that she has always served as his conscience. They prepare to spend the night together in the same room, but when Mary discovers Kay's glasses on the night table she makes Grant sleep on the floor.

Grant, Mary and Spike fly in Grant's plane to Seattle. Grant rejects Spike's speech, retaining the right to ad lib his remarks on the spot. One of Grant's pilots flies by in another plane and chal-

The Films: Credits, Notes, and Synopses

lenges his boss to a daredevil contest. Grant enthusiastically takes over the controls and matches the young pilot stunt for stunt.

Kay orders the editors of her various papers around the country to help deadlock the Republican convention by creating dissension in the press among the various candidates. When they refuse to manipulate the news in this fashion, she fires them. Meanwhile, Grant has delivered a speech in Wichita, which, while pleasing the workers, infuriates labor bosses and their political allies. Jim rushes off to Grant's next stop, Detroit.

Grant and Mary are exhilarated by the popular support they have received following the Wichita speech. Jim argues that Grant has alienated the party bosses, but Grant refuses to budge. That night, addressing an industrial council with a national radio hook-up, he intends to attack the greed of big business, to oppose tax reduction, and to advocate world government based on equal measures of brotherhood and practical responsibility. In between bites of dinner, he meets with various interests groups, bridging a rift between the AFL and the CIO. Mary tries to convince Jim that compromise would destroy her husband. But following a secret meeting with Kay, who has snuck into the hotel suite without Mary knowing, Grant indeed compromises and delivers an innocuous speech over the airwaves that night.

Flying to the next spot on the tour, Grant accepts Spike's revision of a speech despite Mary's protest. Challenged to another aerial contest, Grant is too busy to respond.

Grant agrees to meet with backroom politicos. A senator promises the farm vote in exchange for veto power over the appointment of the secretary of agriculture. A union leader will deliver his constituency for similar power over the secretary of labor. An expert in ethnic voting patterns pushes for a campaign geared to arousing ethnic hatreds. All gather to plot strategy in a dark room. The union leader worries about a rumor linking Grant to Kay, but Jim assures everyone that there will be no problem on this score.

Spike calls on Mary, who has returned to her sunny Long Island home. Mary tries to find out why Grant changed his mind in Detroit, but Spike offers no answers. He has come to ask Mary to invite Kay to a scheduled television broadcast from their home; a photograph of Kay as a "friend of the family," he argues, will silence the gossip. Mary protests; the day of the broadcast is her anniversary. Spike apologizes for asking, kisses her on the forehead, and starts to leave. Mary calls him back.

Grant's patrons assemble at the house on the night of the broadcast. When Kay arrives, Mary manages to keep her cool. A last-minute power play by the union leader threatens the coalition, but Kay fends off his possible defection by promising to smash the man in her papers. Mary learns from a loudmouthed friend who had visited them in Detroit about Kay's visit to the hotel suite on the night of Grant's

The Films: Credits, Notes, and Synopses

compromising speech. Mary quickly gets drunk, giddily mocks the politicians present, and then breaks down in tears. Kay decides to take Mary's place in the family broadcast, but Spike convinces Mary not to give up her role as "first lady." So Mary goes on the air, feigning support for Grant's candidacy and vouching for his integrity. Unnerved by her willingness to lie for him, Grant interrupts Mary. Labeling himself a failure as a leader and as a husband and father, he withdraws his candidacy and is immediately surrounded by family and newly won friends. He goes on to announce that he will stay involved in politics, attacking the corruption of professionals and the laziness of the electorate wherever he finds it. Spike cheers him on. Firing Spike, Kay leaves with Jim in search of another candidate.

48 RIDING HIGH (1950)

Jour de chance (France), La gioia della vita (Italy), Lach und wein mit mir (Germany)

Production Company:	Paramount Pictures Corporation
Producer:	Frank Capra
Director:	Frank Capra
Screenplay:	Robert Riskin, from the story by Mark Hellinger (first filmed as Broadway Bill in 1934); additional dialogue by Melville Shavelson and Jack Rose
Photography:	George Barnes, Ernest Laszlo
Editor:	William Hornbeck
Art Directors:	Hans Dreier, Walter Tyler
Set Decorators:	Emile Kuri, Sam Comer
Costumes:	Edith Head
Makeup:	Wally Westmore
Process Photography:	Farciot Edouart
Musical Director:	Victor Young
Music Associate:	Troy Sanders
Vocal Arrangements:	Joseph J. Lilley
Sound Recording:	John Cope, Hugo Grenzbach (Western Electric Recording)
Assistant Director:	Arthur S. Black
Songs:	"Sure Thing," "Somewhere on Anywhere Road," "Sunshine Cake," and "The Horse Told Me" by Johnny Burke and James Van Heusen; "Camptown Races" by Stephen Foster; and "The Whiffenpoof Song" by Meade Minnigerode, George S. Pomeroy, and Tod Galloway.
Cast:	Bing Crosby (Dan Brooks), Coleen Gray (Alice Higgins), Charles Bickford (J.L. Higgins), Frances Gifford (Margaret Higgins), William Demarest (Happy McGuire), Raymond Walburn (Professor Pettigrew), James Gleason (racing secretary), Ward Bond (Lee), Clarence Muse (Whitey), Percy

The Films: Credits, Notes, and Synopses

Kilbride (Pop Jones), Harry Davenport (Johnson, the butler), Margaret Hamilton (Edna), Paul Harvey (Whitehall), Douglass Dumbrille (Eddie Morgan), Gene Lockhart (J.P. Chase), Marjorie Hoshelle (Mrs. Early), Rand Brooks (Henry Early), Willard Waterman (Arthur Winslow), Marjorie Lord (Mrs. Winslow), Irving Bacon (hamburger man), Joe Frisco (himself), Frankie Darro (Ted Williams, Dan's jockey), Charles Lane (Erickson), Dub Taylor (Joe), Oliver Hardy (horse player), Max Baer (Bertie), Fritz Feld (couturier), Byron Foulger (maitre d'), Percy Helton (pawnbroker), Dorothy Newmann (Dan's secretary), Roger Davis (butler), Victor Romito (barber), Margaret Field (maid), Richard Kipling (jailer), Edgar Dearing and Jim Nolan (deputies), Ann Doran (nurse), Garry Owen (Harry), Tom Fadden (Whitehall's trainer), Stanley Andrews (veterinarian), Ish Kabibble and Candy Candido (musicians), Snug Pollard, Donald Kerr, Wilbur Mack, Gerry Ganzer, Ed Randolph, Charles Sullivan, Laura Elliot, Bob Evans

Filmed at Paramount Studios, and on location at the Tanforan Racetrack near San Francisco and Busch Gardens, Pasadena, in the spring of 1949

Distributor: Paramount Pictures Corporation
Copyright: 9 April 1950 by Paramount Pictures Corporation (LP 22)
Released: 8 April 1950 (Paramount-Hollywood and Paramount-Downtown theaters, Los Angeles)[1]
Running time: 112 minutes

Notes

1. Riding High was previewed at the Paramount Theatre, New York City, on 15 December 1949. A "premiere" was held at the Park Theatre, Front Royal, Virginia, on 1 April 1950 in conjunction with "Bing Crosby Day" in that city.

For this remake of Broadway Bill (1934), Capra brought back several members of the original cast: Clarence Muse, Raymond Walburn, Margaret Hamilton, Douglass Dumbrille, Frankie Darro, Ward Bond, Charles [Levison] Lane, Irving Bacon, and Paul Harvey. Capra's Riding High bears no relation to an earlier Paramount musical by the same title, directed by George Marshall in 1943 and starring Dorothy Lamour and Dick Powell.

The Films: Credits, Notes, and Synopses

Synopsis

For a synopsis of Broadway Bill, the film upon which Riding High is based, see entry 25. The only significant change in the screenplay involves the status of Dan and Margaret's relationship when the film begins. In Broadway Bill they are married, and Dan is already serving as president of the Higgins Paper Box Company. In Riding High they are only engaged, as Margaret awaits a divorce from a previous marriage, and Dan's appointment to the presidency of the Paper Box Company is provisional.

Six musical numbers are also added to the story. "Sure Thing" is sung by Dan to Margaret prior to the first dinner meeting. "Somewhere on Anywhere Road" is sung by Dan, with Whitey accompanying on guitar, as the two drive away from the Higgins mansion after Dan has refused to give up horses for his business career. (This replaces "Headed for the Last Round-Up" in Broadway Bill.) "The Whiffenpoof Song" is sung by Dan and Colonel Pettigrew at the fancy restaurant; when the other customers join in, the commotion permits Dan and his friends to escape without paying their bill. "Sunshine Cake" is sung by Dan, Whitey, and Alice as they prepare dinner in their domesticated barn, just prior to the storm. (This replaces "Going to Heaven" and "The Split Pea Soup and the Succotash" in Broadway Bill.) "The Horse Told Me" is sung by Dan and the crowd at the party on the eve of the big race. "Sure Thing" briefly is reprised by Dan as he and Alice walk back from the party to the barn, and "Camptown Races" is sung by Dan, Whitey, and Alice as they take Broadway Bill from the barn to the track on the day of the race. (These substitute for the reprises of Dan's "Split Pea Soup" song in Broadway Bill.) "Somewhere on Anywhere Road" is briefly heard again at the end of the film as J.L. decides to join Dan, Whitey, and Alice.

49 HERE COMES THE GROOM (1951)

Si l'on mariait Papa (France), E' arrivato lo sposo (Italy), Hochzeitsparade (Germany)

Production Company:	Paramount Pictures Corporation
Producer:	Frank Capra
Associate Producer:	Irving Asher
Director:	Frank Capra
Screenplay:	Virginia Van Upp, Liam O'Brien, and Myles Connolly, from a story by Liam O'Brien and Robert Riskin
Photography:	George Barnes
Editor:	Ellsworth Hoagland
Art Directors:	Hal Pereire, Earl Hedrick
Set Director:	Emile Kuri
Costumes:	Edith Head
Makeup Supervisor:	Wally Westmore
Process Photography:	Farciot Edouart
Musical Director	Joseph J. Lilley

The Films: Credits, Notes, and Synopses

Dance Direction:	Charles O'Curran
Special Orchestral Arrangements:	Van Cleave
Sound:	Harry Mills, John Cope (Western Electric Recording)
Assistant Director:	Arthur S. Black
Songs:	"In the Cool, Cool, Cool of the Evening" by Johnny Mercer and Hoagy Carmichael; "Misto Christofo Columbo," "Your Own Little House," and "Bonne Nuit" by Ray Evans and Jay Livingston; "Caro nome" from <u>Rigoletto</u> by Verdi
Cast:	Bing Crosby (Pete Garvey), Jane Wyman (Emmadel Jones), Franchot Tone (Wilbur Stanley), Alexis Smith (Winifred Stanley), James Barton (Pa Jones), Connie Gilchrist (Ma Jones), Robert Keith (George Degnan), Jacques Gencel (Bobby), Beverly Washburn (Suzi), Walter Catlett (Mr. McGonigle), Ellen Corby (Mrs. McGonigle), H.B. Warner (Uncle Elihu), Ian Wolfe (Uncle Adam), Maidel Turner (Aunt Abby), Nicholas Joy (Uncle Prentiss), Anna Maria Alberghetti (Therese), Alan Reed (Walter Godfrey), Minna Gombell (Mrs. Godfrey), Irving Bacon (Baines), Chris Appel (Marcel), Charles Halton (Cusick), Charles Lane (FBI agent Burchard), Adeline de Walt Reynolds (Aunt Amy), Howard Freeman (governor), Charles Evans (mayor), Ted Thorpe (Paul Pippitt), Art Baker (radio announcer), Laura Elliot (maid), Rev. Neal Dodd (priest), Odette Myrtil (Grey Lady), Michele Lange (French Matron), Donald Kerr (neighbor), Charles Sullivan and Ed Randolph (photographers), Howard Joslin (newsreel cameraman), Walter McGrail (newsreel director), Carl "Alfalfa" Switzer (messenger), James Burke (policeman), J. Farrell MacDonald (man), Chester Conklin, James Finlayson, and Bess Flowers (friends at wedding), Dorothy Lamour, Louis Armstrong, Phil Harris, Cass Daley, and Frank Fontaine (themselves, on plane), Almira Sessions, Frank Hagney, Julia Faye, Franklyn Farnum, and Don Dunning (passengers on plane)
Filmed at Paramount Studios in the winter of 1950-51	
Distributor:	Paramount Pictures Corporation
Copyright:	2 September 1951, by Paramount Pictures Corporation (LP 1147)

The Films: Credits, Notes, and Synopses

Released: 6 September 1951 (Paramount-Hollywood and Paramount-Downtown theatres, Los Angeles)[1]
Running time: 113 minutes

Notes

1. Here Comes the Groom was previewed at a trade show at the Paramount Theatre in Hollywood on 29 June 1951 and in Elko, Nevada, on 30 July 1951. The film did not open in New York until 20 September 1951.

"In the Cool, Cool, Cool of the Evening" received the Academy Award for best song in 1951. Liam O'Brien and Robert Riskin also received Academy Award nominations for best writing-motion picture story. Here Comes the Groom bears no relation to the 1934 Paramount film of the same title, directed by Edward Sedgwick and starring Jack Haley.

Synopsis

Peter Garvey, Paris correspondent for a Boston newspaper, is summoned home by his editor, George Degnan. Having become involved with helping UNESCO orphans, Peter is reluctant to leave Paris, but Degnan entices him away by offering him the highly prized Far East position. A wealthy American, Mrs. Godfrey, arrives at the orphanage to adopt Bobby, a French boy of whom Peter has grown especially fond. Bobby, however, considers Peter to be his "family," and runs off and hides. Peter introduces another orphan, a blind teenage girl, to Mrs. Godfrey and her husband. The girl sings "Caro nome" so beautifully that Mr. Godfrey, a musician, is moved to adopt her immediately. Peter celebrates by singing "Your Own Little House" with the rest of the children. Afterwards he finds Bobby hiding in his closet with the boy's young friend, Suzi. Peter tries to explain to them why he must leave and coaxes the children to bid him farewell by singing. But the kids break down in the middle of "In the Cool, Cool, Cool of the Evening" and run from the room.

Peter receives a record-disk "letter" from his long-time fiancée, Emmadel Jones, who accuses him of deliberately prolonging their engagement. Because her desire for a family is still unfulfilled, she wants to end their relationship. Peter decides to marry Emmadel as soon as he returns to Boston and to bring along Bobby as a start on their family. He writes her about his return, but keeps the news about their son a surprise.

Emmadel runs into Degnan at the airport in Boston, where both await Peter's arrival. Perturbed to learn from Emmadel that his foreign correspondent plans to settle down, Degnan warns her that Peter is untrustworthy. She disagrees, but when Peter does not appear on his scheduled flight, Degnan's appraisal seems confirmed. Emmadel is humiliated and angered.

The Films: Credits, Notes, and Synopses

Peter's journey, however, has been delayed by the paperwork for Bobby's emigration. And when Bobby insists that Suzi come too, Peter has to set out all over again to clear passage for the second youngster. At last all three fly to America, with Peter leading the passengers in a rousing version of "Misto Christofo Columbo." Upon landing, Peter learns from immigration officials that he has only five days to marry or the kids will be returned to France.

Peter arrives at Emmadel's house as a lavish shower for her is ending. But Peter is not the bridegroom-to-be; Emmadel is marrying her boss, Wilbur Stanley, a millionaire scion of a leading Boston family. Emmadel is much taken with Bobby and Suzi, but has no intention of retreating from her storybook marriage. Her father, an ex-fisherman turned down-to-earth drunk, fears he will become imprisoned in the Stanley social elite and welcomes Peter's disruptive presence. But Emmadel's mother, solidly behind the marriage, wants Peter to leave.

Peter plots strategy. Emmadel agrees to help him find a place to stay with the children and takes him to the Stanley office building that night to check the real estate files. By a ruse, he gets her to lease him a house that is already rented and then coaxes her to bid him farewell by singing. They perform a lively duet of "In the Cool, Cool, Cool of the Evening" before she departs in her limousine.

With his lease in hand, Peter engineers a disturbance at the site of the already occupied property. As he roundly condemns the deceitful practices of Stanley as a corporate landlord, Wilbur arrives on the scene. Wilbur is younger and more handsome than Peter expected, but Peter offers a challenge: Wilbur should let him stay at the gatehouse on the Stanley estate until the day of the wedding so that Emmadel has the opportunity to make a genuine choice between the two suitors. Certain of victory, Wilbur accepts.

As the wedding date nears, relatives move into the Stanley estate. Emmadel's parents are tucked away out of sight in special quarters, while their daughter is presented to Wilbur's aunts and uncles, and to a distant cousin, Winifred, who is prim, sullen, and in love with Wilbur herself. A chorus of "In the Cool, Cool, Cool of the Evening," broadcast by Peter over the intercom, interrupts the stuffy proceedings. Emmadel hurries to the gatehouse, where Peter tries to convince her that the children need her as mother. She refuses to back down, but becomes jealous when he notes the attractions of cousin Winifred.

Soaked by a lawn sprinkler turned on by the kids, Winifred seeks shelter in the gatehouse. She and Peter recognize their mutual interest in blocking the wedding and decide to make a pact. Peter proposes that Wilbur is more likely to be enticed by sexual provocation than blueblood propriety, and teaches Winifred, with Degman's assistance, the right way to walk and how to wrestle. Meanwhile Emmadel urges

The Films: Credits, Notes, and Synopses

Wilbur to marry her at once, but he rejects the idea as unbefitting a Stanley.

A sexily dressed Winifred usurps Emmadel's role at the wedding rehearsal, arguing that it is bad form for the bride to participate herself. When it becomes clear, however, that Winifred is playing the scene at the altar for keeps, Emmadel intervenes. A wrestling match ensues with Emmadel the victor. Wilbur, startled, leads her away.

That night Wilbur takes the kids out for an evening of fun. Returning them to the gatehouse, he informs Peter that he plans to adopt the kids when Peter loses control of them tomorrow, their fifth day in America. Peter is discouraged, but hides his worries as he sings "Bonne Nuit" to the children.

The media are out in full force the next day to cover the Cinderella wedding, the social event of the decade. Trying one last trick, Peter gets a fellow reporter to pretend he is an FBI agent arresting Peter for kidnapping the children. A commotion results just as the nuptial vows are about to be spoken. Wilbur publicly announces his intention to adopt the children, but Bobby and Suzi refuse to go with him. Seeing this, Emmadel yields to Peter at last. With Winifred in the wings as an attractive alternative bride, Wilbur gallantly steps aside, and Peter and Emmadel are married. They drive off singing "In the Cool, Cool, Cool of the Evening" with Bobby, Suzi, and Emmadel's parents.

SCIENCE DOCUMENTARIES (1956-58)

The original idea for the Bell System Science Series came from Cleo F. Craig, president of American Telephone and Telegraph, but Capra became involved with the project at an early stage as a consultant and seems to have enjoyed relative freedom in making the films. Working out of a rented studio at Sunset Boulevard and Doheny Drive in Los Angeles between 1952 and 1956, he produced and wrote or (cowrote) all the episodes in the series, and directed all but one. Thirteen episodes were originally planned, but only four were made, each at a cost of approximately $400,000, reportedly the highest budget for a television program up to that time. Capra did not draw a salary, but instead acquired foreign theatrical distribution rights to the series. Copyright on the four films was filed by N.W. Ayer & Son, Inc., the advertising agency assigned to the project by AT&T when the company first decided to become involved in television programming. The first two films were broadcast on CBS-TV, the last two on NBC-TV. After the television showing, 16mm prints of the documentaries became available to schools through local offices of the Bell Telephone Company. In 1958, Capra reportedly reedited 35mm versions of the films for theater circuits, eliminating commercial breaks and adding footage that had been shot but previously not used, but I have found no record of their theatrical exhibition in this country. (In addition to Capra's discussion of this series in The Name Above the

The Films: Credits, Notes, and Synopses

Title, pp. 440-45, see "Capra to Reign at AT&T Vidpix; $2,600,000 cost," Variety, 22 October 1952, and Thomas M. Pryor, "Hollywood Aims," New York Times, 18 May 1958, sec. 2, p. 5.)

Because I have not seen these documentaries since the early 1960s, I have based my synopses on material submitted to the Library of Congress by N.W. Ayer & Son, Inc., for the purpose of securing copyright.

50   OUR MR. SUN (1956)

Bell System Science Series, No. 1

Production Company:	Frank Capra Productions, for N.W. Ayer & Son, Inc.
Producer:	Frank Capra
Assistant Producer:	Donald Jones
Director:	Frank Capra
Script:	Frank Capra
Photography:	Harold Wellman (color)
Animation:	United Productions of America
Editor:	Frank P. Keller
Sets:	Wiard Ihnen
Assistant Director:	Arthur S. Black
Research:	Jeanne Curtis
Advisers:	Drs. Farrington Daniles, Armin Deutsch, Donald Menzel, Walter Orr Roberts, and Otto Struve
Cast:	Frank Baxter (Dr. Research), Eddie Albert (Mr. Fiction Writer); the voices of Lionel Barrymore, Marvin Miller, and Sterling Holloway
Distributor:	Bell Telephone
Copyright:	7 November 1956 by N.W. Ayer & Son, Inc. (LP 9113)
Television premiere:	19 November 1956 (CBS-TV)
Running Time:	59 minutes

Synopsis

Dr. Research and Mr. Fiction Writer discuss the difficulties they are having organizing a vast collection of facts about the sun for presentation on a television show. Mr. Fiction Writer comes up with a solution: out of his imagination he creates a magic screen upon which appear two cartoon characters--Mr. Sun and his companion, Father Time. Much to Mr. Sun's enjoyment, Father Time describes the various religions that have deified the sun. When Dr. Research introduces some facts about the sun, Mr. Sun is disenchanted, but is somewhat mollified when he hears of the efforts scientists have made to understand him. Special instruments, for example, take photographs of him daily, and radio telescopes monitor solar disturbances on his surface. With the aid of a third cartoon figure, Thermo the Magician, Dr. Research

The Films: Credits, Notes, and Synopses

explains the carbon cycle theory of solar energy generation, and a newer proton-proton reaction theory. Then with the aid of a fourth figure, Chloro Phyll, the process of photosynthesis is delineated, although Chloro Phyll hides some of the details behind a "top secret" label. Knowledge of photosynthesis, Dr. Research explains, may help solve the problem of growing food in overpopulated parts of the earth. Finally, Dr. Research tells of how all fuel sources can be traced to the action of sunlight and illustrates various experiments aimed at drawing on the "Sun Power Bank." Speculations by Dr. Research and Mr. Fiction Writer concerning the future of the planet if its fuels are exhausted, and of the limits to atomic energy, convince Mr. Sun that man has proper respect for the sun's importance. Dr. Research expresses concern that the machine age may be running down, but Father Time urges man to use his god-given powers of the mind to seek answers not yet found. Dr. Research ends by thanking Mr. Sun for the glories of nature that he has helped to create.

51   HEMO THE MAGNIFICENT (1957)

Bell System Science Series, No. 2

Production Company:	Frank Capra Productions, for N.W. Ayer & Son, Inc.
Producer:	Frank Capra
Associate Producer:	Joseph Sistrom
Director:	Frank Capra
Script:	Frank Capra
Photography:	Harold Wellman (color)
Animation:	Shamus Culhane Productions
Editor:	Frank P. Keller
Music Supervision:	Raoul Kraushaar
Sound Effects:	Archie Dattelbaum
Assistant Director:	Arthur S. Black
Executive Coordinator:	Donald Jones
Research:	Nancy Pitt
Adviser:	Dr. Maurice B. Virscher
Cast:	Frank Baxter (Dr. Research), Richard Carlson (Mr. Fiction Writer), the voice of Sterling Holloway
Distributor:	Bell Telephone
Copyright:	26 February 1957 by N.W. Ayer & Son, Inc. (LP 9755)
Television premier:	20 March 1957 (CBS-TV)
Running time:	59 minutes

Synopsis

A magic screen with cartoon characters again assists Dr. Research and Mr. Fiction Writer in explaining an area of scientific knowledge, in this case the circulation of blood through the body. Hemo, the animated personification of blood, is the principal character, accompanied by six animal friends: a turtle, alligator, deer, rabbit, squirrel, and bird. The story opens with an account of ancient man's conception of blood as something magical. Modern knowledge, we learn did not begin until 1628 when English scientist William Harvey discovered the circulation of blood through arteries and veins. An animated sequence depicts the operation of the heart, lungs, kidneys, and other organs in this circulation process. The function of the arteries, capillaries, and veins is also detailed.

A theory of the evolution of the composition of blood is presented with the aid of the cartoon animals. In primordial times, all animal life consisted of one-cell organisms, which bathed in and were nourished by warm salt water. As cells aggregated into multicelled animals, they developed simple circulation systems to bring saline fluid to those cells no longer in contact with the sea. Land animals developed their own body fluid to replace the sea water, and each of the millions of cells in the human body is nourished through the passage of blood through capillaries. Motion pictures depict this action under great magnification in a microscope. Extra blood, we learn, is sent to organs involved in the processes of eating, moving, and thinking; muscles have a higher priority than digestive organs, and the brain has the highest priority of all. Knockout and shock result from disruptions in the circulatory control system; with shock a blood transfusion is frequently necessary, but with a knockout the situation is only temporary and readjustments are quickly made. The film closes with hope that some day science will discover the causes of anemia, hardening of the arteries, and other ailments of the circulatory system.

52 THE STRANGE CASE OF THE COSMIC RAYS (1957)

Bell System Science Series, No. 3

Production Company:	Frank Capra Productions, for N.W. Ayer & Son, Inc.
Producer:	Frank Capra
Associate Producer:	Joseph Sistrom
Director:	Frank Capra
Script:	Frank Capra, Jonathan Latimer
Photographer:	Harold Wellman, Ellis Carter (color)
Special Photography:	Edison Hoge
Animation:	Shamus Culhane Productions
Editors:	Frank P. Keller, Raymond Snyder
Music Supervision:	Raoul Kraushaar
Assistant Director:	Arthur S. Black
Research:	Nancy Pitt
Cast:	Frank Baxter (Dr. Research), Richard Carlson (Mr. Fiction Writer), Bill and Cora Baird's marionettes (Edgar Allan Poe, Charles Dickens, Fyodor Dostoyevski)
Distributor:	Bell Telephone
Copyright:	10 October 1957 by N.W. Ayer & Son, Inc. (LP 10426)

The Films: Credits, Notes, and Synopses

Television premiere: 25 October 1957 (NBC-TV)
Running time: 59 minutes

Synopsis

    An award for the best detective story of the twentieth century is under consideration by a panel of marionettes representing Edgar Allan Poe, Charles Dickens, and Fyodor Dostoyevski, past masters of the art. Dr. Research submits the story of the attempt of scientists to investigate the baffling phenomenon of cosmic rays. The story begins with the search for an unknown form of radiation that appears to steal, like a phantom bandit from the Wild West, the electric charge on an electroscope. After many scientific experiments, American Robert A. Millikan confirms the hypothesis of Austrian V.F. Hess that radiation comes from outer space. By checking the effect of cosmic radiation at different spots around the earth, scientists prove that the rays do not come from a single source, such as the sun, a planet, or any single star. German scientists are able to determine that the radiation consists of particles rather than waves. These particles, it is learned, are of two kinds: in the earth's lower atmosphere are <u>secondary</u> particles from air atoms that have been split by the impact of <u>primary</u> particles as they zip from outer space into our atmosphere. By observing the paths of the secondary particles as they move through a cloud chamber, scientists discover that these particles are a mixture of electrons, protons, and neutrons, and they travel fast enough to circle the earth seven times a second. Through measurement and deduction, they also conclude that primary particles are electrically charged protons.

    Further research into cosmic rays, however, reveal particles of matter beyond the previously identified forms of electrons, protons, and neutrons: these include positrons, mu mesons, pi mesons, and many others. Balloon and rocket development after World War II, moreover, has enabled scientists to discover that some primary particles are atoms, stripped of their electrons, which crash into the earth's atmosphere with an effect five million times that of particles from an atom bomb. These, scientists speculate, may be thrown off stars by surface explosions and are bounced back and forth between magnetic fields at tremendous speeds. Scientists are still studying the possible effects of cosmic rays on life on earth. This far from finished detective story is awarded first prize by the panel of judges.

53   **THE UNCHAINED GODDESS (1958)**

    Bell Systems Science Series, No. 4

Production Company:	Frank Capra Productions, for N.W. Ayer & Son, Inc.
Producer:	Frank Capra
Associate Producer:	Joseph Sistrom
Director:	Richard Carlson
Script:	Frank Capra, Jonathan Latimer

The Films: Credits, Notes, and Synopses

Photography:	Harold Wellman (color)
Animation:	Shamus Culhane Productions
Editor:	Frank P. Keller
Music Supervision:	Raoul Kraushaar
Music Editor:	Albert Shaff
Assistant Director:	Stanley Goldsmith
Research:	Nancy Pitt
Advisers:	Drs. Bernhardt Haurwitz and Morris Neiburger
Cast:	Frank Baxter (Dr. Research), Richard Carlson (Mr. Fiction Writer)
Distributor:	Bell Telephone
Copyright:	27 January 1958 by N.W. Ayer & Son, Inc. (LP 11331)
Television premiere:	12 February 1958 (NBC-TV)
Running time:	59 minutes

Synopsis

Dr. Research and Mr. Fiction Writer are again assisted on their magic screen by several cartoon characters: Meteora, goddess of weather; Boreas, god of wind; Cirrus, god of clouds; Thor, god of thunder; and the three Marutas, the Vedic gods of snow, rain, and hail. Dr. Research opens the discussion of the phenomenon of weather with an explanation of what causes wind. As air is heated it rises and cooler air moves in to take its place; this cooler air in turn becomes heated and rises, creating an ongoing circulation. Three loops between the equator and each pole, deflected by the revolution of the earth, constitute the basic circulation pattern of the planet. Winds are also affected by local conditions, such as topographic features and areas of high or low barometric pressure.

Next, the existence of clouds is explained. When the air above the ground cools to the point that its water vapor condenses, water molecules attach themselves to invisible particles of dust, forming cloud droplets. Precipitation is analyzed as an extension of this principle. Fog is cloud cover on the ground, and haze the reduction of visible light by invisible fog particles in the air. When the temperature of the cloud is well below freezing, water vapor crystallizes on the dust particles, which fall of their own weight, collecting other cloud particles to form snowflakes. If the temperature below is above freezing, the snowflakes melt into raindrops. Hail is formed when raindrops are sent back up into clouds by up-drafts, picking up successive coats of moisture which also freeze. Sleet is rain that passes through freezing air before it reaches the ground. Next, lightening is explained as a celestial spark-gap in which reservoirs of positive and negative electricity in clouds become overcharged by turbulence, and electricity leaps between these poles. The sudden expansion of heated air caused by the lightening generates shock waves which are audible as thunder.

Finally, Dr. Research turns to the topic of weather forecasting. Weather maps are drawn from vast data accumulated from local sources.

The Films: Credits, Notes, and Synopses

In an area of high pressure, weather is likely to be fair because air descends, thus becoming warmer and drier. In a low pressure area, the weather is likely to be cloudy and rainy because air masses ascend, where they become cooler. Moreover, wherever two air masses meet, there is usually bad weather. Tornadoes form when cool dry air moves over warm moist air, with a band of strong wind high above the ground. Hurricanes form close to the equator as a result of a combination of weather factors that set up circular air motions of great force. Army and navy fliers track these hurricanes, and long-range weather predictions are now being made by the National Weather Analysis Center. Moreover, the jet stream, a huge river of air that flows up to three-hundred miles per hour at an altitude of thirty-thousand feet, is being studied to determine its effect on weather below.

54   **A HOLE IN THE HEAD (1959)**

Un trou dans la tête (France), Un uomo da vendere (Italy), Ein loch im kopf (Germany)

Production Company: SinCap Productions[1]
Producer: Frank Capra
Director: Frank Capra
Screenplay: Arnold Schulman, from his play[2]
Photography: William H. Daniels (Panavision, Deluxe Color)
Editor: William Hornbeck
Art Director: Eddie Imazu
Set Decoration: Fred MacLean
Costumes: Edith Head
Makeup: Bernard Ponedel
Hair Stylist: Helene Parrish
Music: Nelson Riddle
Orchestrations: Arthur Morton
Songs: "All My Tomorrows"[3] and "High Hopes" by Sammy Cahn and James Van Heusen
Sound: Fred Lau
Production Manager: Joe Cooke
Assistant Directors: Arthur S. Black, Jr., Jack R. Berne
Cast: Frank Sinatra (Tony Manetta), Edward G. Robinson (Mario Manetta), Eddie Hodges (Ally Manetta), Thelma Ritter (Sophie Manetta), Eleanor Parker (Eloise Rogers), Carolyn Jones (Shirl), Keenan Wynn (Jerry Marks), Dub Taylor (Fred), Joi Lansing (Dorine), George De Witt (Mendy), Jimmy Komack (Julius Manetta), Connie Sawyer (Miss Wexler), B.S. Pully (gangster), Joyce Nizzari (Alice), Pupi Campo (master of ceremonies), Benny Rubin (Abe Diamond), Ruby Dandrige (Sally), Robert B. Williams (Cabby), Emory Parnell (sheriff), Billy Walker (Andy)

Filmed in December 1958 and January 1959 at the Samuel Goldwyn Studio

The Films: Credits, Notes, and Synopses

and on location at Miami Beach, Florida, and at Hollywood Beach, Oxnard, California

Distributor: United Artists
Copyright: 17 June 1959 by SinCap Productions (LP 13839)
Released: 17 June 1959 (Fox Beverly Theatre, Los Angeles)[4]
Running time: 120 minutes

Notes

1. SinCap Productions was a company formed by Capra and Frank Sinatra for the purpose of making A Hole in the Head. Sinatra owned two-thirds, Capra one-third; they each had equal voting rights, with Abe Lastfogel of the William Morris Agency deciding disputes.

2. A one-act version of Schulman's play entitled My Fiddle's Got Three Strings played at the Westport (Connecticut) Theatre in the summer of 1950. It was adapted for television as The Heart's a Forgotten Hotel and broadcast live by NBC-TV on the Playwrights '56 series on 25 October 1955. The three-act stage play, A Hole in the Head, opened at the Plymouth Theatre on 28 February 1957 and ran for 157 performances.

3. For a while during postproduction, the slated title for the film was All My Tomorrows. The song plays under the opening credits.

4. The New York opening was delayed until 15 July 1959.

"High Hopes" received the Academy Award for best song in 1959.

Synopsis

Tony Manetta recalls his journey from the Bronx to Miami Beach to make his fortune twenty years before. Two friends came with him: one of them, Jerry Marks, is now a famous promoter; the other, Mendy, is still driving a cab. Tony locates himself somewhere in the middle: he runs a second-class hotel, but is still scheming to make his first million.

Tony returns from a night on the town with his fun-loving girlfriend, Shirl, to learn that he and his son, Ally, face eviction because of unpaid bills. Tony is frustrated: he was just ready to push a $10 million scheme to transform old beachfront properties into a Florida Disneyland. He considers calling his brother, Mario, a successful New York merchant, for financial assistance, but Ally warns him that his uncle and aunt might use this as an excuse to take Ally away, a plan first proposed when his mother died a few years before. Tony assures his son that he won't let this happen.

The next day Tony meets with the bank lawyer and unveils his Disneyland project. The lawyer advises him to stop dreaming and gives him forty-eight hours to come up with $5,000. Tony calls Mario in New

The Films: Credits, Notes, and Synopses

York, but his brother, having bailed Tony out too many times before, refuses to send him any more money. When Tony concocts a story about Ally being ill, however, his sister-in-law, Sophie, decides that she and Mario will take the next plane to Florida. Tony meanwhile learns that Jerry Marks is in town, and his hopes for the Disneyland scheme are raised.

Shirl, a carefree spirit, wants to go with Tony to meet his square brother at the airport that night, but Tony won't let her come. Claiming that Tony is ashamed of her, she picks up her surfboard and threatens to leave. Tony drives her to the beach to calm her down. The time has come, Shirl proposes, for Tony to make up his mind: either he can strive for "respectability" or he can declare himself free to follow his dreams. Arguing for the latter, she suggests they run off together, leaving his troubles, and Ally, behind.

When Mario and Sophie arrive at the airport, Tony is not there. They make it to Tony's hotel where they discover that Ally is, in fact, in good health. Mario's resentment at being tricked by Tony quickens into anger when he witnesses his brother kissing Shirl good night outside. The reunion of the brothers is tense. Mario attacks Tony's life style and his fitness as a father. Ally rises to Tony's defense. Sophie thinks it would be best if she took Ally back to New York, but is willing to reconsider if Tony decides to marry and settle down. Proposing a local widow as a possible match, she exacts a promise from Mario to underwrite a dime store in a small town for Tony should the arrangement work out. Ally wanders outside, worried about his future. Tony follows and promises Ally he will at least meet the widow and see what happens. Father and son sing "High Hopes," a song about optimism.

Shirl is enraged when she hears of the matchmaking the next morning, but Tony appeases her by promising her an excursion-flight date to Cuba that night. The widow, Eloise Rogers, arrives; she is prim, but youthful and attractive, and she and Ally immediately hit it off. Mario, however, spoils the meeting by turning it into business negotiations. Embarrassed, Eloise flees the room. Ally follows and coaxes her back, and Tony tries to salvage the occasion by taking her out for a walk and a cup of coffee.

Both are defensive, and the date starts out rockily, but Eloise ends up inviting Tony to her apartment for dinner. She tells Tony about the death of her husband and young son in a drowning accident two years before, and confesses her fear that no one needs her. Tony admits that his reason for meeting her is not commendable: by pretending to be ready to settle down, he hopes to get enough money from Mario to cover his debts and get back in the action. To his surprise, she invites him to stay for dinner anyhow.

Interrogated upon his return home that evening, Tony says that he and Eloise will likely get married. Sophie, Mario, and Ally are elated. But when Tony makes a pitch for some cash in advance, Mario suspects Tony's true intentions and angrily refuses. Tony's predicament deepens when he learns that Shirl, stood up by him for their scheduled excursion to Cuba, has now left him for good. Tony levels with Ally that he is not marrying Eloise, but refuses to let Mario now take the boy to New York. Mario threatens to go to court to get Ally.

Just then a call comes from Jerry Marks, whom Tony has tried to reach all day. Tony is invited to a lavish party at the Fountainbleau, where Jerry receives him warmly and shows interest in the Disneyland scheme. Invited along to the dog races to discuss plans further, Tony quickly sells his Cadillac to bankroll himself for the evening. He stakes all his money on the first race to keep pace with Jerry's level of betting, and quickly wins the $5,000 he needs to stave off eviction. After calling Ally with the good news, however, he loses everything with a hunch bet on a dog named Lucky Ally. Observing Tony's agitation at the loss, Jerry realizes his old friend is a small-time hustler and backs off from the Disneyland deal. Desperate, Tony pushes hard. Jerry contemptuously gives him some "cigar money." Tony throws it back at him and in return is punched by Jerry's bodyguards.

Tony returns home to the ironic strains of "For He's a Jolly Good Fellow," sung by family, friends, and employees. Mario, at Sophie's urging, offers to pay off the debt, but Tony feels defeated and asks them to take Ally under their wing. When Ally tearfully protests, Tony pretends that he doesn't need him, arguing that in fact the boy has been the source of his failures. A distraught but defiant Ally decides to take off on his own rather than go with his aunt and uncle. Tony slaps Ally, but is immediately shocked by what he has done. Ally claims he will never speak to his father again. Mario follows Tony outside to comfort him.

In the morning, Ally leaves with Mario and Sophie for the airport as Tony watches from behind a tree across the street. In the taxi, Mario worries aloud about Tony's future, noting that he has glimpsed his deserted brother hiding across the street. Hearing this, Ally rushes back to be with Tony; father and son collapse together, laughing, in the ocean. Eloise, who has watched the scene from a distance, joins them and invites them home for dinner. Deciding to take the first vacation of his life, Mario races off with Sophie to join the others on the beach.

55 **POCKETFUL OF MIRACLES (1961)**

Milliardaire pour un jour (France), Angeli con la pistola (Italy), Die unteren Zehntausend (Germany)

Production Company: Franton Productions[1]
Producer: Frank Capra
Associate Producers: Glenn Ford, Joseph Sistrom
Director: Frank Capra

The Films: Credits, Notes, and Synopses

Screenplay: Hal Kanter, Harry Tugend, [and Jimmy Cannon], from Robert Riskin's screenplay for Lady for a Day (1933), based on Damon Runyon's story, "Madama La Gimp"[2]
Photography: Robert Bronner (Panavision, Eastmancolor)
Process Photography: Farciot Edouart
Editor: Frank P. Keller
Art Directors: Hal Periera, Roland Anderson
Set Decorators: Sam Comer, Ray Moyer
Women's Costumes: Edith Head
Men's Costumes: Walter Plunkett
Makeup: Wally Westmore
Hairstyles: Nellie Manley
Musical Score and Conductor: Walter Scharf
Orchestra: Gil Frau
Songs: "Pocketful of Miracles" by Sammy Cahn and James Van Heusen, "The Riddle Song (Until the 12th of Never)"[3]
Choreography: Nick Castle
Sound Recording: Hugo Grenzbach, Charles Grenzbach
Assistant Directors: Arthur S. Black, Jr., Frank Capra, Jr., Ralph Anexes
Unit Production Manager: Kenneth DeLand
Cast: Glenn Ford (Dave the Dude), Bette Davis (Apple Annie), Hope Lange (Queenie Martin), Arthur O'Connell (Count Romero), Peter Falk (Joy Boy), Thomas Mitchell (Judge Henry G. Blake), Edward Everett Horton (butler), Mickey Shaughnessy (Junior), David Brian (governor), Sheldon Leonard (Steve Darcey), Peter Mann (Carlos Romero), Ann-Margaret (Louise), Barton MacLane (police commissioner), John Litel (police inspector), Jerome Cowan (mayor), Fritz Feld (Pierre), Jay Novello (Spanish consul), Frank Ferguson and Willis Bouchey (newspaper editors), Benny Rubin (Flyaway), Ellen Corby (Soho Sal), Jack Elam (Cheesecake), Mike Mazurki (Big Mike), Hayden Rorke (Captain Moore), Doodles Weaver (pool player), Paul E. Burns (Mallethead), Angelo Rossitto (Angie), Edgar Stehli (Gloomy), George E. Stone (Shimkey), William F. Sauls (Smiley), Tom Fadden (Herbie), Snub Pollard (Knuckles), Gavin Gordon (hotel manager), Byron Foulger (manager's assistant), Stuart Holmes, Kelly Thordsen, Romo Vincent

Filmed at Paramount Pictures Studio in the spring of 1961

The Films: Credits, Notes, and Synopses

Distributor: United Artists
Copyright: 18 December 1961 by Franton Productions (LP 21109)
Released: 18 December 1961 (Victoria and Trans-Lux 52nd Street theaters, New York City)[4]
Running time: 136 minutes

Notes

1. Franton Productions was formed by Capra and Glenn Ford for the purpose of making Pocketful of Miracles. Capra and Ford had equal votes in the production company; Abe Lastfogel of the William Morris Agency decided disputes, as he had previously on A Hole in the Head. Capra discusses his discontent with this arrangement at length in The Name Above the Title, pp. 470-75.

2. According to Capra, Jimmy Cannon rewrote the dialogue for the film but was not given credit because of Writers Guild regulations limiting the number of credited writers to two (The Name Above the Title, p. 470). For the published versions of Damon Runyon's "Madame La Gimp," see Lady for a Day (entry 23).

3. According to Steven P. Hill, Capra discovered and wrote special lyrics for "The Riddle Song (Until the 12th of Never)" (see entry 757, p. 54).

4. Pocketful of Miracles was extensively previewed during the late summer and fall of 1961. These screenings included Paramount Theatre, Oakland (18 August); Long Beach (23 September); Grauman's Chinese Theatre, Los Angeles (13 October); and the Directors Guild theatre, Los Angeles (15 October). Capra recounts in his autobiography his dismay at the decision of United Artists to open the film with saturation booking at theaters around the country instead of first showcasing it at select theaters in New York and Los Angeles (The Name Above the Title, p. 482). He is both right and wrong about this: it is true that Pocketful of Miracles opened in Los Angeles on a saturation basis on Christmas Day, 1961 ("in theatres and drive-ins everywhere" the ads proclaimed), but a week earlier it had opened in traditional fashion in New York City at the Victoria and Trans-Lux 52nd Street theaters only. Another aspect of the distribution of the film in southern California might have given Capra pause, however. During the week prior to its Los Angeles release, ads ran in the Los Angeles Times featuring a photograph of a stiffly smiling Richard Nixon. The text beside the photograph was curiously ambiguous: "When Richard Nixon Laughs, Everybody in Los Angeles Laughs! Lucky him! He's just seen Frank Capra's newest picture--and the screen's biggest laugh-getter 'Pocketful of Miracles.'"

Pocketful of Miracles received Academy Award nominations in 1961 for best supporting actor (Peter Falk), best costume design-color, and best song.

The Films: Credits, Notes, and Synopses

Synopsis

A remake of Capra's Lady for a Day (1933), Pocketful of Miracles contains most of the material in the original screenplay. (For a synopsis of that story, see entry 23.) However, the roles of Dave the Dude and Missouri (now "Queenie") Martin have been altered and greatly expanded, and a subplot is introduced concerning Dave's ambition to become a kingpin in the dark criminal world of a Chicago mobster, Steve Darcey, a figure who does not exist in the earlier work.

The impact of these changes is strongest in the first section of the film. As in Lady for a Day, Annie is summoned by Dave, who wants to buy a lucky apple. But Dave is now a bootlegger rather than a gambler and has just paid for the funeral of a heavily indebted speakeasy owner who has been rubbed out by some creditors. With an apple from Annie in hand, Dave immediately gets lucky: the late owner's daughter, Queenie, arrives and gives Dave the lease to the club. Dave's right-hand man, Joy Boy (a more highly strung version of the acerbic Happy in Lady for a Day) points out that with the lease comes a host of old debts to be paid off. But Queenie promises to make good on the debts with the wages she earns as a cafeteria cashier. Instead, Dave decides to promote Queenie as a nightclub star. Two years later, the old speakeasy is the hottest spot in town, and Dave and Queenie are at a turning point in their lives. With all the debts paid, Queenie has sold the club and hopes to settle down with Dave in her hometown in Maryland. Since Prohibition has been repealed, and Dave's bootlegging days are numbered, this is a perfect opportunity for him to go straight. But Dave is lured by the possibility of controlling the entire New York City territory for a new national syndicate, headed by Darcey, which will cater to all human weaknesses. So Dave puts Queenie off. Armed with an apple from Annie, he meets with Darcey in a moving van Dave has provided to steal the notorious mobster into the city. Despite intimations of violent coercion, Dave rejects Darcey's initial terms and brashly makes his counterproposal. The meeting ends in a stalemate.

At this point the story of Annie and her daughter, Louise, commences, unfolding exactly as in Lady for a Day. Unlike Lady for a Day, however, Annie's story serves to highlight Dave's moral dilemma in Pocketful of Miracles. Queenie aligns herself with Annie from the outset, persuading Dave to help solve the old woman's problems. Joy Boy, on the other hand, works tirelessly to keep his boss's attention focused on negotiations with Darcey and frets that Dave's postponement of meetings will provoke the wrath of the ill-tempered mobster. Dave tries to balance both commitments, even as he fears that his chance to own the city may be slipping away. As it turns out, Darcey takes Dave's stalling as a show of strength and offers to meet him at the dock on the night of the reception to make a settlement. But paralleling Dave's commitment to Annie is his domestication by Queenie; swept up in the euphoria of the fairy-tale send-off, he agrees to move her to Maryland. (The event also inspires Joy Boy to express his desire to get home to his pregnant wife, and chauffeur Junior to

The Films: Credits, Notes, and Synopses

request the night off to visit his mother.) At the end of <u>Lady for a Day</u> Dave invites Missouri up to his apartment, and Missouri's efforts to pass herself off as his wife at the reception hints perhaps at a future relationship, but there is no indication in the earlier version that Dave will abandon his career as a gambler, or that such a move would be desirable. In <u>Pocketful of Miracles</u> Dave clearly decides to abandon the city, and his leadership of its underworld, for Queenie's family home.

56   RENDEZVOUS IN SPACE (1964)

Reaching for the Stars

Production Company:	Graphic Films Corporation
Director:	Frank Capra
Script:	Frank Capra
Models:	Gardner Displays
Cast:	Danny Thomas (reporter); Tom Fadden and Benny Rubin (passersby)
Distributor:	Martin-Marietta Corporation
Copyright:	29 July 1965 by Martin-Marietta Corporation (LU 3387)
Released:	September 1964 (Hall of Science, New York World's Fair)
Running time:	19 minutes

Notes

<u>Rendezvous in Space</u> was designed to be seen in conjunction with the presentation of scale-model space vehicles at the New York World's Fair Hall of Science. The film remained a standard feature at the permanent science museum after the fair closed in 1965.

Synopsis

The film opens with a series of still photographs of the earth taken from the Tiros VIII weather satellite. Over these images, astronaut John Glenn is heard describing his view of the earth during his recent orbital mission. Reporter Danny Thomas interviews people in Times Square, New York, about their interest in space travel, and gets a mixed response. An animated passage recounts the discovery of gunpowder and its launching power by the Chinese, and details future plans for manned orbital laboratories. Danny Thomas describes the possible benefits to be had from scientific exploration in space.

IV. Writings about Frank Capra

1922

57   Reid, Laurence. "Ballad of Fisher's Boarding House." <u>Motion Picture News</u> (15 April), p. 2216.
        A short review of Capra's first film. Reid notes that Rudyard Kipling's poem has been transferred to the screen with remarkable fidelity, and that the action is "stirring at all times and unusually rich in characterization." He praises the film as a "masterpiece of realism, carrying dramatic value and a spiritual flavor." No mention of Capra.

1926

58   Anon. "<u>The Strong Man</u>." <u>Photoplay</u> (November), p. 52.
        A brief review. Harry Langdon is seen as entering the front ranks of screen comedians with this film. No mention of Capra.

59   C[laxton], O[liver]. "The Current Cinema." <u>New Yorker</u>, 2, No. 31 (18 September), 50-51.
        A review of <u>The Strong Man</u>. Langdon's comic acting is praised, but the film overall is judged a poor support for his antics. No mention of Capra.

60   Hall, Mordaunt. "The Screen." <u>New York Times</u> (24 May), p. 24.
        A review of <u>Tramp, Tramp, Tramp</u>. No mention is made of Capra's contribution to this film as a screenwriter, but Hall does observe that several episodes are "strongly reminiscent of <u>The Gold Rush</u> and suffer by comparison with the Chaplin comedy. . . . This, of course, is hardly Mr. Langdon's fault, but rather that of the half dozen authors who contributed to the gags in his story." This is of interest in light of Capra's frequent assertion that Langdon came to model himself after Chaplin.

61   _____. "The Screen." <u>New York Times</u> (7 September), p. 44.
        A review of <u>The Strong Man</u>. Hall considers Langdon and Capra to be fine gangsters, but faults the scenario for shifting

abruptly from scene to scene. "If Mr. Langdon would study psychology in constructing his narratives, his films would be more than mere laugh-makers." Brief credits.

62   Rush [Alfred Rushford Grearson]. "The Strong Man." Variety (8 September), p. 16.

A review of the film. "A rich comedy that should take Langdon a step toward the class of stars." No mention of Capra. Brief credits.

63   Sherwood, R[obert] E. "The Silent Drama." Life, 88 (7 October), 26.

A highly favorable review of The Strong Man, focusing on Langdon's capacity for wistfulness, tenderness, and frailty. "In point of construction it represents a tremendous advance over the last Langdon comedy, 'Tramp, Tramp, Tramp'!" No mention of Capra.

1927

64   Abel [Abel Green]. "For the Love of Mike." Variety (24 August), p. 26.

A review of the film. "Lack of expert directorial continuity and allied creative skill counts against 'Mike' which, as a basic idea, had possibilities." The reviewer also notes that Claudette Colbert makes her screen debut but is given "limited opportunity." Very brief credits.

65   Anon. "Biographical Sketch." Motion Picture News (August?), p. 112.

Background information on Capra, written at the time of the release of For the Love of Mike. (On file with Capra clippings at the New York Public Library's Performing Arts Research Center; no month or volume number is given.)

66   Anon. "Long Pants." Film Daily (3 April), p. 6.

The reviewer proposes that "it is purely Langdon's way of doing things that keeps the crowd laughing. The situations aren't consistently mirthful provoking and the repetition of some of the comedy business slows the tempo." Capra is not mentioned, but clearly this is the kind of review that would have encouraged Langdon to assume directorial control of his own films. Very brief credits.

67   Anon. "Long Pants." Photoplay (June).

A brief, favorable review. Harry Langdon is described as "wistful and spiritual." No mention of Capra.

68   C[laxton], O[liver]. "The Current Cinema." New Yorker, 3, No. 5 (2 April), 89.

A review of Long Pants. "As a dispenser of futile and pathetic gestures Langdon is unexcelled, and it would be only more than fair if the Fates deal him a good story." No mention of Capra.

69   Hall, Mordaunt. "The Screen." New York Times (29 March), p. 23.
A review of Long Pants. Although Hall finds some "hilarious passages . . . acted with consummate skill," he faults the film for failing to explore the full implications of its dramatic premise. "Mr. Langdon has once again capitulated to his omnipotent band of gagmen." No mention of Capra. Brief credits.

70   ____. "The Screen." New York Times (2 May), p. 26.
A review of His First Flame, produced by Mack Sennett, directed by Harry Edwards, and written by Arthur Ripley and Capra. Hall judges the comedy of this film to be more sophisticated than the kind with which Sennett is usually associated, and notes that the gags devised by Ripley and Capra are "wonderfully suitable to Mr. Langdon's genius as a silent clown." Brief credits.

71   ____. "The Screen." New York Times (24 August), p. 27.
A review of For the Love of Mike. Hall finds the film neither "a dignified piece of work" nor convincing. No mention of Capra. Brief credits.

71a   ____. Rush [Alfred Rushford Grearson]. "Long Pants." Variety (30 March).
The reviewer finds the Langdon comedy amusing but considers the film something of a let down after The Strong Man. "The sympathetic element is over-developed at the expense of the gags and the stunts." No mention of Capra. Brief credits.

72   Sherwood, R[obert] E. "The Silent Drama." Life, 89 (21 April), 24.
A brief review of Long Pants. Sherwood finds the film "crazily uneven, but in its more commendable moments it manages to be marvelous." Harry Langdon, he concludes, is "badly in need of expert advice in such dull, routine matters as story construction, taste and coherence." No mention of Capra.

1928

73   Anon. "The Matinee Idol." Photoplay (June), p. 82.
A brief review focusing on Bessie Love's performance and lamenting her retirement. No mention of Capra.

74   Anon. "Say It with Sables." Photoplay (September), p. 112.
A brief review primarily synopsizing the film. No mention of Capra.

75   Anon. "So This Is Love." Variety (2 May), p. 15.
A review of the film. "The picture will probably make its way where Columbia has succeeded. . . . From the angle of the second and third-run box-office--not a bad picture." Very brief credits.

1928

Writings About Frank Capra

76   Anon. "Submarine." Photoplay (November), p. 56.
  The reviewer finds the production too mechanical and the performances too "un-human," but suggests that the film is worth seeing for its sense of spectacle and the fine handling of key scenes. No mention of Capra.

77   C[laxton], O[liver]. "The Current Cinema" New Yorker, 4, No. 29 (4 September), 90-91.
  A brief review of Submarine. The film is compared unfavorably with A Girl in Every Port, seen earlier in the year: "Besides lacking the originality of its predecessor, it also lacks the vigor and rough humor." No mention of Capra.

78   Hall, Mordaunt. "'Matinee Idol' Is Gleeful." New York Times (24 April), p. 29.
  A review of Matinee Idol. "This picture makes no pretensions of doing anything save tell a pretty little story, consequently it succeeds quite admirably." No mention of Capra. Brief credits.

79   ____. "The Screen." New York Times (31 August), p. 23.
  A review of Submarine. The film's topical connection to two recent submarine disasters is noted, as is the possible influence of What Price Glory? and Tell It to the Marines, both released in 1926. "Frank R. Capra's direction is especially clever, for not only has he attended to the action of the story, but he has also obtained from his players infinitely better characterization than one is apt to see on the screen, especially in a melodrama." Brief credits.

80   Land [Robert J. Landry]. "Submarine." Variety (5 September), p. 14.
  The reviewer discusses the film in terms of two recent submarine disasters for which navy officials had come under public attack, and suggests that the film tells the story from the navy's point of view. He also notes that Submarine is the second film in a row to be released on Broadway by Columbia, and "will add lustre to the company's standing nationally." Brief credits.

81   ____. "Power of the Press." Variety (5 December), p. 19.
  A review of the film. "Exciting and insistently engaging melodrama with a light touch that lifts it out of the stencil class . . . . The production is good, cast excellent, and Frank Capra's directorial job above average." Very brief credits.

82   Mark [Mark Vance]. "That Certain Thing." Variety (2 May), p. 26.
  A review of the film. "Those who don't think the independents are trying to make good pictures had better take a look at That Certain Thing. . . . Directing is splendid and the work of the small cast immense." Very brief credits.

83   Sherwood, R[obert] E. "The Movies." Life, (28 September), 22.
     A review of Submarine. Sherwood finds the hesitation of the protagonist to rescue his colleagues an improbable dramatic complication. Nevertheless, the film is a "stalwart melodrama" done with "telling realism." Sherwood credits Irvin Willat with the direction; he does not mention Capra.

84   Sid [Sidney Silverman]. "The Matinee Idol." Variety (25 April), p. 29.
     A review of the film, with detailed advice on how it might have succeeded as something more than a "solid laugh and hoke picture." By investing more money in production values and cast, the studio could have released the film at prestige exhibition sites across the country. Moreover, Capra passed up key opportunities as a director to emphasize pathos. "A traveling camera to a close-up in at least one spot might have brought a lump to many a throat, but the film is too concerned with laughs." Brief credits.

85   Williams, Whitney. "'Submarine' Affords Live Interest." Los Angeles Times (16 September), p. 3.
     A review of Submarine, accompanied by an extensive photo spread. Williams calls the film "one of the most agreeable and adroitly directed pictures of the year."

1929

86   Anon. "Amusing Murders." New York Times (29 April), p. 29.
     A review of The Donovan Affair, cited for the merriment with which the subject of murder is treated and for a mystery plot which "is mapped out more intelligently than usual." With minor exception, the "audible angle" of this all-talking film is judged commendable. No mention of Capra. Brief credits.

87   Anon. "At the Colony, 'The Younger Generation.'" New York Post (11 March).
     A synopsis of the film with passing notice that it is dull and unoriginal. No mention of Capra.

88   Anon. "The Donovan Affair." Photoplay (June), p. 57
     The reviewer considers the film to have too little suspense and too much forced comedy for a detective story. "Frank Capra, who directed 'Submarine,' hardly handles Owen Davis' mystery play with as skillful a hand."

89   Anon. "Flight." Moving Picture Stories, 35, No. 836 (10 December), 1-8.
     A short story based on the film.

90   Anon. "Flight." Photoplay (December), p. 55.
     Flight is described as the 'first flying talkie, and one of

the best of the air pictures." The reviewer notes that the "air shots are grand, and credit goes to Frank Capra for direction and dialogue."

91 Anon. "Flight." Screen Book (November), pp. 54-62.
A short story based on the film.

92 Anon. "Pa Goldfish on Screen." New York Times (11 March), p. 22.
A brief review of The Younger Generation. Jean Hersholt's performance in the central role is praised, but the dialogue sequences of this transitional talkie are criticized for adding nothing to the story and containing long, unnecessary pauses. No mention of Capra. Brief credits.

93 "The Power of the Press." Photoplay (January).
A brief review, noting that the film takes an interesting slant on the familiar newspaper story. No mention of Capra.

94 Anon. Submarine." Berlin Film-Magazin (June), pp. 2-3
A feature article describing the film, accompanied by a lavish photo spread.

*95 Beaton, Welford. Review of Flight. Film Spectator (Hollywood), (14 December).
Of the aerial photography in Flight, Beaton comments that Capra "gives us the impression that all the air is his." He also praises Capra's handling of dialogue, noting the lack of stage elocution in the film. In the scene where Lila Lee speaks softly to the injured Ralph Graves, Capra "comes nearer realizing the possibility of dialogue than any director so far" (quoted in Alexander Walker's The Shattered Silents [New York: William Morrow & Co., 1978] p. 196).

96 Evans, Harry. "Movies." Life, 94 (18 October), 28, 34.
A review of Flight. Evans recommends the film mainly for the casting of Ralph Graves and Jack Holt, and for the aerial photography. "Adequate entertainment, but not brilliant." No mention of Capra.

97 Hall, Mordaunt. "The Screen." New York Times (14 September), p. 17.
A review of Flight. Hall finds the film reminiscent of Capra's Submarine, also noting the possible influence of Howard Hawks and Lew Seiler's The Air Circus (1928). Hall praises the aerial footage and stunt flying, but considers the film in general to be bogged down in "melodramatic flubdub, tedious romantic passages and slapstick comedy." Brief credits.

98 Land [Robert J. Landry]. "The Donovan Affair." Variety (1 May), pp. 29, 66.
A review of the film. "Columbia has a strong dialog feature here that can stand the de luxe test anywhere. . . . Capra has

manipulated his story and people with restraint and intelligence." Credits.

99   Reel, Rob. "Film News and Reviews." Chicago American (24 October).
A brief but enthusiastic review of Flight, mainly describing the plot. Credits.

100 Rush [Alfred Rushford Grearson]. "The Younger Generation." Variety (20 March), p. 12.
A review of the film. "Sentimental oil has been spread on thick and often spills over. . . . Another insincere attempt to sell sympathetic syrup to the Jewish public." No mention of Capra. Very brief credits.

101 Sherwood, A.M., Jr. "The Movies." Outlook and Independent, 153, No. 5 (2 October), 193.
A review of Flight. Comedy and adventure compensate for a minor trace of banal sentimentality, according to this reviewer. The film "has so much fun in it, so much he-man stuff, and such good acting and direction that it succeeds in being actually a better picture than most of those it seeks to imitate."

102 Sime [Sime Silverman]. "Flight." Variety (18 September), p. 15.
In a highly favorable review, Flight is judged the best of the recent cycle of airplane films. Credit for the film's fine workmanship is given to Harry Cohn ("who has built a niche of his own among contemporary picture producers"), Capra ("a most skillful and imaginative director"), and the two lead actors, Jack Holt and Ralph Graves. Special mention is made of Capra's handling of the cremation scene. Brief credits.

103 Simpson, Celia. "The Cinema." Spectator, 142, No. 5264 (18 May), 776.
A favorable review of Submarine. The strength of the film is attributed to its use of authentic details concerning airplanes, submarines, and diving contraptions, rather than the acting or plot. No mention of Capra.

1930

*104 Anon. "The Films." Saturday Review (London), 149 (25 January), 108-9.
Review of flight. Cited in Cumulated Dramatic Index, 1909-1949.

105 Anon. "Ladies of Leisure." Screen Romances (June), pp. 42-49, 90-91.
A short story based on the film.

106 "Ladies of Leisure." Photoplay (July), p. 54.
The reviewer credits the film's success to a fortuitous combination of director, writer, and actress. Barbara Stanwyck's performance is praised. "Frank Capra--getting better every picture--directed brilliantly."

107 Anon. "Rain or Shine." Photoplay (October), p. 54.
A brief review, focusing on Joe Cook's background and performance. The film is described as a circus story with a punch finish. No mention of Capra.

108 Bennett, Don. "Radio Becomes a Talkie Prop." Radio News, 11, No. 10 (11 April), 898-901.
Capra's use of radio transmission to direct aerial patterns and ground maneuvers during the filming of Flight is reported here.

109 Evans, Harry. "Movies." Life, 95 (13 June), 20.
A review of Ladies of Leisure. Capra is cited for the care and intelligence with which he adapted the original play, but Evans is less pleased with "the overabundance of tearful emotion in the closing scenes." The acting receives high praise.

110 Hall, Mordaunt. "Miss Stanwyck Triumphs." New York Times (24 May), p. 21.
A review of Ladies of Leisure. The film "stands quite alone for its amusing dialogue, the restrained performances of nearly all the players and a general lightness of handling that commends the direction of Frank Capra." Brief credits.

111 _____. "The Screen." New York Times (8 August), p. 11.
A review of Rain or Shine, centering on the success with which the comic stage performance of Joe Cook has been transferred to the screen. Capra is cited for sustaining the swift pace of the film, and for not allowing serious moments of melodrama to dominate the farce. Brief credits.

112 M[osher], J[ohn] C. "The Current Cinema." New Yorker, 6, No. 26 (16 August), 55-56.
A review of Rain or Shine. Mosher finds the dinner sequence as broadly slapstick as anything in the silent days. The persistent series of comic incidents throughout the film are "a little too obviously manufactured, somewhat too ruthlessly hammered out." No mention of Capra.

112a Rush [Alfred Rushford Grearson]. "Ladies of Leisure." Variety (29 May).
A review of the film, focusing on its relationship to the source play. The casting of Ralph Graves in the lead role is faulted, as are "errors of technical literary treatment in the adaptation and direction." But the reviewer finds vestiges of the power of the original drama, particularly in Barbara Stanwyck's performance late in the film. No mention of Capra. Brief credits.

113   Schallert, Edwin. "Acting in Love Story Attracts." <u>Los Angeles Times</u> 4 April), sec. 2, p. 9.
A review of <u>Ladies of Leisure</u>. "For sheer beauty and sentiment," Schallert finds the film close to a "gem." The acting, especially that of Barbara Stanwyck, is exceptional, and Capra's direction shows "distinct character."

114   Sime [Sime Silverman]. "<u>Rain or Shine</u>." <u>Variety</u> (23 July).
A review of the film. Columbia's decision to strip the stage show of its music and turn the material into a dramatic comedy is judged wise, and the handling of the final mob scene is singled out for praise. "Frank Capra's direction is marked throughout the picture, and it includes comedy too." Credits.

1931

115   Anon. "<u>Dirigible</u>." <u>Film Daily</u> (2 April).
A review of the film. "Showmanship was employed to excellent advantage by Director Frank Capra in this air story. . . . Clever interspersing of beautiful location shots with studio scenes helps to sustain the realism." Brief credits.

116   Anon. "Plays and Pictures." <u>New Statesman and Nation</u>, 1 (20 June), 613.
A review of <u>Dirigible</u>, judged "thrilling entertainment" that is "well told and well photographed." The reviewer is less pleased by a "sentimental thread which hold the story together and an excessive reliance on the unflinching morality of the sailors at the end. But for "variety of incident, beauty of spectacle, and general capacity to lacerate the nerves, <u>Dirigible</u> reaches a very high level of production."

*117   Anon. Review of <u>Dirigible</u>. <u>Week-End Review</u>, 3 (20 June), 919.
Cited in <u>Cumulated Dramatic Index, 1909-1949</u>.

118   Bakshy, Alexander. "Films." <u>Nation</u>, 133, No. 3452 (2 September), 237.
<u>The Miracle Woman</u> is reviewed. Capra is cited for his handling of the sequences in the evangelist's tabernacle, a subject Bakshy considers "striking in its unfamiliarity and well presented." He also finds merit in the film's effort to expose fraudulent evangelism, but adds that the romance between the miracle woman and the blind youth never rings true or convincing.

119   Boehnel, William. Review of <u>Dirigible</u>. New York <u>World-Telegram</u> (6 April).
Capra is praised for constructing "one of the most excitingly realistic airship disasters ever filmed."

120   _____. Review of <u>The Miracle Woman</u>. New York <u>World-Telegram</u> (19 August).

Boehnel faults the film for its simultaneous attack on modern evangelism and its endorsement of "true religion." "Since the aim is vague, and is presented without courage or straightforwardness, the result is both confusing and disappointing." Although the film is expertly directed by Capra, the sermon is "too wishy-washy to make any deep or lasting impression."

121   Char [Roy Chartier]. "Platinum Blonde." Variety (3 November), p. 27.

The film is primarily reviewed as a showcase for rising star Robert Williams, but Capra's direction receives favorable mention, and the newsroom atmosphere of the film is praised for its authenticity. Credits.

122   Evans, Harry. "Movies." Life, 97 (24 April), 22.

A review of Dirigible. Evans finds little merit in the film, either as propaganda for the U.S. Navy or as entertainment. With the exception of the cracking up of the dirigible, and two short passages inside a hangar, the photography is "undistinguished and not to be compared with the spectacular shots in 'Hell's Angels.'" No mention of Capra.

123   ____. "Movies." Life, 98 (11 September), 19.

A review of The Miracle Woman. "This picture is a well directed slam at commercial evangelism with a personal sock at Aimee Semple McPherson and her Los Angeles tabernacle. . . . Director Frank Capra has managed to create several original situations out of a story that is far from new, and the cast behaves entertainingly under his guidance."

124   ____. "Movies." Life, 98 (20 November), 20.

A review of Platinum Blonde. Evan's laudatory remarks center on Robert Williams's performance in the central role, but he also notes that "Frank Capra has shown a delightful sense of surprise in the exploitation of the material."

125   Fleming, Peter. "The Cinema." Spectator, 146, No. 5374 (27 June), 1007.

Dirigible is briefly reviewed as a "monument to Hollywood's limitations," the Antarctic serving as a thrilling background for artless self-glorification and a tired plot. No mention of Capra.

126   Forrest, Mark. "The Films." Saturday Review (London), 151 (20 June), 901.

A review of Dirigible. Capra's handling of both the actors and the action is praised; in the latter category it is found superior to that of the contemporaneous aerial film, Hell's Angels. "The director succeeds in showing his audience not only what the catastrophe looks like from the outside, but what it looks like from the inside--a much more difficult feat." While a good deal of the film's realism arises from the fact that an actual military air base was placed at Capra's disposal, "the use which he has made of it is what really matters."

127   Hall, Mordaunt. "The Screen." New York Times (6 April), p. 24.
        A review of Dirigible. Hall finds the material the film covers a "little bulky," but notes that the action sequences are exciting and directed by Capra with considerable skill. Brief credits.

128   ____. "The Screen." New York Times (17 August), p. 18.
        A review of The Miracle Woman. Hall finds the film "clogged with detail" and illogically plotted, but thinks that the performances are clever. No mention of Capra. Brief credits.

129   M[osher], J[ohn] C. "The Current Cinema." New Yorker, 7, No. 8 (11 April), 91.
        A brief review of Dirigible. Mosher complains that the settings appear faked. No mention of Capra.

130   Peet, Creighton. "The New Movies." Outlook and Independent, 157, No. 15 (15 April), 539.
        Dirigible is reviewed. Peet praises the film for its aerial photography, and for Capra's technical mastery of special effects, but finds the acting and dialogue feeble and irritating.

131   ____. "The Miracle Woman." Outlook and Independent, 159, No. 17 (26 August), 534.
        A brief review of the film, judged an "unusual and decidedly interesting movie." Under Capra's direction the picture moves.

132   Schallert, Edwin. "Air Feature Premiered." Los Angeles Times (9 April), sec. 2, p. 9.
        A review of Dirigible, which is praised for the realism of its spectacular action sequences. "Frank R. Capra's direction reflects the quality of his other recent productions."

133   S[ennwald], A[ndre] S. "Out of His Element." New York Times (31 October), p. 22.
        A brief review of Platinum Blonde. Robert Williams's performance and Robert Riskin's dialogue are found amusing, but no mention is made of Capra. Brief credits.

134   Sid [Sidney Silverman]. "The Miracle Woman." Variety (28 July), p. 14.
        The reviewer praises Capra's talent for working with Barbara Stanwyck, his ability to get immediately into a story, and his skill at handling mob scenes. Silverman also points out that while the film is obviously an expensive one for Columbia Pictures, it probably cost half the amount of a film from a major studio. Brief credits.

135   Sime. [Sime Silverman]. "Dirigible." Variety (8 April), p. 18.
In this review Dirigible is compared with other aerial films of the period, including Capra's own Flight. The crack-up of the dirigible is singled out as the key scene in the film, more spectacular than a similar event in Howard Hughes's Hell's Angels. The story is judged unconvincing, but "Capra did everything he could with the direction." Brief credits.

136   Stern, Seymour. "Cinema Notes of the Quarter." Left, 1, No. 2 (Summer/Autumn), 78-79.
The Miracle Woman is reviewed. According to Stern, the film demonstrates that the possibility for intellectual filmmaking is greater in Soviet Russia than in America: it throws away a golden opportunity to attack religion, and instead concludes with a sentimental glorification of "true religion."

137   Watts, Richard, Jr. Review of The Miracle Woman. New York Herald Tribune (17 August).
Watts briefly notes that the film "is another of those puzzling motion pictures which attempt an important idea and then fails to live up to it."

1932

138   Abel [Abel Green]. "American Madness." Variety (9 August), p. 17.
A review of the film. Describing it as "timely, topical, human, dramatic, punchy and good entertainment at one and the same time," Green notes that American Madness combines effective "propaganda against hoarding, frozen assets and other economic evils which 1932 Hooverism has created" with romance and melodrama. "The mob scenes in the bank run are exceedingly well handled. . . . Capra's direction throughout is big time." Brief credits.

139   Albert, Katherine. "What Happened to Harry Langdon?" Photoplay (February) pp. 40, 106.
Although never mentioned by name, Capra is the villain of the story recounted here. The loser in a power struggle during the making of Long Pants, Capra allegedly uses the movie press to falsely accuse Langdon of being egotistical and impossible to work with. This in turn rapidly leads to the ruin of Langdon's career.

140   Anon. "American Madness." Motion Picture Herald, 108, No. 2 (9 July), 36.
A review of the film. "While it waxes 'preachy' on the depression slant once or twice" the film nevertheless has powerful box-office appeal. Credits.

141   Anon. "The Bitter Tea of General Yen." Daily Variety (18 November).

Writings About Frank Capra   1932

          Review of a preview at the Ritz Theatre, Los Angeles.
"Here is an unusual, queer picture with a story that is questionable
entertainment for American tastes." No mention of Capra. Brief
credits.

142   Anon. Review of American Madness. Times (London), (28
       November).
          A favorable review. The action is "harnessed and con-
trolled by some extremely forceful directing and interpreted by excellent acting."

*143   Anon. Review of American Madness. Week-End Review, 6 (3
       December), 669.
          Cited in Cumulated Dramatic Index, 1909-1949.

144   Anon. Review of American Madness. New York World-Telegram (5
       August).
          The film is distinguished by "one of the most excitingly
realistic mob scenes ever pictured on the screen outside the newsreels." Credit is given to director Frank Capra, "one of Hollywood's
best." Brief credits.

*145   Anon. Review of Forbidden. Gazzetta di Venezia (9 August).
          Cited in Roberto Paolella's "Frank Capra," Bianco e Nero,
20, Nos. 8-10 (August-October 1959), 157-62. See entry 731.

*146   Anon. Review of Forbidden. Il Gazzettino (Venice), (9
       August).
          Cited in Roberto Paolella's "Frank Capra," Bianco e Nero,
20, Nos. 8-10 (August-October 1959), 157-62. See entry 731.

147   Anon. Review of Platinum Blonde. Times (London), (25
       January).
          A mixed review. "Although there are moments when the
camera seems to take too long to do its work and moments, too, when
one could wish that the rich mother-in-law and her relatives had been
drawn by a hand less tempted to caricature, Platinum Blonde, thanks
mainly to the acting of star Robert Williams, is an exceptionally neat
and enjoyable comedy."

148   Bakshy, Alexander. "Madness from Hollywood." Nation, 135,
       No. 3504 (31 August), 198-99.
          A brief review of American Madness. Bakshy considers the
story to be "sheer propaganda for the banks," but finds Capra's direction distinctive. "The scene of the run on the bank is film art at
its best." Reprinted in 1972 (see entry 865).

149   Forrest, Mark. "Films." Saturday Review (London), 153 (5
       March), 246.
          Forbidden is briefly reviewed. Noting that Capra has
scripted a variation on the "eternal triangle," Forrest finds the
story unsatisfying and the final image of Barbara Stanwyck, aged and

alone in a crowd, unpalatable. Stanwyck's acting, however, is praised.

150   ____. "Films." Saturday Review (London), 154 (3 December), 603.
         A review of American Madness centering on Walter Huston's performance. No mention of Capra.

151   Hall, Mordaunt. "The Screen." New York Times (11 January), p. 28.
         A review of Forbidden. Hall finds the behavior of the characters inconsistent and the film "a cumbersome effort at storytelling." This last problem, he proposes, is invariably the case when a director writes his own screenplay, "except, of course, in the case of Chaplin." Brief credits.

152   H[all], M[ordaunt]. "A Bank Robbery." New York Times (6 August), p. 14.
         A review of American Madness. The bank-run sequence and the passages detailing the locking and unlocking of the bank vault are praised, and Walter Huston is cited for his performance in the central role. But the story is faulted for its melodrama and the dialogue for its occasional roughness. Hall also finds the title of the film misleading, in that "the madness, as it is called, might occur in any country." Brief credits.

153   Lusk, Norbert. "New York Sees Superior Film." Los Angeles Times (14 August), p. 17.
         Reporting from New York, Lusk describes American Madness as "by far the strongest drama of the week." Its success demonstrates "the superiority of vehicles written expressly for the screen as opposed to stage adaptations." Moreover, Capra "has directed it with fine authority and a never-failing sense of drama."

154   M[osher], J[ohn] C. "The Current Cinema." New Yorker, 7, No. 48 (16 January), 53-54.
         An unfavorable review of Forbidden. Mosher is especially appalled by the dialogue. No mention of Capra.

155   ____. "The Current Cinema." New Yorker, 8, No. 26 (13 August), 37.
         A brief review of American Madness. Mosher finds the resolution too fanciful and Walter Huston's moralizing wearisome. But the bank run is "spine-shattering," and "the scenes in the bank, the great safes, the truths about tellers it reveals, are of interest." No mention of Capra.

156   Peet, Creighton. "The New Movies." Outlook and Independent, 160, No. 3 (20 January), 87.
         A highly favorable review of Forbidden. "Frank Capra has written and directed a film about suffering womanhood which is so simple, so honest, so entirely unaffected and so completely free from

the gaudy heroics which characterize the inane martyrdom of Constance Bennett, Norma Shearer and Joan Crawford that it finally appears as an especially dramatic and convincing piece of work." Adolphe Menjou and Barbara Stanwyck "give smooth and effortless performances. But Forbidden is chiefly Mr. Capra's triumph."

*157 Q., V. Review of Forbidden. Il Messagero (Rome) (17 August).
Cited in Roberto Paolella's "Frank Capra," Bianco e Nero, 20, Nos. 8-10 (August-October 1959), 157-62. See entry 731.

158 Sid [Sidney Silverman]. "Forbidden." Variety (12 January), p. 24.
A review of the film. As writer, Capra is faulted for having borrowed liberally from a variety of standard stories; as director, he is faulted for a laborious opening passage. Nevertheless, the film is "replete with good workmanship, some laughs, pathos, and is an interesting tale well-played." Brief credits.

159 Skinner, Richard Dana. "The Screen." Commonweal, 16, No. 16 (17 August), 392.
A review of American Madness. Skinner attacks the film for its unrealistic treatment of bank operations and the problem of bank failures. "A grain of truth is distorted into an implied indictment of a whole system." No mention of Capra.

160 Watts, Richard, Jr. Review of American Madness. New York Herald Tribune (6 August).
Watts proposes that several vigorously staged, topical scenes (notably the siege on the bank) have been grafted onto an antique, melodramatic plot. He thus concludes: "You can safely blame Mr. Riskin, who wrote the story, for the defects of 'American Madness' and credit Mr. Capra with the virtues." Brief credits.

1933

161 Anon. Review of The Bitter Tea of General Yen. Times (London) (13 March).
The reviewer criticizes Yen's final gesture of drinking poison as sentimental and melodramatic, but is impressed by the degree to which the film generally avoids the false heroics often found in movies of this kind. This is "thanks partly to the smoothness and subtlety of Mr. Frank Capra's direction and partly to Mr. Nils Asther's playing of the part of Yen."

162 Argus. "On the Screen." Literary Digest, 116, No. 13 (23 (September), 30.
A review of Lady for a Day. "Completely unembarrassed in its assault on the primary emotions, it is, nevertheless, so heartily and completely done that, beautifully acted by the veteran May Robson, it becomes one of the genuinely charming films of the year. But it isn't aristocratic art." No mention of Capra.

163   Boehnel, William. "Love Drama on Radio City's Screen." New York World-Telegram (12 January).
A review of The Bitter Tea of General Yen. "Its intention is better than its achievement." The setting and acting are excellent, and director Capra "has done fairly well with his materials," but the film "slows down and drags so much it must be classed as a handsome and ambitious bore."

164   Caldwell, Cy. "To See or Not to See." New Outlook, 162, No. 4 (October), 48
Lady for a Day is reviewed. "This is simply grand old sentimental hokum, absolutely unbelievable, but delightfully entertaining." Capra's direction is judged faultless.

*165   Cohen, Harold. "Frank Capra." Cinema Digest (10 April), p. 12.
Cited in Mel Schuster's Motion Picture Directors: A Bibliography of Magazine and Periodical Articles, 1900-1972.

166   Cohen, John S. Jr. "'The Bitter Tea of General Yen' and a Sumptuous Stage Show at the Musical Hall." New York Sun (12 January).
A review of The Bitter Tea of General Yen. Cohen notes that the film is timely in light of current news from China and praises it for treating with unusual intelligence a subject frequently betrayed in American movies. He gives credit to the "up and coming Columbia Studios," but does not mention Capra. Brief credits.

167   Crewe, Regina. "'Bitter Tea of General Yen' Is Film of Splendor." New York American (12 January).
A favorable review of the film. "Perforce the tale is told in leisurely fashion, but its pace is soothing rather than not, and its lush oases are superb, both visually and emotionally." Brief credits.

168   Davy, C. "Stage and Screen." Spectator, 151 (29 December), 962.
A review of Lady for a Day. The film's use of modern elements of American city life within a fairy-tale plot is deemed especially interesting. Capra's direction, moreover, receives high praise: "his handling of a fairly complicated plot is a delightful lesson in the art of telling a story swiftly and vividly through the eye of the camera."

169   Delehanty, Thornton. "'The Bitter Tea of General Yen,' with Barbara Stanwyck, Opens at Radio City Music Hall." New York Evening Post (12 January).
A mixed review of The Bitter Tea of General Yen. Despite beautiful photography and authentic atmosphere, "the story is overlong and too deliberate, and the dragged-out dialogue sequences rob the drama of its proper suspense."

170   Dickstein, Martin. Review of The Bitter Tea of General Yen.
      Brooklyn Daily Eagle (30 January).
           Dickstein judges the writing effective and the direction
competent. Moreover, the film "manages to make much more sense than
many stories of this type . . . on the screen."

171   Forrest, Mark. "Films." Saturday Review, 155 (11 March),
      244.
           The Bitter Tea of General Yen is briefly reviewed. Forrest
finds the treatment of the Orient much more judicious than in many
films of this kind. "The more spectacular parts of the picture, which
deal with some aspects of the recent Chinese troubles, are soberly
handled and Mr. Capra's direction throughout is admirably firm."

172   Hall, Mordaunt. "The Screen." New York Times (12 January),
      p. 20.
           An article on the reopening of the Radio City Music Hall as
a movie theater with The Bitter Tea of General Yen as the feature
attraction. Hall describes the film as "scarcely plausible" but
"fairly entertaining." No mention of Capra. Brief credits.

173   ____. "The Screen." New York Times (8 September), p. 22.
           A review of Lady for a Day. Hall sees the film as working
within the dramatic tradition of Barrie's The Old Lady Shows Her
Medals and Shaw's Pygmalion, but set forth in a more popular vein. No
mention of Capra. Brief credits.

174   Land [Robert J. Landry]. "Lady for a Day." Variety (12
      September), p. 17.
           A review of the film. "Hans Christian Anderson stuff
written by a hard-boiled journalist and transferred to the screen by
trick-wise Hollywoodites." Capra is praised for this, but Robert
Riskin's especially cited for "adroit scenario development" and "realistic wisecracks" which divert attention from the improbable twists in
the plot. Brief credits.

175   Lorentz, Pare. "Aside to English Actors." Vanity Fair, 41
      (October), 40. 63.
           A review of Lady for a Day, considered by Lorentz a film of
minor virtues. "The mythical, golden-hearted Broadway in the story is
a realistic fairyland because Capra has learned from the Russians
. . . . He needs only bit players to fill in his fine photography, his
genuine atmospheric feeling of a Broadway teeming with philanthropic
killers and soft-hearted hoofers." Moreover, Capra's previous work on
unpretentious, inexpensive "action" pictures with minor players has
paid off. Lady for a Day "could have been turned into an exaggerated,
blundering, maudlin Broadway sob story. He made it an amusing, sentimental tale." Excerpts are reprinted in 1974 (see entry 939).

176   M[osher], J[ohn] C. "The Current Cinema." New Yorker, 8, No.
      49 (21 January), 47.

The Bitter Tea of General Yen is unfavorably reviewed. Mosher finds Barbara Stanwyck too unglamorous to entice a Manchurian prince. No mention of Capra.

177 _____. "The Current Cinema." New Yorker, 9, No. 31 (16 September), 56.
A review of Lady for a Day. The film is audaciously whimsical, but "you accept the whole thing as quite reasonable human behavior, so nicely has it been handled by Frank Capra."

178 Scheuer, Philip K. "East and West Meet Again." New York World-Telegram (14 January).
A review of The Bitter Tea of General Yen. Scheuer praises the courage that inspired the production and the unerring honesty with which an Oriental viewpoint is captured. Capra's direction, moreover, is labeled a "triumph of repression." "No picture half so strange, so bizarre, has ever before passed outward through the astonishing doors of the Columbia studio. . . . The film is an anomaly among talkies. If you go, go with an open mind."

179 Shan. [Sam Shain]. "Bitter Tea of General Yen." Variety (17 January), p. 14.
The reviewer predicts that audiences will find the romance between a Chinese man and a white woman inherently "unsympathetic." Moreover, General Yen "is a curious and rather questionable human composition of poet, philosopher and bandit. . . . By no means is he a true character." Brief credits.

180 Watts, Richard, Jr. Review of The Bitter Tea of General Yen. New York Herald Tribune (12 January).
Watts considers the film a "slow-paced, but shrewdly-directed melodrama," although he makes no mention of Capra. He finds of chief interest the contrasting ideologies of General Yen and the young woman missionary, noting that the film "insists that the much praised Christian quality of mercy is vastly overrated." Brief credits.

181 _____. "'Lady for a Day'--Radio City Music Hall." New York Herald Tribune (8 September).
A review of Lady for a Day. Watts is charmed by the frank and unashamed sentimentalism of the film. A shrewdly directed version of Damon Runyon's story, it "asks no quarter and gives none in its frontal attack on the more primitive emotions." Brief credits.

1934

182 Anon. "Act by Act." New York Times (2 December), sec. 10, p. 2.
Robert Riskin explains his method of screenplay construction in which the story is divided into three acts, much like a stage play. Lady for a Day and It Happened One Night serve as examples.

183 Anon. "The New Pictures." Time, 24, No. 24 (10 December), 28.
    A review of Broadway Bill. The writer notes that although the story is very familiar, its treatment by Robert Riskin and Capra result in one of the most original comedies of the year. "Difficult to analyze and impossible to imitate, the hallmark of Director Capra's style is his way of turning what for another director would be a commonplace 'gag' into a vital and important incident."

184 Anon. "The New Talkies." New York Sun (23 February).
    A review of It Happened One Night, applauded as not only the best of the "bus talkies," but one of the brightest films of the year. "Mr. Capra, since he always smiles a little at it all, is able to make credible the most preposterous stories. . . . It's not a picture that bears much description. Its values are mainly cinematic, quick inconsequential bits of nonsense and drama." Brief credits.

185 "Strategy." New York Evening Post (22 February).
    Capra's painstaking efforts to obtain the proper sound effects during the bus ride in It Happened One Night are described.

186 Argus. "One the Current Screen." Literary Digest, 117, No. 10 (10 March), 38.
    It Happened One Night is reviewed in terms of the current cycle of films involving long-distance travel by bus. Capra's version is judged a "highly diverting comedy, skillfully directed and attractively played."

187 ____. "On the Current Screen." Literary Digest, 118 (15 December), 37.
    Broadway Bill is reviewed. The writer notes that Capra, long considered a "director's director" within the industry, has now with his third success in a row made his existence known to movie fans as well. The film displays Capra's capacity for making characters and events human, fresh, and sympathetic. Moreover, "the acting is replete with the sort of heart-warming humanity Mr. Capra always manages to infuse into his players."

188 Baskette, Kirtley. "Hollywood's New Miracle Man." Photoplay, 47, No. 1 (December), 31, 82.
    A profile of Capra, inspired by the recent success of It Happened One Night. Capra's immigrant background, rags-to-riches success story, and "mystique" as a director are discussed. He is cited for putting "realism, humaneness, and an understandable naturalness into his pictures." Reprinted in 1971 (see entry 814).

*189 Bernardinelli, Orazio. Review of It Happened One Night. Il Messagero (Rome) (5 August).
    Cited in Roberto Paolella's "Frank Capra," Bianco e Nero, 20, Nos. 8-10 (August-October 1959), 157-62. See entry 731.

190   Bige [Joe Bigelow]. "Broadway Bill." Variety (4 December), p. 12.
A review of the film. "Capra has a fine pair of leads in Warner Baxter and Myrna Loy, and then he has a yarn in which the tempo appears to have been especially suited to his directorial talents. The rest is up to Capra, and the rest is very much okay." Brief credits.

191   Boehnel, William. Review of It Happened One Night. New York World-Telegram (23 February).
Boehnel finds the film Capra's most adroit piece of work to date. "He is an observant student of human nature, and the players, as a result of his cunning advice, behave like real human beings and not like so many actors pretending to be the characters in a make-believe fable."

192   _____. Review of Broadway Bill. New York World-Telegram (30 November).
A favorable review. "Capra has done it again with neatness and dispatch." Broadway Bill is a "gay, polite, literate, and otherwise highly agreeable" screen romance. Brief credits.

193   "It Happened One Night." Variety (27 February), p. 17.
The reviewer is pleased to note that although the film starts out as yet another long-distance bus story, the characters get off the bus before the story palls. Moreover, the absence of a strong, logical plot is compensated for by a smooth blending of acting, dialogue, situations, and direction. The reviewer also notes that the film demonstrates how "a clean story can be funnier than a dirty one," an interesting observation in light of the emergence of an effective Production Code around this time. Brief credits.

194   Creelman, Eileen. "The New Talkies." New York Sun (30 November).
A highly favorable review of Broadway Bill. Comparing it with It Happened One Night, Creelman finds the new film more dramatic, yet marked by the same light touch. "Mr. Capra has a way of winning immediate sympathy for his characters, and of keeping it."

195   Crewe, Regina. Review of Broadway Bill. New York American (30 November).
Crew finds the film "marked by gleeful comedy, appealing romance and some affecting drama attributable to the collaboration of those master movie weavers, Bob Riskin and Frank Capra." Brief credits.

196   Delehanty, Thorton. "The New Films." New York Evening Post (1 December).
A review of Broadway Bill. "Frank Capra is too good a director to miss the drama of the subject, and he has seized all the sidelights of the racing game to build up his climax with the proper amount of thrills."

197   Ferguson, Otis. "Worth Seeing." New Republic, 78, No. 1014 (9 May), 364.

Writings About Frank Capra   1934

          A brief review of It Happened One Night, and one of
Ferguson's early pieces of film criticism. "What the picture as a
whole shows is that by changing such types as the usual pooh-bah
father and city editor into people with some wit and feeling, by
consistently preferring the light touch to the heavy, and by casting
actors who are thoroughly up to the work of acting, you can make some
rather comely and greenish grasses grow where there was only alkali
dust before." He concludes self-consciously: "And now having adjudi-
cated and discriminated and in a word defined the picture with proper
regard for this and that, I am reminded that a picture cannot be
defined at all until we find a way of describing whatever it is that
makes first-rate entertainment what it is." No mention of Capra.
Reprinted in 1971 (see entry 831).

198   ____. "It Happened Once More." New Republic, 81, No. 1046
         (19 December), 167.
          A review of Broadway Bill. Ferguson opens with a general
assessment of Capra as "not the genius of his age, but . . . a careful, talented director who has made a Hollywood success and earns an
office of his own, and still not been taken in by blobs of guilt." He
praises the film for its incidental warmth and naturalness, a sideshow
brightness, and Capra's painstaking supervision of dialogue, incident,
technical attack, and performance. He credits Capra with a mastery of
comic timing and accent, a "precision and instinct for where the swing
of words or of the body should be." Reprinted in 1971 (see entry 831)
and 1975 (see entry 965). Excerpts reprinted in 1974 (see entry 939).
Also see entry 214).

199   Forsythe, Robert. Review of It Happened One Night. New
         Masses (3 July), p. 44.
          The success of the film, and of Capra's career in general,
is attributed to Capra's total control over his productions. It
Happened One Night revives Forsythe's faith in the medium: "For
freshness of treatment and humor of presentation, we have had nothing
to equal it in a long time." Excerpts from his review were reprinted
in 1974 (see entry 939).

200   Hall, Mordaunt. "The Screen." New York Times (23 February),
         p. 23.
          A review of It Happened One Night. "If there is a welter
of improbable incidents these hectic doings serve to generate plenty
of laughter." No mention of Capra. Brief credits.

201   Hills, Beverly. "Mirth, Music, Mystery." Liberty (7 March),
         p. 30.
          It Happened One Night is reviewed. Expert acting and
writing aside, the film is "a director's picture." Capra "has the
knack of making you believe in a story by telling it as thought he
expected you not to. Instead of building his situations up to their
punch lines, he throws them away. With the kind of situations he had
to work with in It Happened One Night, this has the effect of doubling
their impact." Brief credits.

202   Jones, Carlisle. "The Man on the Flying Trapeze." New York
       Herald Tribune (27 May).
           An analysis of the use of the song, "The Man on the Flying
Trapeze," in three new movies: It Happened One Night, Twenty Million
Sweethearts, and The Brass Rail.

203   M[osher], J[ohn] C. "The Current Cinema." New Yorker, 10,
       No. 3 (3 March), 59.
           It Happened One Night is reviewed. Mosher finds the film
unexceptional amid the current crop of movies about overnight bus
trips, save for "natural touches of the habits of the travelers, their
camaraderie, their songs, the etiquette of the ten-minutes-for-lunch
period, the customs."

204   Montagu, Ivor. "Three Films." New Statesman and Nation, 7
       (19 May), 766.
           A highly favorable review of It Happened One Night.
Montagu attributes the success of the film to Capra's selection and
conception of characters. "Whether Colbert and Gable are really nice
is a question not germane. But in this picture character dialogue, an
expressive script, and sensitive direction make them incarnate figures
so irresistible that before the end we are in agony lest their mis-
understanding should continue and they should not find out till too
late--what we know all along--how necessary it is for them to marry
one another."

205   Norton, Helen B. "Fun on a Night Bus." Vanity Fair, 42
       (April), 50.
           A brief review of It Happened One Night. Noting that
Columbia Pictures has begun to produce first-rate pictures in the past
year, Norton describes It Happened One Night as improbable but entertaining, and is pleased with the acting. No mention of Capra.

*206   Pasinetti, Francesco. Review of It Happened One Night.
       Gazzetta di Venezia (5 August).
           Cited in Roberto Paolella's "Frank Capra," Bianco e Nero,
20, Nos. 8-10 (August-October 1959) 157-62. See entry 731.

207   R., D.F. Review of It Happened One Night. Monthly Film Bul-
       letin, 1, No. 8 (September), 65.
           Very brief commentary on the film. "The story scarcely
survives print, but it is exceedingly well told, some of the incidents
being positively brilliant." Brief credits.

*208   Ramperti, Marco. Review of It Happened One Night. Milan
       L'Illustrazione Italiana (12 August).
           Cited in Roberto Paolella's "Frank Capra," Bianco e Nero,
20, Nos. 8-10 (August-October 1959), 157-62. See entry 731.

*209   Sacchi, Fillipo. Review of It Happened One Night. Corriere
       della Sera (Milan) (5 August).

Writings About Frank Capra   1934

           Cited in Roberto Paolella's "Frank Capra," Bianco e Nero, 20, Nos. 8-10 (August-October 1959), 157-62. See entry 731.

210   Sennwald, Andre. "The Screen." New York Times (30 November), p. 22.
       A review of Broadway Bill. Sennwald has high praise for Capra's ability to create satire that is at once painless and engaging, appealing to all segments of the audience. He also cites Capra's special gift for screen comedy: "somehow no scene which he photographs is quite ordinary." Brief credits.

211   Troy, William. "Picaresque." Nation, 138, No. 3584 (14 March), 314.
       Proposing that picaresque narrative is especially well suited to periods in which the social structure is apparently dissolving, Troy notes the current use of the form in a cycle of cross-country bus stories coming from Hollywood. He finds analogies with the picaresque novel especially inescapable in the case of It Happened One Night: motels, hot-dog stands, and gas stations serve the same function as the inns, taverns, and shrines of Smollett and Sterne; Clark Gable is a convincing "rogue" and Claudette Colbert is a reincarnated Dulcinea; modern bourgeois chivalry, as practiced by King Westley, is mocked; events on the road are dynamic, varied, and infused with tart commentary. No mention is made of Capra. Reprinted in 1975 (see entry 996). Also see entry 217.

211a   Tully, Jim. "Frank Capra." Rob Wagner's Script, 11, No. 260 (3 March), 12.
       A profile of Capra and a brief critical assessment of his career. Describing the hardship of Capra's early years as an immigrant youth, Tully stresses the spontaneous, emotional quality of Capra's subsequent work as a film director. Capra is the "intuitive craftsman under control. . . . In his jaw is determination, and in his eyes is pity."

212   Watts, Richard, Jr. "On the Screen." New York Herald Tribune (23 February).
       A review of It Happened One Night. Watts finds the film lively and amusing, but a bit long for complete comfort, and possessing a conclusion that "is just a trifle laborious." The fact that there is nothing particularly dramatic about the bus journey "sets it apart from and . . . considerably ahead of its predecessors in the field. The picture has the advantage of some engaging comedy scenes—when they are not too whimsical—which are played attractively by the two stars." Credits.

213   _____. "On the Screen." New York Herald Tribune (30 November).
       A review of Broadway Bill. Despite Watts's lack of interest in the subject of horse racing, he finds the film "gay, humorous, exciting and vastly human. . . . Directed by Frank Capra, who is just

about the head man in cinema-making right now. 'Broadway Bill' possesses all of that air of racy, informal humanity that is so characteristic of his photoplays." Credits.

1935

214   Ferguson, Otis. "Frank Capra's Latest." National Board of Review Magazine (February).
A review of Broadway Bill. Picking up on the theme of his earlier review of this film for New Republic (see entry 198), Ferguson, discusses Capra's skillful direction of slight story material. Hollywood is at its best, he proposes, when it puts "all its marvelous technical resources into building comedy out of likeable people and familiar situations." Capra demonstrates this in Broadway Bill, where every turn of a familiar plot has had a certain alchemy practiced on it. Capra has a sense for what will be charming and true in people, and now to time the action so that everything moves effortlessly. This leads one to conclude that the director is a crucial figure in the success of a film: photography in and of itself will not make a good movie, and acting is dependent upon skillful casting. Given full authority over his films, Capra has wisely not attempted to ape other art forms. "His material is necessarily restricted and shallow, but he admits it frankly (it is always possible that a good solid plot might faze him) and goes to work; and when at work he shows himself as one of the first artists in the field." Reprinted in From Quasimodo to Scarlett O'Hara: A National Board of Review Anthology, 1920-1940, edited by Stanley Hochman (New York: Frederick Ungar Publishing Co, 1982), pp. 190-91.

215   Jacobs, Lewis. "More about Directors." New York Times (27 October), sec. 9, p. 4.
An attack on major Hollywood directors (Chaplin, Lubitsch, Vidor and DeMille, as well as Capra) who in Jacob's estimation display a facile command of the mechanics of filmmaking while remaining ignorant of the structural use of the "notation and syntax" of the medium. Noting that Capra is the most prized director in the industry today, Jacobs argues that his work is interchangeable with that of a host of efficient craftsmen, all without individualized technique, personal method, or style.

216   Stuart, John. "Fine Italian Hand." Colliers, 96 (17 August), 13, 48-49.
A survey and critical assessment of Capra's career, and a defense of the emerging power of directors within the film industry. Despite the presence of great photography and top-name writers, Stuart proposes, Hollywood recorded flops "until they realized the man who really made the picture was the director" Having escaped an impoverished Italian ghetto and trained in the sciences, Capra has come to command a major position in the movie industry as a director in control of his films. His directorial signature, Stuart notes, is a story that appeals to elemental emotions, told in a "classic rhythm."

217 Troy, William. "On a Classic." Nation, 1940, No. 3640 (10 April), 426-27.

A follow-up review of It Happened One Night on the occasion of the film's revival in New York a year after its initial release. Troy is gratified that the film, despite a lack of extensive publicity, has received widespread recognition "as one of the few potential classics of the recent cinema." He speculates that the success of It Happened One Night is in part a result of the balance it strikes between pure farce and serious social satire. Excerpts reprinted in 1974 (see entry 939). Also see entry 211.

1936

218 Abel [Abel Green]. "Mr. Deeds Goes to Town." Variety (22 April), p. 14.

A review of the film. Green predicts that the film will do well commercially because of its stars, but has reservations about the credibility of Longfellow Deeds and the gun-waving, unemployed farmer who appears midway through the story. In terms of technique the film is judged first-rate, but it is "not as significant as some of Capra's previous efforts." Brief credits.

219 Anon. "All Over the Lot." Stage, 14, No. 3 (December), 73.

This roundup of current productions in Hollywood includes a photograph of Capra directing Lost Horizon. Capra, it is noted, "puts all the pieces together into one of the most anticipated films in production."

220 Anon. "Capra Scores Again." Film Spectator (Hollywood), 2, No. 1 (11 April), 19, 21.

A review of Mr. Deeds Goes to Town. "Just another of those cinematic masterpieces we have been led to expect from Frank Capra when given a script he and Robert Riskin have put on paper." But the reviewer also expresses concern that in Capra's films dialogue rather than depicted action is becoming the central medium of expression.

221 Anon. "Col., Capra, Riskin, Cooper Go to Town with 'Mr. Deeds.'" Hollywood Reporter, 32, No. 26 (25 March), 3.

A review of Mr. Deeds goes to Town. Capra and Robert Riskin are commended for delivering "another sure cure for the depressed or the depression." To give individual credit to one of these collaborators, the reviewer maintains, is impossible: "When Capra and Riskin get together, one never knows where Capra ends and Riskin begins, so perfectly fused are their splendid talents."

222 Anon. "Frank Capra: Star Director Goes to Town with 'Mr. Deeds Goes to Town.'" Newsweek, 7, No. 16 (18 April), 29, 32.

A brief profile of Capra precedes a review of the film. Capra's name on a picture, it is noted, commands the kind of commercial appeal once reserved for D.W. Griffith and Cecil B. DeMille. This reputation is attributed to Capra's skill with actors. As for

Mr. Deeds Goes to Town: "The plot is no world-beater, but Capra's light-hearted additions are."

223   Anon. "Interesting People: Improviser." American Magazine, 121 (June), 77.
A brief profile of Capra, emphasizing his willingness to improvise and his mild-mannered behavior on the set.

224   Anon. "Lost Horizon." Photoplay (October), pp. 42-43.
A photospread on the film prior to its release, depicting and describing individual scenes. The movie is dubbed the "most completely different story ever filmed."

225   Anon. "Man Behind the Stars: Frank Capra." Motion Picture, 52, No. 1 (August), 60, 88.
A career sketch of Capra, now regarded as "one of the foremost directors in the industry."

226   Anon. "Mr. Deeds Goes to Town." Film Daily (27 March), p. 9.
The reviewer has high praise for the film. "Capra has done a grand directorial job and Robert Riskin deserves bouquets for his screenplay." Brief credits.

227   Anon. "Mr. Deeds Goes to Town." Motion Picture Herald, 123, No. 4 (25 April), 37.
The reviewer notes the compatibility of the work of Clarence Budington Kelland with that of Capra, Robert Riskin, and Gary Cooper, all of whom appeal to the same kind of audience. Capra's direction is described as "altogether key, sympathetic, now and then daring, always resourceful, confident, positive." Credits.

228   Anon. "Mr. Deeds Goes to Town." Motion Picture Review Digest, 1, No. 28 (29 June), 87-89.
Reviews are excerpted from a wide variety of sources, including newspapers, magazines, trade papers, and periodicals specializing in rating films for audience suitability.

229   Anon. "The New Pictures." Time, 27, No. 17 (27 April), 36.
A favorable review of Mr. Deeds Goes to Town. Capra and Riskin are described as "co-masters of a unique kind of U.S. comedy, part farce, part fantasy and part hokum." Their "magic" defies analysis on paper, the reviewer notes, "because it fits so perfectly its proper medium, the screen."

230   Anon. "On The Current Screen." Literary Digest, 121, No. 15 (11 April), 19.
A highly favorable review of Mr. Deeds Goes to Town. All Hollywood has tried to repeat the formula of It Happened One Night, the reviewer observes, but the first film to match it comes from Capra and Riskin themselves.

231 Anon. "Plays and Pictures." New Statesman and Nation, 12 (29 August), 289.

A review of Mr. Deeds Goes to Town. The film "has charm, character, comedy, sweetness, and wit in good proportions," and it will also be liked for having something to say. Although it goes only "part of the way in its repudiation of plutocratric values . . . perhaps it is pleasant enough for its message to stick." The reviewer, however, faults Capra for allowing minor characters to overact, weakening an otherwise brilliant film.

232 Anon. Review of Mr. Deeds Goes to Town. Box Office (4 April), p. 57.

A brief review, noting that hilarious humor lightens a highly original story packed with human interest.

233 Anon. Review of Mr. Deeds Goes to Town. Daily Variety (25 March), p. 3.

"Master craftsmen" Capra and Robert Riskin are credited with one of the finest films of the season. Behind the antic comedy, the reviewer notes, "the discerning will see pungent commentary on the manners and the conventions of the times, sometimes caustic, sometimes sympathetic, always deeply comprehending." Credits.

234 Anon. Review of Mr. Deeds Goes to Town. Scholastic (23 May), p. 23.

A brief review, praising the film for its naturalness, humor, and moral strength. Excellent photography and rich settings, moreover, help to offset "a regrettable abundance of conversation."

235 Anon. Review of Mr. Deeds Goes to Town. Stage, 13, No. 8, (May), 10.

Brief and highly favorable. Capra set a high pace for himself with It Happened One Night, but has topped that production here.

236 Anon. "$2,000,000 Worth of Scenes from Lost Horizon." Life, 1, No. 4 (14 December), 30-33.

A photo spread from the film, emphasizing the lavishness of the production.

237 B., O. Review of Mr. Deeds Goes to Town. Monthly Film Bulletin, 3, No. 32 (August), 133.

A plot synopsis and brief commentary on the film. "Frank Capra has made an excellent job of a good story which is allowed to unfold itself in a restrained manner."

238 Boehnel, William. Review of Mr. Deeds Goes to Town. New York World-Telegram (17 April), p. 29.

A favorable review. While Capra has produced many distinguished films, Boehnel observes, none has been more amusing and entertaining. To recount the plot scarcely suggests the rich absurdity of Capra's brand of comedy. The film is "a frankly porous-knit piece of summer weather nonsense" which "makes no pretenses at solving anything."

239   Burdett, Winston. "The Screen." Brooklyn Daily Eagle (18 April).
         A review of Mr. Deeds Goes to Town. Although perhaps not as funny and original as It Happened One Night, the film is directed in Capra's "most adroit and airy manner, and is the brightest piece of nonsense to reach town in several months."

240   Cameron, Kate. "Gary Cooper Toots 'Mr. Deeds' into Town." New York Daily News (17 April).
         A favorable review of Mr. Deeds Goes to Town, focusing on Cooper's performance. The film is "directed by Frank Capra in a sprightly and entertaining manner." Brief credits.

241   Creelman, Eileen. "Picture Plays and Players." New York Sun (15 April).
         An interview with Clarence Budington Kelland in conjunction with the release of Mr. Deeds Goes to Town, based on Kelland's story "Opera Hat." Although he mentions that he thinks Capra's film is a "good picture," most of the commentary concerns his other work. A biographical sketch is included.

242   _____. "Picture Plays and Players." New York Sun (17 April), p. 21.
         A review of Mr. Deeds Goes to Town. While its plot is typical of Clarence Budington Kelland, the film itself has the romantic charm of It Happened One Night. "It is the little things in Capra's productions which prove most effective, a gesture here, a glance there, a word or a phrase, each of them perfectly timed to start an audience chuckling all over again." Brief credits.

243   Crewe, Regina. Review of Mr. Deeds Goes to Town. New York American (17 April).
         The film "mingles burlesque and farce with some pretty serious business about the depression, the unemployed and a public benefactor who has not watched his step." Crewe is not entirely pleased with this mixture: the film is enjoyable as long as Deeds is not taken as "some sort of symbolic character." As director, Capra "spins his tale in an interesting style, speedily, and with stress on laughter." Brief credits.

244   Crisler, B.R. "Film Gossip of the Week." New York Times (26 July), sec 9, p. 3.
         An interview with James Hilton concerning Capra's film version of Lost Horizon. Judging by the rushes, Hilton is satisfied that the film will capture the mood of his novel.

245   Cunningham, James P. "Mr. Deeds Goes to Town." Commonweal, 23, No. 26 (24 April), 724.

A brief review. Although Cunningham does not find the story "outstanding screen material," he grants that the film successfully combines "logical hilarity, satire and light romance."

246   Delehanty, Thornton. "'Mr. Deeds Goes to Town' at Radio City Music Hall." New York Evening Post (17 April).
A review of Mr. Deeds Goes to Town. A "gay and quixotic adventure, full of those light and unexpected twists with which Frank Capra invariably manages to enliven an essentially commonplace story."

247   Early, Dudley. "Mr. Capra and Mr. Riskin Go to Town." Family Circle (23 October), pp. 14-17, 22.
A profile of both Capra and Robert Riskin, incorporating an interview with Riskin. Topics include the recent success of Mr. Deeds Goes to Town, the casting of It Happened One Night, and the working relationship between director and writer. "The reason Frank and I get along so well," Riskin is quoted as saying, "is that we have the same basic story idea. We have some awful battles over how the story should be developed, but we never argue over what constitutes a story."

248   Ellis, Peter [Irving Lerner]. "The Screen." New Masses (28 April), p. 29.
"Peter Ellis" is a pseudonym for Irving Lerner. See entry 257a.

249   Ferguson, Otis. "Mr. Capra goes to Town." New Republic, 86, No. 1116 (22 April), 315-16).
A review of Mr. Deeds Goes to Town. The lesson of both this film and It Happened One Night, Ferguson contends, is that in the hands of the best filmmakers movies can be made out of anything. Capra, for example, "takes a plot with as few restrictions as possible (it has the necessary sentimental angle and forward motion but is fairly empty of anything else) and proceeds to fill it up with situations and characters from life." The effect achieved is "literally too much for words, more to be seen than heard about." Ferguson also likens Capra's comic sensibility and craftsmanship to that of René Clair, but notes that Capra is "more homey . . . closer to the lives of his audience, enlisting more of their belief and sympathy." Reprinted in 1971 (see entry 831) and 1975 (see entry 965).

250   _____. "Odets Takes a Holiday." New Republic, 88, No. 1137 (16 September), 156-57.
Ferguson comments briefly but favorably on The Bitter Tea of General Yen during the course of an unfavorable review of Clifford Odets's script for The General Died at Dawn. Reprinted in 1971 (see entry 831).

251   Greene, Graham. "The Cinema." Spectator, 156, No. 5624 (10 April), 664.
A brief review of If You Could Only Cook, falsely labeled a Capra film by Harry Cohn for its release in Great Britain. Greene is

not overly impressed by the film, but innocently treats it as Capra's work, noting "a few agreeable Capra touches." Reprinted in 1937 (see entry 321), 1971 (see entry 835), and 1972 (see entry 875).

252 _____. "The Cinema." Spectator, 157, No. 5644 (28 August), 343.
A favorable review of Mr. Deeds Goes to Town. Greene compares Capra's comedy to that of other lauded directors of the period: "Capra has what Lubitsch, the witty playboy, has not: a sense of responsibility, and what Clair, whimsical, poetic, a little precious and à la mode has not, a kinship with the audience, a sense of common life, a morality: he has what even Chaplin has not, a complete mastery of his medium, and the medium of sound-film, not the film with sound attached to it." Greene also offers an extensive comparison of Mr. Deeds Goes to Town and Fritz Lang's Fury, proposing that both deal with the fate of goodness and simplicity in a deeply selfish and brutal world. "The pessimist makes a tragedy, the optimist (but how far from sweetness and complacency is Capra's optimism) makes a comedy." Reprinted in 1937 (see entry 321), 1971 (see entry 835), 1972 (see entry 875), 1975 (see entry 969), and 1978 (see entry 1079).

*253 Gromo, Mario. Review of Mr. Deeds Goes to Town. La Stampa (Turin), (1 September).
Cited in Roberto Paolella's Frank Capra," Bianco e Nero, 20, Nos. 8-10 (August-October 1959), 157-62. See entry 731.

254 Hamilton, James Shelley. Review of Mr. Deeds Goes to Town. National Board of Review Magazine, No. 11 (May), pp. 11-12.
Hamilton notes that while Capra had established himself as a director with a unique style by the time of It Happened One Night, one perhaps wished for stories of greater substance (The Bitter Tea of General Yen having been forgotten). With Mr. Deeds that wish has been answered; although the story sounds crazy, "out of the fantastic it creates something touching and moving as well as amusing." Brief credits. Reprinted in From Quasimodo to Scarlett O'Hara: A National Board of Review Anthology, 1920-1940, edited by Stanley Hochman (New York: Frederick Ungar Publishing Co., 1982), pp. 220-22.

255 Hills, Beverly. "Sprightly, Serious, Suave." Liberty (9 May), p. 37.
Mr. Deeds Goes to Town is reviewed. Capra's latest offering is "one of the most hilarious and completely satisfying movies of the season"; it is not only "important cinema" but "a good movie." Brief credits and detailed gossip about the actors are provided.

256 Hilton, James. "Hollywood: the First International City the World Has Ever Seen." Cosmopolitan, 101, No. 5 (November), 22-23, 165-68.
As part of a broader article recounting his experiences in Hollywood, novelist Hilton briefly discusses his meetings with Capra, in Hilton's estimation "one of the greatest of the directors of pictures; an artist whose instinct to produce a work of art has an

Writings About Frank Capra   1936

immortal sureness." Having visited the sets of Lost Horizon, and
having talked with Capra and Robert Riskin extensively about the
project, Hilton is certain that the mood and spirit of his novel is
being preserved. "Capra's conception of the lamasery of Shangri-La
. . . was more visual than mine had ever been; but henceforth it is
part of my own mental conception also."

257   Johaneson, Bland. "Gary Cooper Starred." New York Daily
       Mirror (17 April).
         A review of Mr. Deeds Goes to Town. A "pleasant, gay and
lighthearted comedy which lacks the usual Capra distinctions, but
flaunts the usual Capra elements of wit and fun." Brief credits.

257a   Lerner, Irving ["Peter Ellis"]. "The Screen." New Masses (28
       April), p. 29.
         A review of Mr. Deeds Goes to Town. "Behind its sugar-
coated sentimentality and verbal and physical gags Mr. Deeds
approaches the social film. . . . It isn't often that we get an
American film with such a 'favorable' attitude toward the unemployed
man. Certainly no other Hollywood film has ever had an unemployed
speak his mind with as much warmth and passion as does the farmer of
this film."

258   Melvin, E.F. Review of Mr. Deeds Goes to Town. Boston
       Transcript (11 April), p. 4.
         A favorable assessment of the film. "For a combination of
sentimental imagination with hearty humors Frank Capra is hard to
equal."

259   Meyers, Sidney ["Robert Stebbins"]. "Mr. Capra Goes to Town."
       New Theatre (May), pp. 17-18.
         A review of Mr. Deeds Goes to Town. Meyers is especially
impressed with the film in light of It Happened One Night, the social
premise of which he found indefensible. Underlying the whimsy and wit
of Mr. Deeds, Meyers detects a recognition that great multitudes
suffer for the excesses of the few, and he is particularly pleased
with the farmer's interruption of the boy-girl plot, "the first time
in movies we have been given a sympathetic, credible portrait of a
worker, speaking the language of workers, saying the things workers
all over the country say." Reprinted in 1972 (see entry 896) and 1975
(see entry 995).

260   Mosher, John. "The Current Cinema." New Yorker, 12, No. 10
       (25 April), 37.
         A review of Mr. Deeds Goes to Town. Mosher finds a general
tone of "simple amiability" in the film and admires the fresh handling
of the trial scene.

261   Noble, Lorraine, ed. Four-Star Scripts. Garden City, N.Y.:
       Doubleday, Doran, & Co. pp. 24-212.
         Robert Riskin's screenplays for Lady for a Day and It
Happened One Night are included in this volume, the latter checked

against a transcript of the dialogue taken from the finished film. Noble introduces both screenplays with brief discussions of the films' reception and analysis of the dramatic values contained in the scripts.

262   Nugent, Frank S. "The Screen." New York Times (17 April), p. 17.

A review of Mr. Deeds Goes to Town. Nugent observes that with the sequential successes of It Happened One Night, Broadway Bill, and this film, Capra and screenwriter Riskin have become a "complete production staff in themselves." A mere plot synopsis, he contends, is inadequate to the task of capturing the "gay, harebrained, but entirely ingratiating quality" of Mr. Deeds. Brief credits.

*263   Pasinetti, Francesco. Review of Mr. Deeds Goes to Town. Gazzetta di Venezia (1 September).

Cited in Roberto Paolella's "Frank Capra," Bianco e Nero, 20, Nos. 8-10 (August-October 1959) 157-62. See entry 731.

264   Pelswick, Rose. "Mr. Deeds Goes to Town." New York Evening Journal (17 April).

A laudatory review. "The picture is one sparkling situation after another, for Messrs. Capra and Riskin have used the plot merely as a springboard for a succession of deft directorial twists." Brief credits.

265   Penfield, Cornelia. "Hollywood Helmsmen." Stage, 13, No. 7 (April), 62-64, 66-67.

Background information on Capra's career to date, high praise for the exceptional range of his talents as a director, and a description of his working methods on the set. Special attention is given to his unique concern for actors.

266   Puck. "Galleria: 1.--Frank Capra." Cinema (Rome), No. 1, p. 41.

A career sketch through 1935, emphasizing his background as an Italian immigrant.

*267   Ramperti, Marco. Review of Mr. Deeds Goes to Town. L'Illustrazione Italiana (Milan) (6 September).

Cited in Roberto Paolella's "Frank Capra," Bianco e Nero, 20, Nos. 8-10 (August-October 1959), 157-62. See entry 731.

268   Reid, James. "Lost Horizon--Facts about the Fantasy." Motion Picture, 52 (November), 40-41, 76-77, 79.

Behind-the-scenes information on the production, especially the casting. Describing Capra as "one of Hollywood's few authentic geniuses," Reid stresses the director's central role in the making of the film: "He was the first to envision Lost Horizon as a picture. He had the courage to try to film it, even though it might cost hundreds of thousands of dollars and months--perhaps years--of effort. He worked on every scene of the script with scenarist Robert Riskin.

He helped plan every setting. He cast every role personally. He directed every bit of action, every camera angle." The article concludes with the prediction of an Indian prophetess that Capra "will become the greatest film director of all, then add to his fame by writing a stage-play that will create a world sensation." Reid modifies the prediction by asserting that the first part has already come true.

269   S., E.C. "Monitor Movie Guide." Christian Science Monitor (25 April), p. 15.
       A brief, favorable review of Mr. Deeds Goes to Town. "Frank Capra directed this and his people behave like human beings, not film automatons."

*270   Sacchi, Filippo. Review of Mr. Deeds Goes to Town. Corriere della Sera (Milan) (1 September).
       Cited in Roberto Paolella's "Frank Capra," Bianco 'e Nero, 20, Nos. 8-10 (August-October 1959), 157-62. See entry 731.

*271   Setti, Guglielmina. Review of Mr. Deeds Goes to Town. Il Lavoro (Genova) (2 September).
       Cited in Roberto Paolella's "Frank Capra," Bianco e Nero, 20, Nos. 8-10 (August-October 1959), 157-62. See entry 731.

271a   Stebbins, Robert. [Sidney Meyers]. "Mr. Capra Goes to Town." New Theatre (May), pp. 17-18.
       "Robert Stebbins" is a pseudonym for Sidney Meyers. See entry 259.

272   Van Doren, Mark. Second Comings." Nation, 142, No. 3697 (13 May), 623-24.
       Mr. Deeds Goes to Town is discussed in terms of a messianic tradition in literature. Van Doren locates the strength of the film in its depiction of the central character: innocent, virtuous, rational, yet depleted of spiritual pride upon realizing that the world is corrupt and crazy. He is disappointed by the success of Deed's self-defense at the end, but considers the film "a very intelligent and beautiful affair," no less charming than It Happened One Night and more profound. Reprinted in 1942 (see entry 487).

*273   Vecchietti Giorgio. Review of Mr. Deeds Goes to Town. Lo Schermo (Rome) (September).
       Cited in Roberto Paolella's "Frank Capra," Bianco e Nero, 20, Nos. 8-10 (August-October 1959), 157-62. See entry 731.

274   Watts, Richard, Jr. "On the Screen" New York Herald Tribune (17 April), p. 14.
       A favorable review of Mr. Deeds Goes to Town. Watts describes Capra as "one of the important men in Hollywood. Possessing an unostentatious talent for simplicity, democratic humor, humaneness and the comedy of recognition, he has a thorough-going skill for taking familiar, unexciting material and giving it dexterity and

gayety. He can, in fact, be described with some accuracy as the Lubitsch of homespun hilarity." Credits.

*275   Winter, Alice A. Review of <u>Lost Horizon</u>. <u>St. Nicholas</u>, 64 (November), 19.
        Cited in <u>Cumulated Dramatic Index, 1909-1949</u>.

1937

276   Abel [Abel Green]. "<u>Lost Horizon</u>." <u>Variety</u> (10 March), p. 14.
        The reviewer has high praise for the film, which he considers a difficult story cannily told. Green also notes that although Columbia will likely lose money on the movie because of its $2.5 million price tag, they will make up for this loss in increased prestige. Credits.

277   Agate, James. "<u>Lost Horizon</u>." <u>Tatler</u> (28 April).
        A review of the film. Agate focuses, with an ironic eye, on the effort expended to re-create Tibet on the screen. Nevertheless, by the end of the film he found himself "worked up into a state of genuine excitement." Reprinted in 1946 (see entry 557).

277a   Anon. "Bob Riskin Muses on 'Lost Horizon' and Wisecracking to a Broadway Chorine." <u>Variety</u> (7 April), pp. 4, 57.
        Riskin is described as having nothing left to say about <u>Lost Horizon</u> amid the heated debates the film has aroused in the film industry. Every point of controversy, he explains, was examined by Capra and himself before the film was completed. He has no interest in making a defense of their decisions his life work, but is pleased that <u>Lost Horizon</u> has provoked strong reactions and he is proud of the film itself. Riskin also observes that based upon his experience with <u>When You're in Love</u>, he has decided never to both write and direct a film again.

278   Anon. "Capra's 'Lost Horizon' Great Triumph of Unlimited Appeal."
        <u>Hollywood Reporter</u>, 38, No. 3 (29 February), 2-4.
        A review of <u>Lost Horizon</u>. "It is shattering outdoor spectacle, a thumping adventure tale, an idyllic romance and prophetic tale of a new, better sort of civilization. The picture is all ways a triumph for Frank Capra. . . . It is an audacious production and a master-work of direction."

279   Anon. "Frank Capra in England." <u>Daily Telegraph</u> (London) (19 April).
        A survey of Capra's career on the occasion of his arrival in England together with Robert Riskin.

280   Anon. "Gives the Screen New Dignity: <u>Lost Horizon</u>." <u>Film Spectator</u> (Hollywood), 2, No. 24 (27 February), 8.

Writings About Frank Capra   1937

            A review of Lost Horizon. "An extraordinary demonstration
of the tremendous sweep screen art can attain, a production of magni-
tude and impressiveness, a powerful sermon on right-living, preached
in a fascinating setting and coming at a time when the world badly
needs the lesson it teaches. . . . Capra's direction of his players
reveals outstanding skill."

281   Anon. "London Newspapers Make Frank Capra Something of a
       Paradox: Director Is 'A Plain Business Man' and 'An Idealist
       of the Screen.'" New York World-Telegram (22 May).
            A report on Capra's visit to London, and the contradictory
reactions of the British press to him.

282   Anon. "'Lost Horizon,' at the Tivoli from Monday." New
       Statesman and Nation (17 April), p. 636.
            An ambivalent review of Lost Horizon. Capra, noted for his
delicate handling of sentimental material, has faltered, for James
Hilton's utopia is beyond Capra's power of realization. But "the
comic elements are free from the stink of uplift" and the opening reel
is brilliant.

283   Anon. "Lost Horizon." Film Daily (4 March), p. 5.
            A laudatory review of the film, judged Columbia's most
ambitious screen achievement. "Consistent to the Frank Capra standards, the production has been made with painstaking effort and appreciation of its dramatic values." Brief credits.

284   Anon. "Lost Horizon." Motion Picture Review Digest, 2, No.
       13 (29 March), 66-68.
            Reviews are excerpted from a wide variety of sources,
including newspapers, magazines, trade papers, and periodicals
specializing in rating films for audience suitability. Also see entry
285.

285   Anon. "Lost Horizon." Motion Picture Review Digest, 2, No.
       26 (28 June), 55-56.
            Reviews are excerpted from a wide variety of sources,
including newspapers, magazines, trade papers, and periodicals
specializing in rating films for audience suitability. Also see entry
284.

286   Anon. "Monitor Movie Guide." Christian Science Monitor (17
       April), p. 17.
            A brief review of Lost Horizon. The film combines 'beauti-
ful photography, magnificent settings, and good acting to recreate
through cinematic terms the lost world of Shangri-La."

287   Anon. "The New Pictures." Time, 29, No. 10 (8 March), 54,
       56.
            A review of Lost Horizon. Capra, it is noted, has "devised
one of the most magnificent sets in cinema history." Moreover, he
"has had the good judgement to leave the story almost exactly as it

was written and the skill to match James Hilton's verbal talent with pictorial subtlety." The one flaw is Capra's decision to deviate from the novel and end the film happily.

*288 Anon. Portrait of Frank Capra. <u>Vogue</u>, 89 (1 April), 106.
   Cited in <u>Cumulated Dramatic Index, 1909-1949</u>. It is unclear whether any text is annexed to the portrait.

289 Anon. Review of <u>Lost Horizon</u>. <u>Box Office</u> (6 March), p. 17.
   Brief, but highly favorable. "Capra's inspired production and meticulous direction is a triumph of super-showmanship."

290 Anon. Review of <u>Lost Horizon</u>. <u>Cue</u> (27 February), p. 18.
   The reviewer judges the film to be one of the finest of the decade. "Under the brilliant direction of Frank Capra 'Lost Horizon' grips your attention from first to last."

291 Anon. Review of <u>Lost Horizon</u>. <u>Daily Variety</u> (20 February), p. 3.
   Commercial success and critical favor is predicted.

292 Anon. Review of <u>Lost Horizon</u>. <u>Rob Wagner's Script</u> (13 March), p. 10.
   Primarily a detailed plot synopsis. Capra's direction is described as "fine throughout." With the exception of the opening fanfare, which the reviewer finds overly screeching, the film is judged magnificent.

*293 Anon. Review of <u>Lost Horizon</u>. <u>Theatre World</u>, 27 (June), 91.
   Cited in <u>Cumulated Dramatic Index, 1909-1949</u>.

294 Anon. Review of <u>Lost Horizon</u>. <u>Times</u> (London) (19 April).
   An unfavorable review. Capra is faulted for taking the hint provided by James Hilton's novel "as an index to an inventory." The elaborate scale of the film thus dwarfs the original conception, and the spiritual implications of the theme have been exchanged for "a material realization of a businessman's dream." Although some of the photography is superb and the direction is occasionally admirable, "these have been imposed on a disappointing story."

295 Anon. "Screen: Prize-Winning Team Produces film of Like Caliber." <u>Newsweek</u>, 9, No. 10 (6 March), 30-31.
   The story of the production of <u>Lost Horizon</u> dominates this article, with a brief review appended. The film is seen to differ greatly from the "casual, realistic films that made Capra famous," and hence indicates the director's scope. The opening passages are found most effective; the episodes at Shangri-La are somewhat disappointing in contrast. Extensively illustrated.

296 Anon. "Stage and Screen." <u>Literary Digest</u>, 123, No. 10 (6 March), 20.

A review of Lost Horizon. The film, it is noted, has escaped the disastrous fate of many extravagantly produced movies. "Thanks chiefly to the Capra knowledge of what motion pictures are for and Robert Riskin's expert treatment of a difficult story, 'Lost Horizon' is a stunning, deeply moving film. . . . It has a curious, haunting quality, fetching deep into the emotions."

297 Anon. "Too Much Music for the Film; It May Become a Symphony." New York Herald Tribune (19 September).
An interview with composer Dimitri Tiomkin concerning his work on the score for Lost Horizon. He describes how Capra allows his collaborators freedom yet influences their work.

298 Barnes, Howard. "The Screen." New York Herald Tribune (4 March), p. 7.
A review of Lost Horizon, comparing it with The Good Earth. Barnes decides that although Lost Horizon lacks the "emotional compulsion and epic breath" of the other film, it is more exacting and daring in its reliance on ideas rather than action. Moreover, Capra's ability to make an entertaining film out of a novel little suited for motion pictures augurs well for future enterprises of this kind. Barnes finds the middle section, however, less successful than the beginning and end.

299 _____. "The Screen." New York Herald Tribune (11 April), p. 16.
As part of a larger article on "art versus box-office," Barnes responds to an attack levied against Capra for making Lost Horizon by P.S. Harrison in Harrison's Report. Harrison allegedly argued that Capra could make greater profits by turning out two small films like Mr. Deeds Goes to Town rather than one with a high budget, and that Lost Horizon, unlike Capra's earlier work, was didactic and did not leave the viewer in a happy frame of mind. Barnes replies that Capra's previous films were just as experimental in their way as Lost Horizon; it is only the fact that It Happened One Night has been copied that makes it now seem conventional. Moreover, "whether its offerings are expensive or cheap, the screen's only chance for development . . . is in someone's growing 'artistic' very often." Also discussed are Warner Brother's "social problem" films, and Tabu by Robert Flaherty and F.W. Murnau.

300 Best, Katharine. "See in the Dark." Stage, 14, No. 7 (August), 82.
A review of Lost Horizon. Best admires the attempt to break with standard box-office formulas, but considers the depiction of life at Shangri-La ponderous and the moments of reverence strained and self-conscious. No mention of Capra.

301 Boehnel, William. Review of Lost Horizon. New York World-Telegram (4 March), p. 17.
Highly favorable. The film is "beautifully acted, superbly

directed, oft-times thrilling and compassionate and nearly always entertaining."

302   ____. "Movie Fans to Gain by Capra's Return." New York World-Telegram (30 November).
    The mending of a rift between Capra and Harry Cohn at Columbia provokes the author to survey Capra's life and his work as a film director. He attributes Capra's success to "his genius for supplying the 'business' that goes with the lines the actors speak."

303   Borden, W.T. "Frank Capra of the Cinema." Brooklyn Daily Eagle (7 March), 4F, 8F.
    A feature article on Capra's life and movie career written to coincide with the release of Lost Horizon. The author notes that "in recent years movie audiences have grown more and more director-conscious" and that Capra, whose work has been of consistent quality, has perhaps made the most definite impression on the public.

304   Burdett, Winston. "The Screen." Brooklyn Daily Eagle (4 March).
    A review of Lost Horizon. Burdett notes that Capra handles melodramatic episodes expertly, and natural settings to superb effect, but there are also disturbing shifts in mood, especially involving comedy relief and the love interest. "The result is a film which, despite its many passages of high and awesome fantasy, has a rather difficult time maintaining a unity of tone and atmosphere." Brief credits.

305   Cameron, Kate. "'Lost Horizon' Is a Unique Picture." New York Daily News (4 March), p. 40.
    A review of Lost Horizon. Cameron finds much that is new and beautiful in the film, but also finds the middle section at times talky and overlong. "Mr. Capra's job in transposing the fantastic story to the screen was a painstaking but not an inspired one." Brief credits.

*306   Cecchi, Emilio. "Frank Capra." Cinema (Rome), 2, No. 20 (25 April), 312.
    Cited in Francesco Bolzoni's "Emilio Cecchi, un letterato al cinema," Bianco e Nero, 19, No. 4 (April), 42. See entry 703.

*307   ____. "Frank Capra." Bianco e Nero, 1, No. 4 (30 April), 120.
    Cited in Francesco Bolzoni's "Emilio Cecchi, un letterato al cinema," Bianco e Nero, 19, No. 4 (April), 42. See entry 703.

*308   ____. "Un capolavoro di Frank Capra: Orizzonte perduto." Lo Schermo (Rome), 3, No. 2 (November), 23.
    A review of Lost Horizon. cited in Francesco Bolzoni's "Emilio Cecchi, un letterato al cinema," Bianco e Nero, 19, No. 4 (April), 42. See entry 703.

309   Cook, Alistair. Review of Mr. Deeds Goes to Town, in Garbo and the Nightwatchmen. Edited by Alistair Cooke. London: J. Cape.
       Cook qualifies his previous enthusiasm for Capra's work: "Capra's a great talent all right, but I have the uneasy feeling he's on his way out. He's starting to make movies about themes instead of about people." This review was originally published in an uncited periodical. It was reprinted in 1971 (see entry 829).

310   Creelman, Eileen. "The New Talkies." New York Sun (4 March), p. 29.
       A review of Lost Horizon. Creelman finds the film "as expressive of its times as it is removed from them in plot and atmosphere." Life in Shangri-La strikes her as curiously diluted; hence despite "the humor, the action, the good cheer, the picture's viewpoint has almost a defeatist quality." Whether or not one agrees with the philosophy, however, the work is distinguished and finely acted, skillfully balancing comedy and drama. Brief credits.

311   Crewe, Regina. "'Lost Horizon' Is Masterpiece of Cinema Art, Story Enthralls with Its Gripping Drama." New York American (4 March).
       As the headline suggests, a laudatory review of Lost Horizon. Crewe commends Columbia for risking millions on the film, Capra for the genius to adapt the story to the screen, and Ronald Colman for his central performance. Brief credits.

312   Cunningham, James P. "Lost Horizon." Commonweal, 25, No. 22 (26 March), 612.
       A highly favorable review. Singled out for praise are Capra's direction, the quality of the acting, and the sets. The film is "a striking monument to the courage and vision of Columbia Pictures, its sponsor."

313   Davy, Charles. "Films." London Mercury, 36, No. 212 (June), 187.
       A review of Lost Horizon. Davy finds that the visual energy of the opening flight dissipates when Shangri-La is reached. He also notes that whereas Capra's social conscience gave an edge to the humor of Mr. Deeds Goes to Town, the lama's social principle of kindness is too easy in the utopian world of Shangri-la.

314   Ellis, Peter [Irving Lerner]. "The Screen." New Masses (16 March), pp. 27-28.
       "Peter Ellis" is a pseudonym for Irving Lerner. See entry 328a.

315   F., R.R. Review of Lost Horizon. Monthly Film Bulletin, 4, No. 4 (April), 82.
       Brief credits, a synopsis, and commentary on the film. "The story is Utopian fantasy on a grand scale, but . . . once

Shangri-La is achieved the long passages of philosophical dialogue are not equal to the stupendous excitement of the kidnapping."

316   Ferguson, Otis. "Capra and Tibet." National Board of Review Magazine (March).
A review of Lost Horizon. Ferguson proposes that Capra, having begun to take himself seriously as an artist, saw Lost Horizon as "both a smashing adventure story and an excursion into philosophy that would stun everybody." When he leaves the opening action-spectacle for the romantic utopia of Shangri-La, however, Capra is no longer at ease. "This film was made with obvious care and expense; but it will be notable in the future only as the first wrong step in a career that till now has been a denial of the very tendencies in pictures which this film represents." Reprinted in From Quasimodo to Scarlett O'Hara: A National Board of Review Anthology, 1920-1940, edited by Stanley Hochman (New York: Frederick Ungar Publishing Co., 1982), pp. 239-40. Also see entry 317.

317   _____. "The Earth, the Egg, etc." New Republic, 90, No. 1163 (17 March), 167-68.
A brief assessment of Lost Horizon. Ferguson grants the film some moments of charm and adventure, notes good performances by Ronald Colman and Edward Everett Horton, and speculates that the lavish production may be commercially successful. But he finds the general effect of the film "mawkish, muffed, and . . . mixed up." Reprinted in 1971 (see entry 831). Also see entry 316.

318   Forman, Harrison. "The Hollywood Star You Never See on the Screen." Liberty (April?), pp. 58-59.
A personality profile of Capra at the time of the release of Lost Horizon. As a dreamer himself, Forman proposes, Capra understood the material of the novel. The success of Capra's films is attributed to the fact that his characters are alive, everyday folk, not fanciful puppets. (On file with Capra clippings in the Academy of Motion Picture Arts and Science's Margaret Herrick Library. No date is given.)

319   G., K.M. "Lost Horizon." Scholastic (20 March), pp. 22-23.
A review of the film. Amid real international problems, the reviewer notes, the miracle of Shangri-La may be hard to believe. "But believe it, and you will have one of the experiences of a lifetime in the theatre." Speculating that the film's magnificent architecture, choir music, and heavenly atmosphere are "concessions perhaps to a public attuned to Hollywood romantics," he nevertheless finds the film generally faithful to James Hilton's novel. He links the fiction to traditions of Utopian thought, but assures potential moviegoers that the film is not dry or academic: "Capra has packed his picture with every conceivable variety of thrill."

*320   Gramantieri, Tullio. "Biografia di Capra." Cinema (Rome), No. 29.

Cited in *Filmlexicon degli autori delle opere*. See entry 706.

321 Greene, Graham. Review of *If You Could Only Cook*, in *Garbo and the Nightwatchmen*. Edited by Alistair Cooke. London: J. Cape.
A reprint of Greene's 1937 review (see entry 251). Reprinted again in 1971 (see entry 835).

322 ____. Review of *Mr. Deeds Goes to Town*, in *Garbo and the Nightwatchmen*. Edited by Alistair Cooke. London: J. Cape.
A reprint of Greene's 1936 review (see entry 252). Reprinted again in 1971 (see entry 835).

323 ____. "The Cinema." *Spectator*, 158, No. 5679 (30 April), 805.
A review of *Lost Horizon*. With the exception of the opening aerial evacuation, Graham finds the film a dull, disappointing successor to *Mr. Deeds Goes to Town*. He faults the dialogue, humor, direction, and sets, and is especially disturbed by the decision to have the hero's return to civilization described rather than depicted. Reprinted in 1972 (see entry 875), 1975 (see entry 969), and 1978 (see entry 1079).

324 H., R. Review of *Lost Horizon*. *Manchester Guardian* (16 April), p. 22.
Brief commentary on the film, focusing on the improbability of the design of the lamasery. Supposedly a storehouse of art, the building "resembles nothing so much as 'super-cinema.' Is this Mr. Hilton's fantasy . . . or is it a joke of the director?"

325 Haufler, Charles. "*Lost Horizon*." *Newark Evening News* (4 March), p. 26.
An ambivalent review of the film. Haunting at times, with breathtaking scenery, the film is marred by the intrusion of comedy relief and a Hollywood cuteness. But there were problems in adapting this story, and "Capra merits the highest honors for his remarkable work."

326 Hills, Beverly. Review of *Lost Horizon*. *Liberty* (27 March), p. 49.
Capra (an "ex-Los Angeles newsboy with the touch of Aladdin") is credited with capturing the fragile charm of Hilton's novel. The reviewer notes that there are moments when the story goes "stodgy and moviesque," but for the most part it is singularly beautiful.

327 Johaneson, Bland. "'Lost Horizon' Soon at Globe." *New York Daily Mirror* (1 March).
A brief survey of Capra's career from *The Strong Man* through *Mr. Deeds Goes to Town*.

328 _____. Review of <u>Lost Horizon</u>. New York <u>Daily Mirror</u> (4 March).
Highly favorable. Capra "invokes a witching mood and sustains it through two hours of frantic action and tense suspense."

328a Lerner, Irving ["Peter Ellis"]. "The Screen." <u>New Masses</u> (16 March), pp. 27-28.
A review of <u>Lost Horizon</u>. Ellis notes that Capra, one of the most important Hollywood directors to emerge in the past few years, has been sidetracked by the prospects of a multimillion-dollar spectacle. "Not since the days when Capra made <u>Dirigible</u> and <u>Submarine</u> has any one of his films contained so much that was trite, such little characterization, and such stupid and dangerous philosophy. . . . In a sense, <u>Lost Horizon</u> is an autobiography of Hollywood. It emerges as the apotheosis of escapism."

329 Martin, Mildred. "Camera Angle on Film Folk." <u>Philadelphia Inquirer</u> (8 March).
A highly favorable review of <u>Lost Horizon</u>. Despite the difficulties of translating the book to the screen, Capra succeeds in "capturing the broad beauty, the persuasive philosophy of the Hilton novel."

330 Meyers, Sidney. ["Robert Stebbins"]. Review of <u>Lost Horizon</u>. <u>New Theatre and Film</u> (April), pp. 27-28.
Meyers is alarmed by the drift in Capra's career. <u>Broadway Bill</u> and <u>Mr. Deeds Goes to Town</u> demonstrated Capra's distress with the fact that mass misery is the foundation of the fortunes of the few, but he has been unable to avoid the chauvinism and escapist philosophy of Hilton's novel in <u>Lost Horizon</u>. If, as reports suggest, Capra is solely responsible for the film, the blame he must bear is great. Excerpts from this review were reprinted in 1974 (see entry 939).

331 M[osher], J[ohn] C. "The Current Cinema." <u>New Yorker</u>, 13, No. 3 (6 March), 62.
A brief review of <u>Lost Horizon</u>, which Mosher finds "longish and wearisome." No mention of Capra.

332 Nugent, Frank S. "The Screen." <u>New York Times</u> (4 March), p. 27.
A review of <u>Lost Horizon</u>. With this film, Nugent notes, M-G-M no longer has the corner on the large-scale production market. He is impressed by the opulence of the sets and the attention to large and small detail, but is slightly disappointed by the ending. Photography and set design are judged the best of the year. Brief credits. Also see entry 333.

333 _____. "Scanning <u>Lost Horizon</u>." <u>New York Times</u> (7 March), sec. 11, p. 5.
A followup to Nugent's initial review. He remains fascinated the with technical ingenuity and artistry Hollywood is capable

of deploying, and praises the film for its faithfulness to the spirit of Hilton's novel. Also see entry 332.

334   Orme, Michael. "The World of Kinema." Illustrated London News, 190 (1 May), 762).
    Orme has lavish praise for Capra and Lost Horizon in this review. Capra's recent comedies, Orme proposes, may have obliterated the traces of more vigorous earlier pictures such as Submarine and Dirigible, but Capra's "unerring sense of screen values amounts to genius, and genius is by no means confined to any one particular line of thought." Detailing Capra's efforts in making Lost Horizon, Orme proposes that "the hand of the master is everywhere apparent in a production of enthralling interest. . . . He artfully balances hypothesis with romance and humor, so that philosophy loses its austerity or is, as it were, wreathed in smiles."

335   Pelswick, Rose. "Fantasy & Action Comingle in Story of Tibet Lamasery." New York Evening Journal (4 March).
    A favorable review of Lost Horizon. "Crediting his audience with intelligence, Capra has retained the almost dream-like quality of Hilton's book and enhanced it with breath-taking, lovely sets." Brief credits.

336   Schallert, Edwin. "'Lost Horizon' Limns Rare Utopian Theme." Los Angeles Times (11 March), p. 17.
    A review of Lost Horizon. Schallert is impressed by the romanticism and spirituality of the film. Finding it unlike Capra's previous work (with the possible exception of The Bitter Tea of General Yen), Schallert suggests that it "reveals less of the director's individuality." Capra's craftsmanship, however, is evident in "all the technical phases of the production."

337   Stallings, Laurence. "Four of a Kind." Stage, 14 (April), 53-55.
    Lost Horizon is reviewed. Stallings finds the film a mixture of "Capra-Riskin magic" and "Mr. Hilton's insecure metaphysics." The opening airplane sequence is beautifully shot, but Shangri-La does lend itself to the epic mood established at the outset. Stallings contrasts this with Mr. Deeds Goes to Town, a film in "the true Capra vein," containing more genuine fantasy than Hilton's novel. He speculates that if Capra had allowed Longfellow Deeds, with his soundly quizzical eye, to come upon Shangri-La, the director would have made the film of the year. Excerpts from this review were reprinted in 1974 (see entry 939).

337a   Stebbins, Robert [Sidney Meyers]. Review of Lost Horizon. New Theatre and Film (April), pp. 27-28.
    "Robert Stebbins" is a pseudonym for Sidney Meyers. See entry 330.

*338   Tully, Jim. Commentary on Frank Capra. Cinema Arts (June), p. 42.

Cited in *A Library of Film Criticism: American Film Directors*, edited by Stanley Hochman (New York: Frederick Ungar Publishing Co., 1974), p. 33.

339 _____. "Star Boss." New York *Herald Tribune, This Week Magazine* (14 November), p. 7.
A biographical sketch centering on Capra's early years. Very inaccurate.

340 Van Doren, Mark. "Films." *Nation*, 144, No. 11 (13 March), 305-6.
Lost Horizon is reviewed. A "brilliant beginning and a great deal of wonderful photography throughout do not conceal the fact that the message of the movie is shamefully soft and false." Van Doren chooses to blame James Hilton and Robert Riskin for this rather than Capra, "who after all gave us *It Happened One Night* and *Mr. Deeds*."

341 Winsten, Archer. "Movie Talk." *New York Post* (4 March).
A review of *Lost Horizon*. Noting that separate reviews could be written praising the film itself, comparing it with the novel, or discussing its central theme of kindness, Winsten sketches an outline for all three. He ends the first commending Capra for the courage to deal with an unusual subject: "He believed in the subject and he went a long way with it." Winsten also notes that the action drags somewhat in the middle of the film.

1938

342 Anon. "Capra's Villains Are 'Ideas.'" *Brooklyn Daily Eagle* (27 August).
Commentary on the distinctive qualities of Capra's recent work. Capra is found to eschew flesh-and-blood villains in favor of disembodied ideas against which the forces of righteousness must do battle, forging a conflict between classes rather than individuals. Moreover, he makes plausible improbable situations by treating them matter-of-factly and establishing the actors as real people. He also couches social significance in a story that is never dull. *It Happened One Night*, *Broadway Bill*, and *You Can't Take It with You* are used to illustrate these propositions.

343 Anon. "Columbia's Gem." *Time*, 32, No. 6 (8 August), 35-38.
A cover story on Capra one month before the scheduled release of *You Can't Take It with You*. Capra is now regarded not only as the commercial mainstay of Columbia but as the top director in the industry. His strength is seen as a peculiarly American, kinetic humor marked by adroit bits of business to accent the comic line. While Hitchcock is labeled a master of nightmarish melodrama, Cukor of sentiment, Ford and Fleming of action, Koster of girlish sweetness, and Lubitsch of Continental sophistication, Capra is dubbed a master of pace. A biographical sketch is included.

344 Anon. "Following the Films." Scholastic (1 October), p. 13.
A review of You Can't Take It with You, judged, despite some overlong love scenes, the best screen comedy of the year. The Sycamores are "the grandest, goofiest folks we've ever met on the screen."

345 Anon. "Happiness Offers the Raw Material for His Pictures." New York Herald Tribune (14 August).
An overview of Capra's films during the last five years. Noting that the director has become identified with a certain type of film, the author proposes that Capra has been "building a treatise on the pursuit and capture of happiness." In the process, Capra has endowed entertaining films "with richness of flavor, and a content much more deeply suggestive of reality and the dignity of the human spirit than is at all apparent on their surfaces."

346 Anon. "Life on Display." Brooklyn Daily Eagle (23 October).
A favorable review of You Can't Take It with You and background material on Capra, the latter serving to illustrate how he uses his "knowledge of humans" in his work.

347 Anon. "Lights! Action! Camera!" Canadian Magazine, 90 (October), 55.
You Can't Take It with You is very briefly reviewed. "Last year's Pulitzer Prize-winning stage play picks up speed and plot in its cinema translation to become the top comedy of 1938."

348 Anon. "Monitor Movie Guide." Christian Science Monitor (29 October), p. 17.
A brief review of You Can't Take It with You." "An excellent film comedy with a genuine theme. . . . The cast is in most cases all that could be asked for and Mr. Capra's touches are all over the place."

349 Anon. "Movie of the Week: You Can't Take It with You." Life, 5, No. 12 (19 September), 42-47.
A photo-essay on the film. Great attention is paid to the fact that Capra possesses complete control over his productions and has greater box-office appeal than many stars. Included is a section entitled "How Frank Capra Makes a Hit Picture," in which the director's activity at every stage of the work is detailed. Capra's characteristic touch is defined as "a tender sense of humor, a quick sense of social satire, a glowing faith in human nature."

350 Anon. "The New Pictures." Time, 32, No. 11 (12 September), 44-45.
A laudatory review of You Can't Take It with You. Capra and Riskin are credited with bringing out dramatic conflict and characterization that the comic exterior of Kaufman and Hart's stage play had concealed. Known for his knack of inventing business on the screen, Capra has passed the test of adapting a play already packed

with business and has earned his right to a third Academy Award for direction.

351   Anon. Review of You Can't Take It with You. Box Office (2 September), p. 31.
        The film is found to approach perfection in casting, and to integrate wholesome comedy, romance, pathos, and homespun philosophy.

352   Anon. Review of You Can't Take It with You. Daily Variety (24 August), p. 3.
        Highly favorable. A Capra film "is always a screen event. This one will probably be rated his best."

353   Anon. Review of You Can't Take It with You. Stage, 16. No. 1 (October), p. 63.
        Noting with some irony the growth of Capra's legend in Hollywood ("Mr. Capra's talents seem insurmountable"), the reviewer admits that although the subject matter of the play is dated, Capra's film version gives it a freshness, creating "as deft a sugar-coated pill as will be swallowed nationally."

354   Anon. Review of You Can't Take It with You. Theatre Arts Monthly, 22, No. 11 (22 November), 811.
        The reviewer notes that Grandpa Vanderhof and the Sycamores from the original stage play are, under Capra's understanding direction, as delightful as ever. Moreover, Robert Riskin has made a first-rate scenario from the Kaufman and Hart script, making only careful changes in it.

355   Anon. "'You Can't' Superfine Screen Hit." Hollywood Reporter, 47, No. 16 (24 August), 3.
        A laudatory review of You Can't Take It with You. "With a hand-picked cast studded with No. 1 marquee names, it has been assembled and directed by one of the best megaphonists in the business, Frank Capra."

356   Anon. "You Can't Take It with You." Film Daily (26 August), p. 9.
        A highly favorable review, describing the film as "smoothly directed, naturally acted and carefully produced." Brief credits.

357   Anon. "You Can't Take It with You." Motion Picture Review Digest, 3, No. 39 (26 September).
        Reviews are excerpted from a wide variety of sources, including newspapers, magazines, trade papers, and periodicals specializing in rating films for audience suitability. Also see entry 358.

358   Anon. "You Can't Take It with You." Motion Picture Review Digest, 3, No. 52 (26 December), 103.
        Reviews are excerpted from a wide variety of sources, including newspapers, magazines, trade papers, and periodicals

specializing in rating films for audience suitability. Also see entry 357.

359 Anon. "You Can't Take It with You." Newsweek, 12, No. 11 (12 September), 21-22.
A review of the film, although largely a plot synopsis. Robert Riskin is credited with widening the play's scope and reworking its "wispy plot into a full-bodied narrative." Capra is credited with characteristically inventing bits of business that make the performances more realistic. Together they "have proved that Hollywood can fashion a play into an intelligent movie."

360 Anon. "We Meet a Noisy Family . . . You Can't Take It with You." Film Spectator (Hollywood), 13, No. 16 (3 September), 7-8.
The reviewer claims that You Can't Take It with You is the best talking picture he has ever seen, and praises the film extravagantly. "With keen appreciation of the true values of the story and his extraordinary ability to realize them on the screen, Frank Capra has presented to the world a great human document."

361 Barnes, Howard. Review of You Can't Take It with You. New York Herald Tribune (2 September), p. 10.
A favorable review, focusing on the skill and originality of Capra and Riskin's adaptation. "Instead of merely photographing a sequence of successful stage scenes, they have altered and enlarged the dramatic incident." The resulting work is even more captivating than the original play, and one of the finest films of the year. Credits. Also see entry 362.

362 _____. "The Screen." New York Herald Tribune (4 September).
The success of You Can't Take It with You forces Barnes to go against his long-standing opposition to stage adaptations: Capra and Riskin have enlarged the play's :scope and meaning without destroying its original charm and amusement." Also see entry 361.

363. _____. "The Screen." New York Herald Tribune (9 October).
Barnes proposes that although Capra may be responsible for only one film out of five hundred released by Hollywood during the course of a year, he is in fact the most important figure in motion pictures today, having done more to change the fundamental character and quality of filmmaking than anyone else. Through the example set by his own films, and through his activities as a leader in the industry, he has defined "the importance of the director in the complicated business of turning out a photoplay." Combining the authority of the artist with a shrewd knowledge of the complex business of filmmaking, he has established a model that is likely responsible for the general upswing in the quality of films during the past few years.

364 Boehnel, William. Review of You Can't Take It with You. New York World-Telegram (2 September).

Boehnel praises the film as "one of the most utterly irresistible, delightful, human and entertaining" movies he has ever seen. He finds it superior to the Kaufman and Hart play on which it is based in that Capra and Riskin have emphasized the pertinent social aspects of the material and given the work "a nice homespun philosophy without being maudlin."

365   Brown, John Mason. "Two on the Aisle." New York Post (14 September).

A comparison of Hart and Kaufman's You Can't Take It with You and Capra and Riskin's screen version of it. Noting the many changes in the film, Brown states his preference for the original play.

366   Chamberlin, Jo. "If You Don't Fit a Groove." New York Herald Tribune, This Week Magazine (11 December), p. 2.

Capra's career is discussed as part of a larger article on famous people who experimented with a variety of different jobs before settling into their life work, and who consider themself better off for the experience gained.

367   Char [Roy Chartier]. "You Can't Take It with You." Variety (7 September), p. 12.

An ambivalent review. Chartier finds the film's tempo fast and well sustained, but also thinks the work could be shortened. He considers the comedy suitably wacky, but also notes that it contrasts with a serious, philosophical element that at times seems overstressed. He finds most of the roles well acted, but considers banker Kirby and his establishment a "colossus" of Capra's imagination. Brief credits.

368   Creelman, Eileen. "The New Talkies." New York Sun (2 September).

A review of You Can't Take It with You. Creelman has high praise for Capra and Riskin's adaptation: they have expanded the comedy and philosophy while sacrificing nothing essential. The film is smoother, more subtle, and quite as hilarious as the original play. Brief credits.

369   Dugan, James. "Movies." New Masses (13 September), pp. 28-31.

A review of You Can't Take It with You. Disturbed by the warm reception given the film by an upper-middle-class audience at Radio City Music Hall, Dugan predicts that "the period of big headache is about to begin in the social film." Singled out for special concern is Grandpa's equation of Communism, fascism, and Nazism (a "disenguous bid for reactionary applause") and his subsequent refusal to pay taxes. "The emotional charm that Riskin and Capra have previously commanded becomes hokum and the promise of economic understanding is now demagogy. . . . What Capra and Riskin have done is a good box-office job, an entertaining film, which will just about ruin their enviable position as the screen's foremost exponents of exciting, topical, heartwarming--and honest--material."

370   Ferguson, Otis. "Boys of All Ages." New Republic, 96, No. 1242 (21 September), 188.
       A brief review of You Can't Take It with You. Finding little in the film to suggest Capra's previous charm as a director, Ferguson speculates that the success of Mr. Deeds Goes to Town has given Capra and Riskin a damaging idea of themselves as social philosophers. "The comedy of falls and upsets seems perfunctory though dogged, as though the main business in hand were to make platitude boom like truth." Reprinted in 1971 (see entry 831).

371   Galway, Peter. "The Movies." New Statesman and Nation, 16 (5 November), 724.
       A review of You Can't Take It with You. Galway finds the film exhausting and overly sentimental, but deems the bank scenes "mordantly amusing" and the acting by Edward Arnold, Jean Arthur, and James Stewart "first-rate." No mention of Capra.

*372   Green, E.M. Review of You Can't Take It with You. Theatre World, 30 (October), 184.
       Cited in Cumulated Dramatic Index, 1909-1949.

373   Greene, Graham. "The Cinema." Spectator, 161, No. 5759 (11 November), 807.
       A review of You Can't Take It with You and a reassessment of Capra's career. Greene worries that Capra has emerged as a muddled, sentimental idealist who senses something is wrong with the social system, but offers only vague dissatisfaction and an urge to escape in response. He concedes, however, that Capra has "a touch of genius with a camera," an editing style as brilliant as Eisenstein, and a "popular poetry which is apt to turn wistful." Reprinted in 1972 (see entry 875), 1975 (see entry 969), and 1978 (see entry 1079).

374   Hartung, Philip T. "But Who Wants to Take It with Him?" Commonweal, 28, No. 21 (16 September), 534.
       A brief review of You Can't Take It with You. Hartung considers the film to have greater seriousness and depth than the play on which it is based.

375   Hills, Beverly. "Whimsey Marches On." Liberty (16 October), p. 53.
       A review of You Can't Take It with You. Primarily a plot synopsis, but brief commentary is offered on Robert Riskin's expansion of the original stage play. "Another Frank Capra triumph, with a lot of credit to the authors of the Broadway stage hit, George S. Kaufman and Moss Hart. Has the human touch."

376   Johaneson, Bland. "Capra Product Stars Colbert and Gable." New York Daily News (17 May).

1938   **Writings About Frank Capra**

A revival of It Happened One Night at the Rivoli Theater in New York occasions a brief survey of the history of the film, from Capra's initial problems with casting it through its surprising commercial success and the subsequent career of its stars.

377   ____. "Frank Capra Cast Superb." New York Sunday Mirror (4 September).

A review of You Can't Take It with You, with special attention to the skillful acting in the film.

378   Johnston, Alva. "Capra Shoots as He Pleases." Saturday Evening Post, 210, No. 4 (4 May), 1-9, 67, 69, 71-72.

An overview of Capra's life and career. Johnston places great emphasis on Capra's travels as a "migratory small-time racketeer" after finishing college, a period of "vagabondage" the author finds quintessentially American and a healthy experience for a future movie director. There is also a lengthy passage on Capra's tenure with Walter Montague on Fultah Fisher's Boarding House in 1922, and an unlikely account of the impact of that film on the movie industry in San Francisco. It is difficult to discern which specific details are embellished or fabricated by Johnston for journalistic effect, but the American success-story format and excessively dramatic tone of the piece discourages great confidence in the account. Nevertheless, this article was a standard source of information on Capra for many years.

379   M[osher], J[ohn] C. "The Current Cinema." New Yorker, 14 No. 30 (10 September), 59.

A review of You Can't Take It with You. Mosher objects to the munitions merger subplot and the sermonizing by Lionel Barrymore, both of which are additions to the original stage play. "The effort to explain and expand has been unfortunate here. Reality and humor are not well blended."

380   Nugent, Frank S. "The Screen." New York Times (2 September), p. 21.

A review of You Can't Take It with You. Comparing the film with Kaufman and Hart's original stage play, Nugent proposes that Capra and Riskin have explored the characters more thoroughly, turned a "three curtain" theater piece into a flowing narrative, and widened the drama's viewpoint to encompass that of the Kirby family. By choosing to be serious, and at times moral and sentimental, Capra and Riskin have demonstrated that the characters invented by Kaufman and Hart were not one-dimensional after all. Brief credits. Also see entry 381.

381   ____. "Picking Up the Traces." New York Times (4 September), sec. 10, p. 3.

Nugent briefly follows up on his earlier review of You Can't Take It with You. Noting that the film manages to be as funny as the play without being entirely a comedy, Nugent proposes that "dramatic weight has been added to the Kaufman-Hart skylark." Also see entry 380.

Writings About Frank Capra   1939

382   Orme, Michael. "The World of the Kinema." <u>Illustrated London News</u>, 193 (12 November), 893.
      <u>You Can't Take It with You</u> is reviewed. Orme sees the philosophy of the stage play--that wealth does not lead to happiness-- as one after Capra's own heart, marching "shoulder to shoulder with his unvarying championship of simple joys and brotherly love and the rights of the 'little man.'" Alluding to Capra's previous film, Orme notes that the stage play has enabled Capra "to seek his Utopia at home. There are horizons lost and found in 'You Can't Take It with You.'"

383   P., A. Review of <u>You Can't Take It with You</u>. <u>Monthly Film Bulletin</u>, 5, No. 60 (December), 284.
      Brief credits, a synopsis, and commentary on the film. "Capra's direction is leisurely and meticulous, but he knows the effects he wants to get and get them he brilliantly does."

384   Redman, Ben Ray. "Pictures and Censorship." <u>Saturday Review of Literature</u>, 19, No. 10 (31 December), 3-4, 13-14.
      <u>Mr. Deeds Goes to Town</u> is briefly discussed in terms of Hollywood's effort to ensure that films on contemporary themes are not controversial. Redman argues that although <u>Mr. Deeds</u> was daring in its admission that society is split between rich and poor, comedy blanketed the film's more serious implications. Moreover, it was clear that Deeds himself, however lovable, "was just a bit on the soft and cuckoo side."

385   Winsten, Archer. "Movie Talk." <u>New York Post</u> (2 September).
      A highly favorable review of <u>You Can't Take It with You</u>. "The best comedy with semi-philosophical overtones that the screen has offered in recent memory. It is new and fresh." Credits.

386   Zunser, Jesse. Review of <u>You Can't Take It with You</u>. <u>Cue</u> (10 September), p. 9.
      Zunser finds the film superior to an already entertaining stage play.

1939

387   Anon. "Capra's Latest Is a Bit Too Long." <u>Film Spectator</u> (Hollywood), 14, No. 3 (14 October), 7.
      A review of <u>Mr. Smith Goes to Washington</u>. "Generously splattered with touches of the genius of Frank Capra, but from an entertainment standpoint somewhat below the perfection Frank has attained in previous pictures . . . <u>Mr. Smith</u> is a single idea story, and the single idea is too material and too unemotional to justify the footage it consumes."

388   Anon. "Columbia's Gems." <u>Time</u>, 34, No. 4 (24 July), 43.
      A report on Robert Riskin's split with producer Samuel Goldwyn and his decision to rejoin Capra to form an independent writer-director team under the banner of Frank Capra Productions, Inc.

389   Anon. "Entertainment." <u>Newsweek</u>, 14, No. 17 (23 October), 30, 32.
<u>Mr. Smith Goes to Washington</u> is reviewed. The writer describes Smith's political awakening as "hokum," but concedes that it is "as legitimate as the patriotic preachment is sincere." Capra's talent for shrewd observation as a director is noted.

390   Anon. "Following the Films." <u>Scholastic</u> (30 October), p. 31.
A review of <u>Mr. Smith Goes to Washington</u>. The film's depiction of the Senate is judged timely and accurate, although the ending is found phony and the action in the galleries overly boisterous. But all this is background for "a typical Capra comedy."

391   Anon. "Mr. Smith Goes to Washington." <u>Film Daily</u> (6 October), p. 8.
A favorable review. "Ace box office hit gives Frank Capra another outstanding contender for academy honors." Brief credits.

392   Anon. "Mr. Smith Goes to Washington." <u>Motion Picture Review Digest</u>, 4, No. 52 (27 December), 67-69.
Reviews are excerpted from a wide variety of sources, including newspapers, magazines, trade papers, and periodicals specializing in rating films for audience suitability.

393   Anon. "Mr. Smith Goes to Washington." <u>Variety</u> (11 October), p. 13.
A review of the film. "Typically Capra, punchy, human and absorbing--a drama that combines timeliness with current topical interest and a patriotic flavor."

394   "Movie of the Week: <u>Mr. Smith Goes to Washington</u>." <u>Life</u>, 7, No. 16 (16 October), 67-74.
A photo-essay on the film, focusing on the authenticity with which the "architecture, artifacts, and anthropological curiosities" of Washington, D.C. have been re-created, especially the Senate Chamber and the people who inhabit it.

395   Anon. "The New Pictures." <u>Time</u>, 34, No. 17 (23 October), 51-52.
A highly favorable review of <u>Mr. Smith Goes to Washington</u>. By calling attention to Abraham Lincoln's crucial question "whether that nation or any nation so conceived can long endure," the film has become something more than just another top-ranking work by Capra.

396   Anon. Review of <u>Mr. Smith Goes to Washington</u>. <u>Box Office</u> (14 October), p. 65.
A favorable assessment, predicting commercial success based on the "mastery of the Capra touch." The reviewer notes that the film benefits from not only rich production values but a timely subject matter.

397   Anon. Review of Mr. Smith Goes to Washington. Daily Variety (4 October).
       The film is described as "the most vital and stirring drama of contemporary American life yet told in film."

398   Anon. Review of Mr. Smith Goes to Washington. Hollywood Reporter (8 September), p. 3.
       Capra is praised for bringing the project to the screen. "There is flag waving, but not too much of it. Mr. Capra manages to interpolate it in the picture in just the right dose."

399   Anon. Review of Mr. Smith Goes to Washington. Photoplay, 53 (November).
       Primarily a plot synopsis. The film is described as "a kind of Mr. Deeds Goes to Town with Jimmy Stewart as the naive hero." The success of the film is attributed to Capra's direction.

400   Anon. "Spotlight on Hollywood." Arts and Decorations, 51 (December), 24.
       A photo spread citing Capra as a major Hollywood director along with George Cukor, Alfred Hitchcock, Cecil B. DeMille, and Gregory LaCava.

401   Barnes, Howard. Review of Mr. Smith Goes to Washington. New York Herald Tribune (20 October), p. 14.
       A laudatory review. "Through Mr. Capra's genius the screen has been privileged to state with power and clarity some of the most paradoxical truths which need the most persuasive utterance just now . . . . Once more the great director is dealing with the stuff, rather than the show, of living and the result is the combination of contemporary and eternal values which is the surest trademark of lasting artistry." Credits. Also see entries 402 and 403.

402   _____. "The Screen." New York Herald Tribune (22 October), p. 1.
       A followup to Barnes's original review of Mr. Smith Goes to Washington. He praises Capra for his ability to make ideas an essential part of the dramatic pattern of the film, "moulding the characters and contributing the chief suspense, excitement and entertainment of the drama." In doing so, Capra has demonstrated that "ideas have a place in the cinema." Also see entry 401 and 403.

403   _____. "The Screen." New York Herald Tribune (29 October).
       Further commentary by Barnes on Mr. Smith Goes to Washington. Here he defends the film against recent attacks by politicians, describing the work as "a splendid emotional experience and a straightforward revaluation of democratic methods and ideals." Also see entries 401 and 402.

404   Bell, Nelson B. "'Mr. Smith Goes to Washington' Opens at Earle; Capitol Stage Bill Outpaces Screen Feature." Washington Post (21 October), p. 16.

Bell considers Mr. Smith Goes to Washington a false film given specious authenticity by Capra's wizardry as a director. Capra's keen sense of drama, humor, and melodramatic punch make the filibuster scene on the Senate floor appear more rational and patriotic than it really is. "Mr. Capra frequently has so glossed over falsity to make it appear like truth." Brief credits.

405   Bendslev, W. Leslie. "Movie-Vue: Mr. Smith Goes to Washington." World Horizons, 4 (October), 22-23.
A photo spread reconstructing the plot, and brief, favorable comment. Bendslev praises the acting and Capra's direction. Brief credits.

406   Boehnel, William. "Capra Excels Himself in That Mr. Smith Film" New York World-Telegram (20 October).
A laudatory review of Mr. Smith Goes to Washington, and a defense of its political implications in light of recent attacks upon it. "Mr. Capra is a sentimental and reverent patriot at heart."

407   Cameron, Kate. "Mr. Stewart Goes to Town in 'Mr. Smith.'" New York Daily News (20 October).
A favorable review of Mr. Smith Goes to Washington, focusing on James Stewart's performance in the central role. Brief credits.

408   Cohn, Herbert. "The Sound Track." Brooklyn Daily Eagle (22 October).
A review of Mr. Smith Goes to Washington. Cohn identifies authenticity and simplicity as the distinctive qualities of the "Capra touch," noting that Capra populates his films with genuine types and directs with an eye for dramatic expression free of elaborate camera tricks. Moreover, in Mr. Smith Capra "has put his finger on the weakest spots of the American political system and is caustic and fearless in his criticism."

409   Copeland, Elie. Reel News from Hollywood." Richmond News-Leader (23 October).
A photo-essay on Capra's work on Mr. Smith Goes to Washington. Copeland notes that Capra is familiar to audiences and exercises complete control over his productions.

410   Cunningham, James P. "Press Tells Senate Mr. Smith Insults It, So Senate Is Insulted." Motion Picture Herald (28 October), p. 13.
Cunningham claims that the uproar in Washington over the depiction of the Senate in Mr. Smith Goes to Washington has been largely instigated and exacerbated by the press, and argues that the film, contrary to most reports, is clearly patriotic.

411   Ferguson, Otis. "Mr. Capra Goes Someplace." New Republic 100, No. 1300 (1 November), 369-70.

Writings About Frank Capra   1939

A review of Mr. Smith Goes to Washington. Ferguson laments the direction Capra's work has taken since Mr. Deeds Goes to Town. While he finds the machinery of the Senate admirably depicted, he considers the story "eyewash" politically, and complains that its occasional humor is dispersed by a "slugging, unimaginative sort of direction that Capra became famous for avoiding." Reprinted in 1971 (see entry 831) and 1975 (see entry 965). Excerpts reprinted in 1974 (see entry 939).

412   Griffith, Richard. Review of Mr. Smith Goes to Washington. National Board of Review Magazine (November).
    Griffith argues that the film is an important document of human psychology and index to the temper of the popular mind. Objections to the film emanating from Washington lead him to assume "that the picture has touched a sore spot, that, perhaps, it has even touched the truth." Objections from critics that Capra is repeating himself, Griffith further argues, miss the point. That Capra has poured so much creative energy into retelling the same story suggests that he feels he has something important to say about it, and the popularity of the film suggests that audiences want to hear it. The wish-fulfilling ending is thus more than a movie evasion of truth; it represents the viewpoint of the average voter who knows there are troubles with America, but who passionately believes in the American way of life and government. Individual idealism is the totem people worship as a solution; on this point Capra and his auditors are in accord. Brief credits are included. Reprinted in From Quasimodo to Scarlett O'Hara: A National Board of Review Anthology, 1920-1940 (New York: Frederick Ungar Publishing Co, 1982), pp. 319-22.

413   Hartung, Philip T. "Mr. Capra Goes to Town." Commonweal, 31, No. 1 (27 October), 14.
    A brief review of Mr. Smith Goes to Washington. "Director Capra gives us a sure-fire hit steeped in patriotism, satire, warm humanity and high comedy."

414   Herzberg, Max J., ed. Photoplay Studies: Mr. Smith Goes to Washington, 5, No. 21, 16 pp.
    A study guide to the film. Included is a plot synopsis, production information, and questions for class discussion on American civics, Washington, D.C., and Capra's "cinematic treatment" of the material, especially in relation to Mr. Deeds Goes to Town.

415   Hills, Beverly. Review of Mr. Smith Goes to Washington. Liberty (18 November), p. 55.
    A laudatory review. The film is described as a "true movie--warm, arresting, thrilling."

416   Hoellering, Franz. "Films." Nation, 149, No. 18 (28 October), 476-77.
    A review os Mr. Smith Goes to Washington. Hoellering likens the "pure country Parsifal" formula of Mr. Smith and Mr. Deeds to that of St. George and the dragon. He considers the script taut,

at times reaching the "poetic realism" characteristic of certain French films, and admires Capra's ability to maintain "pace without haste," to convey atmosphere and information through the camera, and to reproduce a mass scene in which the sense of the individual is not lost. Instead of the "fake patriotism which certain business men have been trying to sell in the movie-houses," he finds in Mr. Smith "the spirit of true democracy."

417 Jacobs, Lewis. The Rise of the American Film. New York: Harcourt, Brace & Co., pp. 473-79.
  Jacobs depicts Capra as a sincere and talented director who climbed from obscurity along with Columbia Pictures, and is now in a position to make the kinds of films he chooses. He finds in Capra's best work "a sense of humor, an awareness of American life, and a shrewd use of topical events," all traceable to the director's early experience in silent comedy. Dubbing him the O. Henry of the screen, he also worries that Capra's great commercial success has "obscured his weakness and made a virtue of superficiality." Brief commentary is offered on Lady for a Day, It Happened One Night, Mr. Deeds Goes to Town, Lost Horizon, and You Can't Take It with You. Excerpts were reprinted in 1974. (see entry 939).

*418 Lorentz, Pare. Review of Mr. Smith Goes to Washington. McCalls (December?).
  Extensively quoted without further documentation in Richard Griffith's Frank Capra (see entry 649), p. 27. "Frank Capra's movie . . . has more than news in it; naive, overt, and childish as it is at times, there is a ring of simple honesty in the picture which is more important than the humour, the expert playing, or the punctilious accuracy of the procedure and the settings. Mr. Capra has become heavy-handed in his old days and frankly I groaned inwardly when I heard he had made a picture about Washington and its officials. I expected a great deal of political harangue; I got it. But Mr. Capra is still one of the greatest directors of them all, and by expert editing, by conserving his beautiful shots of the most beautiful monument in the country, the Lincoln Memorial, and by getting more finesse from James Stewart and Claude Raines than they have shown for many a day, he has made an old-fashioned county fair Fourth of July speech into a modern play."

419 Mosher, John. "The Current Cinema." New Yorker, 15, No. 36 (21 October), 73-74.
  A review of Mr. Smith Goes to Washington. Mosher notes Capra's characteristic "homespun touch of sentiment presented with persistent bubbling vivacity," and concludes that Capra's superior showmanship resides in the matter of detail.

420 Nugent, Frank S. "The Screen in Review." New York Times (20 October), p. 27.
  A review of Mr. Smith Goes to Washington. Nugent admires Capra's willingness to express a faith in democratic government through humor, noting that his comedy has become "not merely a

brilliant jest, but a stirring and even inspiring testament to liberty and freedom, to simplicity and honesty and to the innate dignity of just the average man." Brief credits. Also see entries 421 and 422. Reprinted in 1979 (see entry 1111).

421   _____. "Capra Cuts a Caper." New York Times (22 October), sec. 9, p. 5.
   In this followup review of Mr. Smith Goes to Washington, Nugent argues that the success of Capra's satire of the Senate illustrates the strength of democracy and of the American sense of humor that helps sustain it. Also see entries 420 and 422.

422   _____. "Capra's Capitol Defense." New York Times (29 October), sec. 9. p. 5.
   Nugent questions whether he was premature the week before in touting the sense of humor of Americans, considering recent attacks on Mr. Smith Goes to Washington as an affront to representative government in a time of peril. He defends the film as a comic celebration of the spirit, rather than form, of American government. Also see entries 420 and 421.

423   Pelswick, Rose. "Stewart at His Best in 'Mr. Smith' Role." New York Journal-American (20 October).
   A review of Mr. Smith Goes to Washington. Pelswick notes that Capra has turned to examine the contemporary political scene, and that his "cinematic observations are an enormously effective blend of comedy and drama, or romance and human interest and patriotism." Brief credits.

424   Rushmore, Howard. "Capra's Mr. Smith Is Five Star Film of 1939." Daily Worker (November?).
   Rushmore declares Mr. Smith Goes to Washington the best movie of 1939. "It has all the Capra genius and all the instruments by which fine films are built." Capra's greatest achievement, moreover, is the firm grasp he has on the character of Jefferson Smith. (On file with clippings for Mr. Smith Goes to Washington at the New York Public Library's Performing Arts Research Center. No date for the review is given.)

425   Schallert, Edwin. "Capra Hits New High in Latest." Los Angeles Times (4 October), sec. 1, p. 32.
   A highly favorable review of a preview of Mr. Smith Goes to Washington at the Pantages Hollywood Theatre. "Frank Capra goes to town in probably the most hair-raising adventure along political, social and patriotic lines that has ever been conceived for the movies. This is an emotional high point in the singularly gifted director's creative career." Also see entry 426.

426   _____. "'Mr. Smith' Evidences Wizardry of Frank Capra." Los Angeles Times (25 October), sec. 2, p. 15.
   A second, laudatory review of Mr. Smith Goes to Washington following its commercial release. Noting that resentment to the film

in Washington is perhaps not astonishing considering Capra's fictional treatment of congressional proceedings, Schallert argues that the film should not be judged as a documentary. Moreover, because it has a patriotic theme, the film could scarcely have an incendiary effect. As a director, Capra again displays a mastery "in building large panoramas of effects and utilizing numerous people to great advantage, even in bit parts." Also see entry 425.

427   Skolsky, Sidney. "Big Shots as Directors Are Capra and DeMille." New York Post (19 September).

The careers of Capra and Cecil B. DeMille are used to illustrate the importance of the director in the making of a film, although the bulk of Skolsky's commentary concerns Gregory Ratoff and Michael Curtiz.

428   Strout, Richard L. "Washington Sees 'Mr. Smith Goes to Washington' and Is Impressed by Hollywood's Genius for Hokum and Mispresentation." Christian Science Monitor (19 October), p. 1.

Having attended its Washington premier for members of Congress and the National Press Club, Strout sharply criticizes Mr. Smith Goes to Washington for its oversimplification and mispresentation of the activities of the Senate and Washington press. He takes specific objection to (1) Hollywood's caricature of a reporter, a cynical but lovable drunkard; (2) the inordinate power granted a single political boss; and (3) the inaccurate impression made that gallery audiences in the Senate are allowed to applaud. "These departures from reality into a fairyland like that of Oz are the more startling because scenic replicas of the Senate have a fidelity that is almost miraculous." Moreover, the montage of patriotic shrines "is about as tingling as anything ever screened. And at the next moment Mr. Capra plunges into sheer Hollywood hokum."

429   Thorpe, Margaret Farrand. America at the Movies. New Haven: Yale University Press, pp. 146-48.

An account of Capra's effort as president of the Directors' Guild to increase the role directors play within the studio system, and a general endorsement of Capra's notion that films which enjoy the greatest commercial and critical success are those over which the director exercises greatest control.

430   Vreeland, Frank. Foremost Films of 1938. New York and Chicago: Pitman Publishing Co. pp. 129-46.

A chapter is devoted to You Can't Take It with You, including credits, production information, a detailed plot synopsis, an analysis, and very brief biographical sketches of Capra and the major stars. In his analysis, Vreeland stresses the film's kinship with Mr. Deeds Goes to Town (the eccentricities of the characters, the use of musical instruments), and discusses the key points of divergence between the film and the original play by Kaufman and Hart. He considers the strength of Capra's style to be "a remarkable blending of realism with showmanship feeling."

Writings About Frank Capra   1940

431   Zunser, Jesse. "New Films." Cue (21 October), p. 33.
        A review of Mr. Smith Goes to Washington, focusing on the
film's reevaluation of American political liberties at a time when
international tensions have reawakened a dormant patriotism and affection for American government. "Amusing and dramatic by turns, it is a
rare combination, involving a skillful dissection of the American
multi-party system, a character study of machine politics and politicians, and a recapitulation of those remedies lawfully provided for
political abuses." In addition to an exciting climax, there are
"hundreds of human and appealing sidelights skillfully interwoven by
director Frank Capra."

                              1940

432   Anon. "'Lost Horizon' Reviewed at Globe." New York Post (29
        June).
        A review of Lost Horizon, now in revival, focusing on Sam
Jaffe's performance as the high lama.

433   Anon. "Plays and Pictures." New Statesman and Nation, 19 (6
        January), 11-12.
        A review of Mr. Smith Goes to Washington. The reviewer
notes that the film's sentimentality and idealism "are not in any way
offensive; on the contrary they are genuinely moving." Moreover, the
production is filled with brilliant directorial touches by Capra, such
as a dialogue sequence with the camera focused on Smith's nervous
hands, and a passage with MacGann jammed into a telephone booth.

434   Bishop, Allen. "Hollywood Comes of Age." Theatre Arts, No. 2
        (February), 119-29.
        A combined review of Mr. Smith Goes to Washington and
Lubitsch's Ninotchka. Bishop sees in these films evidence of a new
maturity in Hollywood in that both works tackle unconventional political themes with humor, tolerance, and a lack of soapbox oratory. He
admits that Mr. Smith might seem simply "a kind of patriotic debauch"
if subjected to much critical analysis, but admires the film's
emotional appeal, humor, and sincerity, and judges it "the most vivid
example yet seen of the use of the screen as a medium to inform and
arouse public opinion." He contrasts both films with the "Selznick-
International colossus," Gone with the Wind, which he finds "less
photogenic in almost every aspect."

435   Collins, Frederick L. "Hollywood Magician." Liberty (18
        May), pp. 15-16.
        A profile of Capra. Collins surveys Capra's early years
and speculates about the reasons behind his rise to fame as a director. The keynote to Capra's skill on the set, Collins proposes, is
his search for genuineness and realism. Moreover, his insistence on
taking full charge of his productions has encouraged other directors
to free themselves from the interference of producers. In Hollywood
Capra stands for "rebellion against the survival of ignorance, of

phoniness, of impudence, of nepotism, in the making of the nation's films--that and good pictures of his own making."

436   Ferguson, Otis. "While We Were Laughing." Accent, 1, No. 1 (Autumn), 37-43.
      Paying tribute to what he considers to be the neglected, native art of American film comedy, Ferguson cites the lukewarm critical response to It Happened One Night as an example of how intellectual taste often lags behind that of the audience, and cites Capra's direction of that film ("it was a trick of building a whole thing out of little ordinary things, all caught in the shifting eye of the camera") to explain the special style of 1930s comedy. He also observes that now that Capra has been embraced by the critics, the director has "gone off the deep end apparently for good, hunting the wild platitudes of Shangri-La." Reprinted in 1971 (see entry 831).

437   Greene, Graham. "The Cinema." Spectator, 164, No. 5819 (5 January), 16.
      A review of Mr. Smith Goes to Washington. Finding in the film familiar elements of Capra's best work ("exciting close-ups, sudden irrelevant humor, the delight--equal to that of the great Russians--in the ordinary human face"), Greene concludes that the contribution of Robert Riskin to Capra's success was always marginal. Reprinted in 1972 (see entry 875), 1975 (see entry 969), and 1978 (see entry 1079).

438   Heffernan, Harold. "Director Learns How Camera Artist Works." Detroit News (7 April).
      Report on a publicity photo session aimed at capturing the lighter side of Capra's personality, as the director poses on the other side of the camera lens.

439   Hellman, Geoffrey T. "Thinker in Hollywood." New Yorker, 16, No. 2 (24 February), 23-28.
      A New Yorker profile of Capra. The article contains some interesting material on Capra's early years, but Hellman's tone is generally one of amused detachment. The idea of Capra as a "social thinker" and Hollywood celebrant of the poor and humble is a particular source of irony for the author. Reprinted in 1975 (see entry 974).

440   Levin, Meyer ["Patterson Murphy"]. Review of Mr. Smith Goes to Washington. Esquire, 13, No. 1 (January).
      Having been swept away by the film at a preview, Levin is initially prompted to declare it not only Capra's best work but the best film ever made concerning American democracy and its susceptibility to political corruption. Upon reflection, however, he worries that the film fails to suggest any safeguard or remedy to the problem it poses, a weakness reflected in the absence of a convincing resolution. "It may be that Mr. Capra felt it a necessity, in a photoplay, to find a resolution in terms of a single Galahad's heroism. But on afterthought, and the supreme virtue of this photoplay is in

Writings About Frank Capra   1941

its stimulation of afterthought, it appears that he muffs or throws
away a very simple opportunity for an effective, affirmative solution
of the play's crisis." As to the production itself, Capra presents
here "a complete flowering of a style," and the acting has a cohesive-
ness that viewers have come to expect from Capra's stock company of
players. Reprinted in 1972 (see entry 886).

440a   Murphy, Patterson [Meyer Levin]. Review of Mr. Smith Goes to
       Washington. Esquire, 13, No. 1 (January).
          "Patterson Murphy" is a pseudonym for Meyer Levin. See
entry 440.

441   Skolsky, Sidney. "Sidney Skolsky." Hollywood Citizen News
       (19 November).
          Noting that Capra has now reached the enviable position
where he can make films the way he wishes, Skolsky reports on Capra's
control over the production of Meet John Doe. Given autonomy over the
project by Warner Brothers, Capra has decided to return to the sound
stage to shoot additional footage with radio broadcasters and, when
the actors become available, will begin shooting again. "Now that he
can afford to, Frank Capra is making pictures his way."

                                    1941

442   Anon. "Coop." Time, 37, No. 9 (3 March), 78, 80-82.
          A cover story on Meet John Doe. The first half concerns
the making of the film, including Capra and Riskin's problems with the
ending, and includes a brief assessment of the work as "superschmalz."
The second half is a profile on Gary Cooper. (The caption beneath the
cover photo exploits the ambiguous status of Cooper as star and
character outside and inside the film: "Gary Cooper-John Doe/He made
the cover.")

443   Anon. "Frank Capra." Movies and the People Who Make Them,
       No. 2, pp. 39-40.
          A biographical note on Capra.

444   Anon. "Frank Capra Quits Films to Join the Signal Corps."
       New York Times (13 December), p. 24.
          This report on Capra's application for a commission in the
Signal Corps includes a brief note on Capra's reputation for "shrewdly
humorous films on the American scene" and for his antifascist views,
particularly evident in Meet John Doe.

445   Anon. "Movie of the Week: Meet John Doe." Life, 10, No. 10
       (10 March), 43-46.
          A photo spread and brief review of the film. "By pitting
the little man against a corrupt politico-publisher and saucing this
dish with humor and sentimentality, Capra has evolved a movie recipe
that makes him the only U.S. director with the box-office pull of a
star."

446 Anon. "Meet John Doe." Film Daily (13 March), p. 7.
The reviewer finds that effective moments of drama, comedy, and suspense are not always employed to best advantage. "There is a noticeable tendency to unevenness in the telling of the story, and the tempo is not always sustained." Brief credits.

447 Anon. "Meet John Doe." Film Spectator (Hollywood), 15, No. 6 (15 March), 13.
A highly favorable review of the film, "It is by long odds the best thing Capra has done; it raises him to greater heights, gives him new importance, gives the screen new dignity."

448 Anon. Review of Meet John Doe. Daily Variety (13 March), pp. 3, 8.
A highly favorable review. "Like the Capra-Riskin predecessors on the screen, this play deals with the very marrow of significant individual, group and national life." Credits.

449 Anstey, Edgar. "The Cinema." Spectator, 167, No. 5911 (10 October).
A review of Meet John Doe. Anstey finds the film a shocking variation on Capra's familiar story, one that emphasizes the weaknesses in Capra's philosophy while excluding his earlier virtues. Capra's common people, Anstey observes, are now "drooling sentimentalists, looking eagerly for some leader to fool them."

450 Barnes, Howard. "On the Screen." New York Herald Tribune (13 March).
Barnes finds Meet John Doe absorbing and moving. "If it has certain inherent contradictions, a rather confused mysticism and an unwillingness to fit neatly into a dramatic mold, it is because it has more faith than logical political philosophy. In any case, it is burningly sincere and it illuminates an otherwise stunning show in no uncertain manner."

451 Biberman, Herbert. "Frank Capra's Characters." New Masses (8 July), pp. 26-27.
An open letter to Capra concerning what Biberman sees as the ominous turn Capra's political thinking has taken with Meet John Doe. Mr. Deeds Goes to Town and Mr. Smith Goes to Washington, Biberman argues, featured resourceful, honest, and dynamic protagonists "who acted in accordance with and were deeply conscious of the militance and independence of traditional earthy Americanism." Into this gallery now steps John Doe, a declassed derelict, and with him follows the theory that politics is of no use, that unpolitical organized neighborliness holds the best hope for the powerless. The whole of American history, Biberman contends, argues against this; the notion that "politics is a mug's game" is a fascist's gambit, as the film itself acknowledges. Unlike Mr. Smith, Doe does not strengthen himself with the memory of America's political past; he acts simply from animal impulse. He is an expressionless mask, a legal abstraction. The story is not that of John Doe or of the people, but of corporate

treachery out of which Capra has tried to twist a moral for the people without consulting them. That Norton is the most resourceful and convincing character, and that his philosophy dominates the film, is a negation of the best in the American tradition and in the tradition of Frank Capra as represented by Deeds and Smith.

452   Boehnel, William. "*Meet John Doe* is Capra's Finest." New York *World-Telegram* (13 March).
      A brief, laudatory review. "The finest film Frank Capra has ever made, bar none."

453   Bower, Anthony. "Recent Films." *Nation*, 152, No. 13 (29 March), 390.
      A brief review of *Meet John Doe* based on the version in which D.B. Norton reforms at the end. Bower considers *Meet John Doe* deserving of a special Academy Award "for muddled thinking and mawkish sentiment." He finds John Doe lacking the "allegorical robustness" of Capra's earlier Jefferson Smith and Longfellow Deeds. Although Bower is certain the film is designed to deliver a message, "what the message is remains a mystery."

454   Cameron, Kate. Review of *Meet John Doe*. New York *Daily News* (13 March).
      A favorable review. Under Capra's masterful direction, the film "is full of surprise, not the least of which is its spiritual significance."

*455 Campassi, Osvaldo. "Clair, Capra e il denaro." *Il Lambello* (Turin), (May).
      Cited in *Filmlexicon degli autori e delle opere*. See entry 706.

456   Churchill, Douglas W. "News of the Screen." *New York Times* (25 June), p. 17.
      A report on plans by Capra and David O. Selznick to acquire the holdings of Douglas Fairbanks in United Artists.

457   Creelman, Eileen. Review of *Meet John Doe*. New York *Sun* (13 March).
      "The formula is good, the performances splendid, the direction sleek. The formula, however, is beginning to show too clearly."

458   Crow, James Francis. "*Meet John Doe*." *Look*, 5 (11 March), 56-58.
      Background material on *Meet John Doe* and a brief assessment of it. "Perhaps this would have been a better film if John Doe had jumped. But it wouldn't have been box office. Capra blocks no facts and tells no lies, but he is willing to concede the point of a happy ending to keep the audience on his side." Also see entry 459.

459   _____. "Capra: 'John Doe' in Warner Premier." Hollywood *Citizen News* (13 March), pp. 6-7.

A second review of Meet John Doe by Crow. He considers Norton's reformation (not yet deleted from the ending) a grave fault, but also notes the presence of typical Capra elements: a warm, human quality; a fervid championship of little people; and a mixture of comedy and sentiment. Also see entry 458.

460   Crowther, Bosley. "The Screen in Review." New York Times (13 March), p. 25.

A review of Meet John Doe. Tracing the evolution of the Capra hero back to Longfellow Deeds, Crowther notes that this time the protagonist faces a more sinister and persistent foe, one who would obtain dictatorial control by preying upon democratic impulses and goodwill. He considers the film to be of major social importance, and has high praise for Capra's direction, especially the eloquence with which Capra displays affection "for the plain, unimpressive little people who want reassurance and faith." Brief credits. Also see entry 461.

461   _____. "How to Be a Good American." New York Times (16 March), sec. 10, p. 5.

A followup to Crowther's favorable review of Meet John Doe. Crowther admits that the film can be faulted for its reliance on emotion at the expense of straight thinking and for an ending that is illogical and sentimental, but reiterates his contention that the film is politically important. "There will be a lot of talk about this picture," he concludes, "and that's an encouraging thing." Also see entry 460.

462   Evans, Harry. "The Reel Dope." Family Circle (11 April), pp. 14-15, 19.

A review of Meet John Doe, based on the version in which D.B. Norton has a change of heart at the end. Evans objects to this ending ("better to let him remain a villain than clear him up with one line of dialogue"), but otherwise finds the film a "superbly produced, wonderfully acted, beautifully written motion picture" and singles out Capra's reticence with his camera for special praise. Colloquial in tone, with personal asides to Capra, Robert Riskin, and Gary Cooper.

463   Ferguson, Otis. "Who Was That Lady . . . ?" New Republic, 104, No. 1372 (17 March), 372.

During the course of a review of Preston Sturges's The Lady Eve, Ferguson discusses at length the similar comic styles of Capra and René Clair. He sees both directors arriving on the scene at a time when slapstick comedy was becoming increasingly refined and movies were becoming a more personal medium. Capra and Clair, he proposes, adapted "the old standbys of explosive surprise, camera mobility, and chase to the new intimacy of actual people." Moreover, both directors knew how to set up a chain of gags without repeating the same bit of comedy over and over. Reprinted in 1971 (see entry 831).

464 _____. "Democracy at the Box Office." New Republic, 194, No. 1373 (24 March), 405-6.

A review of Meet John Doe. Ferguson still worries that Capra has been distracted by "the business of promoting a thesis" and finds the film almost a replica of Mr. Smith Goes to Washington, which he had reviewed rather harshly two years before (see entry 411). But he is encouraged by the return of "Capra's old felicity" in several comedy sequences in Meet John Doe and notes with pleasure the presence of those moments when one can see "the hand of the loving workman bring out the fine grain." Reprinted in 1971 (see entry 831) and 1975 (see entry 965).

465 Flin [John C. Flinn, Sr.] "Meet John Doe." Variety (19 March), p. 16.

The reviewer finds Capra's attempt to clarify the place of the average American amid the mounting social conflict of the day worthy, but also finds the exposition of this theme "more vehement than conclusive." Of particular disturbance is the change in the hearts and minds of the leading characters. Capra's direction of the "superstructure," however, is judged magnificent. Credits.

466 Hamilton, James Shelley. Review of Meet John Doe. National Board of Review Magazine (April), p. 15.

Hamilton notes that while Capra's overt social conscience has encouraged critics to scrutinize his films carefully, the pattern of the Deeds-Smith-Doe series is almost too apparent. Moreover, having run into a major problem ending Meet John Doe, Capra has experimented with several solutions. Hamilton sees this as "a measure either of weakness in the plot itself or of an unfortunate timidity in resolving the plot, gambling on audience reaction rather than tackling the situation firmly one way or another." Excerpts from this review were reprinted in 1951 (see entry 649) and 1974 (see entry 939).

467 Hamman, Mary. "Meet Frank Capra Making a Picture." Good Housekeeping, 112 (March), 11, 74-76.

A report on the making of Meet John Doe and an analysis of Capra's style of direction. Hamman attributes to Capra an ability to locate significant details that bring an everyday figure or scene to life on the screen. None of these details, she notes, clamors for special attention, "but the sum total of these deft strokes gives his story color, his characters depth and validity." She describes Capra's behavior on the set as authoritative, but quiet and unobtrusive.

468 Harriman, Margaret Case. "Mr. and Mrs. Frank Capra." Ladies Home Journal, 58 (April), 35, 153-55.

A brief analysis of Capra's success as a director, followed by a report on the unassuming domestic life of him and his wife, and a detailed account of his childhood and career in the movie industry. The author attributes the appeal of Capra's work to the touches of realism and comedy he brings to his moral tales, enabling the audience to identify with the characters on the screen.

469   Hartung, Philip T. "Capra and Doe's Little Punks." Commonweal, 33, No. 23 (28 March), 575-76.
     An ambivalent review of Meet John Doe. Hartung faults Capra for allowing the film to become occasionally maudlin and muddled, and for ending on a note of uncertainty and "hokum." But he praises Capra for his superb craftsmanship and his brave protest against the present state of civilization.

470   Hopper, Hedda. "Hedda Hopper's Hollywood." Los Angeles Times (9 March), sec. 3, p. 3.
     A biographical and career sketch of Capra just prior to the release of Meet John Doe.

471   Jacobs, Lewis. "Film Directors at Work, II: Frank Capra." Theatre Arts, 25, No. 1 (January), 43-48.
     A description of Capra's working methods on the set of Meet John Doe, supplemented by some brief remarks by Capra on his selection of story material. Jacobs finds Capra sober, judicious, and completely lacking in directorial exhibitionism. Reprinted in 1975 (see entry 975).

*472   Lewis, J.D. "The Story Man." Colliers, 107 (29 March), 21, 83-84.
     A profile of Robert Riskin following the release of Meet John Doe. Cited in Mel Schuster's Motion Picture Directors, 1900-1972.

473   Leyda, Jay. "Courage in Films." Direction, 4, No. 4 (April-May), 27.
     A review of Meet John Doe. Leyda finds it remarkable that a film backing the American people has found forceful expression in an industrial medium otherwise lending support to the struggle against people. He thus sees it as an American analogue to Fritz Lang's The Testament of Dr. Mabuse, which covertly exposed the true character of Nazi ideology. Where Capra played safe in Mr. Smith Goes to Washington, tackling tiny issues with enormous technique, he and Riskin have now moved further down a dangerous path, revealing the techniques by which Americans are manipulated. Leyda wishes the filmmakers had gone further and illustrated how Americans are fiercely fighting fascism at home, but nevertheless considers the release of Meet John Doe the first great film event of what appears to be an extraordinary year.

474   Mortimer, Lee. Review of Meet John Doe. New York Daily Mirror (13 March), p. 24.
     A highly favorable review of the film, judged Capra's most impressive work to date.

475   Mosher, John. "The Current Cinema." New Yorker, 17, No. 6 (22 March), 64-65.
     A review of Meet John Doe. Mosher notes ironically that it is a "film to delight those worthies who want the Scriptures rewritten

in the language of the streets," but also finds the film inhabited by magnificent character types, especially the cynical colonel.

476   Pelswick, Rose. Review of Meet John Doe. New York Journal-American (13 March).
     Pelswick finds the film a "stirring blend of social consciousness, humor and sentimentality," but thinks that the ending is forced.

477   Rhea, Marian. "The Laws of Averages." Photoplay, 18 (March), 32-33, 35.
     Rhea opens with the assertion that in a world where it is smart to gain individual recognition and impose individual patterns on those around us, we occasionally need a powerful reminder of "the simple but inescapable rules that govern one and all," and that the "human touch" of Capra's Meet John Doe is such a reminder. The rest of the article consists of lengthy quotations, ostensibly from Gary Cooper and Barbara Stanwyck, describing how the philosophy of the film has entered their lives. This is mainly star publicity material.

*478 Riskin, Robert. "Meet the Creators of John Doe; Meet John Doe Himself." Click Photo Parade (March).
     Riskin describes his collaboration with Capra: "A singular experience for a writer is to see his characters come to life on the screen in their true and unmarred form. This, Frank Capra accomplishes for you in his masterful and individual way--and generally, just for good measure, throws in some little tidbit of his own, to heighten and clarify your original conception." Quoted in Scherle and Levy's The Films of Frank Capra (entry 1062), pp. 175-76.

479   Schallert, Edwin. "'Meet John Doe' Hailed as Capra Victory." Los Angeles Times (13 March), sec. 1, p. 16.
     A review of Meet John Doe. Schallert has high praise for everything in the film except its current ending, which involves Ann convincing John not to jump and Norton suddenly becoming kind. "One feels that it is a pity that some more compelling solution was not reached in the picture which is clearly ennobling in its spirit, and which is so deeply moving in many of its scenes, as well as being told with all the Capra vigor, power, and cleverness." Also see entry 480.

480   _____. "Wurtz Will Produce South American Story." Los Angeles Times (15 March), sec. 1, p. 7.
     Noting that the ending of Meet John Doe, released three days before, has already been changed slightly, Schallert proposes that John Doe should die at the end of the film, either accidentally or at the hands of another. "A suicide, of course, is out." Also see entry 479.

481   Skolsky, Sidney. "Sidney Skolsky Writes . . ." New York Post (13 March).
     A personality profile of Capra, covering his working methods as a director, and his tastes and style of living.

1941

482   Strauss, Theodore. "Mr. Riskin Hits the Road." New York Times (26 January), sec. 9, p. 5.
Robert Riskin is interviewed while in New York working on the distribution and promotion deals for Meet John Doe. Riskin explains the reasons behind Capra's and his decision to embark on independent production despite their relative freedom at Columbia, and outlines the procedure he and Capra follow in constructing a script.

483   Winsten, Archer. Review of Meet John Doe. New York Post (13 March).
Winsten notes that "Capra and Riskin have made seven-eights of a great and timely film," but that the ending doesn't work.

1942

484   Anon. "Hollywood Goes to War." Woman's Home Companion, 69 (December), 15, 64, 69.
Capra is very briefly mentioned as part of a larger article on Hollywood's contribution to the war effort.

485   Anon. "Last Cheers of French Audience for Smith Goes to Washington." Hollywood Reporter (4 November).
A report on the selection of Mr. Smith Goes to Washington by French theaters as the final English-language film to be shown before a Nazi ban of American and British films goes into effect.

486   Levitas, Louise. "Movies and the War." PM (30 August), pp. 27-28.
A report on Capra's activities as supervisor of information and morale films for the U.S. Army, including his work on the Why We Fight, Know Your Enemy, and Know Your Ally series, and the army-navy Screen Magazine. "He is doing his best to give them the Capra touch--his knack of dramatizing the humanity of the man in the street."

487   Van Doren, Mark. "The Second Coming," in his The Private Reader: Selected Articles and Reviews. New York: Henry Holt & Co., pp. 130-33.
A reprint of Van Doren's 1936 review of Mr. Deeds Goes to Town (see entry 272).

1943

488   Agee, James. "Films." Nation, 156, No. 24 (12 June), 844-45.
A review of Prelude to War. Agee has an ambivalent response to the way information is presented in the film, but he is pleased with its depiction of fascism, a topic customarily treated in government and Hollywood films "as if it were the hate that dare not speak its name." Reprinted in 1958 (see entry 702) and 1975 (see entry 951).

489   _____. "So Proudly We Fail." Nation, 157, No. 18 (30 October), 509.

Agee urges that The Battle of Britain and The Battle of Russia receive public distribution. "Britain, one hour's calculated hammering of the eye and ear, can tell you more about that battle than you're ever likely otherwise to suspect, short of having been there. Russia, though it is a lucid piece of exposition, is cut neither for fact nor for political needlepoint but purely, resourcefully, and with immensely powerful effect, for emotion." No mention of Capra. Reprinted in 1958 (see entry 702).

490 _____. "Prize Day." Nation, 157, No. 26 (25 December), 768-69.

Agee claims that the Why We Fight films are the only American documentaries that currently excite him, but also tempers his enthusiasm. "Battle of Russia, next to Desert Victory, is the best film of the year. But like the other orientation films it is saturated with words and only begins to use the possibilities of the screen, as such, to show and teach. And like all the others it can make you sick to the very soul with its political timidity." No mention of Capra. Reprinted in 1958 (see entry 702).

491 Anon. "'Battle of Russia' Tells Whole Story." Hollywood Reporter, 75, No. 13 (29 September), 3.

A review of The Battle of Russia. The contributions of Capra, Anatole Litvak, and Anthony Veiller to this army orientation film are noted: "The practiced hands of these valued Hollywood creators have dealt the most comprehensively with the subject."

492 Anon. "The Battle of Russia." Time, 42, No. 22 (29 November), 92.

A review of the film upon its release to civilian audiences, praising it as the most eloquent film yet made concerning Russia's role in World War II. Credit is given to director Anatole Litvak. No mention of Capra.

493 Anon. "Film Preview." Daily Variety (29 September), pp. 3, 5.

A favorable review of The Battle of Russia.

494 Anon. "Prelude to War." Time, 41, No. 22 (31 May), 94, 96.

A review of the film upon its release for civilian audiences. Described as "the first impressive attempt in a U.S. film to present the theory and practice of Fascism," Prelude to War is nevertheless faulted for an overly familiar story, an intricate topic, and a heavy dependence on verbal narration. Brief mention is made of the Hollywood filmmakers working under Capra for the army.

495 Anstey, Edgar. "The Cinema." Spectator, 171 (1 October), 311.

A review of The Battle of Britain. Anstey worries that the film, aimed at instructing American soldiers, is too objective, and that it will leave many British viewers in the dark as to the psychological phenomena that surround them. "Capra is a director of such caliber now that he combines documentary experience with his ability to present screen fiction, that he might well turn to a type of war film which so far has been sadly neglected--the film about the mind at war."

496   ____. "The Cinema." Spectator, 171 (3 December), 527.
         A review of Divide and Conquer, which Anstey sees as limited by its baldly factual March of Time style. While Capra has extracted a wealth of drama and emotion from the newsreel material, Anstey argues, a sense of contact with the suffering of the Nazi victims is missing. Anstey calls for documentaries in which "the work of emotional communication is done by the unassisted image rather than by the bitter turn of a commentary phrase or by rolling drums of doom on the soundtrack."

497   Barnes, Howard. "On the Screen." New York Herald Tribune (15 November).
         A highly favorable review of The Battle of Russia, now being exhibited at commercial theaters. A "comprehensive, tough and explicit documentary film account of the manner in which a whole people fought Nazi invasion. . . . The shrewd editing . . . has seen to it also that the average citizen has been given his due in a brilliant military and social victory."

498   Carmody, Jay. "'Prelude to War' Draws a Gala Premier Audience." Washington Evening Star (27 May).
         A report on the release of Prelude to War to commercial theaters and a review of the film. "More than it teaches you what the war is all about--as if you had not been told--it impresses you with the fact that Lt. Col. Frank Capra is an extraordinarily clever maker of movies."

499   C[rowther], B[osley]. "'Prelude to War' Shown to Public." New York Times (14 May), p. 16.
         Report of a prerelease screening of Capra's first war documentary before its distribution to commercial theaters. Crowther finds Prelude to War emotionally effective, but has doubts about the educational value of the film unaccompanied by the rest of the series. "Its generalizations are vague and it leans heavily on patriotic symbolism to convey a sense of America," he writes. "It leaves many obvious 'why' questions completely unanswered."

500   Crowther, Bosley. "New Film Surveys Soviet Role in War." New York Times (15 November), p. 23.
         A review of The Battle of Russia. Crowther finds the film effective and compelling despite the fact that portions have been taken from Russian documentaries already seen in America. He notes Capra's role as "supervisor," but credits director Anatole Litvak and writer Anthony Veiller with magnificently blending images, words, and music.

501   Farber, Manny. "Education for War." *New Republic*, 108, No. 22 (31 May), 734.

A review of *Prelude to War*. Farber worries that Capra's "ease of thought and technique" have allowed the true causes of fascism to be glossed over and a simplified, idyllic notion of American freedom to be presented. Nevertheless, he finds in the work an accurate interpretation and brilliant visual translation of the ambitions of Americans and the surface aspects of recent history, as well as a vitality that makes Hollywood's version of the 1930's seem "bloodless and inconsequential."

502   Gassner, John, and Dudley Nichols, eds. *Twenty Best Film Plays*. New York: Crown Publishers, pp. 2-59.

A version of Robert Riskin's screenplay for *It Happened One Night* that includes scenes deleted from the final version of the film. Reprinted in 1977 (see entry 1034).

503   Lardner, David. "The Current Cinema." *New Yorker*, 19, No. 14 (22 May), 49.

A review of *Prelude to War*. Capra and the War Department have "succeeded in spicing up the familiar old march of history . . . with all the novel twists you could ask for. Montage and sound effects and the artful use of repetition have done wonders."

504   _____. "The Current Cinema." *New Yorker*, 19, No. 40 (20 November), 72-73.

A review of *The Battle of Russia*. Lardner writes favorably on the release of the *Why We Fight* series to the public and is impressed by the skillful integration of Russian film footage in this segment. No mention of Capra.

505   Maynard, John. "'Battle of Russia' Is a Must Picture at Columbia." *Washington Times-Herald* (11 November).

A highly favorable assessment of *The Battle of Russia*, now exhibited at commercial theaters. Maynard especially praises Capra's painstaking selection of footage and the "practically reverent job of cutting and editing."

506   Schallert, Edwin. "Slavic Courage, Strength Revealed in War Picture." *Los Angeles Times* (13 November), sec. 1. p. 7.

A favorable review of *The Battle of Russia*. Capra and Anatole Litvak "have brought forth an epical impression of how the people of a huge invaded country stood their ground in the face of the fiery and intense attack of a well-accoutred enemy."

507   Whitebait, William. "The Movies." *New Statesman and Nation*, 26 (25 September), 200.

A brief review of *The Battle of Britain*, released for British audiences. "The film goes with a bang from start to finish, and the commentary is more fruity and more embellished with bursts of English song than our own puritan taste would encourage."

1944

508   Agee, James. "Films." Nation, 158, No. 11 (11 March), 316.
    A brief review of The Negro Soldier. The film "is straight and decent as far as it goes, and means a good deal, I gather, to most of the Negro soldiers who have seen it. It is also pitifully mild; but neither the film nor those who actually made it should be criticized for that." No mention of Capra. Reprinted in 1958 (see entry 702).

509   _____. "Films." Nation, 158, No. 13 (25 March), 373-74.
    Tunisian Victory is reviewed. Comparing the film with its British predecessor, Desert Victory, Agee thinks Tunisian Victory suffers from a more complex campaign to cover, the liabilities of collaboration between English and American film units, and the propagandistic concerns of its producers. He also finds the film lacking in "cinematic momentum" and is disturbed by the use of disembodied voices for the soldiers. The latter "give the film the pseudo-democratic, demagogic coloration of most vernacular literature." No mention of Capra. Reprinted in 1958 (see entry 702).

510   Anon. "Arsenic and Old Elderberry." Newsweek, 24, No. 11 (11 September), 110-11.
    A review of Arsenic and Old Lace. "If it isn't one of Capra's best, at least it's one of his funniest. . . . Director Capra has whipsawed a scriptful of bright gags and Halloween hilarity down to the last laugh."

511   Anon. "Arsenic and Old Lace." Film Daily (1 September), p. 8.
    A review of the film. "The Capra trademark, the cast potency, and the publicity that has accrued to the play conspire to assure the success of the production." Capra is mildly criticized for letting the actors get a bit out of hand: "He allows Cary Grant to do everything but bite the camera." Brief credits.

512   "Arsenic and Old Lace." Time, 44, No. 11 (11 September), 95-96.
    A review of the film. Although the film on occasion strives too hard to convulse the audience, the virtues of the play generally have been preserved by Capra.

513   Anon. "'Arsenic' WB Film Wow Now." Hollywood Reporter, 80, No. 2 (1 September), 3.
    A review of Arsenic and Old Lace. The reviewer finds the film extremely funny, but notes that some of the flavor of the original stage play has been sacrificed through overstatement. Capra's direction "is fully worthy of him . . . an excellent effort to bridge the gap until his return to Hollywood."

514   Anon. "Combined Operation." Newsweek, 23, No. 14 (3 April), 94.

A report on the making of Tunisian Victory, and brief critical commentary on the film. It lacks the unity, novelty, and historical immediacy of its British predecessor, Desert Victory, but it may be preferable to American audiences because it depicts American ships and planes in action.

515   Anon. "The Movies." New Statesman and Nation, 27 (25 March), 205.
Although deemed a "notable documentary," Tunisian Victory is measured against Alexander Dovzhenko's The Battle for the Ukraine and found wanting. "It is not merely that the horrors are left out, that we see nothing of Tunisians except at the end lining the streets to cheer; the whole execution of the film is designed to convey the war at a safe distance."

516   Anon. "The New Pictures." Time, 43, No. 13 (27 March), 94, 96.
A review of The Negro Soldier in World War II. Disappointed that some of the bitter facts about racism have been left out of the film, the reviewer nevertheless considers it "a brave, important and hopeful event in the history of U.S. race relations." Credit is given to screenwriter and adviser Carlton Moss. No mention of Capra.

517   Anon. "The New Pictures." Time, No. 16 (17 April), 96.
Tunisian Victory is briefly reviewed. The writer notes that the film has been made with care and skill, but faults it for relating an intricate story "too doggedly, with too much commentary," and for a general tack and politeness which reduces its forcefulness.

518   Anon. "New Pictures You'll Want to See." Cosmopolitan, 117 (October), 85.
Arsenic and Old Lace is briefly reviewed. The cast "has a field day with this wacky comedy."

519   Anon. Review of The Negro Soldier. New York Post (22 April).
An ambivalent assessment. The reviewer laments that although the film aims to stimulate Negro pride and patriotism, and educate whites who are ignorant of the subject, it avoids anything touching controversy, including the discrimination and segregation many Negroes have bitterly resented in this war. "But that is a story which will be told neither by the War Department nor apologists for things as they are. In the meantime, 'The Negro Soldier' should be seen for what it demonstrates positively--pride, ability, courage, and dignity."

520   Anon. "Tunisian Victory." Film Daily, (8 March), p. 6.
A review of the film, judged a "superb achievement" worthy of its predecessor, Desert Victory.

521   Anstey, Edgar. "The Cinema." Spectator, 172 (24 March), 267.
       A review of Tunisian Victory. Anstey faults the film for a sentimental conclusion and a cheapening of the simple direct style of Britain's Desert Victory. Doubting the wisdom of allowing Hollywood to handle film material of this kind, he notes that Capra "has clearly been susceptible to studio influences which have not altogether helped the picture."

522   Barnes, Howard. "On the Screen." New York Herald Tribune (25 March).
       A review of Tunisian Victory, judged a "brilliant war documentary" with "cohesion, depth and engrossing interest." Special note is made of the film's skillful editing and eloquent commentary.

523   ____. "On the Screen." New York Herald Tribune (2 September).
       A favorable review of Arsenic and Old Lace. Capra is cited for the timing and subtle characterizations he provides in adapting this foolproof play to the screen.

524   Benét, William Rose. "The Phoenix Nest." Saturday Review of Literature, 27, No. 12 (18 March), 28.
       A review of The Negro Soldier, which Benét finds absorbing and inspiring.

525   ____. "The Phoenix Nest." Saturday Review of Literature, 27, No. 15 (8 April), 28.
       Tunisian Victory is praised in this review. "This kind of firsthand war reporting is new in our time. The experts have a picture of permanent historical values, and one that gives the man in the street a clear and vivid idea of what went on in Africa."

526   Cameron, Kate. "Wholesale Murder at Strand." New York Daily News (2 September).
       A review of Arsenic and Old Lace. Cameron proposes that although the film has been withheld for three years, it is "escapist entertainment" and therefore has not dated. Viewers who have not seen the play will find it hilarious.

527   Char [Roy Chartier]. "Arsenic and Old Lace." Variety (6 September), p. 10.
       A review of the film, with a highly favorable assessment of its box-office potential. "Capra's production, not elaborate, captures the color and spirit of the play." Credits.

528   Cook, Alton. "Movies." New York World-Telegram (1 September).
       A review of Arsenic and Old Lace. "Violence has been done to the stage version, but the laughter is too substantial to be smothered under its new layer of slapstick."

Writings About Frank Capra   1944

529   Creelman, Eileen. "The New Movies." New York Sun (2
        September).
                A review of Arsenic and Old Lace. Creelman finds the movie
        "fast, funny, but, unlike the play, somewhat gruesome" and speculates
        that the film may seem less tasteful because "the camera makes any
        scene more intimate." Brief credits.

530   C[rowther], B[osley]. "4 Theatres Show Negro War Film." New
        York Times (22 April), p. 8.
                A report on the commercial release of The Negro Soldier.
        Crowther considers it successful as an inspirational document, but
        notes that it skirts the problem of race relations, an issue broader
        than the role of Negroes in the war. No mention of Capra.

531   Crowther, Bosley. "The Screen." New York Times (24 March),
        p. 17.
                A review of Tunisian Victory. Crowther praises the film
        for getting "down to earth with the soldiers in a warmly personal and
        deeply human way," but faults it as a historical document. Also see
        entry 532.

532   _____. "Element of Time." New York Times (2 April), sec. 2,
        p. 3.
                A followup to Crowther's favorable review of Tunisian
        Victory. Surprised by the lukewarm response the film has received,
        Crowther suggests several causes: the lack of drama in the title; the
        time lag between the actual battle and the release of the film; an
        "academic" approach to the topic; and the film's length. He specu-
        lates that films of this kind may not be appropriate for general
        release. Also see entry 531.

533   Faber, Manny. "Men in Battle." New Republic, 10, No. 14 (3
        April), 471.
                A review of Tunisian Victory. Farber faults the film for
        its fragmented style: "It has undoubtedly established a record for
        the number of different commentators used per second and for the
        number of different maps used per inch."

*534   Green, E.M. Review of Arsenic and Old Lace. Theatre World,
        40 (December).
                Cited in Cumulated Dramatic Index, 1909-1949.

535   Hamilton, Sara. "Arsenic and Old Lace." Photoplay, 25
        (November), 21.
                A brief review. "A hilarious screenplay that starts off at
        high tension and maintains a pace that catapults audiences from
        shrieks of laughter to screams of fright."

536   Hartung, Philip T. "Gary and Cary." Commonweal, 40, No. 23
        (22 September), 547-48.
                An ambivalent review of Arsenic and Old Lace. Hartung
        notes that although Capra uses speed and surprise to heighten the

novelty of familiar stage material, he cannot sustain the comic possibilities of murder and insanity.

537   Holmes, Winifred. "Mild or Bitter?" Sight and Sound, 12, No. 48 (January), 81-82.
         A highly favorable assessment of Know Your Ally, Britain. Holmes finds the film fair to the British and a good example of the effective documentary technique Capra has evolved to inform American soldiers of their enemies and allies.

538   Isaacs, Hermine Rich. "War Fronts and Film Fronts." Theatre Arts, 28, No. 6 (June), 343-48.
         Isaacs considers the most interesting new film work to be that of Capra, William Wyler, John Ford, and John Huston for the War Department, and laments the apathy with which their documentaries have been received by the public. Favorable comment is offered on Capra's most recent projects, Tunisian Victory and The Negro Soldier.

539   K[ennedy], P[aul] P. "The Screen." New York Times (2 September), p. 17.
         A review of Arsenic and Old Lace. Kennedy finds the film "good macabre fun," but faults Capra for padding the play with a few "camera capers" which slow it down.

540   Lardner, David. "The Current Cinema." New Yorker, 20, No. 6 (25 March), 63-64.
         Tunisian Victory is reviewed. Lardner finds the documentary polished and engaging, but somewhat derivative of Desert Victory in structure. No mention of Capra.

541   Lardner, John. "The Current Cinema." New Yorker, 20, No. 30 (9 September), 51.
         Arsenic and Old Lace is briefly reviewed. Lardner finds it as funny as the stage play. No mention of Capra.

542   McManus, John T. "Murder Has Its Moment." PM (3 September).
         A review of Arsenic and Old Lace, judged as funny as the play on which it is based. No mention of Capra.

543   Mishkin, Leo. "Screen Present." New York Morning Telegraph (2 September).
         A review of Arsenic and Old Lace. Mishkin finds it an uproarious comedy which has not dated. Brief credits.

544   Mortimer, Lee. "'The Negro Soldier' a Nation's Tribute." New York Daily Mirror (24 April).
         A review of The Negro Soldier. Mortimer criticizes the War Department for turning to Hollywood to make educational films, of which this is the most recent example. "Instead of presenting a straightforward exposition of the Negroes' contribution in war and peace, which is the way a documentary should be made, Col. Capra gets involved with romances, church choirs, parables and clergymen."

Moreover, while the film is "a fine and well-deserved tribute to the race," Negroes have objected to being singled out in the war.

545 Mulvey, Kay. "Hollywood." Woman's Home Companion, 71 (September), 10-11.
  Mulvey reports that the set of Arsenic and Old Lace was a madhouse during production. But she also describes the film as "Frank Capra's latest civilian picture," suggesting that she was never near the set of this prewar production, filmed in 1941. Concerning the finished film, Mulvey notes that the principal performers "work together to make a tidy piece of entertainment."

546 Pelswick, Rose. "'Arsenic' Film at Strand." New York Journal-American (2 September).
  A review of Arsenic and Old Lace, found to be "slick entertainment." Brief credits.

547 Price, Edgar. "Reel Review." Brooklyn Citizen (5 September).
  A review of Arsenic and Old Lace. A hilarious film "directed in his usual able manner by Frank Capra."

548 Ran, Neil. "'Arsenic' Clicks Again as a Film." Los Angeles Examiner (23 September).
  A report on the delay in the release of Arsenic and Old Lace until the end of the stage run of the Lindsay-Crouse play, and a favorable review of the film.

549 Schallert, Edwin. "'Arsenic' Gay Grim Screen Excursion." Los Angeles Times (23 September), sec. 1, p. 7.
  A review of Arsenic and Old Lace. Schallert considers the film less impressive than most of Capra's work; adhering closely to the original play, Capra has not embellished the project with his own brand of social significance. Schallert also finds the pantomime overdone, but attributes this to the difference in audience taste three years ago when the film was made. Arsenic and Old Lace thus appears to him a museum piece.

550 Tyler, Parker. "'John Doe' or, the False Ending," in his The Hollywood Hallucination. New York: Creative Age Press, pp. 168-89.
  Meet John Doe and Hitchcock's Suspicion serve to illustrate Tyler's notion that Hollywood happy endings are "pseudo-divine." As a political fable, he argues, Meet John Doe "is constrained to impose the political reality of democracy as the only 'fate' conceivable, the only 'omnipotent' plot from 'above,' able to determine the end for the hero." Typical of Tyler, the argument is dense. Direct commentary on Meet John Doe is limited to pp. 182-186.

551 Warner, Virginia. "The Negro Soldier: A Challenge to Hollywood." People's World (San Francisco) (8 April).
  Reviewing the film prior to its commercial release, Warner praises The Negro Soldier for overturning old stereotypes about blacks

and laying the groundwork for a new approach to their treatment on the screen. Audience reaction to this film, she proposes, will provide a barometer for their public acceptance in dignified roles. Reprinted in 1971 (see entry 860).

552   Whitebait, William. "The Movies." New Statesman and Nation, 27 (29 January), 76.

A brief, favorable review of The Nazis Strike. Along with other films in the Why We Fight series, "the economical and imaginative use of newsreels provides a new standard for film journalism."

553   Winsten, Archer. "Movie Talk." New York Post (2 September).

A review of Arsenic and Old Lace, judged an entertaining film with many surprises, but not up to Capra's previous high standards nor characteristic of his work. Brief credits.

1945

554   Anon. "War Comes to America." Film Daily (6 June), p. 6.

A review of the film. "Supremely stirring, the picture, produced uncommonly well under the supervision of Col. Frank Capra, covers the events that led to our participation in the conflict with clarity, conciseness, and a breathlessness that is matchless."

554a   Crowther, Bosley. "For the Offensive." New York Times (13 May), sec. 2, p. 1.

As part of a broader discussion of the role commercial theaters have played in the exhibition of instructional films for the government during the war, Crowther praises Two Down, One to Go as "an effective conveyor of public information via the screen." No mention of Capra.

555   Pryor, Thomas M. "Back to Work." New York Times (16 September), sec. 2, p. 3.

Interviewed about his return to motion pictures after the war, William Wyler praises Capra's Why We Fight series as a "new kind of cinematic experience" marking an important advance in the medium.

556   Sadoul, Georges. "Capra ou la rénovation des mythes." Les Lettres Françaises (24 November), p. 7.

A revival of Mr. Smith Goes to Washington in Paris occasions Sadoul's reassessment of the film in light of the events of the past few years. Surveying Capra's career as a "renovator of old myths," Sadoul describes Jefferson Smith as the Don Quixote of democracy in action. Sadoul is therefore baffled why the film was approved in France by Daladier, a man of appeasement at Munich in 1938, and subsequently was allowed to be shown in the southern zone by Vichy after the fall of France in 1940; he notes that in 1941-42 audiences in Marseilles and Toulouse filled the cinemas to see the film and applaud the best passages. Sadoul is also incredulous at rumours that the Hays Office tried to block Mr. Smith on the grounds that it represented an affront to democracy, a fate also contemplated for The

Grapes of Wrath. In their celebration of the right to criticize and denounce hypocrisy, Sadoul argues, these films are among the best instruments democratic America has to make itself known and loved by foreigners.

1946

557 Agate, James. "Lost Horizon," in his Around Cinemas. Amsterdam: Home & Van Thal, pp. 183-85.
     A reprint of Agate's 1937 review. See entry 277.

558 Agee, James. "Films." Nation, 163, No. 26 (28 December), 766.
     Agee briefly notes that It's a Wonderful Life is "one of the most efficient sentimental pieces since A Christmas Carol." (For a followup review, in which Agee discusses his misgivings about the film, see entry 577.) Reprinted in 1958 (see entry 702).

559 Anon. "Capra's Christmas Carol." Newsweek, 23, No. 27 (30 December), 72-73.
     A cover story on It's a Wonderful Life. The first section of the article reviews the film as a successful return by Capra to the kind of moviemaking he enjoyed before the war. The second section concentrates on Jimmy Stewart, providing a career sketch and a discussion of both his and Capra's concerns about resuming their careers in Hollywood. The cover photo is a production still of George Bailey reunited with his family at the end of It's a Wonderful Life; the caption below reads: "The Return of Jimmy Stewart."

560 Anon. "It's a Wonderful Life." Film Daily (19 December), p. 5.
     A laudatory review. Many of the superb films of the season, the reviewer notes, have been made for varying audiences, but this film is for everyone. "Frank Capra has created a grand picture of humanity. . . . With his master hand he has brushed in a gallery of people, places and events that lift the basic story to heights and depths of grandeur and despair." Brief credits.

561 Anon. "Jimmy Stewart Comes Back in New Film." Cue (12 December), pp. 16-17.
     A review of It's a Wonderful Life, encompassing a brief discussion of Capra's typical theme of "David smiting Goliath in the common good," and background information on this production. "Aside from the obvious moralizing . . . excellent drama, fine comedy, filled with the warm and sympathetic directorial touch of Capra and the catalytic, ingratiating performance of Stewart."

562 Anon. "Movie of the Week: It's a Wonderful Life." Life, 21, No. 27 (30 December), 68-73.
     A photo-essay on the film. Noting that it is the first Hollywood movie for Capra and James Stewart since 1941, and the first

released by Liberty Films, the reviewer praises Capra's construction of "a masterful edifice of comedy and sentiment" on a strong plot.

563   Anon. "New Pictures." Time, 48, No. 51 (23 December), 54.
A review of It's a Wonderful Life and a report on Capra's involvement in Liberty Films, Inc. The film is judged a triumphant Hollywood homecoming for Capra and James Stewart, with Capra's inventiveness keeping the moral fable from becoming preachy, and Stewart turning a potentially "goody-goody" role into a constant delight. It is noted that Capra's joint venture in independent production with William Wyler and George Stevens has become a trend in Hollywood and may herald a glorious new era of movies.

564   Anon. Review of It's a Wonderful Life. Daily Variety (19 December), pp. 3, 30.
The film is described as a "highly fortunate blending of fantasy, romance and a measure of realism."

565   Barnes, Howard. "On the Screen." New York Herald Tribune (21 December).
A review of It's a Wonderful Life. Barnes notes that Capra and actor James Stewart have come out of uniform to "collaborate on a large and sentimental film canvas depicting the American way of life." Despite the "mystical nonsense" of the framing fantasy, the story remains "strong and moving." Brief credits.

566   Bert [Bert Briller]. "It's a Wonderful Life." Variety (25 December), p. 12.
A review of the film. Briller welcomes the "wholesomeness and humanness" of It's a Wonderful Life in light of a recent cycle of "psychological" films and "propaganda vehicles." James Stewart has returned from the war to bring a new "maturity and depth" to the central role; Capra has brought back his devotion to detail and characterization, his feeling for dramatic impact, and his deft leavening of drama with humor. Credits.

567   Cameron, Kate. Review of It's a Wonderful Life. New York Daily News (23 December).
Cameron finds the film too sprawling, too noisy, and too obvious in its social message, and suggests that it would be improved by some judicious editing. Nevertheless, "it tells a good story and its conclusion has a heart-warming effect on the audience."

568   Crowther, Bosley. "The Screen in Review: At Three Theatres." New York Times (23 December), p. 19.
A review of It's a Wonderful Life. Noting that Capra has returned to his prewar concern for simple folks, Crowther nevertheless worries that the sentimentality of the film represents an illusory concept of life. He finds that Capra's charming characters, beguiling small town, and optimistic resolution "all resemble theatrical attitudes rather than average realities." Brief credits.

569   Grant, Jack D. "'Wonderful Life' Splendid Start for Liberty
        Films." Hollywood Reporter, 91, No. 36 (19 December), 3.
            A highly favorable review of It's a Wonderful Life. "The
film marks Frank Capra's first production since his return from distinguished service, and he has invested it with the tremendous heart
that always keeps his offerings above average."

570   McCarten, John. "The Current Cinema." New Yorker, 22, No. 45
        (21 December), 85-86.
            A review of It's a Wonderful Life. McCarten describes the
film as "chock-ful of whimsey," and does not mean this kindly. "In
his direction Mr. Capra has seen to it that practically all the actors
involved behave as cutely as pixies."

571   Magnan, Henry. "Le cinéma." Le Monde (27 December), p. 6.
            A review of Arsenic and Old Lace. Magnan notes that while
the film is not a masterpiece by Capra, it is an amusing comedy. The
frenzied pace of the film is memorable.

572   Riley, Nord. "Stewart's Story." This Week (Sunday supple-
        ment) (15 December), pp. 18-19.
            A cover story on It's a Wonderful Life, focusing on the
return of Capra and Jimmy Stewart to Hollywood following World War II.

573   Scott, John L. "Poignant Story of American Life Hailed." Los
        Angeles Times (26 December), sec. 2, p. 3.
            A highly favorable review of It's a Wonderful Life. "Typi-
cal Capra touches of realism and comedy prove once again that he is
indeed a genius at showing life on the screen."

574   Wilkerson, W.R. "Trade Views." Hollywood Reporter, 90, No.
        43, (18 October), 1-2.
            High praise for Capra's career on the occasion of a revival
of The Strong Man in New York.

575   _____. "Trade Views." Hollywood Reporter, 91, No. 30 (11
        December), 1.
            The release of It's a Wonderful Life inspires Wilkerson to
comment on the debt of gratitude the motion picture industry owes
Capra. Wilkerson considers the film to be Capra's greatest work.

576   Wright, Virginia. Review of It's a Wonderful Life. New York
        Daily News (12 December).
            Wright finds the film "an uneven collection of fantasy,
homely philosophy, slapstick, sentimentality and humor."

1947

577   Agee, James. "Films." Nation, 164, No. 7 (15 February), 193-
        94.
            A review of It's a Wonderful Life. Acknowledging the
film's genuine warmth, charm, quality, natural talent, and vigor, Agee

nevertheless is suspicious of its appeal to the heart at the expense of the mind, and mistrusts the film's assumption that people are fundamentally good and turn out well or ill mainly as a matter of outward circumstance. Also see entry 558. Reprinted in 1975 (see entry 952).

578   Anon. "Liberty Picks a Movie Eligible for Top Honors." Liberty (15 February), pp. 64-65, 90.
    A photo spread on It's a Wonderful Life accompanied by a brief review of the film. The blended talents of Capra and James Stewart "have resulted in a film of rare warmth and whimsey. . . . Though the movie might have been a sticky, sentimental sermon, and the hero might have seemed like a disillusioned Boy Scout, it didn't turn out that way with Capra in charge."

579   Anon. "The Price of Liberty." Time, 49, No. 21 (26 May) 88.
    A report on the sale of Liberty Films to Paramount, and the disappointing box-office returns for It's a Wonderful Life.

*580   Anon. Review of It's a Wonderful Life. Photoplay, 30 (March), p. 4.
    Cited in Cumulated Dramatic Index, 1909-1949.

581   Crowther, Bosley. "The Spirits Move." New York Times (12 January), sec. 10, p. 1.
    It's a Wonderful Life is contrasted with Stairway to Heaven (Powell and Pressburger, 1946) to illustrate the differences between Hollywood and British treatment of similar film material. Crowther finds in the former film "a snug and sentimental show of elementary wishful-thinking based on the principle of brotherly love," and faults Capra for rescuing his hero from unreasonable despair through a mechanically fanciful device. In contrast, he finds the flight of fancy in Stairway to Heaven psychologically sound and charged with novelty and wit.

582   Dent, Alan. "The World of the Cinema." Illustrated London News, 210 (19 April), 418.
    It's a Wonderful Life is reviewed. Dent takes pleasure in the welcome return of Capra and James Stewart to the screen, but is greatly embarrassed by the film itself, which he finds "almost brazenly sentimental and almost vulgarly strident."

583   Farber, Manny. "Mugging Main Street." New Republic, 116, No. 1 (6 January), 44.
    A review of It's a Wonderful Life. Farber argues that the film shows Capra's "art at a hysterical pitch." He concedes that Capra's moralizing about the wonders of small-town life "is presented with great talent almost wholly through visual detail," but objects to the contrivance of these details and the unimaginative simplification of the characters. He finds that Jimmy Stewart's traditional character has grown stale, but also notes that the acting of Stewart and

Donna Reed are responsible for some of the film's unsentimental moments.

584   Gable, Clark. "The Role I Liked Best." Saturday Evening Post, 219, No. 46 (17 May), 148.
        Clark Gable recalls working on It Happened One Night: his initial doubts about being loaned to Columbia by M-G-M; his preparation for the part by riding incognito on a night bus from Hollywood to San Francisco; and Capra's emphasis on a "natural" style of acting.

585   Griffith, Richard. Review of It's a Wonderful Life. National Board of Review Magazine, 22 (February-March), 5-8.
        Griffith proposes that his earlier notion of Capra's films as "fantasies of good will" does not apply to the newest work; its depiction of dog-eat-dog methods in business is too grimly accurate. But he worries that Capra has overcompensated for this grimness by interjecting sugarcoated passages, resulting in an abrupt shift between naturalistic and fantastic elements. Reprinted in part in 1950 (see entry 649) and in its entirety in 1975 (see entry 971).

586   Hartung, Philip T. "The Screen." Commonweal, 45, No. 12 (3 January), 305.
        A review of It's a Wonderful Life. Hartung notes that Capra "uses cinema like a master in proving the film's title." The lesson may be pedantic, but Capra and actor James Stewart fashion "an outstanding example of Americana in which humor, sentiment, and good showmanship work well together."

587   I[saacs], H[ermine] R[ich]. "Between Two Years: The Films in Review." Theatre Arts, 31, No. 2 (February), 34-38.
        It's a Wonderful Life is measured against other contemporary films, including Open City, Les enfants du paradis, Henry V, and The Best Years of Our Lives. While Isaacs finds the story of George Bailey absorbing, she is less taken by its sentimentality. "It's a Wonderful Life bears a close resemblance to the pictures Capra was making before the war, even to the point of starring James Stewart. . . . In order to savor a Capra film you have to accept the world as he sees it, which shouldn't be difficult for anyone brought up on fairy tales."

588   M., E.F. "James Stewart at Keith's in Frank Capra Film." Christian Science Monitor (23 January), p. 5.
        A review of It's a Wonderful Life. The film "has characteristic Capra qualities--touches of humor in unexpected places, engaging bits of homely sentiment, and a warm sympathy for little people and their problems. But the story is overdrawn, the fantasy with which it is invested seems at times awkwardly contrived, and the characters are sketched largely in blacks and whites with few modifying shades of gray."

589   Morgansen, Thomas G. "Capra's Thinking." New York Times (19
       January), sec 2, p. 7.
       A letter to the editor, enumerating Capra's strengths and
limitations as a director. Praised as gifted and inspired, with an
individual style and a consistent sympathy for the plain American of
the day, Capra nevertheless disappoints the author because of the
implausibility of his plots.

590   Parsons, Louella. Review of It's a Wonderful Life.
       Cosmopolitan, 122 (January), 67.
       Capra is cited for best direction of the month in this
favorable review.

591   Pudovkin, Vsevolod. "The Global Film." Translated by J[ay]
       L[eyda]. Hollywood Quarterly, 2, No. 4 (July), 327-332.
       Pudovkin uses Prelude to War to illustrate his notion of a
new kind of documentary that will restore to cinema the artistic power
and global audience lost with the passing of the silent era.

592   Rivkin, Allen. "Frank Capra Sticks by the Little Man."
       United Nations World, 1, No. 2 (March), 64.
       A review of It's a Wonderful Life. Rivkin (who worked with
Capra on army orientation films) sees the film as a continuation of
Capra's concern over the years with "the simple, common man, his
essential goodness, and the invariable triumph of that child-like
faith over the forces of evil." He likens Capra's affection for the
"little man" to the political philosophies of Franklin Roosevelt and
Henry Wallace. If Capra's message seems naive and artless to some,
Rivkin contends, it is nonetheless embraced by the audiences and
offers a healthy alternative to the current parade of "heels,"
"killers," and "shady ladies" on the screen.

593   Sadoul, Georges. "Les sourires et les pantins." Les Lettres
       Françaises (17 January), p. 8.
       A review of Arsenic and Old Lace. Sadoul proposes that
Capra evades the booby trap Hollywood has set for him: working with a
celebrated stage play, confined to a studio setting, Capra still makes
cinema through cutting, camera movement, and lighting. Unlike Capra's
previous stage adaptation, You Can't Take It with You, where the
ending had a touching silliness, Arsenic and Old Lace bears no resemblance to the real world; it is a detective farce featuring puppets
in frenetic motion. But Capra and playwright Joseph Kesselring know
what they are doing, obtaining laughs from murder by treating characters as mannequins. One hopes, nonetheless, that Hollywood will allow
Capra to maintain his interest in men more than in puppets, for Capra
has been an incomparable renovator of old myths. During the war, the
chivalry, democratic faith, and idealism of Jefferson Smith sustained
the French in their struggles.

594   Tyler, Parker. Magic and Myth of the Movies. New York:
       Henry Holt & Co. pp. 121-32, 259-60.

A psychoanalytic interpretation of <u>Arsenic and Old Lace</u>. Attributing to Mortimer Brewster an impotence neurosis, Tyler interprets the drama in the home of Brewster's maiden aunts as a pre-bridal night hallucination, with the protagonist caught between a fear of impotence (the dead bodies in the trunk and cellar) and of potency (his frightful brother on the loose). Tyler also proposes that the comic premise of plunging a snobbish drama critic into a world of melodramatic movie conventions is more effectively rendered here than in the original play, simply because it is cast in the medium that inspired it.

595   Wechsberg, Joseph. "Meet Frank Capra." <u>Reader's Digest</u>, 51, No. 306 (October), 80-83.

A biographical and career profile, with a brief description of Capra's working methods and reputation. "Though given to gloomy spells and violent brooding between pictures, on the set he never gets nervous or impatient, and is famous for his courteous treatment of extras and bit players" (condensed from <u>Baltimore Sunday Sun</u>, 17 August 1947).

1948

596   Anon. "Frank Capra." <u>Current Biography</u>, 9, No. 4 (April), 5-7.

A short biography of Capra drawn from a variety of sources.

597   Anon. "Movie of the Week: <u>State of the Union</u>." <u>Life</u>, 24, No. 19 (10 May), 81-82, 84.

A photo spread and review of the film. The film is judged weaker than the play on which it is based; generalities have been substituted for topical satire and the politics are oversimplified.

598   Anon. Review of <u>State of the Union</u>. <u>Cue</u> (24 April).

Despite the difficulties of adapting a Pulitzer Prize-winning play to the screen, the reviewer reports, the film version of <u>State of the Union</u> is a "far better production and eminently more satisfying entertainment" than the original. Moreover, the play's moral--"that people and not politicians should make presidents"--has greater urgency in light of the current presidential election.

*599   Anon. Review of <u>State of the Union</u>. <u>Woman's Home Companion</u>, 75 (July), 10-11.

Cited in <u>Cumulated Dramatic Index, 1909-1949</u>.

600   Anon. "Spencer Tracy for President." <u>Newsweek</u>, 31, No. 18 (3 May), 80.

A review of <u>State of the Union</u>. Capra's film version of the play by Lindsay and Crouse has the humor and emotional appeal of the original and is especially timely during the current election campaign.

601   Anon. "State of the Union." Film Daily (29 March), p. 6.
        A highly favorable review. Capra's direction is cited as worthy of an award. Brief credits.

602   Anon. "State of the Union." Look, 12 (25 April), 108-10.
        A photo spread and brief review of the film, judged superior to the original stage play. "Handsomely produced and perfectly timed for preconvention interest, Capra's film may help halt Hollywood's recent retreat into safe and easy escapism."

603   Anon. "State of the Union." Photoplay, 33 (July), 56-57.
        Behind-the-scenes photos from the production of the film with captions attributed to Van Johnson.

604   Anon. "State of the Union." Screen Stories (June), pp. 28-33, 69-71.
        A short story based on the film.

605   Anon. "State of the Union." Time, 51, No. 18 (3 May), 90, 93.
        A review of the film. Capra is accused of turning the satiric "bludgeons" of the original play into "lollipops" in this screen version. Playwrights Lindsay and Crouse are credited with whatever mild entertainment the work still provides.

606   Anon. "'State of the Union' Strong; Ruthless Wall Street Story." Hollywood Reporter, 98, No. 7 (24 March), 3.
        State of the Union is reviewed. The film overall is considered fast and bright entertainment with a pertinent message, but the comedy is judged unduly stereotypical in contrast to that of the stage play.

607   Anon. "Trade Show." Daily Variety (24 April), pp. 3, 9.
        A review of State of the Union, forecasting great box-office success for the film. Capra has transferred the play to the screen "in a whirlwind pace not unlike that encountered in the noisiest, most headlong George Abbott musical." Credits.

608   Barnes, Howard. "On the Screen." New York Herald Tribune (23 April), p. 18.
        A review of State of the Union. Capra "has worked a minor miracle of transmutation" in adapting the play to the screen. With the help of writers Anthony Veiller and Myles Connolly, old material has been made topical and pertinent, and every shot of the film is alive and arresting. "There is no way of describing the sorcery which an artist such as Capra can effect." Brief credits.

*609   Bianchini, Adelio. "Come Frank Capra conquistò Hollywood." Hollywood (Milan), No. 127.
        Cited in Filmlexicon degli autori e delle opere. See entry 706.

610   Brog [William Brogdon]. "State of the Union." Variety (24 March), p. 8.
   A highly favorable review of the film. "It calls its shots about the political scene in a manner that should prod the voter's conscience, but without using soapbox oratory. Message is adroitly cloaked in good story theatrics that cleverly ladle out drama and humor to make the political sales talk palatable." Moreover, the satire is made stronger by a serious, rather than a slapstick, treatment. Credits.

611   Carroll, Harrison. "Capra Film Satirical Hit." Los Angeles Herald-Express (30 April), p. B8.
   A favorable review of State of the Union. Capra has disproved "an old Hollywood legend that you can't make a satire into a hit picture."

612   Crowther, Bosley. "The Screen in Review." New York Times (23 April), p. 28.
   A review of State of the Union. Crowther speculates that a spontaneous, grass-roots movement may emerge on behalf of Spencer Tracy in this presidential year. He finds the satire sharper here than in the original play, in part because of "more withering commentary" by screenwriters Anthony Veiller and Myles Connolly, and in part because of Capra's sarcastic treatment of backroom politicians. Brief credits.

613   _____. "Favorable Tally." New York Times (2 May), sec. 2, p. 1.
   A followup to Crowther's review of State of the Union. He proposes that while the film is not bold or revolutionary enough to change history, it may have a minor influence on the election.

614   Graham, Virginia. "The Cinema." Spectator, 180 (30 July), 142.
   A review of State of the Union. "Mr. Frank Capra can be complimented on capturing the atmosphere of back-stair political life with its pandering first to one section of the community and then to the other, its seduction and bribery of needed supporters, its jolliness and false bonhomie, its bustle and excitement, its illusion of power which gradually eclipses all other factors, and its eternal exploitation of the ordinary man."

615   Hartung, Philip. "A Movie Must Move." Commonweal, 48, No. 4 (7 May), 79-80.
   A review of State of the Union. "If you don't mind a comedy being stagey instead of cinematic and if you can overlook the story's optimistic faith in the survival of the little man no matter what crooked politicians push him around, you'll get some gay laughs out of this lengthy film."

616   Hatch, Robert. "In Good Faith." New Republic, 118, No. 19 (10 May), 30-31.

As part of a broader article on recent efforts by Hollywood to tackle world problems, Hatch briefly discusses State of the Union, predicting that the film will not please any of the current presidential candidates. He admires the film's insistence on virtue in public office, but faults it for an "ancient, contrived and unlikely plot." No mention of Capra.

617   Kann, Red. Review of State of the Union. Motion Picture Herald, 170, No. 13 (27 February), 27.
   Kann admires the way the film pursues a middle road politically, attacking both right- and left-wing views. He also likes the film's quick pace.

*618   Lambert, Gavin. Review of State of the Union. Sequence.
   Richard Griffith quotes this review at length in his Capra monograph (see entry 649, p. 37). He attributes the review of Sequence #5, but it does not appear in that issue. In Griffith's extract, Lambert notes that whimsey and sentiment in State of the Union are occasionally overplayed, but he considers the film as a whole to show Capra at his most dexterous as a director. Moreover, Spencer Tracy's character—replacing the overworked, diffident figures of James Stewart and Gary Cooper—indicates a new maturity in Capra himself.

619   McCarten, John. "The Current Cinema." New Yorker, 24, No. 10 (1 May), 66-67.
   A brief review of State of the Union. When the film follows the play by Lindsay and Crouse, "it is fairly enjoyable business, but when it lights out on its own, it becomes a sorry spectacle." No mention of Capra.

620   Parsons, Louella. Review of State of the Union. Cosmopolitan, 124 (June), 124.
   Parsons cites Capra's direction as the best of the month. "Frank Capra has always had a missionary spirit which he has put into his pictures, right from the earliest 'flicker' days up to date. He loves people, and he loves idealism, and he never shoots any film that doesn't let him prove his attitude."

621   Redelnig, Lowell E. "Miss Lansbury Heads Acting Performances in State of the Union." Hollywood Citizen News (30 April), p. 9.
   A review of State of the Union, judged inferior to the original stage play.

622   Renzi, Renzo. "Frank Capra." Cinema (Milan), 2 (10 November).
   A biographical sketch, filmography, and critical commentary on Capra's career through 1948. Renzi locates Capra's worldview within liberal, Christian, petit-bourgeois American culture, and Capra's style within mainstream Hollywood cinema. What Renzi finds distinctive in Capra's films, however, is the director's capacity for

imaginative characterization and narrative exuberance, and an assertion of a moral world.

623 Salemson, Harold J. "Mr. Capra's Short Cuts to Utopia." *Penguin Film Review*, 7 (September), 25-34.

A critical and biographical overview of Capra's career. Salemson considers Capra's work the most consistent and original achievement of any commercial filmmaker, marked both by technical mastery and a keen social conscience. But he worries that Capra offers panaceas to the audience rather than analyzing the social problems he raises. Salemson explains this in terms of Capra's rag-to-riches, immigrant background, proposing that while Capra has remained aware of social injustice, he himself cannot imagine radical political solutions, and has therefore restrained "progressive" writers (like Sidney Buchman) with whom he worked. He speculates that the weak reception given *It's a Wonderful Life* may mean that Capra's social message is no longer in tune with the public, and predicts that the popular response to *State of the Union* will signal the direction of Capra's career in the postwar period.

624 Schallert, Edwin. "'State of the Union' Provokes Interest." *Los Angeles Times* (30 April), sec. 1, p. 20.

A review of the film. "Mainly *State of the Union* falls short on the side of significant social implications, and yet its romantic story is to some extent cluttered up by these implications . . . . Capra is at his best when he is just plain excursioning into entertainment."

625 Wright, Virginia. "Film Reviews." New York *Daily News* (30 April).

A review of *State of the Union*. Comparing the film with the play, Wright finds the film's criticism of political compromise more incisive, its comedy more expansive, and its treatment of human relationships warmer.

1949

626 Agee, James. "The Baby." *Life*, 27, No. 10 (5 September), 80-81.

A section of Agee's seminal essay on the major silent comedians, "Comedy's Greatest Era," this account of Langdon's career is largely based on an interview with Capra. Agee thus repeats Capra's version of their relationship, with Capra finding the proper formula for the performer by preserving Langdon's innocence on the screen, and Langdon's career collapsing after breaking with Capra to direct his own pictures. Agee's account, for many years the standard interpretation of Langdon's career, has recently been challenged. The article has been reprinted often. See entries 635, 702, 739, 780, 800, 861, 929, and 1023.

627 Allredge, Charles. "Film That Changed History?" *Variety* (5 January).

Allredge, a former assistant secretary of the interior in the Truman administration and advance man during the 1948 presidential campaign, reports that State of the Union directly influenced Truman's campaign by convincing the candidate to go directly to the people for support.

*628   Anon. "L'oeuvre de Frank Capra et d'autres comédiens." Ciné-Club (Paris), 2, Nos. 8-9 (May-June).
Cited in the Filmlexicon degli autori e delle opere (see entry 706) and in Michel Ciment's bibliography (see entry 824). According to Ciment, articles on Capra by Georges Sadoul, Georges Magnane, and Jean-Georges Auriol are included, as well as a reprint of Capra's 1939 essay, "Ce sont les films qui font les stars" (see entry 1164).

629   Castello, Giulio Cesare. "Contributo alla storia della sophisticated comedy." Bianco e Nero (September), pp. 39-41.
As a part of a larger survey of American "sophisticated comedy" in the sound era, Capra's films from the 1930s are briefly discussed.

630   Griffith, Richard. The Film Till Now. By Paul Rotha in collaboration with Richard Griffith. London: Vision Press, pp. 449-53.
Linking Capra's work to popular fiction of the 1930's, Griffith attributes its success to the nostalgic appeal of small-town individualism and goodwill for middle-class audiences made uneasy by the New Deal. He sees Capra embracing a "fantasy of goodwill" as early as Lady for a Day, although the pattern first appears clearly in Mr. Deeds Goes to Town where recovery occurs not through social reorganization but through the redemption of the individual. Capra's significant films to follow use an American social, political, or economic problem as its springboard. In each case characters, events, and atmosphere are depicted with striking realism, but the solution is always fantastic, as a messianic innocent calls forth the goodwill of the "little people" to triumph over the forces of entrenched greed. "Such a blend of realistic problem and imaginary solution," Griffith proposes, "epitomised the dilemma of the middle-class mind in the New Deal period." This highly influential assessment of Capra's career was reprinted as part of Griffith's B.F.I. monograph on Capra in 1950 (see entry 649).

631   Hovland, Carl I., Arthur Lumsdaine, and Fred D. Sheffield. Experiments on Mass Communication. Princeton, N.J.: Princeton University Press, 345 pp.
A report on a series of experiments conducted by the army during World War II which measured the impact of film and other mass-communication devices on soldiers. Much of the data come from responses to four Why We Fight orientation films: Prelude to War, The Nazis Strike, Divide and Conquer, and especially The Battle of Britain.

*632   MacGowan, Kenneth. Script (February), p. 36.
       State of the Union, and You Can't Take It with You are discussed. Cited in Donald C. Willis's The Films of Frank Capra (see entry 1062), p. 194.

633   Sadoul, Georges. Histoire du cinéma mondial. Paris: Flammarion, pp. 246-48.
       A brief discussion of Capra's work with respect to the prewar tradition of sophisticated comedy in American cinema. Sadoul considers Capra's films during this period to be characteristic of the liberalism of the Roosevelt era, offering covert social critiques and propaganda cloaked as farce.

634   Whitebait, William. "The Movies." New Nation and Statesman, 38, No. 962 (13 August), 171.
       In a review of Magic Town, written by Robert Riskin and directed by William Wellman, Whitebait observes that the film "has provoked everywhere damp murmurs of 'Capra' and as one who has never appreciated Capra I find the insult well merited. This mixture of well-starred sentimentality and politics (or patriotics) seems to me quite unexportable."

1950

635   Agee, James. "L'epoca d'oro della commedia cinematografica." Translated by Paola Ojetti. Bianco e Nero, 11, No. 4 (April), 52-70.
       A translation of Agee's 1949 essay, "Comedy's Greatest Era." See entry 626.

636   Anon. "Der Bingle Rides a Winner." Cue (15 April).
       A favorable review of Riding High, focusing on Bing Crosby's performance.

637   Anon. "Doctored U.S. Film Showing in Moscow." Hollywood Reporter, 112, No. 8 (20 December), 2.
       A report on the exhibition of a pirated print of Mr. Smith Goes to Washington in Moscow under the title Senator. The ending to the film is believed to have been doctored by the Russians, and the satire on American machine politics taken seriously "since it corresponds to what they read in their papers on politics here."

638   Anon. "Great Teamwork by Crosby, Capra." Hollywood Reporter (9 January), pp. 3, 8.
       A highly favorable review of Riding High. Noting that the original story has been altered suitably to meet Bing Crosby's talents, the reviewer reports that under Capra's direction Crosby's "charm, if anything, is magnified" and the songs written for him are "woven artfully into the script."

639   Anon. "Moscow Goes to Town with 'Mr. Deeds' But without Any Payoff." Variety (20 December), pp. 3, 19.

Mr. Smith Goes to Washington is reported to be playing as anti-American propaganda in Moscow. Because of increasing hostility between Russia and the United States, negotiations between the Motion Picture Export Association and the Russians over the distribution of American films have broken down, and Mr. Smith is being shown illegally. The film is said to be drawing crowds in Moscow because of its depiction of machine politics in America. (Although the film title cited in this article is Mr. Deeds Goes to Town, it is clear from the description of the plot that the film in question is in fact Mr. Smith Goes to Washington.)

640   Anon. "Riding High." Film Daily (12 January).
A review of the film. Bing Crosby is dubbed a "natural" for Capra's remake of Broadway Bill. The film is "pleasantly humorous, mildly dramatic and neatly romantic." Brief credits.

641   Anon. "Riding High." Look, 14 (11 April), 106-8.
A photo spread and review of the film, judged the "happiest picture in some time" for both Capra and Bing Crosby.

642   Anon. "Riding High." Time, 55, No. 18 (1 May), 88.
A favorable review of the film. "Like all Capra pictures, it is . . . calculated to delight the largest possible audience by taking potshots at the greedy and the pompous, while letting the meek inherit the earth."

643   Anon. "Trade Show." Daily Variety (9 January), pp. 3, 10.
A favorable review of Riding High. Credits.

644   Barnes, Howard. "On the Screen." New York Herald Tribune (11 April).
A review of Riding High. Barnes proposes that in remaking Broadway Bill as a musical, Capra has "caught every inflection of the original story in terms of humor and dramatic tension" while skillfully interpolating the new songs into the story. Thus Capra has succeeded at the difficult task of maintaining suspense in a musical show. The film is perhaps full of sentiment, but this aspect is nicely restrained. Brief credits.

645   Coffey, Tom. "Horse Laugh on Bing Crosby at Paramount This Week." Los Angeles Mirror (10 April).
A favorable review of Riding High.

646   Crowther, Bosley. "The Screen in Review." New York Times (11 April), p. 26.
A review of Riding High. Crowther likes the film as much as Capra's first version, Broadway Bill, if not more. Capra's decision to cast Bing Crosby in the central role is considered inspired.

647   Farber, Manny. "Capra's Riding High." Nation, 170, No. 23 (10 June), 582-83.

Riding High precipitates an attack on Capra's reputation as a film humorist and social commentator. Farber argues that Capra unwittingly undercuts even his most tired social messages: the "sugary" relationship between Bing Crosby and his black stableboy betrays a deeper kind of prejudice; sympathy for the supposed underdog gets buried in an elegant movie that subtly eulogizes the world of powerful wealth; and Crosby himself seems more a smug, spoiled little boy than an anarchic vagabond. "The chief sensation in Riding High is of a slick, capricious, overtrained life that holds one completely out of the movie as though there were a glass pane between audiences and screen." Reprinted in 1971 (see entry 830).

648 Goodman, Ezra. "Film Review." New York Daily News (10 April).

A review of Riding High. "Capra has directed with a good deal of the flair he evidenced in the original. He knows how to manipulate his actors before the camera and the picture has fluency and feeling."

649 Griffith, Richard. Frank Capra. New Index Series No. 3. London: British Film Institute, 38 pp.

A Capra monograph. Griffith's discussion of Capra as a "fantasist of goodwill"--first spelled out in Paul Rotha's 1949 edition of The Film till Now (see entry 630)--is reprinted here in the prologue. To this Griffith adds a brief paragraph on Capra's special talents, likening his inventiveness with behavior to that of Ernst Lubitsch and his analytical skills as an editor to that of D.W. Griffith and Sergei Eisenstein. A detailed bio-filmography follows, including credits, production information, and excerpts from critical responses. Somewhat fragmentary, this pamphlet nevertheless represents the first full-length study of Capra's career and remained the primary source of information and ideas about his work until the early 1970s.

650 Hatch, Robert. "Revivals, Rewrites and Imports." New Republic, 122 No. 18 (1 May), 21.

A brief review of Riding High. Hatch notes that this is the third film version of Mark Hellinger's play, Broadway Bill, and finds it without "stunning novelties." No mention of Capra.

651 Herb [Herb Golden]. "Riding High." Variety (11 January), p. 6.

A review of Riding High. Capra's decision to remake Broadway Bill is viewed as part of a trend in Hollywood to update past hits; the success of Riding High should further encourage studios to delve into their vaults. According to Golden, Capra's "deft handiwork" in the original is evident again here, and Bing Crosby is perhaps more appropriate for the central role than was Warner Baxter. Moreover, the film offers a "field day for secondary characters." Brief credits.

652   Houston, Penelope. "Mr. Deeds and Willie Stark." Sight and Sound, 19, No. 7 (November), 276-77, 285.

In this survey of Hollywood films dealing explicitly with sociological or political themes, Capra's films are used to illustrate how an audience's concern for political and corporate corruption is first aroused and then relieved through a reassuring solution. "We see corruption at work; we see the little man apparently its victim and then, dramatically, we see that if the hero can once reach the ear of the public he will find in them his support." Mr. Deeds Goes to Town, Mr. Smith Goes to Washington, and State of the Union are cited.

*653   Larsen, Egon. Spotlight on Films. Max Parrish, pp. 106-7.

Commentary on You Can't Take It with You. Cited in Stanley Hochman's A Library of Film Criticism: American Film Directors (see entry 939), p. 35.

654   McCarten, John. "The Current Cinema." New Yorker, 26, No. 9 (22 April), 105.

Riding High is reviewed. "Most of the sequences are fairly familiar ones, but Mr. Capra keeps things moving so slickly that it's hard to object very strenuously when he scatters more corn around the feedbox than is entirely necessary."

655   Schallert, Edwin. "Paramount's 'Riding High' for Holiday." Los Angeles Times (10 April), sec. 3, p. 6.

A review of Riding High. Schallert finds the film erratic, but notes that "Capra can still uniquely contribute the gentle, effective touches to the individual scene."

1951

656   Anon. "'Groom' Merry and Tuneful." Hollywood Reporter, 114, No. 46 (6 July), 3.

A favorable review of Here Comes the Groom. "Capra draws fully on his unique talent for putting real people into impossible situations."

657   Anon. "Here Comes the Groom. Film Daily (7 July), p. 10.

A review of the film. The script is judged "romantically bright and sprightly" and Capra's direction effective. Brief credits.

658   Anon. "Here Comes the Groom." Newsweek, 38, No. 14 (1 October), 88.

A review of the film. "Both Bing Crosby and director-producer Frank Capra have better comedies to their credit. However, Here Comes the Groom is a cozy, professional job of compounding assorted comic felonies into a sure-fire entertainment."

659   Anon. "Here Comes the Groom." Time, 58, No. 16 (15 October), 120, 122.

A review of the film. Capra and Crosby are "up to their oldest tricks" which "ought to amuse all but those optimistic moviegoers who dare to hope for new ones." Capra specifically is to be faulted for leaning heavily on slapstick, and for a frenzied staging of "In the Cool, Cool, Cool of the Evening."

660   Anon. "New Films." Cue (22 September), p. 18.
A brief review of Here Comes the Groom. The film is praised for its hilarity.

661   Anon. Review of Here Comes the Groom. Daily Variety (5 July).
Highly favorable. The reviewer finds in the film "all the charm of the old Capra standouts." Credits.

662   Bauer, Leda. "In the Cool, Cool, Cool of the Evening." Theatre Arts, 35, No. 9 (September), 32-33, 87.
A review of Here Comes the Groom. Bauer finds the film "genuinely gay in conception and handling" and a harbinger of a new vitality in Hollywood. Having labored too long with "dreary tales of the uplift school," Capra brings to the story "a fresh, good-natured approach so disarming that only a carper would bother to point out the hoariness of some of the gags or object to the use of little orphans for pathos."

663   Brady, Thomas F. "Hollywood Agenda." New York Times (8 April), sec. 2, p. 5.
A report on the abrogation of Capra's contract with Paramount by mutual consent of both parties, and a brief history of Liberty Films and its acquisition by Paramount in 1948.

664   Brog [William Brogdon]. "Here Comes the Groom." Variety (11 July), p. 6.
A review of the film, judged greatly superior to recent films involving either Capra or Bing Crosby. Credits.

665   Castello, Giulio Cesare. Review of Frank Capra by Richard Griffith. Bianco e Nero, 12, No. 6 (June), 67-68.
A brief review of Richard Griffith's B.F.I. monograph on Capra (see entry 649). In Castello's estimation, Griffith tends to overrate Capra, who is simply a respectable and representative director.

666   Crowther, Bosley. "The Screen in Review: Two New Films Seen Here." New York Times (21 September), p. 19.
A review of Here Comes the Groom. A "light, breezy item, nicely marked with the genial Capra touch." Brief credits.

667   Deming, Barbara. "Non-Heroic Heroes." Films in Review, 2, No. 4 (April), 32-38.
It's a Wonderful Life is discussed in terms of a group of films from the same period in which a hero dreams of escape but is

thwarted. (The Chase [1946] and None But the Lonely Heart [1944] are also examined.) Deming proposes that while Capra thinks he tells the story of a man realizing that his life has meaning, George Bailey is never shown to accept this basic premise of the angel's argument, and instead is frightened into returning to the secure world in which he has always lived. Reprinted in 1969 (see entry 795).

668 Goodman, Ezra. Review of Here Comes the Groom. New York Daily News (7 September).
  A favorable review. Goodman finds the film reminiscent of It Happened One Night in theme and treatment.

669 Helming, Ann. "New Comedy Entertainment." Hollywood Citizen News (7 September).
  A favorable review of Here Comes the Groom.

*670 MacCann, Richard. "Documentary Film and Democratic Government: An Administrative History from Pare Lorentz to John Huston." Ph.D. dissertation, Harvard University.
  A section of this dissertation containing information on Capra's work for the government on the Why We Fight series was published in 1971 (see entry 841) and 1976 (see entry 1011). A revised version of the dissertation was published in 1973 (see entry 915).

671 McCarten, John. "The Current Cinema." New Yorker, 27, No. 33 (29 September), 101.
  A brief note on Here Comes the Groom, judged satisfactory as light entertainment. No mention of Capra.

672 Proctor, Kay. Review of Here Comes the Groom. Los Angeles Examiner (7 September).
  A favorable review.

673 Scheuer, Philip K. "Capra's 'Here Comes the Groom' Joyful Hit Starring Crosby, Wyman." Los Angeles Times (7 September), sec. 3, p. 9.
  With Here Comes the Groom, the reviewer observes, Capra is "back in stride." The naturalism of the acting under Capra's direction is especially praised.

674 Treadwell, Bill. Fifty Years of American Comedy. New York: Exposition Press, pp. 106-7.
  A brief account of Capra's work with Harry Langdon. "Highbrow writers" are cited as the cause of Langdon's decline.

1952

675 Anon. "Capra to Rein at AT&T Vidpix; $2,600,000 cost." Variety (22 October), p. 21.
  Preparations for a series of thirteen hour-long telefilms sponsored by American Telephone and Telegraph and produced by Frank Capra are dubbed the "most ambitious undertaking in television

history." Capra is slated to continue with the project as production supervisor and editor of the complicated footage, and retains all foreign rights.

676   Crowther, Bosley. "The Screen: Two Newcomers on Local Scene." New York Times (1 January), p. 21.
       A review of Westward the Women, directed by William Wellman from a story by Capra and a screenplay by Charles Schmeer. Crowther considers the film's premise--a wagon train of women bent on marriage arriving in California--farfetched, "even though it is said that Frank Capra got the idea right out of the books." Brief credits.

677   Griffith, Richard. "The Use of Films by the U.S. Armed Services," in Documentary Film. Edited by Paul Rotha. 3d ed. London: Faber & Faber pp. 344-58.
       Griffith surveys documentary films produced by the U.S. Armed Forces during World War II, including Capra's Why We Fight series, the Army-Navy Screen Magazine, and The Negro Soldier. The Why We Fight series is described as "vital to the intelligent prosecution of the war" and a model for films of its kind.

678   Queval, Jean. "Capra, ou l'idéalisme américain." Mercure de France 314, No. 1062 (February), 328-31.
       A review of Richard Griffith's B.F.I. monograph on Capra (see entry 649), essentially summarizing Griffith's interpretation of Capra's career.

1953

*679   Bianchi, Pietro. "Frank Capra." Cinema (Milan), N.S. No. 104.
       Cited in Filmlexicon degli autori e delle opere. See # 706.

680   de Baroncelli, Jean. "Le cinéma." Le Monde (27 June), p. 12.
       The release of Here Comes the Groom in France prompts the author to briefly comment on the American film industry and its relation to cinema art. He considers the film an exclusively American product: "a Paramount cocktail." Its recipe consists of pretty music, stars, and a story of love versus money, all under the direction of the once great Frank Capra who no longer seems to take cinema seriously. Noting that the film, and Bing Crosby's hit song from it, are making money in America, de Baroncelli advises the reader to resist indignation and remember that cinema is an industry that only occasionally attains the status of art. Bing Crosby and "In the Cool, Cool, Cool of the Evening," he concludes, permit the cinema to subsist.

1954

681   Mauriac, Claude. "Eau de rose et vitriol," in his L'amour du cinéma. Paris: Éditions Albin Michel, pp. 262-64.

1954

Part of a chapter by Mauriac on "cinésociologie" in the American film. After noting that Arsenic and Old Lace is a return to the kind of unpretentious light comedy Capra introduced in Lady for a Day and It Happened One Night, Mauriac discusses Meet John Doe as one of Capra's interim "combat" films against capitalism, a mixture of good intentions and banality. Mauriac is struck by some powerful images Capra records and by the spell the film casts despite its puerilities. He hopes for the emergence of a filmmaker who might use the medium as effectively to attack social problems head-on.

682   Montgomery, John. Comedy Films, 1894-1954. London: George Allen & Unwin, pp. 199-200.

A brief discussion of Lady for a Day, It Happened One Night, Mr. Deeds Goes to Town, and Mr. Smith Goes to Washington as "social comedies" in comparison with the work of British director John Baxter.

683   Sennett, Mack. King of Comedy. As told to Cameron Shipp. Garden City, N.Y.: Doubleday & Co., pp. 140-42.

Sennett credits Capra with first recognizing how Harry Langdon's comic personality might come across on the screen and guiding the former vaudevillian to stardom in Keystone two-reelers. Sennett also inaccurately states that Capra had progressed from gagman to director at Keystone before Langdon's arrival, and implies that Langdon failed as a producer as soon as he departed Keystone, ignoring the comedian's successful independent features with Capra.

1955

684   Gallez, Douglas W. "Patterns of Wartime Documentaries." Quarterly Review of Film, Radio and Television, 10, No. 2 (Winter), 125-35.

A survey of World War II documentaries, including the Why We Fight series. Films by Capra and John Huston are seen as working within a "true documentary tradition": socially conscious, evoking compassion, and aimed at molding public opinion.

685   Jeanne, René, and Charles Ford. "Frank Capra," in their Histoire du cinéma. Vol. 2, Le cinéma américain, 1895-1945. Paris: S.E.D.E., pp. 521-24.

This section contains brief, and largely inaccurate, background information on Capra, and commentary on his work from It Happened One Night through Mr. Smith Goes to Washington. The authors credit Capra with a seminal role in the emergence of "comédie américaine" in the 1930s and compare his work with that of John Ford, proposing that Capra and Ford were the directors to most profit from the advent of sound.

1956

686   Anon. "Up with Frank Capra." Newsweek, 48, No. 23 (3 December), 92, 94.

A report on the television presentation of Our Mr. Sun, Capra's first science documentary for Bell Telephone, prior to its distribution to schools and communities.

687 Cincotti, Guido, ed. "Filmografia di Frank Capra." Bianco e Nero, 17, No. 4 (April), 29-34.
A filmography through 1951, with brief credits.

688 Gould, Jack. "Television: 'Our Mr. Sun.'" New York Times (20 November), p. 75.
Reviewing the television broadcast of Our Mr. Sun, Gould finds the work a fruitful experiment in public eduction through entertainment. Although the opening is "on the irritatingly precious and condescending side," once the show turns to the factual material it is genuinely rewarding.

689 Paolella, Roberto. "Ambizioni e vocazioni nell'opera di Frank Capra." Bianco e Nero, 17, No. 4 (April), 13-28.
A survey of Capra's career, focusing primarily on his work in the 1930s. Detailed attention is given to Capra's cycle of films with Barbara Stanwyck, especially The Miracle Woman and Forbidden. It Happened One Night and Lost Horizon are also discussed at length, the former in terms of the development of Capra's comic style and its influence on American comedy, and the latter as Capra's great failure, a film in which his ambition to be philosophical outstripped his vocation.

690 Pryor, Thomas M. "Capra Return to Film Business." New York Times (7 April), p. 12.
A report on Capra's return to Hollywood by way of a one-picture contract with Columbia, the subject of which has not yet been determined.

1957

691 Anon. "Look Applauds." Look, 21 (2 April), 14.
A brief report on Capra adapting his talents as a film director to the Bell Telephone science series for television.

692 Anon. Treasury of Screen Classics. New York: Dell Publishing Co, pp. 21-25, 34-37.
This volume contains plot synopses for It Happened One Night and You Can't Take It with You.

693 Gould, Jack. "TV: The Story of Blood." New York Times (21 March), p. 63.
A highly favorable review of the television broadcast of Hemo the Magnificent. "Under the inspired direction of Frank Capra, the film was a lucid, amusing and highly informative hour for viewers of all ages. . . . Learning and laughter are wonderful companions."

1957

694   Knight, Arthur. *The Liveliest Art*. New York: Macmillan Co. pp. 128-29, 182-83, 260-61.

Commentary on Capra's work appears at several points in this general history. Capra's editing in *The Strong Man* is compared to Eisenstein's montage in its effective extension of time. Capra is praised for understanding the "subtle relationship between dialogue and camera," and the special requirements for directing actors who speak, during the early years of sound. Turning to Capra's "political" films, Knight sees *Mr. Deeds Goes to Town* as an escape from social problems, but *Meet John Doe* as a "daring and angry exposé of American fascism."

695   L[aura], E[rnesto] G. "Riedizioni." *Bianco e Nero*, 18, No. 6 (June), 67-70.

A reassessment of *Lost Horizon*. Speculating that the opening evacuation of Baskul might have shocked viewers accustomed to Capra's "fairy tales," Laura judges it the best sequence in the film. He is less pleased with the message of Shangri-La; while seemingly prophetic of world events, he argues, it cannot be considered anti-fascist since a cultural context is absent, and the notion of peace proposed is vague, if not mystical. He sees the film signaling Capra's abandonment of a natural vocation for comedy and light adventure to pursue message films.

696   Miller, Don. "Films on TV." *Films in Review*, 8, No. 1 (January), 36.

An unfavorable review of Capra's first science documentary, *Our Mr. Sun*. The fictional characters strike Miller as a burlesque of figures associated with Capra's work in the 1930s: Mr. Fiction Writer as an "aw shucks" Deeds or Smith; Mr. Sun as an Edward Arnold tycoon; and Father Time, dubbed by Lionel Barrymore, as Lionel Barrymore.

697   Misurell, Ed. "Science Gets the 'Capra Touch' on TV." Boston *Pictorial Review* (17 March), pp. 4-6.

A report on the Bell Telephone science series prior to the broadcast of Capra's second TV documentary, *Hemo the Magnificent*.

698   Pryor, Thomas M. "Capra to Direct Story from Bible." *New York Times* (18 November), p. 37.

A report on Capra taking over the direction of *Joseph and His Brethren*, a Columbia project with a troubled history.

699   S[hepard], R[ichard] F. "TV Review." *New York Times* (26 October), p. 43.

A brief review of *The Strange Case of the Cosmic Rays*. Capra is commended for again producing an original and entertaining science television show.

700   Thompson, George Raynor, Dixie R. Harris, Pauline M. Oakes, and Dulany Terret. *The Signal Corps: The Test (December 1941 to July 1943)*. Washington, D.C.: Department of the Army, pp. 414-16.

The official military account of Capra's activities with the U.S. Army Signal Corps during the early stages of World War II. The period covered encompasses the solicitation of Capra's services, his commission, the formation of the Capra unit to produce the Why We Fight series, and the group's subsequent work on the Know Your Enemy, and Know Your Ally series. Drawn primarily from memos and correspondence.

701   Webber, Jeanne Curtis. "Science Enlists the Capra Genius." Sign, 36 (June), 18-20.
A survey of Capra's career and background information on his involvement with the Bell Telephone series of science documentaries. Capra's interest in demonstrating the relationship between science and religion is stressed.

1958

702   Agee, James. Agee on Film. Vol. 1. Edited by McDowell Obolensky. New York: McDowell Obolensky, pp. 2-19, 40-41, 56-57, 66, 79-80, 84-85, 233-34.
This anthology includes reprints of "Comedy's Greatest Era" (see entry 626), and Agee's reviews of Prelude to War (see entry 488), The Battle of Britain, and The Battle of Russia (see entries 489 and 490), The Negro Soldier (see entry 508), Tunisian Victory (see entry 509), and It's a Wonderful Life (see entry 558).

703   Bolzoni, Francesco. "Emilio Cecchi, un letterato al cinema." Bianco e Nero, 19, No. 4 (April), 34-35.
Bolzoni discusses writing on Capra from the 1930s by Italian critic and author Emilio Cecchi. Cecchi, Bolzoni observes, held Capra's work in great esteem, recognizing in it a proper conception of life and the world, a moral dimension derived from Capra's Italian background that was jovial and affectionate rather than somber (see entries 307 and 308).

704   Gould, Jack. "RV: Story of Weather." New York Times (13 February), p. 59.
A review of The Unchained Goddess. Gould finds the film informative as a science documentary, but limited in that it addresses children rather than adults.

705   Jacobs, Jack. "Ronald Colman." Films in Review, 9, No. 4 (April), 183.
Brief commentary on Lost Horizon. Jacobs describes Capra's direction as "cinematically inventive and effective."

706   L[aura], E[rnesto] G. "Frank Capra," in Filmlexicon degli autori e delle opere. Rome: Edizione di Bianco e Nero, pp. 1073-80.
A detailed bio-filmography with abbreviated credits and a selected bibliography. Laura's closing assessment is that Capra's work, despite thematic superficiality and a tendency toward pathos, is

central to the evolution of American film comedy for it moves away from the extravagant escapism of Cecil B. DeMille toward psychological refinement, a truthful depiction of small-town life, and a sense of humor that is not cheap.

707   Pryor, Thomas M. "Hollywood Aims." New York Times (18 May), sec. 2, p. 5.
      A report on Capra's return to theatrical filmmaking with A Hole in the Head. His work over the past few years on the Bell Telephone science series and various unrealized projects at Columbia are also discussed.

708   Thomaier, William. "Early Sound Comedy." Films in Review, 9, No. 5 (May), 254-62.
      A survey of thirties screwball comedy, with passing commentary on Capra's films. Thomaier draws a distinction between Capra's attempt to use comedy to point the way toward a better life and the "to hell with everything" premise of true screwball comedy, which Capra only approaches in You Can't Take It with You.

709   Van Horne, Harriet. "Cartoons Hamper Nature Show." New York World-Telegram (13 February).
      A review of The Unchained Goddess. Van Horne criticizes Capra for using "noxious little cartoon characters" to tell a story about weather, and for the overuse of analogies, comparisons, paraphrases, and jokes. While Capra's science programs are full of good intentions, "the finished product is false, vulgar and—worst of all—pretentious."

1959

710   Aaronson, Charles S. "A Hole in the Head." Motion Picture Herald (23 May), p. 276.
      A review of the film, forecasting commercial success. The film is a "slightly mad, whirligig comedy."

711   Anon. "Ein Lock im Kopf [A Hole in the Head]." Filmkritik (Munich), 2, No. 10 (October), 339.
      A synopsis of A Hole in the Head and brief credits.

712   Anon. "A Hole in the Head." Cue (18 July).
      A review of the film, which is found to "wobble just as unevenly as the play between vaudeville humor, dialect comedy, frenetic farce, schmaltzy sentimentalities and wise-cracking gag lines."

713   Anon. "A Hole in the Head." Filmfacts 2, No. 30 (26 August), 171-73.
      Credits, a synopsis, and excerpts from reviews published in the New York Times, Films in Review, Saturday Review, the New York Herald Tribune, Variety, and Time.

Writings About Frank Capra 1959

714   Anon. "A Hole in the Head." Films and Filming, 5, No. 11 (August), 18.
      A photo spread on the film.

715   Anon. "A Hole in the Head." Time, 74, No. 5 (3 August), 65.
      A review of the film. Capra's "sharp, knowing touches about people" cannot salvage this one-act vignette blown up into a two-hour, wide-screen movie.

716   Anon. "Making It Go." Newsweek, 54, No. 1 (6 July), 83-84.
      A brief review of A Hole in the Head accompanied by an interview with Frank Sinatra. The film is described as "a soap opera plot but genuinely entertaining."

717   Beckley, Paul V. "A Hole in the Head." New York Herald Tribune (16 July).
      A review of the film. Beckley finds it "built for warmth rather than logic" and "more sentimental than dramatic," but commends the perfomances of Thelma Ritter and Edward G. Robinson. No mention of Capra. Brief credits.

718   Bogdanovich, Peter. "Hollywood." Frontier, 10, No. 12 (October), 24-25.
      A review of A Hole in the Head. Bogdanovich is greatly disappointed by the film in light of Capra's career. "Where the early movies were clipped, compact, and always to the point," he notes, "this one is overlong, meandering and mawkishly sentimental." He contrasts Capra's sense of comedy here unfavorably with that of The Strong Man, and the motivation and feeling of the central character unfavorably with that of Mr. Smith Goes to Washington. Moreover, he finds in the film a message of middle-class conformity that directly betrays the values, ideals, and crusades of Capra's work in the 1930s and 1940s.

719   Bower, Lynn. "Sinatra's 'Hole in Head' Alters Broadway Script." Los Angeles Examiner (18 June), sec. 2, p. 10.
      A favorable review of A Hole in the Head. "The companionship and devotion of the boy and his dad has the unmistakable stamp of Frank Capra's understanding of kids and men who are still kids." Brief credits.

720   Crowther, Bosley. "Screen: Capra's 'A Hole in the Head.'" New York Times (16 July), p. 31.
      A review of the film. Crowther likens it to Capra's great works of the 1930s: a colloquial American comedy featuring the director's bent for social observation. He predicts the character of Tony, played by Frank Sinatra, will be cherished along with Capra's early protagonists, Deeds and Smith. Brief credits. Also see entry 721.

721   _____. "Return of the Nation." New York Times (26 July), sec. 2, p. 1.

A followup to Crowther's enthusiastic review of <u>A Hole in the Head</u>. If the success of the film is any guide, Crowther speculates, Capra's temporary retirement from feature filmmaking may be an advisable procedure for other directors. In any case, the film is in keeping with Capra's best work. The protagonist is of the same breed as Deeds and Smith, only afflicted with a 1950s version of the American dream. Capra, moreover, has directed with pictorial wit and unremitting verve. Also see entry 720.

722   Dyer, John Peter. "A Hole in the Head." <u>Films and Filming</u>, 5, No. 12 (September), 24.

A review of the film. In a year of comeback films by aging directors, Dyer notes, Capra's contribution lives up to expectations. "The film's surprising degree of unity is a result of warm and arresting characterization, wonderful little touches and catch phrases, and sheer technical control." Credits.

723   Franklin, Joe. "<u>The Strong Man</u>," in his <u>Classics of the Silent Screen</u>. New York: Citadel Press, pp. 94-95.

A synopsis and brief commentary on the film, which Franklin considers to be both Langdon's and Capra's best work. "The best comedy moments are those which have little or no connection with the plot proper."

724   Gene. "<u>A Hole in the Head</u>." <u>Variety</u> (20 May), p. 6.

A review of the film. Arnold Schulman's story is considered flawed, but Capra is cited for his alertness to comic and dramatic values in the screenplay, his direction of the actors, and the pace he sets for the action. Credits.

725   Herbstman. "Reviews of New Films." <u>Film Daily</u> (19 May), p. 6.

<u>A Hole in the Head</u> is favorably reviewed. Credit for the film's success is given to Capra for his direction.

726   Knight, Arthur. "All in Fun." <u>Saturday Review</u>, 42, No. 31 (1 August), 27.

A favorable review of <u>A Hole in the Head</u>. Knight finds Capra's feeling for people and talent for "sensing relationships with the camera" fully evident in the film.

727   Kostolefsky, Joseph. "<u>A Hole in the Head</u>." <u>Film Quarterly</u>, 13, No. 1 (Fall), 50-52.

An ambivalent review of the film. Kostolefsky finds the plot weak and is suspicious of the film's direct appeal to the emotions. But he is pleased by the comedy and makes special note of Capra's control of small gestures and telling expressions by his actors. The sense of space and variety of scenes common to Capra's best work in the 1930s is absent, and good character actors have been replaced by a "platoon of stars," but Capra is still to be welcomed back from "the arid wastes of popular science."

728   McCarten, John. "The Current Cinema." New Yorker, 35, No. 24 (1 August), 61.

   A brief note on A Hole in the Head. Only the appearance of Edward G. Robinson and Thelma Ritter relieves the reviewer's sense of tedium. No mention of Capra.

729   Marcorelles, Louis. "Cinéma." France Observateur (12 November), p. 23.

   A Hole in the Head is reviewed. After an eight-year absence from the screen, Marcorelles observes, Capra has returned to his fundamental obsessions. His optimism remains as indestructible as ever, and neither Cinemascope nor color has changed his extraordinarily relaxed mise-en-scène and direction of actors.

730   Moffitt, Jack. "Capra Production Packs Plenty of B.O. Appeal; Well-Acted." Hollywood Reporter (19 May), pp. 3, 8.

   A highly favorable review of A Hole in the Head. Capra "is back with all his past techniques in full blossom and with a wonderful new ability to capture the flavor of our times." Credits.

731   Paolella, Roberto. "Frank Capra." Bianco e Nero, 20, Nos. 8-10 (August-October), 157-62.

   Plot synopses, credits, and brief excerpts from original Italian reviews are provided for Forbidden, It Happened One Night, and Mr. Deeds Goes to Town. (For reviews of Forbidden, see entries 145, 146, and 157; for It Happened One Night, entries 189, 206, 208, and 209; for Mr. Deeds Goes to Town, entries 253, 263, 267, 270, 271, and 273.)

732   _____. "La retrospectiva 1932-39 e la 'personale' di genina." Bianco e nero, 20, No. 11 (November), 49.

   Brief commentary on Forbidden, It Happened One Night, and Mr. Deeds Goes to Town as significant films during this seven-year period.

733   Powr. "Film Review." Daily Variety (19 May).

   A review of A Hole in the Head. The writer finds the film unevenly paced and senses that Capra has been inhibited by the widescreen format. Instead of using "deft close-ups, skillful cutting and reaction shots to enhance and enlarge his comedy," Capra now resorts to long takes.

734   Scheuer, Philip K. "'Hole in the Head' Pleasant Diversion." Los Angeles Times (18 June), sec. 1, p. 25.

   A review of A Hole in the Head. Scheuer finds the material "overstretched," but is pleased to see Capra's expertise as a director being put to use. "He has at least dressed up a so-so stage comedy with laughs, human interest, a shot of sex and even a surprise of a tear toward the close."

735   Sennett, Ted. "A Hole in the Head." Films in Review, 10, No. 7 (August-September), 424-25.

A review of the film. "The film fails because the protagonist is not a sympathetic character, and because Capra tries to force his individual style on material which resists being stylized." Excesses of sentiment and low comedy remind Sennett of Capra's lesser work.

1960

736   Leyda, Jay. Kino: A History of the Russian and Soviet Film. New York: Macmillan Co. pp. 371, 377, 380.
The influence of Capra's Why We Fight series on Russian filmmakers during the postwar period is briefly discussed.

737   Ranieri, Tino. "Il panoram straniero." Bianco e Nero, 21, Nos. 3-4 (March-April), 141.
A brief review of A Hole in the Head. Ranieri notes in the film a residue of Capra's "message humor." Although Capra's direction occasionally shakes off the rust of the past and appears modern, the story is very repetitious.

738   Stanbrook, Alan. "Ya Gotta Have Heart. Films and Filming, 6, No. 12 (September), 6.
A review of A Hole in the Head. Stanbrook finds signs in the film that Capra may return to top form: as was true of his best work from the 1930s, his philosophy is grounded in the hopes of the common man, and despite a professional veneer the film captures the rhythm of life. But there are also signs that Capra's powers have faded: warmth and humanity glide off into sentimentality, and the hero succeeds not through integrity but by "living off the interest from tomorrow's investments."

1961

739   Agee, James. "Comedy's Greatest Era," in The Open Forum. Edited by Alfred Kazin. New York: Harcourt, Brace, pp. 35-69.
A reprint of Agee's 1949 essay. See entry 626.

740   Anon. "Acting Their Age." Time, 78, No. 26 (29 December), 57.
A review of Pocketful of Miracles, centering on Bette Davis's comeback performance. the film is judged a dated and overlong remake.

741   Anon. "Capra Corn." Newsweek, 58, No. 25 (18 December), 97-98.
A review of Pocketful of Miracles. Capra "has borrowed Runyon's story and characters, thrown out Runyon's dialogue, and gone about his business in his own way. It is happy news that, after 40 years in movies, Capra's way is as sure as ever." An interview with Capra is appended to this review (see entry 1253).

742   Anon. "A Pocketful of Miracles." Film Daily (2 November), p. 9.
A highly favorable review in advance of the film's release. "A large part of the effective quality of the picture which Capra

astutely directed and produced is attributable to the wonderful gallery of supporting characterizations." Brief credits.

743   Beckley, Paul V. Review of Pocketful of Miracles. New York Herald Tribune (19 December).
A favorable review. Capra is judged at top form, mixing sentimentality and impudence, and never letting the sentimentality get heavy.

744   Houston, Penelope. "Pocketful of Miracles." Sight and Sound, 31, No. 1 (Winter), 42.
A review of the film. Houston allows that Capra has earned a license for fantasy, but finds that this project has brought out a maudlin streak in Capra at the expense of honest sentiment. Moreover, the film's sluggishness suggests that his old flexibility has stiffened up.

745   Knight, Arthur. "A Dissertation on Roast Corn." Saturday Review, 44, No. 45 (11 November), 32.
A review of Pocketful of Miracles. Kinght contends that the verve, directness, and lack of pretense that made Damon Runyon's fiction, and the movies it inspired, palatable in the 1930s is absent in this remake of Lady for a Day. He finds the new film overlong, overelaborate, and pretentious, and guilty of "the fundamental error of taking its people seriously."

746   Rothschild, Elaine. "Pocketful of Miracles." Films in Review, 12, No. 10 (December), 624.
A brief, unfavorable review. "A remake of his Lady for a Day ('33), this unbelievable and unfunny comedy proves only that director Frank Capra has learned nothing and forgotten nothing in the 28 years that intervene between the two pictures."

747   Ruddy, Johan M. "Veteran Director Reviews His Forty Years in Pictures." Hollywood Diary (1 July), pp. 4-5.
Background on the remaking of Lady for a Day as Pocketful of Miracles, and a skeletal biography of Capra.

748   Scheuer, Philip K. "Bette Davis, Vivien Leigh Films Viewed." Los Angeles Times (26 December), sec. 4, p. 9.
A review of Pocketful of Miracles, affectionately labeled by Scheuer "Old Home Week Picture of the Year." Noting that at least two reviewers have punned laboriously in describing the film as "Capra-corn," Scheuer proposes that it has been "popped by an expert."

749   Tube [Larry Tubelle]. "Pocketful of Miracles. Variety (1 November), p. 6.
A review of the film. Tubelle speculates that the commercial success of the film will depend on whether or not "unabashed sentiment has gone out of style." He expects that it has, but hedges his bet based on Capra's undiminished "touch." The success of Pocketful of Miracles in fact could launch a renaissance of screen comedy in the 1930s style. Although the film is somewhat long and lethargic,

compensation can be found in Capra's assembling of masterful character actors. Credits.

750 Weiler, A.H. "Capra's 'Pocketful of Miracles' Opens at Two Theatres Here." New York Times (19 December), p. 39.
    A review of Pocketful of Miracles. Weiler considers the Damon Runyon story on which the film is based dated material; thus Capra's energetic performers cannot keep the satire from wearing thin. Credits.

751 Williams, Dick. "Is Sweet Corn of Yore Palatable to Moderns?" Los Angeles Times, Calendar (12 November), pp. 4-5
    A review of Pocketful of Miracles prior to its general release. Williams considers the film an interesting experiment in bringing sentiment back to the screen, but finds the comedy labored, the mugging standard, the pace lethargic, and the ending obvious.

1962

752 Anon. "Capra Is Signed to Direct Two Films for Paramount." New York Times (16 November), p. 27.
    A report on Capra signing a contract to direct Circus and Dear and Glorious Physician.

753 Anon. "Pocketful of Miracles." Filmfacts, 4, No. 49 (5 January), 322-24.
    Credits, a synopsis, and excerpts from reviews published in the New York Herald Tribune, Saturday Review, Films in Review, Variety, Time, and the New York Times.

754 A[rmitage], P[eter]. "Pocketful of Miracles." Film (London), 31 (Spring), 13.
    A brief review. The film marks a genuine comeback for Capra: "no one has ever been able to make the outrageously sentimental so acceptable and the major part of the film has an almost forgotten pace."

755 Baby, Yvonne. "Le cinéma." Le Monde (4 February), p. 15.
    Pocketful of Miracles is reviewed. Baby notes that in the twenty-eight years since he first filmed the story, Capra has aged; his verve and mischievousness have dulled, and digressions now interrupt his narration. Nevertheless, the film has a mysterious charm, attributable in part to the nostalgia of a man who is tempted to return to his dreams and prolong them. Capra lets the miracle of this fairy tale unfold with serenity. Moreover, Bette Davis resists turning the central role into an exercise in virtuosity; she communicates a controlled tension in her double role as beggar and millionaire and, confronted with young actors in the cast, remains the melancholic symbol of the film's return to the past.

756 Cutts, John. "Pocketful of Miracles." Films and Filming, 8, No. 4 (January), 29.

A review of the film. Noting that Capra's general neglect in postwar critical circles has been shameful, Cutts defends his most recent film as open, sunny entertainment. "A film to be accepted on its own terms or not accepted at all." Brief credits.

757   Hill, Steven P. "Le confessioni del 'filibustiere' Frank Capra." Bianco e Nero, 23, No. 5 (May), 49-57.

A review of Pocketful of Miracles and a survey of Capra's career as the "cockeyed optimist of the American cinema." Written at a time when many reviewers were resurrecting the hoariest clichés about Capra's earlier work, this critique is ripe with perceptive cross-references to specific films. Furthermore, Hill makes a case for Pocketful as Capra's most personal film. He argues that while Capra is usually identified with naive, idealized heroes of the Deeds-Smith type, his early films in fact were populated by attractive city slickers and lovable rogues, and that the director has now returned to these heroes in his last two films, perhaps in response to a changing moral climate, or perhaps in memory of his own early years as a con man. He compares Pocketful with Capra's original version, Lady for a Day, noting how elements of post-Deeds Capra have been introduced into the story, and relates comic strategies in this most recent film to those in earlier works, noting where and why he thinks they succeed and fail. He considers the central flaw in Pocketful to be the portrayal of Annie, and the casting of Bette Davis to be a rare mistake of this kind by Capra. He closes with a detailed autobiographical reading of the film: Capra's career is linked to that of Dave the Dude, an ambitious but purposeless gambler who finds meaning in life by assuming the role of Pygmalion, rehabilitating a down-and-out derelict (read Columbia specifically, and cinema generally) into a leader of society. A translation of this article recently has been published in Focus Magazine (University of California, Santa Barbara), 2, No. 2 (June 1982), 6-9.

758   Labarthe, A.-S. "Milliardaire pour un jour." France Observateur (1 February), p. 22.

A review of Pocketful of Miracles. Labarthe sees the film as a comedy in the great tradition of another era, part pastiche, and part hommage by the Capra of today to the Capra of thirty years ago. Capra appears to wax nostalgic not only for a past American cinema but also for the epoch of Roosevelt America. Working with an antiquated style, his mise-en-scène and direction of actors is dazzling.

759   Pechter, William S. "American Madness." Kulchur, 3 No. 12 (Winter), 64-77.

A reassessment of Capra's work, inspired by the release of Pocketful of Miracles. Pechter modifies Richard Griffith's notion of Capra's "fantasy of goodwill" to accommodate a melancholy, if not subversive, strain in the films. The struggle between small-town purity and big-city corruption, he proposes, dramatizes the gap between our childhood selves (and our cultural memory of innocence) and our knowledge of what we have become. The perfunctory, abrupt quality to Capra's "happy endings" (explicitly acknowledged through the deus ex machina in It's a Wonderful Life) betrays Capra's own doubt concerning any easy resolution. Pechter detects in the manic speed and energy of Capra's work a desperation reflecting the gulf between what Capra wishes to say and what he actually succeeds in saying, and values this desperation as Capra's final honesty. He also draws analogies between Capra and Mark Twain as American folk artists, and analyzes Capra's style as one based on editing rather than pictorial composition. Reprinted in 1971 (see entry 848), 1975 (see entry 988), 1977 (see entry 1052), and 1978 (see entry 1087). Excerpts reprinted in 1974 (see entry 939).

760 Quigley, Isabel. "The Gulliver Game." Spectator, 208 (5 January), 18.
 A review of Pocketful of Miracles. Quigley is not surprised that Capra--champion of the underdog, the simple, and the inarticulate--has been carried away into sentimentality by this tale. "The surprise is in how far he has gone, how obvious, even how unprofessional it all seems."

761 Rohrbach, Gunter. "Die unteren Zehntausend." Filmkritik, 6, No. 4 (April), 177-78.
 A review of Pocketful of Miracles. Rohrback finds the film dated as a contemporary work, but comprehensible in light of Capra's career.

1963

762 Calder-Marshall, Alexander. The Innocent Eye: The Life of Robert J. Flaherty. London W.H. Allen & Co., pp. 203-4.
 Robert Flaherty's unproductive tenure with Capra's Signal Corps film unit during World War II is briefly discussed.

763 Connor, Edward. "Revisiting Lost Horizon." Screen Facts, 1, No. 2:50-60.
 A detailed history of Lost Horizon from novel to screen and of the various edited versions subsequently released. Some of Connor's information is inaccurate, and the article unfortunately lacks footnotes, but Connor brings together an impressive body of material.

764 Sarris, Andrew. "The American Cinema." Film Culture, No. 29 (Spring), pp. 18-19.
 Ranking Capra with the "Third Line" of American film directors, Sarris proposes that Capra's political films of the late 1930s implied a belief in the tyranny of the majority, and that with Meet John Doe the director "crossed the thin line between populist sentimentality and populist demagoguery." After years of relative inactivity, Capra then returned with the "new look in conformity" in the person of Frank Sinatra. Sarris links Capra's flair for improvisation with that of Leo McCarey, Gregory LaCava, and other comedy directors of the 1930s, and notes that as a topical director Capra's star rose as Josef von Sternberg's fell. Sarris revised this assessment in 1968 (see entry 792) and 1978 (see entry 1090).

1964

765   Crowther, Bosley. "A Disappointing Science Film." <u>New York Times</u> (10 September), p. 27.
    A review of Capra's documentary short, <u>Rendezvous in Space</u>, screened at the Hall of Science during the New York World's Fair. Crowther reports: "This allegedly scientific exposition of how an orbital laboratory in space would work is, at best, no more exciting or convincing than a cheap science-fiction film. For the most part, it is a juvenile depiction that affronts intelligence."

766   Hill, Steven P. "Frank Capra." <u>Film Society Newsletter</u> (November), pp. 18-19.
    A Capra filmography.

767   Lawson, John Howard. <u>Film: The Creative Process</u>. New York: Hill & Wang, pp. 143-45.
    Brief mention is made of the influence of Capra's <u>Why We Fight</u> series on Russian filmmakers. Drawn mainly from Jay Leyda's <u>Kino</u> (see entry 736).

768   Leyda, Jay. <u>Films Beget Films</u>. New York: Hill & Wang, pp. 58-59.
    Leyda briefly discusses the compilation of various kinds of footage in the <u>Why We Fight</u> series.

*769   Mesnil, Michel. "<u>New York-Miami</u>." <u>Cinéma 64</u> (October).
    A discussion of <u>It Happened One Night</u>. Cited in Jean Mitry's <u>Histoire du cinéma</u>. Vol. 4, <u>1929-1940</u> (see entry 920).

770   Price, James. "Capra and the American Dream." <u>London Magazine</u>, N.S. 3, No. 10 (January), 85-93.
    A recent retrospective leads Price to conclude that Capra's work from the 1930s represents American cinema at its prime, a cinema that has now acquired a poignant quality of futility. Price is most impressed with <u>It Happened One Night</u>, finding its construction impeccable, its observation precise, and its optimism profound. Interpreting <u>Mr. Deeds Goes to Town</u> and <u>Mr. Smith Goes to Washington</u> as Capra's contribution to Roosevelt's New Deal, Price links the straightforward victory of Deeds to an early optimism in this period, and the thorough corruption hanging over Smith's triumph to a darkening perspective at the end of the decade. "Behind his rose-tinted spectacles," Price writes of <u>Mr. Smith</u>, "Capra's gaze takes unwilling account of the cancer of his society. . . . It is at once Capra's most overtly patriotic and most desperately sceptical film."

771   Ranieri, Tino. "<u>Good Neighbor Sam</u>." <u>Bianco e Nero</u>, 25, Nos. 11-12 (November-December), 106-9.
    <u>Good Neighbor Sam</u> (David Swift, 1964) is unfavorably compared with Capra's optimistic comedies of the 1930s.

772   Wiseman, Thomas. *Cinema*. London: Cassell & Co. pp. 72-73.
Capra's films are described in this survey of cinema as modern fairy tales, supplying fanciful, sentimental solutions to real social problems. (*Mr. Deeds Goes to Town* is briefly discussed as an example.) Thus the films, although ostensibly progressive, were in effect reactionary. Nevertheless, Capra's stylish handling of comedy, especially apparent in *It Happened One Night*, was rightly admired and frequently imitated.

1965

773   Halliwell, Leslie. "Frank Capra," in his *The Filmgoers Companion*. New York: Hill & Wang, pp. 75-76.
A brief career sketch and partial filmography. (The entry was slightly revised and a complete filmography included for the fourth edition in 1974.)

774   Lowry, Malcolm. Letter to Priscilla Bonner, in *Selected Letters of Malcolm Lowry*. Edited by Harvy Brett and Margerie Bonner Lowry. Philadelphia and New York: Lippincott, pp. 309-10.
A letter from Lowry to his sister upon reseeing *The Strong Man* in which she has the leading female role. He praises the film and her performance extravagantly, and observes that Capra has continued "to mine that apparently inexhaustible gold mine of the American consciousness of decency and wisdom against the forces of hypocrisy." Reprinted in 1975 (see entry 983).

775   Mallery, David. Review of *It Happened One Night*. *Film Society Newsletter* (February), p. 9.
In this brief reassessment, Mallery remarks that the film has retained its freshness despite our familiarity with the kind of comedy it spawned.

776   Ranieri, Tino. "Trieste: Rassegna utile con qualche incertezza." *Bianco e Nero*, 26, Nos. 10-11 (October-November), 96-97.
Brief commentary on the utopian vision of Shangri-La in *Lost Horizon*. Ranieri finds it naive, irrational, and a dangerous retreat from the problems of the world.

1966

777   Cameron, Evan. "*It Happened One Night* and *Stagecoach*." *Screen Education*, 35 (July-August), 23-45.
Working from the premise that earlier critics had no framework within which to judge the artistic merits of Hollywood comedies or westerns—and hence did not fully appreciate the artistry of films such as *It Happened One Night* and *Stagecoach*—Cameron surveys critical responses to the two films and offers his own analysis. In both cases, he sees the formation of stable director-writer teams (Capra and Riskin, Ford and Nichols) as crucial to the films' success.

Through an analysis of extensive passages of dialogue, he argues that both films reflect the dominant social problems of the day and provide a humanistic message about the essential values of life.

778 Lahue, Kalton C. World of Laughter: The Motion Picture Comedy Short, 1910-1930. Norman: University of Oklahoma Press, p. 162.

Lahue notes that Capra, like Harry Edwards before him, understood better how to nurture and use Harry Langdon's talents than the performer himself.

779 Thompson, George Raynor and Dixie R. Harris. The Signal Corps: The Outcome (Mid-1943 through 1945). Washington, D.C.: U.S. Army, pp. 555-59.

The official military account of Capra's activities with the U.S. Army Signal Corps during the later stages of World War II. The period covered encompasses the success of the Why We Fight series, the decision to abandon the second part of War Comes to America, and the shift to different kinds of morale-building projects such as Your Job in Germany, Two Down and One to Go, and Army-Navy Screen Magazine. Drawn primarily from memos and correspondence.

1967

780 Agee, James. "Comedy's Greatest Era," in The Popular Arts: A Critical Reader. Edited by Irving Deer and Harriet A. Deer. New York: Charles Scribner's Sons, pp. 272-96.

A reprint of Agee's 1949 essay. See entry 626.

781 Bouissinot, Roger, ed. L'encyclopedia du cinéma. Montrouge, France: Bordas, pp. 282-83.

A bio-filmography of Capra. Bouissinot concludes with a brief discussion of the possible influence of Capra's work on Italian neorealism, noting that both possess "an excess of sentimentality saved by naïveté and an elemental taste for enchantment."

782 Jacobs, Lewis. "World War II and the American Film." Cinema Journal, 7 (Winter 1967-68), 1-21.

A brief discussion of the Why We Fight series is included. "Individually and as a series these military films were sharp and quick in impact, penetrating in persuasiveness. They were imbued with a clarity of meaning seldom approached in Hollywood, and set a challenging standard for studio-made products." Reprinted in 1968 (see entry 788).

783 Schonert, Vernon L. "Harry Langdon." Films in Review, 18, No. 7 (October), 470-85, passim.

Schonert's account of Capra's influence on Langdon is drawn mainly from Mack Sennett's autobiography (see entry 683). He proposes, however, that the split between Langdon and Capra after Long Pants may have had less to do with Langdon's inflated ego, as conventional accounts have it, than with the financial burden of Capra's and

Harry Edwards's salaries, and their concern that Langdon might not adapt to sound. A Langdon filmography is appended.

784   Thomas, Bob. King Cohn: The Life and Times of Harry Cohn. New York: G.P. Putnam's Sons, passim.

Capra figures prominently throughout the first half of this anecdotal biography of Harry Cohn. He also is the source of some of the liveliest stories. Capra's rise to power at Columbia is traced, and his evolving love-hate relationship with Cohn provides a major thread of the narrative. Among the early films, Submarine and Donovan's Affair receive special attention, as do all Capra's films at the studio from Lady for a Day onward.

1968

785   Baxter, John. Hollywood in the Thirties. New York: A.S. Barnes & Co.; London: A. Zwemmer, pp. 100-104.

Capra's work in the 1930s is briefly assessed, with specific commentary offered on It Happened One Night, Mr. Deeds Goes to Town, and Lost Horizon. Baxter finds in the films "an almost mystical belief in the ability of man to triumph over the social forces which threaten at every turn to crush him." He considers It Happened One Night and Mr. Deeds to have dated, and Lost Horizon to be Capra's consummate work of the period.

786   Bohn, Thomas William. "An Historical and Descriptive Analysis of the 'Why We Fight' Series." Ph.D. dissertation, University of Wisconsin, 258 pp.

In the first half of this study Bohn outlines the history and function of the documentary war film in America and describes the specific forces responsible for the emergence of the Why We Fight series during World War II. In the second half he discusses the thematic and structural characteristics of the series based on a detailed analysis of the sound and image tracks of each of the seven films. Nine themes are isolated: the people, religion, children, historical tradition, hatred of war, leaders, slavery-machines, courage and intelligence of the Allies, and the Allies' buying time for the world. The effectiveness of the films is attributed to the variety and complex synthesis of structural elements, with editing patterns found to be most important. This dissertation was published in 1977 (see entry 1028).

787   Higham, Charles, and Joel Greenburg. Hollywood in the Forties. New York: A.S. Barnes & Co.; London: A. Zwemmer, pp. 55, 73-74.

The authors briefly comment on It's a Wonderful Life ("magnificent, passionate, full-throated film-making"), Meet John Doe ("a sermon delivered by a master technician"), and State of the Union (less allegorical than Meet John Doe, but still vintage Capra).

788   Jacobs, Lewis. "World War II and the American Film," in The Movies: An American Idiom. Edited by Arthur F. McClure.

Rutherford, N.J.: Fairleigh Dickinson University Press, pp. 68-84.
A reprint of Jacobs's 1967 article. See entry 782.

789   Kael, Pauline. "Arsenic and Old Lace," in her Kiss Kiss Bang Bang. Boston: Little, Brown & Co., pp. 285-86.
A program note for the film, which Kael labels "wholesome black comedy."

790   McCaffrey, Donald W. "A Little Boy in a Big World," in his Four Great Comedians. New York: A.S. Barnes & Co.; London: A. Zwemmer, pp. 104-21.
Capra is credited with gradually tailoring Langdon's material to fit the comic talents of the performer, a process culminating in The Strong Man and Long Pants. According to McCaffrey, Capra's control of the story, camera, and actors makes Long Pants one of the best silent screen comedies, and Langdon's "fateful decision" to dismiss Capra as director spelled the rapid fall of the comedian's career.

791   Robinson, David. Hollywood in the Twenties. New York: A.S. Barnes & Co.; London: A. Zwemer, pp. 112-14.
Robinson notes an early demonstration of an independent directorial approach, an easy craftsmanship, and an instinct for psychological probability in Capra's films with Harry Langdon, but otherwise thinks Capra's silent works do not much anticipate his subsequent career.

792   Sarris, Andrew. The American Cinema: Directors and Direction, 1929-1968. New York: E.P. Dutton & Co., pp. 87-88.
Sarris's 1963 commentary on Capra in Film Culture (see entry 764) is reprinted here with minor revisions. He elevates Capra from "Third Line" status to "The Far Side of Paradise" (Sarris's second echelon), and now notes that "there runs through most of his films a somber Christian parable of idealism betrayed and innocence humiliated. The obligatory scene in most of Capra's films is the confession of folly in the most public manner possible." This assessment was revised once again in 1978 (see entry 1090).

1969

793   Brownlow, Kevin. "We're Not Laughing Like We Used To," in his The Parade's Gone By. New York: Alfred A. Knopf, pp. 438-39.
Brownlow accepts the conventional notion that Capra "understood Langdon's character better than anyone, including Langdon," and judges The Strong Man to be Langdon's masterpiece. He also recounts the version of the Langdon-Capra split reported by Katherine Albert in 1932 (see entry 139).

794   Colombat, Jacques, "Harry Langdon." La Revue du Cinéma/Image et Son, 228 (May), 30-37.

A standard account of Langdon's career and Capra's role as Langdon's director.

795 Deming, Barbara. *Running Away from Myself*. New York: Grossman Publishers, pp. 108-16.
Deming's 1951 essay is reprinted here. See entry 667.

796 Durgnat, Raymond. *The Crazy Mirror: Hollywood Comedy and the American Image*. London: Faber & Faber, pp. 123-30, 198.
Durgnat analyzes *Mr. Deeds Goes to Town* in terms of the politics of the depression and the New Deal. According to Durgnat, the film shifts the blame for economic malfunction from big business to the big city, and to the urban intellectuals who inhabit it. Moreover, Deeds's plan for recovery is based on the charity of private wealth, a solution that serves, on balance, as "propaganda for a moderate, concerned Republican point of view." That the film, along with Gregory LaCava's *My Man Godfrey*, could have seemed to support the New Deal, Durgnat contends, can be explained by a popular mood that allows any radical shake-up, viewed optimistically, to be associated with progressive New Deal attitudes. Durgnat's notion of Capra's Republicanism resurfaces later in the book when he briefly speaks of *State of the Union* as made "on behalf of the Republicans" and complicit with anti-Communist witch-hunts. For a subsequent expansion and clarification of his ideas on Capra's relationship to the New Deal, see entry 910.

797 Robinson, David. *The Great Funnies*. London: Studio Vista; New York: E.P. Dutton and Co, p. 81.
Capra is credited with developing Harry Langdon's screen persona in *Tramp, Tramp, Tramp*, and subsequently directing Langdon's two best films.

798 Swindell, Larry. *Spencer Tracy*. New York and Cleveland: World Publishing Co., pp. 206-8.
Background information on the making of *State of the Union* is provided.

799 Tavernier, Bertrand. "Sidney Buchman." *Positif*, 106 (June), 34-47.
A wide-ranging interview with Buchman, including extensive commentary on Capra. Buchman credits Capra with having an enormous influence on American comedy through his insistence on verisimilitude, his sense of dramatic construction, his inventiveness on the set, and his willingness to sacrifice faultless cinematography for naturalistic effect. He claims that Capra was intellectually and politically unsophisticated: he saw the rich and powerful as wicked and the humble people as good, and required that good be rewarded and evil punished. Capra's strength and weakness was a genuine belief in Shangri-La, the moral of which never applied to real life. Buchman discusses in detail his work as a screenwriter on *Mr. Smith Goes to Washington*, and more briefly his uncredited work on *Broadway Bill* and *Lost Horizon*.

1970

800   Agee, James. "Comedy's Greatest Era," in Film: An Anthology. Edited by Dan Talbot. Berkeley, Los Angeles, and London: University of California Press, pp. 13-47.
         A reprint of Agee's 1949 essay. Seen entry 626.

*801   Kolodjazhnaja, Valentina. History of Foreign Cinema, 1929-1945. Moscow: State Institute of Film.
         According to M. Strotchkov, director of the Gosfilmofond archive, this volume includes research on Capra written by Soviet film historian Kolodjazhnaja.

802   Lahue, Kalton C., and Samuel Gill. "Harry Langdon," in Clown Princes and Court Jesters. South Brunswick and New York: A.S. Barnes & Co.; London: Thomas Yoseloff, pp. 196-206.
         Capra is cited as Langdon's most brilliant writer and director, and Langdon's effort to assume directorial control of his films after Long Pants is seen as an unfortunate mistake.

803   Polonsky, Abraham. "How the Blacklist Worked in Hollywood." Film Culture, Nos. 50-51 (Fall-Winter), p. 44.
         Polonsky makes the point that the most socially aware films in Hollywood during the 1930s and 1940s probably were made not by leftists but by conservative directors like Capra in that "what we consider to be socially aware in America is a sentimental attitude toward the goodness of man, and getting together and working things out right, and getting rid of injustice." Political attitudes of this kind, he notes, are "generalized" (like breathing) rather than "definitive."

804   Quigley, Martin, Jr., and Richard Gertner, eds. Films in America: 1929-1969. New York: Golden Press, passim.
         Capsule commentaries are provided for It Happened One Night, Mr. Deeds Goes to Town, Lost Horizon, You Can't Take It with You, Mr. Smith Goes to Washington, and Meet John Doe.

805   Rhodie, Sam. "A Structural Analysis of Mr. Deeds Goes to Town." Cinema (London), 5 (February), 29-30.
         The second half of a B.F.I. seminar paper on structural anthropology and film analysis. Rhodie delineates an oppositional grid at work in Mr. Deeds Goes to Town, based on the central antinomies of town/country and sophisticated/naive, and briefly discusses the ordinariness of Capra's technical structures and the familiarity and sincerity embodied in the film's stars. He concludes that structural analysis is an inadequate methodology: while it can chart the technical and thematic elements marking the film's banality, it cannot explain what makes the film interesting or powerful. Rhodie's original paper was published in its entirety in 1976 (see entry 1016).

806   Richards, Jeffrey. "Frank Capra and the Cinema of Populism." Cinema (London), 5 (February), 22-28.

Richards proposes that Capra, as an immigrant, was able to distill the essential ingredients of American ideology as expressed in the ideals of the middle class from the time of the Revolution to the New Deal, and to translate these into cinema. He sees this ideology as fundamentally Populist, and the 1930s as marking the last stand of an ethos of self-help against the new federalism waged by the New Deal. Within this framework, Richards analyzes Capra's films from his mature period, discussing in detail the nature of Capra's heroes and heroines, and his thematic treatment of politics, antiintellectualism, wealth, happiness, and good neighborliness. Linking all these to a nostalgia for a fading system of values, Richards reads Capra's decline after the war as a measure of the director's own awareness that populist mythology was no longer workable. This influential essay was reprinted in 1972 (see entry 890), twice in 1973 (see entries 923 and 924), and 1976 (see entry 1017).

807   Rosenberg, Bernard, and Harry Silverstein. The Real Tinsel. New York: Macmillan Co. pp. 232-33.
Actor Edward Everett Horton recounts how he and Capra developed a scene in Lost Horizon through improvisation.

808   Tournes, André. "Harry Langdon." Jeune Cinéma, 51 (December-January), 14-18.
In this commentary on Langdon's career, the author suggests that Capra's screenplay for Tramp, Tramp, Tramp was more suitable for Buster Keaton than Langdon.

809   Zinman, David. 50 Classic Motion Pictures: The Stuff That Dreams Are Made Of. New York: Crown Publishers, pp. 44-49, 50-53, 92-97, 224-29, 249-55.
Films by Capra account for six of Zinman's classics: Mr. Deeds Goes to Town is discussed in terms of Gary Cooper; Mr. Smith Goes to Washington in terms of James Stewart; Lost Horizon as an adventure film; It Happened One Night as romantic comedy; and Meet John Doe as an occasion to sketch Capra's career. Detailed credits and a plot synopsis are provided for each film.

1971

810   Anon. Review of The Name Above the Title. Booklist, 68, No. 4 (15 October), 174.
Publication information concerning Capra's autobiography is provided.

811   Anon. "The Name Above the Title." Journal of the Producers Guild of America (June).
A favorable review of Capra's autobiography. Capra's gift for total recall and the good humor and grace of the prose are found noteworthy.

812   Anon. "The Name Above the Title." Publishers Weekly, 199, No. 8 (22 February), 144.

A brief, highly favorable review of Capra's autobiography.

813   Anon. Review of The Name Above the Title. Kirkus Review, 39 (1 March), 261.
Brief, caustic remarks on Capra's autobiography. "His life was more epic and memorable than his films, and his hot-shot remembrances may place him somewhat near to, if not next to, the immortals."

814   Baskette, Kirtley. "Hollywood's New Miracle Man," in The Talkies: Articles and Illustrations from Photoplay Magazine, 1928-1940. Edited by Richard Griffith. New York: Dover Publications, pp. 165, 339.
A reprint of Baskette's 1934 profile on Capra. See entry 188.

815   Bendow, Burton. "Frank Capra: The Name Above the Title (An Autobiography)." Saturday Review, 54, No. 27 (19 July), 27, 57.
Capra's autobiography, the reviewer notes, demonstrates that one had to be dynamic in Hollywood in the 1930s, but that "it was a disadvantage to be burdened with any quality of mind or spirit usually associated with art." He considers Capra's films to be marred by coyness and in touch with the problems of the depression only in a superficial way; yet they contain comic turns executed with exhilarating briskness.

816   Bergman, Andrew. "Frank Capra and Screwball Comedy, 1931-1941," in his We're in the Money: Depression America and Its Films. New York: New York University Press, pp. 132-48.
Bergman discusses the evolution of Capra's work during the 1930s in terms of the shifting values to be found in movie comedy. He sees Capra affectionately embracing the character types of urban genres in Platinum Blonde and Lady for a Day, and then with It Happened One Night initiating screwball comedy, a genre able to reconcile seemingly irreconcilable tensions in depression America. In Mr. Deeds Goes to Town, Bergman argues, Capra's city turns uglier, and he now extends his "screwball perspective" to allow the idiosyncratic behavior of a small-town hero to melt all social tensions, forging a social unity which parallels the electoral unity of Franklin D. Roosevelt. Bergman sees this social cohesion suffering a sterner test by the end of the decade, noting that in You Can't Take It with You Capra's demonology shifts from the urban shyster to the cold-blooded monopolist, and that in Mr. Smith Goes to Washington and Meet John Doe national political institutions are imperiled, forcing Capra to integrate patriotic symbols into the fabric of the films. For Bergman, Capra's genius throughout this period resided in his ability to manipulate American types to create a social synthesis craved by his audience. Crucial to this was Capra's background as both an "immigrant dreamer" who once worked his way through college and a small-time "con man" who once worked the countryside. Capra's comedy is thus interpreted as "a wide-eyed and affectionate hustle--the master-

work of an idealist and door-to-door salesman." Reprinted in 1975 (see entry 959) and in 1979 (see entry 1098). Excerpts reprinted in 1974 (see entry 939).

817   Bergman, Mark. "The Telephone Company, the Nation, and Perhaps the World." Velvet Light Trap, 3 (Winter), 24-25.

A discussion of It's a Wonderful Life in terms of Capra's readjustment to Hollywood after the war. Bergman argues that while George Bailey's triumph in the film is consistent with Capra's other work, the formula was no longer valid in an era when the violence and fatalism of film noir seemed more to the point. Moreover, Bailey's double role as hardworking hero and suicidal villain is not resolved dramatically, but rather through the intervention of a supernatural agent, an unpopular device at the time. However, he concludes, "one need accept none of Capra's pastoral conventions to be overwhelmed by the film's enthusiasm."

818   Bernds, Edward. "Dear Frank Capra." Film Fan Monthly, 124 (October), 9-11.

Bernds, a former sound man at Columbia, recalls working with Capra on Ladies of Leisure, Rain or Shine, Dirigible, American Madness, and Broadway Bill.

819   Borde, Raymond. "Notes sur trois films muets de Frank Capra." Positif, No. 133 (December), pp. 33-34.

Borde proposes that while the six films Capra churned out for Columbia in 1928 are basically of interest only insofar as they demonstrate Capra's professionalism and readiness for "another destiny," these quickly made films are nevertheless marked by a kind of triumph of naïveté. Borde then offers very brief plot synopses of So This Is Love, The Matinee Idol, and The Younger Generation.

820   Bourget, Jean-Loup. "Frank Capra: The Name Above the Title." Film Comment, 7, No. 4 (Winter), 77-78.

A review of Capra's autobiography. Bourget proposes that in Capra's films sentimentality is undisguised and consistent, and hence valid, and that Capra was capable of grappling with tough subjects, identifying not only with the American dream but with doubts about it.

821   _____. "Capra et la 'Screwball Comedy.'" Positif, No. 133 (December), pp. 47-53.

Noting at the outset the difficulty of precisely defining "screwball comedy," Bourget proceeds inductively from the films of major directors associated with the genre in an effort to delineate its stylistic tendencies and thematic preoccupations. He locates two kinds of comedy at work in these films: slapstick, the roots of which can be traced back to the work of Capra and Leo McCarey in the silent era; and sophisticated or romantic comedy, marked in America by improvisation, unlike the "controlled," European style of, say, Ernst Lubitsch. Bourget discusses the conjunction of screwball comedy and melodrama in the work of Capra and McCarey (which he sees as a

function of the organic link they posit between a crazy and a
sentimental vision of America); the discovery of cinematic pace for
the handling of dialogue scenes; the democratic values inherent in the
figure of a "male Cinderella" to whom a dissatisfied heiress is
romantically attracted; the importance of disguise as a comic device
in an era of social crisis and social fluidity; and the possible
relationship between screwball comedy and the New Deal. With respect
to this last point, Bourget takes issue with Raymond Durgnat's notion
that Capra's celebration of the individual is "Republican" and
"reactionary" (see entry 796), arguing that Capra's attack on ideologies is inscribed within an American tradition that links Abraham
Lincoln and FDR, and that Capra's emphasis as a director on spirited,
spontaneous behavior within a collective context underscores his faith
in potential harmony within a democratic society.

822 Chevallier, Jacques. "Tramp, Tramp, Tramp." Image et Son, No. 247 (February), pp. 120-23.

  The author briefly discusses the importance of considering Harry Langdon's contribution to the mise-en-scène of those films in which he starred and Capra and Harry Edwards directed.

823 Ciment, Michel. "Soleil et pluie sur Frank Capra." Positif, No. 133 (December), pp. 1-10.

  A detailed review of Capra's autobiography and an argument for a reconsideration of Capra's films. Ciment cautions against treating Capra's life story as analogous to the adventures of Mr. Deeds or Mr. Smith, noting that Capra is not as naive as his heroes, and his ending has not been as happy as theirs. Nevertheless, he finds in Capra's account of conquering poverty and achieving success the familiar American myth of Horatio Alger. Synopsizing Capra's career, Ciment pays special attention to Capra's search for an illusion of reality in developing a comic style; his ambivalent attitude toward the power structure in Hollywood; the possible explanations for his decline as a director (Ciment favors the emergence of a gap be-
tween Capra's worldview and the mood of postwar America); and the contradictions within Capra's political philosophy. He commends Capra for dealing in the book with the low points as well as the high points of his career, and notes that despite the darkening tone at the end the book leaves an extraordinary impression of vitality.

824 _____. "Elements de bibliographie." Positif, No. 133 (December), pp.75, 89.

  A selected bibliography of criticism on Capra in French, Italian, and English.

825 Cocks, Jay. "How It Was." Time, 98, No. 5 (2 August), 68.

  A review of Capra's autobiography. Cocks observes that while Capra's early life reads like one of his fairy-tale scenarios, his later life, marked by failure and uneasy retirement, is without a happy, Capraesque ending. Thus while the first section of the autobiography is simply "good, gossipy reading," the latter part provides a "vivid picture of the way Hollywood farms out its once infallible filmmakers."

826 Codelli, Lorenzo. "Liberty Films Inc." Translated into French by Paul-Louis Thirard. Positif, No. 133 (December), pp. 68-75.

An overview of Capra's work during the 1940s, with emphasis on his efforts to establish an independent production company and the waning of his noted optimism. Detailed commentary on Meet John Doe, It's a Wonderful Life, and State of the Union is offered, as well as a general assessment of Capra's politics. Codelli takes issue with Jeffrey Richards's notion that Capra's populism was strictly middle class (see entry 806), arguing that his values emerged from outside the bourgeoisie and can be traced to Capra's immigrant youth. He also proposes that Capra's political naïveté accounts for his ability to reconcile a desire to confront social problems with an obligation to entertain. Brief mention is also made of Arsenic and Old Lace and the Why We Fight series.

827 Cohn, Bernard. "Un général, une blonde, un banquier, des clowns, des explorateurs." Positif, No. 133 (December), pp. 35-46.

Proposing that the themes and character types associated with Capra's films predate his collaboration with Robert Riskin, Cohn discusses Capra's work of the early 1930s in terms of the function of spectacle, melodrama, and comedy. Spectacle, he contends, exists in Capra's work not simply as indulgence of the audience but as an essential part of the subject matter of Rain or Shine, The Miracle Woman, Forbidden, and The Bitter Tea of General Yen. Melodrama and comedy, he notes, function reciprocally in these early films (adding Platinum Blonde, American Madness, and Dirigible to those cited above). He sees Capra's comic style as a philosophical stance: by juxtaposing the socially powerful with simple clowns, the former are made to seem foolish and the latter virtuous. Cohn traces these elements back to the physical and verbal traditions of commedia del l'arte, traditions with which he assumes the Italian-born Capra was familiar.

828 Comte, Olivier, and Olivier Eyquem. "Bio-filmographie de Frank Capra." Positif, No. 133 (December), pp. 76-88.

A brief chronology of major events in Capra's career and a detailed filmography, including shorts, features, television shows, and unrealized projects.

829 Cooke, Alistair, ed. Garbo and the Nightwatchmen. New York, St. Louis, and San Francisco: McGraw-Hill Book Co., pp. 135-37.

This reprint of Cooke's 1937 anthology contains his review of Mr. Deeds Goes to Town. See entry 309.

830 Farber, Manny. "Frank Capra," in his Negative Space. New York and Washington: Praeger Publishers, pp. 105-7.

Writings About Frank Capra 1971

A reprint of Farber's 1950 review of Riding High. See entry 647.

831 Ferguson, Otis. The Films of Otis Ferguson. Edited by Robert Wilson. Philadelphia: Temple University Press, passim.
Ferguson's reviews of the following Capra films are reprinted here: It Happened One Night, pp. 33-34 (see entry 197); Broadway Bill, pp. 58-59 (see entry 198); Mr. Deeds Goes to Town, pp. 127-128 (see entry 249); The Bitter Tea of General Yen, p. 152 (see entry 250); Lost Horizon, p. 169 (see entry 317); You Can't Take It with You, pp. 235-36 (see entry 370); Mr. Smith Goes to Washington, pp. 273-74 (see entry 411); and Meet John Doe, pp. 349-50 (see entry 474). Also reprinted are Ferguson's 1940 essay on comedy, "While We Were Laughing" (see entry 436), pp. 18-24; and a comparison of Capra and Rene Clair (see entry 463), p. 347.

832 Fuller, Edmund. "Capra: Mixing Guts and Stardust." Wall Street Journal (12 July), p. 8.
A review of Capra's autobiography, which the writer finds as lively as Capra's films and valuable to anyone who cares about cinema. A brief overview of Capra's career is included.

833 Furhammer, Leif and Folke Isaksson. "Hollywood and the World," in their Politics and Film. Translated by Kersti French. New York and Washington: Praeger Publishers, pp. 60-61, 64-67.
The authors comment on the relationship of Capra's films to the New Deal ("his new film deal was against crooked capitalism, but was not anti-capitalist"), and discuss the Why We Fight series. They consider the latter to be less restrained and objective than generally reported in film histories and attribute the persuasiveness of the series primarily to its forceful verbal narration. Nevertheless, as "a didactically planned survey of the preliminaries to the war and of its early stages," the series remains unsurpassed. Originally published in Sweden in 1968.

834 Gilliat, Penelope. "Langdon." New Yorker, 47, No. 10 (24 April), 130, 133-34.
Capra is credited with inventing Tramp, Tramp, Tramp, directing Harry Langdon in his two best films, and understanding the performer's comic personality perfectly. Reprinted in 1972 (see entry 874), 1973 (see entry 912), and twice in 1977 (see entries 1035 and 1036).

835 Greene, Graham. Reviews of Mr. Deeds Goes to Town and If You Could Only Cook, in Garbo and the Nightwatchmen. Edited by Alistair Cooke. New York, St. Louis, and San Francisco: McGraw-Hill Book Co., pp. 175, 182-84.
This reprint of the 1937 anthology contains Graham's review of Mr. Deeds Goes to Town (see entry 252) and If You Could Only Cook (see entry 251).

836 H[art], H[enry]. A review of The Name Above the Title. Films in Review, 22, No. 7 (August-September), 433.
    Hart is slightly bothered by the book's inaccuracies and erratic tone, but is generally enthusiastic about this "important autobiography."

837 Hall, Mordaunt. Review of It Happened One Night, in The New York Times Film Reviews: 1913-1970. Edited by George Amberg. New York: Quadrangle Books, pp. 142-43.
    A reprint of Hall's 1934 review. See entry 200.

838 Kozarski, Richard. "Lost and Found." Film Comment, 7, No. 1 (Spring), 70-71.
    Commentary on The Miracle Woman, a rediscovered film. Kozarski finds flaws in the script and Barbara Stanwyck's performance, but thinks that the film, like most "social films" of the 1930s, is much stronger fare than the watered-down descendants today.

839 Lehmann-Haupt, Christopher. "Bad-Tempered Capra-Corn." New York Times (18 June), p. 37.
    A review of Capra's autobiography. "In its perverse way . . . a complete history of Hollywood," Lehmann-Haupt notes, and locates in the work a steady deterioration from lively self-chronicle to self-parody, bombast, and demagoguery. He admires Capra for his persistent struggle to make his own films, but is disturbed by the connection Capra draws between his own loss of courage, the decline of Hollywood, and a "decline" in world taste. "This is an autobiography of an appealing man grown crotchety."

840 Levin, G. Roy. Documentary Explorations. Garden City, N.Y.: Doubleday & Co., pp. 18-19.
    Brief commentary on the Why We Fight series. Levin finds the films dated by their narration and blatant chauvinism, despite an "excellent and even innovative use of sound, editing and visuals."

841 MacCann, Richard Dyer. "World War II: Armed Forces Documentary," in The Documentary Tradition: From Nanook to Woodstock. Edited by Lewis Jacobs. New York: Hopkinson & Blake, pp. 215-19.
    A scholarly study of the interaction between Hollywood and the War Department, and the solicitation of Capra's services for the Why We Fight series. MacCann describes the style of these films as "a combination of a sermon, a between-halves pep talk, and barroom bull session." He argues that Prelude to War was forceful propaganda for soldiers who loosely agreed with its message but had not yet worked out their own ideas. Synopses of Prelude to War and The Battle of Britain are included. Originally part of a Ph.D. dissertation (see entry 670) and reprinted in 1973 (see entry 915).

842 Mast, Gerald. A Short History of the Movies. Indianapolis and New York: Bobbs-Merrill Co., pp. 287-88, 296, 301, 316, 328.

Capra's noted works from the 1930s are seen as "sincere and clever statements of the era's conventional optimism and folksy humanism." Passing comparisons with John Ford and Howard Hawks are offered, and Capra's later films are described as "feeble shadows of his greatest work."

843 Mundy, Robert. "Frank Capra." Cinema (Los Angeles), 7, No. 1 (Fall), 56.

A detailed review of Capra's autobiography. Mundy sees a similarity between Capra's account of his own life and the struggles of the Capra hero on the screen, and argues that the director's unusual power in the 1930s resulted from the exceptional consonance between his own vision of America and that which Hollywood desired to purvey. He is disappointed by the slightness of Capra's commentary on Robert Riskin and Harry Langdon, but pleased with the amount of information provided on lesser-known periods of Capra's career. While Capra is not a man of letters, he concludes, the book is an important testament.

844 Nordell, Roderick. "Shoptalk from a Dream Factory." Christian Science Monitor (29 July), p. 11.

A review of Capra's autobiography. "There really were times like those. Others present might write the scenes with a different slant. But [Capra's] unapologetic patriotism, 'moxie,' self-congratulation, and sentiment were part of it."

845 Nugent, Frank S. The New York Times Film Reviews: 1913-1970. Edited by George Amberg. New York: Quadrangle Books, pp. 162, 170-72, 181-82.

Reprinted here are Nugent's reviews of Mr. Deeds Goes to Town (see entry 261), You Can't Take It with You (see entry 380), and Mr. Smith Goes to Washington (see entry 420).

846 Ophüls, Marcel. "Streben nach Glück: Uber die Filme von Frank Capra." Fersehen/Film, 9 (May), 20-24.

A collage of fragments from various sources--scenes from Capra's movies, an interview for German television, remarks on his work and on topical political events--all centering on the ideological implications of Capra's view of America, with annotations and commentary by Ophüls. In a postscript Ophüls speculates on the possibility of writing about Capra today, and on whether or not his brilliance as a director alone justifies the vision of America he presents.

847 Palmer, Joseph. Review of The Name Above the Title. Library Journal, 96, No. 8 (15 April), 1358.

A synopsis and assessment of Capra's career. "His best films . . . were full of wit, humanity, and an optimistic faith in human nature and America."

848   Pechter, William S. "American Madness," in his <u>Twenty-four Times a Second: Films and Film-makers</u>. New York, Evanston, and London: Harper and Row, pp. 123-32.
       A reprint of Pechter's 1962 essay. See entry 759.

849   Pryor, Thomas M. "Capra's Candid Autobiog Colorful Hollywood Saga." <u>Daily Variety</u> (7 May), pp. 3, 19.
       A review of <u>The Name Above the Title</u> and survey of Capra's career. Pryor describes the autobiography as "the finest, most entertaining book yet written about Hollywood, embracing the whole intricate, complex and generally stormy fusion of art and commerce." It reveals a man of pride and sensitivity, blessed with the perception and innate sense of balance to survive life in Hollywood. For the general reader, Capra offers free-flowing anecdotes and intriguing inside information; for the historian he offers a rich treasure of facts and impressions; for the student he provides the best handbook on the art of communicating through film. Pryor's recapitulation of Capra's career focuses on the years with Harry Cohn at Columbia and on Capra's struggles with <u>A Hole in the Head</u> and <u>Marooned</u> late in his career. Reprinted on 2 June. (see entry 850).

850   _____. "'Frank Capra: Name above the Title' One of Best Books on H'wood That Was." <u>Variety</u> (2 June), pp. 20, 22.
       A reprint of Pryor's 7 May review of <u>Daily Variety</u>. See entry 849.

*851   Swindell, Larry. Review of <u>The Name Above the Title</u>. <u>Book World</u>, 5 (25 July), 7.
       Cited in <u>Book Review Index, 1971</u>.

852   Thomas, Kevin. "Cheery Comedy a la Capra." <u>Los Angeles Times</u> (6 August), sec. 4, p. 10.
       Brief reassessments of <u>Lady for a Day</u> and <u>It Happened One Night</u>, the first two films in a Capra retrospective at the Los Angeles County Museum of Art. Thomas considers both to be "escapist fare at its best, with such verve and good humor that they'll probably remain fresh forever."

853   _____. "Capra Film at Museum." <u>Los Angeles Times</u> (13 August), sec. 4, p. 7.
       Commentary on two more films being shown at the Los Angeles County Museum of Art retrospective. <u>The Bitter Tea of General Yen</u> is judged dated, but having curiosity value and vintage charm. The sentiments of <u>Mr. Deeds Goes to Town</u>, on the other hand, are more timely than ever.

854   _____. "'Lost Horizon' at Museum tonight." <u>Los Angeles Times</u> (20 August), sec. 4, p. 20.
       A reassessment of <u>Lost Horizon</u> on the occasion of its presentation at the Los Angeles County Museum of Art retrospective.

"To see Lost Horizon, a romantic adventure classic that remains a spellbinder, today is to realize that it and a number of other celebrated Capra films of the 30s are not only timeless but timelier than ever."

855 _____. "Capra Classic at Museum Theater." Los Angeles Times (27 August), sec. 4, p. 18.

The timeliness of Capra's work remains Thomas's theme as he comments on the next film in the Los Angeles County Museum series, You Can't Take It with You. Still fresh, in Thomas's estimation, is the film's plea for freedom of expression; its critique of income taxes used for armaments; its attack on greed, materialism, and the dehumanizing effects of big business; and its espousal of "a lively do-your-own-thing philosophy decades before anyone ever heard of the expression."

856 _____. "'Mr. Smith' at Bing Theatre." Los Angeles Times (3 September), sec. 4, p. 14.

Mr. Smith Goes to Washington, screened at the Los Angeles County Museum of Art retrospective, is briefly reassessed. Yet again for Thomas, time has vindicated a Capra film: if modern-day cynicism lessens Mr. Smith's impact, this is only because the truth of its exposé has been borne out.

857 _____. "'Little People' Win the Day." Los Angeles Times, (10 September), sec. 4, p. 18.

Two more Capra films in the Los Angeles County Museum of Art series are reviewed. Meet John Doe is judged an ambitious failure, shrewd in its awareness of the power of the media but unconvincingly resolved. American Madness is considered noteworthy for its pace, construction, acting, and foreshadowing of later Capra-Riskin themes. Both films are timely.

858 _____. "Return of 'Wonderful Life'." Los Angeles Times (17 September), Sec. 4, p. 19.

Reexamining It's a Wonderful Life, the final film in the Los Angeles County Museum of Art series, Thomas finds the work as impressive as he remembered it from his childhood. Although the plot sounds sentimental, he proposes, the film is decidedly tough-minded. Moreover, it richly evokes vanishing small-town Americana and chronicles the life of a generation that grew up with the new century.

859 Vitoux, Frederic. "Harry Langdon et Frank Capra." Positif, No. 133. (December), pp. 25-32.

Vitoux basically accepts Capra's account of his partnership with Harry Langdon, but acknowledges a potential bias in Capra's version and seeks to understand their work together in terms of the intersection of two major talents. His discussion centers on the three feature films, each of which he sees marking a different stage in the relationship: in Tramp, Tramp, Tramp (directed by Harry Edwards) Langdon's performance dominates; in The Strong Man a perfect balance is struck between acting and mise-en scène; in Long Pants

Capra's directorial virtuosity dominates, at times at the expense of the performer. Central to Capra's contribution, Vitoux argues, is his awareness that an improbable persona like Langdon's has to be counterpointed by a scrupulous realism in the selection of subject matter and the direction of secondary characters and bit parts. Quoting liberally from Capra's autobiography, he discusses the contribution of duration, repetition, and hesitation to the psychological richness of Langdon's persona. The films now appear melancholy, he concludes, because they mark the intersection of a career in ascendance (Capra's) and a career about to decline (Langdon's), telling a story of both an encounter and a rupture.

860   Warner, Virginia. "The Negro Soldier: A Challenge to Hollywood," in The Documentary Tradition. Edited by Lewis Jacobs. New York: Hopkinson & Blake, pp. 224-25.
      A reprint of Warner's 1944 review of The Negro Soldier. See entry 551.

1972

861   Agee, James. "Das Baby," in Lotte Reiniger, David W. Griffith, Harry Langdon. Translated by Wolfram Tichy. Frankfurt: Kommunales Kino, pp. 67-68.
      The section on Harry Langdon from Agee's 1949 essay, "Comedy's Greatest Era," in German translation. See entry 626.

862   Anon. "The Name Above the Title." Publisher's Weekly, 201, No. 19 (8 May), 51.
      A brief note concerning Capra's autobiography, now published in paperback.

*863 Anon. Review of The Name Above the Title. Best Sellers, 32 (15 August), 244.
      Cited in Book Review Index, 1972.

*864 Anon. Review of The Name Above the Title. Books and Bookmen, 17 (September), 75.
      Cited in Book Review Index, 1972.

865   Bakshy, Alexander. "American Madness," in American Film Criticism. Edited by Stanley Kauffmann with Bruce Henstell New York: Liveright, p. 268.
      A reprint of Bakshy's 1932 review. See entry 148.

866   Bernds, Edward. "Sound Thinking." Film Fan Monthly, No. 138 (December), pp. 25-38.
      Recollections by Bernds on his career as a Hollywood sound man, including his work at Columbia on Capra's Dirigible, Submarine, and Lady for a Day. Reprinted in 1976 (see entry 1003).

867   Bogdanovich, Peter. "Hollywood." Esquire, 58, No. 4 (October), 87, 92.

Capra's autobiography is reviewed together with <u>Memo from David O. Selznick</u>. Bogdanovich uses the occasion to argue for the greater creative role of the director over that of the producer: "Watching a Capra film we are indeed in the presence of one man—his obsessions, fantasies, dreams; with a Selznick film, we are in the company of a talented executive, influencing others less—and in some cases—more talented than he." He considers Capra's book "the most entertaining and honest memoir ever written by an American filmmaker." Reprinted in 1973 (see entry 907).

868   Brownlow, Kevin. "Harry Langdon, Stummfilmkomiker," in <u>Lotte Reiniger, David W. Griffith, Harry Langdon</u>. Translated by Wolfram Tichy. Frankfurt: Kommunales Kino, pp. 60-63.
   Brownlow's chapter on Harry Langdon from <u>The Parade's Gone By</u> (1969) in German translation. See entry 793.

869   Cawkwell, Tim, and John M. Smith, eds. <u>The World Encyclopedia of Film</u>. London: Studio Vista Publishers, pp. 38-39.
   A biographical sketch and filmography.

870   Coleman, John. "Life Sentences." <u>New Statesman</u>, 84, No. 2161 (18 August), 231.
   A review of Capra's autobiography. Coleman advises the reader to approach the book "with the patience of a prospector, a bushel of salt, and the temporary suspension of hostility toward bad prose. . . . On the in-fighting and cop-outs of Hollywood, this protean bunch of nervous energy is fine. Yet one wants to trust the songs, not the singer, long before the end."

871   Corliss, Richard. "Capra and Riskin." <u>Film Comment</u>, 8, No. 4 (November-December), 18-21.
   A general assessment of Robert Riskin's collaboration with Capra, and detailed commentary on <u>It Happened One Night</u>, <u>Mr. Deeds Goes to Town</u>, and <u>Meet John Doe</u>. Corliss proposes that Riskin was less successful with unfamiliar subjects such as fantasy, mob psychology, and rube psychosis than with his hometown New York milieu and the newspaper comedy. Tracing the evolution of the Capra-Riskin hero from a quick-thinking, charismatic banker in <u>American Madness</u> through a masochistic Deeds and a suicidal John Doe, Corliss also suggests that Riskin was more convincing dramatizing a character's degeneration than winding up a plot effectively. By the time of <u>Meet John Doe</u>, the only solution Capra and Riskin had to offer was an expedient "played-out populism." Reprinted in 1974 (see entry 934).

872   Epstein, Clarence. "Pick of the Paperbacks." <u>Washington Post, Book World</u> (2 July), 13.
   A brief review of <u>The Name Above the Title</u>, published in paperback. "Like many of Capra's films . . . highly entertaining, forthright, spirited, full of snappy dialogue, and blessed with an upbeat ending."

873 Ferguson, Otis. "It Happened One Night," in American Film Criticism. Edited by Stanley Kauffmann with Bruce Henstell. New York: Liveright, pp. 299-300.
A reprint of Ferguson's 1934 review. See entry 198.

874 Gilliat, Penelope. "Ein Machen," in Lotte Reiniger, David W. Griffith, Harry Langdon. Translated by Wolfram Tichy. Frankfurt: Kommunales Kino, pp. 77-78.
Excerpts from Gilliat's 1971 essay on Harry Langdon, in German translation. See entry 834.

875 Greene, Graham. Graham Greene on Film: Collected Film Criticism, 1935-1939. Edited by John Russell Taylor. New York: Simon & Schuster, pp. 64-65, 96-97, 145, 148, 190, 203-4, 260-61.
Contains reprints of Greene's original reviews of If You Could Only Cook (see entry 251), Mr. Deeds Goes to Town, (see entry 252), Lost Horizon (see entry 323), You Can't Take It with You (see entry 373), and Mr. Smith Goes to Washington (see entry 437). (This volume was simultaneously published in Great Britain by Martin Secker & Warburg as The Pleasure Dome.)

876 Handzo, Stephen. "Under Capracorn: A Decade of Good Deeds and Wonderful Lives." Film Comment, 8, No. 4 (November-December), 8-14.
Although no central thesis governs this chronological survey of Capra's feature films between 1936 and 1948, Handzo's commentary is chock-full of insights into the particulars of Capra's style and the tensions at play throughout his work. He places Mr. Smith Goes to Washington at the apex of this period (and of Capra's career), finding in it a directorial assurance not always evident in Mr. Deeds Goes to Town, and a formal richness that has not yet solidified into the formula and ritual of Meet John Doe. He discusses It's a Wonderful Life as a reflective work, with Capra recapitulating the evolution of his film style as well as aspects of his own biography, and interprets Spencer Tracy's confession of having lost faith in his public and himself at the close of State of the Union as a statement by Capra himself. Reprinted in 1975 (see entry 972) and 1978 (see entry 1080).

877 Hitchens, Gordon. "Joris Ivens Interviewed by Gordon Hitchens, November 20, 1968, American Documentaries." Film Culture, Nos. 53, 54, 55 (Sprig), 190-219.
Among a wide variety of topics, Ivens discusses the relationship between his own compilation documentaries and Capra's Why We Fight series for the U.S. government, and traces the troubled history of his involvement with the Know Your Enemy: Japan project for the Capra unit.

878 Hughes, William. "Rites of the Bitch-Goddess." Nation, 215, No. 15 (27 November), 534-35, 537.

Capra's autobiography is reviewed as "a recent installment in that peculiarly American literary phenomenon, the success story," or an exemplary life. As is often true of self-made men, Hughes proposes, Capra's "late-blooming moral imperative" mid-way through the 1930s served to justify his compulsive ambitiousness rather than restrain it. Moreover, the autobiography reveals that Capra was less the master of the symbols and myths of the American dream, as is popularly supposed, than their servant. This servitude, Hughes speculates, placed limits on Capra's development as a filmmaker. Also see entry 1008.

879   James, Clive. "Annals of film-making." <u>Observer</u> (20 August), p. 31.

A favorable review of Capra's autobiography. "Fortunately, the cool and clear-eyed Capra who rode inside the warm and wonderful one has managed to get a word in on his own account, so that the book —while always threatening to be schmaltzy—generates a bracing air of hard-nosed analysis."

880   Kuhns, William. "Frank Capra," in his <u>American in the Movies</u>. Dayton, Ohio: Pflaum/Standard, pp. 154-57.

A standard account of Capra's careen in the 1920s and 1930s, drawn mainly from Richard Griffith, and including brief commentary on <u>It Happened One Night</u>, <u>Mr. Deeds Goes to Town</u>, and <u>Mr. Smith Goes to Washington</u>. Capra's "ultimate importance lies not in advancing the art of the film significantly, but in making visible the relationship between a movie and its audience. . . . Capra did not make movies for all time, but for the people of the Depression-worn thirties. There is no better guide to the mentality of that era than a viewing of Capra's films."

881   Leary, Richard. "Capra and Langdon." <u>Film Comment</u>, 8, No. 4 (September-October), 15-17.

Leary challenges the conventional notion of Langdon as Galatea to Capra's Pygmalion. Langdon's success at Keystone, Leary argues, followed from the freedom he was given to fill out a scene with his unique kind of mime; while he was dependent on firm control in writing and direction, the catalyst was not Capra alone but the effective team formed by Capra, Arthur Ripley, and Harry Edwards. Leary also challenges Capra's notion that Langdon's persona was a "Christian innocent," instead describing him as an inadvertent anarchist. Langdon's error, he concludes, came not in firing Capra but in not entrusting his direction to another professional, although his downfall was in any case assured by the coming of sound and the changing taste of depression audiences.

882   Mahoney, Jon C. "Mr. Smith Goes to Cairo." <u>Performing Arts</u>, 6, No. 1 (January), 9-15.

Working from the premise that Capra captured and crystallized the mood and ideals of America during the 1930s and 1940s, Mahoney surveys contemporary politicians as to the influence of <u>Mr. Smith Goes to Washington</u> on their lives or careers, only to find that few are willing to respond. Mahoney reports, however, that, according to Capra, former Egyptian president Nassar claimed the film influenced his decision to move from a military career to politics. Mahoney further speculates that Nasser's efforts to democratize Egypt in the first years of his presidency may also be traced to his memory of the film.

883   Maltin, Leonard. The Great Movie Shorts. New York: Crown Publishers, pp. 68-69.
       A standard account of Capra's work with Harry Langdon in the 1920s.

884   Manvell, Roger, general ed. The Encyclopedia of Film. New York: Crown Publishers, p. 121.
       A Capra bio-filmography.

885   Merritt, Russell. "Frank Capra, The Name Above the Title." Cinema Journal, 11, No. 2 (Spring), 37-40.
       A review of Capra's autobiography. Merritt notes that Capra has taken biographical facts and "irresistibly cast them into the shape of the latest Frank Capra movie" with the author cast as a Capra hero. Capra's candidness, Merritt speculates, may in fact be a salesman's strategy to create a genial self-portrait, but it also serves to reveal something more: "his amiability and charm have behind them the pressure of a harsh environment which it required courage to meet." Proposing that the weakness of Capra's films is a patronizing attitude toward the "little man," Merritt finds this element in the autobiography as well. "If the book cannot be taken seriously as historical source, it is of inestimable value as the self-portrait of a key American filmmaker."

886   Murphy, Patterson [Meyer Levin], "Mr. Smith Goes to Washington," in American Film Criticism. Edited by Stanley Kauffmann with Bruce Henstell. New York: Liveright, pp. 377-83.
       A reprint of Levin's 1940 review. See entry 440.

887   Murphy, William Thomas. "The Methods of Why We Fight." Journal of Popular Film, 1, No. 3 (Summer), 185-96.
       Murphy proposes that Capra's proven ability with the medium of the fiction film and his understanding of American ideals made him especially suitable for the Why We Fight series. He then analyzes specific strategies used in the documentaries: voice-over commentary, music, animation, and editing for rhythmic, graphic, and dialectical effect. Special attention is also given to the assemblage of various kinds of footage--theatrical, controlled documentary, and newsreel. Murphy sees the series as the model for compilation films that appeared after the war.

888   Orsoni, Mario. "Le candide follie di Harry Langdon." Filmcritica, 224 (April-May), 187-92.

Passing reference to Capra is made in this overview of Langdon's film career. For Orsoni, those films directed or written by Capra compose Langdon's best work.

889   Palmer, Tony. "Rehearsing the Old Movie Magic." Spectator, 229, No. 7539 (30 December), 1048-49.
Capra's autobiography sparks a mild diatribe on Hollywood. Capra is included in the attack, but Palmer appears to be unfamiliar with any of Capra's films.

890   Richards, Jeffrey. "Frank Capra and the Cinema of Populism." Film Society Review, 7, No. 6 (February), 38-46; and 7, Nos. 7-9 (March-May), 61-71.
Richards's 1970 essay is reprinted here in two parts. See entry 806.

891   Sadoul, Georges. Dictionary of Films. Translated, edited, and updated by Peter Morris. Berkeley and Los Angeles: University of California Press, passim.
Capsule commentaries are provided for The Strong Man, Long Pants, The Miracle Woman, Lady for a Day, It Happened One Night, Mr. Deeds Goes to Town, Mr. Smith Goes to Washington, and A Pocketful of Miracles.

892   _____. "Frank Capra," in his Dictionary of Film Makers. Translated, edited, and updated by Peter Morris. Berkeley and Los Angeles: University of California Press, pp. 36-37.
Capra's entry centers on the films of the 1930s. "Capra, who himself had many of Mr. Smith's traits, possessed great faith in the myth of the New Deal and reflected his Rooseveltian beliefs in his somewhat utopian films." A filmography is included.

893   Sennett, Mack. "Ein unschuldiges Baby," in Lotte Reiniger, David W. Griffith, Harry Langdon. Translated by Wolfram Tichy. Frankfurt: Kommunales Kino, pp. 64-65.
A German translation of Sennett's account of Capra's work with Harry Langdon at the Sennett studios. Taken from Sennett's autobiography. See entry 683.

894   Shales, Tom. "Frank Capra," in The American Film Heritage: Impressions from the American Film Institute Archive. Washington, D.C.: Colortone Press, pp. 115-23.
In this career sketch, Capra is described as a populist artist whose films were made for audiences rather than award committees or critics; his work thus constitutes a significant part of the national literature. Special attention is given to The Younger Generation, Platinum Blonde, American Madness, and Mr. Deeds Goes to Town. Excerpts from Shales's commentary were reprinted in 1974 (see entry 939).

895   Shindler, Colin. "Capra Revisited." Sight and Sound, 42, No. 1 (Winter 1972-73), 56.

A response to Elliott Stein's review of Capra's autobiography (see entry 897). Shindler accuses Stein of falsely saddling Capra's films with the egocentricity and literary pretentiousness he finds in the book, and is dumbfounded by Stein's preference for Capra's work before 1935 and dismissal of all his work thereafter.

896   Stebbins, Robert [Sidney Meyers]. "Mr. Deeds Goes to Town," in American Film Criticism. Edited by Stanley Kauffmann with Bruce Henstell. New York: Liveright, pp. 300-301.
A reprint of Meyers's 1936 review. See entry 259.

897   Stein, Elliott. "Capra Counts His Oscars." Sight and Sound, 41, No. 3 (Summer), 162-64.
A review of Capra's autobiography and a reassessment of his career. Stein challenges the notion that Capra's best work was done after 1935 (a position he ascribes to the official histories), arguing that after that date Capra lost a "lovely luminescent touch" as a director and came to embrace a philistine, populist politics closer to the status-quo values of the American middle class than to any libertarian New Dealism. He offers an ironic retelling of Capra's explanation for the change in his work during this period and detects in Capra's bitter, homophobic attack on the immorality of contemporary films and filmmakers the oppressive "underbelly" of the director's own "fantasies of goodwill." Capra-as-autobiographer is also criticized for his neglect of cinematographer Joseph Walker, his account of Harry Langdon's career, and various erroneous and misleading passages in the text. For a response to this review see entry 895.

898   Truscott, Harold. "Harry Langdon." Silent Picture, 13 (Winter-Spring), 14-17.
Within a larger essay aimed at establishing Langdon's credentials as a great creative artist, Truscott refutes the account of Langdon's film career offered by Mack Sennett in his autobiography (See entry 683). Truscott proposes that Harry Edwards would have been more likely to have influenced Langdon as a director than Capra, and argues that the continuity of Langdon's film work suggests that the performer himself played a major role in shaping his screen comedy.

899   Vidor, King. On Film Making. New York: Douglas McKay Co., pp. 40-41.
Vidor briefly speculates on the connection between Capra's immigrant youth and his decision to champion the outsider on the screen.

900   White, David Manning, and Richard Averson. The Celluloid Weapon: Social Comment in the American Film. Boston: Beacon Press, pp. 28, 35-36, 67-69, 84-86, 88, 116, 261.
Passing references to Capra's films appear throughout the text, but there are two concentrated sections of discussion. The first deals with Capra's work from The Miracle Woman through Lost Horizon, stressing his role as populist social commentator in both comedy and serious films. The second deals with Mr. Smith Goes to

Washington and Meet John Doe in light of the political tensions of the prewar period.

1973

901 Andersson, Willmar. "Arsenick och gamla spetsar/Arsenic and Old Lace." Filmrutan, 16, No. 3. 120-24.
Included here are credits, a synopsis, a history of the film's censorship in Sweden, career sketches for Capra and the principal actors, and a provocative analysis of the film. Andersson places Arsenic and Old Lace in a special position amid Capra's mature period, arguing that while the film does not attempt to mediate a social or political message and makes no allusions to a topical issue like fascism, it nonetheless reflects the madness of the times through its black humor and sense of the macabre. Although these elements are present in the original stage play, they are given a murderous pace through Capra's direction. Andersson also finds it interesting that in Sweden objections were raised that mass murderers should not look like nice old ladies, considering future revelations about the ordinariness of the most brutal Nazis. A summary of Parker Tyler's psychoanalytic reading of the film (see entry 594) is appended.

902 Anon. "Frank Capra." Filmihullu (Helsinki), No. 6, pp. 29-32.
A Capra filmography.

903 Anon. "Frank Capra Receives SMPTE Award." Journal of the SMPTE, 82, No. 5 (May), 414.
A report on Capra's receipt of an achievement award from the Society of Motion Picture and Television Engineers, and a summary of his career. Also see entry 1279.

*904 Anon. Review of The Name Above the Title. Audience, 6, No. 6 (July).
Cited in Film Literature Index, 1973.

*905 Anon. Review of The Name Above the Title. Choice, 10 (March), 37.
Cited in Book Review Index, 1973.

906 Barsam, Richard Meran. "Military Training Films," in his Nonfiction Film: A Critical History. New York: E.P. Dutton & Co., pp. 182-92.
Barsam surveys Capra's orientation films for the army during World War II, with special focus on the Why We Fight series. This series, Barsam concludes, "is not only the best group of films to come out of the war, but also the best film record of the reasons behind that war, the most dramatic account of the battles in it, and the most eloquent tribute to the civilian and military men and women who fought and died in it." Reprinted in 1975 (see entry 958).

907 Bogdanovich, Peter. "Capra v. Selznick," in his *Pieces of Time*. New York: Arbor House/Esquire Books, pp. 199-203.

A reprint of Bogdanovich's 1972 review of Capra's autobiography. See entry 867. (*Pieces of Time* was published in Great Britain by George Allen & Unwin, as *Picture Shows*.)

908 Bogle, Donald. *Toms, Coons, Mulattoes, Mammies, and Bucks: An Interpretative History of Blacks in American Films*. New York: Viking Press, pp. 53-54, 56.

Bogle briefly discusses Capra's use of black actor Clarence Muse, which he finds sensitive.

909 Cargin, Peter. "National Film Theatre, Bun[u]el and Capra—Two Men and Their Art." *Film* (London), 2, No. 6 (September), 21.

Briefly reviewing a National Film Theatre retrospective of Capra's films, Cargin observes that he does not share the audience's taste for sentimentality. "Capra's weakness is his determination to draw a happy ending out of thin air; this brings a touch of absurdity to films which express serious views notwithstanding story elements of comedy." He considers *State of the Union* to be Capra's best film, in part because of the "greater depth of characterization" provided by the stage play.

910 Durgnat, Raymond, and Tom Flinn. "Correspondence." *Velvet Light Trap*, No. 9 (Summer), pp. 58-60.

In an earlier review of Durgnat's *The Crazy Mirror* (see entry 796), Flinn objected to Durgnat's characterization of *Mr. Deeds Goes to Town* as Republican propaganda. This exchange followed. Durgnat now proposes that Capra's blend of Populism, Progressivism, and "Middletown" middle-class morality allowed him to go along with the first New Deal (before 1935), with its utopian and moral cast of mind, but kept him removed from the second New Deal, with its intensive hostility toward big business and its combativeness, energy, and cynicism. Flinn counters that *Mr. Deeds* espouses neither a Republican nor a New Deal viewpoint, but is instead informed by the agrarian idealism of Jeffersonian democracy. To depict Capra as pro-big business in light of the populist demonology of *Mr. Smith Goes to Washington* and *Meet John Doe*, Flinn argues, is to distort the political implications of Capra's work.

911 Fleming, Alice. "Frank Capra," in her *The Moviemakers*. New York: St. Martin's Press, pp. 110-113.

A survey of Capra's career drawn primarily from his autobiography. Fleming credits Capra with proving that moviegoers in the 1930s would "pay money to see pictures about ordinary people like themselves."

912 Gilliat, Penelope. "Harry Langdon," in her *Unholy Fools*. New York: Viking Press, pp. 137-42.

A reprint of Gilliat's 1971 essay. See entry 834.

913   Goldstein, Ruth M. "The Feature Film in 16MM." <u>Film News</u>, 30, No. 4 (September), 22-23.
A reassessment of <u>Mr. Smith Goes to Washington</u>, focusing on its usefulness in the classroom amid the current political scandal of Watergate.

914   Löthwall, Lars-Olaf. "Profiler I Cannes." <u>Chaplin</u>, No. 123, p. 143.
A brief report on Capra's appearance at the Cannes Film Festival and a review of <u>The Miracle Woman</u>. Löthwall finds Stanwyck's performance and Capra's handling of crowd scenes noteworthy, but does not consider the film on a par with Capra's best work.

915   MacCann, Richard Dyer. "World War II: Armed Service Documentary," in his <u>The People's Films: A Political History of U.S. Government Motion Pictures</u>. New York: Hastings House, pp. 152-59.
MacCann's study of the <u>Why We Fight</u> series is reprinted. See entries 670 and 841.

916   McCaffrey, Donald W. <u>The Golden Age of Sound Comedy: Comic Films and Comedians of the Thirties</u>. South Brunswick and New York: A.S. Barnes & Co.; London: Tantivy Press, pp. 136, 156-58.
<u>It Happened One Night</u> and <u>You Can't Take It with You</u> are briefly discussed as films that successfully blended "sophisticated" and "sentimental" styles of comedy in the 1930s.

917   Madsen, Axel. <u>William Wyler</u>. New York: Thomas Y. Crowell Co., pp. 223-28, 279-83.
Madsen describes Capra's association with William Wyler, first as officers in the Army Signal Corps film unit during World War II and then as partners in Liberty Films after the war.

918   Mariani, John. "The Missing American Hero." <u>New York</u> (13 August), pp. 34-38.
Lamenting the loss of an American idealism embodied by former movie stars such as Gary Cooper, Henry Fonda, and Jimmy Stewart, Mariani argues that <u>Mr. Smith Goes to Washington</u> is an especially instructive film in light of the current Watergate scandal. "While the film was just another Frank Capra masterpiece when it appeared in 1939, today it takes on allegorical implications. The light-heartedness of the Capra style is a salve for the withered spirit of a Watergate generation, and one can easily imagine Jefferson Smith growing into the role of Sam Ervin in 1973."

919   Mast, Gerald. <u>The Comic Mind: Comedy and the Movies</u>. Chicago: University of Chicago Press, pp. 168-74, 259-65.
In a section on Harry Langdon, Mast challenges Capra's claim that Langdon never understood his comic persona, noting that the strangeness of the performer's comic situations cuts across his early and later features. But Mast also locates Capraesque elements in the

films made with Langdon: warmhearted, unaffected, uncallous "little people" who triumph over selfish, money-hungry, power-mad "city rats"; the thematic simplicity and banality of good versus evil in The Strong Man; and the foregrounding of the back of Langdon's head and neck during the climactic scene in Long Pants. Later Mast turns to Capra's sound films, dismissing the early work at Columbia as drab and undistinguished, but considering the comedies made between 1933 and 1941 as valuable documents of American hopes, beliefs, and ideals during the period. The intellectual weakness of these films, according to Mast, follows from Capra's inability to divorce moral character and ideological principle. Nevertheless, the natural warmth, internal logic, and vitality of the characters create a world saturated with comic if not moral truth. These values, Mast proposes, were squashed in Capra's work after the war by a banal self-consciousness and glossy production values.

920   Mitry, Jean. Histoire du Cinéma. Vol. 4, 1929-1940. Paris: Éditions Jean-Pierre Delarge, pp. 206-14.

A critical survey of Capra's work in the 1930s with emphasis on the evolving relationship between comic structures and social comment. Platinum Blonde is cited as the first "comédie américaine"; American Madness as the film marking Capra's arrival as a first-rank director; and Lady for a Day for its perfection of Capra's comic style, a style rendered definitive by the great success of It Happened One Night. The social critique of Mr. Deeds Does to Town, Mitry observes, is a populist defense of individualism, and Capra's style here is alertly casual and elliptical. Mr. Smith Goes to Washington pursues the political direction of Deeds. Farfetched parody in You Can't Take It with You, Capra's funniest film, suggests that utopia is realizable only in the imagination, a point confirmed through fantasy in Lost Horizon.

921   Pells, Richard. Radical Visions and American Dreams. New York: Harper & Row, pp. 278-82.

Pells argues that while Capra's "social trilogy" (Mr. Deeds Goes to Town, Mr. Smith Goes to Washington, and Meet John Doe) may seem to commemorate the natural wisdom and benevolence of the common man, the films also lay bare the stupidities of the average citizen and the perils of mass conformity. Pells therefore sees these films as closer in spirit to the individualism of the nineteenth century than to the collectivist dream of the 1930s. He notes, however, that Capra's screwball comedies, though often labeled escapist, might be more correctly read as satiric critiques of established institutions and ideals.

*922 Poague, Leland. "The Cinema of Frank Capra." Ph.D. dissertation, University of Oregon, 384 pp.

An early version of Poague's 1975 book on Capra. See entry 989.

923   Richards, Jeffrey. "Capra och den populistiska filmen." Filmhaftet, 1:16-32.

A reprint of Richards's 1970 essay. No translator is cited. See entry 806.

924 _____. "Frank Capra: The Classic Populist," in his Visions of Yesterday. London: Routledge & Kegan Paul, pp. 234-53.
Richards's 1970 essay is reprinted with minor changes: the sections on "The Populist Context" and "The Doctrine of Self-Help" have been deleted; his analysis of thematic elements has been expanded slightly to accommodate more films; and Populism has been changed to populism. See entry 806.

925 Rose, Tony. "Capra at the NFT." Movie Maker, 7 (August), 514.
A report on Capra's lecture at the National Film Theatre in England, and a brief assessment of Capra's career. "His films were popular but never cheap. They were full of optimism and sentiment but were saved from sentimentality . . . by his ever present sense of humor."

926 Rosen, Marjorie. Popcorn Venus. New York: Coward, MacCann, & Geoghagen, pp. 136-138.
Rosen briefly discusses Jean Arthur's role in Capra's films in terms of the matriarchal myth "of the diminutive mother hen who arranged men's lives, was responsible for their success, thrived as the women behind their democratic thrones. And, of course, basked in their world accomplishments, not her own."

927 Simsolo, Noël. L'athlète incomplet [The Strong Man]." La Revue du Cinema/Image et Son, 269, 9-13.
A study of The Strong Man. Simsolo cites Capra's neglect in France as one of the great oversights of la politique des auteurs, arguing that while the ideology reflected in Capra's work may remain a perfect example of "Rooseveltian liberalism" an interesting play with sexuality and sexual taboo has been generally ignored. In this early work with Langdon, Simsolo observes, not only does Capra unify the gags throughout the film; he develops a style designed to highlight the ambiguity of Langdon's persona: on the one hand a poet of the idée fixe, on the other a little boy almost obscenely arrested in puberty. Capra thus discovers a terrain here that he will return to throughout his career, bypassing censorship by comically alluding to the forbidden. A synopsis, credits, and skeletal biographies for Capra and Langdon are included.

928 Thomas, Kevin. "Frank Capra Films Analyzed in KCET." Los Angeles Times (17 November), sec. 2, p. 5.
Reviewing Richard Schickel's television segment on Capra in The Men Who Made the Movies (see entry 1310), Thomas notes: "Capra's name is synonymous with those tumultuous years between the onslaught of the Depression and the outbreak of World War II . . . [yet the films] seem timelier than ever. That the times are probably much too cynical for such pictures to be made now simply makes them all the more appealing."

1974

929 Agee, James. "Comedy's Greatest Era," in Film Theory and Criticism. Edited by Gerald Mast and Marshall Cohen. New York: Oxford University Press, pp. 438-57.
A reprint of Agee's 1949 essay. See entry 626.

930 B[adder], D[avid] J. "Frank Capra." Film Dope, No. 6 (November), pp. 14-16.
A bio-filmography, including a well-researched account of Capra's work on silent shorts. Badder also provides a summary assessment of Capra's work, lamenting that from Mr. Deeds Goes to Town onward Capra became enslaved by a sentimental populism, but conceding that the simple faith in people and contagious optimism of It's a Wonderful Life make for "an emotionally and spiritually uplifting experience." Additions and corrections to the bio-filmography appeared in 1975 (see entry 953).

931 Barnouw, Eric. Documentary: A History of the Non-Fiction Film. New York: Oxford University Press, pp. 155-62.
Barnouw recounts Capra's version of his assignment to the Why We Fight project, and analyzes the films in terms of their formal strategies and social impact. He sees the long-range significance of the series to be its broad acceptance as a tool for political education and speculates that potential opposition from civil libertarians at the time was mitigated by the liberal positions the films took with respect to the Spanish civil war, isolationism, and the Soviet Union.

932 Bauche, Freddy. Le cinéma américaine, 1955-1970. Lausanne: Éditions l'Age d'Homme, pp. 413-14.
An unfavorable review of A Hole in the Head. Bauche considers Capra, once representative of the most celebrated American comedy, to have lost his imagination as a filmmaker, settling in old age for the insipid, prewar sentimentality of Shirley Temple and Mickey Rooney.

933 Coombs, Richard. "Platinum Blonde." Monthly Film Bulletin, 41, No. 482 (March), 58-59.
Credits, a synopsis, and commentary on the film. Noting that Capra saw both Platinum Blonde and Arsenic and Old Lace as safe, diversionary projects, Coombs proposes that the supposed split in Capra's career between pre-Deeds entertainment and post-Deeds seriousness is in fact an ambivalence running through most of the films. In Platinum Blonde, both the comedy and the protagonist's dilemma anticipate works to follow.

934 Corliss, Richard. "Robert Riskin," in his Talking Pictures. Woodstock, N.Y.: Overlook Press, pp. 217-224.
Corliss's earlier essay on Robert Riskin's work with Capra (see entry 871) is reprinted here with a few minor alterations.

(Capra and Riskin's "played-out populism" in Meet John Doe now becomes a "demagogic populism.") A Riskin filmography is included.

935 Eyquem, Olivier. "Frank Capra," in Dossiers du cinéma: Cinéastes III. Tournai: Éditions Casterman, pp. 21-28.
A critical survey of Capra's career emphasizing the social implications of his films. Eyquem traces a principle of innocence in Capra's universe back to the films with Harry Langdon and finds in the work between 1928 and 1936 an emerging social orientation. This orientation becomes overtly political beginning with Mr. Deeds Goes to Town, read by Eyquem as a populist response to the infringement of personal enterprise augured by the New Deal. He analyzes Mr. Deeds and Mr. Smith Goes to Washington as a diptych in which Capra dramatizes the conquest of modern urban reality by outdated rural ideals, displacing the problem of social reform onto the terrain of personal morality. The social model sketched by these films, however, was never fully defined; World War II interrupted the search, and with the advent of the cold war, Capra found himself isolated in his longstanding commitment to the credo of his heroes and a faith in the people. In retrospect, Eyquem concludes, what is most moving in Capra's films from the 1930s is not their certitude but their disquiet; it is in the moments where Capra finds himself helpless before a state of affairs beyond repair that he speaks to us most sincerely and truly. A bibliography and filmography is appended.

936 Grogg, Sam L., Jr. "Irving Wallace and Hollywood: An Interview." Journal of Popular Film, 3, No. 1 (Winter), 59-62.
Wallace recounts his experience working as a writer under Capra for the Signal Corps Motion Picture Unit during World War II. He claims that despite the efforts of Capra to push Know Your Enemy: Japan in an implicitly racist direction, Carl Foreman and he were able to use the testimony of outside experts to establish a foreign policy that separated the Japanese people from General Tojo's fascist military clique.

937 Haskell, Molly. From Reverence to Rape: The Treatment of Women in the Movies. New York: Hold, Rinehart & Winston, pp. 122-23.
Brief commentary on Capra's women, as a mediator between idealism and corruption in Mr. Smith Goes to Washington, and as visionaries--by virtue of "woman's intuition"--in The Miracle Woman and Lady for a Day.

938 Higham, Charles. The Art of the American Film; 1900-1971. Garden City, N.Y.: Doubleday & Co. pp. 32, 34, 188-95.
Higham briefly discusses Capra's early career as a "tough and resilient" director for Harry Langdon in the silent era, observing that Capra later pursued a theme first expressed in these films: "the shrimp defeats the bigwigs." He comments at greater length on Capra's work from the 1930s and 1940s, describing it as "fast-moving, energetic and brashly directed." While Capra and Riskin cannot be taken seriously as political or moral thinkers, the execution "is such that

while the films are being watched, they must sweep away all but the most cautious judgment."

939   Hochman, Stanley, ed. A Library of Film Criticism: American Film Directors. New York: Frederick Ungar Publishing Co., pp. 29-37.

A collection of excerpts from the following articles and books: "Aside to English Actors" by Pare Lorentz, Vanity Fair, October 1933 (see entry 175); a review of It Happened One Night by Robert Forsythe, New Masses, 3 July 1934 (see entry 199); "It Happened Once More" by Otis Ferguson, New Republic, 19 December 1934 (see entry 198); "On a Classic" by William Troy, Nation, 10 April 1935 (see entry 217); a review of Lost Horizon by Robert Stebbins, New Theatre, April 1937 (see entry 330); a review of Lost Horizon by Laurence Stallings, Stage, April 1937 (see entry 337); Jim Tully on Capra, Cinema Arts, June 1937 (see entry 338); Lewis Jacobs on Capra, The Rise of the American Film, 1939 (see entry 417); "Mr. Capra Goes Someplace" by Otis Ferguson, New Republic, 1 November 1939 (see entry 411); a review of Meet John Doe by James Shelley Hamilton, National Board of Review, April 1941 (see entry 466); Egon Larsen on You Can't Take it with You from Spotlight on Films, 1950 (see entry 653); "American Madness" by William S. Pechter, Kulchur, Winter 1962 (see entry 759); "Frank Capra and Screwball Comedy, 1931-1941" by Andrew Bergman from We're in the Money, 1971 (see entry 816); "Frank Capra" by Tom Shales from The American Film Heritage, 1972 (see entry 894). Also reprinted in this volume are excerpts from Capra's autobiography (see entry 1176) concerning the following directors: John Ford (p. 132), Henry King (p. 227), Stanley Kramer (p. 231), Gregory LaCava (p. 244), Ernst Lubitsch (pp. 289-90), Leo McCarey (p. 304), Mack Sennett (pp. 391-92), and George Stevens (pp. 411-12).

940   Jameson, Richard T. "Platinum Blonde." Movietone News, 29 (January-February), 11-12.

A program note for a revival of the film. Jameson notes that the pace of Platinum Blonde matches its Warner Brothers contemporaries during the early sound era. The film, moreover, is marked by "Capra's inimitable, collateral sense of browsy improvisation and disarmingly unexpected tenderness," having "somewhat the air of a rehearsal for the later, more celebrated Mr. Deeds Goes to Town." Credits.

941   Kaminsky, Stuart. "History and Social Change: Comedy and Individual Expression," in his American Film Genres. Dayton, Ohio: Pflaum Publishing, pp. 158-59.

The Strong Man is analyzed in terms of its "intentionally Biblical structure, a fundamentalist form which comes as much from director Frank Capra as it does from Langdon's character."

942   Leish, Kenneth W. Cinema. New York: Newsweek Books, pp. 84-85.

A brief discussion of Capra's work in the 1930s. "At a time when Americans wanted to believe that the individual still mattered and that the average man could still control his own destiny, Capra's films found receptive audiences."

943   Manvell, Roger. Films and the Second World War. South Brunswick and New York: A.S. Barnes and Co.; London: J.M. Dent & Sons, pp. 155-56, 167-76.
        Commentary on Capra's work for the government during World War II, especially the Why We Fight series. Manvell observes that Capra "understood the 'common audience,' and knew how to appeal to the emotions in a way directors who had worked solely in the documentary field might have failed to do." He also compares Tunisian Victory unfavorably with the British Desert Victory, suggesting that the optimistic view of smiling children at the end of the former film is a "Capra-like touch of 'pie in the sky'" and a "grave miscalculation."

944   Milne, Tom. "The Bitter Tea of General Yen." Monthly Film Bulletin, 41, No. 481:56-57.
        Credits, a synopsis, and high praise for the film as a sui generis work within Capra's career. "With its exalted emotions and gestures, its glowingly muted lighting, its caressing dissolves and glittering ornamentation, it is a masterpiece escaped from the Sternberg filmography." Moreover, unlike Capra's later works, the film bows to neither audience nor moralist.

945   Nelson, Joyce. "Mr. Smith Goes to Washington": Capra, Populism and Comic-Strip Art." Journal of Popular Film, 3, No. 3 (Summer), 245-55.
        Nelson proposes that the comic-strip quality of Mr. Smith Goes to Washington underlies both the political opposition it aroused and the popular response it enjoyed; it "is at once the source of the film's power to engage its audience as well as its means for avoiding the deeper political and ideological issues it might raise." Included in her analysis is a discussion of character types, Populist and popular folk heroes, the iconography of historical monuments, the spatio-temporal freedom of montage editing, audience identification with Saunders, and the visual positioning of Smith in alignment with patriotic figures from the past. The ending might be construed as ambiguous, she argues, but the style of the film (which does not ask for logic) nevertheless fosters a simplified notion of the workings of democracy and the villains and heroes who threaten and save it.

946   Parish, James Robert. "State of the Union," in his Hollywood's Great Love Teams. New Rochelle, N.Y." Arlington House Publishers, pp. 552-54.
        Background information on the making of the film and a summary of critical reviews at the time of the film's release. Today, Parish proposes, State of the Union "holds up well as an interesting reflection of pre-New Frontier politicking."

*947   Suominen, T. "Amerikkalaisen idealismin kasvot." Filmihullu (Helsinki), No. 3, pp. 20-23.
        Cited in Film Literature Index, 1974.

948   Watz, Edward. "Langdon, the Unsung Genius." Classic Film Collector, 43 (Summer), 33, 38-39.
Watz proposes that while Langdon's six features between 1926 and 1928 are his most impressive achievement, The Strong Man and Long Pants are overrated, suffering from weak story development and average direction. He also contrasts Capra's version of the breakup with Langdon in his autobiography with that of Katherine Albert in 1932 (see entry 139).

949   ____. "Langdon, Silent and Sound (Part 1)." Classic Film Collector, 45 (Winter), X9-X10, X12, 55.
In this survey of Harry Langdon's silent shorts for Mack Sennett, Watz disputes Capra's account of having discovered a persona for newcomer Langdon, noting that prior to Capra's arrival at the studio Langdon had starred in several two-reelers featuring the "baby" character.

950   Willis, Donald C. The Films of Frank Capra. Metuchen, N.J.: Scarecrow Press, 214 pp.
In his introduction Willis outlines a critical profile of Capra's work in the 1930s and 1940s: the "good early talkies" are dissimilar, except in their "wit, feeling, and technical élan"; the films fall off between Mr. Deeds Goes to Town and the filibuster scene in Mr. Smith Goes to Washington as Capra tries to assimilate a new altruistic impulse into his refined technique; the gap between message and technique then closes, resulting in Capra's two great films, Meet John Doe and It's a Wonderful Life. In this section Willis also traces a suicide motif running through Capra's films, and briefly discusses their politics, concluding that for all their political frenzy they are not definable in political terms. Unfortunately, these introductory remarks serve only to stitch together the material that follows in a very loose way. Willis admits in the introduction that after his opening discussion of Mr. Deeds, Mr. Smith, Meet John Doe, and It's a Wonderful Life, his organization of material is arbitrary. Each film inspires some commentary, but many of the later passages appear hastily written and bear little relation to the work overall. Moreover, Willis tends to work through his reactions, developing arguments in their behalf; consequently the history of his own responses takes precedence over a systematic analysis of the films themselves. The book, however, is filled with information and is well researched: Willis's credits are far more thorough than anything previous; excerpts from a variety of contemporaneous reviews run throughout the text; and a section of appendices include data on films tangential to Capra's career, a listing of Oscar nominations and awards given to Capra's films, and a review of Capra's autobiography. In short, a potentially provocative and useful book in need of a good editor.

1975

951 Agee, James. "Prelude to War," in Frank Capra: The Man and His Films. Edited by Richard Glatzer and John Raeburn. Ann Arbor: University of Michigan Press, pp. 155-56.
A reprint of Agee's 1943 review. See entry 488.

952 ____. "It's a Wonderful Life," in Frank Capra: The Man and His Films. Edited by Richard Glatzer and John Raeburn. Ann Arbor: University of Michigan Press, pp. 157-58.
A reprint of Agee's 1947 review. See entry 577.

953 Anon. "Additions and Corrections: Frank Capra." Film Dope, No. 8 (October), pp. 24c-24d.
Additions and corrections to the magazine's 1974 biofilmography of Capra (see entry 930), supplied by Capra and Wolfram Tichy.

954 Anon. "AFI Comes to the Rescue." Variety (9 April), p. 28.
A report on the American Film Institute's recent efforts to restore and preserve Capra's films. The information is drawn from a current AFI newsletter (see entry 955).

955 Anon. "From the Archives: Lost and Found--the Films of Frank Capra." AFI News, 5, No. 1:7.
A report on recent efforts to locate and preserve prints of Capra films. Specific information is provided for the following: Fultah Fisher's Boarding House, Say It with Sables, That Certain Thing, Submarine, Ladies of Leisure, Lady for a Day, Broadway Bill, Lost Horizon, Meet John Doe, and It's a Wonderful Life. Reprinted in Film, No. 27 (see entry 957).

956 Anon. "Hollywood anni '50--il modo di produzione." Filmcritica, Nos. 258-260 (October-December), p. 326.
Brief commentary is offered on Capra's attempt to control all stages of the production of his films in the 1930s and 1940s.

957 Anon. "Lost and Found: The Films of Frank Capra." Film, No. 27 (June), p. 10.
A report on recent efforts to locate and preserve Capra films, reprinted from the AFI News (see entry 955).

958 Barsam, Richard. Why We Fight," in Frank Capra: the Man and His Films. Edited by Richard Glatzer and John Raeburn. Ann Arbor: University of Michigan Press, pp. 149-54.
A reprint of Barsam's discussion of Capra's war documentaries in Nonfiction Film. See entry 906.

959 Bergman, Andrew. "Frank Capra and Screwball Comedy," in Frank Capra: The Man and His Films. Edited by Richard Glatzer and John Raeburn. Ann Arbor: University of Michigan Press, pp. 68-82.

A reprint of Bergman's chapter on Capra from We're in the Money. See entry 816.

960   Bohn, Thomas, Richard L. Stromgren, and Daniel H. Johnson. Light and Shadow. Sherman Oaks, Calif.: Alfred Publishing Co., pp. 76, 100, 186, 212-13, 264-66, 176.
The authors offer passing commentary on Capra's relationship with Langdon, the middle-class ethic and depression appeal of his films with Riskin at Columbia, and the influence of the Why We Fight series on the Soviets.

961   Brown, Kent R. A review of Frank Capra: The Man and His Films. Journal of Popular Film, 4, No. 2:185-86.
A favorable review of the Glatzer and Raeburn anthology. See entry 966.

962   Buscombe, Edward. "Notes on Columbia Pictures Corporation 1926-41." Screen, 16, No. 3 (August), 65-82.
Using the Keynesian rhetoric of American Madness as a starting point, Buscombe investigates the possible correlation between the presence of A.H. Giannini as a major figure in the corporate hierarchy of Columbia Pictures in the 1930s and a political slant favorable to the New Deal in Columbia's films. He concludes that while Columbia remained relatively independent of the conservative Wall Street establishment during this period, there is no evidence to suggest any deliberate policy favoring the New Deal or leftist causes, and that Capra's path toward "social comment" in his films was not followed by other directors working for the studio. Framing this study is an argument by Buscombe for more rigorous historical research into the complex role of the movie industry as a mediating structure between films and society.

963   Casty, Alan. Development of the Film. New York, Chicago, San Francisco, and Atlanta: Harcourt, Brace, Janovich, pp. 90, 147-48, 169, 198.
Casty comments briefly on Capra's work in silent comedy with Harry Langdon, on the Why We Fight series, and on It's a Wonderful Life. He discusses at greater length Capra's dramatic comedies of the 1930s. "Capra's satire and his expert editing for both comical and emotional points are softened by rosy sentimentality and a cracker-barrel populist political naïveté."

964   Cohen, Hubert I. Review of Frank Capra: The Man and His Films. Cinema Journal, 15, No. 1 (Fall), 63-65.
Cohen briefly discusses the possible reasons for Capra's aversion to the films of Orson Welles; the neglect of Capra's work in the 1960s and its revival in the 1970s; cultural explanation for the power the films still hold; and the darkening aspect to Capra's work as World War II approached. Cohen is generally pleased with the Glatzer and Raeburn anthology, but regrets the continued emphasis on those films made between 1933 and 1947 at the expense of those from before and after. See entry 966.

965   Ferguson, Otis. "The Business of Promoting a Thesis," in Frank Capra: The Man and His Films. Edited by Richard Glatzer and John Raeburn. Ann Arbor: University of Michigan Press, pp. 101-9.
Reprinted here are four reviews by Ferguson: Broadway Bill (see entry 198), Mr. Deeds Goes to Town (see entry 249), Mr. Smith Goes to Washington (see entry 411), and Meet John Doe (see entry 464).

966   Glatzer, Richard, and John Raeburn, eds. Frank Capra: The Man and His Films. Ann Arbor: University of Michigan Press, 190 pp.
An anthology of reviews, essays, and interviews, with a brief filmography and bibliography appended. (Each of the articles is annotated in this volume separately under the author's name.)

967   No entry.

968   _____. Meet John Doe: An End to Social Mythmaking," in Frank Capra: The Man and His Films. Edited by Richard Glatzer and John Raeburn. Ann Arbor: University of Michigan Press, pp. 139-48.
Glatzer argues that while Capra intended Meet John Doe to reaffirm small-town American values at a time when they were in danger of being eclipsed, the strategies he had established as a social mythmaker in Mr. Deeds Goes to Town and Mr. Smith Goes to Washington could not contain the dark vision of American democracy that erupts in this film. He notes several key changes from the earlier films: a shift in scale from city to nation; the disappearance of a rural-urban dichotomy; the magnification of evil; and, most especially, John's initial amorality and its symbolic implication that ordinary Americans are ethically blank slates. The source of the film's darkness, Glatzer proposes, follows from this last point: Capra's little people are now ripe for fascist control. Moreover, Meet John Doe can be read autobiographically, with Capra calling into question his own role as media manipulator and American mythmaker, and moving toward the more personal cinema of It's a Wonderful Life.

969   Greene, Graham. "A Director of Genius: Four Reviews," in Frank Capra: The Man and His Films. Edited by Richard Glatzer and John Raeburn. Ann Arbor: University of Michigan Press, pp. 110-20.
Reprints of four reviews by Greene: Mr. Deeds Goes to Town (see entry 252), Lost Horizon (see entry 323), You Can't Take It with You (see entry 373), and Mr. Smith Goes to Washington (see entry 437).

970   Griffith, Richard. "Capra's Early Films," in Frank Capra: The Man and His Films. Edited by Richard Glatzer and John Raeburn. Ann Arbor: University of Michigan Press, pp. 49-56.
An excerpt from Griffith's 1950 monograph covering Capra's career through 1931. See entry 649.

971   _____. It's a Wonderful Life and Post-War Realism," in Frank Capra: The Man and His Films. Edited by Richard Glatzer and John Raeburn. Ann Arbor: University of Michigan Press, pp.160-63.
       A reprint of Griffith's 1947 review of the film. See entry 985.

972   Handzo, Stephen. "Under Capracorn," in Frank Capra: The Man and His Films. Edited by Richard Glatzer and John Raeburn. Ann Arbor: University of Michigan Press, pp. 164-76.
       A reprint of Handzo's 1972 essay. See entry 876.

973   _____. "Platinum Blonde.' Thousand Eyes Magazine, 1, No. 3 (October), p. 3.
       Commentary on the film. Noting that Stew Smith in Platinum Blonde is both a "regular guy" reporter confronting a strong-minded heiress and a "Cinderella man," Handzo links the character with the later figures of Peter Warne (It Happened One Night) and Longfellow Deeds. He finds the pacing of Platinum Blonde more awkward and slow than that of Capra's later work, but notes several Capra "touches," and warns that the visual virtuosity of cameraman Joseph Walker is largely lost in standard 16mm prints of the film.

974   Hellman, Geoffrey T. "Thinker in Hollywood," in Frank Capra: The Man and His Films. Edited by Richard Glatzer and John Raeburn. Ann Arbor: University of Michigan Press, pp. 3-13.
       A reprint of Hellman's 1940 New Yorker profile of Capra. See entry 439.

975   Jacobs, Lewis. "Capra at Work" in Frank Capra: The Man and His Films. Edited by Richard Glatzer and John Raeburn. Ann Arbor: University of Michigan Press, pp. 40-41.
       A reprint of Jacob's 1941 article. See entry 471.

976   Kael, Pauline. "The Man from the Dream City." New Yorker, 51, No. 21 (14 July), 65-66.
       During the course of a profile on Cary Grant, Kael asserts that after the success of It Happened One Night Capra "lost his instinct for sex scenes, and his comedies became almost obscenely neuter, with clean friendly grandpas presiding over blandly retarded families." Consequently, Grant "was turned into a manic neuter in Arsenic and Old Lace." Reprinted in 1980 (see entry 1125).

977   Kay, Karyn. "Part-time Work of a Domestic Slave." Film Quarterly, 24, No. 1 (Fall), 52-57.
       Arguing that screwball comedies, like medieval Noah plays, conventionally close with a reiteration of a man-above-woman world order, Kay illustrates her point with a capsule reading of It Happened One Night. An exchange with Leland Poague followed in 1976 (see entry 1013). Reprinted in 1977 (see entry 1040).

978   Kerr, Walter. "Who Was Harry Langdon?" American Film, 1, No. 2 (November), 11.
      In a passage deleted from this essay when it was reprinted as a chapter in The Silent Clowns (see entry 979), Kerr comments that Capra made the most of Langdon's sweetness, "developing 'the principle of the brick' under an umbrella provided by God."

979   _____. The Silent Clowns. New York: Alfred A. Knopf, pp. 270-72, 276-78, 279, 281-82, 284.
      Kerr agrees that principal credit for shaping Langdon's film image should be given to Capra, but doubts if that image could have been entirely imposed, suggesting instead that Capra and his associates watched Langdon for distinctive mannerisms and lured him into his persona. He attributes the structural soundness of The Strong Man to Capra's writing and direction, and finds evidence in Langdon's later films to confirm Capra's assertion that Langdon never understood his own character.

980   Lambert, Gavin. "The Fortune Cookie Stylist." Films and Filming, 21, No. 8 (May), 53.
      The publication of Willis's critical study (see entry 950) occasions a reassessment of Capra's career by Lambert. He argues that while Capra tried to convince us that we live in the best of all possible worlds, his depiction of the corrupt and ruthless was usually more persuasive than that of the innocent and homespun. Capra emerged as a leading director during the depression, swept away by the collective feeling that the power of big business and dictatorships would crumble in the face of simple integrity. But when this mood was challenged in the 1940s, the threat of suicide or withdrawal became directly stated in his work; at the end of Meet John Doe he can only try to bluff his way out of a real world. Lambert thus reads the last shot of Lost Horizon as autobiographical, "the projection of never-never land where all problems are solved in fortune cookie style."

981   Larkin, Rochelle. "The Capra Years," in her Hail, Columbia. New Rochelle, N.Y.: Arlington House Publishers, pp. 41-87.
      This survey of Capra's tenure at Columbia is mainly drawn from Capra's autobiography and Bob Thomas's King Cohn (see entry 784). Larkin concludes that while a "revolution in public morality" has dated the very best of Capra's films, his legacy is major. A filmography with credits is included.

982   Leab, Daniel J. From Sambo to Superspace: The Black Experience in Motion Pictures. Boston: Houghton Mifflin Co., pp. 127-28.
      The Negro Soldier in World War II is briefly discussed. Capra, rather than the director Stuart Heisler or writer Carlton Moss, is credited with the final shape of the project. The film is judged a respectful but superficial depiction of the role of blacks in the U.S. history.

983 Lowry, Malcolm. "Capra's Idealism," in *Frank Capra: The Man and His Films*. Edited by Richard Glatzer and John Raeburn. Ann Arbor: University of Michigan Press, pp. 47-48.

A reprint of a letter by Lowry concerning *The Strong Man*. See entry 774.

984 Mack. "Partly Insightful Book on Capra." *Variety* (29 January), p. 34.

A review of *The Films of Frank Capra* by Donald C. Willis (see entry 950). The reviewer finds some of Willis's observations fresh, but is skeptical of his notion that it is impossible to abstract a political philosophy from the films and hard to make sense of the emotional shifts within individual films. "The feeling persists throughout the book that if Willis had looked harder and exercised more intellectual discipline on his own part he could have found more coherence in Capra. It's an absurd cop-out to argue, as he does, that Capra is a 'nihilist.'"

985 Maland, Charles J. "American Visions: The Films of Chaplin, Ford, Capra, and Welles, 1936-41." Ph.D. dissertation, University of Michigan, pp. 191-294.

Maland devotes two chapters to Capra's work from this period. He outlines a formula struck by Capra in response to the social turbulence of the depression in which screwball comedy is wedded to the traditional middle-class novel of reform, and charts the variations of the formula to be found in *Mr. Deeds Goes to Town*, *Lost Horizon*, *You Can't Take It with You*, *Mr. Smith Goes to Washington*, and *Meet John Doe*. When he affirmed small-town piety in *Mr. Deeds*, Maland argues, Capra was reflecting a middle-class viewpoint of the times, but when he championed national causes in *Mr. Smith* and *Meet John Doe*, Capra was helping to create a new emphasis in that culture's view of reality. Extending the range of his discussion to include *It's a Wonderful Life*, Maland also proposes that it was not until Capra divorced religion from nationalism, and abandoned his concern for social relevance, that he was able to perfect his formula and express what he wanted to say. The relationship of these works to changes in American culture is of central importance to Maland throughout his analysis. This dissertation was published in 1977 (see entry 1047).

986 N[ichols], B[ill]. Review of *Frank Capra: The Man and His Films*. *Women & Film*, 2, No. 7:115.

A short, largely favorable review of the Glatzer and Raeburn anthology. See entry 966.

987 O'Connor, John J. "TV: WNET Panorama--30 Years after V-E Day." *New York Times* (8 May), p. 79.

Surveying a group of wartime propaganda films broadcast by the Public Broadcasting System, O'Connor notes of *Prelude to War*: "The distortions are glaring. The emotional justifications are accurate and startling."

988   Pechter, William S. "American Madness," in Frank Capra: The Man and His Films. Edited by Richard Glatzer and John Raeburn. Ann Arbor: University of Michigan Press, pp. 177-85.
       A reprint of Pechter's 1962 essay. See entry 759.

989   Poague, Leland. The Cinema of Frank Capra. Cranbury, N.J.: A.S. Barnes and Co.; London: Tantivy Press, 252 pp.
       In the first half of this book, a strategy is mapped for the studying of Capra's work as a complete entity; in the second half, nine feature films are analyzed. Poague's primary assertion is that Capra's work must be examined within the context of literary history, an approach he sees as a necessary corrective to sociological accounts of the films and best able to explain their enduring power. Using work on ritual, myth, and literature by Francis Cornford and Northrop Frye, Poague connects traditional forms of comedy and romance, illustrated largely through the plays of Aristophanes and Shakespeare, with dramatic patterns discernible in Capra's cinema. These patterns, he argues, cut across four sequential periods: Capra's city films, country films, political films, and a final period of retrospection. Thus That Certain Thing, You Can't Take It with You, and Here Comes the Groom are all read as literary comedies, and Dirigible, American Madness, and It's a Wonderful Life as literary romances, with the two forms collapsing together in many of the other films. Critics have been led astray, Poague contends, by focusing on the political trilogy (Mr. Deeds Goes to Town, Mr. Smith Goes to Washington, and Meet John Doe) and stressing the topical issues dealt with in them. Capra's popularity, he proposes, is not explainable simply in terms of the audience's desire to escape the problems of the depression or their willingness to respond to the evocation of American myths; these elements comprise a "surface structure" beneath which resides a "deep comic structure" involving fertility, moral integrity, and community, a "comic mythos" of which the American populist-agrarian myth is simply one version. In a chapter on Capra's style, moreover, Poague proposes that the overriding stylistic concern of these works is an accurate rendition of this comic world, and that through cinematography this world matches up with "actual reality." The great success of Capra's films, he concludes, is attributable both to Capra's mastery of literary forms and to the emotional experience Capra affords the audience through the actions of realistic characters. Singled out for detailed analysis are The Strong Man, Long Pants, The Bitter Tea of General Yen, It Happened One Night, Mr. Deeds Goes to Town, Mr. Smith Goes to Washington, Meet John Doe, It's a Wonderful Life, and Pocketful of Miracles. Portions of this book appeared as a dissertation in 1973 (see entry 922).

990   Raeburn, John. "Introduction" in Frank Capra: The Man and His Films. Edited by Richard Glatzer and John Raeburn. Ann Arbor: University of Michigan Press, pp. vii-xiv.
       Raeburn charts the fall and rise of Capra's reputation and discusses at length the attraction Capra's films hold for contemporary, college-age audiences. He attributes the latter in part to a

new appreciation of Capra's formal virtuosity. But he considers of even greater importance the fact that Capra's work offers a legacy of valuable American modes and tradition, a social criticism positing that the insidious designs of the rich and powerful can be thwarted, and a vision of middle-class life that is invested with vitality and style. Raeburn closes with an appeal for close, formal analysis of Capra's films, as well as those of other major American directors.

990a _____. "American Madness and American Values," in Frank Capra: The Man and His Films. Edited by Richard Glatzer and John Raeburn. Ann Arbor: University of Michigan Press, pp. 57-67.

An analysis of American Madness as a social document of depression American and as American myth. Raeburn argues that by placing the figure of Tom Dickson—benevolent, resolute, exemplar of an individualist ethic and nineteenth-century small-town ideals—within the contemporary context of urban corporate power, Capra gives dramatic shape to the fears and confusions of depression audiences while holding out hope for a better future rooted in traditional American values. Finding little in Capra's early work to suggest the talent for social observation and penchant for social analysis demonstrated in this film, Raeburn considers it the first in which Capra displayed his maturity as an artist. Close attention is paid to formal strategies at work in American Madness, including camera movement, cutting, and sound.

991 Reitz, Carolyn. "Mr. Deeds Goes to Town." CinemaTexas Program Notes, 8, No. 21 (17 February), 1-6.

An analysis of comic elements that temper the film's resemblance to a social morality play. Detailed credits, filmography, and bibliography.

992 Sklar, Robert. "The Imagination of Stability: The Depression Films of Frank Capra," in Frank Capra: The Man and His Films. Edited by Richard Glatzer and John Raeburn. Ann Arbor: University of Michigan Press, pp. 121-38.

Sklar argues for a framework to account for the appeal of Capra's depression films that is more precise than conventional criticism has supplied. He objects to the populist label often affixed to Capra's work on both historical and critical grounds, and places the films from this period within the genteel tradition of middle-class popular fiction. He contends that stories of upward mobility and romantic love, in which a hero of uncommon will and imagination makes his way up the social hierarchy, are modified by Capra and Robert Riskin for depression audiences. The drawing room is exchanged for more commonplace settings, and heiresses replaced by working women. The power of the popular press to publicize private lives is examined, and the hero is made to seem vulnerable and incomplete without a community to support him. As the genteel forms become increasingly unconvincing during the course of the decade, Capra's heroes begin to openly oppose wealth and power. By the time of Meet John Doe, this opposition ends in a stalemate. Also see entry 993.

993 _____. "The Making of Cultural Myths: Walt Disney and Frank Capra," in his *Movie-Made America: A Cultural History of American Movies*. New York: Random House, pp. 195-215.

Films by Capra and Disney are used by Sklar to illustrate the increasing willingness of Hollywood to revitalize and refashion national cultural mythology as the 1930s progressed. Sklar distinguishes between Capra's early "fantasies," in which viewers were encouraged to imagine a world they could never enter, and his later 'idealizations," in which viewers were invited simply to accept a prepackaged network of myths. The latter, he proposes, were a conscious response to domestic turmoil caused by the rise of Nazism abroad. *The Bitter Tea of General Yen* and *It Happened One Night* figure prominently in the first half of his discussion; the second half on the overtly political films is drawn mainly from the concluding section of Sklar's article in Glatzer and Raeburn (see entry 992).

994 Sobchak, Thomas. Review of *Frank Capra: The Man and His Films*. *Western Humanities Review*, 29, No. 3 (Summer), 304-6.

Sobchak finds little in the Glatzer and Raeburn anthology (see entry 966) to convince him that Capra is an auteur. "The simple fact that he had control over all aspects of his films does not make him a director with a distinctive style or a distinctive temperament: his themes are merely the commonplaces of Americana."

995 Stebbins, Robert [Sidney Meyers]. "Mr. Capra Goes to Town," in *Frank Capra: The Man and His Films*. Edited by Richard Glatzer and John Raeburn. Ann Arbor: University of Michigan Press, pp. 117-20.

A reprint of Meyers's 1936 review of *Mr. Deed's Goes to Town*. See entry 259.

996 Troy, William, "Capra and the Picaresque," in *Frank Capra: The Man and His Films*. Edited by Richard Glatzer and John Raeburn. Ann Arbor: University of Michigan Press, pp. 99-100.

A reprint of Troy's 1934 review of *It Happened One Night*. See entry 211.

997 Truffaut, François. "Frank Capra, le guerisseur," in his *Les films de ma vie*. Paris: Flammarion, pp. 94-95.

Capra, according to Truffaut, brought the secrets of Italian commedia del l'arte to Hollywood. He steered his characters through tragic human situations before providing the miracle that restored a comic balance. The growing harshness of life after the war made his miracles seem even more improbable, but Capra remained the kind of healer who is an enemy of official medicine. Truffaut's book was translated into English in 1978 (see entry 1094).

998 Walker, Kathleen. "The Strong Man." *CinemaTexas Program Notes*, 8, No. 13 (3 February), 1-4.

Walker finds Capra's influence on the film unmistakable in its pitting of the hero "against cunning, cruelty and general moral decay." But unlike his later comedies, the plot is weak and underdeveloped, and the moral ascendancy of the hero eerily inappropriate. Credits, bibliography, and filmography.

999   Willson, Robert. "Capra's Comic Sense," in *Frank Capra: The Man and His Films*. Edited by Richard Glatzer and John Raeburn. Ann Arbor: University of Michigan Press, pp. 83-98.

Willson proposes that in Capra's best films his social sense, a faith in the power of goodness and the courage to defend right causes, is served by his comic sense, forging a comprehensive comic vision that engages the hearts and heads of the audience. Tracing Capra's comic style back to his early experiences as an immigrant youth and his professional training at the Hal Roach and Mack Sennett studios, Willson charts the evolution of that style across seven films: *It Happened One Night*, *Mr. Deeds Goes to Town*, *You Can't Take It with You*, *Mr. Smith Goes to Washington*, *Meet John Doe*, *It's a Wonderful Life*, and *Pocketful of Miracles*. He sees Capra moving away from comic genre pieces like *It Happened One Night* toward an engagement with social issues and an articulation of social philosophy. By the time of *Meet John Doe*, Wilson contends, Capra was so adept at depicting social villainy his comic sense faltered; thus beginning with *Its a Wonderful Life*, Capra turned to "fairy-tale fantasy" as a way of providing solutions to social problems.

1976

1000   Anon. "Frank Capra," in *The Oxford Companion to Film*. Edited by Liz-Anne Bowden. New York and London: Oxford University Press, pp. 110-111.

A Capra bio-filmography.

1001   Balio, Tino. *United Artists: The Company Built by the Stars*. Madison: University of Wisconsin Press, pp. 176-77, 181-82.

Balio describes Capra's negotiations with United Artists in 1939 and 1941 to become a partner in the company.

1002   Barbaro, Nick. "*It Happened One Night*." *CinemaTexas Program Notes*, 10, No. 2 (9 March), 89-94.

Barbaro recounts Capra's version of the making of *It Happened One Night* and analyzes the film in terms of a thematic interplay between individualism and social concern. Detailed credits, a filmography, and a brief bibliography are included.

1003   Bernds, Edward. "Sound Thoughts," in *Hollywood: The Movie Factory*. Edited by Leonard Maltin. New York: Popular Library, pp. 97-104.

A reprint of a 1972 interview with Bernds. See entry 866.

1004   Beylie, Claude. "Capra." <u>Ecran</u>, 48 (June), 73.
         Capra's autobiography, now published in French, is favorably reviewed.

1005   Brown, Geoff. "The Strong Man." <u>Monthly Film Bulletin</u>, 43, No. 511 (August), 179-80.
         Credits, a synopsis, and commentary on the film. Brown finds the film structurally and stylistically disjunctive, but thinks it holds together thematically, presaging Capra's later interest in stories of perennial innocents embroiled in big-city vice and of small towns saved from corruption.

1006   Eder, Richard. "Re-examining the 'State of the Union.'" <u>New York Times</u> (29 October), p. C8.
         A reassessment of <u>State of the Union</u> during its revival during the last week of the 1976 presidential campaign. Eder finds the political speeches, which functioned as "yeast" in <u>Mr. Smith Goes to Washington</u>, to be simply "gassy" here, and that long expository passages bog the film down. He also notes that Spencer Tracy's inspired litany to occupants of the White House has lost its poetry amid the contemporary political scene.

1007   Grisola, Michel. "Le roi des villes et le roi des champs." <u>Le Nouvel Observateur</u>, 613 (9 August), 52.
         The publication of French translations of autobiographies by Capra and Raoul Walsh provokes a comparative look at the two directors. Grisola proposes that Walsh depicts an America of open spaces, Capra one of great cities; that Walsh is a cowboy, Capra an advocate; that Walsh offers virile vitality, Capra passionate idealism. That Capra is an auteur and Walsh a metteur-en-scène, moreover, is confirmed by their memories of their careers: Capra remembers themes, Walsh his pals.

1008   Hughes, William. "The Evaluation of Film as Evidence," in <u>The Historian and Film</u>. Edited by Paul Smith. Cambridge: Cambridge University Press, pp. 68-69.
         Capra's career is used to illustrate the author's contention that American filmmakers generally share a national commitment to a dream of success. Hughes finds in Capra's autobiography evidence that the director was less the master of the symbols and values of American life than their servant. Also see entry 878.

1009   Jowett, Garth. "Hollywood Goes to War, 1939-1945," in his <u>Film: The Democratic Art</u>. Boston and Toronto: Little, Brown & Co., pp. 300, 320-21.
         Jowett describes <u>Meet John Doe</u> as an "especially effective exposé of the possibility of fascism in America," and briefly discusses Capra's role in the <u>Why We Fight</u> series.

1010   Kozarski, Richard. "Frank Capra, 1897-," in his <u>Hollywood Directors: 1914-1940</u>. London, Oxford, and New York: Oxford University Press, p. 180.

An introduction to a reprinting of Capra's 1927 essay, "The Gag Man" (see entry 1158). Kozarski connects Capra's experience as a silent comedy writer, styling material to the personality of Harry Langdon, with Capra's later skill at creating comic masks for James Stewart, Gary Cooper, and Cary Grant.

1011 MacCann, Richard Dyer. "World War II--Armed Forces Documentary," in <u>Nonfiction Film: Theory and Criticism</u>. Edited by Richard Meran Barsam. New York: E.P. Dutton & Co., pp. 136-57.
Reprinted from MacCann's 1973 book. See entry 916.

1012 Nesteby, James R. Review of <u>The Cinema of Frank Capra</u> by Leland Poague. <u>Journal of Popular Film</u>, 5, No. 2:168.
A favorable review of Poague's 1975 book. See entry 989.

1013 Poague, Leland A., and Karyn Kay. "Controversy and Correspondence." <u>Film Quarterly</u>, 29, No. 4 (Summer), 62-64.
This exchange concerning the ideological implications of medieval Noah plays and screwball comedy films includes opposite readings of <u>It Happened One Night</u> by Poague and Kay. Poague (responding to a brief analysis of the film by Kay in a previous issue) proposes that Ellie's victimization involves not male domination of women but parental domination of children, and that in the end she is liberated to marry a man who respects her spunk, drive, and independence. Kay counters that Ellie is depicted as a shrew--a bored, bratty heiress unable to take care of herself--and that Peter intervenes as paternal surrogate, a function that Ellie's father acknowledges when he aggressively conspires to have the two marry. Also see entry 977. Reprinted in 1977 (see entry 1040).

1014 Ray, Robert. "Moving On: The Road Motif in American Cinema (part 1)." <u>Media Montage</u>, 1, No. 1:25-28.
<u>It Happened One Night</u> is discussed as a seminal work in the absorption of the picaresque tradition into American movies. "With its almost documentary style and its charmingly plausible characters, Capra created a particular American addition to the age-old concept of the road as the ultimate teacher."

1015 Rhode, Eric. <u>A History of the Cinema</u>. New York: Hill & Wang, pp. 321-22, 339-42, 413-15, 445.
Rhode discusses <u>American Madness</u> and <u>Lady for a Day</u> as harbingers of the New Deal's message of confidence; <u>It Happened One Night</u> as initiating a series of adult romances in the 1930s; <u>Mr. Deeds Goes to Town</u> and <u>Mr. Smith Goes to Washington</u> in terms of American heroes and an emerging nationalistic temper as the war approaches; the <u>Why We Fight</u> series as reductionist propaganda (sometimes trenchant, sometimes simplistic); and <u>It's a Wonderful Life</u> as a postwar fairy tale that cheats the audience. Throughout Rhode emphasizes the likely influence of Sicilian poverty and Catholicism on Capra's work.

1016   Rhodie, Sam. "Totems and Movies," in *Movies and Methods*. Edited by Bill Nichols. Berkeley, Los Angeles, and London: University of California Press, pp. 466-81.

A B.F.I. seminar paper on structural anthropology and film analysis, written in 1969. The first section discusses the theoretical problems of applying structural analysis to movies; the second section tests those problems through a structural analysis of *Mr. Deeds Goes to Town*. The latter section was published on its own in 1970 (see entry 805).

1017   Richards, Jeffrey. "Frank Capra and the Cinema of Populism," in *Movies and Methods*. Edited by Bill Nichols. Berkeley, Los Angeles, and London: University of California Press, pp. 65-77.

A reprint of Richards's 1970 essay. See entry 806.

1018   Rose, Brian Geoffrey. "An Examination of Narrative Structure in Four Films of Frank Capra." Ph.D. dissertation, University of Wisconsin, Madison, 233 pp.

Proposing that *Mr. Deeds Goes to Town*, *Mr. Smith Goes to Washington*, *Meet John Doe*, and *It's a Wonderful Life* together form a "natural narrative unit," Rose closely analyzes the structure of all four films, comparing and contrasting specific aspects of their narrative design. In doing so he seeks to pinpoint the specific narrative causes of thematic problems attributed to the later films by culturally oriented critics. He finds in *Mr. Deeds* a perfectly balanced conflict between protagonist and antagonist, culminating in a climax whereby all principal issues are resolved in favor of the community values the hero (and Capra) extols. Rose sees this form as ideal for the presentation of Capra's thematic concerns and argues that the next three films, although greatly indebted to the *Deeds* model, deviate from it in ways that result in dramatic impasse and structural collapse. In *Mr. Smith Goes to Washington*, for example, the increased powers of the antagonist within a drama of expanded political scope and conflict cause a structural imbalance the ending cannot wholly resolve. In *Meet John Doe* irresolution is exacerbated by a villain of even greater power and a hero of diminished authority and strength. Capra reduces the scope of the conflict and restores the power of the protagonist in *It's a Wonderful Life*, but an exclusive focus on a hero of unsettling contradictions and disruptive impulses results in a narrative so imbalanced that resolution can only be effected through the unconvincing device of a deus ex machina. Prefacing Rose's dissection of the four films is a section on methodology in which he drafts a system for formal narrative analysis derived in part from the writings of Victor Shklovsky, Boris Tomashevsky, Vladimir Propp, and Claude Brémond. This dissertation was published by the Arno Press in 1980 (see entry 1130). Also see Rose's 1977 article on *It's a Wonderful Life* (entry 1060).

1019   Thomas, Kevin. "1926 Classic Still Tickles." *Los Angeles Times* (21 July), sec. 4, p. 14.

A review of <u>The Strong Man</u>, screened as part of a "Mirth of a Nation" retrospective at the Los Angeles County Museum of Art. The silent comedy classic marks "the full-fledged directorial debut of one of Hollywood's greats, Frank Capra."

1020   Thomson, David. "Frank Capra," in his <u>A Biographical Dictionary of Film</u>. New York: William Morrow & Co., pp. 75-76.
Thomson attacks Capra's work after 1936 as politically dangerous and artistically stunted. "His politics have the rosy, witless complacency that might turn to authoritarianism when put under pressure. . . . The little man's paranoia prompts his first depiction of a rotten world; but his instinct for sentimental bigotry always pretends that the rottenness can be neatly excised. The inability to understand that our flaws are organic is a crucial failure of artistic intelligence, very close to the damaging simplicity of Chaplin's vision." Thomson contrasts the post-1936 work with Capra's earlier films at Columbia, which he finds lively and sexually alert. A filmography is included.

1021   Watz, Edward. "<u>The Strong Man</u>." <u>Classic Film Collector</u>, 50 (Spring), 46-47.
A reassessment of the film. Watz describes the relationship between Capra and Langdon as one "more of coach and comedy creator than that of director and star." Watz finds much of Langdon's performance hilarious, but considers the plot to be mawkish and the last-minute heroics demanded by Capra to exceed the limitations of Langdon's personality.

1022   _____. "<u>Long Pants</u> and a Pair of Shorts." <u>Classic Film Collector</u>, 52 (Fall), 47-48.
Background information on <u>Long Pants</u>, and a plot synopsis of the film. Watz finds the plot development weak but Langdon's performance superbly controlled.

1977

1023   Agee, James. "Comedy's Greatest Era." <u>Awake in the Dark</u>. Edited by David Denby. New York: Vintage Books, pp. 23-48.
A reprint of Agee's 1949 essay. See entry 626.

1024   Amoruso, Mario A. "<u>It's a Wonderful Life</u>—It's a Wonderful Movie." <u>Grand Illusions</u> (Publication of the Emerson College Film Society), 1, No. 1 (February), 6-7.
An overview of Capra's career and a critique of the film. "Out of all Capra's films, <u>It's a Wonderful Life</u> expresses his prevalent theme of individual triumph in a more personal and localized scope. . . . Due to its smaller premise it could more easily be related to the viewers' own conflicts and situations."

1025   _____. "Retrospect: <u>Mr. Deeds Goes to Town</u>." <u>Grand Illusions</u> (Publication of the Emerson College Film Society), 2, No. 1 (Winter), 36-37.

A brief discussion of Capra's career in general and of Mr. Deeds Goes to Town in particular. Capra is described as the filmmaker of the people, paying tribute to the dignity of the common man and giving people hope in the heart of the depression. Mr. Deeds is considered the first film in which Capra fully realized his goals as a filmmaker.

1026 Bernds, Edward. "Cross Fire on the Director-Writer Front." Los Angeles Times Calendar (10 July), p. 11.

A letter from Capra's sound engineer at Columbia in response to the Capra-Rintels controversy (see entries 1057, 1058, and 1192). Bernds reports that Capra's contribution to many of the scripts for which Riskin got credit was sufficient to warrant joint screenplay credit by current Writers Guild rules, and that the two worked well together and respected and liked each other. Moreover, he finds Capra's heated self-defense justified: "It's small-minded to attempt to diminish Capra by pitting Riskin against him. From what I saw of Riskin in those great days at Columbia, I don't think he'd approve of it." Bernds also refutes Rintels's contention that Capra's pre-Riskin work was minor, noting that several were hit pictures of their time.

1027 Black, Louis. "Meet John Doe." CinemaTexas Program Notes, 13, No. 2 (24 October), 71-78.

Black provides background information on Meet John Doe, briefly discusses the limitations placed on Capra criticism by the director's explanations and clarifications of his work, and offers a tentative ideological reading of the film. In this last section Black proposes that the intended message of the film is undercut by its depiction of injustice and the Colonel's compelling attack on populism and the American dream. Detailed credits, a bibliography, and a filmography are included.

1028 Bohn, Thomas William. An Historical and Descriptive Analysis of the "Why We Fight" Series. New York: Arno Press, 258 pp.

Publication of Bohn's 1968 Ph.D. dissertation. See entry 786.

1029 Byron, Stuart, and Elisabeth Weis. Movie Comedy. New York: Grossman Publishers, pp. 42, 78.

In an introduction to 1930s comedy, the authors briefly relate Capra's screwball comedies to his work overall; screwball characters, they propose, serve as mouthpieces for Capra's special brand of optimistic populism. In a later section on contemporary trends in comedy, You Can't Take It with You is cited as the archetype for modern films celebrating eccentricity.

1030 Connor, Edward. "Print Report." Thousand Eyes Magazine, 2, No. 7 (March), 12.

A detailed account of the differences between the original version of Lost Horizon released in 1937 and the edited version, Lost Horizon of Shangri-La, released in 1942. Also see entry 763.

1031   Everson, William K. *Claudette Colbert*. New York: Pyramid Publications, pp. 37-38, 71-80.
    Early in this monograph, Everson speculates that *For the Love of Mike* may not have been as mediocre as Capra and Colbert both claim. Later he provides a concise history of the making of *It Happened One Night* and its subsequent influence. He credits Capra with giving this otherwise conventional project a special charm and attributes the great popular success of the film to its rural as well as metropolitan appeal and to a felicitous choice of title.

1032   Flaherty, Joe. "Jimmy Carter: John Doe Born Again." *Soho Weekly News* (3 February), pp. 8-9.
    Flaherty proposes that the 1976 presidential campaign of Jimmy Carter parallels with chilling accuracy the plot of Capra's *Meet John Doe*, and that by imagining a darker ending to the 1941 movie the current government of avowed populists surrounded by moneybrokers can be fully understood.

1033   Frank, Sam. "Lost Footage of 'Lost Horizon.'" *Los Angeles Times* (25 February), sec. 4, p. 13.
    A report on the efforts of the AFI to restore *Lost Horizon* to its original length, a survey of the various versions that have appeared over the years, and a brief assessment of the film as a "fantasy classic."

1034   Gassner, John, and Dudley Nichols, eds. *Twenty Best Film Plays*. Garden City, N.Y.: Doubleday, Doran, & Co., pp. 2-59.
    A reprint of Gassner and Nichols's 1943 anthology (see entry 502), including a version of Robert Riskin's screenplay for *It Happened One Night* containing scenes deleted from the final version of the film.

1035   Gilliat, Penelope. "Langdon," in *Awake in the Dark*. Edited by David Denby. New York: Vintage, pp. 356-61.
    A reprint of Gilliat's 1971 article. See entry 834.

1036   _____. "Harry Langdon," in *Movie Comedy*. Edited by Stuart Byron and Elisabeth Weis. New York: Grossman Publishers, pp. 6-10.
    A reprint of Gilliat's 1971 essay. See entry 834.

*1037   Greico, David. "Frank Capra conferenziere smemorato." *L'Unita* (20 April).
    Cited in a bibliography compiled by the Bulgarska Nacional Filmoteka, Sofia, Bulgaria. See entry 1391.

1038   Handzo, Stephen. "Capra: Big Man on the Columbia Lot." *Thousand Eyes Magazine*, 2, No. 6 (February), 4-5, 24.
    A collection of program notes for *Dirigible*, *Platinum Blonde*, *American Madness*, *The Bitter Tea of General Yen*, *Lost Horizon*, and *Mr. Smith Goes to Washington*, and a useful supplement to Handzo's more detailed study of Capra's work from *Mr. Deeds Goes to Town*

through State of the Union (see entry 876). Of particular interest is Handzo's brief analysis of possible autobiographical elements in Mr. Smith, including Capra's early loss of his father and his later struggles to free himself of big-studio compromise.

1039 _____. "Columbia Pictures Presents." Thousand Eyes Magazine, 2, No. 6 (February), 3, 10.

In this overview of the history of Columbia Pictures during the sound era, Handzo suggests that although Capra did more than anyone else to establish dramatic comedy as the studio's specialty, the genre became a Columbia tradition transcending individual directors.

1040 Kay, Karyn. "Part Time Work of a Domestic Slave, or Putting the Screws to Screwball Comedy," in Women and Cinema: A Critical Anthology. Edited by Gerald Peary and Karyn Kay. New York: E.P. Dutton, pp. 311-23.

A reprint of Kay's 1975 article on screwball comedy, incorporating further commentary on It Happened One Night from a subsequent exchange with Leland Poague. See entries 977 and 1013.

1041 Kozarski, Richard. "Frank Capra, 1897-," in his Hollywood Directors: 1941-1976. London, Oxford, and New York: Oxford University Press, p. 82.

An introduction to a reprinting of Capra's 1946 essay, "Breaking Hollywood's 'Pattern of Sameness'" (see entry 1168). Kozarski briefly discusses Capra's loss of contact with his audience in the postwar period despite the optimism expressed in his article.

1042 Kreuger, Myles, ed. Souvenir Programs of Twelve Classic Movies, 1927-1941. New York: Dover Publications.

The original souvenir program for Lost Horizon is reprinted in this volume.

1043 Leach, Jim. "The Screwball Comedy," in Film Genre: Theory and Criticism. Edited by Barry K. Grant. Metuchen, N.J., and London: Scarecrow Press, pp. 75-89.

Leach argues that Capra's "populist comedies" are not truly "screwball comedies," but rather an offshoot of that tradition. "Capra takes the screwball formula and gives it a political twist by relating the process by which the screwball wins over an initially cynical partner to the process by which divisive forces of a corrupt society are ousted by the constructive ability of the screwball individual to realize the American ideal of a classless and egalitarian society." His endings are thus less tentative than in screwball comedy where openness to experience substitutes for a trust in norms or ideals. Placing the sexual conflicts of screwball comedy in a social context, Capra appears deeply ambivalent about this comic mode: "On the one hand, it represents an attractive freedom from inhibitions and reinforces the American distrust of European sophistication; on the other, it suggests irresponsibility and an alarming lack of social concern."

1044   Littlefield, Walt. "Capra for the Defense." Grand Illusions
        (Publication of the Emerson College Film Society), 1, No. 1
        (February), 6, 8.
        A brief analysis of Prelude to War as propaganda.

1045   Lowry, Ed. "The Battle of Britain." CinemaTexas Program
        Notes, 12, No. 2 (f April), 41-45, 49.
        Lowry ascribes the enduring appeal of the Why We Fight
series to the fact that its call to arms was geared to America's self-
image as a peace-loving nation, a paradox Capra had already captured
in fictional films where the hero embodies both a simple pragmatism
and a deeply felt idealism, and is slow to anger but ferocious when
stirred. Bibliography, filmography, and brief credits.

1046   McKee, G. "More Golden Oldies!" Film-Making, 14 (January),
        39.
        A report on a twenty-minute super-8 version of Mr. Deeds
Goes to Town available for rental in England.

1047   Maland, Charles J. American Visions: The Films of Chaplin,
        Ford, Capra, and Welles, 1936-1941. Dissertations on Film
        Series. New York: Arno Press, pp. 191-294.
        A reprint of Maland's 1975 dissertation. See entry 985.

1048   Mellen, Joan. Big Bad Wolves: Masculinity in the American
        Film. New York: Pantheon Books, pp. 23, 70, 97-111.
        Mellen links the role of the Capra hero in the 1930s to
social upheaval in depression America. "The Capra protagonist is
rarely domineering or overbearing. A homely down-to-earth everyman,
his appeal is to a down-and-out audience whose faith in America he
gently restores without belligerence or hostility." Discussions of It
Happened One Night, Mr. Deeds Goes to Town, Mr. Smith Goes to
Washington, and Meet John Doe follow, with particular emphasis placed
on the channeling of male initiative and aggression away from sexual
relationships toward heroic, individual action in the social sphere.

1049   Moberly, Michael. "Cross Fire on the Director Writer Front."
        Los Angeles Times Calendar, (10 July), p. 11.
        A letter in defense of Capra inspired by the Capra-Rintels
controversy (see entries 1057, 1058, and 1192). Noting that "Capra
has never been a modest man--nor need he be," Moberly credits Capra
with Harry Langdon's success (long before meeting Riskin), and with
bringing out the best work in writers Sidney Buchman, Myles Connolly,
and Albert Hackett and Frances Goodrich. "When a director works as
intimately on the scripting, shooting and editing as Capra did, and
the results (good or bad) always carry the unmistakable Capra look and
sound, then they are Capra films."

1050   Molitor, Douglas. "Directeur Theory--More Correspondence."
        Los Angeles Times Calendar, (26 June), p. 47.
        Responding to David Rintels's attack on the auteur theory
by way of questioning Capra's authorship of his films with Robert

Riskin (see entry 1057), the writer suggests that Rintels has selected a poor example in light of Capra's close collaboration on scripts, his background as a writer, and the consistency to be found throughout his work.

1051 Neale, Steve. "Propaganda." *Screen*, 18, No. 3 (Autumn), 20-25.

In this section of a longer essay on propaganda and cinema, Neale analyzes the way in which Populist ideology is inscribed within the "classical realist texts" of *Mr. Deeds Goes to Town* and *Mr. Smith Goes to Washington*, as well as *Ruggles of Red Gap* by Leo McCarey, and *The Prisoner of Shark Island* and *Young Mr. Lincoln* by John Ford. Building upon previous critical work by Jeffrey Richards (see entry 806) and *Cahiers du Cinéma* ("John Ford's *Young Mr. Lincoln*," *Cahiers du Cinéma*, No. 223, 1970), Neale proposes that the terms necessary for establishing a new social equilibrium at the end of Capra's films are explicitly drawn from historical figures important to the Populist tradition, and that contradictions in Populist ideology are made more manageable in comedies by Capra and McCarey than in *Young Mr. Lincoln*, where contradictions remain disturbing. A provocative analysis, marred by several factual errors about the films.

1052 Pechter, William S. "Frank Capra," in *Movie Comedy*. Edited by Stuart Byron and Elisabeth Weiss. New York: Grossman Publishers, pp. 63-70.

A reprint of his 1962 essay, "American Madness." See entry 759.

1053 Poague, Leland. "*As You Like It* and *It Happened One Night*: The Generic Pattern of Comedy." *Literature/Film Quarterly*, 5, No. 4 (Fall), 346-50.

Drawing heavily upon the genre theory of Northrop Frye, Poague proposes that *It Happened One Night* partakes of the conventions of traditional literary comedy. His specific point of reference is *As You Like It*; both works, he suggests, share a concern with the fate of comic lovers who, freed from the envy and self-centeredness associated with sophisticated urban environments, triumph in a productive relationship symbolized by marriage. Differences between the play and the film are traced by Poague to different resources of each medium; similarities are seen as analogous to "deep structures" of language, subject to varying transformational rules based on the different "surface structures" required of plays and films.

1054 Quart, Leonard. "Frank Capra and the Popular Front." *Cineaste*, 8, No. 1 (Summer), 4-7.

Quart traces the intersection of Capra's career in the middle and late 1930s with concerns of the political Left, as the latter moved away from sectarian militancy toward the broad democratic consensus of the Popular Front. Despite obvious differences in philosophy, Quart argues, Capra and the Popular Front shared a rhetoric and an imagery grounded in a new fusion of populism and nationalism; leftists critics were thus able to ignore Capra's commitment to petty bourgeois capitalism and enthusiastically embrace Capra for his social conscience.

1055 _____. "Mr. Smith Goes to Philadelphia: Capra and Stallone." Intellect, 106, No. 2391 (December), 245.
Quart proposes that scriptwriter-star Sylvester Stallone in Rocky has made a modern version of Capra's sentimental fables of the 1930s, featuring a hero who, if less intelligent, articulate, and pure than the Smith-Deeds-Doe archetype, is nevertheless an ordinary man who triumphs over cynicism and contempt.

1056 Rabinovitz, Lauren. "It's a Wonderful Life." CinemaTexas Program Notes, 13, No. 2 (31 October), 89-98.
Rabinovitz offers a detailed comparison of It's a Wonderful Life and Mark Twain's unfinished novel, The Mysterious Stranger, arguing that although the two works are similarly structured they move toward opposite conclusions. "Capra concludes . . . that even though it is a deterministic world populated with intrinsically evil men who cannot be vanquished (symbolized by Potter), one's own goodness, love and need for others can be their own reward." For Twain, on the other hand, "knowledge of the deterministic world does not strengthen the significance of man's moral acts, but rather shows up the ludicrousness of a social or spiritual morality." Detailed credits, a bibliography, and a filmography are included.

1057 Rintels, David W. "Someone's Been Sitting in His Chair." Los Angeles Times Calendar, (5 June), p. 42.
In the closing section of an attack on the auteur theory, Rintels illustrates his concern for the neglect of the Hollywood screenwriter by discussing Capra's collaboration with Robert Riskin. Rintels claims that because critics in the 1930s and 1940s referred to the "small town point of view and/or warmly sentimental moments" in Riskin's scripts for Capra as "the Capra touch," the director came to believe he had indeed authored these moments and thus touted his style and vision to the press. Riskin, the story goes, one day responded by bringing Capra 120 pages of blank paper and saying, "Here, Frank, put a few of the famous touches on this." Yet today Capra is famous, while Riskin, a giant among screenwriters is not, a fate Rintels attributes to critics, film schools, French snobs, and the "final Capra touch" of a autobiography entitled The Name Above the Title. This article by Rintels (at the time the president of the Writers Guild of America, West) provoked a heated controversy, with Capra himself responding. (See entries 1058 and 1192).

1058 _____. "Someone Else's Guts--The Rintels Rebuttal." Los Angeles Times Calendar, (26 June), p. 12-13.
Responding to Capra's defense of his authorship of the films he directed (see entry 1192), Rintels asserts that until Capra met Robert Riskin he had directed B pictures to which no one paid any attention, and that after they split Capra only had three or four

commercial hits, two of which were based on smash Broadway plays. Moreover, all the writers Capra worked with did better films with other directors. That Capra and Riskin did their best work together suggests that their chemistry was special; perhaps (as writer Philip Dunne has proposed) Riskin's sharpness and acidity combined perfectly with Capra's schmaltz and treacle for a perfect blend. Rintels closes with an attack on Capra's long-standing desire for full credit, accusing him of "a mean defensive spirit which has made him belligerent." Certain that Capra's reputation is assured, Rintels expresses concern for Riskin's. (Also see entries 1057 and 1192).

1059   Rodowick, David. "Long Pants." CinemaTexas Program Notes, 12, No. 1 (3 March), 83-86.
        Rodowick focuses on Harry Langdon's persona and film career, relying heavily on Capra's account of their working relationship. A brief bibliography, credits, and filmographies for both Langdon and Capra are included.

1060   Rose, Brian. "It's a Wonderful Life: The Last Stand of the Capra Hero." Journal of Popular Film, 6, No. 2 (Spring), 156-68.
        This article is largely based on Rose's chapter on It's a Wonderful Life from his 1976 dissertation (see entry 1018), but he is more greatly concerned here with cultural explanations for the evolution of Capra's work. Rose proposes that the idealism, responsibility, and rustic charm of the Capra hero represented a nostalgic challenge to modern times in the 1930s, but that during the turbulent years surrounding World War II his battles became harder to fight and more difficult to accept. Hence, in It's a Wonderful Life George Bailey now must face opposing instincts within himself, and at the end of this unconvincing story Capra is left with little room to further explore his hero's role.

1061   Sayre, Nora. "Did Cooper and Stewart Have to Be So Stupid? New York Times (7 August), sec. 2, pp. 11-12.
        Investigating male roles in old movies, Sayre finds the Capra hero embodied by Gary Cooper and James Stewart to be particularly unflattering and disturbing. "Granted . . . that the rustic who triumphs over the treacheries of the city is an American favorite, the fact that Cooper and Stewart persisted as stars throughout the sophistications of the 1930s and 1940s seems quite amazing today. Probity and purity can be appreciated; these are men you can't bribe. But must they be so stupid?" Mr. Smith Goes to Washington is singled out for detailed discussion.

1062   Scherle, Victor, and William Turner Levy. The Films of Frank Capra. Secaucus, N.J.: Citadel Press, 278 pp.
        Neither a critical study nor a scholarly work, this book is an homage to Capra from the first page to the last. Tributes from various directors, writers, and actors, as well as Justice William O. Douglas and cinematographer Joseph Walker, are collected in the first section of the book. This is followed by a biographical sketch and

full credits and a plot synopsis for every Capra film, supplemented by recollections of people involved on each project. (Among these remarks, the periodic commentary of Columbia sound man Edward Bernds is the most informative.) The book is also replete with carefully annotated photographs, few of which have been previously published.

1063   Shiffrin, Bill. "Cross Fire on the Director-Writer Front." Los Angeles Times Calendar, (10 July), p. 11.

Responding to the Capra-Rintels controversy (see entries 1057, 1058, and 1192), Shiffrin criticizes Capra for not acknowledging the uncredited contribution of writer Myles Connolly to the scripts of Lost Horizon, Mr. Deeds Goes to Town, Meet John Doe, and A Hole in the Head. He proposes that Connolly was responsible for most of the homey philosophy that evolved into the Capra trademark. (Shiffrin was Myles Connolly's agent.)

1064   Winogura, Dale. "Directeur Theory--More Correspondence." Los Angeles Times Calendar, (26 June), p. 47.

Responding to David Rintels's questioning of Capra's authorship of films written for him by Robert Riskin (see entry 1057), Winogura suggests that in light of the mediocrity of Riskin's films without Capra "the possibility exists that Capra added something to them that made the works his own."

1065   Wood, Robin. "Ideology, Genre, Auteur." Film Comment, 13, No. 1 (January-February), 46-51.

In an effort to synthesize various critical methodologies, Wood proposes that Hollywood genres, usually treated discretely, can be seen as interlocking across a series of unresolvable tensions in American capitalist ideology, and that these tensions come to particular focus through the medium of the individual auteur, taking on aesthetic as well as sociological interest. He then offers a comparative analysis of It's a Wonderful Life and Shadow of a Doubt, finding in both films a disturbing influx of film noir into the world of small-town domestic comedy, and a similar ideological project based on the reaffirmation of family and small-town values. In the case of Capra's film, Wood concludes, that reaffirmation is precarious but convincing, while in the case of Hitchcock's, it is hollow, leaving a bitter taste.

1978

1066   Allen, Tom. "Revivals: Sequels of Summer." Village Voice (3 July), p. 42.

In a review of a Capra retrospective in New York, Allen notes that the difference between the comic genius of Ernst Lubitsch and Capra can perhaps be best discerned in Heaven Can Wait (Lubitsch) and It's a Wonderful Life (Capra): "the first defines his protagonist through an urbane devil and the second through a redneck angel."

1067   Anon. "Lost Capra Films Found, Restored, and Duplicated." Box Office, 113, No. 16 (24 July), NC4.

A report on a project undertaken by Kit Parker Films to locate, restore, and circulate prints of Capra films made between 1928 and 1930.

*1068 Anon. Review of Arsenic and Old Lace. Cinématographe, No. 40, p. 82.
Cited in the UCLA Theatre Arts Library card catalogue of film reviews.

1069 Belton, John. "James Stewart: Homegrown," in Close-Ups: The Movie Star Book. Edited by Danny Peary. New York: Workman Publishing, pp. 537-42.
Belton credits Capra with both shaping Stewart into a figure of popular mythology and demythologizing that image by playing up the actor's physical frailty and psychological vulnerability, tapping an underlying desperation and paranoia. These latter elements, he proposes, become an integral part of Stewart's screen persona, one that embodies all the contradictions of American culture and its ideals.

1070 Beylie, Claude. "Sur trois films de Capra." Écran, 71 (July), 5-7.
Despite Capra's celebrated reputation, Beylie proposes, he may in fact be a neglected director only now being rediscovered. In the past critics scoffed at his soothing optimism, his anachronistic conservatism, his heavy-handedness in comparison with McCarey, Cukor, or Hawks. But this Capra concealed another, one more profound and sincere, whose true register was romanticism, sustained through a sparkling, sculpted mise-en-scène. Capra made comedies, but ones infiltrated by purely tragic motifs. Beylie is led to this reassessment by a specific Positif number on Capra (December 1971), the publication in French of Capra's autobiography, and the recent revival of three films--The Miracle Woman, The Bitter Tea of General Yen, and State of the Union--each of which Beylie briefly discusses in terms of romantic themes. In the ideal cinematheque, he concludes, Capra would be placed somewhere between Frank Borzage and Douglas Sirk.

1071 Braudy, Leo, and Morris Dickstein. "Frank Capra," in Great Film Directors: A Critical Anthology. Edited by Leo Braudy and Morris Dickstein. New York: Oxford University Press, pp. 145-46.
In this introduction to a series of reprinted articles, the authors survey Capra's career, stressing his role as a social and political fabulist whose stories grew increasingly dark in the 1940s. The ideas expressed here are developed much more fully in a later essay by Dickstein (see entry 1122).

1072 Brown, Geoff. "It Happened One Night." Monthly Film Bulletin, 45, No. 529 (February), 33.
Credits, a synopsis, and commentary on the film. Brown notes that subsequent films by Capra develop elements presented in embryonic form here (the Capra-Riskin hero, the song session), but

prefers the "improvisational ease in intimate surroundings" of this film to the "extravagant set-pieces" of Capra's later work.

*1073   Colpart, G. "Frank Capra: Un rêveur éveillé." Téléciné, No. 228 (May), pp. 57-58.
Cited in Film Literature Index, 6.

1074   Cripps, Thomas. Black Film as Genre. Bloomington and London: Indiana University Press, pp. 108-14.
An analysis of The Negro Soldier in World War II. Capra's contribution is considered minor. For an expanded discussion of this film by Cripps and David Culbert, see entry 1104.

1075   Crowther, Bosley. "Lost Horizon," in his Re-run: 50 Memorable Films. New York: G.P. Putnam's & Son, pp. 36-50.
Crowther recalls the impact of Lost Horizon at the time of the film's release, attributing the appeal of Shangri-La to a widespread anxiety that no purely tranquil places were left in the world.

1076   Everson, William K. American Silent Film. New York: Oxford University Press, pp. 237, 276, 358-59.
Everson briefly discusses the Why We Fight series in terms of Hollywood documentary films, and attributes the success of Tramp, Tramp, Tramp, The Strong Man, and Long Pants to Capra's and Harry Edwards's ability to keep Harry Langdon from slipping into a tasteless infantilism. In an appendix on film scholarship, Everson also attacks Capra's autobiography for its gross inaccuracies, and for the egotism and vindictiveness it reveals, but nevertheless finds the book an evocative and accurate picture of how a director worked under varying conditions of power and freedom in Hollywood.

1077   _____. "Rediscovery." Films in Review, 29, No. 9 (November), 555-58.
A reassessment of Flight upon the discovery of a sound version of this early talkie. Everson finds the film much more interesting than available silent prints previously had suggested, noting that aeronautical sound effects create a rhythm for the film, and that the dialogue has a casual, naturalistic flavor. He suggests that Capra's treatment of political intervention in Nicaragua anticipates the unquestioning Americanism and skill at propaganda with which the director later became associated. He also proposes that Capra, like Robert Wise, became locked into safe projects once his career was established, but that he brought to his early films an enthusiasm and love of craft that resulted in some of his best and most personal work.

1078   Gehring, Wes D. "McCarey vs. Capra: A Guide to American Film Comedy of the '30s." Journal of Popular Film and Television, 7, No. 1:67-84.
Gehring divides American film comedy of the 1930s according to opposing archetypes: the "comic antihero" found in the films of Leo McCarey and the "cracker-barrel Yankee" found in the films of

Capra. Tracing the roots of the latter back to nineteenth-century American fiction, he sees Capra filling a void in this tradition after the death of Will Rogers. As defined by Gehring, the antihero has boundless leisure time, while the Yankee maintains a profession; the antihero is apolitical and nonintellectual, while the Yankee dispenses political wisdom; the antihero is frustrated by domestic life and often sexually dominated, while the Yankee is competent and sexually dominant; the antihero is a child figure, while the Yankee is a father or grandfather figure; the antihero is urban, while the Yankee is rural but able to bring provincial wisdom to the city. After the 1930s, Gehring proposes, the antihero emerged as the prevailing archetype, while Capra's Yankee receded from the national scene, but because McCarey's later work ironically came to resemble Capra's, critics mistakenly assume that the directors shared similar comic temperaments in the 1930s as well.

1079   Greene, Graham. "A Director of Genius: Four Reviews," in Great Film Directors: A Critical Anthology. Edited by Leo Braudy and Morris Dickstein. New York: Oxford University Press, pp. 147-52.
        Reprints of four reviews by Greene: Mr. Deeds Goes to Town (see entry 252), Lost Horizon (see entry 323), You Can't Take It with You (see entry 373), and Mr. Smith Goes to Washington (see entry 437).

1080   Handzo, Stephen. "Under Capracorn," in Great Film Directors: A Critical Anthology. Edited by Leo Braudy and Morris Dickstein. New York: Oxford University Press, pp. 160-72.
        A reprint of Handzo's 1972 essay. See entry 876.

1081   Hart, Nancy K. "Frank Capra," in Close-Up: The Hollywood Director. Edited by Jon Tuska. Metuchen, N.J.: Scarecrow Press, pp. 75-91.
        A mixture of critical commentary on Capra's career, a review of his autobiography, and an account of his visit to the University of Wisconsin at Madison. Under the guise of correcting the inaccuracies of the autobiography, Hart offers a reconstruction of this biographical material that is itself inaccurate. Several of the films also are misdescribed; in the case of The Younger Generation (a film she claims stands out in her mind), she repeats the severe inaccuracies to be found in the American Film Institute Catalogue. In general she finds the films to be dated dramatizations of the false optimism and platitudes of the New Deal: "the motion picture has matured, though, and today much of what Capra sought to convey in his films is relegated to the opium confined to the small screen." At one point she describes the style of the films as "stage-bound and garrulous." Later she notes that despite the films' ideological problems, "there is no denying that they are almost always interesting, and that they move." In short, contradictory and unreliable. A filmography by Maxine Fleckner is appended.

1082   Harvey, Stephen. "Jean Arthur: Passionate Primrose," in Close-Ups: The Movie Star Book. Edited by Danny Peary. New York: Workman Publishing, pp. 431-34.
Harvey considers the collaboration between Capra and Jean Arthur inspired: her astringency in Mr. Deeds Goes to Town and Mr. Smith Goes to Washington provides "a welcome antidote to Capra's patriotic treacle"; her relative sanity in You Can't Take It with You provides "a poignant center to the movie's aggressively playful spirit."

*1083   Hosman, H. "Frank Capra: En charmante patriot met een scherp oogvoor de Kassa." Skoop, 14 (November), 41-44.
Cited in Film Literature Index, 6.

1084   Lefèvre, Raymond. "Arsenic et vieilles dentelles [Arsenic and Old Lace]." La Revue du Cinéma/Image et Son, No. 330 (July/August), p. 128.
Noting that 1978 has marked the rediscovery of Capra's work in France, Lefèvre has high praise for Arsenic and Old Lace. The film is a model for its genre in its comic structure and interpretation, and its intelligent use of allusions to other movies.

1085   Maland, Charles. "Mr. Deeds and American Consensus." Film and History, 8, No. 1 (February), 9-13.
Noting that the cure for the depression offered by the hero in Mr. Deeds Goes to Town is benevolent leadership within the framework of capitalism, Maland argues that the film is a watershed work in the emergence of a new nationalism in the mid-1930s, not only reflecting the cultural values of the period, but helping to create a cultural consensus. In large part drawn from Maland's 1975 dissertation (see entry 985).

1086   Maltin, Leonard. "Harry Langdon," in his The Great Movie Comedians. New York: Crown Publishers, pp. 59-66.
Capra's version of his relationship with Langdon is included in Maltin's commentary here.

1087   Pechter, William S. "American Madness," in Great Film Directors: A Critical Anthology. Edited by Leo Braudy and Morris Dickstein, pp. 153-59.
A reprint of Pechter's 1962 essay. See entry 759.

1088   Pym, John. "Tramp, Tramp, Tramp." Monthly Film Bulletin, 45, No. 529 (February), 33-34.
Credits, a synopsis, and brief commentary on the film. Pym focuses on Langdon's comic persona and the variety and pace of the film's action which helps keep the pathos of Langdon at bay.

*1089   Rosar, William H. "Lost Horizon: An Account of the Composition of the Score." Film Music Notebook, 4.

A study of Dimitri Tiomkin's score for <u>Lost Horizon</u>. Cited in Rudy Behlmer's <u>America's Favorite Movies: Behind the Scenes</u> (New York: Frederick Ungar Publishing Co., 1982), p. 39.

1090 Sarris, Andrew. "Scratch DeMille: New Pillars in the Pantheon." <u>Village Voice</u> (3 July), p. 39.

Reevaluating his earlier ranking of American directors (see entries 764 and 792), Sarris indicates that Capra (along with Preston Sturges and Billy Wilder) might now be raised to top-line status in the pantheon. Sarris now considers <u>It's a Wonderful Life</u> to be an American masterpiece.

1091 _____. "The Sexy Comedy without the Sex." <u>American Film</u>, 3, No. 5 (March), 8-15.

In this essay on screwball comedy, Sarris notes: "Frank Capra tended to inflate the screwball comedy, first with populist vaudeville (in <u>It Happened One Night</u>) and then gradually with populist melodrama (in <u>Mr. Deeds Goes to Town</u>, <u>You Can't Take It with You</u>, and <u>Mr. Smith Goes to Washington</u>). Finally, by the time of <u>Meet John Doe</u> in 1941, the melodrama had completely engulfed the comedy."

*1092 Schmidt, Sanford Michael. "The Theme of Class Confrontation in Hollywood's Romantic Comedies, 1934-1942." Ph.D. dissertation, New York University.

This dissertation deals in part with a series of romantic comedies from the 1930s that maintained traditional values by reaffirming the dream of a classless society. <u>It Happened One Night</u>, is seen as the first of this series, and Capra's work from the period is examined as "the most notable example of Hollywood's attempt to provide Americans with an idealized view of their national character." (Cited in <u>Dissertation Abstracts Index</u>, October 1978.)

1093 Spoto, Donald. <u>Camerado: Hollywood and the American Man</u>. New York, and Scarborough, Ont.: Plume Books, pp. 5-11.

Spoto discusses Capra's ideal "democratic man" in <u>Mr. Deeds Goes to Town</u> and <u>Mr. Smith Goes to Washington</u>, proposing that a black-and-white portrait of male characters has a crippling effect on <u>Mr. Smith</u>. "Like the other arts, cinema doesn't lend itself especially well to the alternative functions of podium or pulpit, and in retrospect it seems [Capra] was trying to corner the market on a soft and maudlin chauvinism."

1094 Truffaut, François. "Frank Capra, the Healer," in his <u>The Films in My Life</u>. Translated by Leonard Mayhew. New York: Simon & Schuster, p. 69.

An English translation of Truffaut's 1975 book. See entry 997.

1979

*1095 Anon. "Frank Capra: Immigrant in sprookjesland." Film en Televise (Brussels), No. 270 (November), pp. 28-34.
Cited in the International Index to Film Periodicals, 1979.

1096 Anon. Review of Rain or Shine. Classic Images, No. 66 (November), pp. 62, 74.
A favorable reassessment of the film on the occasion of its nontheatrical release in 16mm by Kit Parker Films. The only fault found by the reviewer (who recalls seeing Rain or Shine when it was first released in 1930) is the length of Joe Cook's monologues.

1097 Anon. "The Talk of the Town." New Yorker, 54, No. 48 (15 January), 25-26.
A report on an annual party held in New York in conjunction with the holiday showing of It's a Wonderful Life on television. Also see entry 1135.

1098 Bergman, Andrew. "Frank Capra and Screwball Comedy, 1931-1941," in Film Theory and Criticism. 2d Ed. Edited by Gerald Mast and Marshall Cohen. New York and Oxford: Oxford University Press, pp. 761-77.
A reprint of the chapter on Capra from We're in the Money, 1971. See entry 816.

1099 Bohnenkamp, Dennis R., and Sam L. Grogg, eds. Frank Capra Study Guide. Washington, D.C.: American Film Institute, 31 pp.
A study guide designed to accompany a videotape of a seminar with Capra, part of the AFI's larger Dialogue on Film project. The pamphlet contains a short biography, a detailed filmography with complete credits, a bibliography, and a selection of study questions.

1100 Brown, Geoff. "Long Pants." Monthly Film Bulletin, 46, No. 543 (April), 82.
Credits, a synopsis, and brief commentary on the film. "The plot provides an early instance of Capra's fondness for pitting rural small-town virtues against big-city vice. In outline it is also well suited to Langdon's persona. . . . [But] Capra and his writers develop the plot incoherently, and it fails to provide sufficient support for the varying set-pieces."

1101 Browne, Nick. "The Politics of Narrative Form: Capra's Mr. Smith Goes to Washington." Wide Angle, 3, No. 3:4-11.
Browne investigates the relationship between political power and comic narrative form in Mr. Smith Goes to Washington, focusing on the function of "representation" within both the institutional structures of American politics and the cinematic structures of classical Hollywood filmmaking. Proposing that Smith's central mission in the film is to animate the dead letter of American political tradition by investing it with true speech within an encrusted legislative

apparatus. Browne carefully traces the hero's apprenticeship as a public speaker and links this trajectory to Smith's maturation within a romance plot resolving kinship ties. He interprets the climactic exchange between Smith and Paine as an Oedipal and Christian drama that allows Capra to bring together a self-validating configuration of comic form, Christian mythology, and American ideology. Capra's repeated use of this form, Browne concludes, and the increasing problems he confronts resolving it underscore the director's own assumption of the role of spokesman, and martyr, for a past political tradition within a contemporary media apparatus.

1102 Brownlow, Kevin. Hollywood Pioneers. New York: Alfred A. Knopf, p. 145.
A retelling of Capra's version of his work with Harry Langdon.

1103 Chapman, Ross, "The Craft of a Capra Film." Spectrum (SUNY, Buffalo) (27 April), pp. 7, 12.
Chapman locates the significance of Capra's work historically in the director's persistent belief that a film should be made by one man, and in his ability to provide an appealing populism and folksy humanism for an economically depressed nation. He considers Capra to have faltered in pulling away from the "black realism" of his villains, providing unlikely rescues for his protagonists. All in all, however, Capra's "artistry lies not in his message but in the craft with which he gives his message feeling and life."

1104 Cripps, Thomas, and David Culbert. "The Negro Soldier (1944): Film Propaganda in Black and White." American Quarterly, 31, No. 5 (Winter), 615-40.
A scholarly account of the complicated history of The Negro Soldier in World War II, and an assessment of its long-range impact on the use of film to promote racial tolerance in America. The authors conclude that, although the film officially was supervised by Capra under the aegis of his army film unit, his role in the making of the work was minor.

1105 Fell, John. "Frank Capra," in his A History of Films. New York: Holt, Rinehart & Winston, pp. 232-34.
According to Fell, Capra's forte as a director was humorous, sentimental drama, supportive of American ideals and aligned with New Deal aspirations and values. That the design of the films accommodated the needs of a particular decade, he notes, is suggested by the fact that Capra and Riskin were unable to resolve the drama in Meet John Doe. Partial filmography.

1106 Graham, Olive. "You Can't Take It with You." CinemaTexas Notes, 17, No. 2 (16 October), 17-21.
Noting that the film has been critically neglected in favor of other Capra films of the period, Graham offers a brief commentary on a variety of elements in the work, including the deemphasizing of the conventional Capra hero, the centrality of the relationship

between Grandpa Vanderhof and Kirby, Sr., and Capra's stock company of actors. Detailed filmography, bibliography, and credits.

1107 Katz, Ephraim. "Frank Capra," in his The Film Encyclopedia. New York: Thomas Y. Crowell Publishers, pp. 203-4.

A biographical survey and filmography. Katz's final assessment is that Capra's formula was appropriate for the depression era but proved too naive and sentimental for postwar audiences.

1108 Kittredge, William, and Steven M. Krauzer. "Night Bus (It Happened One Night)," in Stories into Film. Edited by William Kittredge and Steven M. Krauzer. New York, Hagerston, San Francisco, and London: Harper Colophon Books, pp. 32-34.

In an introduction to a reprint of the short story upon which It Happened One Night was based, the editors discuss the translation of the story into film and the impact of the movie version on depression audiences. They note the similarities between story and film and find Capra's direction on the whole cautious, but propose that the film is satisfying because it is a "fantasy cloaked in a finely wrought created reality, peopled by strong personalities, centering on people made plausible." Moreover, the decision to change the hero from high-class gadabout to a working reporter is typical of Capra in its "affirmation of the American myth of egalitarian democracy." Disputing the notion that the film is a screwball comedy, the authors link it instead with the "sophisticated light romances" of William Powell-Myrna Loy and Fred Astaire-Ginger Rogers.

1109 McCarthy, Todd. "AFI Screens Results--So Far--of Search for Lost 'Horizon' Scenes." Daily Variety (22 October), pp. 4, 9.

On the occasion of the presentation of a restored version of Lost Horizon at Mann's Chinese Theatre in Hollywood, McCarthy outlines current efforts to completely reassemble the 1937 print, and the severe problems archivists have encountered. Included is a brief summary of major changes made in the film for its 1942 rerelease as Lost Horizon of Shangri-La.

1110 Mariani, John. "The Intelligent Heart." Film Comment, 15, No. 5 (September-October), 34-39.

Writing on sentiment in the movies, Mariani proposes that Capra is able to bring off a potentially cloying tale in It's a Wonderful Life by alternating visions of sentimentality with a troubling cynicism, of a Norman Rockwell America with one in which belief in traditional virtues "is constantly corrupted by the very money that sustains it." Rescued from near tragedy, George Bailey is not assured a happy life thereafter. "But, says Capra, at least Bailey has an epiphany--a moment of intense realization about life's basic values."

1111 Nugent, Frank S. Review of Mr. Smith Goes to Washington, in The New York Times at the Movies. Edited by Arleen Keylin and Christine Bent. New York: Arno Press, pp. 145-46.

Nugent's 1939 review is reprinted together with an advertisement for the film. See entry 420.

1112 Phelps, Glenn Alan. "The 'Populist' Films of Frank Capra." Journal of American Studies, 13, No. 3 (December), 377-92.

Phelps examines Mr. Deeds Goes to Town, Mr. Smith Goes to Washington, Meet John Doe, and It's a Wonderful Life in terms of current debate in political theory over pluralist and elitist explanations for the nature and distribution of power in America. Phelps challenges the notion that Capra's work is embued with an optimistic populism, arguing that the final victory of the Capra hero does not carry with it the kind of structural change needed to alter the powerful plutocracy Capra depicts throughout most of the films. But he concedes that a genuine populism perhaps surfaces in Capra's conviction that democracy will result when individuals become aware of their political responsibilities, and admits that Capra's "illogical" endings make more sense if we view the Capra hero as a model for this new democratic man in an America yet untested and unfulfilled.

1113 Rheuban, Joyce. "The Comedian as Metteur-en-scène: A Critical Analysis of the Silent Film Comedies of Harry Langdon." Ph.D. dissertation, New York University.

Rheuban argues that Langdon should be considered the author of his film comedies, not on the basis of their narrative values, for which Capra can be given credit, but rather on the basis of Langdon's consistent comic style and formal mise-en-scène, which can be traced back to his career in vaudeville. Rheuban's discussion of Capra figures most prominently in chapter 1, in which she offers a detailed critique of the conventional accounts of Langdon's film career, and in chapter 4, in which she analyzes Langdon's comic conception as elaborated in the mise-en-scène of specific film passages.

1114 Silver, Alain, and Elizabeth Ward, eds. Film Noir. Woodstock, N.Y.: Overlook Press, pp. 331-32.

In an appended article on the relationship between film noir and Hollywood genres, Capra's films are used to illustrate the impact of a bleak, noir sensibility on American comedy. Meet John Doe and Arsenic and Old Lace are specifically cited.

1115 Skagow, Michael. "Mythic-America Revisited." Los Angeles Herald-Examiner (7 December), pp. B1, 10.

Reassessing It's a Wonderful Life, Skagow argues that the appearance of an angel to rescue George Bailey does not simply signal a desperate belief in goodwill, but rather allows Capra to push dramatic conflict to its limits, capturing "the agony and frustration of a first encounter with accidental misfortune and injustice with an acuteness and authenticity missing from most of his other films." But Skagow also finds evidence in Capra's autobiography that behind the director's career resided neither a vision of America nor a personal code of behavior, but simply technical curiosity, ebullience, and drive. He proposes that where John Ford has a poetic style flowing from a unified vision, Capra uses a "pushy style to sell his content."

1116 Sloan, Kay. "It's a Wonderful Life." CinemaTexas Program Notes, 18, No. 1 (13 December), 7-13.

Strongly influenced by Robin Wood's 1977 essay, "Ideology, Genre, Auteur" (see entry 1065), Sloan's discussion focuses on the integration of film noir styles and themes into small-town comedy, and the ideological implications of this interplay between varying genre elements in It's a Wonderful Life. Detailed credits, bibliography, and filmography are included.

1117 Steele, Richard W. "'The Greatest Gangster Movie Ever Made': Prelude to War." Prologue: The Journal of the National Archive, 11, No. 4 (Winter), 221-35.

Steele first traces the prehistories of the Office of War Information (a civilian agency) and the Armed Services' Morale Branch during World War II. He then discusses Capra's assignment to the Why We Fight series and analyzes Prelude to War in terms of official attitudes and popular prejudices toward American foreign policy. Steele attributes the film's failure to deal with the Nazi racial policy toward Jews to a general concern not to antagonize Americans with similar racial attitudes. He also sees the film's focal concern with the apathy of ordinary citizens as a calculated attack on isolationist sentiment in America, with long-range implications for postwar foreign policy. He thus finds it unsurprising that Prelude to War eventually was shown to the public, despite opposition from the OWI. Based on studies made at the time, however, Steele questions whether the film functioned as effective propaganda. Very thorough and well documented.

1118 Tibbetts, John. "The Wisdom of the Serpent: Frauds and Miracles in Frank Capra's The Miracle Woman." Journal of Popular Film and Television, 7, No. 3:293-309.

Tibbetts analyzes The Miracle Woman in terms of the popular tradition of the huckster-evangelist in America and the special appeal of salvation-on-earth messages for depression audiences. He sees Florence Fallon's ambiguous blend of fraud and sincerity as a measure of the public's confused response to popular evangelists of the period, most notably Aimee Semple McPherson. He links Fallon's romantic redemption to the conventional notion that female activism was rooted in sexual frustration, and Fallon's gospel of hope cloaked in theatrical spectacle to the inspirational political rhetoric of the period. Ten years later in Meet John Doe, Tibbetts notes, Capra places this thematic material in an overtly political arena. Well documented with respect to the role of theatrical evangelism in American life and entertainment.

1980

1119 Anon. "Frank Capra Given Masquers' Tribute as 'Great Director.'" Daily Variety (3 March), p. 3.

A report on a tribute given to Capra at which a series of testimonials are presented. Hal Kanter describes Capra as "the second Italian to have discovered America." Rouben Mamoulian recalls recognizing Capra's directorial talent during the late 1920s and characterizes Capra's work as bearing a "bright, humane radiance" and

1126   Karr, Lawrence F. "The American Film Institute and the Library of Congress." <u>Quarterly Journal of the Library of Congress</u>, 37, Nos. 3-4 (Summer/Fall), 358-59.
   Karr describes efforts to restore <u>Lost Horizon</u>, a project undertaken by the American Film Institute in 1973.

1127   Kupferberg, Audrey F. "Films from the Archives." <u>Preview</u> (Washington, D.C.), 1, No. 12 (April), 22-23.
   Background information on efforts to restore five Capra films made in 1928: <u>So This Is Love</u>, <u>Way of the Strong</u>, <u>Submarine</u>, <u>That Certain Thing</u>, <u>Power of the Press</u>, and <u>Say It with Sables</u>. Brief synopses and credits are given.

1128   Maland, Charles J. <u>Frank Capra</u>. Boston: Twayne Publishers, 218 pp.
   A useful introduction to Capra's work for general readers. Of primary concern to Maland in this chronological study is the relationship of Capra's films to cultural changes in America between the 1920s and the 1950s, but he skillfully integrates this line of inquiry with biographical material and a close reading of specific works. The first three chapters ("Backing into Movies," "Learning the Craft," and "Making It") cover Capra's career through 1935, focusing on the highs and lows of his experience as an ambitious immigrant, his gradual mastery of film form, and the emergence of those elements associated with the "social vision" of his major period to follow. Drawing in part on his previous writing on Capra (see entry 985), Maland discusses the films between 1936 and 1941 in terms of broader efforts to refashion a national cultural mythology, linking Capra's "ecumenical church of humanism" to a revival of the notion of America as a sacred land, and discerning in <u>Meet John Doe</u> Capra's self-doubt about his own role as national mythmaker. Maland then traces Capra's involvement in wartime documentaries for the government, his return to Hollywood, and his waning fortunes after 1947, a decline Maland attributes to Capra's tempering of his depiction of domestic tycoons in response to the cold war and the new prosperity. The centerpiece of this section, however, is a chapter devoted to <u>It's a Wonderful Life</u>, analyzed from stylistic, cultural, and autobiographical perspectives. Maland sees the film as Capra's culminating work, one that powerfully crystallizes Capra's obsession with the competing values of personal achievement and social commitment, a conflict that in turn has deep roots in American culture. In his conclusion, Maland briefly discusses Capra's style in terms of directorial effacement in classical Hollywood cinema and develops further the connections he has made between Capra's work and American literary traditions. A filmography and selected bibliography is included.

1129   Mitry, Jean. <u>Histoire du cinéma</u>. Vol. 5, <u>1940-1950</u>. Paris: Éditions Jean-Pierre Delarge, pp. 544-45.
   A synopsis of <u>Meet John Doe</u> and brief critical commentary on it. Mitry sees the film as marking the beginning of Capra's decline in spirit, a pseudocritique directed against "isms" rather than concrete facts which betrays a latent conformism.

1130   Rose, Brian Geoffrey. *An Examination of Narrative Structure in Four Films of Frank Capra.* New York: Arno Press, 233 pp.
        The publication of Rose's 1976 dissertation. See entry 1018.

1131   Sarris, Andrew. "Kurosawa in Capraland." *Village Voice* (27 August-2 September), p. 39.
        Noting the possible influence of Capra on Kurosawa's 1950 film, *Scandal*, Sarris suggests that Western audiences "may not yet have come to terms with the emotional masochism and spiritual grandeur of Frank Capra's masterpiece, *It's a Wonderful Life* (1946), a film that resembles *Scandal* in its wholehearted concern for self-respect."

1132   Stein, Elliot. "Frank Capra," in *Cinema: A Critical Dictionary.* Vol. 1. Edited by Richard Roud. New York: Viking Press, pp. 181-88.
        In evaluating Capra's work, Stein follows a pattern he first outlined in his 1972 review of Capra's autobiography (see entry 897), greatly favoring the early films for their energy, visual sophistication, and thematic range, and dismissing all the work after 1935. He has heightened his attack, however, on Capra's personality and politics. Opening with quotations from Irving Wallace on Capra's alleged racism and George Orwell on Christian demagoguery, Stein proceeds to construct an image of Capra as xenophobic Christian demagogue. As a bright college student Capra tinkers with bombs to burn people; as a director of silent comedies he spitefully vilifies the talented Harry Langdon; as a director in the 1930s he grows rich preaching the moral inferiority of the rich to the man on the street; by the time of *Mr. Deeds Goes to Town* a "quack benignity" has set in which prefigures the politics of the McCarthy and Nixon eras. There are factual errors in the background information Stein provides (ironic in light of Stein's chastising of Capra for mistakes in his autobiography), and his plot descriptions are occasionally inaccurate and frequently misleading.

1133   Walker, Marjorie. "*Lost Horizon* Returns--SRO." *Hollywood Studio Magazine*, 13, No. 9 (March), 6-7, 21.
        A feature article on the presentation of a restored version of *Lost Horizon* at Mann's Chinese Theatre in October 1979 and on the efforts of the AFI to locate and assemble missing footage from the 1937 version.

1134   Weales, Gerald. "Frank Capra against the Sandinists." *Nation*, 230 No. 6 (16 February), 184-87.
        Weales analyzes the depiction of the first Nicaraguan Sandinist rebellion in *Flight*, proposing that "the ideological implications and the historical situation in the film provide an eccentric backdrop to an ugly civil war around which Washington tiptoed in search of a safe spot to shelter American interests." The treatment of the rebellion in the American press of the period is also discussed.

1141   Gerster, Patrick. "The Ideological Project of <u>Mr. Deeds Goes to Town</u>." <u>Film Criticism</u>, 5, No. 2 (Winter), 35-48.

Situating Capra's "social-message" films within a broader cultural effort to repair national mythology at a time of great social stress, Gerster analyzes the "ideological deep structure" of <u>Mr. Deeds Goes to Town</u>. He uses as an interpretive frame Van Wyck Brooks's observation that cultural thought in America often establishes an opposition between two discrete character types, "the poet" and the "man of the world." "Longfellow Deeds"--part poet, part man of action--mediates these roles, as the narrative trajectory of the film maps the integration of his "poetical" and "practical" selves. During the scene at Grant's Tomb (which Gerster examines closely), Deeds emerges as a Seer; then through his relationship with Babe Bennett, a marriage of opposites, full wisdom is made available to him. This is given public expression at the trial: when Deeds speaks, poetry and pragmatism are synthesized, and American ideals are renewed as plain common sense.

1142   Giannini, Louis. "The Individualist Mystique: The Cinema of Frank Capra," in his <u>Masters of the American Cinema</u>. Englewood Cliffs, N.J.: Prentice-Hall, pp. 141-62.

A biographical and critical survey. The biographical material is efficiently condensed from Capra's autobiography. The critical section synthesizes material from a variety of sources, with an emphasis on Richard Griffith (see entry 649), Jeffrey Richards (see entry 806), and Stephen Handzo (see entry 876). Giannini concurs with those commentators who see Capra's social movies as Populist, but resists the notion that this fully accounts for their appeal, noting that "the millions who thronged to Capra's Populist parables included many of the same millions who overwhelmingly supported the New Deal." Surveying Capra's working methods as a director, he briefly discusses Capra's flexibility with scripts; his emphasis on casting and acting; his unobtrusive camera style and skill with tempo and editing; and his reliance on the responses of preview audiences. He finds Capra weakest when working outside the comic range, where sentiment often turns maudlin, a vice afflicting directors of similar sensibilities such as D.W. Griffith and John Ford. He judges Capra to have had an incalculable influence, not only on American directors of his own day but also on the international "humanist cinema" of disparate filmmakers such as Ermanno Olmi, Milos Forman, Satyajit Ray, and Yasujiro Ozu. A bibliography is appended.

1143   Jameson, Richard T. "Stanwyck & Capra." <u>Film Comment</u>, 17, No. 2 (March-April), 37-39.

A reconsideration of the four films Capra made with Barbara Stanwyck between 1930 and 1932, with special attention to their first collaboration, <u>Ladies of Leisure</u>. In this film, where the heroine's earthly vitality is exchanged for abstract transcendence, Jameson detects Capra's closest confrontation with "the sinister contradictions in the visionary posture he and his heroes habitually adopt." While in later films suicidal desperation leads to the spiritual rejuvenation of a male protagonist, here the protagonist is female;

while later Capra will identify with Gary Cooper or James Stewart, here "he projects his lethally loving fascination onto a luminous Other." Jameson also traces this pattern through The Miracle Woman, Forbidden, and The Bitter Tea of General Yen.

1144   Karp, Walter. "The Patriotism of Frank Capra." Esquire, 95, No. 2 (February), 33-35.
        Karp discusses the nature of Capra's patriotism, focusing on the controversy aroused by Mr. Smith Goes to Washington in 1939 and incorporating a recent interview with the director. He argues that Capra's devotion to America was not that of the flagwaver, schoolmarm, or public official, but instead followed from an immigrant's love of freedom and rejection of the stifling fatalism of his peasant background. Indifferent to the politics of the New Deal, Capra was nevertheless fascinated by the faith Americans displayed when faced with the depression. In the best tradition of American politics, he was willing to tell a dark truth about corruption in high political places, and while authorities attacked him, audiences cheered. But Capra lost faith himself after witnessing the brutality of World War II, a brutality Americans shared in, and his career as patriotic filmmaker went into eclipse. Also see entry 1307.

1145   McCarthy, Todd. "Weekend with Frank Capra Proves Full of Surprises." Daily Variety (10 March), pp. 6, 22.
        A report on a weekend tribute to Capra at Indian Wells, California, sponsored by the Directors Guild of America. Reminiscing about the early years of his long collaboration with Capra, cinematographer Joseph Walker recounts that he was displeased at being assigned to Capra's first film at Columbia in 1928, but had a change of heart when he saw the touches Capra put in the film. For Capra's remarks on the occasion, see entry 1308.

1146   _____. "Capra, Walker Star at Directors Guild Weekend." Variety (18 March), p. 84.
        A reprint of McCarthy's article from Daily Variety on 10 March. See entry 1145.

1147   Phelps, Glenn A. "Frank Capra and the Political Hero: A New Reading of Meet John Doe." Film Criticism, 5, No. 2 (Winter), 49-57.
        Challenging the notion that Capra's heroes serve as spokesmen for petit bourgeois political philosophy, Phelps analyzes Meet John Doe in terms of the protagonist's transformation within a complex moral matrix. Phelps delineates three ideological focal points--Norton's secular materialism, Doc Mitchell's Christian communalism, and the Colonel's asocial individualism--and traces Willoughby's evolution from a figure of ideological and moral uncertainty into John Doe, bearer of Doc Mitchell's message. Phelps cites three epiphanies marking this process: first, John speaks over the radio, reciting "The Word" passed down from Doc Mitchell through Ann; second, he learns from the Millville Club members that his leadership is necessary; third, he is kept from killing himself by the notion that mass

action rather than personal heroism is the only hope for a reformed society. This promise of a new America, Phelps concludes, owes little to nineteenth-century agrarianism or turn-of-the-century populism; rather a radical Christian communalism is espoused, even as the beliefs and powers threatening the realization of that vision are acknowledged.

1148   Pogue, Leland. "Book Review." Film Criticism, 5, No. 2 (Winter), 70-74.

A review of Allen Estrin's 1980 monograph on Capra (see entry 1124). Poague commends Estrin for responding to two recurring problems in Capra criticism: how to define the shape of the canon, and the relationship of style to theme. By placing Capra's populist films within the context of the early works, Poague notes, Estrin is able to discern a thematic complexity that has often escaped critics who treat the later films in a vacuum. Poague also cites Estrin's attempts at linking theme to specific mise-en-scène and editing patterns, elements of style he feels have been handled in overly simple ways by previous critics, including himself (see entry 989). Poague disagrees, however, with Estrin's notion that Capra's editing is "undemocratic," proposing that the dominant impression of the montage passages is less one of manipulation than confession.

1149   Roffman, Peter, and Jim Purdy. The Hollywood Social Problem Film. Bloomington: Indiana University Press, pp. 48-50, 57, 98-102, 179-90, 268-73.

In a chapter entitled "Frank Capra's Super-Shysters and Little People," the authors discuss the dramatic structure and ideological import of Mr. Deeds Goes to Town, You Can't Take It with You, Mr. Smith Goes to Washington, and Meet John Doe. They attribute the emotional power of these films to Capra's skill at building the audience's own doubts into the structure of the plot whereby characters convert to just causes, and offer a detailed analysis of John Doe's first speech to illustrate the complexities of Capra's handling of political rhetoric. The limitation of Capra's work, they propose, is that emotional effectiveness is not matched by intellectual credibility; in the end Capra has nothing new to offer politically. They also trace the evolution of the Capra villain from the shyster lawyer through fascist dictator, and while they worry that the dependency of the little people on a charismatic leader defeats Capra's ostensibly antiauthoritarian message in Meet John Doe, they credit Capra with facing the specter of fascism head-on. In other sections of the book, American Madness, Mr. Deeds, and You Can't Take It with You are discussed in terms of the tendency of films in the 1930s to offer laissez-faire solutions to social problems, and It's a Wonderful Life in terms of the darkening view of the relationship of the individual to society in postwar cinema.

1150   Sarris, Andrew. "The One and Only Lady Eve." Village Voice (22-29 April), p. 43.

In this critical survey of Barbara Stanwyck's career, Sarris notes that with Capra the actress hit the "directorial jackpot" early on. "If Capra and Stanwyck had made an accomplished movie like The Miracle Woman at a major studio like Metro, they would have been immediately lionized. As it was, Capra had to wait for It Happened One Night in 1934 and Stanwyck for King Vidor's Stella Dallas in 1937, for the big breakthroughs."

1151   Schatz, Thomas. "The Screwball Comedy," in his Hollywood Genres: Formulas, Filmmaking, and the Studio System. New York: Random House, pp. 150-85.

Defining screwball comedy as romantic comedy in which sexual confrontation and courtship works through the socioeconomic conflicts of depression America, Schatz sees Capra and Riskin as establishing the basic terms of the genre in It Happened One Night. Later comedies of this type, including Capra's own Mr. Deeds Goes to Town, extend socioeconomic distinctions to the point where the kind of credible reconciliation of classes offered in It Happened One Night becomes strained. While the preoccupation with the depression diminishes in these comedies during the late 1930s and early 1940s, Capra moves in an opposite direction, growing increasingly obsessed with ideological conflicts. In a separate section on Capra and Riskin's work between 1934 and 1941, Schatz develops this notion, proposing that from Mr. Deeds onward they turned the strategy of using ideological disparities to motivate romantic conflict back on itself; now the lovers' attraction is used to investigate the values and beliefs that separate them. For reasons similar to those outlined by Stephen Handzo in 1972 (see entry 876), Schatz finds Mr. Smith Goes to Washington the most effective film in the political trilogy, more skillfully made than Mr. Deeds, less predictable and overstated than Meet John Doe. He also finds the crucial distinction between enlightened and unenlightened capitalism blurred in the last film, with Capra so adept at articulating the contradictions in American ideology that he can't resolve the problem. This signals the end of Capra's widespread popularity with the American mass audience.

1152   Self, Robert, and Lois Self. "Adaptation as Rhetorical Process: It Happened One Night and Mr. Deeds Goes to Town." Film Culture, 5, No. 2 (Winter), 58-69.

Contrasting each film with the short story from which it was adapted, the authors argue that the hierarchy of social relationships constructed by Capra and Riskin in each instance is similar. In It Happened One Night, a simple romance of two like-minded people is developed into a story of class conflict where the attractive male hero is made to seem the rightful manager of the heroine. These values are transposed in Mr. Deeds Goes to Town; cynicism and aggression is attributed to the heroine, a character who does not appear in the original story. But she too must subsume her identity under that of the hero, affirming the small-town virtues of Longfellow Deeds. In both cases, the authors contend, the complication and resolution of a romantic relationship serve as the key to the unraveling of all other plot tensions, including economic conflict. Public confessions by the heroine function ritualistically, reaffirming the middle-class values upheld by the hero and reinforcing normative sexual roles. Thus, while social commentary in Mr. Deeds has become more overt and self-conscious, the deep structure of social politics implied by the representation of sexual difference remains constant.

1153 Silverman, Kaja. "Male Subjectivity and the Celestial Suture: It's a Wonderful Life." Framework, No. 14 (Spring), pp. 16-22.

Drawing upon Louis Althusser's theory of the interpellation of the subject within ideology, Silverman analyzes the mechanisms through which a male subject is required to identify with a "weak" or "castrated" father in It's a Wonderful Life. The Oedipal drama informing mainstream Hollywood cinema, she proposes, here is challenged in that a male subject participates in the passivity and masochism usually associated with female subjects. The institutional support to effect this is Christianity: by means of a "celestial suture" between Bedford Falls and heaven, a paradigm is established aligning Joseph and Clarence in heaven with Peter and George Bailey on earth, all of whom are low mimetic versions of God, the symbolic father or Absolute Subject. Moreover, a transcendental point of view is aligned with the cinematic apparatus as Clarence witnesses through a celestial viewfinder the events of George's life. As the story unfolds, George resists identification with his economically castrated father, but is repeatedly "hailed" by others to renunciate personal desire and fill his father's position, thereby assuming the debts of others. It is only after the nightmare sequence that George learns to take pleasure in this renunciation; deprived of his past subjectivity, inserted into the narcissistic position of Potter (the figure of George's own repressed desire), he is terrorized and welcomes a return to weak paternity. Through Christian paradox, plenitude is then assured. The viewing-subject, Silverman concludes, is asked to identify both with George and the celestial viewfinder that inflicts pain and pleasure upon him. Like Clarence, we exercise no control over what that celestial gaze reveals; we expose ourselves to lack and insufficiency, confident of integration into celestial plenitude and sufficiency.

1154 Tone. "High Hopes: The Capra Years." Daily Variety (24 December).

A television documentary on Capra is favorably reviewed. The generous use of clips from Capra's celebrated films creates for the reviewer the sense of an hour well spent with old friends.

1155 Valenti, Peter. "The Theological Rhetoric of It's a Wonderful Life." Film Criticism, 5, No. 2 (Winter), 230-34.

Valenti locates the unique power of It's a Wonderful Life in the secular religious sentiments of the central characters and their interaction on behalf of one another and the community at large. Noting that the presence of a Heavenly Father (and a divine order) is evoked at the outset through a physical absence, he argues that while all subsequent events are understood as governed by God's agency, the drama unfolds in terms of secular generation—the family in time. Valenti illustrates this through a close analysis of the dining room scene between Peter Bailey and his son George. A hierarchy of paternal power is established, with Peter as God's emissary on earth, passing on a sacred trust to his son at a ritualistic Last Supper. But the specific elements of the exchange are secular: a building and loan company must be preserved to protect the people from Potter's exploitation. Thus Christian theology is linked to benevolently democratic capitalism. This process of secular generation, Valenti proposes, also informs the scene where Vi strolls before George, Ernie, and Bert at the taxicab; a comic acknowledgement of sexual desire skillfully opens the way for the sublimation of desire within the domestic sphere. In both scenes sublimated feelings are captured under a transcendent force.

1156   Wead, George, and George Lellis. <u>Film: Form and Function</u>. Boston: Houghton Mifflin Co. pp. 302-4.

    Brief commentary on Capra's collaboration with Robert Riskin, based on Philip Dunne's notion that their combined narrative voice consisted of a perfect blend of Capra's optimism and Riskin's cynicism (see entry 1058). <u>Mr. Deeds Goes to Town</u> and <u>Meet John Doe</u> are used to illustrate the complex tone that results.

1157   Wineapple, Brenda. "The Production of Character in <u>It's a Wonderful Life</u>." <u>Film Criticism</u>, 5, No. 2 (Winter), 4-11.

    Wineapple argues that by making the life history of George Bailey the subject of the film, <u>It's a Wonderful Life</u> points to the way character is defined within the structure of a classic Hollywood cinema. At first a "divine" voice-over commands the world we see, telling us where to look to construct George's character. But the camera eventually becomes an autonomous instrument of knowledge, subsuming Clarence's point of view, and the audience takes on the function of the voice-over, embracing the illusory power to interpret and organize the significance of events. This occurs only when George accepts the meaning of his life projected from above, one in which character is defined within a specific social and ideological system made to see the "natural" order of things. Confronting the horror of his own absence, George appropriates the role given to him within the community; at the same time he is invited to see that role as integral to the order of things. An illusion of individual uniqueness is thus affirmed, with no mediating force visible to rob George (or the audience) of a sense of mastery.

V. Writings by and Interviews with Frank Capra

ARTICLES AND BOOKS

1927

1158   "The Gag Man," in <u>Breaking into the Movies</u>. Edited by Charles Reed Jones. New York: Unicorn Press, pp. 164-71.

Capra describes the work of a gagman behind the scenes on comedies and dramatic films. He recommends the field to talented newcomers on the grounds that comedy specialists are in short supply, entry into the craft can be made simply by serving a probationary period, and advancement to the role of director or scenario writer--positions offering greater recognition and higher pay--is a natural step. Reprinted in 1976 (see entry 1190).

1931

1159   "The Cinematographer's Place in the Motion Picture Industry," in <u>Cinematographic Annual</u>. Vol. 2. Edited by Hal Hall. Hollywood: American Society of Cinematographers, pp. 13-14.

Defending the American cinematographer as a crucial contributor to the art of the motion picture, Capra enunciates an aesthetics of cinematography in which the look of the film is subordinate to the appeal of an engaging story. In the silent era, he proposes, the story was relatively unimportant, but today the success of a movie depends on a credible drama with characters who hold the audience's attention. "Reality is what is wanted, not symbolic touches and beautiful settings for mere beauty's sake." Thus "good photography merges itself in the atmosphere of the story. Photography that is not calling attention to itself is the finest photography." The same rule applies for directorial touches and the performance of the actors. Because American cameraman generally have eschewed "pictorial exploitation," Capra adds, they have not received the praise afforded their foreign counterparts; yet they are the finest in the world.

1934

1160 "Frank Capra Tells All." New York Times (16 December), p. 4.
Capra discusses his working methods: the care he devotes to preparing a script, the freedom he gives actors, his policy of previewing a film with a large audience before making a final cut, and his effort to achieve a simple film style. He also expresses concern that the public's appetite for big-name stars in the cast lessens the possibility of a film being a well-rounded production.

1936

1161 "A Sick Dog Tells Where It Hurts." Esquire, 5, No. 1 (January), 87, 130.
Capra argues that while film is the most magnificent medium of expression ever afforded artists, its growth has been severely stunted by the system established to manufacture and market it as a product. He proposes as remedies the divorcement of theater chains from the studios in favor of an open marketplace; the rejection of high salaries and long-term contracts by writers, actors, and directors in favor of a commitment to specific films based on their merit; and the rejection of censorship in favor of free expression. He places the blame for the state of affairs squarely on the shoulders of creative talent who have lost a sense of perspective in Hollywood's "pseudo-land." Directors, he argues, are in the best position to follow the example of Chaplin and Disney and lead films out of the "factory wilderness," but in most cases their hunger to do something worthwhile has been appeased by money. Concluding with a call for courage and artistic honesty, he notes ironically that he himself has recently signed a long-term contract. (For Capra's reworking of this theme ten years later, see entry 1168.)

1162 "Mr. Capra (Humanist) Shares a Bow." New York Times (19 April), sec. 9, p. 4.
Capra draws a distinction between two schools of film directors: those who appeal to the audience intellectually, and those who appeal emotionally. Directors of the first school (Lubitsch, Von Stroheim, Mamoulian, Korda, and Howard) strive for effects and moods that call attention to the presence of the filmmaker. Those of the second school (Borzage, Cukor, Ford, LeRoy, Van Dyke, and himself) efface themselves in favor of the actor and seek to make the audience forget they are watching a movie.

1163 "Sacred Cows to the Slaughter." Stage, 13, No. 10 (July), 40-41.
Capra attributes his success as director since Lady for a Day to his willingness to break rules in Hollywood, and notes that his current project, Lost Horizon, has stirred the greatest controversy of all. Plot in novels, plays, and movies, he explains, is unimportant; he is most interested in characterization. In selecting a story and making a picture, he abides by three rules: the story must have

charm; the characters must be interesting and human; the actors must be similar to the characters they portray.

1939

1164   "Ce sont les films qui font les stars." Cinémonde (4 January).
     Capra proposes that while a good film can make a star, a star can never save a bad film. Stars are simply the natural consequence of the combined effort of all sectors of the studio working to shape a good film. A prerequisite for stardom is proper casting: actors should be given roles where they can be "themselves" on the screen, for the camera possesses an infallible gaze, and a natural attitude, when compared to laborious pantomime, is like pure gold compared to unpolished dross. The performances of Gary Cooper in Mr. Deeds Goes to Town, Clark Gable in It Happened One Night, and Ronald Colman in Lost Horizon confirm Capra's theory that the success of his films has much to do with the fact that they are perfectly cast. Every actor attains his summit when he is able to express himself in a character who resembles him like a brother. But in attempting to discern what goes into the making of a successful film, Capra cautions, it must be remembered that cinema has not yet produced a work to rival that of genius in other art forms. Cinema is not mature enough for us to be able to establish artistic standards similar to those that exist in literature and the other arts. Moreover, the collaborative nature of the medium makes it difficult to effectively criticize a film. So we must content ourselves with empirical signs of success. A director should find a good subject, cast it well, and permit the actors to be themselves. Glory will naturally fall on the shoulders of the stars, but it is the film that makes the star, not the star that makes the film. This essay was reprinted in 1946 (see entry 1167) and 1949 (see entry 1171). An English translation by Charles Wolfe was published in Focus (University of California, Santa Barbara), 2, No. 2 (June, 1982), 10-12.

1165   "By Post from Mr. Capra." New York Times (2 April), sec. 10, p. 4.
     Responding to an article in which the role of Hollywood directors in the filmmaking process had been depicted as primary, Capra complains that in fact studios sharply curtail directorial activities and describes the efforts of the Directors Guild to change this. Reprinted in 1975 (see entry 1187).

1166   "Just What Is the Capra Touch? Its Possessor Attempts to Explain." New York Herald Tribune (5 November).
     Capra outlines his working methods and attempts to define the "Capra touch--the knack of putting a slice of life on the screen." He hopes that his films reflect not himself but life, and that people recognize themselves in them. While conscious techniques are involved in making a film, they are difficult to describe, and he relies on instinct to make decisions at each stage of the process. In selecting material, he looks for believable, attractive characters and

situations that are familiar. In developing and focusing a story, a top writer is necessary. On the set, Capra becomes the audience, reacting to the actors as a viewer might in hopes of discovering the proper way to play the scene. Finally, the editing stage entails a rigorous selection and elimination of elements in order to construct the completed version.

1946

1167   "Ce sont les films qui font les stars," in <u>Anthologie du cinéma</u>. Edited by Marcel Lapierre. Paris: La Nouvelle Édition, pp. 333-36.
        A reprint of Capra's 1939 article. See entry 1164.

1168   "Breaking Hollywood's 'Pattern of Sameness.'" <u>New York Times Magazine</u> (5 May), pp. 18, 57.
        A continuation of Capra's argument, outlined ten years before (see entry 1161), against a mass-production system in Hollywood that fails to accommodate the creative side of filmmaking. He now is encouraged, however, by the sharp increase in independent production the postwar period has fostered. He predicts that audiences will soon detect a refreshing break with Hollywood's "pattern of sameness" as films marked by individual style and subject matter are produced. The path to quality films, he notes, also has been cleared by government action halting block booking; now all movies, whether produced by independents or major studios, will have to stand on their own merit in the marketplace. Reprinted in 1977 (see entry 1191).

1169   "Il faut un film avant de la commencer." <u>Cinémonde</u>, No. 621 (25 June).
        Addressing French readers, Capra discusses his working methods. He argues for the importance of a carefully composed screenplay, noting that it is only through the difficult labor of construction that an appearance of ease is born. He advises directors to make sure that actors do not overplay their roles, for only a "natural" performance touches the viewer and truly conveys the ideas of the author. Casting, moreover, must follow from the specific demands of the subject, and the impact of the supporting actors on the performance of the principals and the vitality of the setting cannot be overlooked. Acknowledging his great debt to Robert Riskin, Capra claims that they still consult each other about story problems. He proposes that character development is the most important element of a screenplay, followed by theme, and then plot. He concludes with an optimistic forecast for independent production in Hollywood; mass-produced films will soon be replaced by works on a variety of subjects, in a variety of styles, bearing the personal stamp of the individual creator. Reprinted in 1971 (see entry 1180).

1170   "We Should All Be Actors." <u>Silver Screen</u>, 16, No. 11 (September), 54, 85-86.
        Capra recommends dramatic training as an aid to any professional or social endeavor. "In this day of intensified training

and education and in this era of specialized skills, any one of a hundred men or women may be equally capable performing a given task or assignment. But the one person who gets the assignment is the one who can put his best foot forward. Acting can be your ace in the hole."

1949

1171   "Ce sont les films qui font les stars." Ciné-Club, Nos. 8-9 (May-June).
A reprint of Capra's 1939 article. See entry 1164.

1172   On Riding High. Los Angeles Mirror (5 September).
Capra describes the problems he faced attempting to get a rooster to crow during the shooting of Riding High. (Reprinted in The Name Above the Title, pp. 412-14.)

1961

1173   "Anything for a Laugh." Los Angeles Examiner (24 December).
An anecdote concerning a practical joke pulled on Mack Sennett by his writers at the Keystone Studio, and a brief discussion of Capra's own use of slapstick in Pocketful of Miracles.

1962

1174   "Do I Make You Laugh?" Films and Filming, 8, No. 12 (September), 14-15.
Although edited as an article authored by Capra, this appears to be an interview with comments by Capra stitched together. Topics include Harry Langdon's desire to direct his own films (a problem recurring with stars today); the imperiled hero on the screen and the imperiled individual in modern society; contemporary film production (independents, state subsidy, television, film schools); and the persistence and significance of comedy.

1969

1175   "Directors Still Dominate." Making Films, 3, No. 5 (October), 44.
Capra argues that the dominant figure in film production historically has been the director, but that during the 1950s the role of the director and producer was eclipsed by that of the star. Recent trends, however, suggest that the pendulum has slowly swung back, and before long talented new directors will receive the credit they deserve.

1971

1176   The Name Above the Title: An Autobiography. New York: Macmillan Co., 513 pp.
As Capra cautions in his preface, this autobiography is less a scholarly document than a dramatization of his life as he

recalls it. Capra casts himself as protagonist of an immigrant saga, struggling with poverty, power brokers, and titanic egos, including his own. Moments of euphoria are juxtaposed with those of despair, of hubris with those of humility. Successes are recounted with great pride; failures with varying mixtures of irony, anger, and guilt. The structure of the book is delineated by the title of its four sections: "Struggle for Success" (migration to America through receipt of an Academy Award nomination in 1933); "Struggle with Success" (the Oscar sweep of It Happened One Night through an attempt at independent production with Meet John Doe); "The Great Struggle" (self-doubts supplanted by the epic crisis of World War II); "An Entirely New Ball Game, With Entirely New Rules" (the hot-and-cold relationship with Hollywood during his last twenty years as a filmmaker). Capra's bitterness is most disturbing in the latter passages where, tending to wounds that are still fresh and facing premature retirement, he links the decline of his career to a collapse of a moral base in Hollywood and in society overall; the book at this point seems motivated by a desire to vent acute frustration. But, like a Capra hero, he is back on his feet at the end, summoned from the brink of despair when his life is put into perspective by the death of his brother, Ben, a man of no fame but many friends. This not only allows Capra to conclude on an inspirational note; it provides a certain closure to the book, as Ben's departure to America opened the immigrant saga at the outset. The Name Above the Title has been criticized for a lack of accuracy and equanimity, but Capra's decision to write with aggressive candor has likely resulted in a more revealing work. For a factual record and balanced appraisals of his colleagues and his films, one should turn to other sources. But as an account of a director's perception of his career in Hollywood, of the willfulness required to sustain a single project, let alone a career, of the strain placed on friendships and the unique kinds of friendships forged, this is a remarkably informative and compelling book. Translated into French in 1976 (see entry 1189).

1177 "Casting Couch Is Not Just a Bed of Roses." Los Angeles Times (30 May), pp. 14, 16.
An excerpt from chapter 23 of Capra's autobiography on the filming of Pocketful of Miracles.

1178 "The Name Above the Title." Action, 6, No. 3 (May-June), 5-11.
Two excerpts from Capra's autobiography are reprinted here: a description of several fellow film directors (pp. 244-48), and an account of his activities as president of the Directors Guild in 1939 (pp. 266-71).

1179 "Amère epoque et thé amer." Translated by Jeannine Ciment. Positif, No. 133 (December), pp. 11-21.
An excerpt from chapter 8 of Capra's autobiography, "Bitter Times and Bitter Tea."

Writings by and Interviews with Frank Capra 1973

1180   "Il faut un film avant de la commencer." Positif, No. 133 (December), pp. 22-24.
       A reprint of Capra's 1946 article. See entry 1169.

1972

1181   "Foreword" in The Man Who Invented Hollywood: The Autobiograpy of D.W. Griffith. Louisville, Ky.: Touchstone Publishing Co., pp. vii-xii.
       In this survey of Griffith's career, Capra emphasizes Griffith's struggle for artistic autonomy and eventual neglect by the Hollywood studio system his own work spawned. He credits Griffith with fashioning film as an art form and pioneering the "one man, one film" concept which Capra was later to adopt.

1182   On It Happened One Night. Yale Alumni Magazine (June), p. 16.
       An excerpt from a talk by Capra at Yale University in which he recounts the problems of casting Clark Gable in It Happened One Night.

1183   "Frank Capra on Movies." Saturday Evening Post, 244, No. 4 (Winter), 22-25, 100.
       Capra attributes declining movie attendance to the audience's boredom with depravity and violence on the screen. He is encouraged by a recent tour of universities and colleges where students have responded enthusiastically to his work and the values of heroism, love, and comic victory he sought to affirm in it. He argues against the reestablishment of government or industry censorship, trusting instead in the "natural censorship of the box office."

1973

1184   "Introduction" in Directors in Action: Selections from Action! The Official Magazine of the Directors Guild of America. Edited by Bob Thomas. Indianapolis and New York: Bobbs-Merrill Co., pp. vii-x.
       Capra briefly traces the history of the Directors Guild of America. He defines the special gift of the director as the ability to keep the development of a story clearly in mind even as the film is being shot out of sequence.

1185   "Introduction" in Light Your Torches and Pull Up Your Tights by Tay Garnett. New Rochelle, N.Y.: Arlington House, pp. 7-10.
       An introduction to Tay Garnett's autobiography. Capra praises the Irish for their wit and poetry, and surveys Garnett's career.

1186   On William Wellman. Action, 8, No. 2 (March-April), 36-37.
       An excerpt from Capra's introduction to William Wellman on the occasion of Wellman's receipt of the Directors Guild D.W. Griffith Award. Offering a brief summary of Wellman's career, Capra praises

his colleague's courage, complex passions, and fierce independence. Because Wellman had no independent production company to shield him from the "heavy-handed overlordship of many superegos," Capra considers his colleague's ability to make films his own way especially extraordinary.

1975

1187   "Directors without Power," in Frank Capra: The Man and His Films. Edited by Richard Glatzer and John Raeburn. Ann Arbor: University of Michigan Press, pp. 14-15.
A reprint of a 1939 letter by Capra to the New York Times. See entry 1165.

1188   "What Directors Are Saying." Action, 10, No. 2 (March-April), 23.
Capra's remarks to Richard Glatzer (see entry 1286) on filmmaking as a decision-making process are quoted.

*1189   Hollywood Story. Paris: Éditions Stock, 440 pp.
A French translation of Capra's autobiography. See entry 1176.

1190   "The Gag Man," in Hollywood Directors: 1914-1940. Edited by Richard Kozarski. London, Oxford, and New York: Oxford University Press, pp. 181-85.
A reprint of Capra's 1927 article. See entry 1158.

1977

1191   "Breaking Hollywood's 'Pattern of Sameness,'" in Hollywood Directors: 1941-1976. Edited by Richard Kozarski. London, Oxford, and New York: Oxford University Press, pp. 83-89.
A reprint of Capra's 1946 article. See entry 1168.

1192   "'One Man, One Film'--The Capra Contention." Los Angeles Times, Calendar (26 June), p. 12.
Capra replies to an article in which David Rintels asserted that Robert Riskin was the creative source of the famous "Capra touch," and that Capra helped foster his screenwriter's unfortunate neglect (see entry 1057). Capra counters with a point-by-point summary of his collaboration and friendship with Riskin. He agrees that Riskin was, in Rintels's phrase, a "giant among screenwriters," but argues that Riskin's reputation was earned for his work with Capra instead of for his nine other scripts at Columbia, his one attempt at direction at Columbia, or his later independent productions. Moreover, Capra is uncertain whether the films he made with Riskin are necessarily his own best work; he favors It's a Wonderful Life and State of the Union, neither of which were scripted by Riskin. In any case, whatever original material Capra used, the final film "expressed dreams, hopes, and angst that came from my guts, for better or worse." Capra also denies the old story (recounted by Rintels) that Riskin

once handed him a sheaf of blank pages and advised him to try to put his famous Capra touch on it; Riskin was too much a gentleman for that, Capra claims. (For Rintels's response see entry 1058.)

1980

1193   "Frank Capra, Director," in Sound and the Cinema: The Coming of Sound to American Film. Edited by Evan William Cameron. Pleasantville, N.Y.: Redgrave Publishing Co., pp. 76-84.
   A transcript of a talk delivered at a symposium on sound held in Rochester, N.Y., in 1973. Capra relates his experiences at Columbia Pictures during the transitional period from silent film to talkies. He also discusses at length the crucial relationship between director and actor in the making of a film, one that must be based, he proposes, on "great trust and great love."

1194   "The Great Days of Hollywood Are Over." U.S. News and World Report, 89, No. 8 (25 August), 66.
   Capra discusses the current state of film and television, and offers some optimistic predictions for the future of these media. Noting that most people making movies in Hollywood today are solely interested in money, he predicts that simpler and smaller equipment will free new filmmakers to abandon Hollywood for small-scale location filmmaking around the country. Moreover, despite the cultural bias against movies in America, the medium's power to inspire and educate is recognized by many countries around the world. The interaction of film and television, a medium with far-reaching clout, may also result in new markets for movies and a flowering of moviemaking in the next decade. Capra attributes the decline in female stars to the emphasis on obscenity and nudity in recent films. He concludes with an assertion of faith in the future of America and in the principle of American freedom.

1195   Capra, Frank. "Unforgettable Jimmy Durante." Reader's Digest, 119, No. 715 (November), 115-20.
   Capra reminisces about Jimmy Durante, whose life story Capra learned while preparing an unrealized film on the performer in the late 1950s.

PUBLISHED INTERVIEWS

1931

1196   Babcock, Muriel. "'Best Performances' Just Player Being Self." Los Angeles Times (16 August), sec. 3, p. 13.
   Capra is cited as an exponent of a naturalistic style of acting. He describes his discovery of Barbara Stanwyck in Ladies of Leisure, and his current work on Gallagher (later to be retitled Platinum Blonde). Babcock notes that because Capra works at Columbia ("a small studio which turns out pictures rapidly at the least possible cost") he has not yet attracted the kind of attention afforded directors of similar talent.

1932

1197 Haid, Liane. "Wie man es austellen muss . . ." *Theatre Leben* (Germany), (March), p. 6.
    An interview with Capra who is on vacation in Europe. *Dirigible*, *Submarine*, and *Forbidden* are briefly discussed.

1198 Morris, Ruth. "Capra Forsees Satirical Cycle; Many Subjects Ripe for Ridicule." *Variety* (2 February), p. 2.
    According to this report, Capra predicts that a great comic film will soon emerge out of the depression. "Satirical treatment of a plutocrat, insanely trying to conserve wealth and finding happiness only when he is reduced to the breadline, will strike a responsive note in the mass mind. . . . The Man in the Street has had so many dogmas crammed down his throat that he is prepared to revolt against current underestimation of his intelligence. He's fed up. Politics, prohibition, patriotism, big business, highpowered advertising, are subjects ripe for ridicule." Moreover, small-scale dramas, shorn of theatricality and projecting a deep and true love, will also be popular. Turning to the question of authorship, Capra reportedly refutes the notion that the director is best equipped to direct his own story on the grounds that a director who authors his own film lacks judgment and perspective. (It is interesting to note here that Capra's most recent film, *Forbidden*, had been written by him.) Collaboration, however, should be limited to the writer and director and not spread to other sections of the studio. Finally, a recent trip to Europe has convinced Capra that British film producers are undercutting their ability to compete against American movies by basing their productions on West End stage shows that are "ingrown and emotionless" rather than "down to earth."

1933

1199 Freedman, Leo. "Frank Capra Thinks Audience Should Help Create Film Story." New York *Herald Tribune* (3 September).
    Interviewed in conjunction with the release of *Lady for a Day*, Capra speaks at length about the function of dialogue in movies. Instead of curtailing dialogue passages on the screen, as some critics have proposed, Capra favors using more dialogue, but of a different kind than found in novels and plays. Cinema, he argues, does not require that everything be translated into action: "The real action, the important action, is not what takes place on the screen, but what happens in the mind of the audience. . . . The imagination is a greater artist than either the writer or director." Consequently he and Robert Riskin have experimented with a different kind of dialogue in *Lady for a Day*, one aimed at stimulating the imagination and suggesting action that is never shown.

1934

1200 Anon. "A Film Director's Guiding Rule: He Seeks Actors Who Don't Act." New York *Herald Tribune* (25 November).

Interviewed about the role of acting in motion pictures, Capra stresses the necessity of a naturalistic style. Unlike theater, he proposes, where there are curtains and intermissions, in films the battle of the actor to hold the audience's interest is constant. "From the first frame to the last dissolve you must let nothing detract from the story."

1201 Creelman, Eileen. "Picture Plays and Players." New York Sun (13 September).

Capra briefly discusses The Bitter Tea of General Yen, Lady for a Day, and It Happened One Night, as well as his current work on Broadway Bill, now being edited. He also announces his desire to make a musical and a film on the Soviet Union.

1935

1202 Harrison, Paula. "The Master of the Human Touch." Motion Picture, 49 (July), 55, 76.

Capra is depicted in this interview as wearied by endless rags-to-riches stories about himself. But he becomes animated when asked to talk about the craft of film direction: how to make characters seem "real"; how to inject "life touches" into the drama.

1937

1203 Anon. "Capra Puts Films First, Stars Next." New York World-Telegram (25 September).

A report on Capra facing the French press in Paris. He is said to claim that in filmmaking the importance of the scenario is primary, that of the actors secondary, and that he has no intention of using color. He also observes that French films, unlike British, retain a national character and therefore are well received in America.

1938

1204 Creelman, Eileen. "Picture Plays and Players." New York Sun (6 October).

An interview with Capra concerning the postpreview editing of You Can't Take It with You, and his plans for Mr. Smith Goes to Washington. Lady for a Day, Creelman reports, is Capra's favorite film.

1205 Crowther, Bosley. "Such Guys as Capra and Wellman." New York Times (16 October), sec. 9, p. 5.

Interviewed by Crowther, Capra attacks the major Hollywood studios for stifling new ideas and blocking attempts at independent production, including his own.

1206 Daugherty, Frank. "He Has the Common Touch." Christian Science Monitor Weekly Magazine (9 November), p. 5.

1938

An interview with Capra and a career sketch by Daugherty. Capra expresses concern that Lost Horizon offered a solution to current problems that was too distant from home and claims to be more comfortable with the familiar setting of You Can't Take It with You. Other topics include altering the tone of satirical material to please wider audiences, the depth of American actors, the greater commitment of time involved when a director assumes full responsibility for the making of a film, and plans for Mr. Smith Goes to Washington.

1939

1207   Churchill, Douglas W. "Mr. Capra Girds (Mildly) at the Government." New York Times (14 May), sec. 10, p. 3.
Capra is interviewed concerning production plans for Mr. Smith Goes to Washington.

1208   Mok, Michael. "Mr. Capra Comes to Town." New York Post (24 October).
An interview with Capra in conjunction with the release of Mr. Smith Goes to Washington. Capra claims that luck is the most important element in making a film, and that the theme of Mr. Smith is that American democracy is indestructible no matter how severely it is buffeted. A biographical sketch by Mok is included.

1941

1209   Anon. "Capra Links 'Mr. Deeds,' 'Mr. Smith.'" Los Angeles Herald-Express (6 June), p. B1.
Testifying at a plagiarism suit filed against Columbia concerning the screenplay to Mr. Smith Goes to Washington, Capra reportedly claims that he was inspired to make the film by a one-page synopsis that reminded him of Mr. Deeds Goes to Town, and that he first wanted Gary Cooper to play the role of Mr. Smith, but Cooper was unavailable.

1210   Anon. "Work Is 'Fun' to Frank Capra." New York World-Telegram (1 March).
An interview with Capra prior to the release of Meet John Doe, centering on his collaboration with Robert Riskin and the "fun" Capra allegedly has on the set.

1211   Churchill, Douglas W. "Murder in Hollywood." New York Times (9 November), sec. 10, p. 5.
Production information on Arsenic and Old Lace is supplied by Capra in this interview. He also comments briefly on the film's lack of social significance ("With the world in its present state, what's the good of a message?"), and on his recent decision not to join United Artists as a partner.

1212   Coons, Robbin. "Capra Urges More Humor for Movies." Richmond News-Leader (20 November).

Writings by and Interviews with Frank Capra 1944

An interview with Capra, who claims he will be making Arsenic and Old Lace "just for laughs."

1213   Keller, Allan. "Capra Set for Poison Film." New York World-Telegram (6 September).
   Interviewed just prior to the shooting of Arsenic and Old Lace, Capra announces his intention not to preach a sermon but simply to have fun with the film. He also expresses resentment over the fact that Hitler has been said to count It Happened One Night among his favorite films, and declares his opposition to movie censorship.

1942

1214   Anon. "Signal Corps Calls Capra." New York Times (10 February), p. 24.
   Capra announces that, having completed work on Arsenic and Old Lace, he has now received word to report to the Signal Corps in Washington, D.C.

1215   Benedict, Paul. "Frank Capra's Secret!" Silver Screen, 12, No. 3 (January), 34-35, 75-77.
   The "secret" unearthed here is Capra's approach to acting. He discusses the importance of effacing the artistry of the camera in favor of the actors, of actors effacing their own art in favor of credible characters, or eliminating makeup, of correct casting, and of creating an atmosphere on the set ripe for improvisation. The plot of the film, Capra proposes, is far less important than "human touches." He also relates numerous anecdotes concerning stars with whom he has worked.

1943

1216   Anon. "War Movies Criticized." New York Times (26 September), sec. 1, p. 41.
   Interviewed in England, Capra is critical of Hollywood war movies, speculating that the people who made them are ignorant of the real situation. He reportedly considers Desert Victory and Report from the Aleutians the best war films.

*1217   Davidson, Bill. "They Fight with Film." Yank Magazine (5 March), p. 21.
   Capra is interviewed concerning the Why We Fight series. Cited by Thomas Bohn in An Historical and Descriptive Analysis of the "Why We Fight" Series (see entry 786), p. 118.

1944

*1218   Anon. Interview with Frank Capra. Salient, No. 3.
   Cited in Positif, No. 133 (December 1971), p. 75.

1945

1219   Pryor, Thomas M. "Mr. Capra Comes to Town." New York Times (18 November), sec. 2, p. 3.
Interviewed concerning his return to commercial filmmaking after a four-year absence for the war, Capra expresses concern about making the transition smoothly. He discusses his future projects, including the formation of Liberty Films as an independent production company and the filming of It's a Wonderful Life. He also predicts that the day of specialized audiences is coming, but worries that the structure of the industry will not accommodate the making of specialized films.

1946

1220   Brady, Thomas. "Unrest in Hollywood." New York Times (30 June), sec. 2, pp. 1, 3.
In this interview Capra complains about a lack of effort and enthusiasm in Hollywood at all levels of production, which has resulted in delays in the making of It's a Wonderful Life. He also discusses the financial arrangement behind Liberty Films.

1221   Muir, Florabel. "Florabel Muir Reports: Capra, Stewart Planning Sequel to Mr. Smith." Hollywood Citizen News (25 February).
Capra is interviewed about the formation of Liberty Films and his plans to make It's a Wonderful Life. Muir provides a brief career sketch.

1222   Schallert, Edwin. "Emotional Appeal Capra's Goal." Los Angeles Times (3 March), pp. 1, 3.
Capra discusses with Schallert his return to commercial filmmaking after the war and his plan to make "human interest" movies.

1947

1223   Norton, Eliot. "Jimmy Stewart and Capra in Hub." Boston Post (29 January).
An interview centering on Capra's war experiences and his return to commercial filmmaking with It's a Wonderful Life. Capra also recounts the story of the disastrous preview screening of Lost Horizon.

1224   Pryor, Thomas M. "Sounds of Alarm." New York Times (26 January), sec. 2, p. 5.
According to this report, Capra denounces as anti-Hollywood propaganda allegations by the British Board of Trade that British films do not have a decent chance to play in American theaters (a controversy much in the news at the time).

1225   Scheuer, Philip K. "'State of Union' to Pace Election." Los Angeles Times (28 September), sec. 2, pp. 1, 2.

An interview with Capra focusing on the production of State of the Union and the possible political impact of the film. "I do believe in putting up a fight for whoever happens to be the underdog at the time," Capra is quoted as saying. "If there is anything 'leftist' in this, it's in what people read into it. I am against the inequalities of this world, but I think that sooner or later they will be resolved under a system like ours."

1948

1226   Anon. "Interviewed on Location Shooting." Variety (14 April), pp. 1, 55.

Capra is interviewed concerning his thoughts on television. He welcomes the new technology, seeing it as a means of attracting nonhabitual filmgoers to the movies, and as an aid to the director in determining correct camera placement without having to wait for rushes. "I'm completely sold on television. I wish I had some television plans of my own that I could talk about now."

1227   Brady, Thomas F. "Hollywood Thrift." New York Times (15 February), p. 5.

Brady reports that M-G-M is delighted that Capra has finished State of the Union fifteen days ahead of schedule and interviews the director concerning the film. Capra expresses concern that it may be attacked as unpatriotic. "Far from undercutting democracy," he argues, "the picture merely reaffirms the precept of eternal vigilance and points out the danger of apathy in the electorate."

1949

1228   Anon. "All's Well, Etc." New York Times (10 April), p. 5.

Background information on the making of Riding High, including a brief interview with Capra, who is pessimistic about his future prospects at Paramount in light of the studio's excessive caution in approving projects.

1950

1229   Anon. "Fewer, Better Films Rather than Sliced Costs Sez Capra." Variety (26 April), p. 2.

A report on Capra's proposals for a more efficient use of limited finances in the film industry.

1230   McCrary, Tex, and Jinx Falkenburg. "New York Close-Up." New York Herald Tribune (30 April).

An interview with Capra at the time of the release of Riding High. Capra discusses his experiences working with Mack Sennett.

1952

1231   Anon. "Frank Capra Returns from India Film Festival." Hollywood Reporter (3 March).
    Interviewed upon his return from a film festival in India, Capra announces that international film festivals are being used by the Communists to spread propaganda.

1232   St. John, Ann. "On the Town." Hollywood Citizen News (16 October).
    Capra is interviewed concerning his retirement from the film industry. "When I left Hollywood I felt dried up inside. Each picture became more and more an effort. Then too, with the way things are now, a lot of fun has gone out of movie-making." He claims to have taken naturally to farming on his new ranch, where for the past year he has grown oranges, lemons, and avocadoes. But he also admits that he has a few scripts around the house. "If I do come back, it will be with something entirely different."

1956

1233   Gardella, Kay. "Capra Goes to Town on Sun." New York Sunday News (18 November), sec. 2, p. 10.
    An interview with Capra concerning Our Mr. Sun prior to its television premiere. Capra describes the challenge and fascination the science programs hold for him.

1234   Minoff, Philip. "Frank Talk from Capra." Cue, 25, No. 47 (14 November), 16.
    Capra talks about his work on the Bell Telephone science documentaries, his opposition to interrupting old films with commercials on television, his fear that producers in Hollywood are more interested in widening the screen than working with good stories, and his fondness for actors.

1235   Torre, Marie. "TV-Radio Today." New York Herald Tribune (12 November).
    An interview with Capra concerning the Bell Telephone science series. Capra announces his intention to return to Hollywood after a four-year absence.

1957

1236   Pryor, Thomas M. "School Gets a New Look." New York Times (17 November), sec. 1, p. 81.
    A report on efforts to revise the study of science in secondary schools, including information on Capra's activities as chief consultant for the project's film program. Interviewed concerning the program, Capra asserts that the marriage of films and textbooks opens up a new frontier in education, solving the problem of teacher shortages and the inability of high school instructors to keep abreast of the latest thinking in the field. The introductory film,

he announces, will be What Is Physics?; fifteen others are currently being drafted.

1958

1237 Anon. "Capra Agrees It's Tough for Yanks at 'Art Fests.'" Variety (16 July).
An interview with Capra concerning his experiences as a juror at the Berlin Film Festival. He claims it is unfair to match the films of young native industries with those from Hollywood. He also notes that jury voting never reflects the sentiment of the audiences watching the films, and that political considerations dictate the distribution of prizes to films from different countries.

1238 Anon. "Capra of Mr. Deeds, Mr. Smith Sees Hollywood Now Overintellectualized." Variety (16 July), pp. 1, 15.
Capra outlines plans for the making of A Hole in the Head, and discusses current problems in the film industry.

1239 Garrison, Omar. "Scientific Films Given Personality." Los Angeles Mirror News (17 June), sec. 1, p. 6.
An interview with Capra concerning his work on The Strange Case of the Cosmic Rays. Capra proposes that science teachers have not been able to arouse the enthusiasm of students for science because the material is presented in too abstract a way. He also relates the story of his receipt of a "Smiley" award from a trophy-maker in Ohio for his work on Hemo the Magnificent.

1240 Hyams, Joe. "Capra's Back after 7 Years." New York Herald Tribune (24 November).
An interview with Capra on the set of A Hole in the Head. Capra briefly discusses his television science series. He also suggests that the only way motion pictures will survive is by joining forces with pay television.

1959

1241 Anon. "Capra Sounds Off on Sex." Daily Variety (1 September), pp. 1, 15.
Interviewed at a Brazilian film festival, Capra expresses concern for the "hard-selling" of sex in movies and speculates about his own plans for a film biography of Jimmy Durante.

1242 Anon. "No Major Improvement in Direction Since D. W. Griffith--Frank Capra." Hollywood Reporter, 156, No. 48 (25 September), 4.
In this interview Capra discusses the contribution of D.W. Griffith to film direction: "Of course there have been the strictly technical improvements--many. But as far as sheer creative direction is concerned, no one has advanced beyond the achievements of Griffith." Capra's plans to film a biography of Jimmy Durante are

also discussed. He reiterates a credo never to "glorify the negative side of humanity," nor to make a film "awash with violence."

1243 Bacon, James. "Self-Exiled Frank Capra Returns to Screen." Baltimore Sun (25 January).
An interview with Capra during the making of A Hole in the Head. Topics include Walter Wanger's I Want to Live! (which Capra thinks makes a mockery of the American judicial system), Harry Cohn, and It Happened One Night. A brief biographical sketch is provided by Bacon.

1244 Scott, John L. "Frank Capra Returns, Resumes Career." Los Angeles Times (14 June), sec. 5, pp. 3, 5.
An interview with Capra concerning his return to theatrical filmmaking with A Hole in the Head. He discusses working with Frank Sinatra, directing within a restricted budget, and shooting on location. Queried about the Bell Telephone science series, he advises: "Give filmgoers an experience, not a lecture."

1245 Scott, Vernon. "Frank Capra Scores Stars' Avarice in Film Industry." New York Morning Telegraph (5 February), p. 2.
Capra reportedly denounces the power-broker status stars now enjoy in the making of films, arguing that it has undermined the authority of the director.

1960

1246 Anon. "Capra Outlines 3 Film Projects." New York Times (28 April), p. 30.
Capra announces that three new theatrical films are in the works, all sharing "the idea of the value of the individual man dramatically triumphing over adversity." These include a remake of Lady for a Day, and screen adaptations of The Meaning of Treason by Rebecca West and The Best Man by Gore Vidal.

1247 Anon. "Mutilation of Films on TV Hit by Frank Capra." Los Angeles Times (19 October), sec. 3, p. 2.
Speaking as president of the Directors Guild before a Federal Communications Committee hearing on television, Capra castigates TV producers for "slashing and mutilating" feature films in order to squeeze a work into a specified time slot.

1248 Anon. "TV Mutilation of Film Rapped by Frank Capra." Hollywood Citizen News (19 October), p. 7.
A report on Capra's attack on the policy of television stations to edit films in order to squeeze them into fixed blocks of time.

1249 Luther, Marylou. "So You Want to Be a Director? Think of Fans, Not Self--Frank Capra." Los Angeles Times (11 August), sec. 2, pp. 1, 5.

An interview with Capra concerning his advice to aspiring directors. He defends the happy ending as part of the director's responsibility to reaffirm the positive qualities of humanity and recommends both a mastery of the basic tools of the medium and a familiarity with good writing. There is no prescribed route to the top, he advises, and a wide variety of directorial styles can be studied. The primary task of a director is to provide the actors with a complete understanding of their character, for "there's no such thing as a bad actor, only bad directors."

1250 Margulies, Harriet. "Impact of Capra TV Protest Exactly." Film Daily (19 October).
As president of the Directors Guild of America, Capra is reported to express opposition to the current practice of showing old films on television. Not only are the films mutilated, he argues, but television competes unfairly with movie theaters, filling up program hours that could be devoted to new material.

1251 Ross, Don. "Frank Capra's New Projects." New York Herald Tribune (28 August), pp. 1, 3.
An interview with Capra concerning his ideas for new film projects, including a life of William Joyce, a remake of Lady for a Day, and a biblical drama based on the Sermon on the Mount.

1961

1252 Anon. "Let's Keep U.S. Only Major Producer of Film Not Subsidized--Capra." Variety (22 November), pp. 5, 20.
Capra is reported to oppose government subsidies to Hollywood to compete with foreign films, and to favor pay television as a solution to current economic problems in the industry.

1253 Anon. "Capra Corn." Newsweek, 58, No. 25 (18 December), 97-98.
A brief interview with Capra is incorporated into this favorable review of Pocketful of Miracles. He discusses the advantages of editing a film based on the taped reactions of preview audiences, and his desire to bring a harder edge to his remake of Lady for a Day. Also see entry 741.

1254 Morgenstern, Joseph. "Capra Prefers to Exit Laughing." New York Herald Tribune (3 December).
An interview with Capra prior to the release of Pocketful of Miracles. He describes the story as a fairy tale, set in the 1930s which could not take place today. He also discusses his taping of preview reactions to the film before making a final cut, and recounts the disastrous preview experience he had with Lost Horizon.

1255 Schumach, Murray. "Hollywood Maverick." New York Times (28 May), sec. 2, p. 7.
Interviewed on the set of Pocketful of Miracles, Capra discusses the current lack of comedy films and good scripts, and

expresses concern for how future directors will learn their craft in light of the current state of the industry.

1256   Zunser, Jesse. "Frank Capra Returns." Cue, 30, No. 51 (23 December), 11.

    A brief survey of Capra's career, and an interview with the director at the time of the release of Pocketful of Miracles. Capra comments briefly on remakes ("no good story should be allowed to die"), censorship, television, film subsidies, and the impact of It's a Wonderful Life on a group of prison inmates at a recent screening.

1962

1257   Anon. "Capra Interviewed at Czech Film Festival." Variety (11 July), p. 36.

    At a press conference at the 13th Carlevy Vary Film Festival, Capra reportedly observes that "I have always hankered to make classics as films or do more ambitious production but have usually ended up doing a comedy." Lost Horizon, he notes, reflected that ambition. An American-Soviet coproduction of Anna Karenina, staring Sophia Loren and directed by Capra, is announced.

1258   Anon. Interview with Capra. Films in Review, 13, No. 3 (March), 131-32.

    Capra is briefly quoted concerning his decision to burn the first two reels of Lost Horizon prior to its official release, and his tape recording of preview reactions before making a final cut of Pocketful of Miracles.

1963

1259   Stein, Herb. "'Circus' Is First Movie Made Abroad by Capra." New York Morning-Telegraph (22 June).

    An interview with Capra in Madrid as he prepares to direct Circus for Samuel Bronston. Capra reportedly claims that it is now necessary to make "big" films to survive in the business, and that he is impressed with the optimism and enthusiasm of the people with whom he is now working. (He was later to depart from the project.)

1964

1260   Anon. "Capra Gives Writers Guild Off-Record Report on Reds." Daily Variety (24 January).

    A report on a talk given by Capra to the Writers Guild upon his return from the Soviet Union. He is quoted as observing that the only change for filmmakers working in Russia today is that while Stalin once ordered certain kinds of film to be made, Khrushchev now cajoles.

1965

1261 Madsen, Axel. "Brève rencontre avec Frank Capra." Cahiers du cinéma, 166-67 (May-June), 114-15.

Capra discusses his current work on Marooned, the madhouse atmosphere at Sennett's Keystone studio in the 1920s, visual as opposed to verbal comedy, humor as opposed to satire, Robert Riskin, Charlie Chaplin, D.W. Griffith, and the future of the film industry.

1969

1262 Anon. "Capra Predicts Turn from Sex Shockers." Box Office, 95, No. 12 (7 July), SW4.

An account of a discussion with Capra following a speech he delivered in San Antonio, Texas. Capra reportedly asserts that religion will help keep America free of dictatorship, and that while much of what young people are questioning today is not without cause, they should be wary of forces that do not have their best interest in mind. He also is said to predict that once the public realizes sex scenes are simply stuck into films for shock value, viewers will return to "good dramatic stories."

1970

1263 Hendrick, Kimmis. "The Capras Retire to a Joint Literary Effort." Christian Science Monitor (9 March), p. 12.

Capra and his wife are interviewed as part of a series of articles on how people use their retirement years creatively. Capra explains that he knew it was time to stop making movies when he no longer could make decisions quickly, and that working on his autobiography (with his wife's assistance as critic) has allowed him to fulfill a long-standing ambition to write. Hendrick briefly profiles the entire Capra family and sketches Capra's background.

1971

1264 Amory, Cleveland. "Trade Winds." Saturday Review, 54, No. 28 (10 July), 4.

A short interview with Capra following the publication of his autobiography, marked by Amory's ironic distance from his subject.

1265 Anon. "Capra on His 'Roots.'" Daily Variety (21 September).

Having recently revisited his birthplace in Sicily, Capra reports that his return sparked no emotion. "Who the hell cares where you are born. That town meant nothing to me." People who love to live in ethnic ghettoes, he asserts, are happy to rush back to them once they get out. "I wasn't interested in making films about them. My roots are in America."

1266 Anon. "Eye Too." Women's Wear Daily (9 June), p. 10.

A brief interview with Capra in conjunction with the publication of his autobiography. Capra comments on the response of young people to his work: "Maybe I can't communicate with them as a person, but I do in my films of the '30s." He also describes the reasons for his retirement after Pocketful of Miracles.

1267   Anon. "Hollywood." New York Daily News (14 June).
       An interview with Capra in conjunction with the publication of his autobiography. Topics include the importance of intuition in creative decision making, Harry Cohn, and the bright future for young filmmakers amid current experimentation.

1268   Champlin, Charles. "Apostle of the Individual." Los Angeles Times (7 May), sec. 4, p. 1.
       Champlin interviews Capra about the approaching release of his autobiography, and briefly discusses Capra's career as a "maverick" in the film industry.

1269   M[ount], D[ouglas] N. "Authors & Editors." Publisher's Weekly, 200, No. 5 (August), 31-33.
       A brief interview with Capra inspired by the publication of his autobiography. Topics include Capra's bitterness over the recent acquisition of power by stars, the work of current directors, tackling controversial themes, pace in American Madness, and motion pictures as a young man's game. Mount touts Capra as an "unsung authentic auteur."

1270   Sweeney, Louise. "Capra Makes Two Hours in the Dark Count." Christian Science Monitor (4 October), p. 15.
       An interview with Capra in conjunction with the publication of his autobiography. Capra discusses the nature of comedy, his recovery from a mysterious illness in the mid-1930s, the search for values among young film viewers today, and the power of cinema. A brief biographical sketch is provided by the author.

1271   Tallmer, Jerry. "Frank Capra: Murder on the Late Show." New York Post (3 July), sec. 2, p. 13.
       An interview with Capra in conjunction with the publication of his autobiography. Topics include Harry Cohn, the disadvantages of government subsidies to filmmakers, the mindless slashing of old movies to conform to television scheduling, student audiences today, and his symbiotic relationship with screenwriters.

1272   Thompson, Howard. "Capra, 74, Looks Back at Film Career." New York Times (24 June), p. 32.
       A brief interview in conjunction with Frank Capra Day at the Museum of Modern Art and the publication of Capra's autobiography. Capra discusses the value of laughter, his "improbable hero," his insistence on directorial autonomy, and the lack of form and discipline he finds in movies today. He also describes his working relationship with various stars.

1273   Zito, Tom. "Capra Recalls the Old, Somewhat Better Days." Chicago Sun-Times (3 January), sec. 5, p. 10.

An interview with Capra on the occasion of screenings of Mr. Smith Goes to Washington at the American Film Institute and the Why We Fight series at the National Archives in Washington. Capra discusses his retirement, his childhood, his entry into the film business, and the script problems he had with Meet John Doe. (This syndicated article also appeared in the Washington Post and the Hartford Times on 3 January, and in the New York Post and the Boston Sunday Globe on 22 March.)

1972

1274   Berggren, Noel. "Arsenic and Old Directors." Esquire, 77, No. 4 (April), 132.
Invited to comment on the current state of movies, Capra attacks the tasteless treatment of sex and violence on the screen, and proposes that he could turn the current crop of pornographic films into comedies "by just putting a reactive character in there watching them and wondering."

1275   Bressan, Arthur, and Michael Moran. "Mr. Capra Goes to College." Andy Warhol's Inter/View, 22 (1 June), 25-30.
Of all interviews conducted with Capra, this delves the deepest into the ambiguities of Capra's politics, especially with respect to his simultaneous espousal of individualism and social action. Capra admits to an ambivalent attitude toward capitalism ("Things own you. With communism and fascism--ideas own you"); discusses the paradoxes of his work for the military and the Directors Guild ("to fight conglomerates you have to build a union as I did . . . but I was doing that as an individual"); and clarifies the attack he made in his autobiography on youth protest (demonstrations seem to him faddish media events, as contrasted with the direct action of Ralph Nader). Other topics include favorable student response on his campus tours, laughter and sadness in his films, religious faith, General Yen as a Capra hero, and the problem of ending Meet John Doe.

1276   Childs, James. "Capra Today." Film Comment, 8, No. 4 (November-December), 22-23.
In this interview Capra discusses the importance of individualism, hope, and sentiment; the arguments for idealism and pragmatism offered in Mr. Smith Goes to Washington; his pacificism; his respect for young people who question war and bad politics; and his "mother complex" as a possible source of strong female characters in his films.

1277   Prelutsky, Burt. "West View." Los Angeles Times (West), (10 September), p. 6.
Capra briefly discusses the popularity of his autobiography and the problems that beset the making of Pocketful of Miracles.

1278   Silke, James R., and Bruce Henstell, eds. Frank Capra: "One Man--One Film." Discussion No. 3. Washington, D.C.: American Film Institute, 17 pp.

An interview conducted at the American Film Institute's Center for Advanced Film Studies on 26 May 1971. Topics include the direction of actors, Lost Horizon and preview reactions, editing, pace, collaboration, bit parts, production on Mr. Smith Goes to Washington, the transition to talkies, the use of reactive characters, casting, the Capra hero, script problems with Meet John Doe, directorial control, budgeting, and the nature of comedy. A selected bibliography and filmography are appended. Excerpts from the interview were reprinted in 1975 (see entry 1292). This discussion should not be confused with a later interview conducted by the AFI and published in American Film in 1978 (see entry 1299).

1973

1279   Anon. "Frank Capra Receives SMPTE Award." Journal of the SMPTE, 82, No. 5 (May), 414.
In this account of Capra's receipt of an achievement award from the Society of Motion Picture and Television Engineers, Capra is reported to have informed the gathering of the value of his engineering background to his career as a director and producer, particularly during the period of transition to sound. Also see entry 903.

1280   MacCaffrey, Donald W. "Frank Capra: The Ideal and the Real," in The American Cinema. Edited by Donald E. Staples. Washington, D.C.: Voice of America, pp. 127-43.
Most of the topics discussed in this detailed interview are drawn from Capra's autobiography: improvisation, pace, and storytelling through actors; Harry Langdon and silent comedy; the first talkies and Capra's later use of live music at Paramount; cold weather effects for Dirigible and Lost Horizon; the problem of ending Meet John Doe; and the principle of "one man, one film." Capra also discusses the appeal of his films for audiences today.

1974

1281   Anon. "Frank Capra Interviewed at the Second Tehran International Film Festival." American Cinematographer, 55, No. 2 (February), 168-69, 210-13.
Capra discusses his motive for writing an autobiography, the importance of comedy, pace in movies, Harry Langdon, the film industry past and present, and his confidence in cinema's future.

1282   Anon. "'True Golden Age Ahead'--Capra." Variety (1 May), p. 3.
A report on an address delivered by Capra to the convention of the Society of Motion Picture and Television Engineers. Capra proposes that the best motion pictures remain to be made, and briefly discusses his welcoming of talkies when the industry made the transition to sound in the late 1920s.

1975

1283 Anderson, Nancy. "Trends Change Because Trends Stink!" Photoplay, 88, No. 5 (November), 16, 58.

Capra denounces the tendency of producers to follow trends, describes the difficulties involved in making a film, discusses the emergence of film schools and new young directors, and provides background information on It's a Wonderful Life. The interview is preceded by a brief career summary by Anderson.

1284 Bailey, George. "Why We (Should Not) Fight." Take One, 4, No. 11 (September), 10-12.

An interview concerning the Why We Fight series, supplemented by excerpts from a television interview in Milwaukee by Dominique Noth. Capra describes the political problems involved in making films about Russia and China during the war, the need to simplify issues when survival is at stake, and his experiences working with John Grierson, Robert Flaherty, and Pare Lorentz during this period. He explains that he became a pacifist after witnessing firsthand the death and destruction of the war years, and notes that long before Vietnam Gen. George C. Marshall warned against getting involved in a land war in Asia. Capra observes that had he been requested to make a film about Vietnam, he would have called it Why We Should Not Fight.

1285 Colman, Juliet Benita. Ronald Coleman: A Very Private Person. New York: William Morrow & Co., pp. 174-78.

Capra recounts his experiences working with Ronald Colman on Lost Horizon.

1286 Glatzer, Richard. "A Conversation with Frank Capra," in Frank Capra: The Man and His Films. Edited by Richard Glatzer and John Raeburn. Ann Arbor: University of Michigan Press, pp. 24-39.

An extensive interview, conducted by Glatzer in August and September 1973. Capra discusses the control he exercised over his films, his memories of Power of the Press, the transition to sound, editing and cinematography, improvisation and pace, A.P. Giannini and American Madness, the script for Soviet at M-G-M, his early years as a drifter, the autobiographical component in his work, his use of songs to break up action, screenwriting and the ending to Meet John Doe, dramatizing factual material in the war documentaries, It's a Wonderful Life and the postwar period, love scenes and reactive characters, and current responses to his work. Capra also comments on assorted actors (Cooper, Stewart, Arthur, Colbert, and Stanwyck) and directors (Ford, McCarey, Hawks, Wellman, and Welles).

1287 McBride, Joseph. "Frank Capra Sees Emerging Sense of Comedy and Idealism among Student Filmmakers." Daily Variety (16 April), p. 3.

Interviewed upon returning from a film festival in Montreal, Capra speaks optimistically about the future of cinema. He reports a renewed interest in comedy and a hunger for idealism among young filmmakers, and advises them not to follow trends. He also speculates that audiences are growing tired of "sick comedy." Among current Hollywood films, he favors American Graffiti and Godfather II, and respects the ability of William Friedkin to hold an audience's interest. He also discusses idealism and entertainment, his interest in people, his hatred of the rich, and his bitter experiences working in the industry in the 1960s.

1288 _____. "Capra Conks Creepy Pic Heroes." Variety (23 April), p. 24.
A reprint of McBride's interview with Capra in Daily Variety on 16 April. See entry 1287.

1289 Murphy, Mary. "Movie Call Sheet." Los Angeles Times (19 November), sec. 4, p. 14.
Briefly interviewed, Capra takes issue with current commentators who feel the motion picture industry is in decline, asserting that the best films are yet to be made.

1290 Schickel, Richard. "Frank Capra," in his The Men Who Made the Movies. New York: Atheneum, pp. 57-92.
A detailed interview, chronologically surveying Capra's career. Capra discusses life as an immigrant youth, breaking into movies, his early work with Mack Sennett, Harry Langdon, and Harry Cohn, and the transition to sound. He then comments on all the feature films from American Madness through State of the Union (Broadway Bill excepted), with passing remarks on Jean Arthur and Jimmy Stewart, and on the formation of Liberty Films. The interview concludes with a discussion of comedy and tragedy, unrealized "dream films," and the changing industry that forced his retirement. In his introduction, Schickel stresses the enduring authenticity of Capra's work from the 1930s, and the director's admirable response to his fate in the industry later on. This interview should not be confused with the compilation documentary by Schickel bearing the same title (see entry 1310), although selected portions from his discussion with Capra do appear in that film.

1291 Sherman, Eric. Directing the Film: Film Directors on Their Art. Boston and Toronto: Little, Brown & Co., passim.
Capra is quoted at various points on rehearsing actors, film editing, and the importance of the audience.

1292 Silke, James R. "Frank Capra--'One Man, One Film,'" in Frank Capra: the Man and His Films. Edited by Richard Glatzer and John Raeburn. Ann Arbor: University of Michigan Press, pp. 16-23.
A condensed version of the 1971 AFI interview with Capra. See entry 1278.

1976

1293 Bishop, Harv. "Frank Capra Profile." Classic Film Collector, 53, (Winter), 36, 30.
   An interview with Capra at his home in La Quinta, California. Capra describes D.W. Griffith's visit to the set of Mr. Smith Goes to Washington, and comments on his stock company of actors, his use of faces as background, and the pacing of his films.

1977

1294 Flatley, Guy. "The Sound That Shook Hollywood." New York Times Magazine (25 September), pp. 84-85.
   Capra describes his memories of the film industry's transition to sound fifty years before.

1295 Gardner, P.A. "Capra Deplores Today's 'Decisions' by Young Trend-Prone Officials." Variety (28 September), pp. 3, 30.
   Interviewed at the opening of the Canadian National Film Theatre season, Capra attacks current thinking in Hollywood, noting that the industry now produces too many sequels and remakes, and that the studios are "owned by conglomerates and run by young people who just follow trends."

1296 Leyda, Jay, ed. Voice of Film Experience: 1894 to the Present. New York: Macmillian Co., pp. 60-61.
   Brief excerpts from various sources are reprinted here; Capra comments on Barbara Stanwyck, casting Clark Gable in It Happened One Night, and the accelerated pace of American Madness.

1297 Livingston, Guy. "Vidor, Capra Tell of Good Old Days at Boston Tribute." Daily Variety (22 June), p. 9.
   A report on a tribute given to Capra and King Vidor at Boston University. Both directors reminisce about their careers.

1298 Mariani, John F. "Frank Capra." Focus on Film, 27:41-47.
   Capra is interviewed on a wide range of topics, including student response to his work, film study and academia, D.W. Griffith, improvisation and sight gags, Gary Cooper's persona, the logistics of the stadium sequence in Meet John Doe, the Red Scare, America's potential for fascism, and Robert Riskin's Magic Town. In his introduction, Mariani emphasizes the dark side of Capra's vision of America.

1978

1299 Anon. "Dialogue on Film: Frank Capra." American Film, 4, No. 1 (October), 39-50.
   An interview conducted by the American Film Institute on 5 April 1977 and published in American Film as part of its Dialogue on Film series. Capra discusses Mack Sennett, Harry Langdon, Harry Cohn, The Bitter Tea of General Yen as an "art film," Lost Horizon and preview reactions, Clark Gable and It Happened One Night, comedy,

pacing, naturalistic acting, the making of the Why We Fight series and It's a Wonderful Life, retirement, and his unrealized film projects. A videotape of this interview is available from the AFI (see entry 1311).

1979

1300   Bishop, Harv. "The Directors: Frank Capra." Hollywood Studio Magazine 12, No. 11 (February), 25-26.
   This interview with Capra focuses on his approach to film direction. Included are brief comments on the delicate balance of power between stars and directors, Capra's fondness for actors, his approach to shooting a scene and respect for the values of the first take, and his subordination of the machinery of filmmaking to the central task of involving the audience in the lives of the characters.

1301   Drew, William M. "A Lighthouse in a Foggy World." American Classic Screen, 3, No. 6 (July-August), 14-16.
   Capra discusses his decision to switch from a career in science to filmmaking, his working agreement with Harry Cohn at Columbia, films about contemporary Americans, city versus country life, screenwriting and screenwriters, the polarization of politics, and his faith in the individual.

1302   McLellan, Joseph. "Reel Veneration at the Archives: Feting 2 Fathers of Film." Washington Post (13 October), p. B1.
   Interviewed on the occasion of being honored by the National Archives, Capra relates a series of anecdotes concerning Mr. Smith Goes to Washington, Lost Horizon, and State of the Union.

1980

1303   Anon. "Frank Capra Given Masquers' Tribute as 'Great Director.'" Daily Variety (3 March), p. 3.
   A report on a tribute given to Capra at which he observes that film is America's contribution to the world of art, and that his own strategy as an artist was to entertain the audience before saying what he wanted. Brief testimonials from colleagues are also reported. See entry 1119.

1981

1304   DuBrow, Rick. "A Master of Movies Speaks Out on TV." Los Angeles Herald Examiner (13 December), p. E7.
   Capra is interviewed at the time of the broadcast of "High Hopes: The Capra Years" concerning his thoughts on current television. Noting that he is disturbed by the cynicism that permeates television programming, Capra reiterates his faith in the audience. "It's the guys who are strictly out to make money rather than use the medium for something entertaining. TV's a powerful medium and it's not being used. It's being unused." Were he working in television today, Capra notes, he would do the same kinds of things he has done

all his life. He considers "M.A.S.H." the best program in the brief history of the medium, and also has kind words for "Gunsmoke," "Lou Grant," "Barney Miller," "Archie Bunker's Place," "Little House on the Prairie," and "The Waltons." Background information on "High Hopes: The Capra Years" (see 1312) is also provided by DuBrow.

1305 Hargrave, Harry A. "Interview with Frank Capra." Literature/ Film Quarterly, 4, No. 3:189-204.
Topics covered in this interview include Capra's early work in silent comedy, the transition to sound, the "one-man, one-film" concept, cinematography and editing, location shooting, his fascination with people and faces, and sexuality in the movies. Capra also discusses his collaboration with Robert Riskin, Dimitri Tiomkin, Joseph Walker, and Barbara Stanwyck. Preceding the interview is a biographical sketch which is riddled with inaccuracies.

1306 Hurley, Neil. "Frank Capra." New Orleans Review (Winter), pp. 64-75.
An interview conducted with Capra in La Quinta, California, in January 1980. Capra discusses his association with Harry Cohn at Columbia, The Bitter Tea of General Yen and his desire for an Oscar, the casting of It Happened One Night, his illness and revival prior to Mr. Deeds Goes to Town, working with actress Jean Arthur, the value of a relaxed set, adapting stage plays to the screen, music and musicals, the social value of humor, and the recurring motifs of suicide and Christmas in his works. A sketch of Capra's career precedes the interview.

1307 Karp, Walter. "The Patriotism of Frank Capra." Esquire, 95, No. 2 (February), 33-35.
Woven into this discussion of Capra's patriotism are comments by Capra elicited by Karp in an interview. Capra describes his desire to escape an ethnic ghetto and mingle with Americans, and the faith he came to have in the common man. Uncertain about the politics of the New Deal, he nevertheless was fascinated by the response of the people: "They were down, very down, but they didn't panic; they never quite lost the faith." He recounts the controversial reception given Mr. Smith Goes to Washington, and links the decline of his career to the terrible shock the war years registered upon his faith in the human race. "I began to think that maybe I really was a Pollyanna." Also see entry 1144.

1308 McCarthy, Todd. "Weekend with Frank Capra Proves Full of Surprises." Daily Variety (10 March), pp. 6, 22.
A report on a weekend tribute to Capra at Indian Wells, California, sponsored by the Directors Guild of America. Capra is interviewed on a range of topics, including contemporary movies, the reasons behind his retirement, and the idea of "one man, one film." Noting that audiences today seem to get more from his films than did those when the films were first released, he reaffirms his faith in the appeal of human comedy despite the excessive sex and violence in current films. He also discusses his lack of sentiment for his

Sicilian roots, and the responsibility held by filmmakers to unite rather than fragment their audience. Also see entry 1145.

1309 _____. "Capra, Walker Star at Directors Guild Weekend." Variety (18 March), p. 84.
A reprint of McCarthy's article from Daily Variety on 10 March. See entry 1308.

INTERVIEWS ON FILM AND VIDEOTAPE

1975

1310 "Frank Capra" episode of The Men Who Made the Movies. Director-Writer-Producer: Richard Schickel. Produced under the auspices of WNET/13, New York City. Narrated by Cliff Robertson. 88 minutes.
A compilation documentary incorporating excerpts from two interviews (one at Capra's home, the other at West Point, New York) and clips from American Madness, The Bitter Tea of General Yen, It Happened One Night, Mr. Deeds Goes to Town, Lost Horizon, Mr. Smith Goes to Washington, Meet John Doe, Arsenic and Old Lace, the Why We Fight series, and It's a Wonderful Life. First broadcast in 1975 in conjunction with the publication of Schickel's book of the same title (see entry 1290). A 16mm film of this episode is now available for rent from the Museum of Modern Art.

1979

*1311 "Frank Capra" interview from Dialogue on Film: A Seminar Series with Master Filmmakers. Produced by the American Film Institute. 3/4 inch, color videotape. 60 minutes. Recorded at the American Film Institute on 5 April 1977. Available for purchase for $200 from the American Film Institute, John F. Kennedy Center, Washington, DC 20566. A study guide has been published to be used in conjunction with this tape (see entry 1099). A partial transcript of the interview appeared in American Film in October 1978 (see entry 1299).

1981

1312 "High Hopes: The Capra Years." Production Company: Columbia Pictures-TV. Producers: Carl Pingitore, Frank Capra, Jr. Director: Vincent Sherman. Script: Richard Schickel. Cameras: Al Francis, Chuck Wheeler, and Travers Hall. Editor: Michael Luciano. Sound: John de Grazzio, Dean Hodges, and Don Rush. Music: Jimmy Haskell. Hosts: Carl Reiner, Lucille Ball, and Burt Reynolds, with a special appearance by James Stewart. Shot at Burbank Studios, Burbank, California. Broadcast by NBC-TV on 24 December 1981. Commentary by Schickel is narrated by Reiner, Ball, and Reynolds, and Capra is interviewed by Reiner. Clips are presented from It Happened One Night, Mr. Deeds Goes to Town,

Lost Horizon, You Can't Take It with You, Mr. Smith Goes to Washington, Arsenic and Old Lace, It's a Wonderful Life, State of the Union, and *A Hole in the Head.*

VI. Other Film-Related Activity

1922–1923

1313   Walter Ball Film Lab, San Francisco
       Capra worked for a year and a half as a lab assistant for Walter Ball, developing, printing, and editing footage, primarily for newsreels and advertising films.

1314   Robert Eddy Comedies
       Capra worked as a prop man, editor, and gag writer for Eddy, a Los Angeles-based producer of two-reel comedies who was filming the Toonerville Trolley series in the San Francisco area in 1923.

1924

1315   Hal E. Roach Studios
       For six months Capra was employed as a writer on the Our Gang series under the supervision of director Robert McGowan. Capra did not receive official credit, so it is difficult to determine on which films he worked. In compiling a Capra filmography, David Badder has assumed that those Our Gang films released between 1924 and January 1925 were in part written by Capra, and thus credits the following titles to him: High Society (August), The Sun Down Limited (September), Every Man for Himself (October), Fast Company (November), The Mysterious Mystery (December), and The Big Town (January 1925) (see entry 930). In his compilation of "peripheral" Capra films, Donald C. Willis attributes the screenplay to Every Man for Himself to Capra; he also speculates that Official Officers (released 28 June 1925) was a Capra project, but does not say why (see entry 950, p. 197).

1316   Mack Sennett Studio
       Capra arrived at the Sennett studio in the latter months of 1924. Leland Poague has suggested that all of Harry Langdon's films directed by Harry Edwards were probably scripted by Capra and Arthur Ripley (see entry 989, p. 235). But for this to be true Capra would have had to have been working with Edwards by late summer, 1924, which is unlikely in light of Capra's assertion that he spent six months as

a general gagman before becoming a staff writer of original comedies (see The Name above the Title, p. 50). It is also important to note that Capra did not work exclusively with Langdon, nor with Edwards and Ripley, and that Langdon made successful films during this period with other directors and writers. Capra's first official credit came on A Wild Goose Chaser, filmed at the end of 1924, but not released until January 1925 (see entry 1317).

1925

1317   A WILD GOOSE CHASER

Production Company:	Mack Sennett Studio
Producer:	Mack Sennett
Supervisor:	J.A. Waldron
Director:	Lloyd Bacon
Screenplay:	Frank Capra
Titles:	Felix Adler, A.B. Giebler
Editor:	William Hornbeck
Cast:	Ben Turpin (Hunter), Madeline Hurlock (Hunter's wife), Jack Cooper (divorce specialist), Eugenia Gilbert (vamp actress)
Distributor:	Pathé Exchange Inc.
Released:	January 18, 1925
Length:	2 reels

1318   PLAIN CLOTHES

Production Company:	Mack Sennett Studio
Producer:	Mack Sennett
Director:	Harry Edwards
Screenplay:	Frank Capra, Arthur Ripley
Cast:	Claire Cushman, Jean Hathaway, Vernon Dent, Harry Langdon, William McCall
Distributor:	Pathé Exchange Inc.
Released:	March 29, 1925
Length:	2 reels

1319   BREAKING THE ICE

Production Company:	Mack Sennett Studio
Producer:	Mack Sennett
Screenplay:	Frank Capra, Jefferson Moffitt
Cast:	Ralph Graves, Marvin Lobach, Alice Day
Distributor:	Pathé Exchange Inc.
Released:	April 5, 1925
Length:	2 reels

1320   THE MARRIAGE CIRCUS

Production Company:	Mack Sennett Studio

Other Film-Related Activity 1925

Producer:	Mack Sennett
Directors:	Reggie Morris, Ed Kennedy
Screenplay:	Frank Capra, Vernon Smith
Cast:	Ben Turpin (dutiful son), Louise Carver (aggressive mother), Madeline Hurlock (vamp), Sunshine Hart, William C. Lawrence, Christian J. Frank
Distributor:	Pathé Exchange Inc.
Released:	April 12, 1925
Length:	2 reels

1321 GOOD MORNING, NURSE!

Production Company:	Mack Sennett Studio
Producer:	Mack Sennett
Director:	Del Lord
Screenplay:	Frank Capra, Jefferson Moffitt
Cast:	Ralph Graves (hypochondriacal millionaire), Olive Borden (nurse), Marvin Lobach
Distributor:	Pathé Exchange Inc.
Released:	May 31, 1925
Length:	2 reels

1322 SUPER-HOOPER-DYNE LIZZIES

Production Company:	Mack Sennett Studio
Producer:	Mack Sennett
Director:	Del Lord
Screenplay:	Frank Capra, Jefferson Moffitt
Cast:	Billy Bevan, Andy Clyde, Lillian Knight, J.J. Richardson
Distributor:	Pathé Exchange Inc.
Released:	June 14, 1925
Length:	2 reels

1323 HIS FIRST FLAME

Production Company:	Mack Sennett Studio
Producer:	Mack Sennett
Director:	Harry Edwards
Screenplay:	Frank Capra, Arthur Ripley
Photography:	William Williams, Ernie Crockett
Cast:	Harry Langdon (Harry Howells), Ruth Hiatt (Mary Morgan), Natalie Kingston (Ethel Morgan), Vernon Dent (Amos McCarthy), Bud Jamison (Hector Benedict), Dot Farley (Mrs. Benedict)
Distributor:	Pathé Exchange Inc.
Released:	May 3, 1927
Length:	6 reels

His First Flame, Harry Langdon's first (and only) feature film for Mack Sennett, had a curious history at the Sennett studio. In January 1925, Exhibitors Herald noted that Langdon was considering a switch to features, a move apparently requested by exhibitors. In June, the magazine reported that His First Flame had been completed, but that Langdon was to go back to two-reelers before undertaking another feature. Then in July it reported that His First Flame was being cut and edited. Copyright on the film, however, was not taken out until 6 February 1926. On 27 March 1926--the same week that First National Pictures advertised Langdon's appearance in "his first feature length comedy," Tramp, Tramp, Tramp--Pathé advertised the release of His First Flame, "your first choice in feature comedy." In the same issue of Exhibitors Herald it was reported that Sennett had several new Langdon films in the offing, including Fiddlesticks (a two-reeler), The Soldier Man (a four-reeler, see entry 1327), and His First Flame ("the comedian's initial five-reel comedy feature"). His First Flame, however, was not released until a year later, on 3 May 1927, following the success of Langdon's first three independent features, Tramp, Tramp, Tramp, The Strong Man, and Long Pants.

It is logical to assume that Sennett's withholding of His First Flame, and his apparent restriction of Langdon to shorts, motivated the performer's decision to form an independent production company, taking Edwards, Capra, and Ripley with him. But it would be interesting to know whether Sennett held up the film because he was genuinely displeased with its quality, or because he was trying to keep Langdon from becoming too powerful a star (much as Sennett had tried to arrest Chaplin's career, with similar results, more than ten years before). In any case, Sennett (or perhaps Pathé) delayed the releases of His First Flame until Langdon had already proven himself as a feature film star on his own. (See Exhibitors Herald, 3 January 1925, p. 40; 20 June 1925, p. 46; 18 July 1925, p. 66; and 27 March 1926, pp. 22, 75.)

1324   CUPID'S BOOTS

Production Company: Mack Sennett Studio
Producer: Mack Sennett
Director: Ed Kennedy
Screenplay: Frank Capra
Cast: Ralph Graves (bookkeeper), Thelma Hill (his girlfriend)
Distributor: Pathé Exchange Inc.
Released: July 26, 1925
Length: 2 reels

1325   LUCKY STARS

Production Company: Mack Sennett Studio
Producer: Mack Sennett
Director: Harry Edwards
Screenplay: Frank Capra, Arthur Ripley
Photography: George Crocker

Other Film-Related Activity 1926

Editor: William Hornbeck
Cast: Harry Langdon (hero), Natalie Kingston
                     (vampish senorita), Vernon Dent (quack
                     doctor)
Distributor: Pathé Exchange Inc.
Released: August 16, 1925
Length: 2 reels

1926

1326   SATURDAY AFTERNOON

Production Company: Mack Sennett Studio
Producer: Mack Sennett
Director: Harry Edwards
Screenplay: Frank Capra, Arthur Ripley
Titles: A.H. Giebler
Cast: Harry Langdon, Vernon Dent, Ruth Hiatt, Peggy
                     Montgomery
Distributor: Pathé Exchange Inc.
Released: January 31, 1926
Length: 2 reels

1327   THE SOLDIER MAN

According to Leland Poague, this Langdon short was written by Capra and Arthur Ripley, directed by Harry Edwards, and released in May 1926 (see entry 989, p. 236). All other references to the film that I have come across have been extremely sketchy. David Turconi, in the filmography appended to Mack Sennett: Il 're delle comiche' (Rome: Edizioni dell'Ateneo Roma, 1961), simply lists it as a Langdon two-reeler and speculates that it was released in April 1926. Kalton Lahue in World of Laughter describes it as a Langdon three-reeler released in May 1926 (see entry 778, p. 197). Donald C. Willis indicates that it was a three-reeler that may have been written by Capra, but says nothing more about the film (see entry 950, p. 198). In March 1926 Exhibitors Herald described The Soldier Man as a Langdon four-reeler scheduled to be released later in the year, but I have been unable to locate any further information concerning the participants in the film or its actual date of release (see Exhibitors Herald, 27 March 1926, p. 75, and the notes to entry 1323).

1328   TRAMP, TRAMP, TRAMP

Production Company: Harry Langdon Corporation
Producer: Harry Langdon
Director: Harry Edwards
Screenplay: Frank Capra, Arthur Ripley, Tim Whelan, Hal
                     Conklin, J. Frank Holliday, Gerald Duffy,
                     Murray Roth
Photography: Elgin Lessley

1926   Other Film-Related Activity

Cast: Harry Langdon (Harry Logan), Joan Crawford
                          (Betty Burton), Edwards Davis (John
                          Burton), Alec B. Francis (Harry's father),
                          Tom Murray (Nick Kargas, the Argentine),
                          Carlton Griffin (Roger Caldwell), Brooks
                          Benedict (taxi driver)
Distributor: First National Pictures, Inc.
Copyright: March 7, 1926 by First National Pictures,
                          Inc. (LP 22515)
Released: April 1926
Running time: 62 minutes at 24 fps

Tramp, Tramp, Tramp was Harry Langdon's first independent feature film. In addition to working on the screenplay, Capra claims to have directed several of the scenes when Harry Edwards, exasperated with Langdon, left the set (interview with author, 23 July 1981). Edwards broke with Langdon permanently after the making of the film, and Capra took over the direction of Langdon's next two features, The Strong Man and Long Pants.

1928

Following a split with Harry Langdon on Long Pants, and an unsuccessful attempt to sustain his budding career as a director on For the Love of Mike, Capra returned to the Sennett studio as a writer in 1928.

1329   THE SWIM PRINCESS

Production Company: Mack Sennett Studio
Producer: Mack Sennett
Director: Alf Goulding
Screenplay: James Tynan, Frank Capra
Editor: William Hornbeck
Cast: Daphne Pollard, Andy Clyde, Carole Lombard
Distributor: Pathé Exchange Inc.
Release: February 26, 1928
Length: 2 reels

1330   THE BURGLAR

        Also known as Smith's Burglar

Production Company: Mack Sennett Studio
Producer: Mack Sennett
Director: Phil Whitman
Screenplay: Dick Barrows, Frank Capra
Editor: William Hornbeck
Cast: Raymond McKee, Ruth Hiatt, Billy Gilbert
Distributor: Pathé Exchange Inc.
Released: December 9, 1928
Length: 2 reels

1933

1331   SOVIET

After Lady for a Day, Columbia loaned Capra to M-G-M where he worked for several months with producer Irving J. Thalberg on a film about the building of a Soviet dam. The film was nearing its production date when Thalberg left for Europe for health reasons and Louis B. Mayer canceled the project. Capra then returned to Columbia to make It Happened One Night. In 1973 Capra described the screenplay to Richard Glatzer as follows:

> Wally Beery was going to play the role of a commissar who was given the job of building this great dam. He didn't know anything about engineering, but was a man in charge who had made his way up from the bottom of the Bolshevik regime. Marie Dressler was his wife, and a very patient, loving wife she was. Joan Crawford was the assistant commissar. Clark Gable was an American engineer, sent over to help them build this dam. The conflicts were personal and ideological: the American wants to get things done and the commissar wants to get them done in his own way. Gable falls in love with Joan Crawford, and they have a running battle: she hates anything that is not Communistic, and he hates anything that is Communistic--all this plus the drama of building this dam. . .The Wally Beery character was particularly complex. One of his hands had been cut off, and on his remaining hand he wore a handcuff--with an empty handcuff dangling--as a symbol of his slavery under the Czarist system that had cut off his hand--he never took this handcuff off. During the celebration [of the completion of the dam] the camera pans down the enormous face of the dam and then moves into a close-up and there is this handcuff sticking out of the cement--Beery had been buried inside the dam.

Capra also reported that at the end of the story Clark Gable was to return to America without Joan Crawford (see the Glatzer interview with Capra, entry 1286, pp. 29-30, and The Name Above the Title, pp. 160-61).

1934

1332   FRISCO FURY

On 5 December 1934, Edwin Schallert reported in the Los Angeles Times that Capra was to go to Palm Springs to work on the script for a new film, adapted by Robert Riskin from a story by Hy Craft, to star Walter Connolly. The title, "Frisco Fury," as well as the casting of Connolly, is perhaps reminiscent of Capra's Broadway Bill, released the week before. However, I have found no other references to this project. Schallert also noted that Capra had recently suffered a relapse following an appendicitis operation and had returned to the hospital, hence the project may well have been abandoned because of

Capra's health (see Schallert, "Capra to Work in Palm Springs," <u>Los Angeles Times</u>, 5 December 1934, sec. 1, p. 19, and <u>The Name Above the Title</u>, pp. 172-82).

1935

1333   VALLEY FORGE

Harry Cohn purchased the rights to Maxwell Anderson's play for Capra in 1935, but Capra decided to make <u>Mr. Deeds Goes to Town</u> instead because he feared that "<u>Valley Forge</u> was beyond my competency. I wanted a story closer to our times; about people that I knew" (<u>The Name Above the Title</u>, p. 179). Capra nevertheless kept the project in mind over the years, and in the late 1960s he tried to buy the rights to the play from Columbia, which still owned them. He claims that the studio refused to sell the rights because of its plan to make a film version of the Broadway musical, <u>1776</u>, a refusal that left Capra extremely bitter (see Joseph McBride's 1975 interview with Capra, entry 1287).

1938

1334   THE LIFE OF CHOPIN

According to Axel Madsen, this project originated with William Wyler, who attempted to sell Samuel Goldwyn on the idea of filming a biography of Chopin with Marlene Dietrich as George Sand. When Goldwyn refused, Wyler reportedly went to Harry Cohn with the project; they never came to terms, but Cohn purchased the rights (Madsen, <u>William Wyler</u> [New York: Thomas Y. Crowell Co., 1973], p. 197). Bob Thomas, in his biography of Cohn, does not mention Wyler, but states that Cohn purchased the right to a German film as the basis for a Chopin script when Capra became enamored with the project. Sidney Buchman then composed a shooting script; a cast was selected; Capra requested to shoot the film in color and Cohn agreed. But Columbia's New York office, led by Jack Cohn, vetoed the project, and Capra, who had spent a year on the project, left Columbia vowing never to return. Joe Walker was sent as an emissary to lure Capra back with an offer of 50 percent of the profits in addition to complete financing of his next film, but Warners had already offered a lucrative deal to Capra and Riskin for the making of <u>Meet John Doe</u> (Thomas, <u>King Cohn</u>, entry 784, p. 152). Capra's version in his autobiography is somewhat different. He claims Harry Cohn blocked the project because he felt Marlene Dietrich, who Capra wanted for the George Sand role, was box-office poison. Moreover, Capra places the fight with Cohn <u>prior</u> to the making of <u>Mr. Smith Goes to Washington</u>, and does not bring the Chopin project into his discussion of his decision to leave Columbia for independent production at Warners. (<u>The Name Above the Title</u>, p. 253). In any case, the film was finally made at Columbia in 1945 as <u>A Song to Remember</u>. Sidney Buchman produced the film and wrote the screenplay, based on a story by Ernst Marischka. Charles Vidor

Other Film-Related Activity 1945

directed. Merle Oberon starred as George Sand and Cornel Wilde as Chopin.

1940

1335   CAVALCADE OF ACADEMY AWARDS

Producer: Academy of Motion Picture Arts and Sciences
Supervisor: Frank Capra
Director: Ira Genet
Screenplay: Owen Crump
Photography: Charles Rosher
Commentary: Carey Wilson
Distributor: Warner Brothers
Premiere: April 4, 1940 (Ciro's, Los Angeles)
Running time: 30 minutes

I have been unable to ascertain what Capra contributed to this film.

1941

1336   TOMORROW NEVER COMES

In May 1941 Capra purchased the rights to a story by Hugh Wedlock and Howard Snyder entitled "Tomorrow Never Comes," and hired the authors to write a screenplay based upon it. Reportedly a modern comedy, it was announced as Capra's next production. The price of the rights and the nature of the plot were not disclosed. Capra, however, ended up directing Arsenic and Old Lace for Warner Brothers instead. The project may bear some relation to It Happened Tomorrow, a 1944 film directed by René Clair; source material for that film's screenplay by Dudley Nichols and Clair is credited in part to Wedlock and Snyder (see Douglas W. Churchill, "Screen News Here and in Hollywood," New York Times, 20 May 1941, p. 27).

1943-1945

1337   ARMY-NAVY SCREEN MAGAZINE

This series was the offshoot of a suggestion made by Capra shortly after he was appointed head of the army's orientation film unit in 1942. It was launched in April 1943 under the supervision of Leonard Spigelgass, with Henry Berman as editor and Don Etlinger as chief scriptwriter. Seventy biweekly issues of the newsreel followed; most were incorporated within a forty-five minute program called G.I. Movie Weekly. Footage filmed by all branches of the military were included in the newsreel, as well as sequences from commercial motion pictures, and cartoons featuring the popular animated character, Private Snafu. "By Request," a segment in which soldiers were shown requested views of hometown life, was also frequently part of the program (see The Signal Corps: The Outcome [mid-1943 through 1945], edited by George Raynor Thompson and Dixie Harris [Washington, D.C.: U.S. Army, 1966], p. 556, and Thomas Bohn's An Historical and Descriptive Analysis of the 'Why We Fight' Series [New York: Arno Press, 1977], pp. 61-63).

1338   THIS IS THE PHILIPPINES

Although not cited in Capra filmographies, this orientation film made for invasion forces in the Philippines in 1944 was assembled by the Army Pictorial Service during the period that Capra supervised its film unit. Whether or not he played any direct or indirect role in the making of the film is uncertain.

1339   ON TO TOKYO

Although not cited in Capra filmographies, this film also was produced by the Army Pictorial Service while Capra was in charge of the film unit. It was released two weeks after Two Down, One to Go (see production notes for entry 45) and had the similar purpose of informing military and civilian audiences about the shift in military strategy from Europe to the Pacific following V-E Day. But while Two Down, One to Go was made in the fall of 1944 and its release held up until 10 May 1945, On to Tokyo appears to have been made very close to its release date, at which time Capra was attempting to wind down his activities with the film unit. In his autobiography, he mentions the film in passing while describing his attempt to extricate himself from further work at the time of his discharge in June (The Name Above the Title, p. 366).

1945

1340   THE FLYING YORKSHIREMAN

In May 1941 Capra bought the rights to this novel by Eric Knight from Frank Lloyd for $40,000, but he did not seriously consider making the film until he returned to civilian life in 1945. RKO held an option on the rights during the war years, but never used them. Once Liberty Films had been established, Capra tentatively scheduled The Flying Yorkshireman as his second film for the new company (after It's a Wonderful Life), but the project was considered a difficult one because of the amount of preparation involved in the production. When Liberty Films was sold to Paramount, Capra tried to interest his new studio in the project without success. He eventually sold the rights to Stanley Kramer (see Douglas W. Churchill, New York Times, 20 May 1941, p. 27; Thomas M. Pryor, "Mr. Capra Comes to Town," New York Times, 18 November 1945, sec. 2, p. 3; and The Name Above the Title, pp. 375, 404, 424).

1341   NO OTHER MAN

Capra had Liberty Films buy the rights to Alfred Noyes's novel as a possible project after the war. He described it to Thomas Pryor of

Other Film-Related Activity 1948

the New York Times as a "prophecy of the utter destruction of the Continent of Europe" and a "smashing melodrama with a deeply religious angle to it, something like Lost Horizon." Planned as a Technicolor film, to be shot on location, the project appears to have gone the way of many of Capra's ambitious plans amid the economic constrictions he faced in the postwar period (see Thomas M. Pryor, "Mr. Capra Comes to Town," New York Times, 18 November 1945, sec. 2, p. 3).

1342   IT HAPPENED ON FIFTH AVENUE

Capra: "I also had Liberty buy It Happened on Fifth Avenue, a comedy about a tramp who found the secret of living the life of Riley: He lives in rich men's homes in New York in winter, and in their Florida homes in summer" (The Name Above the Title, pp. 375-76). The film was eventually made by Monogram Pictures in 1947, produced and directed by Roy del Ruth, starring Victor Moore.

1343   PIONEER WOMAN

See Westward the Women (entry 1347).

1947

1344   FRIENDLY PERSUASION

While involved with preproduction activities on State of the Union, Capra had a writer working on a screenplay of Friendly Persuasion, Jessamyn West's novel about a Quaker family during the Civil War. When Liberty Films was sold to Paramount a year later, Capra proposed that Friendly Persuasion be his first film at the studio with Bing Crosby and Jean Arthur in the central roles. But Paramount vetoed the project because of its expense. Capra sold the rights to William Wyler, who made the film for Allied Artists in 1956 with Gary Cooper and Dorothy McGuire (see The Name Above the Title, pp. 386, 403-4, 424).

1948

1345   ROMAN HOLIDAY

Capra hoped to direct this story of a runaway princess and an American newsman, written by Ian McClellan Hunter, as his second film at Paramount, and tried to line up Elizabeth Taylor and Cary Grant for the central roles. But Paramount vetoed the project because of its expense. Capra sold the rights to William Wyler, who was permitted to make the film at Paramount in 1953. Gary Cooper and Audrey Hepburn starred in Wyler's version (see The Name Above the Title, pp. 403-4, 424).

1948   Other Film-Related Activity

1346   A WOMAN OF DISTINCTION

   While at Paramount, Capra bought the rights to this comic story by Hugo Butler and Ian McClellan Hunter concerning a dignified dean of a New England's girls' school and a visiting British astronomer. Capra hoped to get Katharine Hepburn and Ray Milland to star in the film, but Paramount deemed the project too expensive. Capra traded the rights to Harry Cohn at Columbia in exchange for the remake rights and original negative to Broadway Bill; he was thus able to make Riding High at Paramount. Columbia released A Woman of Distinction in 1950, with Rosalind Russell and Ray Milland in the starring roles, and Edward Buzzell directing (see The Name Above the Title, pp. 404-6).

1951

1347   WESTWARD THE WOMEN

Production Company:	Metro-Goldwyn-Mayer
Producer:	Dore Schary
Director:	William A. Wellman
Screenplay:	Charles Schnee, from the story "Pioneer Woman" by Frank Capra
Photography:	William Mellor
Editor:	James E. Newcome
Art Directors:	Cedric Gibbons, Daniel B. Cathcart
Set Decorators:	Edwin B. Willis, Ralph S. Hurst
Costumes:	Walter Plunkett
Sound:	Douglas Shearer
Music:	Henry Russell
Technical Adviser:	Jim Launch
Cast:	Robert Taylor (Buck Wyatt), Denise Darcel (Fifi Danon), Hope Emerson (Patience Hawley), John McIntire (Ray Whitman), Julie Bishop (Laurie Smith), Lonore Lonergan (Margaret O'Malley), Beverly Dennis (Rose Meyers), Marilyn Erskine (Jean Johnson), Renata Vanni (Mrs. Moroni), Guido Martufi (Antonio Moroni), Henri Nakumura (Ito), Bruce Cowling ("Cat")
Distributor:	Metro-Goldwyn-Mayer
Released:	December 31, 1951 (Capitol Theatre, New York City)
Running time:	118 minutes

   Long interested in directing a western, Capra wrote "Pioneer Woman" when he returned to civilian life after the war and included it in his stock of possible projects for Liberty Films. When Liberty was sold to Paramount, Capra offered to film "Pioneer Woman" with Gary Cooper in the starring role as part of his three-picture contract, but the studio rejected the project because of its expense. When Capra's friend and neighbor William Wellman expressed interest in the story,

Other Film-Related Activity   1957

Capra sold it to Dore Schary at M-G-M for Wellman to direct. Capra was not especially pleased with the completed film (interview with author, 23 July 1981).

1957

1348 PHYSICAL SCIENCE STUDY FILMS

In the fall of 1957 Capra was appointed chief consultant on a series of twenty-minute science films made for use in high schools around the country. The project was part of a new program in science instruction developed by the Physical Science Study Committee, a group formed by Dr. James R. Killian, special assistant for science and technology in the Eisenhower administration, and headed by Professor Jerrold R. Zacharias of MIT. Funding came from the National Science Foundation, the Ford Foundation, the Fund for the Advancement of Education, and the Alfred P. Sloan Foundation. Capra was undoubtedly appointed to the committee because of his recent work on the Bell System science series, but his precise role in the making of the films remains unclear. In November 1957 it was reported that he would serve as consultant on fifty to seventy of these short educational films, with top scientists assigned to work closely with directors, producers, and writers on each subject. Capra announced at the time that his introductory film was to be What Is Physics? and that fifteen others were scheduled to be completed by the following September. In his autobiography, Capra notes that while he was waiting for Frank Sinatra to become available for production on A Hole in the Head in early 1958, he "went to Cambridge, Massachusetts, to see how M.I.T.'s Professor Zacharias's 'five-year physics plan' was coming along, and to supervise a couple of the seventy twenty-minute color films I had helped Zacharias lay out" (see Thomas M. Pryor, "School Science Gets a New Look," New York Times, 19 November 1957, sec. 1, p. 81, and The Name Above the Title, p. 451).

1349   JOSEPH AND HIS BRETHREN

Following the success of The Robe in 1953, Harry Cohn undertook this project at Columbia, a biblical story adapted by Clifford Odets from the novel by Thomas Mann. The film's original director, William Dieterle, spent several months on location in Egypt in 1954 photographing background sequences, but Rita Hayworth, who Cohn wanted for the starring role, balked at appearing in the film. A court case resulted, with Hayworth finally agreeing to appear in Pal Joey instead. Otto Preminger took over the direction of the film for a brief period, but abandoned the project when casting problems remained unresolved. In November 1957 Cohn invited Capra to return to Columbia to produce and direct the film; Capra, who had not made a commercial feature since 1951, accepted. Capra claims to have worked excitedly on the script over the Christmas holidays that year. But the production came to a halt in the spring when Harry Cohn died and Columbia's New York office, which had never favored the project, canceled it. During this period Capra also discussed remaking Lady for a Day at

Columbia, but these talks also stopped after Cohn's death (see Thomas M. Pryor, "Capra to Direct Story from Bible," New York Times, 18 November 1957, p. 37, and The Name Above the Title, p. 451).

1959

1350   THE JIMMY DURANTE STORY

According to Capra, Frank Sinatra proposed that he and Capra form a partnership to film the life story of Jimmy Durante following their collaboration on A Hole in the Head. Bing Crosby and Dean Martin were also to be copartners, with ownership of the production company being divided four ways. A tentative deal was struck when Columbia agreed to coproduce and distribute the film, and Capra completed a seventy-five-page treatment in the fall of 1959. But the project was abandoned by Capra in January 1960 when a draft of an agreement prepared by Sinatra's lawyers made it clear that Capra would not have control over the making of the film (see "Capra Sounds Off on Sex," Daily Variety, 1 September 1959, pp. 1, 15, and The Name Above the Title, pp. 464-67).

1960

1351   THE BEST MAN

Capra first announced his intention to film Gore Vidal's play about presidential politics in April 1960; at the time he hoped to acquire Spencer Tracy, with whom he had worked on State of the Union, for the starring role. After completing Pocketful of Miracles, Capra returned to the project, but soon dropped it because of disagreements with Vidal concerning the screenplay. The film was eventually made by Franklin Schaffner in 1964, with Henry Fonda in the central role (see "Capra Outlines 3 Film Projects," New York Times, 30 April 1960, p. 30, and The Name Above the Title, pp. 469, 487).

1352   THE MEANING OF TREASON

In 1960 Capra announced that he was interested in making a film based on Rebecca West's account of the trial of William Joyce, an Irishman who delivered pro-Nazi broadcasts during World War II and was eventually executed for treason. Capra claimed that he was attracted to the story because of the character's change of personality and conversion to democratic principles during the course of the trial. No actual work on the project seems to have been done (see "Capra Outlines 3 Film Projects," New York Times, 30 April 1960, and The Name Above the Title, p. 469).

1962

1353   CIRCUS

In 1962 Capra was hired by Paramount and producer Samuel Bronston to direct Circus, replacing Nicholas Ray, who had suffered a heart

Other Film-Related Activity   Undated

attack while filming Bronston's 55 Days in Peking. Capra spent several months in Madrid working on a script with Joseph Sistrom, and as late as June 1963 expressed optimism about the project. He claims that his role in the production came to an end when John Wayne arrived on the scene and rejected the script. However, according to Paul N. Lazarus, Jr., executive vice president for Samuel Bronston Productions at the time, it was the producers who were displeased with the script and Wayne himself never saw it. Henry Hathaway replaced Capra as director and Ben Hecht was hired to quickly rewrite the screenplay. The film was released as Circus World in 1964 (see "Capra is Signed to Direct Two Films for Paramount," New York Times, 16 November 1962, p. 27; Herb Stein, "'Circus' Is First Movie Abroad by Capra," New York Morning-Telegraph, 22 June 1963; and The Name Above the Title, pp. 489-90).

1354   ANNA KARENINA

At a press conference at the Carlevy Vary Film Festival in Czechoslovakia in July 1962, plans were announced for an American-Soviet coproduction of Anna Karenina, with Sophia Loren in the central role and Capra directing, but no further work seems to have been done on the project. Capra claims to have contemplated directing either Anna Karenina or Crime and Punishment in 1935, but that he had felt at the time he was not competent to direct Russian actors. At the Czech festival in 1962 he reiterated a long-standing interest in making film versions of the classics (see "Capra Interviewed at Czech Film Festival," Variety, 11 July 1962, p. 36, and The Name Above the Title, p. 179).

1964

1355   MAROONED

While working on Rendezvous in Space, Capra picked up an option on a novel by Martin Caidin about an American astronaut marooned in space. Mike Frankovich, the new head of Columbia Pictures, agreed to back the project, and a script was prepared by Walter Newman. After three years of trying to get the film made, however, Capra lost out in a power struggle with Frankovich and was replaced by John Sturges. Marooned was eventually released in 1969. (see Thomas M. Pryor's review of Capra's autobiography in Daily Variety [entry 849], and The Name Above the Title, pp. 492-93).

Undated

1356   "DREAM FILMS"

In a 1975 interview with Richard Schickel, Capra described some of the films he dreamed about making over the years:

> I wanted to make Cyrano very much throughout my whole life, but I had no chance to. I wanted to make Don Quixote, Cervantes'

show. I never got the opportunity to make that. I've always
wanted to make those two. I read them over and over at times. I
also wanted to make the story of Saul who later became Paul,
which to me is one of the greatest stories ever told: a man, a
Hitler-type guy, suddenly becomes converted and becomes the
thirteenth apostle--a great story of an individual, great story
of clashes of ideas. I wanted to make the story of Luke, a
Greek, a born slave of the Romans, who worked his way up and
becomes a great physician--doesn't believe all that mystical
nonsense about religions--he's a complete scientist--how he gets
converted and becomes an apostle--what happens to him. (entry
1290, p. 88).

In his autobiography, Capra speaks of toying with the notion of filming Edmond Rostand's Cyrano de Bergerac in 1940, before settling on Meet John Doe as his first independent production. In 1959 he considered making a film about St. Paul with Frank Sinatra. When Capra was signed to direct Circus in 1962 (see entry 1353), Paramount agreed to let him film Taylor Caldwell's novel about St. Luke, Dear and Glorious Physician, once he had completed the circus film. None of these projects, however, progressed beyond the "dream" stage (see "Capra Is Signed to Direct Two Films for Paramount," New York Times, 16 November 1962, p. 27, and The Name Above the Title, pp. 295, 463, 490-91).

VII. Archival Sources

AMES, IOWA

1357   The American Archives of the Factual Film, Iowa State University Library, Ames, IA 50011. Curator: Dr. Stanley Yates. Phone: (515) 294-6672.
   Researchers should write for appointments; screening dates should be scheduled at least one week in advance. A small fee per hour is charged.

Prints: <u>Prelude to War, The Nazis Strike, Divide and Conquer, The Battle of Britain, The Battle of Russia, War Comes to America, Our Mr. Sun, Hemo the Magnificent, The Strange Case of the Cosmic Rays, The Unchained Goddess</u>

AMSTERDAM

1358   Stichting Nederlands Filmmuseum, Vondelpark 3-1071 AA, Amsterdam, Netherlands. Director: Jan de Vall. Phone: 020-83 16 46. Telegrams: Filmmuseum Amsterdam.
   Prints from the museum's collection are available for study purposes on a viewing table only after the authorization of the copyright owner has been acquired.

Prints: <u>Long Pants, Lost Horizon, You Can't Take It with You, Divide and Conquer, War Comes to America, The Negro Soldier, Know Your Enemy: Japan, It's a Wonderful Life</u>

BERKELEY

1359   Pacific Film Archive, University Art Museum, University of California at Berkeley, 2625 Durant Avenue, Berkeley, CA 94720. Public Service Coordinator: Linda Artel; Assistant: Nancy Goldman. Phone: (415) 642-1437.
   The Film Study Center at the Pacific Film Archive is a research screening facility and library for scholars and educators. In a ten-seat theater or screening room with 16mm and 35mm flatbed viewers, researchers can view any film from the PFA collection.

Archival Sources

Screenings are scheduled weekdays by reservation only. Fees are charged on a sliding scale. The study center also includes a library of two-thousand books, one-hundred periodicals, newsletters, and extensive clippings files of film reviews, biographical articles, and subject files.

Prints: <u>Prelude to War</u>
Scripts: <u>It Happened One Night</u>, <u>Mr. Smith Goes to Washington</u>

BERLIN

1360 Stiftung Deutsche Kinemathek, Pommernalle 1, 1000 Berlin 19, West Germany. Phone: 3036-233/234.

Print: <u>Arsenic and Old Lace</u> (in German)

BUDAPEST

1361 Magyar Filmtudományi Intézet És Filmarchívum, Népstadion út 97, Budapest, Hungary. Director: Dr. Sándo Papp. Phone: 429-599. Telegram: Hungarchiv, Budapest.

Stills: <u>Mr. Deeds Goes to Town</u>, <u>Mr. Smith Goes to Washington</u>

CANBERRA

1362 National Film Archive, National Library of Australia, Parkes Place, Canberra Act 2600, Australia. Reference Officer: Kate McLoughlin. Phone: (062) 62 1359. Telex: 62100. Telegram: Natlibaust Canberra. Open: 9:30 A.M.-4:45., Monday to Friday.
   Archive films may be viewed on the library premises by private individuals for bona fide research purposes. Viewing machines and projection theaterettes are available for use only by prior appointment, free of charge. Copies of stills, posters, news clippings, and other documentation materials are available in accordance with the library's standard scale of photographic charges. Prior copyright clearance may be necessary before material can be supplied. Information on costs and availability will be supplied upon request.

Stills: <u>Flight</u>, <u>Ladies of Leisure</u>, <u>Dirigible</u>, <u>The Miracle Woman</u>, <u>The Bitter Tea of General Yen</u>, <u>Lady for a Day</u>, <u>It Happened One Night</u>, <u>Broadway Bill</u>, <u>Mr. Deeds Goes to Town</u>, <u>Lost Horizon</u>, <u>You Can't Take It with You</u>, <u>State of the Union</u>, <u>Riding High</u>, <u>Here Comes the Groom</u>, <u>A Pocketful of Miracles</u>
Lobby Card: <u>The Younger Generation</u>

1363 National Film Lending Collection, National Library of Australia, Parkes Place, Canberra ACT 2600, Australia. Telex: Libaust AA62100. Telegraph: Natlibaust Canberra. Open: 9:30 A.M.-4:45 P.M., Monday to Friday.

Archival Sources

        Films from the collection are available to groups or organizations in Australia. Individual viewing of films or videocassettes at the library can be arranged subject to the prior needs of the lending service. Prior appointment is necessary to ensure availability of staff and facilities.

Prints: Prelude to War, The Nazis Strike, Divide and Conquer, The Battle of China, The Negro Soldier

COPENHAGEN

1364   Det Danske Filmmuseum, Store Sondervoldstraede, 1419 Copenhagen K., Denmark. Librarian: Lars Olgaard. Phone: (01) 57 65 00. Telex: 31465. Telegram: Filmatheque.

Prints: The Way of the Strong (35mm safety print with Danish titles)
Mr. Deeds Goes to Town (35mm safety print with German subtitles)
Meet John Doe (16mm print with Danish subtitles)
The Nazis Strike (35mm nitrate print with Danish commentary)
Tunisian Victory (35mm nitrate print with Danish commentary)

Scripts: Lady for a Day (Danish dialogue list)
Mr. Deeds Goes to Town (sound continuity sheet and Danish dialogue list)
You Can't Take It with You (sound continuity and dialogue list in English and Danish)
Mr. Smith Goes to Washington (English spot titles, cutting continuity, dialogue continuity, and Danish dialogue list)
It's a Wonderful Life (cutting continuity and Danish dialogue list)
A Hole in the Head (cutting continuity and dialogue continuity)

Stills: The archive holds 42 portrait stills of Frank Capra. Production stills are held for the following Capra films: The Strong Man (9), Long Pants (18), The Younger Generation (4), Dirigible (9), Platinum Blonde (9), The Bitter Tea of General Yen (2), Lady for a Day (13), It Happened One Night (11), Broadway Bill (2), Mr. Deeds Goes to Town (83), Lost Horizon (126), You Can't Take It with You (66), Mr. Smith Goes to Washington (50), Meet John Doe (8), Arsenic and Old Lace (42), Prelude to War (2), The Nazis Strike (15), The Battle of Britain (32), The Battle of Russia (35), Tunisian Victory (24), It's a Wonderful Life (46), State of the Union (11), Riding High (78), Here Comes the Groom (39), A Hole in the Head (74), A Pocketful of Miracles (50)

Files: Files containing Danish newspaper clippings, press materials, and souvenir programs are held for the following Capra films: The Strong Man, Long Pants, That Certain Thing, So This Is Love, The Way of the Strong, Submarine, Flight,

Archival Sources

Dirigible, Platinum Blonde, Forbidden, American Madness, The Bitter Tea of General Yen, Lady for a Day, It Happened One Night, Broadway Bill, Mr. Deeds Goes to Town, Lost Horizon, You Can't Take It with You, Mr. Smith Goes to Washington, Meet John Doe, Arsenic and Old Lace, Prelude to War, The Nazis Strike, Divide and Conquer, The Battle of Britain, The Battle of Russia, Tunisian Victory, The Negro Soldier, It's a Wonderful Life, State of the Union, Riding High, Here Comes the Groom, A Hole in the Head, Pocketful of Miracles

HELSINKI

1365   Suomen Elokuva-Arkisto (The Finnish Film Archive), P.O. Box 216, SF-00181, Helsinki 81, Finland. Director: Seppo Huhtala.

Prints: Mr. Deeds Goes to Town (35mm acetate)
You Can't Take It with You (35mm acetate)
Mr. Smith Goes to Washington (35mm nitrate)
Tunisian Victory (35mm nitrate)

Scripts: Mr. Deeds Goes to Town (English spotting list, 55 pp.)
You Can't Take It with You (dialogue continuity, 53 pp.; and English spotting list, 54 pp.)
Mr. Smith Goes to Washington (dialogue continuity, 50 pp.)

LONDON

1366   British Film Institute, Library Services, 127 Charing Cross Road, London WC2H OFA, England. Head: Gillian Hartnoll. Phone: 01-437 4355. Open: Tuesday, Thursday and Friday, 11 A.M.-6 P.M.; Wednesday, 11 A.M.-9 P.M.
    All services are accessible to the public by letter, telephone, or personal visit, but regular users are expected to take out membership in the BFI.

Scripts: Lady for a Day, It Happened One Night, You Can't Take It with You, Mr. Smith Goes to Washington, Pocketful of Miracles

Files: Microfiche cards containing newspaper clippings are held for the following Capra films: The Strong Man, Long Pants, The Matinee Idol, The Way of the Strong, The Power of the Press, Dirigible, The Miracle Woman, Platinum Blonde, Forbidden, American Madness, The Bitter Tea of General Yen, Lady for a Day, It Happened One Night, Broadway Bill, Mr. Deeds Goes to Town, Lost Horizon, You Can't Take It with You, Mr. Smith Goes to Washington, Meet John Doe, Arsenic and Old Lace, Prelude to War, The Nazis Strike, Divide and Conquer, The Battle of Britain, The Battle of Russia, Know Your Ally: Britain, Tunisian Victory, It's a Wonderful Life, State of the Union, Riding High, Here Comes the Groom, A Hole in the Head, Pocketful of Miracles

Archival Sources

Other: The library's periodical index contains bibliographical references to articles on the following Capra films: <u>The Strong Man</u>, <u>Long Pants</u>, <u>For the Love of Mike</u>, <u>That Certain Thing</u>, <u>The Matinee Idol</u>, <u>The Way of the Strong</u>, <u>Submarine</u>, <u>The Power of the Press</u>, <u>The Younger Generation</u>, <u>The Donovan Affair</u>, <u>Flight</u>, <u>Ladies of Leisure</u>, <u>Rain or Shine</u>, <u>Dirigible</u>, <u>The Miracle Woman</u>, <u>Platinum Blonde</u>, <u>Forbidden</u>, <u>American Madness</u>, <u>The Bitter Tea of General Yen</u>, <u>Lady for a Day</u>, <u>It Happened One Night</u>, <u>Broadway Bill</u>, <u>Mr. Deeds Goes to Town</u>, <u>Lost Horizon</u>, <u>You Can't Take It with You</u>, <u>Mr. Smith Goes to Washington</u>, <u>Meet John Doe</u>, <u>Arsenic and Old Lace</u>, <u>Prelude to War</u>, <u>The Nazis Strike</u>, <u>Divide and Conquer</u>, <u>The Battle of Britain</u>, <u>The Battle of Russia</u>, <u>Know Your Ally: Britain</u>, <u>The Battle of China</u>, <u>Tunisian Victory</u>, <u>War Comes to America</u>, <u>The Negro Soldier</u>, <u>Two Down, One to Go</u>, <u>It's a Wonderful Life</u>, <u>State of the Union</u>, <u>Riding High</u>, <u>Here Comes the Groom</u>, <u>A Hole in the Head</u>, <u>Pocketful of Miracles</u>

1367 National Film Archive, 81 Dean Street, London W1V 6AA, England. Curator: David Francis. Phone: 01-437-4355.

Prints: <u>Long Pants</u>, <u>Dirigible</u> (trailer), <u>Platinum Blonde</u>, <u>It Happened One Night</u>, <u>Mr. Deeds Goes to Town</u>, <u>Lost Horizon</u>, <u>You Can't Take It with You</u>, <u>Mr. Smith Goes to Washington</u>, <u>Meet John Doe</u>, <u>Divide and Conquer</u>, <u>The Battle of Britain</u>, <u>The Battle of Russia</u>, <u>Tunisian Victory</u>, <u>It's a Wonderful Life</u>

1368 Imperial War Museum, Lambeth Road, London SE1 6HZ, England. Keeper of the Department of Film: Clive Coultass. Phone: 01-735 8922.
There are no restrictions on access to these films for researchers and scholars.

Prints: 35mm – <u>Prelude to War</u>, <u>The Nazis Strike</u>, <u>Divide and Conquer</u>, <u>The Battle of Britain</u>, <u>the Battle of Russia</u>, <u>The Battle of China</u>, <u>Tunisian Victory</u>, <u>War Comes to America</u>
16mm – <u>Know Your Ally: Britain</u>, <u>Know Your Enemy: Japan</u>

LOS ANGELES (AND VICINITY)

1369 The Louis B. Mayer Library, The American Film Institute, 2021 North Western Avenue, Los Angeles, CA 90027. Director: Anne G. Schlosser. Open: Monday to Friday, 10:30 A.M.–5:30 P.M.

Prints: The American Film Institute's print collection is held at the Library of Congress in Washington, D.C. (see entry 1400). Copies of the following films, however, are also held at the AFI-West for study purposes: <u>It Happened One Night</u>, <u>Mr. Deeds Goes to Town</u>, <u>Lost Horizon</u>, <u>Mr. Smith Goes to Washington</u>, and <u>It's a Wonderful Life</u>.

Archival Sources

Scripts: The Miracle Woman, American Madness, It Happened One Night, Mr. Deeds Goes to Town, Lost Horizon, You Can't Take It with You, Mr. Smith Goes to Washington, Meet John Doe, It's a Wonderful Life, Pocketful of Miracles

Stills: The Columbia Stills Collection (1930-50) includes photographs from all the films made by Capra at Columbia in the 1930s.

Files: The clipping files tend to be thin; program notes for retrospectives and recent news items are the dominant material. There is a biography file for Capra, and separate film files for Lost Horizon, Mr. Smith Goes to Washington, Meet John Doe, and State of the Union.

Other: The library has transcripts of three seminars with Capra held at the AFI Center for Advanced Film Studies on 11/6/74 (T 220), 4/5/77 (T 402), and 5/23/78 (T 509). There is also a transcript of a seminar on Mr. Deeds Goes to Town held at the center on 11/12/71 (T 86.5).

1370 The Margaret Herrick Library, Academy of Motion Picture Arts and Sciences, 8949 Wilshire Boulevard, Beverly Hills CA 90211. Head Librarian: Terry T. Roach. Archivist, Special Collections: Sam Gill. Coordinator of Photographic Services: Robert Cushman. Phone: (213) 278-4313. Open: Monday, Tuesday, Thursday, Friday, 9 A.M.-5 P.M.

The library's resources and services are open to the public. Xerox and photographic services are available.

Scripts: Lady for a Day, It Happened One Night, Lost Horizon, Mr. Smith Goes to Washington, Meet John Doe, It's a Wonderful Life

Stills: Long Pants, Submarine, The Young Generation, The Donovan Affair, Flight, Ladies of Leisure, Dirigible, The Miracle Woman, American Madness, The Bitter Tea of General Yen, Lady for a Day, It Happened One Night, Broadway Bill, Mr. Deeds Goes to Town, Lost Horizon, You Can't Take It with You, Mr. Smith Goes to Washington, Meet John Doe, Arsenic and Old Lace, It's a Wonderful Life, Riding High, Here Comes the Groom, A Hole in the Head

Files: Files at the library are divided into two categories: biography and production. Holdings related to Capra are extensive in both categories. There are ten biography files entered under Capra's name. "Studio Biography and Credits File #1" contains studio handouts for Lady for a Day, Meet John Doe, State of the Union and Riding High. "Studio Biography and Credits File #2" contains a research guide to Capra's work compiled by the Academy, and Xeroxed articles concerning Capra's appearance at SUNY, Buffalo, in 1979. There are also three files of magazine articles (-1939, 1940-1969, 1970-), and five files of newspaper clippings (-1959, 1960-1969, 1970-1975, 1975-1977, 1978-). In addition to clippings, these latter files include an introductory program note by Bob Epstein for the Los

Archival Sources

Angeles County Museum of Art Capra retrospective in 1971; program notes by David Mallery for a Walnut Street Theatre (Philadelphia) retrospective in May 1978; and program notes for the AFI screening of a restored print of <u>Lost Horizon</u> at Mann's Chinese Theatre in October 1979.

Production files are held for individual films. These files contain a variety of material, including reviews, Motion Picture Call Bureau Cast Service listings, programs, pressbooks, lobby cards, press releases, and program notes for retrospective screenings. As might be expected, files for films after 1936 tend to be more voluminous than those for earlier works. A separate production file exists for <u>every</u> <u>commercial</u> <u>feature</u> <u>film</u> directed by Capra. In addition, there are production files for <u>Prelude to War</u>, <u>Divide and Conquer</u>, <u>The Battle of Britain</u>, and <u>The Battle of Russia</u>.

Other:
- The Mack Sennett Collection contains stills and script material on most of the Harry Langdon shorts on which Capra worked in 1924 and 1925.
- The Paramount Production Facts File contains information relating to <u>Riding High</u> and <u>Here Comes the Groom</u>.
- The Lincoln Quarberg Collection contains RKO studios handbooks for publicity issued at the time of the release of <u>It's a Wonderful Life</u>.
- The Edward Manson Collection contains Warner Brothers publicity material issued at the time of the release of <u>Arsenic and Old Lace</u>.
- A copy of "Frank Capra: A Research Guide," compiled by the library's research staff, is available through the mail for $1.00.

1371   Department of Special Collections, Occidental College, Mary Norton Clapp Library, 1600 Campus Road, Los Angeles, CA 90041. Librarian: Michael C. Sutherland. Phone: (213) 259-2852. Open: Monday to Friday, 1 P.M.-5 P.M.

The Bill Henry Collection Contains correspondence between Henry and Capra. Material may be viewed only through special arrangement.

1372   UCLA Theater Arts Library, University Research Library, University of California at Los Angeles, Los Angeles, CA 90024. Head: Audree Malkin. Phone: (213) 825-4880. Open: Monday to Thursday, 9 A.M.-11 P.M. (during regular academic session); Friday, 9 A.M.-6 P.M.; Saturday, 9 A.M.-5 P.M.; Sunday, 1 P.M.-10 P.M.

The library is open to scholars and researchers with a valid Research Library reference card. All Xeroxing and photographic reproductions are subject to Library regulations. Photographic reproduction is available through University Photographic Services.

Archival Sources

Scripts: It Happened One Night (dialogue continuity)
Mr. Deeds Goes to Town (dialogue continuity)
You Can't Take It with You (dialogue continuity)
Meet John Doe (treatment entitled "The Life and Death of John Doe" by Richard Connell and Robert Presnell; and a dialogue continuity)
It's a Wonderful Life (dialogue continuity)
State of the Union ("file copy," dated 9/16/47, with numerous changes indicated for dates ranging from 8/21/47 to 12/6/47)
Riding High (undated, but with changes indicated for 3/7/49, 3/10/49, and 4/9/49)
Here Comes the Groom ("final white" copy, date 11/16/50, with changes indicated for 12/11/50, 1/5/51, 1/6/51, and 1/8/51)

Files: The library holds a general clipping file on Capra, and individual files for the following films (the latter files tend to be thin, usually containing a few reviews): The Strong Man, For the Love of Mike, Mr. Deeds Goes to Town, You Can't Take It with You, Mr. Smith Goes to Washington, Meet John Doe, It's a Wonderful Life, State of the Union, A Hole in the Head, Pocketful of Miracles.

Other: - The Stuart Heisler Collection, housed by the Department of Special Collections of the University Research Library, contains Lillian Hellman's story for The Negro Soldier. It may also contain other material on the film among Heisler's papers.
- The recently acquired RKO Collection, which is not yet catalogued, is likely to include material on It's a Wonderful Life.

1373 UCLA Film Archives, Department of Theatre Arts, University of California at Los Angeles, Los Angeles, CA 90024. Curator: Robert Epstein. Phone: (213) 206-8013. Open: Monday to Friday, 9 A.M.-5 P.M.

Prints: With the exception of Broadway Bill, all the prints listed below are acetate and viewable on the UCLA campus. Broadway Bill is a nitrate print and must be viewed at the archive's Hollywood vaults. The archive has: That Certain Thing, The Bitter Tea of General Yen, Broadway Bill, Mr. Deeds Goes to Town, Mr. Smith Goes to Washington, Meet John Doe, Prelude to War, The Nazis Strike, The Negro Soldier, War Comes to America, It's a Wonderful Life

1374 ATAS/UCLA Television Archives, Department of Theatre Arts, University of California at Los Angeles, Los Angeles, CA 90024. Curator: Dan Einstein. Phone: (213) 206-8013. Open: Monday to Friday, 9 A.M.-5 P.M.
  The archive holds 3/4-inch videocassette copies of Our Mr. Sun and Hemo the Magnificent. These programs are not available for

Archival Sources

loan or rent; they can be screened only at the archive's viewing facility at UCLA.

1375   USC Department of Special Collections, Archives of Performing Arts, Doheny Library, University of Southern California, Los Angeles, CA 90007. Head: Robert Knutson. Phone: (213) 741-6058.

Arrangements for the use of materials should be made in advance. This is especially true of files from the Warner-Burbank collection, which is not housed in the library building.

Scripts: In addition to the department's general holding of scripts, copies can be found in individual collections, as noted below.
Platinum Blonde (typescript draft, Fay Wray Collection)
American Madness (draft, Fay Wray Collection)
Lady for a Day (draft, Fay Wray Collection; final, general collection)
It Happened One Night (draft, James Boyle Collection; typescript draft, Fay Wray Collection; final, general collection)
Broadway Bill (typescript final, Fay Wray Collection; final, general collection)
Mr. Deeds Goes to Town (fourth draft, 10/14/35, general collection; final, 12/10/35, Fay Wray Collection)
You Can't Take It with You (third draft, 3/17/38, Fay Wray Collection; final, general collection)
Meet John Doe (final, Fay Wray Collection; dialogue transcript and revised transcript with handwritten corrections, Warner-Burbank collection)
Arsenic and Old Lace (draft, 10/10/41, with revisions on 10/16/41, 10/23/41, 10/24/41, 10/29/41, 12/3/41, and 12/5/41)
State of the Union (final, general collection)
Pocketful of Miracles (final, 3/6/61, Jack Oakie Collection)

Files: The library has a clipping file for Capra and for many of his films.

Other: - The Warner-Burbank Collection contains West Coast production files for Meet John Doe and Arsenic and Old Lace. For Meet John Doe there is a Research Department file, a Picture File (containing memoranda, contracts, a shooting schedule, a daily progress and production report), a Copyright and Censorship File (containing memoranda, a dialogue transcript, and revised transcript with handwritten corrections), and a Publicity File. For Arsenic and Old Lace there is a Research Department File, a Picture File (containing memoranda and contracts), a Legal Department File, a Daily Progress and Production Report, and two separate files (384-1 and 384-2) containing casting and production information, including staff and cast sheets, a budget, and a script.

Archival Sources

- The Fay Wray Collection contains a 16mm print of Meet John Doe, screenplays for many of Robert Riskin's films with Capra (see above), and scrapbooks, contracts, and photographs that may relate to these films.
- The Dimitri Tiomkin Collection contains musical scores for Lost Horizon, It's a Wonderful Life, and the Why We Fight series. Some of the personal papers and correspondence in this collection also likely relate to Capra.
- The Oral History Collection includes two tapes of Capra (a lecture at Cal Tech on 4/17/72; and a discussion with Arthur Knight at USC on 10/31/72). It also includes a tape of Joseph Walker, Capra's long-time cinematographer.

MADISON, WISCONSIN

1376   The Wisconsin Center for Film and Theater Research. Administrative Offices, 6039 Vilas Communication Hall, University of Wisconsin, Madison, Madison, WI 53706. Director: Tino Balio. Phone: (608) 262-9706. Film Archive, State Historical Society, 816 State Street, Madison, WI 53706. Film Archivist: Maxine Fleckner. Reference Archivist: Josephine L. Harper. Phone: (608) 262-0585. Hours: Monday to Friday, 8:30 A.M.-4:30 P.M.

The collection is available to scholars engaged in serious research upon consent from the Wisconsin Center for Theater Research. Researchers are urged to write or telephone in advance. Manuscript holdings may be examined at the Archives-Manuscript Reading Room at the State Historical Society. There are restrictions on photocopying and on publication of some materials in the United Artists Collection. The center's Film Archive, also located at the State Historical Society, has Steenbeck viewing machines for individual screening of films in the collection.

Prints: Broadway Bill, Arsenic and Old Lace
Scripts: Arsenic and Old Lace (shooting script, and dialogue transcript: United Artists Collection)
           Pocketful of Miracles (second draft, 7/19/60; final shooting script; Hal Kanter Collection)
Files: - Contract file for Arsenic and Old Lace (UA Collection)
           - Contract negotiations UA held with Capra and Robert Riskin in 1941 (O'Brien Legal file, UA Collection)
Other: - Pressbooks for For the Love of Mike and Arsenic and Old Lace (on microfilm: UA Collection)
           - Costume drawings for A Hole in the Head (11 watercolor sketches; Edith Head Collection)

MIDDLETOWN, CONNECTICUT

1377   The Frank Capra Collection, Cinema Archives, Wesleyan University, Middletown, CT 06457. Curator: Jeanine Basinger. Phone: (203) 347-9411, ext. 2259.

Archival Sources

Capra donated this major collection to Wesleyan University in 1981. According to curator Jeanine Basinger, the archive will include: a massive collection of correspondence; scripts to almost all of Capra's films, including the Why We Fight series; stills from most films, as well as personal photographs, many from World War II; costume and set design sketches for most films (including the set designs for Lost Horizon); pressbooks, and other advertising and promotional material; scrapbooks of newspaper clippings; Columbia Pictures Annuals; drafts from Capra's autobiography, his speech for the American Film Institute tribute to Jimmy Stewart, and an unpublished novel; memorabilia (including plaques, awards, and tributes from fans); and a host of personal items (including books, records, and prints). In short, this collection promises to be an extraordinarily rich archive, not only for future work on Capra, but also for research on his colleagues and the institutions with which they were associated.

MOSCOW

1378 Gosfilmofond, Stansia Bielye Stolby, Moskovskaia oblast, U.S.S.R. Director: M. Strotchkov.

Scripts: The archive holds Russian translations of the scripts to the following Capra films: It Happened One Night (published in 1939), Lady for a Day (published in 1940), Mr. Deeds Goes to Town (published in separate editions in 1940 and 1943), Lost Horizon (published in 1940).

Other: The archive also holds the State Institute of Film's History of Foreign Cinema (1970), the second volume of which contains a section on Capra written by Soviet film historian Valentina Kolodjazhnaja.

NEW YORK CITY

1379 The Billy Rose Theatre Collection, New York Public Library, Lincoln Center for the Performing Arts, 111 Amsterdam Avenue, New York, NY 10023. Curator: Dorothy Swerdlove. Phone: (212) 799-2200. Open: Monday and Thursday, 12 P.M.-8 P.M., Tuesday, Wednesday, Friday, and Saturday, 12 P.M.-6 P.M.

Scripts: It Happened One Night (dialogue continuity, Robert Gessner Collection)
Mr. Deeds Goes to Town (dialogue continuity, Robert Gessner Collection)
Lost Horizon ("Final Draft," 3/23/36 with pp. 82-122 added 4/7/36)
You Can't Take It with You ("Third Draft," 3/17/38, with revisions 3/30/38 and 5/9/38)
Meet John Doe (dialogue continuity, Robert Gessner Collection)

Stills: Long Pants, For the Love of Mike, Flight, Ladies of Leisure, Rain or Shine, Dirigible, American Madness, The

Archival Sources

Bitter Tea of General Yen, Lady for a Day, It Happened One Night, Broadway Bill, Mr. Deeds Goes to Town, Lost Horizon, You Can't Take It with You, Mr. Smith Goes to Washington, Meet John Doe, Arsenic and Old Lace, The Battle of Russia, Tunisian Victory, It's a Wonderful Life, State of the Union, Riding High, Here Comes the Groom, Pocketful of Miracles

Files: The library has two Capra clipping files, each of which are packed with articles and interviews spanning his entire career in motion pictures. There also are clipping files for individual films; these typically contain prerelease publicity, reviews, advertising, and related material published in newspapers and magazines. In addition to a clipping file, some files also are indexed separately for "reviews"; this usually leads you to a special collection or scrapbook in which a review is contained. Souvenir programs can also be found in some of the clippings files. (There is also a separate program card file for several titles, as indicated below.) All the films to follow have a clippings file, a review file, or both: The Strong Man, Long Pants, For the Love of Mike, That Certain Thing, The Young Generation, The Donovan Affair, Flight, Ladies of Leisure, Rain or Shine, Dirigible, The Miracle Woman, Platinum Blonde, American Madness, The Bitter Tea of General Yen, Lady for a Day, It Happened One Night, Broadway Bill, Mr. Deeds Goes to Town, Lost Horizon, You Can't Take It with You, Mr. Smith Goes to Washington, Meet John Doe, Arsenic and Old Lace, Prelude to War, Divide and Conquer, The Battle of Russia, Tunisian Victory, The Negro Soldier, It's a Wonderful Life, State of the Union, Riding High, Here Comes the Groom, Our Mr. Sun, A Hole in the Head, Pocketful of Miracles.

Pressbooks: The library holds pressbooks, press sheets, or both, for the following Capra films: The Strong Man, Long Pants, For the Love of Mike, Ladies of Leisure, Rain or Shine, Dirigible, The Miracle Woman, Platinum Blonde, American Madness, The Bitter Tea of General Yen, Lady for a Day, It Happened One Night, Broadway Bill, Mr. Deeds Goes to Town, Lost Horizon, You Can't Take It with You, Mr. Smith Goes to Washington, Meet John Doe, Arsenic and Old Lace, Divide and Conquer, The Battle of Russia, Tunisian Victory, It's a Wonderful Life, State of the Union

Programs: Say It With Sables, Lady for a Day, Broadway Bill, Mr. Deeds Goes to Town, Lost Horizon, You Can't Take It with You, Meet John Doe, State of the Union

Posters: Mr. Deeds Goes to Town, Arsenic and Old Lace, Tunisian Victory

Other: As part of the library's drama collection, the following source plays for Capra's films can be found: Rain or Shine by James Gleason (prompt book); You Can't Take It with You by Moss Hart and George S. Kaufman (original prompt book);

Archival Sources

<blockquote>

Arsenic and Old Lace by Joseph Kesselring, and the teleplay adapted by Robert Harung for the Hallmark Hall of Fame in 1962; and A Hole in the Head by Arnold Schulman (typescript for its presentation at the Plymouth Theatre in 1957).

</blockquote>

1380   Donnell Film Library, New York Public Library, 20 West 53rd Street, New York, NY 10019. Phone: (212) 621-0609. Open: Monday to Saturday, 12:30 P.M.-5:30 P.M.

Feature films are restricted to viewing at the library's study center. Capra's World War II documentaries can be viewed at the library or taken out with a New York Public Library card.

Prints: Lost Horizon, It's a Wonderful Life, Prelude to War, The Nazis Strike, Divide and Conquer, The Battle of Britain, The Battle of Russia, The Battle of China, War Comes to America, The Negro Soldier, Know Your Enemy: Japan

1381   Film Study Center, Museum of Modern Art, 11 West 53rd Street, New York, NY 10019. Supervisor: Charles Silver. Phone: (212) 708-9614. Open: Monday to Friday, 1 P.M.-5 P.M.

Material is made available only to qualified scholars working on specific research projects. Students who wish to view films must present a letter from their instructor requesting permission, stating the nature and validity of the project, and listing the films required. Writers who present a similar letter from their editor or publisher may also obtain permission to view films. Requests for viewing films should be made at least a week in advance. Morning appointments can be arranged for out-of-town visitors. The Film Stills Archive is open 1:30 P.M. to 5 P.M.; an appointment must be made in advance with Mary Corliss, Curatorial Assistant, at (212) 956-4209.

Prints: American Madness, The Bitter Tea of General Yen, It Happened One Night, Mr. Deeds Goes to Town, Mr. Smith Goes to Washington, Prelude to War, The Nazis Strike, Divide and Conquer, The Battle of Britain, The Battle of Russia, The Battle of China, War Comes to America, Know Your Ally: Britain, The Negro Soldier, Two Down, One to Go

Scripts: Mr. Deeds Goes to Town (cutting continuity)
You Can't Take It with You ("Test Scene," Alice and Tony in the park, included in clipping file for the film)
Meet John Doe (cutting continuity)
Arsenic and Old Lace (dialogue continuity)
It's a Wonderful Life (final, 5/18/46, with revisions)

Stills: The museum has stills for every commercial feature film Capra directed. In addition it has stills for Prelude to War, The Nazis Strike, Divide and Conquer, The Battle of Britain, The Battle of Russia, and The Negro Soldier.

Files: The Film Study Center has a general file on Capra, which contains Richard Griffith's BFI monograph (see entry 649); program notes for a Capra retrospective by the Cinema Guild in Ann Arbor, Michigan, in February, 1973; correspondence between Capra and the Vermont Film Center; and an assortment of news clippings and interviews. There also are individual clipping files for many Capra films; these usually contain recent clippings and program notes (including those for the Museum of Modern Art by Charles Silver, Mary Corliss, and Leonard Maltin, and those for the New School by William K. Everson). Most older reviews are stored on microfiche cards, which have a separate index. Material on the following films is held: The Strong Man (microfiche), Long Pants (file, microfiche), So This is Love (file), The Matinee Idol (microfiche), Submarine (file, microfiche), The Younger Generation (file), The Donovan Affair (microfiche), Flight (file and microfiche), Ladies of Leisure (microfiche), Rain or Shine (file, microfiche), Dirigible (file, microfiche), The Miracle Woman (file, microfiche), American Madness (file, microfiche), The Bitter Tea of General Yen (microfiche), Lady for a Day (microfiche), It Happened One Night (file, microfiche), Broadway Bill (file, microfiche), Mr. Deeds Goes to Town (file, microfiche), Lost Horizon (file), You Can[t Take It with You (file), Meet John Doe (file), Arsenic and Old Lace (file, microfiche), Prelude to War (file), The Battle of Britain (file), The Battle of Russia (file), Tunisian Victory (file), War Comes to America (file), Two Down, One to Go (file), It's a Wonderful Life (file, microfiche), Riding High (file, microfiche), Here Comes the Groom (file, microfiche), A Hole in the Head (file, microfiche), Pocketful of Miracles (microfiche).

1382   The Museum of Broadcasting, 1 East 53d Street, New York, NY 10022. Director of Library Services: Douglas Gibbons. Phone: (212) 752-4690. Open: tuesday to Saturday, 12 P.M.-5 P.M.; Thursday, 5-7:30 P.M.
       The museum's collection includes a tape of Capra's appearance on "Bing Crosby: His Life and Legend," a program aired by ABC on 25 May 1978.

OSLO

1383   Norsk Filminstitutt, Aslakveien 14 B, Postboks 5 Roa, Oslo 7, Norway. Phone: (02) 24 29 94. Telegram: Filminstitutt.
       There are no special restrictions on access to the material by scholars.

Prints: It Happened One Night, Lost Horizon, Mr. Smith Goes to Washington
Stills: In addition to Capra portraits, the archive holds stills for the following Capra films: Dirigible, It Happened One Night, Mr. Deeds Goes to Town, Lost Horizon, You Can't Take It with You, Mr. Smith Goes to Washington, Meet John Doe, Arsenic and Old Lace, It's a Wonderful Life, Here Comes the Groom, A Hole in the Head, Pocketful of Miracles

Archival Sources

Programs: The Way of the Strong, American Madness, The Bitter Tea of General Yen, Lady for a Day, It Happened One Night, Mr. Deeds Goes to Town, Lost Horizon, You Can't Take It with You, Mr. Smith Goes to Washington, Meet John Doe, Arsenic and Old Lace, Riding High, Here Comes the Groom, A Hole in the Head

Files: The archive holds a file of publicity material on Capra's career and clipping files for the following Capra films: Ladies of Leisure, American Madness, It Happened One Night, Lost Horizon, You Can't Take It with You, Arsenic and Old Lace, A Hole in the Head, Pocketful of Miracles

1384 Sonja Henies Ob Neils Onstads Stiftelser, 1311 Kunstesentret Hovikodden, Oslo, Norway. Director: Old Henrik Moe. Curator: Per Hovkenakk.

The Henie-Onstad Art Institute has a Capra file containing Scandinavian newspaper clippings and a few program sheets. There are no restrictions on access to the material by researchers.

PARIS

1385 Service Des Archives Du Film Du Cente National De La Cinématographie, Rue Alexandre Turpault, 78390 Bois D'Arcy, Paris, France. Curator: Nicole Schmitt. Phone: 460-20-50.

Prints: Flight (one reel only), Arsenic and Old Lace, Prelude to War, The Nazis Strike, Divide and Conquer, The Battle of Britain, The Battle of Russia, It's a Wonderful Life

Other: The archive also has a collection of "appréciations"--brief excerpts from reviews in French newspapers and periodicals --for the following Capra films: It Happened One Night, Mr. Deeds Goes to Town, Lost Horizon, You Can't Take It with You, Mr. Smith Goes to Washington, Meet John Doe, Arsenic and Old Lace, It's a Wonderful Life, State of the Union, Riding High, Here Comes the Groom, A Hole in the Head, Pocketful of Miracles.

PHILADELPHIA

1386 Free Library of Philadelphia, Theatre Collection, Logan Circle, Philadelphia, PA 19103. Theatre Librarian: Geraldine Duclow. Phone: MU 6-5427. Open: Monday to Friday, 9 A.M.-5 P.M.

The collection includes a newspaper clippings file on Capra and reviews of individual films by him. The material does not circulate, but photocopies are available through the mail, or in person, on a limited basis.

POCATELLO, IDAHO

1387 Speech and Drama Department, Idaho State University, Pocatello, ID 83209. Phone: (208) 236-3695.

Archival Sources

The Edward Stevenson Collection includes watercolor costume drawings for The Bitter Tea of General Yen. Material may be viewed through special arrangement.

POONA, INDIA

1388 National Film Archive of India, Ministry of Information and Broadcasting, Law College Road, Pune 411 004, India. Curator: P.K. Nair.

Prints: It Happened One Night, Mr. Smith Goes to Washington, Meet John Doe
Scripts: Forbidden, Lost Horizon, A Hole in the Head, Pocketful of Miracles
Other: The archive also holds a number of press clippings, brochures, pamphlets, folders, and magazine articles on Capra.

PRETORIA

1389 South African National Film Archives, National Film Board, P.O. Box 600, Silverton, Pretoria, South Africa. Director: J.H. de Lange.

Prints: Prelude to War, The Nazis Strike, Divide and Conquer, The Battle of Britain, The Battle of Russia, The Battle of China

ROCHESTER, NEW YORK

1390 George Eastman House, International Museum of Photography, Department of Film, 900 East Avenue, Rochester, NY 14607. Director: John B. Kuiper. Phone: (716) 271-3361. Open: Tuesday to Sunday, 10 A.M.-4:30 P.M.

Prints: Divide and Conquer, The Battle of Russia, Tunisian Victory
Stills: The museum reports "scattered coverage" of stills from Capra films. The Warner Brothers New York City stills library, which the museum holds, would likely include stills from The Strong Man, Long Pants, For the Love of Mike, and Arsenic and Old Lace.

SOFIA, BULGARIA

1391 Bulgarska Nacionalna Filmoteka, Ul. Gourko 36, 1000 Sofia, Bulgaria. Director: Todor Andreykov.
No restrictions are placed on access to the material by scholars.

Prints: It Happened One Night, Mr. Deeds Goes to Town, Arsenic and Old Lace
Stills: Long Pants, Platinum Blonde, It Happened One Night, Mr. Deeds Goes to Town, Arsenic and Old Lace

Archival Sources

STOCKHOLM

1392 Svenska Filminstitutet, Filmhuset, Borgagen, Box 27 126, 192 52 Stockholm 27 Sweden. Phone: 08-63 05 10. Telex: 13326 Filmins S. Telegram: Filminstitutet.
    There are no special restrictions on access to the material, but the screening of films is expensive.

Prints: American Madness, The Bitter Tea of General Yen, Lady for a Day, It Happened One Night, Mr. Deeds Goes to Town, Lost Horizon, You Can't Take It with You, Mr. Smith Goes to Washington, Meet John Doe, Arsenic and Old Lace, The Nazis Strike, Divide and Conquer

Scripts: Mr. Smith Goes to Washington, Arsenic and Old Lace, A Hole in the Head, Pocketful of Miracles

Stills: The Strong Man, Long Pants, Submarine, Flight, Ladies of Leisure, Rain or Shine, Dirigible, The Miracle Woman, Platinum Blonde, American Madness, The Bitter Tea of General Yen, Lady for a Day, It Happened One Night, Mr. Deeds Goes to Town, Lost Horizon, You Can't Take It with You, Meet John Doe, Arsenic and Old Lace, It's a Wonderful Life, State of the Union, Riding High, Here Comes the Groom, A Hole in the Head, Pocketful of Miracles

Files: Files of newspaper clippings are held for the following Capra films: The Strong Man, Long Pants, The Way of the Strong, Submarine, Flight, Ladies of Leisure, Dirigible, American Madness, The Bitter Tea of General Yen, Lady for a Day, It Happened One Night, Broadway Bill, Mr. Deeds Goes to Town, Lost Horizon, You Can't Take It with You, Mr. Smith Goes to Washington, Meet John Doe, Arsenic and Old Lace, Prelude to War, Tunisian Victory, The Negro Soldier, It's a Wonderful Life, State of the Union, Riding High, Here Comes the Groom, A Hole in the Head, Pocketful of Miracles.

TORONTO (VICINITY)

1393 The Ontario Film Institute, 770 Don Mills Road, Don Mills, Ontario, Canada. Director: Gerald Pratley. Phone: (416) 429-4100.
    The Ontario Film Institute's library is open to the public for reading, study, and research on the premises. Included in the library's holding is a file of press clippings on Capra.

TOULOUSE

1394 Cinémateque de Toulouse, 3 rou Roquelaine, Toulouse, France. Curator: Raymond Borde.
    Because of budget limitations, the archive is not open to students.

Archival Sources

Prints: *Lady for a Day*, *You Can't Take It with You* (both nitrate)

TURIN

1395   Museo Nazionale Del Cinema, Palazzo Chiablese, Piazza S. Giovanni 2, 10122 Torino, Italy. Director: Maria Adriana Prolo. Librarian: Roberto Radicati.
    There are no restrictions on access to the material by scholars.

Prints: *State of the Union* (16mm, in Italian)
Stills: *Dirigible* (2), *Forbidden* (1), *American Madness* (1), *The Bitter Tea of General Yen* (1), *Mr. Deeds Goes to Town* (6), *Lost Horizon* (3), *You Can't Take It with You* (4)
Other: The museum's collection also contains Italian posters and lobby cards for the following Capra films: *Mr. Deeds Goes to Town*, *You Can't Take It with You*, *Mr. Smith Goes to Washington*, *Meet John Doe*, *Arsenic and Old Lace*, *It's a Wonderful Life*, *State of the Union*, *Riding High*, *Here Comes the Groom*.

VIENNA

1396   Österreichisches Filmmuseum, Augustinerstrasse 1, 1010 Vienna, Austria. Curators: Peter Konlechner, Peter Kubelka. Phone: 52 34 26, 52 62 06. Telegram: Filmmuseum Wien.

Prints: *Prelude to War*, *The Nazis Strike*, *Divide and Conquer*, *The Battle of Britain*, *The Battle of Russia*, *War Comes to America*, *The Negro Soldier*, *Two Down, One to Go*
Stills: *The Strong Man*, *Say It with Sables*, *The Power of the Press*, *Dirigible*, *Forbidden*, *The Bitter Tea of General Yen*, *Lady for a Day*, *It Happened One Night*, *Broadway Bill*, *Mr. Deeds Goes to Town*, *Lost Horizon*, *You Can't Take It with You*, *Mr. Smith Goes to Washington*, *Arsenic and Old Lace*, *A Hole in the Head*, *Pocketful of Miracles*.

WASHINGTON, D.C. (AND VICINITY)

1397   Army Audio-Visual Agency, DAVA/PSPD-ACD, 5A518, Pentagon, Washington, DC 20310.
    Stills from the army orientation films supervised by Capra during World War II are held at this agency.

1398   Federal Records Center, Washington National Records Center, Suitland, Maryland. c/o Mr. Paul Taborn, Security Specialist, HQDA (DAAG-AMR), Room GA076, Forrestal Building, 1000 Independence Avenue, SW, Washington, DC 20314.
    The Federal Records Center holds twenty-two cartons of film records, including film production files for Capra's *Why We Fight* series. Written permission from Paul Taborn is required for access to this material at the Washington National Records Center in Suitland.

Archival Sources

Maryland. According to David Culbert, who was perhaps the first film scholar to use this material, the Why We Fight files are indexed according to their production numbers in the 6000 series. For further information see Culbert's "Note on Government Paper Records" in Bonnie G. Rowans's Scholar's Guide to Washington, D.C., Film and Video Collections (Washington, D.C.: Smithsonian Institution Press, 1980), pp. 235-43.

1399   Manuscript Division, Library of Congress, Manuscript Reading Room, Thomas Jefferson Building, Washington, DC 10540. Acting Chief Librarian: Paul T. Heffron. Phone: (202) 287-5387. Open: Monday to Friday, 8:30 A.M.-5:00 P.M.
       The May Robson Collection contains newspaper clippings and magazine articles concerning Lady for a Day (carton 10).

1400   Motion Picture, Broadcasting and Recorded Sound Division, Library of Congress, Thomas Jefferson Building, Room 1053, Washington, DC, 20540. Chief: Erik Barnouw. Reference Librarian: Barbara Humphreys. Phone: (202) 426-5840. Open: Monday to Friday, 8:30 A.M.-4:30 P.M.
       Viewing facilities may be used free of charge, but viewing times must be scheduled in advance. The facilities are open to serious researchers only. Undergraduate college and university students must provide a letter from their professor endorsing their project; high school students cannot be accommodated. The division's reading room is open to the public, although high school students again are not permitted. Here card files, by title, of all the films in the collection can be consulted. The files include a shelflist, a dictionary catalogue, a nitrate film file, a directors file, a chronological and company files for silent films. The staff will answer written and telephone inquiries about the holdings and make appointments for the use of reference facilities by individual scholars. Copies of film footage not restricted by copyright, by provision of gift or transfer, or by physical condition may be ordered through the division. Those requesting this service are responsible for the search of copyright records held by the Register of Copyrights, Library of Congress.

Prints: Fultah Fisher's Boarding House (16mm acetate)
         That Certain Thing (16mm acetate)
         Say It with Sables (35mm nitrate trailer)
         Submarine (35mm acetate)
         The Power of the Press (16mm acetate, cut version)
         The Younger Generation (35mm acetate)
         The Donovan Affair (35mm acetate)
         Ladies of Leisure (35mm acetate sound; 16mm acetate silent)
         Dirigible (35mm acetate; 35mm nitrate trailer)
         The Miracle Woman (35mm acetate)
         Platinum Blonde (35mm acetate)
         Forbidden (35mm acetate; 16mm acetate)
         American Madness (35mm acetate; 16mm acetate)
         The Bitter Tea of General Yen (35mm acetate)

Archival Sources

<u>It Happened One Night</u> (35mm acetate)
<u>Broadway Bill</u> (35mm acetate)
<u>Mr. Deeds Goes to Town</u> (16mm acetate)
<u>Lost Horizon</u> (35mm nitrate; 35mm acetate)
<u>You Can't Take It with You</u> (16mm acetate)
<u>Mr. Smith Goes to Washington</u> (16mm acetate)
<u>Meet John Doe</u> (35mm nitrate; 35mm acetate)
<u>Arsenic and Old Lace</u> (16mm acetate)
<u>Prelude to War</u> (16mm acetate)
<u>The Nazis Strike</u> (16mm acetate)
<u>Divide and Conquer</u> (16mm acetate)
<u>The Battle of Britain</u> (16mm acetate)
<u>The Battle of Russia</u> (16mm acetate)
<u>Two Down, One to Go</u> (16mm acetate)
<u>It's a Wonderful Life</u> (35mm acetate; 16mm acetate)
<u>State of the Union</u> (16mm acetate)
<u>Here Comes the Groom</u> (35mm acetate)
<u>Our Mr. Sun</u> (16mm acetate)
<u>Hemo the Magnificent</u> (16mm acetate)
<u>The Strange Case of the Cosmic Rays</u> (16mm acetate)
<u>The Unchained Goddess</u> (16mm acetate)
<u>A Hole in the Head</u> (35mm acetate)
<u>Pocketful of Miracles</u> (35mm acetate)
<u>Rendezvous in Space</u> (16mm acetate)

Scripts: <u>It's a Wonderful Life</u>, <u>State of the Union</u>. (Both of these are cutting continuities submitted to the Library of Congress as copyright material. See below.)

Other: Copyright files contain printed material submitted to the Library of Congress for the purpose of establishing copyright on individual films. The content of these files vary from film to film; most of the early submissions are simply brief synopses. The contents of copyright files for Capra's films are described below:
<u>Fultah Fisher's Boarding House</u> (1-paragraph synopsis)
<u>The Strong Man</u> (2-paragraph synopsis)
<u>Long Pants</u> (2 1/2-page synopsis)
<u>For the Love of Mike</u> (7-paragraph synopsis)
<u>That Certain Thing</u> (2-page synopsis)
<u>So This Is Love</u> (1 1/2-page synopsis)
<u>The Matinee Idol</u> (2-page synopsis)
<u>Say It with Sables</u> (exhibitors publicity material)
<u>The Power of the Press</u> (5-page synopsis)
<u>The Donovan Affair</u> (2 1/2-page synopsis)
<u>Flight</u> (exhibitors pressbook)
<u>Ladies of Leisure</u> (exhibitors campaign book; 5-page synopsis)
<u>Rain or Shine</u> (exhibitors campaign book)
<u>Dirigible</u> (1 1/2-page synopsis)
<u>The Miracle Woman</u> (exhibitors pressbook)
<u>Platinum Blonde</u> (8-paragraph synopsis)
<u>Forbidden</u> (7-paragraph synopsis)
<u>American Madness</u> (3-paragraph synopsis)

Archival Sources

<u>The Bitter Tea of General Yen</u> (6-paragraph synopsis)
<u>Lady for a Day</u> (press sheet; 9-paragraph synopsis)
<u>It Happened One Night</u> (exhibitors pressbook; press sheet)
<u>Broadway Bill</u> (press sheet; 6-paragraph synopsis)
<u>Mr. Deeds Goes to Town</u> (press sheet; 8-paragraph synopsis)
<u>Lost Horizon</u> (press sheet; 7-paragraph synopsis)
<u>You Can't Take It with You</u> (exhibitors pressbook)
<u>Mr. Smith Goes to Washington</u> (2-page synopsis)
<u>Meet John Doe</u> (2-page synopsis)
<u>Arsenic and Old Lace</u> (8-paragraph synopsis)
<u>It's a Wonderful Life</u> (cutting continuity; assorted reviews)
<u>State of the Union</u> (cutting continuity)
<u>Riding High</u> (exhibitors pressbook; assorted reviews)
<u>Here Comes the Groom</u> (exhibitors pressbook)
<u>Our Mr. Sun</u> (5-page synopsis)
<u>Hemo the Magnificent</u> (4-page synopsis)
<u>The Strange Case of the Cosmic Rays</u> (7-page synopsis)
<u>The Unchained Goddess</u> (7-page synopsis)
<u>A Hole in the Head</u> (exhibitors pressbook)
<u>Pocketful of Miracles</u> (exhibitors pressbook)

Note: Copyright materials from <u>The Way of the Strong</u>, <u>Submarine</u>, and <u>The Younger Generation</u> were being microfilmed at the time of my research at the library.

1401 Motion Picture and Sound Recording Branch, National Archives and Records Service, Office 20E, Pennsylvania Avenue between 7th and 9th Streets, NW, Washington, DC 20408. Chief: William Murphy. Phone: (202) 523-3267 or 3294.

Material relating to Capra's work for the army during World War II is voluminous, although not always easy to locate. Prints of all the orientation films made by the army's film unit under Capra's supervision are available for viewing by appointment. In addition, the archive holds files for each of the films; these contain shot lists, scripts, sources, and some notes and correspondence relating to the gathering of footage. Unfortunately there is no general index to policy-level correspondence and records concerning Capra, but material relating to Capra or Capra films can be found in at least four Record Groups:

RG 111: Office of the Chief Signal Officer, 1909-1954 (Production Files)
RG 165: War Department General and Special Staffs, Public Relations Division, 1921-1949
RG 208: Office of War Information, 1941-1945
RG 330: Office of the Secretary of Defense

Research assistance is available at the archives. Because the material is spread about in various locations, it is wise to contact in advance the Chief of the Motion Picture Branch, the Chief of Modern Military Records, and the Chief of State Department Records. For a bibliographic guide to use of the National Archives, see David Culbert's "Note on Government Paper Records" in Bonnie G. Rowan's

Archival Sources

Scholars' Guide to Washington, D.C., Film and Video Collections (Washington, D.C.: Smithsonian Institution Press, 1980), pp. 235-43.

1402   Prince George's County Memorial Library System, Films Division, 6532 Adelphi Road, Hyattsville, MD 20782. Coordinator: Kent A. Moore. Phone: (301) 699-3500.
     The collection is available to holders of adult library cards from any public library in the state of Maryland. A nonresident card is available for a fee. Films may not be shown where any admission is charged or for fund-raising. Films may not be copied or shown on television. Films may not be borrowed for classroom use in any elementary or high school. Fees range from $1.00 to $4.00.

Prints: The Strong Man, It Happened One Night, Meet John Doe, Arsenic and Old Lace, Prelude to War, The Nazis Strike, Divide and Conquer, The Battle of Britain, The Battle of China, War Comes to America, It's a Wonderful Life, Hemo the Magnificent, The Unchained Goddess

WEISBADEN

1403   Deutsches Institut Für Filmkunde, Schloss, 6200 Weisbaden-Biebrich, West Germany. Directors: Theo Fürstenau, Ulrich Poschke; Deputy: Eberhard Spiess.

Prints: Arsenic and Old Lace
Other: Stills and printed material (including reviews, press books, programs, censorship cards, and publicity material) are held for specific Capra films. Information is available upon request from the directors.

The following archives reported no Capra holdings: Freunde der Deutschen Kinemathek e.V., Welserstrasse 25, 1000 Berlin 30, West Germany; Bundesarchiv-Filmarchiv, Am Wöllershof 12, 5400 Koblenz, West Germany; München Stadtmuseum, Filmmuseum Postfach, 8000 Munich 1, West Germany; and Czechoslovokak Film Archive, Národní 40, Prague 1, Czechoslovakia.

VIII. Film Distributors

Listed below are films directed or supervised by Frank Capra that currently are available for 16mm, nontheatrical rental in the United States. A key to rental sources follows the list of film titles. Both the film title and distributor lists are alphabetically arranged.

American Madness (1932)	COR, SWA
Arsenic and Old Lace (1944)	UA
The Battle of Britain (1943)	BUD, FI, IMA, KIT, MUS, NAT, ROA, TRA, TWY, VIE
The Battle of China (1944)	BUD, FI, IMA, KIT, MUS, NAT, TRA, TWY, VIE
The Battle of Russia (1943)	BUD, FIL, FI, IMA, KIT, MUS, NAT, ROA, TRA, TWY, VIE
The Bitter Tea of General Yen (1933)	ADE, FI, IMA, JEN, KIT, SWA, TWY, WEL, WES, WHO
Dirigible (1931)	ADE, JEN, KIT, SWA, WEL, WES
Divide and Conquer (1943)	BUD, FI, IMA, KIT, MUS, NAT, TRA, TWY, VIE
Flight (1929)	KIT
Forbidden (1932)	KIT
Here Comes the Groom (1951)	FI, PAR
Here Is Germany (1945)	NAT
A Hole in the Head (1959)	UA
It Happened One Night (1934)	BUD, CLW, LU, SWA, WEL

Film Distributors

It's a Wonderful Life (1946) — ASF, BAU, BUD, CIN, CLA, EM, FI, IMA, IVY, JEN, KIT, NW, SWA, TWY, VCI, WEL, WES, WHO

Know Your Ally: Britain (1943) — BUD, NAT

Know Your Enemy: Japan (1945) — NAT

Ladies of Leisure (1930) — KIT

Long Pants (1927) — TWY

Lost Horizon (1937) — ADE, ASF, CLW, FI, IMA, INS, IVY, JEN, KIT, ROA, SEL, SWA, TWY, VCI, WES, WHO

Meet John Doe (1941) — BUD, CLA, EM, FC, FI, IMA, INS, IVY, KIT, SEL, VCI, WHO

The Miracle Woman (1931) — KIT

Mr. Deeds Goes to Town (1936) — ADE, ASF, BUD, CLW, FI, IMA, INS, IVY, JEN, KIT, ROA, SEL, SWA, TWY, VCI, WES, WHO

Mr. Smith Goes to Washington (1939) — ADE, ASF, CLW, FI, IMA, INS, IVY, JEN, KIT, SWA, TWY, VCI, WEL, WES, WHO

The Nazis Strike (1943) — BUD, FI, IMA, KIT, MUS, NAT, TRA, TWY, VIE

The Negro Soldier (1944) — FI, IMA, MUS, NAT

Platinum Blonde (1931) — ADE, FI, KIT, SWA, TWY, VCI

Pocketful of Miracles (1961) — BUD, FI, ROA, UA, WEL, WHO

Prelude to War (1942) — BUD, FI, IMA, KIT, MUS, NAT, TRA, TWY, VIE, WHO

Rain or Shine (1942) — KIT

So This Is Love (1928) — KIT

State of the Union (1948) — U16

The Strong Man (1926) — TWY

Submarine (1928) — KIT

Film Distributors

That Certain Thing (1928)	KIT
Tunisian Victory (1944)	BUD
Two Down, One to Go (1945)	KIT
War Comes to America (1945)	BUD, FI, IMA, KIT, MUS, NAT, ROA, TWY, VIE
The Way of the Strong (1928)	KIT
You Can't Take It with You (1938)	ADE, FI, IMA, INS, JEN, KIT, ROA, TWY, VCI, WES, WHO
The Younger Generation (1929)	KIT
Your Job in Germany (1945)	NAT

Distributor Key

ADE   Adelphia Cinema Enterprises, Inc.
        580 Lancaster Ave., Bryn Mawr, PA 19010; (215) 525-5650

ASF   Association Films, Inc.
        866 Third Avenue, New York, NY 10022; (212) 935-4210

BAU   Bauer International Pictures
        695 West 7th St., Plainfield, NJ 07060; (201) 757-6090

BUD   Budget Films
        4590 Santa Monica Blvd., Los Angeles, CA 90029; (213) 660-0187

CIN   Cine-Craft Films
        1720 N.W. Marshall, P.O. Box 4126, Portland, OR 97208; (503) 228-7484

CLA   Classic Film Museum, Inc.
        4 Union Square, Dover-Foxcroft, ME 04426; (207) 564-8371

CLW   Clem Williams Films, Inc.
        2240 Noblestown Road, Pittsburgh, PA 15205; (412) 921-5810

COR   Corinth Films
        410 East 62nd St., New York, NY 10021; (212) 421-4770

EM   EM Gee Film Library
        6924 Canby Ave., Suite 103, Reseda, CA 91335; (213) 981-5506

FC   "The" Film Center
        938 K St., N.W., Washington, DC, 20001; (202) 393-1205

FI   Films Incorporated

Film Distributors

	1144 Wilmette Ave., Wilmette, IL 60091; (312) 256-4730
FIL	Film Images (A Division of Radim Films, Inc.) 1034 Lake St., Oak Park, IL 60301; (312) 386-4826
IMA	The Images Film Archive 300 Phillips Park Road, Mamaroneck, NY 10543; (914) 381-2993
INS	Institutional Cinema Inc. 10 First St., Saugerties, NY 12477; (914) 246-2848
IVY	Ivy Film 165 West 46th St., New York, NY 10036; (212) 765-3940
JEN	Jensen's Cinema 16 4524 Howard Ave., Western Springs, IL 60558; (312) 246-6116
KIT	Kit Parker Films Carmel Valley, CA 93924; (408) 659-3474 or 659-4131
LU	Louisiana State University, 16mm Film Library Instructional Resource Center, 118 Himes Hall, Baton Rouge, LA 70737; (504) 380-1135
MUS	The Museum of Modern Art, Department of Film 11 West 53rd St., New York, NY 10019; (212) 956-4205
NAT	National Audiovisual Center National Archives and Records, Service, General Services Administration, Order Section DL, Washington, DC 20409; (301) 763-1891
NW	Northwest Film Study Center, Portland Art Museum 1219 Southwest Park Ave., Portland, OR 97205; (503) 221-1156
PAR	Paramount Non-Theatrical 5451 Marathon St., Hollywood, CA 90038; (213) 462-0700
ROA	ROA Films 1696 North Astor St., Milwaukee, WI 53202, (414) 271-0861
SEL	Select Films 115 West 31st St., New York, NY 10001; (212) 564-4457
SWA	Swank Motion Pictures, Inc. 6767 Forest Lawn Drive, Los Angeles, CA 90068; (213) 851-6300
TRA	Trans-World Films, Inc. 382 South Michigan Ave., Chicago, IL 60604; (312) 922-1530
TWY	Twyman Films, Inc. 4700 Wadsworth Road, Box 605, Dayton, OH 45401; (513) 276-5941

Film Distributors

UA   United Artists Entertainment
          729 Seventh Ave., New York, NY 10019; (212) 575-4715

U16   Universal 16
          8901 Beverly Blvd., Los Angeles, CA 90048; (213) 550-7461

VCI   V.C.I. Films
          6555 East Skelly Drive, Tulsa, OK 74145; (918) 583-2681

VIE   Viewfinders, Inc.
          800 Custer Avenue, P.O. Box 1665, Evanston, IL 60204; (312) 869-0600

WEL   Welling Motion Pictures
          454 Meacham Ave., Elmont NY 11003; (516) 354-1066

WES   Westcoast Films
          25 Lusk St., San Francisco, CA 94107; (415) 362-4700

SHO   Wholesome Film Center, Inc.
          20 Melrose, St., Boston, MA 02116; (617) 426-0155

Author Index

Aaronson, Charles S., 710
Abel. See Green, Abel
Agate, James, 227, 557
Agee, James, 488-89, 508-9, 558, 577, 626, 635, 702, 739, 800, 861, 929, 951, 1023
Albert, Katherine, 139
Allen, Tom, 1066
Allredge, Charles, 627
Amoruso, Mario A., 1024-25
Amory, Cleveland, 1264
Anderson, Nancy, 1283
Andersson, Willmar, 901
Andrew, Dudley, 1134a
Anstey, Edgar, 449, 495-96, 521
Argus, 162, 186, 187
Armitage, Peter, 754
Averson, Richard, 900

B.O., 237
Babcock, Muriel, 1196
Baby, Yvonne, 755
Bacon, James, 1243
Badder, David J., 930
Bailey, George, 1284
Bakshy, Alexander, 118, 148, 865
Balio, Tino, 1001
Barbaro, Nick, 1002
Barnes, Howard, 298-99, 361-63, 401-3, 450, 497, 522-23, 565, 608, 644
Barnouw, Eric, 931
Barsam, Richard, 958
Baskette, Kirtley, 188, 814
Bauche, Freddy, 932
Bauer, Leda, 662
Baxter, John, 785

Beaton, Welford, 95
Beckley, Paul V., 717, 743
Bell, Nelson B., 404
Belton, John, 1069, 1136
Bendow, Burton, 815
Bendslev, W. Leslie, 405
Benedict, Paul, 1215
Benét, William Rose, 524-25
Bennett, Don, 108
Berggren, Noel, 1274
Bergman, Andrew, 816, 959, 1098
Bergman, Mark, 817
Bernardinelli, Orazio, 189
Bernds, Edward, 818, 866, 1003, 1026, 1137
Bert. See Briller, Bert
Best, Katharine, 300
Beylie, Claude, 1004, 1070
Bianchi, Pietro, 679
Bianchini, Adelio, 609
Biberman, Herbert, 451
Bige. See Bigelow, Joe
Bigelow, Joe, 190
Bishop, Allen, 434
Bishop, Harv, 1293, 1300
Black, Louis, 1027
Boehnel, William, 119-20, 163, 191-92, 238, 301-2, 364, 406, 452
Bogdanovich, Peter, 718, 867, 907
Bogle, Donald, 908
Bohn, Thomas William, 786, 1028
Bohnenkamp, Dennis R., 1099
Bolzoni, Francesco, 703
Borde, Raymond, 819
Borden, W.T., 303
Bouissinot, Roger, 781

Author Index

Bourget, Jean-Loup, 820-21
Bower, Anthony, 453
Bower, Lynn, 719
Brady, Thomas F., 663, 1220, 1227
Braudy, Leo, 1071
Bressan, Arthur, 1275
Briller, Bert, 566
Brog. See Brogdon, William
Brogdon, William, 610, 664
Brown, Geoff, 1005, 1072, 1100
Brown, John Mason, 365
Brown, Kent R., 961
Browne, Nick, 1101, 1138
Brownlow, Kevin, 793, 868, 1102
Burdett, Winston, 239, 304
Buscombe, Edward, 962
Byron, Stuart, 1029

Calder-Marshall, Alexander, 762
Caldwell, Cy, 164
Cameron, Evan, 777
Cameron, Kate, 240, 305, 407, 454, 526, 567
Campassi, Osvaldo, 455
Cargin, Peter, 909
Carmody, Jay, 498
Carroll, Harrison, 611
Castello, Giulio Cesare, 629, 665
Casty, Alan, 963
Cavell, Stanley, 1121, 1139
Cawkwell, Tim, 869
Cecchi, Emilio, 306-8
Chamberlin, Jo, 366
Champlin, Charles, 1268
Chapman, Ross, 1103
Char. See Chartier, Roy
Chartier, Roy, 1121, 367, 527
Chevallier, Jacques, 822
Chic, 193
Childs, James, 1276
Churchill, Douglas W., 456, 1207, 1211
Ciment, Michel, 823-24
Cincotti, Guido, 687
Claxton, Oliver, 59, 68, 77
Cocks, Jay, 825
Codelli, Lorenzo, 826
Coffey, Tom, 645
Cohen, Harold, 165
Cohen, Hubert I., 964
Cohen, John S., Jr., 166
Cohn, Bernard, 827

Cohn, Herbert, 408
Coleman, John, 870
Collins, Frederick L., 435
Colman, Juliet Benita, 1285
Colombat, Jacques, 794
Colpart, G., 1073
Comte, Olivier, 828
Connor, Edward, 763, 1030
Cook, Alton, 528
Cooke, Alistair, 309, 829
Coombs, Richard, 933
Coons, Robbin, 1212
Copeland, Elie, 409
Corliss, Richard, 871, 934
Creelman, Eileen, 194, 241-42, 310, 368, 457, 529, 1201, 1204
Crewe, Regina, 167, 195, 243, 311
Cripps, Thomas, 1074, 1104
Crisler, B.R., 244
Crow, James Francis, 458-59
Crowther, Bosley, 460-61, 499-500, 530-32, 554a, 568, 581, 612-13, 646, 666, 676, 720-21, 765, 1075, 1205
Culbert, David, 1104
Cunningham, James P., 312, 410
Cutts, John, 756

Daugherty, Frank, 1206
Davidson, Bill, 1217
Davy, C., 168, 313
de Baroncelli, Jean, 680
Delehanty, Thornton, 169, 196, 246
Deming, Barbara, 667, 795
Dent, Alan, 582
Dickstein, Martin, 170
Dickstein, Morris, 1071, 1122
Draper, Ellen, 1123
Drew, William M., 1301
DuBrow, Rick, 1304
Dugan, James, 369
Durgnat, Raymond, 796, 910
Dyer, John Peter, 722

Early, Dudley, 247
Eder, Richard, 1006
Ellis, Peter. See Lerner, Irving
Epstein, Clarence, 872
Estrin, Allen, 1124
Evans, Harry, 96, 109, 122-24,

Author Index

462
Everson, William K., 1031, 1076-77
Eyquem, Olivier, 828, 935

F., R.R., 315
Falkenburg, Jinx, 1230
Faber, Manny, 501, 533, 583, 647, 830
Fell, John, 1105
Ferguson, Otis, 197-98, 214, 249-50, 316-17, 370, 411, 436, 463-64, 831, 873, 965
Flaherty, Joe, 1032
Flatley, Guy, 1294
Fleming, Alice, 911
Fleming, Peter, 125
Flin. See Flinn, John C., Sr.
Flinn, John C., Sr., 465
Flinn, Tom, 910
Ford, Charles, 685
Forman, Harrison, 318
Forrest, Mark, 126, 149, 150, 171
Forsythe, Robert, 199
Frank, Sam, 1033
Franklin, Joe, 723
Freedman, Leo, 1199
Fuller, Edmund, 832
Furhammer, Leif, 833

G., K.M., 319
Gable, Clark, 584
Gallagher, Brian, 1140
Gallez, Douglas W., 684
Galway, Peter, 371
Gardella, Kay, 1233
Gardner, P.A., 1295
Garrison, Omar, 1239
Gassner, John, 502, 1034
Gehring, Wes D., 1078
Gene, 724
Gerster, Patrick, 1141
Gertner, Richard, 804
Giannini, Louis, 1142
Gill, Samuel, 802
Gilliat, Penelope, 834, 874, 912, 1035-36
Glatzer, Richard, 966, 968, 1286
Golden, Herb, 651
Goldstein, Ruth M., 913
Goodman, Ezra, 648, 668
Gould, Jack, 688, 693, 704

Graham, Olive, 1106
Graham, Virginia, 614
Gramantieri, Tullio, 320
Grant, Jack D., 569
Greason, Alfred Roshford, 71a, 112a, 62, 100
Green, Abel, 64, 138, 218, 276
Green, E.M., 372, 534
Greenburg, Joel, 787
Greene, Graham, 251-52, 321-23, 373, 437, 835, 875, 969, 1079
Greico, David, 1037
Griffith, Richard, 412, 585, 630, 649, 677, 970-71
Grisola, Michel, 1007
Grogg, Sam L., 936, 1099
Gromo, Mario, 253

H., R., 324
Haid, Liane, 1197
Hall, Mordaunt, 60-61, 69-71, 78-79, 97, 110-11, 127-28, 151-52, 172-173, 200, 837
Halliwell, Leslie, 773
Hamilton, James Shelley, 254, 466
Hamilton, Sara, 535
Hamman, Mary, 467
Handzo, Stephen, 876, 972-73, 1038-39, 1080
Hargrave, Hary A., 1305
Harriman, Margaret Case, 468
Harris, Dixie R., 700, 799
Harrison, Paula, 1202
Hart, Henry, 836
Hart, Nancy K., 1081
Hartung, Philip T., 374, 413, 469, 536, 586, 615
Harvey, Stephen, 1082
Haskell, Molly, 937
Hatch, Robert, 616, 650
Haufler, Charles, 325
Heffernan, Harold, 438
Hellman, Geoffrey T., 439, 974
Helming, Ann, 669
Hendrick, Kimmis, 1263
Henstell, Bruce, 1278
Herb. See Golden, Herb
Herbstram, 725
Herzberg, Max J., 414
Higham, Charles, 787, 938
Hill, Steven P., 757, 766

Hills, Beverly, 201, 255, 326, 375, 415
Hilton, James, 256
Hitchens, Gordon, 877
Hochman, Stanley, 939
Hoellering, Franz, 416
Holmes, Winifred, 537
Hopper, Hedda, 470
Hosman, H., 1083
Houston, Penelope, 652, 744
Hovland, Carl I., 631
Hughes, William, 878, 1008
Hurley, Neil, 1306
Hyams, Joe, 1240

Isaacs, Hermine Rich, 538, 587
Isaksson, Folke, 833

Jacobs, Jack, 705
Jacobs, Lewis, 215, 417, 471, 782, 788, 975
James, Clive, 879
Jameson, Richard T., 940, 1143
Jeanne, René, 685
Johaneson, Bland, 257, 327-28, 376-77
Johnston, Alva, 378
Jones, Carlisle, 202
Jowett, Garth, 1009

Kael, Pauline, 789, 976, 1125
Kaminsky, Stuart, 941
Kann, Red, 617
Karp, Walter, 1144, 1307
Karr, Lawrence F., 1126
Katz, Ephraim, 1107
Kay, Karyn, 977, 1013, 1040
Keller, Allan, 1213
Kennedy, Paul P., 539
Kerr, Walter, 978, 979
Kittredge, William, 1108
Knight, Arthur, 694, 726, 745
Kolodjazhnaja, Valentina, 801
Kostolefsky, Joseph, 727
Kozarski, Richard, 838, 1010, 1041
Krauzer, Steven M., 1108
Kreuger, Myles, 1042
Kuhns, William, 880
Kupferberg, Audrey F., 1127

Labarthe, A.-S., 758

Lahue, Kalton C., 778, 802
Lambert, Gavin, 618, 980
Land. See Landry, Robert J.
Landry, Robert J., 80-81, 98, 174
Ladner, David, 503-4, 540
Lardner, John, 541
Larkin, Rochelle, 981
Larsen, Egon, 653
Laura, Ernesto G., 695, 706
Lawson, John Howard, 767
Leab, Daniel J., 982
Leach, Jim, 1043
Leary, Richard, 881
Lefèvre, Raymond, 1084
Lehmann-Haupt, Christopher, 839
Leish, Kenneth W., 942
Lellis, George, 1156
Lerner, Irving, 248, 257a, 314, 328a
Levin, G. Roy, 840
Levin, Meyer, 440-40a, 886
Levitas, Louise, 486
Levy, William Turner, 1062
Lewis, J.D., 472
Leyda, Jay, 473, 736, 768, 1296
Littlefield, Walt, 1044
Livingston, Guy, 1297
Lorentz, Pare, 175, 418
Löthwall, Lars-Olaf, 914
Lowry, Ed, 1045
Lowry, Malcolm, 774, 983
Lusk, Norbert, 153
Luther, Marylou, 1249

M., E.F., 588
McBride, Joseph, 1287-88
McCaffrey, Donald W., 790, 916, 1280
MacCann, Richard Dyer 670, 841, 915, 1011
McCarten, John, 570, 619, 654, 671, 728
McCarthy, Todd, 1109, 1308-09, 1145-46
McCrary, Tex, 1230
MacGowan, Kenneth, 632
Mack, 984
McKee, G., 1046
McLellan, Joseph, 1302
McManus, John T., 542
Madsen, Axel, 917, 1261
Magnan, Henry, 571

Author Index

Mahoney, Jon C., 882
Maland, Charles J., 985, 1047, 1085, 1128
Mallery, David, 775
Maltin, Leonard, 883, 1086
Manvell, Roger, 884, 943
Marcorelles, Louis, 729
Margulies, Harriet, 1250
Mariani, John, 918, 1110, 1298
Mark. See Vance, Mark
Martin, Mildred, 329
Mast, Gerald, 842, 919
Mauriac, Claude, 681
Maynard, John, 505
Mellen, Joan, 1048
Melvin, E.F., 258
Merritt, Russell, 885
Mesnil, Michel, 769
Meyers, Sidney, 259, 271a, 330, 337a, 896, 995
Miller, Don, 696
Milne, Tom, 944
Minoff, Philip, 1234
Mishkin, Leo, 543
Misurell, Ed, 697
Mitry, Jean, 920, 1129
Moberly, Michael, 1049
Moffitt, Jack, 730
Mok, Michael, 1208
Molitor, Douglas, 1050
Montagu, Ivor, 204
Montgomery, John, 682
Moran, Michael, 1275
Morgansen, Thomas G., 589
Morgenstern, Joseph, 1254
Morris, Ruth, 1198
Mortimer, Lee, 474, 544
Mosher, John C., 112, 129, 154-55, 176-77, 203, 260, 331, 379, 419, 475
Mount, Douglas N., 1269
Muir, Florabel, 1221
Mulvey, Kay, 545
Mundy, Robert, 843
Murphy, Mary, 1289
Murphy, Patterson. See Levin, Meyer
Murphy, William Thomas, 887

Neale, Steve, 1051
Nelson, Joyce, 945
Nesteby, James R., 1012

Nichols, Bill, 986
Nichols, Dudley, 1034
Noble, Lorraine, 261
Nordell, Roderick, 844
Norton, Eliot, 1223
Norton, Helen B., 205
Nugent, Frank S., 262, 332-33, 380-81, 420-22, 845, 1111

Oakes, Pauline M., 700
O'Connor, John J., 987
Ophüls, Marcel, 846
Orme, Michael, 334, 382
Orsini, Mario, 888

P., A., 383
Palmer, Joseph, 847
Palmer, Tony, 889
Paolella, Roberto, 689, 731-32
Parish, James Robert, 946
Parsons, Louella, 590, 620
Pasinetti, Francesco, 206, 263
Pechter, William S., 759, 848, 988, 1052, 1087
Peet, Creighton, 130-31, 156
Pells, Richard, 921
Pelswick, Rose, 264, 335, 423, 476, 546
Penfield, Cornelia, 265
Phelps, Glenn Alan, 1112, 1147
Poague, Leland, 922, 989, 1013, 1053, 1148
Polonsky, Abraham, 803
Powr, 733
Prelutsky, Burt, 1277
Price, Edgar, 547
Price, James, 770
Proctor, Kay, 672
Pryor, Thomas M., 555, 690, 698, 707, 849-50, 1219, 1224, 1236
Puck, 266
Pudovkin, Vsevolod, 591
Purdy, Jim, 1149
Pym, John, 1088

Q., V., 157
Quart, Leonard, 1054-55
Queval, Jean, 678
Quigley, Isabel, 760
Quigley, Martin, Jr., 804

Author Index

R., D.F., 207
Rabinovitz, Lauren, 1056
Raeburn, John, 966, 990-90a
Ramperti, Marco, 208, 267
Ran, Neil, 548
Ranieri, Tino, 737, 771, 776
Ray, Robert, 1014
Redelnig, Lowell E., 621
Redman, Ben Ray, 384
Reel, Rob, 99
Reid, James, 268
Reid, Laurence, 57
Reitz, Carolyn, 991
Renzi, Renzo, 622
Rhea, Marian, 477
Rheuban, Joyce, 1113
Rhode, Eric, 1015
Rhodie, Sam, 805, 1016
Richards, Jeffrey, 806, 890, 923-24, 1017
Riley, Nord, 572
Rintels, David W., 1057-58
Riskin, Robert, 478
Rivkin, Allen, 592
Robinson, David, 791, 797
Rodowick, David, 1059
Roffman, Peter, 1149
Rohrbach, Gunter, 761
Rosar, William H., 1089
Rose, Brian Geoffrey, 1018, 1060, 1130
Rose, Tony, 925
Rosen, Marjorie, 926
Rosenberg, Bernard, 807
Ross, Don, 1251
Rothschild, Elaine, 746
Ruddy, Jonah M., 747
Rush. See Grearson, Alfred Rushford
Rushmore, Howard, 424

S., E.C., 269
Sacchi, Fillipo, 209, 270
Sadoul, Georges, 556, 593, 633, 891, 892
St. John, Ann, 1232
Salemson, Harold J., 623
Sarris, Andrew, 764, 792, 1090-91, 1131, 1150
Sayre, Nora, 1061
Schallert, Edwin, 113, 132, 336, 425-26, 479-80, 506, 549, 624, 655, 1222
Schatz, Thomas, 1151
Scherle, Victor, 1062
Scheuer, Philip K., 178, 673, 734, 748, 1225
Schickel, Richard, 1290
Schmidt, Sanford Michael, 1092
Schonert, Vernon L., 783
Schumach, Murray, 1255
Scott, John L., 573, 1244
Scott, Vernon, 1245
Self, Lois, 1152
Self, Robert, 1152
Sennett, Mack, 683, 893
Sennett, Ted, 735
Sennwald, Andre S., 133, 210
Setti, Guglielmina, 271
Shain, Sam, 179
Shales, Tom, 894
Shan. See Shain, Sam
Shepard, Richard F., 699
Sherman, Eric, 1291
Sherwood, A.M., Jr., 101
Sherwood, R.E., 63, 72, 83
Shiffrin, Bill, 1063
Shindler, Colin, 895
Sid. See Silverman, Sidney
Silke, James R., 1278, 1292
Silver, Alain, 1114
Silverman, Kaja, 1153
Silverman, Sidney, 84, 134, 158
Silverman, Sime, 102, 114, 135
Silverstein, Harry, 807
Sime. See Silverman, Sime
Simpson, Celia, 103
Simsolo, Nöel, 927
Skagow, Michael, 1115
Skinner, Richard Dana, 159
Sklar, Robert, 992-93
Skolsky, Sidney, 427, 441, 481
Sloan, Kay, 1116
Smith, John M., 869
Sobchak, Thomas, 994
Spoto, Donald, 1093
Stallings, Laurence, 337
Stanbrook, Alan, 738
Stebbins, Robert. See Meyers, Sidney
Steele, Richard W., 1117
Stein, Elliott, 897, 1132
Stein, Herb, 1259
Stern, Seymour, 136

Author Index

Strauss, Theodore, 482
Strout, Richard L., 428
Stuart, John, 216
Suominen, T., 947
Sweeney, Louise, 1270
Swindell, Larry, 798, 851

Tallmer, Jerry, 1271
Tavernier, Bertrand, 799
Terret, Dulany, 700
Thomaier, William, 708
Thomas, Bob, 784
Thomas, Kevin, 852-58, 928, 1019
Thompson, George Raynor, 700, 779
Thompson, Howard, 1272
Thompson, David, 1020
Thorpe, Margaret Ferrand, 429
Tibbetts, John, 1118
Tone, 1154
Torre, Marie, 1235
Tournes, André, 808
Treadwell, Bill, 674
Troy, William, 211, 217, 996
Truffaut, François, 997, 1094
Truscott, Harold, 898
Tube. See Tubelle, Larry
Tubelle, Larry, 749
Tully, Jim, 211a, 338-39
Tyler, Parker, 550, 594

Valenti, Peter, 1155
Vance, Mark, 82
Van Doren, Mark, 272, 340, 487
Van Horne, Harriet, 709
Vecchietti, Giorgio, 273
Vreeland, Frank, 430
Vidor, King, 899
Vitoux, Frederic, 859

Walker, Kathleen, 998
Walker, Marjorie, 1133
Ward, Elizabeth, 1114
Warner, Virginia, 551, 860
Watts, Richard, Jr., 137, 160, 180-81, 212-13
Watz, Edward, 948-49, 1021-22
Wead, George, 1156
Weales, Gerald, 1134
Webber, Jeanne Curtis, 701
Wechsberg, Joseph, 595
Weiler, A.H., 750
Weis, Elisabeth, 1029

White, David Manning, 900
Whitebait, William, 507, 552, 634
Wilkerson, W.R., 574-75
Williams, Dick, 751
Williams, Whitney, 85
Willis, Donald C., 950
Willson, Robert, 999
Wineapple, Brenda, 1157
Winogura, Dale, 1064
Winsten, Archer, 341, 385, 483, 553
Winter, Alice A., 275
Wiseman, Thomas, 772
Wood, Robin, 1065
Wright, Virginia, 576, 625

Zinman, David, 809
Zito, Rom, 1273
Zunser, Jesse, 386, 431, 1256

Film-Title Index

The Air Circus, 97
All My Tomorrows. See A Hole in the Head
American Graffiti, 1287
American Madness, 21, 138, 140, 142-44, 148, 150, 152-53, 155, 159-60, 818, 827, 857, 865, 871, 894, 920, 962, 989, 990a, 1015, 1038, 1124, 1149, 1269, 1286, 1290, 1296, 1364, 1366, 1369, 1375, 1379, 1381, 1383, 1392, 1395, 1400
Anna Karenina, 1257, 1354
Army-Navy Screen Magazine, 486, 677, 779, 1337
Arsenic and Old Lace, 31, 510-13, 518, 523, 526-29, 534-36, 539, 541-43, 545-49, 553, 571, 593-94, 681, 789, 826, 900, 933, 976, 1068, 1084, 1114, 1211-14, 1310, 1312, 1336, 1360, 1364, 1366, 1370, 1375-76, 1379, 1381, 1383, 1385, 1390-92, 1395-96, 1400, 1402-3

The Ballad of Fisher's Boarding House. See Fultah Fisher's Boarding House.
The Battle for the Ukraine, 515
The Battle of Britain, 36, 489, 495, 507, 631, 702, 841, 1045, 1357, 1364, 1366, 1368, 1370, 1380-81, 1385, 1389, 1396, 1400, 1402
The Battle of China, 39, 1363, 1366, 1368, 1381, 1389, 1402
The Battle of Russia, 37, 489-93, 497, 500, 504-6, 702, 1357, 1364, 1366, 1368, 1370, 1379, 1380-81, 1385, 1389-90, 1396, 1400
The Best Man, 1246, 1351
The Best Years of Our Lives, 46, 587
The Big Town, 1315
The Bitter Tea of General Yen 22, 141, 161, 163, 166-67, 169, 170-72, 176, 178-80, 250, 254, 336, 827, 831, 853, 944, 989, 993, 1038, 1070, 1124, 1143, 1201, 1299, 1306, 1310, 1362, 1364, 1366, 1370, 1373, 1379, 1381, 1383, 1387, 1392, 1395-96, 1400
The Brass Rail, 202
Breaking the Ice, 1319
Broadway Bill, 25, 48, 183, 187, 190, 192, 194-96, 198, 210, 213-14, 262, 330, 342, 640, 644, 646, 650-51, 799, 818, 831, 955, 965, 1201, 1332, 1346, 1362, 1364, 1366, 1370, 1373, 1375-76, 1379, 1381, 1392, 1396, 1400
The Burglar, 330

Cavalcade of Academy Awards, 1336
The Chase, 667
Circus. See Circus World
Circus World, 752, 1259, 1353, 1356

Film-Title Index

Crime and Punishment, 1354
Cupid's Boots, 1324
Cyrano de Bergerac, 1356

Dear and Glorious Physician, 752, 1356
Desert Victory, 40, 490, 509, 514, 520-21, 540, 943, 1216
Dirigible, 17-18, 115-17, 119, 122, 125-27, 129-30, 132, 135, 328, 334, 818, 827, 866, 989, 1038, 1120, 1197, 1280, 1362, 1364, 1366-67, 1370, 1379, 1381, 1383, 1392, 1395-96, 1400
Divide and Conquer, 34, 496, 631, 1357-58, 1363-64, 1366-68, 1370, 1379-81, 1385, 1389-90, 1392, 1396, 1400, 1402
The Donovan Affair, 13, 86, 88, 98, 784, 1366, 1370, 1379, 1381, 1400

Les Enfants du paradis, 587
Every Man for Himself, 1315

Fast Company, 1315
Fiddlesticks, 1323
55 Days in Peking, 1353
Flight, 14, 89-91, 95-97, 99, 101-2, 104, 108, 135, 1077, 1134, 1362, 1364, 1366, 1370, 1379, 1381, 1385, 1392, 1400
The Flying Yorkshireman, 1340
Forbidden, 20, 145-46, 149, 151, 154, 156-58, 689, 731-32, 827, 1124, 1143, 1197-98, 1364, 1366, 1370, 1381, 1388, 1395-96, 1400
For the Love of Mike, 4, 64-65, 71, 1031, 1366, 1370, 1372, 1376, 1379, 1381, 1390, 1400
Friendly Persuasion, 1344
Frisco Fury, 1332
Fultah Fisher's Boarding House, 1, 57, 378, 955, 1400
Fury, 252

Gallagher. See Platinum Blonde
The General Died at Dawn, 254
A Gentleman Goes to Town. See Mr. Deeds Goes to Town
G.I. Movie Weekly, 1337
A Girl in Every Port, 77
The Godfather, Part II, 1287
The Gold Rush, 60
Gone with the Wind, 434
The Good Earth, 298
Good Morning, Nurse!, 1321
Good Neighbor Sam, 771
The Grapes of Wrath, 556
Heaven Can Wait, 1066
Hell's Angels, 126, 136
Hemo the Magnificent, 51, 693, 697, 1239, 1357, 1374, 1400, 1402
Henry V, 587
Here Comes the Groom., 49, 656-62, 664, 666, 668-69, 671-73, 680, 989, 1362, 1364, 1366, 1370, 1370, 1372, 1379, 1381, 1383, 1385, 1392, 1395, 1400
Here Is Germany, 42
"High Hopes: The Capra Years," 1304, 1312
High Society, 1315
His First Flame, 70, 1323
A Hole in the Head, 54, 55, 707, 710-22, 724-30, 733-35, 737-38, 849, 932, 1034, 1063, 1238, 1240, 1243-44, 1312, 1348, 1350, 1364, 1366, 1370, 1372, 1376, 1379, 1381, 1383, 1385, 1388, 1392, 1396, 1400

If You Could Only Cook, 251, 321, 835, 875
I Remember Mama, 46
It Happened One Christmas, 46
It Happened One Night, 24-25, 182, 184-86, 188-89, 191, 193-94, 197, 199, 200-209, 211-12, 217, 230, 235, 239, 242, 247, 249, 254, 259, 261-62, 272, 299, 340, 342, 376, 417, 436, 502, 584, 668, 681-82, 685, 689, 692, 731-32, 769-70, 772, 775, 777, 785, 804, 809, 816, 831, 837, 852, 871, 873, 880, 891, 916, 920, 939,

Film-Title Index

973, 976-77, 989, 993, 996, 999, 1002, 1013-15, 1031, 1040, 1048, 1053, 1072, 1091-92, 1108, 1121, 1125, 1139, 1150-52, 1164, 1176, 1182, 1201, 1213, 1243, 1296, 1299, 1306, 1310, 1312, 1331, 1359, 1362, 1364, 1366-67, 1369-70, 1372, 1375, 1378-79, 1381, 1383, 1385, 1388, 1390, 1392, 1396, 1400, 1402
It Happened on Fifth Avenue, 1342
It Happened Tomorrow, 1336
It's a Wonderful Life, 46, 558-70, 572-73, 575-83, 585-88, 590, 502, 623, 667, 702, 787, 817, 826, 858, 876, 930, 950, 952, 955, 963, 968, 971, 989, 999, 1015, 1018, 1024, 1056, 1060, 1065-66, 1090, 1097, 1110, 1112, 1115-16, 1122, 1128, 1131, 1135, 1149, 1153, 1155, 1157, 1192, 1219-21, 1223, 1256, 1283, 1286, 1299, 1310, 1312, 1340, 1358, 1364, 1366-67, 1369-70, 1372, 1375, 1379-81, 1383, 1385, 1392, 1395, 1400, 1402
I Want to Live!, 1243

The Jimmy Durante Story, 1350
Joseph and His Brethren, 698, 1349

Know Your Ally: Britain, 35, 537, 1366, 1368, 1381
Know Your Enemy: Germany. See Here Is Germany
Know Your Enemy: Japan, 43, 877, 936, 1358, 1368, 1380
Ladies of Leisure, 15, 105-6, 109-10, 113, 818, 955, 1137, 1143, 1196, 1362, 1366, 1370, 1379, 1381, 1383, 1392, 1400
The Lady Eve, 463
Lady for a Day, 23, 55, 162, 164, 168, 173-75, 177, 181-82, 261, 417, 630, 681-82, 745-47, 757, 784, 816, 852, 866, 891, 920, 937, 955, 1015, 1199, 1201, 1204, 1246, 1251, 1253, 1331, 1349, 1362, 1364, 1366, 1370, 1375, 1378-79, 1381, 1392, 1394, 1396, 1399-1400
The Life of Chopin. See A Song to Remember
Long Pants, 3, 66-69, 72, 139, 783, 790, 802, 859, 891, 919, 948, 989, 1022, 1059, 1076, 1100, 1323, 1358, 1364, 1366-67, 1370, 1379, 1381, 1390-92, 1400
Lost Horizon, 22, 27, 219, 224, 236, 244, 256, 268, 275-78, 280-87, 289-301, 303-5, 308, 310-13, 315-19, 322, 324-37, 340-41, 417, 432, 557, 689, 695, 705, 763, 776, 785, 799, 804, 807, 809, 831, 854, 875, 900, 920, 939, 955, 969, 980, 985, 1030, 1033, 1038, 1042, 1063, 1075, 1079, 1089, 1109, 1123-24, 1126, 1133, 1163-64, 1206, 1223, 1254, 1257-58, 1278, 1280, 1285, 1299, 1302, 1310, 1341, 1358, 1362, 1364, 1366-67, 1369-70, 1375, 1377-81, 1383, 1385, 1392, 1395-96, 1400
Lucky Stars, 1325

Magic Town, 634, 1298
The March of Time, 496
Marooned, 849, 1261, 1355
The Marriage Circus, 1320
The Matinee Idol, 7, 73, 78, 84, 819, 1366, 1370, 1381, 1400
The Meaning of Treason, 1246, 1352
Meet John Doe, 30, 441-42, 444-54, 457-62, 464-67, 469-80, 482-83, 550, 681, 694, 764, 787, 804, 809, 816, 826, 831, 857, 871, 876, 900, 910, 921, 934, 939, 950, 955, 965, 968, 980, 985, 989, 992, 999, 1009, 1018, 1027, 1032, 1048, 1063,

Film-Title Index

1091, 1105, 1112, 1114,
1118, 1122, 1128-29, 1140,
1147, 1149, 1151, 1156,
1176, 1210, 1273, 1275,
1278, 1280, 1286, 1298,
1310, 1334, 1356, 1364-67,
1369-70, 1372-73, 1375,
1379, 1381, 1383, 1385,
1388, 1390, 1392, 1395,
1400, 1402
The Miracle Woman, 18, 118, 120,
123, 128, 131, 134, 136-37,
689, 827, 838, 891, 900,
914, 937, 1070, 1118, 1124,
1143, 1150, 1362, 1366,
1369-70, 1379, 1381, 1392,
1400
Mr. Deeds Goes to Town, 25-27,
29, 218, 220-22, 226-28,
230-35, 237-43, 245-47, 249,
252-55, 257-60, 262-64, 267,
269-74, 299, 309, 313, 322-
23, 327, 330, 337, 340, 370,
384, 399, 411, 414, 416-17,
430, 451, 487, 630, 652,
682, 694, 731-32, 770, 772,
785, 796, 804-5, 809, 816,
831, 835, 845, 853, 871,
875-76, 880, 891, 894, 896,
910, 920-21, 930, 935, 940,
950, 965, 968-69, 985, 989,
991, 995, 999, 1015-16,
1018, 1025, 1038, 1047-48,
1051, 1063, 1079, 1082,
1085, 1091, 1093, 1112,
1122, 1132, 1141, 1149,
1151-52, 1156, 1164, 1209,
1238, 1306, 1310, 1312,
1333, 1361-62, 1364, 1366-
67, 1369-70, 1372-73, 1375,
1378-79, 1381, 1383, 1385,
1390, 1392, 1395-96, 1400
Mr. Smith Goes to Washington, 25,
29, 387-99, 401-16, 418-26,
428, 431, 433-34, 437, 440,
451, 464, 473, 485, 556,
637, 639, 652, 682, 685,
718, 770, 799, 804, 809,
816, 831, 845, 856, 875-76,
880, 882, 886, 891, 900,
910, 913, 918, 920-21, 935,
937, 945, 950, 965, 968-69,

985, 989, 999, 1006, 1015,
1018, 1038, 1048, 1051,
1061, 1079, 1082, 1091,
1093, 1101, 1111-12, 1138,
1140, 1144, 1149, 1151,
1204, 1206-9, 1221, 1238,
1273, 1276, 1278, 1293,
1302, 1310, 1312, 1334,
1359, 1361, 1364-67, 1369-
70, 1372-73, 1379, 1381,
1383, 1385, 1388, 1392,
1395-96, 1400
My Man Godfrey, 796
The Mysterious Mystery, 1315

The Nazis Strike, 33, 552, 631,
1357, 1363-64, 1366, 1368,
1373, 1380-81, 1385, 1389,
1392, 1396, 1400, 1402
The Negro Soldier, 38, 508, 516,
519, 524, 530, 538, 544,
551, 677, 702, 860, 982,
1074, 1104, 1358, 1363-64,
1366, 1372-73, 1379-81,
1392, 1396
The Negro Soldier in World War
II. See The Negro Soldier
Ninotchka, 434
None But the Lonely Heart, 667
No Other Man, 1341

Official Officers, 1315
On to Tokyo, 1339
Our Gang, 1315
Our Mr. Sun, 50, 686, 688, 696,
1233, 1357, 1374, 1379, 1400

Pioneer Woman. See Westward the
Women
Plain Clothes, 1318
Platinum Blonde, 19, 121, 124,
133, 816, 827, 894, 920,
933, 940, 973, 1038, 1196,
1364, 1366-67, 1370, 1375,
1379, 1381, 1390, 1392, 1400
Pocketful of Miracles, 23, 55,
740-51, 753-61, 891, 989,
999, 1173, 1253-56, 1258,
1266, 1277, 1351, 1362,
1364, 1366, 1369, 1370,
1372, 1375-76, 1379, 1381,
1383, 1385, 1388, 1392,

Film-Title Index

1396, 1400
The Power of the Press, 11, 81, 93, 488, 494, 498-99, 501, 503, 1127, 1286, 1366, 1370, 1381, 1396, 1400
Prelude to War, 32, 591, 631, 702, 841, 951, 987, 1044, 1117, 1357, 1359, 1363-64, 1366, 1368, 1370, 1373, 1380-81, 1385, 1389, 1392, 1396, 1400, 1402
The Prisoner of Shark Island, 1051

Rain or Shine, 16, 107, 111-12, 114, 818, 827, 1096, 1366, 1370, 1379, 1381, 1392, 1400
Reaching for the Stars. See Rendezvous in Space
Rendezvous in Space, 56, 765, 1355, 1400
Report from the Aleutians, 1216
Riding High, 25, 48, 636, 638, 640-48, 650-51, 654-55, 830, 1172, 1228, 1230, 1346, 1362, 1364, 1366, 1370, 1372, 1379, 1381, 1383, 1385, 1392, 1395, 1400
The Robe, 1349
Rocky, 1055
Roman Holiday, 1345
Rome, Open City, 587
Ruggles of Red Gap, 1051

Saturday Afternoon, 1326
Say It with Sables, 9, 74, 955, 1127, 1370, 1379, 1381, 1396, 1400
Scandal, 1131
Shadow of a Doubt, 1065
Smith's Burglar. See The Burglar
The Soldier Man, 1323, 1327
A Song to Remember, 1334
So This Is Love, 6, 75, 819, 1127, 1364, 1370, 1381, 1400
Soviet, 1286, 1331
Stagecoach, 777
Stairway to Heaven, 581
State of the Union, 46-47, 597-608, 610-21, 623-25, 627, 632, 652, 787, 796, 798, 826, 876, 909, 946, 1006, 1038, 1070, 1192, 1225, 1227, 1290, 1302, 1312, 1344, 1351, 1362, 1364, 1366, 1369-70, 1372, 1379, 1381, 1385, 1392, 1395, 1400
Stella Dallas, 1150
The Story of G.I. Joe, 43
The Strange Case of the Cosmic Rays, 52, 699, 1239, 1357, 1400
The Strong Man, 2, 58-59, 61-63, 327, 574, 694, 718, 723, 774, 790, 793, 859, 891, 919, 927, 941, 948, 979, 983, 989, 998, 1005, 1019, 1021, 1076, 1323, 1364, 1366, 1370, 1372, 1379, 1381, 1390, 1392, 1396, 1400
Submarine 10-11, 76-77, 79-80, 83, 85, 94, 97, 103, 328a, 334, 784, 866, 955, 1120, 1127, 1197, 1364, 1366, 1370, 1381, 1392, 1400
The Sun Down Limited 1315
Super-Hooper-Dyne Lizzies, 1322
Suspicion, 550
The Swim Princess, 1329

Tabu, 299
Tell It to the Marines, 79
The Testament of Dr. Mabuse, 473
That Certain Thing, 5, 82, 955, 1124, 1127, 1364, 1366, 1370, 1373, 1379, 1381, 1400
This is the Philippines, 1338
Tomorrow Never Comes, 1336
Toonerville Trolley, 1314
Tramp, Tramp, Tramp, 60, 797, 808, 822, 833-34, 859, 1076, 1088, 1323, 1328
Tunisian Victory, 40, 509, 514-15, 517,520-22, 525, 531-33, 538, 540, 702, 943, 1364-68, 1379, 1381, 1390, 1392
Twenty Million Sweethearts, 202
Two Down, One to Go, 45, 554a, 779, 1339, 1366, 1381, 1396, 1400

The Unchained Goddess, 53, 704, 709, 1357, 1400, 1402

Film-Title Index

Valley Forge, 1333
War Comes to America, 41, 554, 779, 1357-58, 1366, 1368, 1373, 1380-81, 1396, 1402
The Way of the Strong, 8, 1127, 1364, 1366, 1370, 1381, 1383, 1392, 1400
Westward the Women, 676, 1347
What Is Physics?, 1236, 1348
What Price Glory?, 79
Why We Fight, 486, 490, 504, 552, 555, 631, 670, 677, 684, 700, 736, 767-68, 779, 782, 786, 826, 833, 840-41, 877, 889, 906, 915, 931, 943, 958, 960, 963, 1009, 1015, 1028, 1045, 1076, 1117, 1124, 1217, 1273, 1284, 1299, 1310, 1375, 1377, 1398. See also individual titles in this series
A Wild Goose Chaser, 1316-17
The Wizard of Oz, 1123
A Woman of Distinction, 1346
The Yes Man. See The Strong Man
You Can't Run Away from It, 24
You Can't Take It with You, 27-28, 342-44, 346-62, 364-65, 367-75, 377, 379-83, 385-86, 417, 430, 593, 632, 653, 692, 708, 804, 816, 831, 845, 854, 875, 916, 920, 939, 969, 985, 989, 999, 1029, 1079, 1082, 1091, 1106, 1139, 1149, 1204, 1206, 1312, 1358, 1362, 1364-67, 1369-70, 1372, 1375, 1379, 1381, 1383, 1385, 1392, 1394-96, 1400
The Younger Generation, 12, 87, 92, 100, 819, 894, 1081, 1124, 1362, 1364, 1370, 1381, 1400
Young Mr. Lincoln, 1051
Your Job in Germany, 42, 44, 779